The American Governor in Behavioral Perspective

The American Governor in Behavioral Perspective

EDITED BY

Thad Beyle

The University of North Carolina
AND

J. Oliver Williams

North Carolina State University

Harper & Row, Publishers
NEW YORK, EVANSTON, SAN FRANCISCO, LONDON

THE AMERICAN GOVERNOR
IN BEHAVIORAL PERSPECTIVE

CONTENTS

PREFACE

The American governorship presents an interesting political paradox. The governor is undoubtedly the most important participant in the subnational politics of the federal system. Within the political systems of the individual states, he is the key political figure; his role as chief legislator, chief administrator, and chief policy-maker is as pervasive at the subnational level as that of the president at the national level. And, as states become more active in urban problems and in the implementation of domestic programs at the state and local levels, the governor is assuming a more important intergovernmental role.

Yet, the governorship emerged in the 1960s as a vulnerable political office that increasingly leads to dead-end political careers. The incumbent governor faces a greater likelihood of defeat and has fewer opportunities for advancing to higher political office than politicians who bypass the governorship for other state and national political jobs.

We became aware of this and other perspectives of gubernatorial politics while serving as consultants and research associates for two institutes on state politics in the late 1960s—"A Study of the American States," conducted by former Governor Terry Sanford of North Carolina, and "The Institute on State Programming for the 70s," led by former Governor Jack Campbell of New Mexico. Our experience with these institutes, for which we conducted field research in most of the states, has led us to develop a systematic, behavioral study of gubernatorial leadership and politics in the context of the American federal system.

Despite the significance of the office, the governorship has been relatively unstudied, except from a descriptive standpoint. For this volume, we have selected and commissioned articles that describe the contemporary political roles and behavior of the governor. Many of the selections stress the role of the governor in the implementation of national programs at the state and local levels. It is our belief that the essence of state politics can be obtained by focusing on the politics of the governor's office. The section on the "Politics of Leadership" broadens the scope to include administrative and legislative politics in the states. Hopefully, this volume will be useful in courses in executive politics as a comparison of leadership at the subnational level and the presidency.

Several of the articles deal with previously un-published data on the governor. These data were made available by the two institutes and by the Southeast Survey at the University of North Carolina, which collected national public opinion data on the governor. In the section, "Implementing Policies in the States," we have attempted to highlight new policy areas which are emerging in the states.

We are indebted to the authors who have written articles for this volume: Nancy Anderson, Robert Chartrand, James Clodfelter, William R. Hamilton, John N. Kolesar, John W. Lederle, Robert G. Lehnen, Harvey D. Miller, and Deil S. Wright. We are also indebted to the authors who have allowed us to republish articles which seemed appropriate to this volume. We are particularly indebted to Malcolm E. Jewell who has written extensively on state legislative politics and who contributed a special article, "The Governor as Legislative Leader."

And foremost we are indebted to Luther Wilson and the editors of Harper & Row for the interest they have shown in this volume.

T.L.B.
J.O.W.

BIOGRAPHIES
OF
AUTHORS

Clark D. Ahlberg is President of Wichita State University, Wichita, Kansas.

Nancy N. Anderson is Director, Health Systems Division, Institute for Interdisciplinary Studies, Minneapolis, Minnesota.

Thad L. Beyle is Associate Professor of Political Science, University of North Carolina, Chapel Hill, North Carolina.

Earl Black is Assistant Professor of Political Science, University of South Florida, Tampa, Florida.

Robert L. Chartrand is Specialist in Information Sciences for The Legislative Reference Service of The Library of Congress, Washington, D.C.

James Clotfelter is Assistant Professor of Political Science, Emory University, Atlanta, Georgia.

Thomas R. Dye is Chairman and Professor of Political Science, Florida State University, Tallahassee, Florida.

Leon D. Epstein is Professor of Political Science, University of Wisconsin, Madison, Wisconsin.

William R. Hamilton is President of William R. Hamilton and Staff, Political Polling and Counseling, Washington, D.C.

Malcolm E. Jewell is Chairman and Professor of Political Science, University of Kentucky, Lexington, Kentucky.

John N. Kolesar is an Associate at the Center for Analysis of Public Issues, Princeton, New Jersey,

John W. Lederle is Joseph B. Ely Professor of Government, The University of Massacusetts, Amherst, Massachusetts.

Robert G. Lehnen is Assistant Professor of Political Science, University of North Carolina, Chapel Hill, North Carolina.

Norton E. Long is Director, Center of Community and Metropolitan Studies, University of Missouri—St. Louis, St. Louis, Missouri.

Sarah P. McCally is Assistant Professor, Department of Political Science, Hunter College, New York, New York.

Harvey Miller is Director, Dept. of Public Safety, County of Newcastle, Delaware

Daniel P. Moynihan is Professor, Graduate School of Education, Harvard University, Cambridge, Massachusetts.

Robert E. O'Connor is Assistant Professor of Political Science, Pennsylvania State University, State College, Pennsylvania.

Gerald M. Pomper is Chairman and Professor of Political Science, Rutgers, The State University, New Brunswick, New Jersey.

Alan Evan Schenker is Assistant Professor of Political Science, University of Wyoming, Larimee, Wyoming.

Joseph A. Schlesinger is Professor of Political Science, Michigan State University, East Lansing, Michigan.

Ira Sharkansky is Professor of Political Science, University of Wisconsin, Madison, Wisconsin.

Donald R. Sprengel is Associate Professor of Political Science, Saint Louis University, St. Louis, Missouri.

J. Stephen Turett is a graduate student in Political Science, University of California, Berkeley, California.

John L. Wickman is Director, Dwight D. Eisenhower Presidential Library, Abilene, Kansas.

J. Oliver Williams is Assistant Professor of Politics, North Carolina State University, Raleigh, North Carolina.

Deil S. Wright is Professor of Political Science, University of North Carolina, Chapel Hill, North Carolina.

Alan J. Wyner is Assistant Professor of Political Science, University of California, Santa Barbara, California.

CHAPTER
1
CHANGING PERSPECTIVES ON THE AMERICAN GOVERNOR

J. Oliver Williams

As the American federal system moves into the 1970s, the politics of state governors need to be reassessed in the light of some new perspectives. In the past several decades governors have moved from low visibility and low activity to positions of more positive executive leadership within the states and the nation. And trends within the federal system indicate the possibility of even more visibility for governors both politically and programmatically.

At the same time, the governor's political role and the office remain ambiguous in the politics of some states and within the national political process. The governorship is a valuable political prize; but where do governors go after serving limited terms as state executives? The increased vulnerability of recent incumbents seems to indicate shorter political careers even within states that have lengthened the statutory term of office. This vulnerability seems to be coupled with a decline in the importance of the office as a steppingstone to national leadership. At the same time that more attention is being given to national revenue sharing with the states and the call for more political and administrative decision-making at the state and local levels in national domestic programs, questions are also raised about the effectiveness of state and local leadership in coming to grips with domestic problems and in managing the conflicting interests.

VICTIM OF AN UNBALANCED SYSTEM

At the center of reverberations in the federal system is the governor. It is the governor today who is caught in a crossfire between growing demands for services and protests against rising taxes, between the problems of cities and legislatures that are often dominated by rural and suburban representatives. More than chief executives at other levels, he is the principal victim of an unbalanced federal system, with local governments demanding state aid faster than the national government, with its heavy commitment to military spending, can expand its grants to the states.

Yet, it is the executive leadership at the state level that provides the link between people and their problems and the resources that government can bring to bear on these problems. States, as V. O. Key, Jr., pointed out in the late 1950s, have come to occupy a new and pivotal administrative and fiscal position in the federal governmental structure.[1] Not only is this true with the services traditionally provided for by the states, but trends indicate that it is likely also to be the case with regard to other national resources. The governor is becoming the federal systems officer at the subnational level—the coordinator and administrator of increased federal grants-in-aid for state and local services.

These trends call for new perspectives on the governor's political and programmatic roles. The selections in this volume were developed around a number of questions concerning the governor's role and office in the context of the federal system. First, are the politics of the governorship changing? Are new demands being placed on the office producing a different type of occupant? Have recent incumbents become more vulnerable politically in domestic politics? How successful have governors been with traditional state services which increasingly call for greater governmental outlays? How successful are governors in new policy proposals and in performing the federal systems role of planning and administering national domestic programs?

About half of the articles were written for this volume to develop the thesis that the governor is the prime mover of significant politics and administration at the state level and that much of intergovernmental politics can be interpreted through the gubernatorial role. Other previously published research was selected to complement this thesis. The criteria for new and existing research were that it (1) bear directly on the theme and (2) evaluate the governor's role and performance critically or empirically. The articles selected all have a policy focus or bear on the policy-making process.

From this collection we have been able to develop what appear to be changing perspectives of both the governor and the federal system. In no respect are the perspectives clear cut. In most cases there are conflicting interpretations of trends of the past decade. Whether these trends prove to be short-lived, "peripheral" phenomena or are institutionalized—become orthodoxy of the federal system—depends on continuing developments.

[1]V. O. Key, Jr., *American State Politics: An Introduction* (New York: Knopf, 1956), p. 7.

THE VULNERABILITY AND VISIBILITY OF GOVERNORS

As several articles will show, incumbency guarantees neither reelection nor postgubernatorial political career opportunities. Whether the governorship has merely become more visible, and thus a more competitive political office, or if indeed it has become a more vulnerable office, where incumbents face a greater risk of defeat because of negative images of gubernatorial performance, is somewhat problematical.

Political folklore has it that most vulnerable governors were those who found it necessary to enact—or propose—a new form of taxation or a substantial increase in the level of taxation. But to date, empirical evidence does not uphold this bit of political wisdom.

An article in this collection suggests that the governorship has become a more vulnerable office because of high political visibility. But does it necessarily follow that a visible political office will develop an "anti-incumbent" posture? Besides a more visible role, it may be that governors, like big-city mayors, are viewed by voters as executives who are hamstrung by the system and are unable to change policies and solve problems.

Recently, strident critiques of New Deal-Great Society liberalism have questioned whether government can effectively resolve major "people" problems and have suggested that, more often than not, government action deepens or exacerbates, the problems it seeks to solve.[2] Thomas Cronin suggests that, despite these reassessments of political liberalism, the orthodox view that a President can change policies and resolve public problems still exists.[3]

The first national survey data on public views of gubernatorial effectiveness, presented in this volume, suggest that this may also be the case with governors. But governors rank much below the

[2]Representative of this genre are Edward C. Banfield, *The Unheavenly City* (Boston: Little, Brown, 1968); Theodore Lowi, *The End of Liberalism: Ideology, Policy and the Crisis of Public Authority* (New York: Norton, 1969); and Daniel P. Moynihan, *Maximum Feasible Misunderstanding* (New York: Macmillan, 1969).

[3]Thomas E. Cronin, "The Textbook Presidency and Political Science," unpublished paper delivered at the Sixtysixth Annual Meeting of the American Political Science Association, Los Angeles, California, September 7–12, 1970.

President in the public's confidence for providing positive political leadership.

THE "NEW POLITICS" IN GUBERNATORIAL ELECTIONS

A new style of politics has come to characterize gubernatorial elections in diverse state political systems. The so-called new politics—with a professional political manager, and an issue-oriented campaign, mass-media appeal, and computerized voter profiles—actually is over thirty years old. And since the mid-1960s, it has become almost a *modus operandi* of gubernatorial campaigning. In most gubernatorial races in 1970, some new-politics techniques were employed; and the major party candidates reported spending nearly $9 million for radio and television advertising alone.[4]

Perhaps this is to be expected in an office where a low recognition factor apparently is as much—or a greater—advantage as being a visible incumbent. The new politics has invigorated the politics of the highest state political office, and perhaps has been a component of vulnerability as well. Issue-oriented, mass-media campaigning places the burden of defending unresolved problems on the incumbent.

CONSUMER AND URBAN ISSUES OF THE SIXTIES

New trends are emerging also in the programmatic roles of state chief executives. While governors still play the salesman-constituency role, the issues and programs that enable incumbents and the new-politics candidates to succeed in state politics are changing. From the industrial and economic development roles of the 1950s, the politics of election and constituency maintenance of the sixties and the early seventies have often evolved around a coterie of new consumer issues—the environment and quality of life and urban services.

But what the system demands now, the governor cannot easily give. Unlike economic development and promotional roles, urban services require large money outlays and taxes. Environmental programs have electoral and constituency appeal, but they also antagonize traditional state power bases—the people who pollute.

Faced with increasingly volatile and vocal pro-

[4]U.S., Federal Communications Commission, report issued June 17, 1971, in the *New York Times*, June 18, 1971, p. 13.

grammatic demands, governors have several political alternatives, none of which is particularly inviting. The easiest is to anticipate retribution at the polls, particularly if taxes are involved, and duck the issues. But to take no action can bring on a new-politics challenge.

Or governors can champion these issues and face the gale of protest that accompanies the rise in state taxes. The effect of raising taxes on prospects for reelection is an empirical question discussed in several of the articles. Certainly, increasing taxes does not automatically doom an incumbent, but taxing at the state level does provoke a reaction unequalled at either the local or national levels in terms of where blame is laid.

The nature of state taxes—largely regressive and narrow in base—leaves most governors no alternative but to consider additional taxation to finance any increase in the level of services or any new programs. State tax sources provide little of the growth revenue that makes governmental expansion possible without increasing old or imposing new taxes.

The dilemma the governor faces in raising taxes is quite clear: He can increase the return from existing taxes, that is, sales taxes, which most likely will antagonize the state's voting power base, or he can suggest a broader tax base, that is, income and corporate taxes, which most likely will antagonize the economic power base. Obviously, neither of these alternatives is attractive politically, and the governor may look elsewhere before making these hard decisions.

THE STATE'S FEDERAL SYSTEMS OFFICER

There is another and increasingly utilized alternative to skirting the new issues of the seventies or meeting them head on with new taxes and antagonized power bases. More and more, governors are going outside the state to encourage action at the national level and secure for the governor a larger role in channeling federally financed programs and services through the states. This might be called the federal-systems-officer role at the state level.

Increasingly, governors seem to be playing this role to a greater extent than the traditional textbook roles assigned to chief executives. The governor, his staff, and the administrative agencies most susceptible to his influence become the chief coordinators-planners for federal grant-in-aid programs. Often it is the federal programs that give the governor the wherewithal to act—the finances to meet new constituency and consumer demands, control over fragmented and autonomous programs, and the legitimacy to act—all under the aegis of available federal funds.

The federal-systems-officer role has led to several changes in gubernatorial-constituency and gubernatorial-administrative relations. In gubernatorial-constituency relations, the federal-systems-officer role enables the governor to dispense a new style patronage—one not merely of jobs and offices, but of services and programs to key and influential groups and to units of local government. The rise of departments of local affairs and gubernatorial coordinators of local programs in the 1960s is the most obvious indicator of the programmatic and patronage mileage that governors have gained as a federal systems officer. Like the departments of administration in the 1950s, which were designed to accomplish the function of giving governors greater administrative control over fragmented state administrative arrangements, departments of local and urban affairs have been executive-oriented to enable governors to perform better the role of delivering federal services and programs to constituents.

At the same time, these federal programs provide the governor with the greatest headaches. He must grapple with guidelines from Washington, with "runaway" agencies or programs that can maneuver without his acquiesence, and with faits accomplis as previously federal-funded activities lose federal sources of dollars and turn to the governor for their livelihood. And often he must struggle with a severely distorted set of priorities because the state is induced to embrace programs and activities for which federal money is available, and not necessarily those the state needs.

Governors predictably have been more successful with federal programs when they have had access to the new policy tools of planning, budgeting, and systems information. While these tools are normally a part of federal programs, due largely to the built-in requirements of the grant-in-aid system, the governors who have utilized them most and who have forseen the need for emphasizing them in staffing administrative departments have been most successful in the federal systems role.

But, the real impact of the federal systems role for the governor lies in his increasing involvement in the various programs conducted at the state and local levels of government. The governor has moved beyond being the chief administrator, the chief budget officer, and the chief planner at the state level—all these with administrative connotations—to being the chief educator, the chief health officer, the chief social services officer, and the chief law enforcement officer in the state, or better, at the subnational level. There are obviously other areas into which the governor has moved in his responsibilities. These titles are only symbolic of his expanding role, which is now seen more in programmatic than administrative terms. He is perforce active in politics and policy throughout the state, with his impact increasingly being felt at the local level.

His greatest concerns have to be the state's educational system from kindergarten to postgraduate levels; the various welfare and antipoverty programs struggling with our social and economic inequities; the development of a transportation system, which is more than just linking urban areas with concrete; *and*, of course, obtaining the funds state and local governments need to provide these services.

It is in this context of pressures and counterpressures that the governors have become the prime supporters of a federal revenue-sharing plan—with the states and local governments being the recipients of this federal largesse. In fact, the governors support almost any proposal that would move the financial responsibilities up to the federal level, while maintaining program responsibility at the state level. Equally attractive are the various proposals for a "decentralization of the federal system, again with the states (and not federally devised regions) as the loci of the devolved power.

Governors relish and strive to maintain and enhance their various roles in subnational politics. By gaining and holding on to policy and program activities, while relieving themselves of some of their fiscal problems, they can foresee an even greater role for the state chief executives. It should not surprise that a major roadblock to these proposals lies in Congress, whose members attain their status and role in subnational politics—the governor's domain. In politics, one does not cheerfully "beef up" potential rivals, no matter how great a statesman the politician may be.

The other major block lies within the federal system's programmatic bureaucracies which are wary of the governor's increasing strength and power in the various functional areas. The bureaucracies need the money and the governor's imprimatur to carry out their programs and therefore welcome the possibilities of some form of revenue sharing. But they also wish to maintain their professionalism. The governor's newer roles intrude into the world of the bureaucracy, and proposals making him an even more significant "intruder" do not elicit enthusiastic bureaucratic support.

THE GOVERNOR: LED OR LEADER?

Recent studies of politics and public policy have suggested that social and economic differences explain the significant variations among political systems. An equally strong and perhaps countervailing view is that elite influence is also an important dimension.

This collection of articles is intended to explore the latter perspective. The underlying theme is that governors are the prime movers of state politics. Much of what happens within the states, and increasingly between the states and national government, revolves around state executive leadership. Although a number of articles examine state legislatures and bureaucracies, the perspective is mostly from the governor's office.

The intent is not to give an unbalanced view of state political systems or to discount the importance of other state political actors, but to depict what appears to be central to state politics and policy-making. Nor is there an intent to discount the importance of social and economic differences among the states; many of the following analyses do take these factors into account in examining the governor's role in state and federal politics. A governor may be led into many situations and decisions by events and developments beyond his control or direction; but he, in turn, is the leader of government and politics at the subnational level, and as such the impact of his action or inaction is significant.

SECTION
1
GUBERNATORIAL
POLITICS

From the results of recent elections it has become clear that governors, like big-city mayors and even county commissioners, cannot possibly please enough people to win reelection very often. Voters seem to be looking for leaders who can follow projects to completion and get results—but not raise taxes. And increasingly, governors rate high among the casualties.

To be sure, some governors, such as Nelson Rockefeller in New York and Ronald Reagan in California, have built tenure into the gubernatorial office. But the first election of the 1970s continued to highlight a trend that appears to be a dominant characteristic of the politics of American governors: Governors do not necessarily have long careers and the office is not always a stepping stone to national leadership. This trend has been noted not only by scholars but also by incumbent governors, any number of whom in recent elections have observed that the candidate with a new face and no record enters races with an advantage over the man in office.

Unlike many generalities of the federal system, the visibility of gubernatorial politics and the vulnerability of incumbent governors is not limited to either party or region. Even in the South, which V. O. Key, Jr., characterized as a region that had not developed executive leadership adequate to cope with its problems, voters increasingly are looking for new faces and presumably governors who can show results in manpower training, education, employment, housing—the general range of problems that confronts the American voter.

The articles in this section deal with emerging trends in gubernatorial politics, but the focus here, as in other sections, is on policy and how the politics of election affect state public policies.

CHAPTER 2

THE CAREERS OF GOVERNORS

The political careers of American governors have long been of interest to students of American politics. In earlier years of the American federal system, governors were prime candidates for presidential and vice-presidential nominations, and quite a few Presidents and Vice-Presidents began their political careers as governors of states. The U.S. Senate has been another outlet for gubernatorial advancement in the federal system.

There are several explanations of why governors have been a source of political talent for the federal system. The governorship has always been a conspicuous position—probably the number two political executive position, and until recently it has been one of little controversy where a political leader could build a reputation as an able politician. In addition, governors wield considerable political power in the nomination and election of Presidents, which has made them attractive choices and compromises for the presidential and vice-presidential positions on national party tickets.

In the past three decades, however, the political careers of governors have undergone a reassessment. Students of subnational politics are beginning to seek new answers to and explanations for the questions of where governors come from and where they go. The reason stems from a belief that the governorship has changed. It is now a more controversial position and a more difficult place for politicians to make a good name. In a few words, the political nature of the office has changed.

But how has this affected the political careers of governors, or, to phrase it in a different manner, has it affected where governors come from and where they go? Do fewer men seek the governorship today and do fewer governors go on to higher political offices in the American federal system? Are those who occupy governor's offices in the midtwentieth century more vulnerable; that is, do they face decreasing margins of victory and defeat?

Political scientists have now begun to explore the matter of political careers as a critical element in recruitment to office, and the governorship has been a source of considerable study. In this chapter, Joseph A. Schlesinger reassesses the governor's place in American politics—his tenure in office and his potential for political advancement. He concludes that the politics of the governorship has not changed as much as the offices to which governors once advanced. Stephen Turrett examines competition for the gubernatorial office in all twentieth-century elections to determine (1) if governors, in fact, have become more vulnerable; (2) if vulnerability varies with certain economic and demographic factors; and (3) how presidential elections impinge upon gubernatorial races. He finds that governors, compared to the same party's candidates for the U.S. House of Representatives, are running better than ever before.

So, are governors more vulnerable in career pattern and opportunities today or are they just more visible?

THE GOVERNOR'S PLACE IN AMERICAN POLITICS
Joseph A. Schlesinger

More than ten years ago Louis Harris wrote a prophetic article entitled, "Why the Odds are Against a Governor's Becoming President."[1] Harris argues that the principal reason why governors had been so prominent among presidential candidates in the past was their ability to combine a conspicuous position, they too were executives, with lack of controversy. But in recent national politics governors have had greater difficulty than senators or Vice-Presidents in developing a national following; at the same time the increasing burdens of state government have made them controversial. Thus, Harris concluded, the odds had shifted against the governor. The three following presidential elections appear to have confirmed his prophecy.

On the face of it, change appears to have taken place in the careers of our chief politicians. It is therefore worthwhile for us to reconsider the place of the governor in the American political system. Of the nine men who obtained a major party nomination for President or Vice-President in 1960, 1964, and 1968, only one, Spiro Agnew of Maryland, was a governor. In contrast the three preced-

ing elections had produced two governors as presidential candidates, Dewey and Stevenson, and one for the vice-presidency, Warren, again out of a total of nine men. Whether this is a short- or long-run trend we cannot tell, but it does invite us to probe systematically the reasons for possible shifts in career lines.

The question is of more importance than a passing one to specific governors or senators. Patterns of political careers, I have argued, are a critical guiding element to the activities of politicians, in any political system.[2] They provide whatever order exists for the expectations of politicians, not only about their own prospects but those of others, multiple expectations which guide much of the behavior of all politicians. Only a few men in any generation can reasonably plan and act on the proposition that they might become President; many more can have the idea in mind. Surrounding each of these men are many others, their retinues, would-be replacements, and their retinues who act in response to the arousal of presidential expectations. Thus even a small change in career patterns can produce a substantial reorientation of expectations throughout the political system. Changes in the expectations spur the ambitions of some while they dampen those of others; senators act like presidential candidates; governors try to make a career of that office.[3]

If, as I have argued, career patterns are central to politics, then we should attempt some systematic examination of why they come about and why they change. Here, therefore, I want to examine the relationship between the governor and the presidency with the purpose of laying out the prin-

Source: Reprinted by permission of the authors and publisher from Joseph A. Schlesinger, "The Governor's Place in American Politics," *Public Administration Review*, 5, (January–February 1970), pp. 2–10.

[1] Louis Harris, "Why the Odds Are Against a Governor's Becoming President," *The Public Opinion Quarterly*, Vol. XXIII, No. 3 (Fall 1959), pp. 361–370.

[2] Joseph A. Schlesinger, *Ambition and Politics: Political Careers in the United States* (Chicago: Rand McNally, 1966).

[3] The proposition that politicians respond to their office ambitions has received some empirical support in recent studies. See, for example, E. Nelson Swinerton, "Ambition and American State Executives," *Midwest Journal of Political Science*, Vol. XII, No. 4 (November 1968), pp. 538–549. Administrators with ambitions for higher office saw their proper roles as more closely related to those of the governor and his party than did those who were content to remain at their current level. Similarly, San Francisco Bay Area councilmen who were ambitious had policy views different from their less ambitious colleagues, Kenneth Prewitt and William G. Nowlin, "Political Ambitions and the Behavior of Incumbent Politicians," *Western Political Quarterly*, Vol. XXII, No. 2 (June 1969), pp. 298–308.

cipal variables which produce changes in such patterned movement. I do not claim that explanations
which do not fit this scheme are necessarily invalid. The changes taking place in American politics explain almost any phenomenon.

Patterned movement between elective offices
takes place within three distinct yet related aspects
of the political system: the structure of political
opportunities, the party system, and party organization. When I say these aspects are distinct I
mean that each develops its own patterns and that
each can change without being prodded by the
other. But they are related, because when change
in one aspect does take place, it will affect the
other two. By *structure of political opportunities* I
mean the total number of political offices and the
rules, both formal and informal, for their attainment. The *size* of the structure of political opportunities is affected by the rate of turnover of men
in office; its *shape* is affected by the routes men
take to higher office.[4] The *party* system is the
statement of each party's relative chances within
the opportunity structure. The concept, therefore,
encompasses both the number of parties and the
level of party competition for various offices.
Party organization constitutes the ways in which
men cooperate to capture positions within the
structure of opportunities. Knowledge of these
three factors can never tell us precisely who will
advance to any office; individual idiosyncrasies as
well as issues of the moment can always eliminate
one person and inject another. But the three variables do encompass the persistent or systematic
influences which create patterns of movement
through offices.

Each of the three variables invokes a different
explanation for the development of a promotional
pattern. The structure of political opportunities
invokes a "structural" explanation arising out of
rules and past experiences. Since the rules for
officeholding, formal and informal, are never
impartial to officeholders, we expect some pattern
of promotion simply because some people are
more obviously placed in any race. The party
system on the other hand invokes "rational" reasons, or those which assume each party makes its
nominations in terms of the men most likely to

win. A promotional pattern emerges here in response to a persistent strategic need which can be
met by nominating a particular type of officer
such as the governor. Finally, party organization
invokes explanations of influence and control.
Here promotional patterns will emerge if an officer
such as the governor has exceptional resources
within the organization. The three factors may be
cumulative or contradictory; they also interact
upon each other. Let us examine each in relation
to the problem of the governor and his party. It is
important here to keep in mind that by talking of
"the governor" we are glossing over 50 quite diverse situations.

The elements which make up the structure of
political opportunities tend to be quite stable over
time. Rules are set; men respond; and the circular
process whereby human activities become self-
perpetuating occurs. The governorship becomes a
way of attaining the presidency; and many would-
be Presidents aim first at the governorship. We can
note only two periods of major change in the
opportunity structure. The first was the formative
period between 1820 and 1840 when many of the
offices and the procedures surrounding them were
established.[5] The second was the Progressive Era
at the turn of the century, which introduced such
basic changes in the ground rules for officeholding
as direct election of senators, the direct primary,
and women's suffrage.

It may well be that the reapportionment decisions of the last decade will mark a third period of
change. If the Electoral College were to be substantially altered and a system of primary nominations for the presidency adopted, it is likely that
this too will lead to a period of major change in
the opportunity structure.

At this point, however, we can detect little
change in the general patterns of advancement
since the Progressive Era. Governors of the 1950s
and 1960s have come from very much the same
kinds of offices and in the same proportions as
they did in the 1920s, 1930s, and 1940s. No great
changes have taken place in the careers they have
followed after the governorship: most have not
gone on in office politics, but a goodly number,
much the same share, have gone to the U.S. Senate

---

[4] Schlesinger, *op. cit.*, deals more fully with the concept
of the political opportunity structure.

[5] Richard McCormick, *The Second American Party
System* (Chapel Hill, N.C.: University of North Carolina
Press, 1966).

TABLE 1. Tenure in Office of Governors
(Figure is percentage of all governors who served during the decade.)

Number of Years Spent in Office of Governor	1800–1809	1820–1829	1850–1859	1870–1879	1900–1909	1920–1929	1950–1959
10 plus	14.3	3.5	0.8	0.0	1.3	1.0	4.0
5–9	16.1	14.0	5.6	11.8	8.5	15.1	26.5
3–4	30.3	40.2	40.4	49.1	54.5	53.5	50.3
1–2	39.3	42.3	53.2	39.1	35.7	30.4	19.2
N	56	92	124	154	154	185	151

or to high-level federal appointments. Indeed the most noteworthy departure from the past in career opportunities has not been in the governor's chances for higher office but in the reawakening of the vice-presidency as an independent route to the presidential nomination. Two cases, Nixon and Humphrey, hardly make a pattern. Their significance lies rather in the sharp break they represent in the well-established character of the office as a dead end.

While the shape of the opportunity structure as defined by career lines has not changed much over time, there has been a long-run secular trend for the number of opportunities to decline. This has been due to the trend toward greater longevity in office. Starkly evident in the U.S. Congress is the fairly continuous trend shown by Polsby's figures for the average number of terms served to increase every two years.[6] But the trend has been evident for the governorship as well. While it remains true that the governorship is a transitory position which most governors hold for four years or less, the evidence is that those spending more time in office is increasing. This trend, of course, is obviously related to the trend toward the adoption of the four-year governorship in many states. But there is also evidence that where there are no constitutional restraints, enough governors are being reelected one or more times to produce a degree of longevity in the position unequaled since the early days of the Republic.

What, if any, difference has the change in the size of the structure of opportunities made in the

[6]Nelson W. Polsby, "The Institutionalization of the U.S. House of Representatives," *The American Political Science Review*, Vol. LXII, No. 1 (March 1968), pp. 144–168.

chances of governors to become President? The historical evidence indicates that it has worked against the governor; it has been the relatively new governor who has walked off with the presidential and vice-presidential nominations. Note (Table 2) that close to 80 percent of the governors who achieved these nominations had served four years of less. Spiro Agnew's year and a half experience as governor when he was nominated for Vice-President, therefore, was well within the norm of gubernatorial experience. The contrast with the other great source of nominations for the presidency and vice-presidency, senators, and representatives, is clear. Most senators and representatives had eight or more years of office experience; most senators were at least in their second term and representatives in their fourth at the time of their nomination. In this context note that two of the three principal unsuccessful gubernatorial aspirants for the presidency in 1968 were outside the norm, George Romney had held office for six years and Nelson Rockefeller ten; Ronald Reagan, with two years in office, was within the norm.

The norm, however, tells us little about why it came to be. It may simply be the statistical product of governors' spending fewer years in office than senators or representatives. Or it may be that historically governors emerged as candidates primarily when the parties resorted to persons who were least likely to have national reputations or followings. For the proposition that the fewer the years in gubernatorial office the more obscure the nominee, there is some evidence in the number of ballots required to nominate nonincumbent presidential candidates at the national conventions. A disproportionate number of governors required more than one ballot for nomination compared with nongovernors. Most of the governors nomi-

TABLE 2. Length of Time in Office Before Nomination for President
or Vice-President (1848–1968)
(Figure is percentage of those in group)

Number of Years Spent in Last Office Before Nomination	Governors	U.S. Senators	U.S. Representatives
12 plus	0.0	39.1	36.4
8–11	4.2	17.4	45.4
5–6	16.7	21.7	0.0
4	37.5	8.7	18.2
2–3	41.6	13.1	0.0
N	24.0	23.0	11.0

nated on the first ballot, McKinley in 1896, Smith in 1928, and Dewey in 1944, had been active candidates in the previous convention; Landon in 1936 was the exception.

In recent years the trend has been toward first-ballot nominations, running parallel to the trend to longevity in the governorship. Should the first-ballot trend continue, the change in the size of the structure of opportunities may well facilitate instead of deter the governor who would seek the presidency. Since 1952 neither party has gone beyond a first-ballot nomination. At that time the Democrats needed more than one ballot to nominate the first-term governor of Illinois, Adlai Stevenson. On the other hand, Romney and Rockefeller, despite their disappointments, were at least the two leading gubernatorial contenders for the Republican presidential nomination of 1968. Since first-ballot nominees have generally been men who developed a sizable national following before the convention, time in office is probably the most efficient way for governors to achieve first-ballot nominations. In the long run, then, the trend toward longevity in office may well prove essential to the governor's advance.

TABLE 3. Number of Ballots Required for a Presidential Nomination (Republican and Democratic Parties, 1896–1968)

Number of Ballots	Governors	Nongovernors
	(percentages)	
1	31.0	62.5
2–4	38.0	12.5
5 and over	31.0	25.0
N	13.0	24.0

Note here that while the structure of opportunities and party organization have changed independently, changes in one aspect of the political system have had clear implications for the other. The number of ballots needed to nominate a President is an organizational question, depending upon the variety of forces which influence the way a party reaches decisions. At the same time, the structure of political opportunities plays a significant part in determining what resources party officials may have at hand. Change in the structure of opportunities changes the range of choice for the party. On the other hand, the party's organizational procedures may well affect the shape or the place of offices in the structure of opportunities.

THE PARTY SYSTEM

The party system I have defined as a statement of each party's chances at winning office, producing promotional patterns only when they are the most rational choices for the party's strategic needs. Here it is critical that we recognize the substantial changes which the existing party system has undergone. Current scholarship indicates that the Republican-Democratic contest has gone through at least two phases: in the period from the Civil War to 1896 the two parties were closely balanced in presidential contests; in the second phase, from 1896 to 1932, the Republicans dominated; after 1932 the Democrats emerged as the majority party.[7]

The question which concerns us is what strategic

[7]The concept of a succession of party systems has been laid out most fully in William Chambers and Walter Dean Burnham (Eds.), *The American Party System* (New York: Oxford University Press, 1967).

value the governor has had for the parties in each of these periods. The use of the governor in party strategy has always appeared to rest upon the specific importance of one or more states in the party's calculations. Certainly the state identification has been the primary asset which governors have brought to the presidential contest. In using the governor the party's leaders have had to see the winning of New York or Ohio or California as of such clear importance that the primary qualification in a candidate was the ability to win that state and hopefully others in its region.

In the pre-1896 period each party had a large bloc of strongly committed states. The few states in the middle which could be tipped, therefore, loomed exceedingly large. In that period New York and Indiana were the most flexible of the states, while Ohio went Republican only by the narrowest margins. During that period each party nominated governors for President or Vice-President, the Republicans nominating two from Ohio; the Democrats three from New York, one from Indiana, and one from Missouri. The large number of men nominated from these states by both parties simply reflects rational party strategy.

When, on the other hand, the party system tipped in favor of one of the two parties, as has been true since 1896, the governor strategy became primarily the strategy of the minority party. For this strategy to be reasonable, the distribution of party strength must be regional, as it has been. In order for the minority to win it must capture states in the dominant party's region of strength. Thus any governor the minority party has been able to elect in that area has great strategic value. The Brookings Institution study has shown that gubernatorial nominations for the presidency have been an "out-party" phenomenon.[8] But more particularly they have been the "out-party" phenomenon of the minority party of the period. From 1896 to the present, minority Democrats and minority Republicans nominated seven governors. During the same period the majority parties nominated only one governor, Adlai Stevenson in 1952. The two "critical" elections of 1896 and 1932 were won by governors, McKinley and Roosevelt, men whose victories transformed their parties to majority status.

[8] Paul David, Ralph Goldman, and Richard Bain, *The Politics of National Party Conventions* (Washington, D.C.: The Brookings Institution, 1960).

The rationality of the minority nominations of governors in regional terms is evident. Strong in the South and West but weak in the industrial Northeast, the post-1896 Democrats went to New Jersey for Wilson, Ohio for Cox, and New York for Smith and Roosevelt. After 1932 the Republicans, having shown their strength in the Midwest and West, moved toward the Northeast which was now critical to their victory. In 1944 and again in 1948 they nominated New York's Governor Thomas Dewey. The Republicans' nomination of Kansas Governor Alfred Landon in 1936 was not, I would argue, the result of rational strategy but rather the desperate act of a party bereft of officeholders.

But before a party can act in anything like a rational manner it, or rather the party's leaders, must be able to see clearly what the party's electoral position is. With the advantages of hindsight and sophisticated research we can now tell that 1896 and 1932 produced electoral realignments.[9] But when did the Democrats after 1896 and Republicans after 1932 realize not only that they were in difficulty, but just what the nature of the difficulty was? It seems to me that at least two and more likely three presidential elections must pass before the new party alignment becomes self-evident. A second defeat for the party can be attributed, as it usually is, to the advantage of the incumbent. Thus we would not expect the out-party to begin rationally nominating governors on a regional basis with any regularity until three elections had established its minority status.

The experience after 1896 bears out this argument. The minority Democrats in 1900, 1904, and 1908 nominated no governor for President or Vice-President. But in 1912, and almost exclusively thereafter during their minority, the party took to governors for its presidential nominees. Once we agree that the Landon nomination was the nomination of a party with very few choices, the Republicans began to use the regional gubernatorial strategy in 1944, after three elections had clearly indicated the nature of their minority position.

The interesting question which remains is the

[9] As, for example, in V. O. Key, Jr., "A Theory of Critical Elections," *Journal of Politics*, Vol. 17 (1955), pp. 3-18; and Duncan MacRae, Jr., and J. A. Meldrum, "Critical Elections in Illinois, 1888-1958," *The American Political Science Review*, Vol. 54 (1960), pp. 669-683.

fate of the gubernatorial strategy in the 1960's. A good case can be made that the party system is once again in a state of change. Just what realignments will mark the future are not yet clear. But the disposition of state strength in the presidential election of 1964 was markedly different from that of 1960, and though the 1968 election produced a different partisan result, it resembled 1964 more than it did any of the previous elections in the post-1932 period.[10] Republican gains in the South and West coupled with improvements in Democratic strength in the Northeast were omens of a geographic shakeup of the proportions of 1896. At this writing, however, with only two elections behind us, we cannot tell whether these changes will have a durable effect upon the party system. Will there again be a minority party and if so will it be a party with strong regional weaknesses?

Given this situation, would it not be irrational for the parties to base their presidential strategy on the governorship at a time when the evidence of the usefulness of that strategy is not at all clear. In 1968 Nelson Rockefeller invoked the Republicans' past regional strategy to support the claim that his nomination was essential to victory. But his evidence was not convincing and his argument was destroyed by the election results which followed. As we pointed out earlier, the changes in the structure of opportunities by no means precluded Rockefeller's advance. On the other hand, we would not project a return to the gubernatorial strategy which he represented until the contours of the party system are once again clear and once again clearly require it.

PARTY ORGANIZATION

Party organization I defined earlier as the various ways in which men cooperate to gain office in the structure of opportunities. The question we should ask here is what additional advantages organized cooperation gives to governors in the contest for the presidency beyond those provided by the structure of opportunities and the party system. For much of party organization is in effect a response to the other two variables. The organization of office-seeking parties cannot stray far from the office structure. Thus the governor is important in state parties because his office, which is set

up by the state constitution not the party, is one of the primary reasons for the existence of the party itself. Similarly, the party system influences party organization. We need only recall the changing character of state party systems, a condition now well recognized. This implies that the governor's influence within his party depends upon his strategic value to the party. That value depends upon politicians' perceptions of the governor's place in the future as defined by the party system.

The relevance of the party system in defining the governor's influence within his state party has recently been demonstrated in a study by McCally of several state legislatures.[11] Using support of the governor's vetoes as the test of influence, she demonstrated that a party majority in the legislature was helpful to the governor, but as the size of the majority in the legislature grew, gubernatorial influence upon his own legislative party declined rapidly. Perhaps even more significant, and certainly less to be expected, was her finding that the size of a governor's victory in the primary following the legislative session correlated better with his influence over his legislative party than any other measure, including the size of his majority in the election which coincided with that of the legislature. Such a finding is subject to various interpretations, but I would propose that the party's legislators in this case were responding to their fairly accurate assessment of the governor's future staying power.

The governor's influence within party organization, beyond that attributable to the opportunity structure and the party system, is difficult to determine. One of the more pervasive views of presidential nominations is their control by "bosses" and functionaries with an eye to their private interests, using patronage and jobs as their means of control. From this standpoint the governor's advantage in a presidential nomination must be limited to his control over the votes of his state's delegation to the national convention. That governors do exercise some control over their state delegations is certainly true, but it is far from the authoritarianism often pictured. Table 4 shows the votes of the state delegations in the nine Republican conventions of this century where there was a

[10]Walter Dean Burnham, "American Voting Behavior and the 1964 Election," *Midwest Journal of Political Science*, Vol. XII, No. 1 (February 1968), pp. 1–40.

[11]Sarah P. McCally, "The Governor and His Legislative Party," *The American Political Science Review*, Vol. LX, No. 4 (December 1966), pp. 923–942.

TABLE 4. Cohesions in State Delegations Voting at Republican National Conventions
(Figures are percentages of states with and without a Republican governor at the time of the convention.)

Cohesiveness on a Key Vote	1912 With	1912 W/out	1916 With	1916 W/out	1920 With	1920 W/out	1940 With	1940 W/out	1948 With	1948 W/out	1952 With	1952 W/out	1964 With	1964 W/out	1968 With	1968 W/out
Solid	42.9	37.1	50.0	25.0	41.4	15.8	23.6	9.7	33.3	8.4	44.0	39.1	46.7	42.8	38.5	29.2
Moderate (1–24 percent defection)	28.6	44.4	10.0	3.6	13.8	26.4	23.6	9.7	12.6	20.8	28.0	47.8	53.3	20.1	30.7	12.5
Split (25 percent or more defection)	28.5	18.5	40.0	71.4	44.8	57.8	52.8	80.6	54.1	70.8	28.0	13.1	0.0	37.1	30.8	58.3
Number of states	21.0	27.0	20.0	28.0	29.0	19.0	17.0	31.0	24.0	24.0	25.0	23.0	15.0	35.0	26.0	24.0

significant division. The Democratic conventions are less useful for this purpose because of the widespread use of the unit rule. There is certainly a clear tendency for delegations from states which had a Republican governor to be more cohesive than those without a governor. Yet there were two conventions, 1912 and 1952, when states without Republican governors showed more cohesion; these were the two conventions in which the Tafts played their southern strategy. Moreover, close to a third of the states with Republican governors revealed defections of 25 percent or more of the delegations. Only one convention, 1964, produced no such sizable defections among the states with governors. By any measure that convention would have to be considered the one in which the Republican governors had the least influence. Thus factional conflict within the party seems as significant in determining the cohesion of state delegations as the presence of the governor.

Even if every governor had complete control over his own delegation, it is hard to see how this would give governors much of an advantage in amassing a convention majority, or at least enough of an advantage to produce a gubernatorial promotion pattern. Only if one could demonstrate that governors were a cohesive group, interested in advancing one of their own, would this be true. Yet on the rare occasions when governors have acted together in support of a presidential nominee they have been as likely to support a non-governor, as was true of the Republican governors' role in the Eisenhower nomination. Certainly a sizable and cohesive state delegation could contribute to the nomination of its governor. But unless the delegates' contribution supported the strategic needs of the party system, it is highly unlikely that they could impose their choice upon the convention.

CONCLUSIONS

I have attempted to define the conditions which determine the place of the governor in American politics by emphasizing the pattern of promotion of governors to the presidency. No effort has been made to compare the governorship with other modes of advancement, although a similar analysis could be made for senators, generals, businessmen, or ideologues. Nevertheless, the movement of any one of these other groups, frequent enough to warrant description as a pattern, would have to be explained within the context of the three components of the American political system which give rise to regularized movement and which have dominated my discussion of the governorship.

Of the three components, party organization, in the limited sense of internally derived influence, appears least significant in explaining the promotion of governors. While governors have some control over their own state delegations to national conventions, this in itself is not enough to give any one governor commanding control and there is little evidence of any special organizational interest in promoting governors as such. Indeed, the fact that few governors gain nominations when internal influences might be expected to have the freest play, when the party is dominant or the majority party, testifies to the weakness of the organizational explanation.

The structure of opportunities, on the other hand, does appear relevant to the promotion of governors, but essentially in a permissive way. Governors have functions similar to Presidents, and procedures such as the Electoral College link the state to the presidency. These factors certainly help place governors within the ring of presidential hopefuls; but they by no means make clear what proportion of presidential candidates we ought to expect to be governors. All we can say is that we would expect some governors to become presidential nominees. Thus if there were no governors nominated for over a hundred years, as was the case with Vice-Presidents, we would have to go beyond the structure of opportunities for an explanation.

It is the party system which provides a positive explanation for both the existence of the gubernatorial pattern of promotion to the presidency and its periodic decline. The sectional strength of the two parties has meant that the strategic problem of meeting the opposition has often been defined in sectional terms. This has given particular states, and thus their governors, a strategic prominence. But as we have noted, strategy requires knowledge, and knowledge rests upon the experience of several elections. Thus we have noted the drop in the governor's presidential fortunes after the periodic realignments of party strength. If this analysis is correct, then the future of the governor's pattern of promotion, as distinct from the success of an exceptional governor who has gained a national following, rests upon the future of regional distributions of strength within the party system.

THE VULNERABILITY
OF AMERICAN GOVERNORS,
1900-1969
J. Stephen Turett

A number of scholars have held that American governors are more politically vulnerable now than was true in earlier years, and, furthermore, that this increasing vulnerability is related to characteristics inherent in the office and not shared by other major elected officials.[1] This has occurred,

Source: Reprinted from "The Vulnerability of American Governors: 1900-1969," *Midwest Journal of Political Science*, 15, No. 1 (February 1971) by J. Stephen Turett by permission of the Wayne State University Press.

[1] The thesis has been stated and most critically examined by Lattie Finch Coor, Jr., "The Increasing Vulnerability of the American Governor" (unpublished Ph.D. dis-

we are led to believe, concurrently with—and despite—the continuous growth of gubernatorial power.[2] Most significant among the several supporting elements upon which the thesis is based are these: (1) The states have inadequate revenue sources, but (2) their populations demand more and more public services, because (3) increasingly they are urbanized and industralized. Voters more frequently are making extravagant and sometimes impossible demands on the governor. Or, put somewhat differently, voter expectations have begun to run far ahead of any reasonable level in action or accomplishment. The governor, therefore, is placed in the unenviable and precarious position of being held responsible for that over which he has little or no control. "A governor today," warned Malcolm Jewell,

is caught in the crossfire between growing demands for services and a chorus of protests against rising taxes, between the problems of the sprawling metropolis and the stubbornness of a rural legislature. He is a victim of midcentury federalism, with local governments demanding state aid faster than the national government . . . can expand its grants to the states. The governor is blamed for the lagging economy, depressed areas, and spreading unemployment, none of which he can control, and every move on his part to expand state services and revenues is criticized on the grounds that it will drive industry away.[3]

sertation, Department of Political Science, Washington University, 1964). See also Austin Ranney, "Parties in State Politics," in Herbert Jacob and Kenneth N. Vines (Eds.), *Politics in the American States* (Boston: Little, Brown, 1965), pp. 90-91. "The reason for the new political vulnerability of governors," he wrote, "is plain: most state governments . . . now face enormously increased demands for more and better schools, highways, welfare, recreational facilities, and so on—but most face them armed with very inadequate revenue sources."

[2] The development of gubernatorial power is concisely treated in William H. Young, "The Development of the Governorship," *State Government*, Vol. XXXI (Summer 1958), pp. 178-183. For an earlier more detailed study see Leslie Lipson, *The American Governor: From Figurehead to Leader* (Chicago: University of Chicago Press, 1939). The best description of the constitutional powers of the governors can be found in Coleman B. Ransone, Jr., *The Office of Governor in the United States* (Alabama: University of Alabama Press, 1956). See also Thad L. Beyle, "The Governor's Formal Powers: A View from the Governor's Chair," *Public Administration Review*, Vol. XXVIII (November-December, 1968), pp. 540-546.

[3] "State Decision-Making: The Governor Revisited," in Aaron Wildavsky and Nelson W. Polsby (Eds.), *American Governmental Institutions* (Chicago: Rand McNally, 1968), pp. 545-546.

The governor, then, whether or not he has the formal authority or power, is forced to fight on all fronts—and is expected to emerge victorious. The disorders at the public university, a rise in tax rates, or a drop in employment are visible problems of importance; but they are only a fraction of the total. Governors are faced with a whole galaxy of problems, all of which are within their sphere of influence, few within their orbit of command. As the population has grown and the problems of a complex society proliferate, the solutions of an earlier era become mere palliatives. In the words of two students: "Occasionally, they actually solve problems; more often, they simply enable the state government to live with the problems. Though these actions are satisfactory to other political leaders, they seldom please the public."[4] As a result, the argument goes, more governors are being sent into involuntary retirement. Incumbents suffer; challengers benefit.

The governor whose continuance in office is doubtful must act differently than one whose tenure is secure. Any approaching election may turn the former into a lame duck: his hand in policy-making, legislative leadership, and administrative management could be seriously impaired. Those seeking reelection might hesitate to alienate even small segments of the population; instead, they would go slow, let things ride—or, at worst, do nothing. A pall of uncertainty might straitjacket even the most ambitious of governors.

And certainly not least in importance is the impact this would have on the recruitment of qualified and talented individuals to serve in the office. The challenge might not be worth the time, effort, and money; the office itself could decline in prestige. While probably not the principal cause, high electoral vulnerability could contribute to the decline of governors as presidential timber. In earlier years the governorship was looked upon as a stepping-stone to the presidency. Since 1876 thirteen governors—two via the vice-presidency— have become national standard-bearers of their

party. Recently, however, governors have lost out to senators as presidential candidates. "A senator," as one perceptive journalist has written, "can lay siege to the presidency; a governor must seize it on the run."[5] Delay for a governor may be tantamount to defeat, while time is a senator's ally.

The governorship route to the nomination is far riskier, far less likely to succeed. It should appeal only to the gambler who wants to chance it all on one roll of the dice. If he delays his bid more than two years after taking office, he is tempting fate.[6]

Eleven of the thirteen governors who became their party's candidate were nominated prior to 1940; and it has been almost 40 years since the state capitals produced a White House winner. Moreover, since 1952 the vice-presidential nominees of both major parties have, with only two exceptions, come exclusively from the Congress.[7]

For the ambitious office-seeker the prospects for advancement are not particularly appealing. Today governors encounter many of the same problems— only usually on a more intensified scale—as faced by big city mayors. And the latter, according to the best work on the subject, face poor prospects for advancement.[8] Commenting on the difficulties of the governorship, one observer summed up the situation: "If the governor is very fortunate he may get by for two years with his reputation in-

[4] Robert C. Wood and Bradbury Seasholes, "The Image of the Governor as a Public and Party Leader: The Disintegration of an Image—Reflections of Five Governors," in Robert R. Robbins (Ed.), *State Government and Public Responsibility, 1961: The Role of the Governor in Massachusetts,* Papers of the 1962 Tufts Assembly on Massachusetts Government (Melford, Mass.: The Lincoln Filene Center for Citizenship and Public Affairs, Tufts University, 1961), p. 80.

[5] See the excellent article by David S. Broder, "What's the Best Road to the White House," The *New York Times Magazine,* September 22, 1963, p. 93. He further commented: "The point is obvious but frequently overlooked. No one stands taller on the political horizon than the governor of a big state on the day he is first elected. But unfortunately for governors, their moment of glory tends to be brief " (p. 28).

[6] *Ibid.,* p. 93.

[7] Joseph E. Kallenbach, *The American Chief Executive* (New York: Harper & Row, 1966), pp. 175–176; Russell Baker, "Best Road to the White House—Which?" The *New York Times Magazine,* November 27, 1960, pp. 22 ff.; Broder, pp. 28 ff.; and Paul T. David, Ralph M. Goldman, and Richard C. Bain, *The Politics of National Party Conventions* (Washington: The Brookings Institution, 1960), pp. 145–163, 485–488. A brief discussion of the relative positions of senators and governors over the years can be found in Louis Harris, "Why the Odds are Against a Governor's Becoming President," *Public Opinion Quarterly,* Vol. IV (July 1959), pp. 361–370.

[8] Banfield and Wilson attribute these prospects to the cleavage between the hinterland and the city. See Edward C. Banfield and James Q. Wilson, *City Politics* (Cambridge: Harvard University Press and The M.I.T. Press, 1963), p. 35.

tact. If he lasts longer than that, he's either a genius or the luckiest damn fool alive."[9]

The plight of a governor is even more complicated given the fact that consistency and coherence in attitudes and activities by state voters can easily deteriorate into contradiction. Thus, "taxation to finance welfare programs meets opposition among those who favor welfare programs even more frequently than among those who oppose them. . . . The same people simultaneously want increased expenditures and reduced taxes."[10] High spending, then, may provide only an evanescent protection to the charge of high taxes.[11]

Given that the proposition concerning vulnerability is verifiable, it is surprising that little empirical evidence can be gathered in its support. Three salient questions will therefore be examined. (1) Have governors, in fact, become more vulnerable? (2) Does vulnerability vary with certain economic and demographic factors? (3) How do presidential elections impinge upon gubernatorial races?

I

Several criteria of vulnerability have been employed in this analysis: (1) the election outcome, (2) the change in a governor's winning margin, (3) the relative change in a governor's winning margin, and (4) a compared margin of victory. Each measures a slightly different aspect of vulnerability.

At the lowest level, vulnerability can be measured by the election outcome itself—that is, the victory or defeat of an incumbent. A comparison of the defeat rate over time is revealing, but hardly decisive: fluctuations in turnout or a popular head of the ticket can too easily spell the difference between winning and losing. Under these circumstances, it becomes more difficult to measure vulnerability accurately.

More importantly, a "winning percentage"[12] can be computed. We can then compare the governor's current margin of victory to his margin in the election immediately preceding. If the winning percentage for the two successive elections is the same, the change in the winning percentage is zero; if the previous winning margin exceeds the present one, the change is negative.[13] These electoral margins are, in a sense, a measure of vulnerability as a potential for defeat. Shrinking pluralities, in other words, can plausibly be equated with higher vulnerability.

National or statewide movements should also be taken into account in measuring gubernatorial vulnerability. In some elections it might be misleading, indeed incorrect, to consider a governor more vulnerable simply because there was a decline in his winning margin. What we need in effect is to compare the change in the governor's winning margin to the change in his party's fortune in general.[14] If they vary together, the governor per se is

---

[9] An anonymous political scientist quoted in Broder, p. 90. "The problems that confront governors today," Broder wrote, "are too familiar to require much detailing. In many of the big city states, a rapidly increasing population and an accumulating demand for education and other public services collide with rigid and inadequate tax systems. In others, the shock of technological change cripples key industries, creating pockets of continuing unemployment and inflating welfare costs" (p. 28).

[10] V. O. Key, Jr., *Public Opinion and American Democracy* (New York: Knopf, 1965), pp. 168–169. Also see Robert Axelrod, "The Structure of Public Opinion on Policy Issues," *Public Opinion Quarterly*, Vol. XXXI (Spring 1967), pp. 51–60.

[11] The relationship between taxes and electoral results has been the object of much speculation but little investigation. For the speculation aspect see Theodore H. White, *The Making of a President 1960* (New York: Atheneum, 1961), pp. 213–215; and Harris, pp. 366–369. White notes that of the twenty-seven governorships up for reelection in 1960, twelve changed hands, "largely because of grass-roots tax revolts." A more systematic analysis is undertaken by Gerald M. Pomper, *Elections in America* (New York: Dodd, Mead, 1968), Chapter 6. His conclusion was that there was "no strong and unidirectional relationship between tax or spending increases and electoral results. Voters do not evidence a consistent concern for fiscal issues" (p. 137).

[12] The concept is defined as "the difference between the percentage of total votes gained by the victor and that gained by the candidate with the next largest number of votes." Joseph A. Schlesinger, *How They Became Governor* (East Lansing: Governmental Research Bureau, Michigan State University, 1957), p. 27.

[13] The figure is calculated by subtracting the previous winning margin from the present one. The former will always be positive. Should a governor be defeated, however, in his bid for reelection, his current "winning" margin will be negative, and the change in this margin will, of course, be an even lower negative number.

[14] Donald Stokes in an unpublished paper reports the informative experience of a British Member of Parliament which should accentuate the significance of using a comparative measure: "One of my parliamentary respondents . . . wistfully reported that he had been delighted by the increase of his majority until he realized that his swing was dead on the national average." "The Nationalization of Political Attitude" (Survey Research Center, University of Michigan, 1967), p. 11.

not becoming more vulnerable. Free from the contamination of distracting trends and movements, the relative change in a governor's winning margin will enable us to determine the extent to which the electorate singles out the governor for special treatment. The resulting figure is a comparison of changes and, as such, may be considered the "critical change."[15] For example, when the change in a governor's winning percentage stands at -5 percent and that for his party at -7 percent, the critical change is +2 percent.

Since the governorship is more competitive than other state offices,[16] voting for the latter cannot be expected to yield a valid indicator of general party strength. As V. O. Key observed:

The special role of the governor in our politics accounts in part for the divergence between results of elections of governors and elections of other officials. The prominence of the governor in the field of public attention and the tendency of popular discontent and hope to center upon him often make candidates for that office either weaker or stronger than the general strength of the party, if such a generalized party following may be supposed to exist. Crusades tend to form behind personalities, not parties.[17]

To approximate the political milieu of an incumbent governor after an election the statewide congressional (U.S. House of Representatives) vote can serve as a barometer of a state's present political temperament. The advantages of a figure based on congressional voting are as follows: (1) Congressional races are likely to be somewhat more competitive than races for most statewide offices; hence they should more closely resemble the competition for governor than would lesser state offices.[18] (2) The voting for congressional seats would be more likely to reflect national (or statewide) trends—not only detecting them but also indicating their relative strength. It would thus at least indirectly control for "extraneous" forces influencing the vote for governor. (3) Unlike data on state races, the congressional data are readily available.

Finally, to ascertain the present standing—and not merely the change in standing—of governor vis-à-vis his party's candidates in House races, we can compare the two pluralities. A compared margin of victory will measure whether or not the governor ran ahead or behind his party's congressional candidates. Zero on this scale would not necessarily correspond to absolute uniformity in the partisan division of the vote for the two offices, but it would indicate identical pluralities.

For present purposes a "gubernatorial incumbent" may be defined as the person holding the office of governor, provided that he has served at least one year. Those, therefore, succeeding to the office may, at times, be treated as incumbents.[19] There are many reasons for proceeding in this manner. Among the most significant is the fact that the nomination itself would be expected to

[15] The critical change may be thought of simply as the relative change in a governor's winning percentage. It can, of course, take on both positive and negative values. Nelson Polsby effectively uses a similar measure to test the hypothesis that McCarthy was instrumental in bringing about the defeat of Senator William Benton. See "Towards an Explanation of McCarthyism," *Political Studies*, Vol. VIII (October 1960), pp. 264–268.

[16] Empirical confirmation of this proposition can be found in Joseph A. Schlesinger, "The Structure of Competition for Office in the American States," *Behavioral Science*, Vol. V (July 1960), pp. 197–210. He concluded: "Much of the cyclical character of the minor state offices reflects not only one-party control for long periods but also control of the office by a single person. In other words, there is the tendency for the electorate (and party organizations) to treat the lesser state offices as though they were careers, and to permit a person, regardless of the flow of party fortunes, to retain the seat. Thus there is a built-in lag in party turnover for these positions" (p. 208). Also see his, "The Politics of the Executive," in Jacob and Vines, pp. 208–209, 219. By contrast, he reported in another study, "the margins for the electoral security for the governorships are today as low as they have ever been." Stability in the Vote for Governor, 1900–1958." *Public Opinion Quarterly*, Vol. XXIV (Spring 1960), p. 91.

[17] *American State Politics* (New York: Knopf, 1956), p. 205. Additionally, see the statement by Jewell, "State Decision-Making: The Governor Revisited," in Wildavsky and Polsby, p. 564: "When demands are made on government, they are made on the governor."

[18] This is probably true notwithstanding the contention that most of the seats in Congress are safe for one party or the other. See Lewis A. Froman, Jr., *Congressmen and Their Constituencies* (Chicago: Rand McNally, 1963), pp. 61–62. But outside the South, according to Wolfinger and Heifetz, less than 40 percent of the Democratic seats are safe. Raymond E. Wolfinger and Joan Heifetz, "Safe Seats, Seniority, and Power in Congress," *American Political Science Review*, Vol. LIX (June 1965), pp. 339–341.

[19] Incumbency in most instances was ascertained from *The Governors of the States 1900–1966* (Chicago: Council of State Governments, 1966). The latter factor in the definition is negligible, comprising less than 5 percent of all the elections with incumbents. If a successor's party affiliation differed from that of his predecessor—a not too uncommon situation in the earlier years—he was not considered an incumbent.

indicate some fairly high level of political strength. It is noteworthy that about 40 percent of those persons succeeding to the office did not, for one reason or another, receive the nomination of their party in the subsequent election.

Some successors will be considered incumbents because those benefits which traditionally accrue to an incumbent would also, even if in a lesser degree, be available to an incumbent's successor if he had served a long enough time. We would expect, for example, that a large amount of publicity would have surrounded his activities—something which most challengers could not be expected to have received over such an extended period of time. Of recognition, Stokes and Miller maintain: "In the main, recognition carries a positive valence; to be perceived at all is to be perceived favorably."[20]

Nineteen states with at least moderately competitive gubernatorial elections in both the pre- and post-Depression years,[21] and in which a gover-

[20] Donald E. Stokes and Warren E. Miller, "Party Government and the Saliency of Congress," in Angus Campbell, Philip E. Converse, Warren E. Miller, and Donald E. Stokes, *Elections and the Political Order* (New York: John Wiley, 1966), p. 205. The statement was specifically made in regard to congressional candidates but probably has general applicability for most offices below President and Vice-President.

[21] This does not mean of course that there would have been no utility in examining noncompetitive states. What is crucial for a study of this type, however, is the place where the actual decision is made. In some states—especially, but not exclusively, the South—the crucial point for decision has been the primary. In these states the primary has been the election—the latter being, for all practical purposes, merely a ratification of a previous decision. On this point see Cortez A. M. Ewing, "Primaries as Real Elections," *Southwestern Social Science Quarterly*, Vol. XXIX (March 1949), pp. 293–298; V. O. Key, Jr., *Southern Politics in the State and Nation* (New York: Vintage Books, 1949), Chapters 19–20; and Coleman B. Ransone, Jr., *The Office of Governor in the South* (Alabama: Bureau of Public Administration, University of Alabama, 1952), Chapter 2. The importance of primaries is indicated by the statement made some time ago by Merriam and Overacker: "The fact is that the primary is the election in about one-half of the states, one-half of the counties, and one-half of the legislative congressional districts of the nation." Charles E. Merriam and Louise Overacker, *Primary Elections* (Chicago: University of Chicago Press, 1928), p. 269. Perhaps the framework of this study could be extended to primaries. However, to equate primary results in some states with general election results in others could be misleading. One study of congressional primaries in all regions of the country con-

nor could constitutionally succeed himself at least once, constitute the universe for this analysis.[22] These states, representing all regions with the single exception of the South, have held a total of 505 gubernatorial elections over the last 70 years. For analytical purposes the data[23] were examined in seven periods, each covering a decade of the twentieth century. Ten year intervals have a dual advantage: They are usually long enough to provide a large enough number of cases from which to generalize, and they are short enough to discern trends. As a check, three other intervals (seven, fourteen, and twenty-three years) were also examined, none of which altered the general findings.

II

At the outset, two things are immediately noticeable. In the first place, the number of gubernatorial elections (Table 1) has steadily decreased over the last 50 years. The decline can be attributed to an increase in the number of states adopting four-year terms of office. Whereas in 1920 more than half of the nineteen states had two-year terms for

TABLE 1. Governors Seeking Reelection, by Period

Period	Number of Elections Held	Elections with Incumbents	
		Number	Percent
I (1900–09)	76	35	46.1
II (1910–19)	77	44	57.1
III (1920–29)	77	37	48.1
IV (1930–39)	75	44	58.7
V (1940–49)	72	49	68.1
VI (1950–59)	68	44	64.7
VII (1960–69)	59	43	72.9

cluded that "there are few districts in the country where the primary serves as an effective alternative to two-party competition." Julius Turner, "Primary Elections as the Alternative to Party Competition in 'Safe' Districts," *Journal of Politics*, Vol. XV (May 1953), pp. 197–210.

[22] All of the following remarks are confined to these states. States were first ranked according to the average margin of victory for governors from 1900–1928 and 1929–1969. This was then combined with a won-lost criterion to determine competitiveness. The status of each state (excluding Alaska and Hawaii) is given in the appendix.

[23] Electoral data were made available through the Inter-University Consortium for Political Research. From 1900–1969 there have been a total of 1,246 gubernatorial elections.

TABLE 2. Partisan Affiliation of Governors Seeking Reelection, by Period

	Number of Elections With Incumbents		Percent of Incumbents	
Period	Democratic	Republican	Democratic	Republican
I (1900–09)	9	26	25.7	74.3
II (1910–19)	21	23	47.7	52.3
III (1920–29)	18	19	48.6	51.4
IV (1930–39)	32	12	72.7	27.3
V (1940–49)	24	25	49.0	51.0
VI (1950–59)	20	24	45.4	54.6
VII (1960–69)	21	22	48.8	51.2

governor, by 1968 less than a quarter of them had such short terms. The steep drop in the number of elections in Period VII is the result of state constitutional revisions in the 1950s and early 1960s.

Secondly, the percentage of elections with incumbents has correspondingly increased—despite the fact that three of the states have now made changes which limit their governors to only two consecutive terms. Slightly less than half of the races had incumbents in them in the first decade of this century, while in the sixties nearly three-fourths did. Incumbents, as Table 2 makes clear, have been evenly divided between the two parties in five of the seven periods, including the final three. Only in the religiously Republican years of period I and the equally dominant Democratic years of period IV do the party balances differ significantly. And even these two periods are strikingly similar in one respect: the controlling party at the national level fields three-fourths of the incumbents—no doubt due, in great part, to high rates of defeat for candidates of the other party in the earlier years of both decades.

Turning from the preliminaries to the various indicators of vulnerability, we find that they lead to remarkably similar conclusions. There is no difference in the rate of defeat (Table 3) for the last three decades; in each, the proportion defeated hovers around one-third. Neither the percentage nor the number defeated has changed. For five of the seven periods the defeat rate falls within a 10 percent range—between 28 and 38 percent. Periods II and IV, by contrast, are at the polar positions: From 1910 to 1919, 45 percent of all incumbents were defeated, but from 1930 to 1939 only 25 percent lost.

The percentage of incumbents with a negative change in their plurality is uniformly higher than the percentage defeated. Between 60 and 70 percent of all incumbents do less well in their bids for reelection (Table 3), and the coefficient of variation for this second measure is even smaller than that for the percentage defeated. In fact, the changes in the percentages in the second set of figures in Table 3 closely parallel similar shifts in the percentage defeated (Figure 1). In period IV, that with the lowest rate of defeat, the percentage of governors with a decreased plurality was also the lowest. Nevertheless, only two-fifths of the incumbents could improve upon their previous pluralities. Somewhat surprisingly, perhaps, governors in period VII fared nearly as well.

The critical change complements the other indicators. With a major exception in period IV, when most incumbent Democratic governors did not benefit as greatly by the Roosevelt candidacy and program as did Democratic House nominees, the critical change figures tend to oscillate in much the same way as the previous two measures. Compar-

TABLE 3. Three Measures of the Vulnerability of Incumbent Governors, by Period

			Negative			
	Defeated		Change in plurality		Critical change	
Period	%	(N)	%	(N)	%	(N)
I (1900–09)	28.6	(35)[a]	69.0	(29)	57.1	(14)
II (1910–19)	45.5	(44)	68.2	(44)	60.6	(33)
III (1920–29)	29.7	(37)	67.6	(37)	51.4	(35)
IV (1930–39)	25.0	(44)	59.1	(44)	67.4	(43)
V (1940–49)	34.7	(49)	65.3	(49)	49.0	(49)
VI (1950–59)	36.4	(44)	68.2	(44)	61.4	(44)
VII (1960–69)	34.9	(43)	62.8	(43)	48.8	(43)

[a]Numbers in parentheses refer to the bases upon which percentages are calculated.

FIGURE 1. Comparison of Measures of Vulnerability, by Period[a]

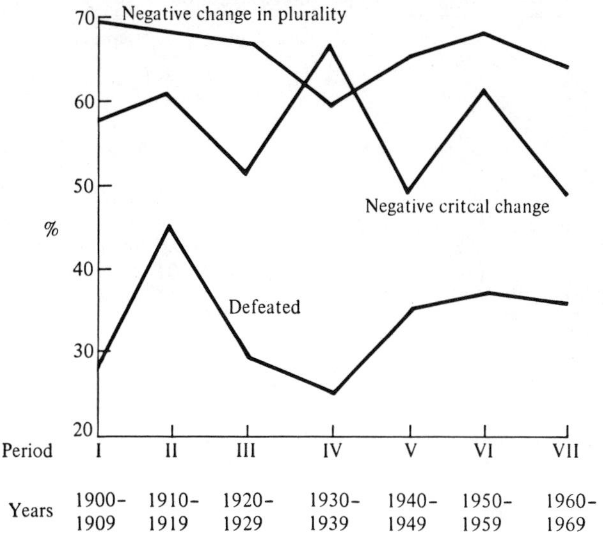
Negative change in plurality
Negative critcal change
Defeated
%
70
60
50
40
30
20
Period
I
II
III
IV
V
VI
VII
Years
1900–1909
1910–1919
1920–1929
1930–1939
1940–1949
1950–1959
1960–1969

[a]Data from Table 3.

ing the percentages with a negative critical change lends no credence at all to the thesis of increased vulnerability. Quite the contrary. They show that governors, as compared to House candidates of the same party, are running better now than ever before. For only the second time in seven decades, less than half of the governors had a negative critical change. Additional evidence is provided by the accompanying figures in Section A of Table 4. To facilitate comparisons, a mass of data has been telescoped into Figure 1.

The compared margin of victory conveys the same impression. Section C of Table 4 demonstrates, as did the last column of percentages in Table 3, that the position of governors is improving rather than deteriorating. Especially in period VII is the improvement manifest: incumbent governors are today, on the average, running 9 percent ahead of the statewide House vote for their party. Through the 1950s a very different pattern prevailed.

The above characteristics suggest the conclusion that governors, perceived in perspective, are no more vulnerable today than they have been in previous years. What we are witnessing, it appears, and what has caught the eye of political scientists, is increasing visibility, not vulnerability.

Despite the fact that governors do not seem to have become *more vulnerable*, it would nevertheless be interesting to ascertain what factors, if any,

TABLE 4. Incumbent Governors and House Races: Mean Scores on Comparative Measures, by Period

Period	A. Critical Change	B. Difference in Critical Change for Winners and Losers	C. Compared Margin of Victory
I (1900–09)	0.29	2.17	-2.22
II (1910–19)	-3.46	5.64	-0.12
III (1920–29)	-0.71	2.03	-1.00
IV (1930–39)	-5.28	1.64	-2.72
V (1940–49)	-0.41	7.59	2.07
VI (1950–59)	-3.40	7.02	1.27
VII (1960–69)	-0.48	12.83	9.02

TABLE 5. Coefficients of Simple Correlation Between Economic, Demographic, and Vulnerability Measures[a]

Variable[b]		Base Values		Rate of Change	
		Change in plurality	Critical change	Change in plurality	Critical change
1. Urbanization	(+)	.06	.03	−.06	−.03
2. Industrialization	(+)	.11	.05	−.16	−.09
3. Crime	(+)	.02	.10	.02	−.02
4. Unemployment	(+)	.13	.06	−.01	−.04
5. Tax Burden[c]	(+)	−.09	0.0	.02	.09
6. Expenditure effort	(−)	−.04	−.01	−.03	.17
7. Educational effort	(−)	−.12	−.12	.03	.29

[a]The individual vulnerability scores were multiplied by −1 in order that high positive scores would be more vulnerable than low negative scores.

[b]The proposed relationships between independent variables, nos. 1–7, and the two measures of vulnerability are shown in parentheses.

[c]Burden and effort are defined in terms of taxes or expenditures per $1000 of personal income.

are related to *vulnerability itself.* Although vulnerability has not varied, there still could be merit in explanations which relate vulnerability to diverse demographic characteristics, disparities in economic wealth, or differences in the level of governmental activity and the nature of public services provided.[24] To test for such a relationship, the forty-three elections with incumbents in the 1960s were selected for study. Data for each of these elections were collected for seven variables: urbanization, industrialization, crime, unemployment, tax burden, total expenditure effort, and educational expenditure effort.[25]

[24]See, for example, the above questions: Jewell, p. 109; Ranney, note 1; and Broder, note 9. The concern of these writers, as in comparative state policy studies in general, has not been with short-term or purely political variables, which, perhaps, might better explain declines in support for governors. These few paragraphs merely make some initial tests on these writers' assertions.

[25]There were no significant differences in the analysis when per capita expenditure and revenue data were substituted for the burden and effort variables. Ideally, the nature of public services provided rather than merely the level of expenditures should have been examined. The former, however, are not easily assessable. The expenditure and revenue data examined here are for both state and local governments since the extent to which services have been centralized at the state level or supported by state grants is not uniform. Ira Sharkansky in assessing the relationship between spending and services has proceeded in a similar manner "because of technical problems which preclude the assessment of services supported by *state agencies, per se. . . .*" He found that "the levels of state

An attempt was also made to explain vulnerability in terms of intrastate changes on the above variables. For example, crime rates per 100,000 inhabitants, while greater in highly urbanized states, are increasing rapidly in some less urbanized, western states.[26] Thus, the rate of change was used as the independent variable rather than the base figures. Rates of change were calculated over two-year periods (e.g., the change from 1960 to 1962) since they coincide with the terms of office in some of the states.

Table 5 emphasizes the point that there is no linear relationship between any of the independent variables and vulnerability. Most of the simple correlations are close to zero and none is statistically significant at the .05 level. Although the correlation with the variable of percentage change in educational expenditure effort approaches statistical significance, it is not in the expected direction. In

and local government spending do not exert pervasive influence upon the nature of public services." *Spending in the American States* (Chicago: Rand McNally, 1968), Chapter 7. Others though (cited by Sharkansky) have claimed that governmental expenditures reflect the "scope and character" or the "alpha and omega" of public services.

[26]The crime data are significant in at least one respect. The mean rate of increase in crime under Democratic incumbents seeking reelection (21 elections) was only 10.6 percent, while that for Republicans (22 elections) was 24.9 percent. Cf. Thomas R. Dye, *Politics, Economics, and the Public* (Chicago: Rand McNally, 1966), pp. 233–234.

short, changes within states in crime, unemployment, taxes, expenditures, and so on, are—like the prevailing levels themselves—not crucial determinants of vulnerability.[27]

III

Since "the American states operate, not as independent and autonomous political entities, but as units of the nation," it would be valuable to determine the manner in which nationwide trends and presidential elections affect gubernatorial races. Although federal theory "presuppose[s] a political capacity congruent with the constitutional competence of each federated unit,"[28] the states obviously do not operate in a political vacuum. The affairs of states and the outcomes of state elections might be inundated by the prevailing presidential politics. With certain major exceptions there is, concluded Key,

a striking interlocking of state and national voting. . . . When a region shifts its political preferences from Democratic to Republican, the presidential result, the elections to the House of Representatives, and the choices of governors tend to move in the same direction. Republicans replace Democrats, or vice versa, in about the same proportions. While both state and national voting may, in these great swings, be responsive to common causes, to some extent voting on state and local offices represents a more or less automatic extension of strong preferences or dislikes in national politics. The pervasive effect of national politics becomes patent when inconspicuous state and local candidates, hidden away far down the ballot, ride into—or are ousted from—office with the movement of the national pendulum.[29]

Regarding the influence of presidential elections on gubernatorial races, it is interesting to note that some states have attempted, in Key's words, to shield state politics from the blasts of national conflict by scheduling gubernatorial elections in the off-years. There has thus been a secular decline in the number of gubernatorial elections held in presidential years.[30] Of those states switching from two-year to four-year terms for governor in the fifties and sixties, none have made them concurrent with the presidential election. The changes through the century are summarized in Table 6. In the 1960s, for only the second time when there were three presidential elections in a decade, more than half of all gubernatorial elections with incumbents were held in the two off-years. About 60 percent of the elections were held in the presidential years in the two comparable periods (III and V).[31]

While the sharp decrease of gubernatorial elections in presidential years makes an historical evaluation of the relationship of presidential and gubernatorial voting more difficult, Figure 2 is nevertheless revealing.[32] Attenuated correlation coefficients in presidential years suggest a dissociation of presidential and gubernatorial voting.[33] The close

[30]See Nelson W. Polsby and Aaron B. Wildavsky, *Presidential Elections* (2nd ed.; New York: Scribner's, 1968), pp. 187–188.

[31]Period I, which also had three presidential elections, is not strictly comparable because two states then held annual elections.

[32]Correlations may have been higher had percentages of the two-party vote been examined. To increase the number of elections, and to embellish with more credibility, the simple correlations (based again on the total vote) for the examined states can be compared to those for all nonsouthern states. The trend is basically unchanged, as the following table indicates:

PRESIDENTIAL AND GUBERNATORIAL VOTING

	Simple Correlations	
Year	Examined states	All nonsouthern states*
1944	.72	.77
1948	.54	.73
1952	.67	.77
1956	.56	.13
1960	.35	.46
1964	−.53	−.23
1968	−.13	−.09

*Excludes elections in North Dakota (1944) and Utah (1956) because of exceedingly strong showings by third-party candidates.

[33]Key makes a similar observation in a note of the fifth edition of *Politics, Parties, and Pressure Groups*, p. 307.

[27]A more comprehensive examination of nearly 90 elections from 1950 to 1969, employing some of the same variables, led to the same conclusion.

[28]Key, *American State Politics*, pp. 18–19.

[29]*Politics, Parties, and Pressure Groups* (5th ed.; New York: Thomas Y. Crowell, 1964), pp. 304–305. See also Louis H. Bean, *How to Predict Elections* (New York: Knopf, 1948); Malcolm C. Moos, *Politics, Presidents, and Coattails* (Baltimore: Johns Hopkins Press, 1952); Warren E. Miller, "Presidential Coattails: A Study in Political Myth and Methodology," *Public Opinion Quarterly*, Vol. XIX (Winter 1955–56), pp. 353–368; Angus Campbell and Warren E. Miller, "The Motivational Basis of Straight and Split Ticket Voting," *American Political Science Review*, Vol. LI (June 1957), pp. 293–312.

TABLE 6. Incumbent Governors Running in Presidential Years

Period	Elections (#)		% Pres. Yrs. of Total	Incumbents (#)		% Pres. Yrs. of Total
	Total	Pres. yrs.		Total	Pres. yrs.	
I	76	41	53.9	35	13	37.1
II	77	30	39.0	44	18	40.9
III	77	49	63.6	37	22	59.5
IV	75	33	44.0	44	18	40.9
V	72	44	61.1	49	29	59.2
VI	68	26	38.2	44	18	40.9
VII	59	31	52.5	43	21	48.8

FIGURE 2. Declining Relationship Between Percentage of Total Vote Democratic for Governor and Percentage of Total Vote Democratic for President

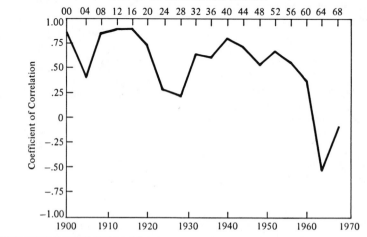

articulation of presidential and gubernatorial voting, evident especially in periods I and II, has apparently given way to a greater separability of national and state politics.[34]

One way of discussing the problem of national or statewide trends is to calculate the differences

[34] The relationship between gubernatorial and presidential voting has probably always been weaker than that between House and presidential voting. While only about 25 percent of the incumbent Democrats in 1932 and 1936 had a smaller plurality, almost 75 percent had a negative critical change. Democratic incumbent governors ran behind their party's nominees for the House by an average of over 3 percent. Republican incumbent governors ran over 5 percent ahead of their party's House nominees. For a discussion of presidential and congressional voting see, in addition to the sources cited in note 29, Milton C. Cummings, Jr., *Congressmen and the Electorate* (New York: The Free Press, 1966), Chapter 7.

in the critical change for winning and losing incumbents. As the figure diverges from zero, the salience of factors common to both governor and House races decreases. If, in other words, the critical changes for winners and losers were the same, then the changes in winning margins for gubernatorial candidates would be equal to those of their party's House candidates. This could easily be the result of a national movement toward one party; on the other hand, it is possible that the effects are peculiar to a single state. At any rate, it would be impossible to argue that characteristics inherent in the governor's office are responsible for fluctuations in both gubernatorial and House voting. Section B of Table 4 shows, not unexpectedly, that trends were most important in periods IV and II, precisely the decades in which presidential winners won by the largest pluralities. By contrast, trends

TABLE 7. Vulnerability of Incumbent Governors in Presidential Years, by Outcome of Presidential Election

Governor's Presidential Party	Defeated		Decreased Plurality		Negative Critical Change	
	%	(N)[a]	%	(N)	%	(N)
Won	19.7	(76)	51.4	(74)	63.0	(73)
Lost	42.9	(63)	73.8	(61)	44.8	(58)

[a]Numbers in parentheses refer to the bases upon which percentages are calculated.

TABLE 8. Vulnerability of Incumbent Governors in Off-Years, by Presidential Party

Party	Defeated		Decreased Plurality		Negative Critical Change	
	%	(N)[a]	%	(N)	%	(N)
In	42.0	(100)	77.6	(98)	57.5	(80)
Out	26.3	(57)	54.4	(57)	61.7	(47)

[a]Numbers in parentheses refer to the bases upon which percentages are calculated.

were least prominent in period VII, the decade with two of the closest presidential elections in history.

Characteristically, members of the party winning the White House have done better than members of the defeated presidential party, and, further, suffer a loss in the ensuing off-year election.[35] As is evident from Table 7, incumbents of the losing presidential party are twice as likely to be defeated in presidential years; and whereas only half of the incumbents of the presidential party had decreased pluralities, three-fourths of the incumbents of the party losing the Presidency suffered such declines. But in the off-years the roles are reversed (Table 8).[36] This pattern repeats itself in virtually every period (Tables 9 and 10). With only two exceptions in presidential years (periods III and VII), the percentage of incumbents of the defeated presidential party with a negative change in their plurality has exceeded that for the winning presidential party. In the off-years members of the party previously losing the presidency consistently run stronger than incumbents of the President's party.

In most instances the above alternating advantage is probably a function of differentials in voter participation. Upsurges in turnout, as both Key

[35] See Key, *American State Politics*, pp. 41–49.

[36] In determining the relationship between presidential outcome and gubernatorial voting, the only two measures of importance are the number defeated and the number with a negative change in their plurality. The critical change, which functions as a trend controlling measure, would be expected to negate any relationship. In the off-years, for example, the ϕ relating previous success of presidential party to negative change in plurality dims perceptibly—increasing from −.24 to .04—when critical change in substituted; similarly, Yules Q goes from −.34 to .09. The limitations of ϕ and its comparison to Q are discussed in John H. Mueller and Karl F. Schuessler, *Statistical Reasoning in Sociology* (Boston: Houghton Mifflin, 1961), pp. 252–258.

TABLE 9. Defeat Rates of Incumbent Governors in Presidential and Off-Years, by Period and National Success of the Governor's Presidential Party

	Governor's Presidential Party							
	Won				Lost			
	Presidential years		Off years		Presidential years		Off years	
Period	%	(N)	%	(N)	%	(N)	%	(N)
I	33.3	(9)[a]	17.6	(17)	50.0	(4)	40.0	(5)
II	42.9	(7)	50.0	(14)	45.0	(11)	41.7	(12)
III	16.7	(12)	28.6	(7)	40.0	(10)	37.5	(8)
IV	0.0	(15)	42.9	(21)	33.3	(3)	20.0	(5)
V	27.3	(11)	38.5	(13)	44.4	(18)	14.3	(7)
VI	0.0	(10)	62.5	(16)	50.0	(8)	20.0	(10)
VII	33.3	(12)	50.0	(12)	33.3	(9)	20.0	(10)

[a]Numbers in parentheses refer to the bases upon which percentages are calculated. In this table and Table 10 the number of elections in most cells is so small that the percentages should be regarded as no more than suggestive.

TABLE 10. Incumbent Governors with a Decreased Plurality in Presidential and Off-Years, by Period and National Success of the Governor's Presidential Party

	Governor's Presidential Party							
	Won				Lost			
	Presidential years		Off years		Presidential years		Off years	
Period	%	(N)	%	(N)	%	(N)	%	(N)
I	71.4	(7)[a]	66.7	(15)	100.0	(2)	60.0	(5)
II	57.1	(7)	71.4	(14)	81.8	(11)	58.3	(12)
III	66.7	(12)	85.7	(7)	60.0	(10)	62.5	(8)
IV	26.7	(15)	76.2	(21)	100.0	(3)	60.0	(5)
V	45.5	(11)	76.9	(13)	83.3	(18)	28.6	(7)
VI	40.0	(10)	93.8	(16)	75.0	(8)	50.0	(10)
VII	66.7	(12)	75.0	(12)	44.0	(9)	60.0	(10)

[a]Numbers in parentheses refer to the bases upon which percentages are calculated.

and Campbell have found, are accompanied by an exceptionally high rate of increase in the vote for one party with little or no change in the vote for the other.[37] The electorate responds differently to the stimuli of different elections. Surge and decline is thus a cyclical process—one in which the peripheral voters, drawn into the active voting universe by the stimulation of some specific short-term election situation, recede from it upon the removal of the stimulus.[38] "As long as there is no significant shift in the distribution of standing party attachments within the electorate," Campbell wrote, "the decline in turnout will almost certainly be associated with a decline in the proportion of the vote received by the presidential party."[39]

The success of incumbents would also be expected to depend on the magnitude of the presidential victory in the governor's state. To some extent this is the case, although the relationship is

[37]*Politics, Parties, and Pressure Groups*, pp. 590–591; and Angus Campbell, "Surge and Decline: A Study of Electoral Change," *Public Opinion Quarterly*, Vol. XXIV (Fall 1960), pp. 397–418.

[38]Peripheral voters form what Campbell calls "a rather inert reservoir of voters, available for service under conditions of high stimulation but not highly notivated by an intrinsic interest in politics." Campbell, "Surge and Decline," p. 409. See also Walter Dean Burnham, "The Changing Shape of the American Political Universe," *American Political Science Review*, Vol. LIX (March 1965), pp. 7–28; and William A. Glaser, "Fluctuation in Turnout," in William N. McPhee and William A. Glaser (Eds.), *Public Opinion and Congressional Elections* (New York: The Free Press, 1962), pp. 19–51.

[39]Campbell, "Surge and Decline," p. 417.

certainly not as clear-cut as might have been anticipated. State political shifts, as Table 11 suggests, may lag—perhaps considerably—behind shifts in presidential party preference. Approximately 40 percent of the incumbents whose party's nominee for the presidency polled less than 45 percent of the two-party vote actually won; however, only 25 percent of them had improved winning margins. At the other extreme, about 15 percent of the incumbents were defeated when their party's presidential nominee polled at least 60 percent of the two-party vote, and fully half had smaller pluralities. For the most part, the deviant elections occurred in periods III and VI—two periods in which voter preference for Republicans at the

TABLE 11. Articulation of Presidential and Gubernatorial Voting

% of State Vote[a] for Governor's Presidential Party	Defeated		Decreased Plurality	
	%	(N)[b]	%	(N)
Under 45	58.1	(31)[c]	76.7	(30)[d]
45–49.9	46.2	(26)	80.0	(25)
50–54.9	16.0	(25)	54.2	(24)
55–59.9	11.5	(27)	44.0	(25)
60 or more	16.1	(31)	51.6	(31)[e]

[a]Two-party vote.
[b]Numbers in parentheses refer to the bases upon which percentages are calculated.
[c]Seven of the 13 deviant elections in this cell occurred in periods III and VI.
[d]Five of the 7 deviant elections in this cell were also in periods III and VI.
[e]Seven of the 15 deviant elections in this cell occurred in period III.

TABLE 12. Indicators of Vulnerability in Landslide and Nonlandslide Presidential Years, by Outcome of Presidential Election

Governor's Presidential Party	Landslide				Nonlandslide			
	Defeated		Decreased plurality		Defeated		Decreased plurality	
	%	(N)	%	(N)	%	(N)	%	(N)
Won	7.1	(42)[a]	38.1	(42)	35.3	(34)	68.8	(22)
Lost	40.0	(20)	70.0	(20)	44.2	(43)	75.6	(31)

[a]Numbers in parentheses refer to the bases upon which percentages are calculated.

presidential level did not extend to the state level. Throughout the 1920s the national Democratic party was in disarray,[40] and in the 1950s Republicans could not entirely capitalize on Eisenhower's popularity.[41]

When presidential years are separated into two types—landslide and nonlandslide—the differences in party success are more distinct. Landslide years may be defined as those in which the presidential winner polls over 55 percent of the total national vote. Incumbents of the winning presidential party in landslide years run far ahead of incumbents of the defeated presidential party (Table 12).[42] Surprisingly, though, for incumbents of the losing presidential party the type of presidential election is not important: Their rate of defeat and their percentage with a smaller plurality are the same in both landslide and nonlandslide years. Moreover, in nonlandslide years the party differences are not large. Marked differences in Table 7, therefore, must be attributed almost solely to landslide years. On both measures of vulnerability, the ϕ expressing the relationship between the success of a governor's presidential party and the results of governors' races in nonlandslide years is very close to zero. The fact that both presidential elections in periods IV and VI were landslides accounts for the strength of incumbent governors of the winning presidential party in these decades (Tables 9 and 10). Just as significantly, it would seem to explain the relative weakness of presidential party incumbents in the 1960s.

IV

Some of the findings which emerge from this study are at variance with apparently widely held suppositions. In the first place, it was shown that governors, historically viewed, have not become more vulnerable. Briefly, gubernatorial visibility—not vulnerability—has increased. There has been,

[40]An excellent account of the plight of the Democratic party in the twenties is given in Wilfred E. Binkley, *American Political Parties* (4th ed.; New York: Knopf, 1962), pp. 349–356. See also Frank R. Kent, *The Democratic Party: A History* (New York: Century, 1928), pp. 436–517.

[41]See Herbert H. Hyman and Paul B. Sheatsley, "The Political Appeal of President Eisenhower," *Public Opinion Quarterly*, Vol. XXVII (Winter 1953–54), pp. 443–460; Angus Campbell, Gerald Gurin, and Warren E. Miller, *The Voter Decides* (Evanston, Ill.: Row, Peterson and Co., 1954); and Angus Campbell, Philip E. Converse, Warren E. Miller, and Donald E. Stokes, *The American Voter* (New York: John Wiley, 1960).

[42]The differences between the results in landslide and nonlandslide years are even more sharply delineated when Key's definition of a landslide is employed. He limits landslides to votes of lack of confidence which clearly express "a widespread unhappiness with past performance." In these elections, "the party in power, in comparison with the preceding election, loses voting strength in most counties of the nation. Though the data are lacking, the odds are that the decline in strength also permeates most social and economic classes." *Politics, Parties, and Pressure Groups*, p. 522. Three presidential elections—1920, 1932, and 1952—are classified as landslides. No incumbent of the party winning the White House in these years was defeated and only about 10 percent had a smaller winning margin. Conversely, more than half of the incumbents of the party losing the presidency were defeated, and virtually all had a negative change in their

plurality. Frank Lausche (D-Ohio) ran a somewhat stronger race in 1952 than he had in 1950, even though General Eisenhower swept the state. The electorate appears to have acted consistently though, since Lausche's Republican opponent was widely considered the more liberal of the two candidates, a kind of Republican New Dealer. Lausche, explains John Fenton, "was a Democrat, but the policies he pursued were as conservative as those advocated by any of his Republican opponents." *Midwest Politics* (New York: Holt, Rinehart, and Winston, 1966), p. 148. For an extension of the rationality argument in presidential voting see V. O. Key, Jr., *The Responsible Electorate* (Cambridge: Harvard University Press, 1966).

particularly in the past three decades, no detrimental change in the status of governors seeking reelection. In fact, today they are running farther ahead of their party's congressional nominees than ever before. The contention, therefore, that vulnerability has increased cannot be advanced to explain the weakened position of governors in contending for presidential nominations. Recent senatorial accession to the presidency is the result of other factors.

Secondly, economic and demographic differences between states are not related to vulnerability. Changes within states on these characteristics are likewise not decisive determinants of vulnerability. Urbanization, crime, unemployment, expenditures, and taxes exhibit no discernible agreement with gubernatorial vulnerability. No pattern of vulnerability was found.

And finally, the impact of presidential elections on governor's races is dependent, in general, upon the type of presidential election, and, probably more directly, upon the state vote for a governor's presidential party nominees. Incumbents of the party winning the White House do significantly better than incumbents of the defeated presidential party only in landslide presidential years. In other presidential years, the success of a governor's presidential party is not the controlling factor. States are now making an effort to isolate their politics from national political conflict; fewer are scheduling governor's elections in presidential years. In those states still holding gubernatorial elections in presidential years, however, there is strong evidence that the previous close articulation of presidential and gubernatorial voting has, to some extent, deteriorated. Keen competition in presidential elections in the 1960s, and continuing constitutional revisions by states, have recently reduced the influence which presidential candidates have been able to exert on state races.

APPENDIX

State	Examined	Not Competitive, 1900–28	Not Competitive, 1929–69	No Consecutive Reelection Permitted at Some Time Since 1900	State	Examined	Not Competitive, 1900–28	Not Competitive, 1929–69	No Consecutive Reelection Permitted at Some Time Since 1900
Alabama		X	X	X	Nebraska	X			
Arizona	X				Nevada	X			
Arkansas		X	X		New Hampshire	X			
California		X	X		New Jersey				X
Colorado	X				New Mexico	X			
Connecticut	X				New York	X			
Delaware	X				North Carolina		X	X	X
Florida		X	X	X	North Dakota		X		
Georgia		X	X	X	Ohio	X			
Idaho	X				Oklahoma			X	X
Illinois	X				Oregon			X	
Indiana				X	Pennsylvania		X		X
Iowa		X			Rhode Island	X			
Kansas		X			South Carolina		X	X	X
Kentucky				X	South Dakota		X	X	
Louisiana		X	X	X	Tennessee		X	X	X
Maine		X	X		Texas		X	X	
Maryland	X				Utah	X			
Massachusetts	X				Vermont		X	X	
Michigan		X			Virginia		X	X	X
Minnesota		X			Washington	X			
Mississippi		X	X	X	West Virginia				X
Missouri			X	X	Wisconsin		X		
Montana	X				Wyoming	X			

CHAPTER 3

GUBERNATORIAL CAMPAIGNS

There are two major themes in gubernatorial campaigning today. One is an old issue—the effect of increased taxing and spending on an incumbent's prospects for reelection. The other—new politics—has come about more recently, and it involves campaign styles and the type of issues raised in gubernatorial elections. Several of the authors in this section believe that the two themes are closely related. A governor who proposes new taxes and new programs often faces the wrath of angry voters on election day. (We explained in Chapter 1 why it is so necessary for governors to propose new taxes and new tax sources.) Yet, a governor who does not propose new taxes and new programs is often subject to a new-politics-style, issue-oriented campaign. And some governors have gone down to defeat this way. These issues are the two sides of the vulnerability question which has resulted in short tenures and fewer career opportunities for governors (Chapter 2).

The articles in this chapter explore the effect of tax issues on governors and other complexities of gubernatorial campaigns. Several questions are raised about the new politics.

What is the new politics and how new is it? The new politics has two alternative meanings. In one sense, it is a method of "scientific" campaigning; in another, it is a participatory style of politics, most recently employed by Eugene McCarthy.

The scientific methodology of new politics—employing professional mass media techniques, direct mailing to potential voters, extensive opinion polling, and even campaign simulation—was first employed over 30 years ago in the California politics. Hence, the new politics is *really* not so very new.

By the 1960s, however, new politics trends had spread to gubernatorial campaigns in all areas of the country, including, finally, the South and Rocky Mountain states. This style of campaigning is expensive and requires the talents of professionals and experts. Its utilization is thus an indication that the governor's office remains *the* important office in most states.

This in itself raises important political questions. What effect have the new campaign styles had on the type of men who seek the governorship? To what extent has the increased competition which the new politics injects into campaigning for the governor's office contributed to the vulnerability of the office? And, most important, is this new-politics phenomenon an "elitist" attempt to manipulate the voter, or is it rather an attempt to allow the voter to participate more effectively in the campaign?

ELECTING A GOVERNOR
IN THE SEVENTIES
James Clotfelter
and
William R. Hamilton

In gubernatorial campaigns, as in limited wars, the objective is "not to lose." And, as in limited wars, not losing is easier for the insurgent who has no bridges to protect and who can be on the offensive constantly. Guerilla forces, in limited-war strategy, attempt to bleed their more powerful opponents until they accept defeat; the positive build-up of their own position can take place only after their opponents' credibility with the people has been undercut.

Gubernatorial politics has not yet become as dangerous as Indochina, but the analogy has some merit. Negative politics characterizes all campaigns, of course, but gubernatorial elections are peculiarly susceptible, and the place of the incumbent is becoming increasingly difficult. In the 1970s the governorship, like big-city mayoralties, may become the seat of almost mandatory unpopularity—so much so that ambitious politicians, recognizing that it is less valuable as a stepping-stone to the Senate or presidency, avoid running for governor.

At present, however, the governor's office remains a valued electoral prize in most states, and is pursued with the full panoply of new-politics methodology: professionally-manicured television spots (either structured agency ads—for Republicans—or newsreel style *cinema verité*—for Democrats); computer simulation; carefully programmed direct-mail campaigns; and extensive polling. According to the press, the record of political image-makers was tarnished by erratic results in 1970 campaigns. "I don't think there are any geniuses," one image-maker commented after the election. Geniuses or not, gubernatorial candidates around the country—including areas such as the South and the Rocky Mountains, which had lagged behind new politics trends—increasingly are depending upon professional campaign guidance.

What does the campaign advisor have to work with? Who runs for governor? As in the past,[1] gubernatorial candidates come from the state legislature, state and federal elective offices, law enforcement positions, and sometimes administrative positions. The new consumer issues have made offices such as attorney general and comptroller general visible, and state legislative leaders and lieutenant-governors continue to be frequent candidates.

Most of state politics has been characterized as a setting with "low visibility"[2] and "low salience."[3] But the governor's electoral problem is quite the reverse. It is a vulnerable office because of the incumbent governor's high political visibility. A governor's record is often more visible and salient to voters than a U.S. senator's record. Even as well-publicized a figure as Vice-President Spiro Agnew was recognized by fewer Georgians than were the two gubernatorial candidates to be discussed below. In October 1970, less than 1 percent of a state sample failed to recognize the names of Jimmy Carter and ex-Governor Carl Sanders, and only 10 to 15 percent had no opinion of them, whereas 3.5 percent failed to recognize the controversial Vice-President, and 25 percent had no opinion of him. A governor, increasingly, is likely to have a higher unfavorable performance rating than a senator and therefore is more likely to be defeated. In 1970, in almost all of the more than 20 states surveyed by William R. Hamilton and Staff, the governor had a higher negative rating than the incumbent U.S. senators—regardless of whether they were of the same party or whether the governor or senator was up for reelection. The two most important characteristics of gubernatorial contests, then, as contrasted with other

[1] Joseph A. Schlesinger, *How They Became Governor* (East Lansing: Michigan State Governmental Research Bureau, 1957), and his more recent work. Gubernatorial candidates apparently have continued to be younger than their previous-generation counterparts, with more formal education, and a large percentage of lawyers. See Schlesinger, *Ambition and Politics: Political Careers in the United States* (Chicago: Rand McNally, 1966).

[2] James W. Fesler (Ed.), *The 50 States and Their Local Governments* (New York: Knopf, 1967), pp. 202 ff.

[3] M. Kent Jennings and Harmon Zeigler, "The Salience of American State Politics," *American Political Science Review*, Vol. LXIV (June 1970), pp. 523–535.

major elections, are:

1. The governor's program is highly visible, especially regarding taxes. Daniel R. Grant and H. C. Nixon point out that a governor's fate increasingly is tied to "the one big tax battle" at some point during his term.[4] Because of the heightened demands for schools, highways, recreation, and other services, and because of most states' inadequate revenue sources, few governors can avoid this battle for four years.

2. There is an "anti-" flavor to campaigns and voters' attitudes. Governors, even those former governors who (as in most southern states) are forced by state laws to wait four years before seeking reelection, find election to a second or third term difficult. What analysts call the "classic anti-incumbent campaign"—"it's time for a change"—is proving more successful in gubernatorial than in senatorial races.

Any governor has to make decisions. The decisions he makes will more closely involve the individual than many of the decisions made by U.S. senators—sales taxes on food versus Vietnam and HEW appropriations. Where a senator votes on a vast range of complex subjects far off in Washington, a governor must decide on a smaller range of better understood subjects close to home.

A candidate planning to run against a governor or ex-governor can count on attracting voters antagonized by his opponent on each of a number of decisions any governor must make. Sometimes, it resembles a "coalition of intense minorities" situation, or an "Arrow problem," where the incumbent cannot possibly please a stable majority because of the range and type of decisions he must make. Further, most pollsters agree that "anti" voters have more motivation to participate actively and vote than "pro" voters.

Because of these characteristics of gubernatorial campaigns, some campaign consultants are finding that running a candidate from a nonvisible office such as state senator or representative, or a candidate with no meaningful political experience, is preferable to running a candidate with a high recognition factor—and the vulnerabilities that go with such recognition. Any man who has held an executive position has a record that he cannot avoid, and has made enemies across the state, in his party, and among important groups; a relatively unknown fig-

[4] *State and Local Government in America* (2nd ed.; Boston: Allyn & Bacon, 1968), p. 303.

ure has not yet accumulated such enemies. An unknown is easier for the image-builders to deal with; because of the absence of publicly-recognized past behavior, the candidate does not have to be defensive. He can attack the incumbent with little fear of having to defend his own flank: He has no flank. Arkansas Governor Winthrop Rockefeller, defeated for reelection in 1970 by a self-styled "country lawyer," said of his opponent's strength: "He was new. He was fresh. He had no record."

The independence of gubernatorial politics from national political trends varies by states and, of course, by whether state elections are held in presidential election years. Just as most gubernatorial campaigns are in large part independent of national factors, the day of the local community opinion-molder is over in most regions. Gubernatorial candidates cannot be content with winning the support of key individuals or organizations, and then letting them "deliver" the votes in their constituencies. Today, as the political merchandisers tell candidates, voters by-pass local "influentials" and rely upon their visual impressions of candidates as perceived through the mass media. Less well-known candidates, therefore, are urged to go over the heads of party bosses, ethnic leaders, and economic bloc leaders—straight to the voters through television, radio, print media, billboards, or computer-typed letters. This type of "mass politics," of course, requires that the candidate and his managers understand how average voters and target groups feel. Polls are used to answer these questions about the voters:

1. What are the most important issues, and how strongly do voters feel about them? How are candidates (especially the opponent) perceived to stand on these issues?

2. What specific issues are important enough to a majority of voters to affect their voting decision, and can these issues be welded into a campaign theme?

3. How many and which voters recognize and approve of the opposing candidates?

4. How does the overall political climate of the constituency, including campaigns of other candidates on both sides, affect the race?

5. What are the damaging images that voters have of the candidate or party, and what are the favorable images? What is the image of the incumbent administration, or of the opponent's previous administration?

Before the campaign begins, the candidate should be alerted by polls to his chances of winning against alternative opponents and to the "state of the market" (the issue and partisan orientations of important voting groups). The fear is sometimes expressed that polls interfere with the democratic process by discouraging candidates who fare poorly in initial polls from even offering themselves to the voters (e.g., George Romney in the 1968 presidential primaries). However, the 1970 experiences of underdogs in Arkansas, Florida, Georgia, and other states show that it is the polls' suggestions of voter *movement* (actual and potential) that are most important to a determined candidate. Issues—and the images that issue positions help to build—are important to candidates, Dan Nimmo points out,[5] because candidates have more control over issues and images than they do over the partisan distribution of their constituency. Despite widespread voter indifference on many issues, then, candidates still find it advantageous to "run on the issues," to appear well informed; they try to talk about issues without taking stands. The media, Nimmo also points out, are more willing to publicize issue positions than calls for party loyalty, although it should be added that the media prefer dramatic-style campaigning (e.g., senatorial candidate Lawton Chiles' 1,003 mile walk through Florida) to most discussion of issues.

To illustrate the methods of gubernatorial campaigning, we shall examine the 1969–70 Jimmy Carter campaign for governor in Georgia. (One of the authors, William Hamilton, conducted five statewide polls for the Carter campaign between September 1969 and October 1970. He served as an advisor on strategy to both Mr. Carter and his advertising agency.)

THE CARTER CAMPAIGN: PEANUTS, POPULISM, AND "ANTI-ISM"

This is the door to an exclusive Country Club, where the big money boys play cards, drink cocktails, and raise money for their candidate: Carl Sanders." (Country club door opens; closeup of man writing check.) "People like us aren't invited. We're busy working for a living." (Footage of Carter talking with "average man.") "That's why our votes are going for Jimmy Carter. Vote Jimmy Carter, *Our* kind of man, *Our* kind of governor.

This twenty-second television commercial was part

[5] *The Political Persuaders* (Englewood Cliffs, N.J.: Prentice-Hall, 1970), p. 24.

of the anti-Carl Sanders thrust of the last three weeks of Jimmy Carter's primary campaign for the Georgia Democratic gubernatorial nomination. With a carefully prepared "average man" campaign, Carter moved from 32 percent behind widely-respected former Governor Sanders in September 1969 (when Carter was known by only half of the electorate) to an upset 48–38 percent primary lead the next September and a 60–40 percent runoff victory two weeks later. In the general election he held most of his supporters and won back some of Sanders's for a 59–41 percent victory over Republican Hal Suit. In a state where the Republican candidate had led the balloting in 1966 (but lost the governorship in the General Assembly), the Republicans lost every statewide office up for election and suffered losses in the legislature.

Carter's victory was one of personal campaign style rather than a mandate to change specific policies. In a state whose rural gallus-snappers have had little claim to be called populists, Carter campaigned as a Populist, what we would call a *stylistic Populist*. His symbols were his own expressed concern for the workingman and his identification of Sanders as too wealthy to understand the average man, too citified and sophisticated ("Cufflinks Carl") and too liberal for Georgians, too closely tied to the political and economic "power structure" of Atlanta and Washington. Carter appealed to the anti-Establishment feelings of his target groups: rural whites and urban blue-collar whites. Eighty-one percent of his February 1970 supporters agreed that "the average man today doesn't have any control over what goes on in government," and it was control and understanding that Carter promised. To defeat Sanders, who had the support of most black leaders, he had to put together the Wallace-Maddox coalition. But because of Carter's own racial attitudes and the belief that black voters might be needed in the general election, this coalition had to be constructed *without* an antiblack appeal.

To see how this voting group was put together, we should go back to the beginning of the campaign. For Carter, a two-term state senator, the contest began at the end of the 1966 gubernatorial campaign; he entered that race late, ran as a moderate against former Governor Ellis Arnall (a liberal), Lester Maddox, and others, and barely missed the primary runoff. Maddox, who placed second, went on to win the runoff and became governor despite trailing the Republican candidate in popular votes, and Carter spent the next two and one-half years speaking to every civic and women's club he could find.

Eighteen months before the fall of 1970 the Carter advisors began laying groundwork for the direct campaigning aspects of the governor's contest: How could he defeat (1) the then popular former governor and (2) the Republican candidate in November?

Their strategy, based partially on poll results and partially on the candidate's political acumen and philosophy, had three parts:

1. to build a generally favorable image of Carter as a man capable of handling the job of governor;
2. to build the image of Carter as "our kind of man," a man who understands the problems of the working man;
3. to "unmake a governor," to show the sophisticated, wealthy, Northeastern Establishment liberalism of Carl Sanders as contrasted to Carter.

Strategy number one was fairly obvious. Sanders was seen as a man who had "done a good job" as governor—one who had brought credit to Georgia. To become an acceptable alternative, Carter had to show that he could at least handle the job adequately.

The second strategy was a little longer in coming to the fore. In the September 1969 poll both Sanders and Carter were seen by the voters as more liberal than themselves. At that time it was unclear as to which, if any, segregationist candidate would enter the race to claim a large chunk of the rural and small-town vote on the race issue alone.

Blacks already were supporting Sanders. So Carter made the decision to approach the Wallace-Maddox "agrarians," not on the race issue but as a Populist—a man who understood their problems, was of them, and therefore would treat them right in terms of their traditional values and economic well-being. This Populism was intended to be a large enough umbrella for blacks to come under should they want (at least after the primary) and also to appeal to the blue-collar workingman in Atlanta and other urban areas. Groups whose votes were not being depended upon included blacks and urban professional and white-collar classes, except insofar as a "Middle American" campaign would attract members of these groups.

In 1969 rural Georgians who were concerned about integration and agreed with Populistic alienation statements thought both Sanders and Carter were too liberal. But Sanders was better known, and as he said after his defeat, "I was frozen in. Everybody knew what I was and what I stood for. I couldn't get out there on the streets in June and start waving my arms and saying, 'Hooray for George Wallace.' People knew me too well. It wouldn't have worked." By taking a Populistic approach and by not publicizing his moderate racial views, Carter hoped to keep a serious segregationist candidate out of the race. He hoped to appeal to a large part of the Wallace vote—as was charged by Sanders and other critics—but he hoped to attract that vote on a dimension other than race.

The third part of the campaign strategy had two purposes. First, if Sanders was shown to be the antithesis of the small town, rural, and working Georgian, it could only make Carter look better in these voters' eyes. Also, early polls showed that Sanders would probably win the primary without a runoff if it "were held today." Thus, some candidate, either a minor candidate (there were eventually eight candidates) or Carter had to begin to cut into Sanders' vote. Poll results also showed that at least 20 to 25 percent of Sanders' existing support was "soft," meaning that they did not care for Sanders on at least one dimension. The dimensions on which Sanders appeared most vulnerable were his affluence since leaving the governor's office, his big-city ways and his ties to the Atlanta "bigwigs" and limousine liberals, and his closeness to Washington.

To run as a neo-Populist against the wealth and exposure of a former governor, a candidate needs certain personal qualities which Carter possessed, and he needs *not* to have certain qualities. He had some money, but his affluence came from his peanut farm and warehouse in Plains, Georgia, a small town far from the corrupting influences of Atlanta. He was a former nuclear physicist and submarine officer, but he looked, dressed, and acted like a friendly Georgia boy, not a city-slicker professional. His campaign could be tailored for stylistic Populism because he had no public record through service in a visible state office. He could choose his issues—issues and styles on which his opponent was vulnerable.

Because many of the local party leaders were

pledged to support Sanders, Carter chose two other methods of getting his messages to the voters: his own personal campaigning *and* television.

Beginning in the fall of 1969 Carter began ranging about central and south Georgia where the majority of his target groups lived. While he attempted to set up county organizations and still speak to civic clubs, he concentrated more on getting out on Main Street or to the country store or gas station and meeting the folks. In the Atlanta area he spent his time almost exclusively at factory gates during shift changes and at shopping centers located in the heart of working-class precincts; he campaigned, he said, "where the people are," and claimed to have met half a million Georgians personally.

The new politics was not totally new to Georgia. These techniques had been used in the Republican gubernatorial campaign of 1966 and were being used by Sanders in 1970. Sanders was spending a large amount for media advertising, while Carter was having difficulty raising funds from the usual corporate sources. Despite a tight budget, Carter also used many new-politics techniques. But he usually kept the polls quiet, and according to his advertising man, Gerald Rafshoon, "slickness was avoided—if we got a rough cut on a film we let it stay." Using the experts is not what the voters might expect from a Populist candidate.

Carter's advertising and personal campaigning was aimed at middle- and lower-middle-income whites, housewives, and blue-collar families generally. Country-music programs, television movies, and soap operas received much of the estimated quarter-million-dollar Carter television budget. The first wave of pro-Carter "image-building" commercials began in March 1970 and dealt with the candidate's Georgia background ("The Carters have lived and farmed in Sumter County since 1840 . . . "), his various careers ("After the death of his father . . . the young lieutenant returned to his native Plains . . . and on a shoestring started a successful peanut and cotton warehouse . . . "), and specific issue areas (urban problems, conservation, and taxes). A 30-minute program with Carter talking to 50 people about various issues was used for image-building at this point, but later the campaign went to 20-, 30-, and 60-second spots. In July some of these spots hinted at the stronger anti-Sanders campaign to follow; one, for example, showed Carter on a tractor in the fields helping with the peanut harvest:

Jimmy Carter knows what it's like to *work* for a living. He still puts in twelve hours a day in his shirt sleeves on the farm at Plains during peanut harvest. . . . Can you imagine any of the *other* candidates for governor working in the hot August sun? No wonder Jimmy Carter has a special understanding of the problems facing everyone who works for a living. . . ."

The picture chosen for his billboards ("Isn't it time somebody spoke up for you?") fit into his "rough" media image; a campaign aide said an intentionally "ugly" picture of the somewhat "Kennedyesque" Carter was chosen. "It made Jimmy look like an average workingman," the aide said. "He had a little fear in him. He was proud, a little wary perhaps."

Carter's fund-raising spots emphasized that other candidates were supported by "*big* money asking *big* favors," and that "Jimmy Carter made it the *hard* way." Carter was shown talking to laborers at an Atlanta manhole, hunting, and with his family: "Your kind of man," the commercial said. At least one program was scheduled after a Billy Graham television revival, and viewers were urged to see both. A specific appeal for "Middle American" support said: "You're a good citizen. You work hard, pay your taxes, respect the law. Isn't it time somebody in government did something about *your* problems?" On panels where other candidates talked about busing or taxes, Carter said the real issue was "who will control the government— the people or a small band of men?"

Carter's polls showed a gradual slippage in support for Sanders while Carter stayed at slightly below a third of the Democratic support. Sanders dropped from 55 to 50 percent to slightly below 50 percent in early August. While continuing to say they supported Sanders, some voters came to agree that Carter would be more likely than Sanders to "give the average man a voice in government," and others became concerned about Carter's charge of Sanders' misuse of his office. To make it into the runoff in an impressive manner, however, Carter had to cut further into Sanders' near majority. As of early August, Sanders was still hanging on to many of his latent defectors. In the final three weeks of the primary the Carter campaign was devoted largely to relieving Sanders of this "soft" support.

Now strongly anti-Sanders television commercials were used, including the country club ad mentioned earlier. Spots showed Sanders and Hubert Humphrey laughing and asked, "Why are these men laughing?" Another asked why Sanders should be elected *again:*[6] "So he can wheel and deal with his Washington buddies and the big money boys? You and I say *never again.*" Although lack of finances forced Carter to curtail radio and newspaper ads, Sanders' support slipped away precipitously in the final three weeks, as Carter ran up a surprising 48 percent plurality.

Runoff commercials claimed that Carter supporters had "voted to run our lives *without* outside interference." The rest of the themes were unexceptional: for clean government and law and order, against "the old pay-off politics" and unfair taxes. During the two weeks between the primary and the runoff election, Sanders attempted desperately to shift his image away from that of the cool, sophisticated, upper-middle-class attorney in a business suit—which his own expensive and slickly-edited advertising had helped to create—to that of a gut-issue man of the people. But some of Sanders' local political leaders—looking for a winner—went over to Carter, and Sanders failed to pick up much of the other candidates' votes. Carter won the runoff by a three-to-two margin.

Winning the Democratic nomination for governor used to be, in the pundit's words, "tantamount to election" in Georgia. But in 1966 the Republicans gave "tantamountcy" a bad scare, and in 1968 five Democratic members of the state cabinet switched to the Republican party.

Carter faced former Atlanta newsman Hal Suit, who had never held public office, and who was to receive little support from the state Republican organization. Suit had defeated one of the party switchers for the Republican gubernatorial nomination. His main theme was that he was a "concerned citizen" and Carter, like Suit's primary opponent, was the professional politician. The *Atlanta Constitution's* editor wrote, "Carter's primary campaign was an elemental, visceral appeal to the voters to distrust politicians. Lo and behold, now he is one." After he won the primary, college students began to give Carter a hard time across the state: "Now I'm the Establishment candidate," Carter explained. Suit's campaign attempted to play upon these new uncertainties about Carter—uncertainties born of being a winner, the man on top. Suit also sought to portray himself as a man of the people in south Georgia, scorning the big-city "asphalt jungles" and extolling the glories of game-hunting.

Where the Carter-Sanders primary campaign had been mean and protracted, the six-week Carter-Suit campaign was to be relatively mellow, with each accusing the other of being a "liberal" and each praising Maddox, who was running an easy race for lieutenant-governor. (Maddox, according to Carter, was "the essence of the Democratic party. . . . He has compassion for the ordinary man.") Maddox, in turn, agreed that *both* candidates were liberals and charged them with supporting the 1964 Civil Rights Act.

The most important factors in the general election campaign were (1) Carter's retention of the "average man" image, and (2) the revived strength of the Democratic party. Carter's "common man" image was not hurt by his association with Maddox.[7] Fifty-two percent in an October state survey agreed that "Jimmy Carter seems to care more about average working people than Hal Suit does," while only 28 percent disagreed. Among blue-collar classes, Carter's "sensitivity to the average man" was mentioned as a positive characteristic as often as all other characteristics of his "performance profile" combined.

Despite some predictable difficulty in combining the Sanders and Carter forces because of the rough primary campaign, the Democratic party appeared more unified than a dominant party usually is. Even Senator Richard Russell, whom Suit had eulogized in a biography and television documentary, and who usually stayed out of campaigns other than his own, endorsed the straight Democratic ticket and said he was confident that Carter

---

[6] "Again" was a major word used in all Sanders advertising. The Carter campaign sought to make their opponents work for them in other ways too. In a "Br'er Rabbit and the Briar Patch" episode during the summer, Carter goaded the Atlanta newspapers into attacking him. "We loved all those scurrilous cartoons," a Carter campaign manager said. To rural Georgians, the newspapers represented the Atlanta liberal and moneyed Establishment.

[7] Campaign advertisements for Maddox claimed he had "provided the first pipeline from the Statehouse to the People in our lifetime" through his "Little Man's Day" at the governor's mansion. He was accused by the Republican candidate for lieutenant-governor of being a liberal Populist.

would win. Carter also called for straight-ticket voting, and felt sufficiently confident of party loyalties to utter such traditional accusations as, "The last time the Republicans had power in Georgia they burned Atlanta." Maddox made contradictory statements regarding endorsement of Carter, but of seventeen questions he directed at both candidates, most reflected unfavorably on the Republicans. Suit, despite his hopes of encouraging Suit-and-Maddox votes, appeared to lose his patience with the governor and criticized him publicly.

"Two years ago and six years ago," Carter said, "it was hard to get people to admit they were Democrats. One of the reasons was that people like myself had nothing to say about the operations of the party." He proposed extensive reforms of party machinery for delegate selection and other functions. Despite widespread assumptions about the erosion of Democratic ties to the party of their fathers, Georgians continued to vote in the Democratic primary. Only 10 percent in October 1970 said they considered themselves Georgia Republicans, compared with 67 percent who said they were Georgia Democrats. (In terms of national self-identification, the Democrats also held an overwhelming advantage: 61%–14%.) The voters saw themselves as moderate conservatives (14 percent liberal, 39 percent moderate, and 32 percent conservative), and they saw Carter and the Georgia Democratic party in the same terms (the latter was 15–32–25 percent). The Georgia Republican party was still a mystery, with 42 percent being unable to identify it by ideology.

On the other side, Suit received visits from the President and Vice-President, but was apprehensive that Vice-President Spiro Agnew's visit would hurt him rather than help him. He told Georgians that he had not invited Agnew and that the Vice-President would not "say one word against the Democrats." He urged Agnew not to attack Georgia Democrats or to urge voters to support Suit. Carter had been saying that Georgians did not like to be told how to vote by "big shots" from the national administration, and later claimed that an anti-big-shot reaction increased his winning margin. Carter even used the visits to support his Populist image, telling rallies that he had defeated the "Atlanta power structure" in the primary, and that in the general election he had a "fight on my hands with the Washington power structure."

The press talked of a last-minute Suit surge, but Carter won with 59 percent of the vote. Carter won almost every county outside the Atlanta metropolitan area where Suit was well known as a television personality. Every Democratic candidate for statewide administrative position was elected as two more "turncoats" were turned out of office and straight-ticket voting was widespread.

CONCLUSION

Although this case study involves a southern state, it is somewhat idiosyncratic, not in the usual southern sense (one-party dominance), but because Carl Sanders was as popular as any former governor could hope to be. But, much as Florida's Leroy Collins, a popular former governor, discovered when he ran for the U.S. Senate in 1968, initial popularity did not protect Sanders from erosion of support. Sanders' central weakness, ironically, was his visible *success* in economic and national political affairs, and this record of "success" became Carter's target for criticism. Further, even a popular former governor is vulnerable to the "Arrow problem"[8] strategy discussed above.

Polls in 1970 showed that most governors who had been in office two years or more were generally unpopular. Take two Republican governors, for example: Florida's Claude Kirk was highly controversial and his performance rating was poor, but Pennsylvania's nationally-respected Raymond Shafer also had an unimpressive performance rating. Seven nominated incumbents were defeated for reelection that year, and other former governors were defeated in primaries or in races for other offices.

The unpopularity of these defeated state executives was often attributed, in polls, to voter antagonism toward their tax programs—or, in some cases, to their failure to tax the right people (e.g., the absence of a Florida corporate tax). Worse, the tax issue is only part of the governor's "buck-stops-here" problem: The plethora of issues conspires against him. For the 1970s it appears that governors will face a difficult battle for election after having spent two to four years in office, especially against opponents without records of their own. A governor, in such a contest, always will start out ahead in preference polls: He is better known than his opponents, and his "errors" have yet to be focused on. But part of his support,

[8] Anthony Downs, *An Economic Theory of Democracy* (New York: Harper & Row, 1957), pp. 60–61.

such as the blue-collar workers who said they supported Sanders, is "soft" and will leave him as the campaign intensifies.

The Georgia situation also illustrates points that may be peculiar to the South and to this time period: (1) A "new face" gubernatorial candidate can exert a powerful influence in bringing together a factionalized party for electoral purposes, if he has ties to no entrenched (especially "national") faction; (2) "outsiders," no matter how popular, cannot be used against a gubernatorial candidate, because the governor is supposed to run his own state for the benefit of his own people; and (3) stylistic Populism may have become a campaign theme particularly suited to anti-incumbent races.

SOUTHERN GOVERNORS AND POLITICAL CHANGE: CAMPAIGN STANCES ON RACIAL SEGREGATION AND ECONOMIC DEVELOPMENT, 1950-1969*
Earl Black

Writing in the late 1940s, V. O. Key predicted that such factors as urbanization, Negro out-migration, and the spread of commerce and industry would gradually "create conditions favorable to [political] change"[1] in the American South. In the interval since Key wrote, the southern economy has been steadily moving "from rural-agricultural to urban-industrial."[2] Only a tenth of the region's labor force were employed in agriculture by 1960, a decline of almost 60 percent since 1940. Out-migration reduced the percentage of blacks in the 1960 southern population to 21 percent, and majorities of both blacks (58 percent) and whites (56 percent) resided in urban areas. Socioeconomic changes such as these, together with a series of challenges to the South's caste system of race relations, have produced a "slow-moving social revolution of significant proportions."[3]

*Reprinted by permission from the *Journal of Politics*, Vol. 33 (August 1971), pp. 703-734.

[1] V. O. Key, Jr., *Southern Politics in State and Nation* (New York: Knopf, 1949), pp. 674-675.

[2] James G. Maddox *et al.*, *The Advancing South: Manpower Prospects and Problems* (New York: The Twentieth Century Fund, 1967), p. 22. Statistics used in the first paragraph are drawn from this source, pp. 23-27.

[3] *Ibid.*, p. 19.

Concentrating on the period 1950-69, this paper attempts to document and assess the views of one set of white politicians in the South concerning two dimensions of this "social revolution," racial segregation and the role of state governments vis-à-vis economic development. The theoretical importance of elite studies is readily apparent from Key's research. In *Southern Politics* he argued persuasively that the region had constructed "no system or practice of political organization and *leadership* adequate to cope with its problems."[4] A decade later Key reached the general conclusion that "the critical element for the health of a democratic order consists in the beliefs, standards, and competence of those who constitute the influentials, the opinion-leaders, the political activists in the order."[5] The broad question raised here concerns the ways in which white politicians, in an era of rapid socioeconomic change, have dealt with two policy areas of great substantive importance. To oversimplify somewhat, we are investigating the extent to which the South has begun to acquire "leadership adequate to cope with [some of] its problems."

Our focus on white elites is also designed to help fill a gap in the literature of contemporary southern politics. White politicians possess a relevant but comparatively neglected perspective on political change.[6] Much has been written regarding the political activities of black southerners at both the

[4] Key, *Southern Politics*, p. 4. Emphasis added.

[5] V. O. Key, Jr., *Public Opinion and American Democracy* (New York: Knopf, 1961), p. 558.

[6] The most comprehensive history of white political activists during the 1950s is Numan V. Bartley, *The Rise of Massive Resistance* (Baton Rouge: Louisiana State University Press, 1969). There are several useful but specialized studies of white southern politicians. See, e.g., Marshall Frady, *Wallace* (New York: World, 1968); Robert Sherrill, *Gothic Politics in the Deep South* (New York: Grossman, 1968); J. Harvie Wilkinson III, *Harry Byrd and the Changing Face of Virginia Politics, 1945-1966* (Charlottesville: The University Press of Virginia, 1968); James R. Soukup, Clifton McCleskey, and Harry Holloway, *Party and Factional Division in Texas* (Austin: University of Texas Press, 1964); James W. Silver, *Mississippi: The Closed Society* (New York: Harcourt Brace Jovanovich, 1964); Walter Lord, *The Past That Would Not Die* (New York: Harper & Row, 1965); Howard H. Quint, *Profile in Black and White* (Washington: Public Affairs Press, 1958); William C. Havard, Rudolf Heberle, and Perry H. Howard, *The Louisiana Elections of 1960* (Baton Rouge: Louisiana State University Press, 1963); and A. J. Liebling, *The Earl of Louisiana* (New York: Simon and Schuster, 1961).

elite and mass levels,[7] but there has been no systematic, long-range study of white political elites. These politicians deserve scrutiny, if for no better reason than that they have monopolized state offices in the past and seem likely to do so indefinitely. The white elite under consideration consists of all politicians elected governor from 1950–69 in the eleven ex-Confederate states.[8] Governors were chosen for study because their role as chief executive has frequently made them central figures in racial conflict and in matters affecting economic development.

To reduce the topic to manageable proportions and to facilitate longitudinal and cross-sectional comparisons, the orientations of white politicians concerning racial segregation and economic development will be ascertained through an examination of their campaign rhetoric. Since all governors campaign for public office, campaign rhetoric may be utilized as a common and accessible indicator of the elite policy views we wish to assess. It must be stressed, however, that the concern of this paper is *not* with political campaigns as such, but rather with two analytic dimensions—racial segregation and economic development—assumed to be present in campaigns and to vary over time. These particular issues were selected for analytic purposes—that is, because the caste system and the comparative lack of economic development have

long been recognized as fundamental regional problems. Because of the difficulty of devising typologies applicable to politicians across eleven states over a twenty-year period, our analysis will be confined to two policy dimensions considered especially pertinent for an understanding of white elites. Clearly, racial segregation and economic development have not been the only important issues in southern campaigns, but they have been significant ones, with implications for the nature of race relations and for the allocation of economic resources.

Although our interest is limited to two policy fields, we shall try to compensate for this narrow focus by examining all of the region's governors over a reasonably lengthy and highly eventful period in southern history. The specific question we are researching may be expressed as follows: Among those white southern politicians who have won governorships, what changes on the racial segregation and economic development dimensions may be mapped out since 1950?

Using terms employed by Matthews and Prothro, regional findings will be controlled for differences between two subregions, the Deep South (Alabama, Georgia, Louisiana, Mississippi, and South Carolina) and the Peripheral South (Arkansas, Florida, North Carolina, Tennessee, Texas, and Virginia).[9] Previous research has established the importance of subregional comparisons. With regard to white political behavior, Matthews and Prothro used survey data to show that Deep South whites were more committed to "strict segregation" and less aware of the true racial attitudes of blacks than Peripheral South whites.[10] Cosman, analyzing the 1964 presidential election, found Peripheral South whites less willing to vote on the basis of racial prejudice than whites in the Deep South.[11] Distinctive subregional patterns, it will be demonstrated, exist for white politicians as well as for whites generally.

Since any conclusions rest upon the accuracy of the original classifications, the procedures used to code individuals need to be elaborated. Data on the governors' campaign stances have been gath-

[7]See, e.g., Donald R. Matthews and James W. Prothro, *Negroes and the New Southern Politics* (New York: Harcourt Brace Jovanovich, 1966); Harry Holloway, *The Politics of the Southern Negro* (New York: Random House, 1969); H. D. Price, *The Negro and Southern Politics* (New York: New York University Press, 1957); Everett C. Ladd, *Negro Political Leadership in the South* (Ithaca: Cornell University Press, 1966); William Keech, *The Impact of Negro Voting* (Chicago: Rand McNally, 1968); Andrew Buni, *The Negro in Virginia Politics, 1902-1965* (Charlottesville: The University Press of Virginia, 1967); Stokely Carmichael and Charles V. Hamilton, *Black Power* (New York: Random House, 1967); Pat Watters and Reese Cleghorn, *Climbing Jacob's Ladder* (New York: Harcourt Brace Jovanovich, 1967); and Howard Zinn, *SNCC: The New Abolitionists* (Boston: Beacon Press, 1964).

[8]This paper is drawn from a larger study, now in progress, of southern governors and the Negro since 1950. Here our attention will be limited to *successful* southern politicians. No attempt will be made in this paper to compare the policy orientations of successful with unsuccessful candidates, delve into the intricacies of campaign strategy, or relate the views of campaigners to their performance in office.

[9]Matthews and Prothro, *New Southern Politics*, p. 169.
[10]*Ibid.*, pp. 355–357.
[11]Bernard Cosman, *Five States for Goldwater* (University: University of Alabama Press, 1966), pp. 120-125 *et passim*.

ered primarily from state newspapers.[12] Because southern newspapers vary widely in terms of the frequency, comprehensiveness, and biases of their campaign coverage, the more elaborate techniques of content analysis were not considered appropriate. No attempt has been made to produce generalizations on the order of "Governor A advocated defiance of the *Brown* decision in twice as many speeches as Governor B." We are essentially concerned with the substance of a politician's references to racial segregation and economic development. To determine these policy orientations, two newspapers were selected for each state and all articles pertaining to a given gubernatorial election, including reports of stump speeches, television addresses, profiles of candidates, and the like, were read. For Arkansas, Louisiana, and Mississippi, where coverage seemed adequate or where a second newspaper was unobtainable, a single source was used. Campaign reportage was followed on a day-by-day basis for each stage (Democratic first primary, Democratic second primary, and, when closely contested, the general election) of the southern electoral process. Coverage typically began some six weeks before the first primary. Depending upon whether a second primary was necessary to determine the Democratic nominee and whether a Republican actively sought the office, each campaign was followed for a period of six to fourteen weeks. As stories were read, notes (ranging from lengthy quotations to brief comments) were taken on the policy stances of each politician. Using these notes and applying criteria to be specified shortly, southern governors were then classified according to their campaign stances on racial segregation and economic development. Classifications of individual governors are listed in the appendix.

[12] The following newspapers were used: Birmingham *News* and Montgomery *Advertiser* (Alabama); *Arkansas Gazette* (Arkansas); Miami *Herald*, Tampa *Tribune*, and St. Petersburg *Times* (Florida); Atlanta *Constitution* and Atlanta *Journal* (Georgia); New Orleans *Times-Picayune* (Louisiana); Raleigh *News and Observer* and Charlotte *Observer* (North Carolina); Jackson *Clarion-Ledger* (Mississippi); Columbia *State* and Charleston *News and Courier* (South Carolina); Nashville *Banner*, Nashville *Tennessean*, and Memphis *Commercial Appeal* (Tennessee); Dallas *Morning News*, Houston *Post*, and *Texas Observer* (Texas); and Richmond *Times-Dispatch* and Washington *Post* (Virginia).

SOUTHERN GOVERNORS AND RACIAL SEGREGATION

With respect to southern electoral politics, the Supreme Court's 1954 school desegregation decision ultimately accomplished what the white primary and FEPC controversies of the 1940s failed to achieve: the revival of an extraordinarily divisive issue—the "place" of the Negro—that most white southerners had assumed or considered settled beyond challenge. There might be differences of style, tone, and emphasis, but white politicians in the years before *Brown v. Board of Education* were united by "a common resolve indomitably maintained—that it shall be and remain a white man's country."[13] It seems worthwhile, therefore, to examine systematically the white politician's historic commitment to racial segregation during the years in which the legal basis for the caste system was destroyed. If southern racial traditions *have* been appreciably altered since 1954, change should be discernible over time in the rhetoric of successful candidates for the governorship.

In terms of racial segregation, governors will be categorized as *strong* or *militant segregationists, moderate segregationists,* or *nonsegregationists.* Since the purpose of the analysis is to gauge change (or continuity) in southern racial norms, the typology has been designed to identify the point at which winning candidates for a major state office, as a practical matter, cease to campaign as racial segregationists. Failure to advocate and defend the caste system will be regarded as a significant break with tradition, whether or not such politicians openly align themselves with efforts to end racial segregation. No nominal classification of this sort, relying on newspaper accounts of campaign rhetoric, can aspire to complete objectivity, but his typology is offered as one means of comparing the campaign racial stances of governors over time and between subregions. The results appear to be, to borrow one of Key's phrases, "within shouting distance of the realities."

Slightly less than half (45 percent) of the southern governorships settled between 1954 and 1969 were won by politicians whose campaigns were characterized by a militant defense of racial segregation. (Percentages mentioned here and in the following paragraphs are taken from Table 4.) Cam-

[13] Ulrich B. Phillips, "The Central Theme of Southern History," *American Historical Review*, Vol. 34 (October 1928), p. 31.

paigners who satisfied *at least one* (most met more) of the following criteria have been considered *strong* or *militant segregationists:*

1. The candidate expresses unambiguous, emphatic, and more or less unqualified opposition to racial desegregation and support for racial segregation. No countervailing values (e.g., the duty to comply with federal court orders) are recognized that would dilute this commitment to the maintenance of a caste system.
2. The candidate makes his defense of racial segregation (or opposition to desegregation, HEW guidelines, etc.) a leading campaign theme. The segregation issue is discussed incessantly and can be traced in most campaign speeches.
3. The candidate appeals to racial prejudice (e.g., designating an opponent as the "NAACP candidate") to discredit his opposition.

Though found in far greater proportion in the Deep South (70 percent from 1954–69) than in the Peripheral South (30 percent), militant segregationists were elected governor of every southern state at some point after the *Brown* decision. Representative strong segregationists include Mississippi's Ross Barnett, Alabama's George Wallace, and Virginia's Lindsay Almond. Typical statements from Barnett's 1959 campaign illustrate, in an extreme form, the militants' opposition to racial change: "I don't believe God meant for the races to be integrated," he told Mississippi audiences. "God placed the black man in Africa and separated the white man from him with a body of water." Barnett described himself as a "firm and unwavering believer in the complete segregation of the races" and believed even token school desegregation would have disastrous consequences. "Integration has ruined every community in which it has been practiced," he asserted. "I would rather lose my life than see Mississippi schools integrated."[14]

Approximately one-third (32 percent) of the post-*Brown* governors shared the militants' antipathy for racial desegregation without treating segregation as an issue of commanding importance. Governors who described themselves as racial segregationists in their campaigns but who did not meet the criteria established for strong segregationists have been designated *moderate segregationists.* The adjective "moderate" is employed for want of a better term. Since the word is frequently used by militant segregationists to describe a white who seems insufficiently committed to the caste system, it should be noted that no such connotation is implied in this paper. Here all moderates are segregationists. The following statements apply to most moderates:

1. The candidate favors racial segregation and opposes desegregation, but these preferences are usually qualified by other values and commitments. While promising to do his best to preserve segregation or limit desegregation, he often expresses his intention to respect decisions of the federal judiciary.
2. The candidate does not make the defense of racial segregation a leading campaign issue. Racial segregation is supported primarily as a matter of regional tradition, a commitment routinely expected of serious officeseekers. References to segregation tend to be brief and perfunctory; campaign speeches typically focus on nonracial issues.
3. The candidate avoids appealing to racial prejudice to discredit his opposition. On the contrary, more militant opponents may be attacked for race-baiting.

Victorious moderate segregationists include Georgia's Carl Sanders (in 1962), Florida's LeRoy Collins, and Louisiana's Earl Long. Sanders' 1962 campaign against former Governor Marvin Griffin, a strong segregationist of the Eugene Talmadge school, exemplifies the approach of the moderate segregationist. The candidate called for law and order and denounced Griffin as an "agitator." While Sanders promised to employ "every legal means to preserve segregation of the races in Georgia," he would never "put a padlock on a schoolhouse." "I am a segregationist," Sanders said. "I believe in equal opportunity but if I am elected governor I will not tolerate race-baiting or race-mixing."[15]

Southern officeseekers traditionally supported the region's caste system. Depending upon the situation, racial segregation might or might not become an explicit issue in pre-*Brown* campaigns,

[14] Jackson *Clarion-Ledger*, June 14; July 2, 15–16, 1959.

[15] Atlanta *Constitution*, July 13, 27; August 8, 16, 1962.

but it could safely be assumed that all serious politicians regarded themselves as racial segregationists. Candidates who doubted the justice of the social order did not ordinarily share their reservations with the electorate. In view of the tenacity of southern racial norms, the emergence of *nonsegregationists* is a development of considerable significance. Nonsegregationists won nearly one-quarter (23 percent) of the governor's races from 1954 to 1969. This category is purposively inclusive. The nonsegregationist classification might have been subdivided into racial neutrals or indifferents, moderate integrationists, and strong integrationists, but too few nonsegregationists have been elected governor to justify such a detailed breakdown. Nonsegregationists range from a minority of governors who adopted fairly specific pro-civil rights stances to politicians who simply chose, for varying reasons, not to identify themselves publicly as racial segregationists. Many of these governors, then, were essentially indifferent to the merits of segregation versus desegregation in their campaigns and sought generally to be as noncommittal as possible concerning the caste system. These politicians usually fell into one of the following varieties:

1. Whatever his private beliefs, the candidate does not campaign openly as a segregationist. For all practical purposes, he seeks to avoid explicit stands on racial issues; he champions neither segregation or desegregation.
2. The candidate does not describe himself as a segregationist or as an integrationist, but he expresses qualified support for some black demands. Statements concerning race tend to be indirect and highly abstract (e.g., the candidate favors "equality of opportunity"). Black support is welcomed.
3. The candidate explicitly and unambiguously favors various Negro rights. Racial segregation may be explicitly repudiated; black support is welcomed.

No more than a curiosity in the Deep South,[16]

nonsegregationists won a third of the Peripheral South governorships from 1954 to 1969. Examples include Tennessee's Buford Ellington (in 1966), Texas' John Connally, Arkansas' Winthrop Rockefeller, and Virginia's Linwood Holton. While Ellington's remarks in his 1966 campaign are *not* representative of most nonsegregationists, they serve as a concrete example of political change. The self-proclaimed "old-fashioned segregationist" of the 1958 gubernatorial campaign told Tennesseans that he had changed his mind concerning racial segregation:

Change is an ever constant factor in men's culture. Values change. Standards change. Convictions change. Change is the theme of social growth.

I say this by way of making a frank face-up to the matter of discrimination on account of race and color. I am sure that all Americans are agreed that the word segregation . . . based on race . . . is a term that is obsolete.

. . . Let's bury the word and practice of segregation. Let's stay in step with the times.[17]

The rise and partial decline of the segregation controversy in recent southern electoral politics is evident in Figure 1, which graphs the campaign racial stances of Deep South and Peripheral South governors since 1950.[18] For most governors in the pre-*Brown* years, racial segregation was a latent or, at most, secondary issue. No one was elected governor who questioned the merits of the caste system, yet only a small minority, unevenly distributed even within the Deep South, campaigned as militant segregationists. The average governor (86 percent) ran as a moderate segregationist. These politicians would affirm their loyalty to southern racial customs if circumstances required it; otherwise, they ignored the topic or minimized the relevance of the segregation issue by arguing that the Negro's "place" was a closed question. Southern apologists have often contended that the *Brown* decision undermined race relations in the region and that southerners were slowly "working out the problem" on their own. An examination

---

[16]The sole Deep South nonsegregationist in this period was a borderline case. Louisiana's John McKeithen avoided racial issues in his 1967 campaign for reelection. After the election was over McKeithen told a New Orleans civic group that "We believe in equal opportunity for all. We want Negroes in state government and jobs, the state police. Thank goodness for this old Southern state—it has

finally turned the clock and got into the twentieth century." New Orleans *Times-Picayune*, November 16, 1967.

[17]Nashville *Banner*, June 24, 1966.

[18]Graphs used in this paper are based on five intervals of four years, beginning in 1950. Because all of the southern states except Arkansas and Texas (and Tennessee until 1954) elect governors for four-year terms, each interval includes data on two governors for those states with two-year terms and on one governor for the remaining states.

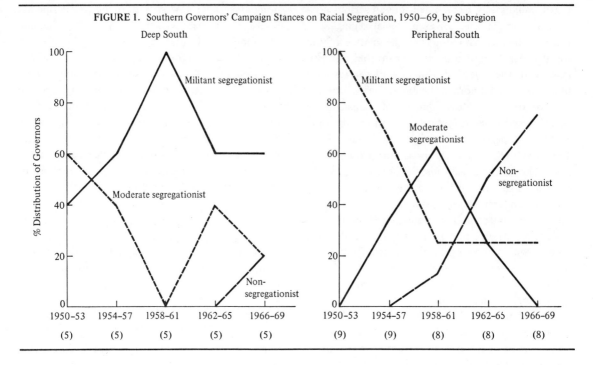

FIGURE 1. Southern Governors' Campaign Stances on Racial Segregation, 1950–69, by Subregion

of the tone and content of campaign rhetoric in the early 1950s indicates the mythic nature of this belief. The relative absence of stemwinding racist oratory in southern campaigns did not signify any gradual internal transformation of a segregated social order. A few white politicians did propose that steps be taken to improve the quality of black education, but certainly no successful candidate argued against the principle of racially segregated public schools. The belated interest in Negro education was mainly an effort to put a measure of equality into the "separate but equal" doctrine.[19]

Southern campaigners responded predictably once the Supreme Court ordered school desegregation. Ambitious politicians, to put it mildly, perceived few incentives to advocate compliance. In the mid-1950s, blacks were generally ill-organized politically; whites did most of the voting and preferred racial segregation; and neither the President nor the Congress appeared anxious to help the Supreme Court implement school desegregation. Campaigners consequently denounced the *Brown*

decision. Militants won 43 percent of the southern governorships from 1954 to 1957, again outnumbered by moderate segregationists (57 percent). Had the Supreme Court ordered immediate desegregation, instead of compliance "with all deliberate speed," the percentage of strong segregationists would doubtless have been considerably higher.

Militant segregationists reached the height of their regional influence in the late 1950s and early 1960s, often in specific response to the 1957 school desegregation crisis in Little Rock. The political rewards of conspicuously defying federal authority were demonstrated to white politicians across the South by Arkansas Governor Orval Faubus's landslide reelection in 1958. Seventy-seven percent of the gubernatorial contests from 1958 to 1961 were won by militants, a showing approached by no other type of candidate at any time after 1954. Only two moderate segregationists were successful during the period, and, for the first time, a borderline nonsegregationist was elected.[20]

To an inordinate degree, elections for governor during the first eight years after the *Brown* deci-

[19] For an analysis of the segregation issue in pre-*Brown* gubernatorial campaigns, see Earl Black, "Southern Governors and the Negro: Race as a Campaign Issue since 1954" (unpublished Ph.D. thesis, Harvard University, 1968), pp. 52–80.

[20] Compared to his previous campaigns, Texas Governor Price Daniel in 1960 did not discuss racial segregation.

sion reflected the white South's determination to perpetuate racial segregation. Three-fifths (59 percent) of the governorships were captured by strong segregationists, another third went to moderate segregationists, and the remaining contest was won by a nonsegregationist. Militancy was particularly evident in the Deep South, where 80 percent of the governors from 1954 to 1961, compared to 47 percent in the Peripheral South, campaigned as strong segregationists.

Despite the Wallace movement, the consensus among white southern politicians concerning racial segregation increasingly evaporated in the 1960s. Half as many strong segregationists (38 percent) were elected in the South from 1962 to 1965 as were chosen during the previous four years. The percentage of moderate segregationists doubled (31 percent), and, more significantly, there was a four-fold rise (31 percent) among nonsegregationists.

The regional trend toward fewer winning segregationists (whether militants or moderates) accelerated in the last half of the 1960s. Data on the thirteen governorships decided from 1966 to 1969 clearly indicate the erosion of the white South's traditional solidarity regarding racial segregation. Militant segregationists won 23 percent of the elections, less than one-third of their victories in the late 1950s, and moderates accounted for another 23 percent. For the first time in the history of the modern South, half of the region's governors campaigned as nonsegregationists. The ability of nonsegregationists to *survive* the electoral process is one indication that significant political change is occurring in the South.

Two factors—the role of the federal government and Negro voting—appear of central importance in the decline of segregationist campaign rhetoric in the 1960s. The occasional intervention of the federal executive to impose school desegregation gradually expanded the arena of racial conflict from small, isolated southern constituencies to Washington, thus making it more difficult for local whites to preserve total racial segregation.[21] A series of

federal-state confrontations, all lost by the militants, ultimately suggested to many politicians the futility of continued defiance on the *principle* of racial desegregation, and passage of the Civil Rights Act of 1964 and the Voting Rights Act of 1965 meant that white southerners could no longer claim that racial change lacked a congressional mandate. With the enactment of federal aid to education in 1965, funds being contingent upon some degree of desegregation, local school districts were given a strong economic incentive to integrate.[22] Once *widespread* (though generally token) school desegregation began, most campaigners outside the more recalcitrant Deep South states came to accept some measure of racial integration as a political reality.

The rise in black political participation in the 1960s, while one of the most dramatic accomplishments of the civil rights movement, must be seen in the perspective of white participation patterns. On the assumption that higher levels of black voter registration vis-à-vis white registration indirectly reflects the strength of black political organization within a state, differences in statewide voter registration *rates* were calculated by subtracting the percentage of eligible Negroes registered to vote in a given year from the comparable white figure. As Table 1 indicates, the magnitude of these differences in registration rates is strongly associated (gamma = .79 and lambda b = .53) with the campaign racial stances of governors elected in the 1960s. The more blacks have been mobilized in rough proportion to whites, the more likely candidates have been to avoid militantly segregationist postures. In elections where the difference in registration rates was lower than 15 percentage points, 90 percent of the winners were nonsegregationists.

As long as decisions affecting Negroes were confined to the local level, blacks could expect little sympathy for their grievances. *Private Power and American Democracy* (New York: Knopf, 1966), pp. 91–118, 176–178. On the application of federal pressure for (limited) racial change, see, e.g., Anthony Lewis *et al.*, *Portrait of a Decade* (New York: Random House, 1964), pp. 104–124; and Harold C. Fleming, "The Federal Executive and Civil Rights: 1961–1965," in Talcott Parsons and Kenneth B. Clarke (Eds.), *The Negro American*, (Boston: Houghton Mifflin, 1966), pp. 371–399.

[22] For a detailed account of the politics of the HEW school desegregation guidelines, see Gary Orfield, *The Reconstruction of Southern Education* (New York: John Wiley-Interscience, 1969).

[21] E. E. Schattschneider has argued that "the scope of a conflict determines its outcome" and that Negro civil rights is a kind of issue that benefits from broad attention. *The Semisovereign People* (New York: Holt, Rinehart & Winston, 1960), pp. 7–8 *et passim*. More recently, Grant McConnell has stressed the importance of constituency size as a factor in resolving racial (and other) issues.

TABLE 1. Southern Governors' Campaign Stances on Racial Segregation and Differences in White and Black Voter Registration Rates, 1960–69 (%)

	Differences in Registration Rates*				
Campaign Racial Stance	High	Medium	Low	Totals	*N*
Strong segregationist	70	27	10	35	(11)
Moderate segregationist	20	55	0	26	(8)
Nonsegregationist	10	18	90	39	(12)
Totals	100	100	100	100	(31)
Number of cases	(10)	(11)	(10)	(31)	

*High = 30 or more percentage point difference between percentage of eligible whites registered to vote and percentage of eligible blacks registered; Medium = 15–29.9 percentage points difference; Low = less than 15 percentage points difference. Where data was not available for exact election year, the average of the preceeding and succeeding years was used. For the 1969 Virginia election, 1968 estimates were employed.

Sources of voter registration estimates: U.S. Commission on Civil Rights, *1961 Report*, Vol. I, *Voting*, (Washington, D.C.: U.S. Government Printing Office, 1961), pp. 252–307; Pat Watters and Reese Cleghorn, *Climbing Jacob's Ladder* (New York: Harcourt Brace Jovanovich), Appendix II; and "Voter Registration in the South, Summer, 1968" (Atlanta: Voter Education Project, Southern Regional Council, 1968), n.p.

Where whites have registered at vastly higher rates than blacks, successful campaigners have commonly emphasized traditional segregationist views. Seventy percent of the elections in which differences exceeded 30 percentage points were won by strong segregationists. If blacks within a state become sufficiently well organized to approximate white registration levels, they may influence campaign rhetoric (by raising the costs of race-baiting) even while constituting a small percentage of the total electorate.[23] Outside the Peripheral South, however, Negroes have been unable to narrow the registration gap appreciably. The difference between the registration rates of whites and blacks in the Deep South declined from 41.9 percentage points in 1964 to 26.4 points in 1968. Comparable figures for the Peripheral South are 7.4 in 1964 and 9.1 in 1968.[24]

Thus the rise of the nonsegregationist governor has been limited primarily to the Peripheral South. Sixty percent (compared to 13 percent in the Peripheral South) of the winning Deep South candidates from 1962 to 1969 were militants and

[23]There is no comprehensive analysis of the relationship of black voter organizations to statewide politics. For a recent study of black organizations in several large southern cities, see Holloway, *Southern Negro*, chaps. 7–10.

[24]These estimates were computed from voter registration data found in the sources listed in Table 1.

only 10 percent (63 percent in the Peripheral South) were nonsegregationists. The Goldwater sweep in 1964, George Wallace's ability to carry the Deep South (South Carolina excepted) in 1968, and Wallace's renomination for the Alabama governorship in 1970 indicate the persistence of racial segregation as a significant campaign issue in much of the Deep South. While unadulterated segregationist oratory may give way to comparatively subtle, euphemistic language, the transition from segregationist to nonsegregationist, if it occurs at all, will be extremely difficult in states like Alabama and Mississippi. On the other hand, the principle of racial segregation is now virtually dead as an explicit campaign issue in the Peripheral South. No politician campaigning as a militant segregationist has been elected governor in that subregion since 1964, and nonsegregationists have won the governorship at least twice in Tennessee, Texas, Virginia, and Arkansas.

SOUTHERN GOVERNORS AND ECONOMIC DEVELOPMENT

Politicians throughout the South have encouraged the development of economic systems grounded less on agriculture and more on commerce and industry. "Southern governors have become the de facto executive directors of the state chambers of commerce," Dunbar has written, "and spend their time competing with each other as suppliants for new plants."[25] But if the goal of economic development has been universally shared, there has been less agreement concerning what southern state governments should do to expedite economic growth. (We take for granted that southern politicians routinely support various state-authorized subsidies for new industry and invariably claim to be better qualified than their opponents to attract new payrolls into their states.) Differing conceptions of the state government's role regarding economic development are particularly significant because of the long-standing deficiencies of public education in the South. A recent analysis of the southern labor force emphasizes the relationship between economic development and quality education and concludes that:

The shortages of skilled workers, of technicians, of scientists, of managerial ability among small businessmen, and of risk-taking entrepreneurs are serious stumbling blocks to further industrialization and technological development of the South. Education and training that sufficed for the southern agricultural labor force are not adequate to meet the demands of today's manpower market and certainly will not be adequate in the years to come in the industries of the South and elsewhere in the nation.[26]

Given comparatively low standards of living and inadequate educational systems, what roles have white politicians envisioned for state government regarding economic development? On the basis of the governor's stance toward (1) public education and (2) class-oriented politics, four responses will be differentiated: *marginalist*, *adaptive*, *neo-Populist/marginalist*, and *neo-Populist/adaptive*. Although we are primarily interested in how politicians have related public education to economic development, we also wish to isolate the few successful southern candidates who have generally favored the expansion of redistributive economic programs.

Nearly half (45 percent) of the gubernatorial elections held from 1954 to 1969 were won by campaigners whose approach to education and economic development minimized the financial responsibilities of the state. *Marginalists* have been defined as follows:

1. The candidate does not advocate substantially increased state spending for public education.

Although marginal improvements in the educational system may be favored, the candidate's campaign rhetoric reflects overriding concern with the present costs of state government. Economy in government is commonly stressed; budget-cutting may be advised.

2. The candidate's speeches do not reflect a view of politics as (more or less) a struggle between "haves" and "have-nots." Redistributive economic programs are not emphasized.

Marginalist campaigners rarely advocated a significant expansion of social welfare programs (e.g., old-age pensions) or aligned themselves noticeably with "have-not" groups within the state. Virginia's A. S. Harrison, Texas's Allan Shivers, and Louisiana's Jimmie Davis exemplify the marginalist. Harrison, the Byrd Organization's candidate in 1961, attacked his opponent's "ultraliberal approach to state finances" and promised to preserve Virginia's "sound, economical, constructive, progressive, honest government." The root issue for Harrison was whether the state would "abandon the sound political philosophies we have followed for 50 years." If the national business community thought Virginia was becoming a "free-wheeling, free-dealing, socialist, spending state, we might as well fold up our tents and steal away as far as getting new industry is concerned."[27]

A growing number of successful candidates (34 percent of the post-*Brown* governors) have taken the position that long-range economic growth requires an assumption of far greater financial support for public education by the states themselves. By proposing the expansion or creation of trade schools, community colleges, state university systems, and the like, *adaptives* have attempted to enhance job opportunities for individuals and to make their states more attractive to industry. Politicians who met the following criteria have been considered adaptives:

1. The candidate favors substantially increased state support for public education and commonly describes the improvement of education as having a high priority in his administration. Increased expenditures for education may be explicitly defended as an investment in future economic development.

2. The candidate's rhetoric does not reflect a view

[25] Leslie W. Dunbar, "The Changing Mind of the South: The Exposed Nerve," *Journal of Politics*, Vol. 25 (February 1964), p. 20.

[26] Maddox *et al.*, *The Advancing South*, p. 208.

[27] Richmond *Times-Dispatch*, June 6–7, 1961.

of politics as (more or less) a struggle between "haves" and "have-nots."

Redistributive economic programs are not emphasized. Like the marginalists, adaptives have typically been indifferent, if not hostile, to increased spending for social welfare programs. Representative adaptives include Texas's John Connally (in 1964 and 1966), North Carolina's Terry Sanford, and Georgia's Carl Sanders. Campaigning for reelection in 1964, for example, Connally described his fundamental goal as an improvement of the state's educational system so that more Texans might "share in the economic fruits of the technological space age."[28]

A dwindling fraction of southern governorships (15 percent since 1954) were won by *neo-Populist/ marginalists*. The campaign rhetoric of these politicians, unlike that of marginalists and adaptives, is grounded in a more or less articulate conception of politics as conflict between "haves" and "have-nots." Neo-Populist/marginalists have urged the redistribution of state resources in directions calculated to benefit "have-not" groups, and this redistributive orientation distinguishes them from adaptives and marginalists. Neo-Populist/marginalists may be characterized as follows:

1. The candidate does not advocate substantially increased state support for public education. Marginal improvements (e.g., higher teacher salaries, hot lunch programs for schoolchildren) may be vigorously supported.
2. The candidate's rhetoric reflects a view of politics as (more or less) a struggle between "have" and "have-nots" (e.g., "special interests" versus "the people"). The candidate emphasizes his willingness to expand such social welfare programs as old-age pensions.

Few campaigners of this type have been elected governor since 1954. Arkansas's Orval Faubus, who accounts for six of the eight governorships won by neo-Populist/marginalists, was the only politician of this category to succeed in the 1960s, and Faubus defies easy classification. While he originally ran as a neo-Populist/marginalist in the Sid McMath tradition, he later established close ties with leading segments of the Arkansas business community. Since his campaign rhetoric, which emphasized the redistributive achievements of his administrations, remained basically consistent over

the years, he has been considered a neo-Populist/ marginalist.[29] Alabama's James Folsom and Louisiana's Earl Long, both elected in the mid-1950s, were the other victorious neo-Populist/marginalists. With the exception of Faubus in his 1958 and 1960 campaigns, these politicians have run as moderate segregationists.

Over time neo-Populists have become more aware of developmental questions, so that it is possible to identify a small but influential group of *neo-Populist/adaptives*. This category combines the redistributive perspective of the neo-Populist/ marginalist with the adaptive's concern for public education. Neo-Populist/adaptives, who won 6 percent of the post-*Brown* governorships, may be described as follows:

1. The candidate favors substantially increased state support for public education and commonly describes the improvement of education as having a high priority in his administration. Increased expenditures for education may be explicitly defended as an investment in future economic development.
2. The candidate's rhetoric reflects a view of politics as (more or less) a struggle between "have" and "have-nots" (e.g., "special interests" versus "the people"). The candidate emphasizes his willingness to expand such social welfare programs as old-age pensions.

Georgia's Lester Maddox and Alabama's George and Lurleen Wallace, all of whom were militant segregationists, were the only successful neo-Populist/adaptives from 1954 to 1969. As George Wallace's career illustrates, the fusion of racism with welfare politics has been a potent combination in Alabama.[30] Though his economic proposals received far less attention than his bizarre views on race, Maddox wanted to double educational expenditures in Georgia and denounced his Republican opponent as a rich man who "would be a lot better off if he knew about people as well as dollars." While he led Georgia, Maddox said, there would be "no more of the rich getting richer and the poor poorer."[31]

[28] Dallas *Morning News*, April 25, 1964.

[29] On Faubus's career, see Roy Reed, "Another Face of Orval Faubus," *New York Times Magazine*, October 9, 1966, pp. 44 ff.; and Sherrill, *Gothic Politics*, pp. 110–114.

[30] See Frady, *Wallace*.

[31] Atlanta *Constitution*, October 11, 15, 17; November 1, 1966.

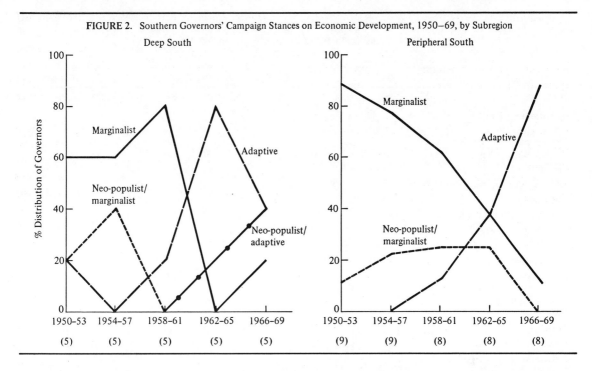

FIGURE 2. Southern Governors' Campaign Stances on Economic Development, 1950–69, by Subregion

Figure 2 graphs the economic development position of successful gubernatorial candidates by subregion for the period 1950–69. Roughly three-quarters of the southern governors chosen during the 1950s campaigned as marginalists, politicians who believed the state could best encourage economic growth by limiting its own spending and, using tax advantages as bait, by energetically recruiting new industry. Neo-Populist/marginalists won all but one of the remaining governorships, and campaigners like Long and Folsom were less interested in economic development per se than in redistributing existing resources to benefit "have-not" groups directly. Price has summarized the policy consequences of this situation:

The politics of black belt vs. nonblack belt or of agrarian protest vs. Big Mules is fascinating to behold, but essentially a merry-go-round. The most interesting thing is the campaign itself, not any substantive policy results. Such politics is cyclic, if not plain static.[32]

White politicians in the 1950s were generally more interested in defending racial segregation in the

[32]Hugh Douglas Price, "Southern Politics in the Sixties: Notes on Economic Development and Political Modernization" (a paper read at the annual meeting of the American Political Science Association, Chicago, September 1964; mimeographed), p. 10.

public schools than in proposing or supporting any innovative, expensive role for the state regarding long-term economic development. At a time when many politicians contemplated closing the public schools to prevent desegregation, it made little political sense to advocate substantially higher investments in public education.

In the 1960s, as the region's need for a better educated, more skilled labor force became more obvious and, at least in the Peripheral South, as the school desegregation controversy waned, southern campaigns grew somewhat less "static." Adaptives emerged as a relatively progressive voice in southern politics, winning a majority of the governorships contested in the decade. Marginalists won less than a third as many elections (19 percent) from 1962 to 1969 as they had in the previous eight years (70 percent). The rise of the adaptives and the decline of the marginalists occurred in both subregions.

Separate examinations of the racial segregation and economic development dimensions, two fundamental components of the South's "social revolution," have demonstrated that important changes have taken place within each policy area since the *Brown* decision. If white politicians are beginning to respond to a vastly more complex socioeconomic and political environment, these

TABLE 2. Distribution of Racial Segregation and Economic Development Categories, pre-*Brown* and post-*Brown*, Among Southern Governors, by Region and Subregion (%)

| | Pre-*Brown* | | | Post-*Brown* | | | | | | | | |
| | 1950–53 | | | 1954–61 | | | 1962–69 | | | 1954–69 | | |
Campaign Stance	DS	PS	Reg	DS	PS	Reg	DS	PS	Reg	DS	PS	Reg
Strong segregationist												
Marginalist	20	0	7	70	35	48	10	13	12	40	24	30
Neo-populist/marginalist	20	0	7	0	12	7	0	0	0	0	6	3
Neo-populist/adaptive	0	0	0	0	0	0	30	0	12	15	0	6
Adaptive	0	0	0	10	0	4	20	0	8	15	0	6
Moderate segregationist												
Marginalist	40	89	71	0	29	19	0	6	4	0	18	11
Neo-populist/marginalist	0	11	7	20	12	15	0	13	8	10	12	11
Neo-populist/adaptive	0	0	0	0	0	0	0	0	0	0	0	0
Adaptive	20	0	7	0	6	4	30	6	15	15	6	9
Nonsegregationist												
Marginalist	0	0	0	0	6	4	0	6	4	0	6	4
Neo-populist/marginalist	0	0	0	0	0	0	0	0	0	0	0	0
Neo-populist/adaptive	0	0	0	0	0	0	0	0	0	0	0	0
Adaptive	0	0	0	0	0	0	10	56	38	5	27	19
Total	100	100	100	100	100	100	100	100	100	100	100	100
Number of cases	(5)	(9)	(14)	(10)	(17)	(27)	(10)	(16)	(26)	(20)	(33)	(53)

Key: DS = Deep South; PS = Peripheral South; Reg = Region.

changes in elite orientations should be complementary.

THE POLICY DIMENSIONS COMPARED

The changing policy stances of southern governors are suggested by Table 2, which shows the distribution of the combinations of racial segregation and economic development categories before and after the *Brown* decision. While the typical pre-*Brown* governor (71 percent from 1950 to 1953) campaigned as a moderate segregationist and marginalist, since 1954 the modal governor across the South has been the militant segregationist/marginalist (30 percent), followed by the nonsegregationist/adaptive (19 percent). Moderate segregationists who were marginalists or neo-Populist/marginalists each accounted for a tenth of the governorships. Other possible combinations occurred rarely or not at all. For example, a handful of strong segregationist/adaptives (all from the Deep South) and nonsegregationist/marginalists (both from Texas) were elected. Of greater significance for southern politics, *no* nonsegregationist/neo-Populist (whether marginalist or adaptive) won a governorship during the years 1954–69. A white politician might succeed as either a nonsegregationist or a neo-Populist (marginalist or adaptive), but the combination was considered radical by southern standards. Such politicians as Texas' Don Yarborough, Florida's Robert King High, and Alabama's Richmond Flowers were repeatedly assailed as "ultraliberal" and defeated.

Marginalists with militantly segregationist views, the dominant southern combination in the late 1950s (winning 48 percent of the governorships from 1954 to 1961), clearly declined in the 1960s as a regional force (12 percent from 1962 to 1969). Mississippi remains the most obvious stronghold for this type of politician. The racial stances of adaptives have shifted over time. During the early 1960s, winning adaptives were segregationists (militant or moderate) more frequently than nonsegregationists, but as the salience of the segregation issue lessened, they increasingly assumed nonsegregationist stances. The modal southern governor in the last half of the 1960s, unlike his predecessors, campaigned both as a nonsegregationist and as an adaptive.

Cross-tabulation of the variables indicates that, despite subregional differences, the racial segregation and economic development dimensions are associated. Across the South in the years 1954–69,

TABLE 3. Campaign Economic Development Stances of Southern Governors, 1954–69, by Racial Segregation Position and Subregion (%)

Campaign Stance on Economic Development	Campaign Stance on Racial Segregation											
	Deep South				Peripheral South				Region			
	SS	MS	NS	T	SS	MS	NS	T	SS	MS	NS	T
Marginalist	57	0	0	40	80	50	18	48	67	35	17	45
Neo-populist/marginalist	0	40	0	10	20	33	0	18	8	35	0	15
Neo-populist/adaptive	21	0	0	15	0	0	0	0	13	0	0	6
Adaptive	21	60	100	35	0	17	82	33	13	29	83	34
Totals	100	100	100	100	100	100	100	100	100	100	100	100
Number of cases	(14)	(5)	(1)	(20)	(10)	(12)	(11)	(33)	(24)	(17)	(12)	(53)

Key: SS = Strong Segregationist; MS = Moderate Segregationist; NS = Nonsegregationist; T = Totals.
Tau beta values: Deep South = .45; Peripheral South = .50; Region = .45.

TABLE 4. Campaign Racial Segregation Stances of Southern Governors, 1954–69, by Economic Development Position and Subregion (%)

Campaign Stance on Racial Segregation	Campaign Stance on Economic Development														
	Deep South					Peripheral South					Region				
	M	NP/M	NP/A	A	T	M	NP/M	NP/A	A	T	M	NP/M	NP/A	A	T
Strong segregationist	100	0	100	43	70	50	33	0	0	30	67	25	100	17	45
Moderate segregationist	0	100	0	43	25	38	67	0	18	36	25	75	0	28	32
Nonsegregationist	0	0	0	14	5	13	0	0	82	33	8	0	0	55	23
Totals	100	100	100	100	100	100	100	0	100	100	100	100	100	100	100
Number of cases	(8)	(2)	(3)	(7)	(20)	(16)	(6)	(0)	(11)	(33)	(24)	(8)	(3)	(18)	(53)

Key: M = Marginalist; NP/M = Neo-Populist/Marginalist; NP/A = Neo-Populist/Adaptive; A = Adaptive.
Tau beta values: Deep South = .45; Peripheral South = .50; Region = .45.

two-thirds of the successful militant segregationists were also marginalists and over four-fifths of the winning nonsegregationists were adaptives. (See Table 3.)

The data in Tables 3 and 4 show basic subregional variations concerning the economic development positions associated with particular stances on racial segregation. In the tradition-bound Deep South, the most significant differences with respect to economic development are those separating militant from moderate segregationists. Nearly three-fifths of the Deep South militants were marginalists, but none of the successful moderate segregationists campaigned as undiluted marginalists. By contrast, in the comparatively open political culture of the Peripheral South, differences are more apparent between segregationists (of whatever variety) and nonsegregationists. While four-fifths of the Peripheral South's militants and half of its moderates were marginalists, adaptives comprised 82 percent of the nonsegregationists there. An examination of subregional differences be-

tween the percentage of elections won by strong segregationists and nonsegregationists reveals, again, fundamental contrasts. For the post-*Brown* period, the Deep South figure (65) is over 20 times greater than that of the Peripheral South (−3).

Consideration of the economic development dimension suggests that, with several qualifications, similarities are more striking than differences. Governors in both subregions who adopted "traditional" (i.e., marginalist or neo-Populist/ marginalist) positions on economic development generally held "traditional" views on racial segregation (i.e., strong or moderate segregationist). (See Table 4.) Deep South adaptives were mainly militants or moderates (both 43 percent), but the relationship between adaptive orientations and segregationist stances was reversed in the Peripheral South: four-fifths of the adaptives there were nonsegregationists. Aside from the inability of neo-Populist/adaptives to win Peripheral South governorships, economic development types have done about as well in one subregion as in the other, and the difference between the percentage of elections won by marginalists and adaptives is actually smaller for the Deep South (5) than for the Peripheral South (15). Primarily because racial segregation has been the inherently more controversial and divisive issue, distinctive subregional patterns have been more apparent for racial segregation than for economic development.

CONCLUSIONS

We have argued that a growing percentage of successful contenders for southern governorships may be described as nonsegregationists and that the appearance of these candidates is one indication of meaningful political change in the South. Compared to the political atmosphere of the late 1950s and early 1960s, considerable progress has been made, in many states, toward eliminating or reducing the explicitness of the more blatant forms of race-baiting. In most Peripheral South campaigns the principle of racial segregation is a dead or dying issue; and truculent demands for the preservation of racial segregation have frequently been replaced by more euphemistic language in the Deep South. The spectrum of politically feasible expression on matters concerning the caste system has broadened significantly, especially in the Peripheral South, since the *Brown* decision.

At the same time, it must be emphasized that the decline of segregationist oratory, where it has occurred, has not been accompanied by much specific attention to the socioeconomic needs of black southerners. Progress in civil rights, as measured by the campaign rhetoric of white politicians, has been more verbal than substantive. Because of the minority position of blacks and the indifference or hostility of many whites, it seems improbable that many white candidates will use campaigns to articulate fundamental problems—employment, education, housing, law enforcement, and welfare—of blacks in the South. Black gains have been associated more with "Liberty" than with "Equality."[33] The right to participate in politics has largely been won, but the concept of "equal results" has not been seriously raised in state campaigns. Moreover, the decline of explic-

itly segregationist rhetoric does not necessarily mean that white politicians have given up "race" as a campaign issue. Our concern has been to trace changing elite attitudes toward racial segregation, an important but not the sole indicator of the race issue. Many white candidates have and will find ways to appeal to antiblack prejudices without describing themselves as segregationists.

While the shifts that have occurred in the campaign rhetoric of many governors are less than monumental and fall exceedingly short of the region's needs, they should not be dismissed as trivial. As Dunbar has suggested, southern history provides a perspective for evaluating the events of the last two decades:

... [W]e can note that any government has but three possible postures toward the question of racial equality: in favor, opposed, or neutral. The political theory of the South has for more than three centuries been grounded on the principle of white supremacy. It has been the cardinal doctrine. If ... southern state governments were to follow the lead already given by some municipalities, and move from opposition to neutrality, this would be a truly historic change.[34]

A systematic analysis of racial segregation as a campaign issue indicates that, particularly in the Peripheral South, signs of a shift by white elites "from opposition to neutrality" have become more and more visible.

During the 1960s many governors also reached a new understanding of the state's role regarding economic development. Numerous white politicians have become less concerned with the size of the state budget per se and more willing to support substantially higher state spending for public education as a long-range investment in economic development. By the end of the 1960s, then, many southern governors could be differentiated from their predecessors by a comparatively reduced preoccupation with the principle of racial segregation and by a heightened interest in adaptive economic development policies. A sizeable proportion of white politicians, in short, were *beginning* to frame issues of greater relevance to the needs of the contemporary South.

[33] See Daniel Patrick Moynihan, "Employment, Income, and the Ordeal of the Negro Family," in Parsons and Clark, *Negro American*, pp. 134–135.

[34] Dunbar, "The Changing Mind of the South," p. 18.

Southern Governors' Campaign Stances on Racial Segregation and Economic Development, 1950–69

Deep South				Peripheral South		
Governor	Year elected	Classification		Governor	Year elected	Classification
Alabama					**Arkansas**		
G. Persons	1950	MS	M	S. McMath	1950	MS	NP/M
J. Folsom	1954	MS	NP/M	F. Cherry	1952	MS	M
J. Patterson	1958	SS	M	O. Faubus	1954	MS	NP/M
G. Wallace	1962	SS	NP/A	O. Faubus	1956	MS	NP/M
L. Wallace	1966	SS	NP/A	O. Faubus	1958	SS	NP/M
Georgia				O. Faubus	1960	SS	NP/M
H. Talmadge	1950	SS	NP/M	O. Faubus	1962	MS	NP/M
M. Griffin	1954	SS	M	O. Faubus	1964	MS	NP/M
E. Vandiver	1958	SS	M	W. Rockefeller	1966	NS	A
C. Sanders	1962	MS	A	W. Rockefeller	1968	NS	A
L. Maddox	1966	SS	NP/A	**Florida**			
Louisiana				D. McCarty	1952	MS	M
R. Kennon	1951–52	MS	M	L. Collins	1954	MS	M
E. Long	1955–56	MS	NP/M	L. Collins	1956	MS	M
J. Davis	1959–60	SS*	M	F. Bryant	1960	SS	M
J. McKeithen	1963–64	SS*	A	H. Burns	1964	SS	M
J. McKeithen	1967	NS	A	C. Kirk	1966	MS	M
Mississippi				**North Carolina**			
H. White	1951	SS*	M	W. Umstead	1952	MS	M
J. Coleman	1955	SS	M	L. Hodges	1956	MS	M
R. Barnett	1959	SS	M	T. Sanford	1960	MS	A
P. Johnson	1963	SS	A	D. Moore	1964	SS*	M
J. Williams	1967	SS	M	R. Scott	1968	MS	A
South Carolina				**Tennessee**			
J. Byrnes	1950	MS	A	R. Browning	1950	MS	M
G. Timmerman	1954	SS	M	F. Clement	1952	MS	M
E. Hollings	1958	SS	A	F. Clement	1954	MS	M
D. Russell	1962	MS	A	B. Ellington	1958	SS	M
R. McNair	1966	MS	A	F. Clement	1962	NS	A
				B. Ellington	1966	NS	A
				Texas			
				A. Shivers	1950	MS	M
				A. Shivers	1952	MS	M
				A. Shivers	1954	SS	M
				P. Daniel	1956	SS*	M
				P. Daniel	1958	MS	M
				P. Daniel	1960	NS	M
				J. Connally	1962	NS	M
				J. Connally	1964	NS	A
				J. Connally	1966	NS	A
				P. Smith	1968	NS	A
				Virginia			
				T. Stanley	1953	MS	M
				L. Almond	1957	SS	M
				A. Harrison	1961	SS	M
				M. Godwin	1965	NS	A
				L. Holton	1969	NS	A

*Indicates governors who switched from a moderate segregationist position in the Democratic first primary to a strong segregationist stance in the Democratic second primary.

Key: SS = Strong Segregationist; MS = Moderate Segregationist; NS = Nonsegregationist; M = Marginalist; A = Adaptive; NP/M = Neo-Populist/Marginalist; NP/A = Neo-Populist/Adaptive.

GOVERNORS, MONEY, AND VOTES
Gerald M. Pomper

State politics affords another opportunity to discover the impact and significance of elections. In contests for the presidency, the voters' intervention crucially affects the party balance, but their influence on governmental policy is neither direct nor obvious. Contests for governor involve fewer voters and more familiar issues. Perhaps the ballot has a more immediate impact in state elections. When government is close to the grass roots, politicians may be forced to keep their ears to the ground. In this chapter, we will test the existence of direct popular control of policy in postwar gubernatorial elections.

Voter control might be expected in regard to fiscal policy. State taxes and spending affect every voter in a very personal way. His income, purchases, and even fishing rights are taxed to provide his schools, roads, and license plates. Even before the United States came of age, the economic basis of politics had been evident to political theorists from Aristotle to Marx. . . . Most voters in the United States . . . view the parties in terms of the group benefits they provide.[1] National balloting also has been found to be related to the swings of the business cycle. The party in power gains presidential votes and congressional seats in times of prosperity, but loses both in times of recession.[2]

A direct popular concern for fiscal policy is often posited in state politics. Taxes are seen as crucial to the voters. In particular, according to a widespread belief, the electoral fate of governors clearly follows from their budget practices: Governors who increase taxes lose elections; governors who hold the tax line also hold their offices. If this relationship truly exists, the mystery of elections would be lessened considerably. Aware of the voters' demand, politicians would know how to behave and governmental policy would be popularly and directly controlled.

The presumed connection between taxes and votes has been emphasized recently, as both state taxes and spending have increased sharply. The states "face enormously increased demands for more and better schools, highways, welfare, recreational facilities, and so on—but most face them armed with very inadequate revenue sources. . . . The governor is to a great extent the most visible state official and therefore the logical scapegoat for the state's apparent inability to solve its problems."[3]

Many specific examples exist of the threat to governors from increased taxes. Before the 1960 election, Louis Harris found Democrat Albert Rosselini of Washington to be trailing in his bid for reelection. As one citizen complained, "I just think Rosselini is taking it out of the taxpayer's pocket. He raised the sales tax, and the tax on food, too—the poor man just can't make it. I say he's done a poor job." For similar reasons, Nebraska's Democratic governor was also found in danger. On the other hand, Democrats in Iowa and South Dakota, who had succeeded in restricting taxes, were seen as likely to be reelected.[4]

Governors find it difficult to convince the public of the need for increased public services. As an aide to Governor Gaylord Nelson of Wisconsin despaired in 1960, "You can't get attention. You can't get attention for schools, or for taxes, for problems of aging, or mentally retarded children. . . . You can reach them one by one and make them understand. But how do you make them all understand?" His reporter, Theodore White, found it "noteworthy that the chief casualties in both parties in the fall elections later in 1960 were the governors beset by such problems as these." Half of the governorships changed party hands, "largely because of grass-roots tax revolts," while Nelson "squeaked through with 51.6 percent."[5]

Presumed taxpayer resistance continues to worry government officials. Up to the present time, "as taxpayer resistance to state and local tax increases has stiffened, and as the demands of a burgeoning

Source: Reprinted by permission of Dodd, Mead & Company, Inc., from *Elections in America* by Gerald M. Pomper. Copyright ©1968 by Dodd, Mead & Company, Inc.

[1] See . . . Angus Campbell *et al.*, *The American Voter* (New York: John Wiley, 1960), chap. 10.

[2] Louis H. Bean, *How to Predict Elections* (New York: Knopf, 1948), chap. 6.

[3] Austin Ranney, in Herbert Jacob and Kenneth N. Vines, *Politics in the American States* (Boston: Little, Brown, 1965), p. 91.

[4] "Why the Odds Are against a Governor Becoming President," *Public Opinion Quarterly*, Vol. XXIII (Fall 1959), pp. 367-368.

[5] *The Making of the President 1960* (New York: Atheneum, 1961), pp. 214-215.

population for more governmental services has mounted, governors, mayors, and county supervisors alike have searched with mounting desperation for 'a way out.' "[6] Politicians evidently believe that voters seek direct control of policy through their ballots.

Although the relationship between taxes and electoral results is commonly assumed, it is not clearly proven. Obviously, many high-spending governors are politically successful. They gain enough support from the beneficiaries of state services to offset the lost votes of disgruntled taxpayers. This strategy, too, has some standing in the conventional wisdom of politics. Philosophers emphasizing direct control in elections feared that the populace would mandate high spending. In modern times, the opponents of Franklin Roosevelt complained, "You can't beat Santa Claus," as they explained the political success of vast increases in federal budgets. An apocryphal remark, erroneously attributed to Harry Hopkins, summarizes this tactic: "We shall tax and tax, spend and spend, elect and elect."[7] Even on the basis of political aphorisms, therefore, there is reason to doubt the electoral consequences of state taxation.

Further skepticism about "tax revolts" is aroused when we consider the specific examples cited to demonstrate the theory. Governors Rosselini and Nelson won reelection in 1960, in the face of reported discontent with their financial records. Moreover, both ran ahead of their party's presidential candidate, John Kennedy, and both surpassed the national average vote for Democratic gubernatorial candidates in 1960. Contrary to Harris's expectations, moreover, the Democrats won in Nebraska, but lost in Iowa and South Dakota.

The superficially "obvious" relationship between taxes and elections is not so "obvious" when we begin to look at the contradictory strategies suggested by political folklore or at individual state results. The policy implications of state elections require more thorough exploration. It would therefore be useful to attempt more rigorous tests of the relationships between taxes, spending, and votes, through statistical operations performed on a computer.

Even if we find a statistical relationship, however, we still cannot be sure that we have found a direct causal relationship. At most we could conclude that tax increases and electoral losses are associated with one another. On the other hand, the absence of a statistical association would clearly disprove, or severely qualify, this alleged direct impact of voting. In a science of politics, disproving hypotheses is as important as their confirmation.

MONEY AND VOTES: TESTING HYPOTHESES

Three steps are needed to test an hypothesis through statistical methods: (1) State the hypothesis precisely; (2) define the terms or variables quantitatively; (3) use an appropriate test for deriving a measure of association. The first step is simple and implicit in the previous discussion. Our precise hypothesis is that political success is associated with low tax increases. We will test this hypothesis by examining postwar elections in 37 states, excluding only the southern states, which were overwhelmingly one-party, and the new states of Alaska and Hawaii.

In the second step, we must define political success and tax increases. Two different measurements of political success are used. It is first defined as *victory* for the incumbent party in a state, whether through the reelection of a governor or the victory of a new candidate of his party. This definition, however, may be too broad. An incumbent in one state might be reelected in a runaway contest, while another governor won by a hair. A more precise indicator of political success would be the party's *vote change* from one election to the next. The most successful state party would show the greatest increase in its percentage of the vote since the last polling; the least successful would show the greatest decline.

To isolate the particular influence of state politics, we also must control the national trend. Therefore, for each candidate, the vote change is measured in comparison to all of his party's gubernatorial candidates.[8] The procedure is explained more fully in the Appendix.

[8]The voting data were obtained from Richard M. Scammon (Ed.), *American Votes 6: 1964* (Washington: Congressional Quarterly, 1966). Where 1944 figures were needed, they were obtained from *The World Almanac and Book of Facts* (New York: New York World Telegram 1945), pp. 721–745. Because Earl Warren won both parties' nominations in 1946, the California figures for this year are actually those from the 1942 election.

[6]U.S. Advisory Commission on Intergovernmental Relations, *Eighth Annual Report* (1967), p. 4.

[7]Robert E. Sherwood, *Roosevelt and Hopkins*, rev. paper ed. (New York: Bantam, 1950), Vol. I, p. 124.

Five measures of tax increases are used: (1) Absolute, or dollar, increase in per capita state taxes since the last election; (2) percentage increase; (3) annual percentage increase; (4) increase in "personal tax burden"—defined as per capita tax divided by per capita personal income; and (5) first-year taxes.[9] The last figure is the percentage of tax increases occurring in the first year of a governor's term. This measure is useful for testing another common political maxim, that new taxes should be concentrated at the beginning of an administration. By such action, governors presumably win time for the voters to forget their burdens before a new election looms. If this maxim is true, then governors who concentrate their tax increases in the first year should enjoy greater political success than those who follow a different course.

We now have two measures of relative political success and five measures of relative tax increases. The hypothesis to be tested is that they are inversely related, so that greater success will follow from lesser tax burdens.[10] For this test, each of the political measures is correlated separately with each of the tax indexes for the nine elections from 1948 to 1964.[11] The coefficient of association employed is known as the Goodman-Kruskall *gamma*. It can range as high as 1.0, which would fully support the folklore rule that political gains are related to limited new taxes. A coefficient of − 1.0 would indicate that governors gain votes from large increases; lower coefficients would demonstrate lower association. The statistical procedure used is explained in the appendix.

The assumed relationships between money and votes concern expenditures as well as taxes. For a fuller test, state spending is also analyzed, using the same methods. Paralleling the analysis of taxes, the indexes of spending increases are: (1) Absolute increase in per capita general expenditure since the last election; (2) percentage increase; (3) annual percentage increase; (4) increase in "personal benefit"—defined as per capita spending divided by per capita personal income; and (5) last-year spending. The last figure is the percentage of the spending increase which occurred in the last year of a governor's term. If the voters indeed have short memories, it would be politically wise to concentrate new benefits in the period immediately preceding the balloting. Finally, the increases in spending and taxes are compared by the use of ratios. The *gamma* measure of association is used in all cases. A positive coefficient would indicate that restraints in spending lead to political success. A negative coefficient would suggest the opposite conclusion, that spending increases are more likely to yield electoral benefits.

MONEY AND VOTES: THE RESULTS

If citizens seek control of fiscal policy through their votes, our various statistical measures should reflect their concern. Association of the vote with gubernatorial taxing and spending programs will be evidenced by high correlations, within limits of 1.0 to − 1.0. The lack of voter concern will be evidenced in lower coefficients. These are our standards. What are the results?

Table [1] summarizes the correlations obtained when we compare political success with increases in taxes and spending. The minus sign preceding the first figure in the 1948 column shows that low absolute tax increases in 1948 were associated not with victory, but with defeat. (Alternately, we can say victory was associated with high tax increases.) The second figure in the column indicates, however, that low absolute tax increases were associated positively with favorable vote change. In both cases, the low coefficients, −.16 and .27, indicate weak relationships.

The bulk of the table does not disguise the low coefficients obtained. The dominant impression from these figures is the absence of any meaningful association between these factors. The coeffi-

[9] The financial data were obtained from U.S. Bureau of the Census, *Compendium of State Government Finances*, published annually. The data for state spending and personal income, discussed subsequently, are also from this source. Per capita taxes include all sources of revenue Calculations are based on the per capita tax in the fiscal year beginning in the same calendar year as a given election. The fiscal year begins for most states six months before the calendar year. Thus, for the election of 1964, the tax increases of greatest impact are those which begin July 1, 1964, the start of fiscal year 1965. The political assumption here is that voters will be most affected by recent increases in taxes, rather than those already familiar to them, or only threatening in the future.

[10] The variations among states in the absolute level of taxes is not examined here. These differences result from many political and historical factors, fully considered by Clara Penniman, in Jacob and Vines, chap. 8.

[11] New Jersey and Kentucky, which hold gubernatorial elections in odd-numbered years, are included with the elections of the preceding years for purposes of analysis.

TABLE [1] Political Success and Financial Policies

Political Variable	Index of Increases	Election Years								
		1948	1950	1952	1954	1956	1958	1960	1962	1964
		(coefficients of correlation)								
Victory	Absolute tax	-.16	.19	.21	.34	.00	.14	-.48	-.38	.26
Vote change	Absolute tax	.27	.29	.24	-.36	-.28	.13	.00	.00	.42
Victory	Absolute spending	.30	.19	.21	.00	.17	-.29	-.46	-.42	-.26
Vote change	Absolute spending	.62	.14	.24	.15	.00	-.13	-.08	.19	.09
Victory	% tax	-.31	.19	.41	.17	-.16	.14	-.32	-.38	-.26
Vote change	% tax	.14	.29	.30	-.41	-.28	.07	.08	-.07	.28
Victory	% spending	.14	.19	.40	.00	.17	-.29	-.60	-.55	-.26
Vote change	% spending	.34	.14	.16	.15	.15	-.06	-.07	.14	.09
Victory	% annual tax	-.58	.19	.20	.00	.17	.14	-.28	-.14	.00
Vote change	% annual tax	-.08	.44	.07	-.37	-.08	.00	.00	-.21	.26
Victory	% annual spending	-.46	.19	.21	.00	.17	-.14	-.48	-.55	-.26
Vote change	% annual spending	.15	.14	.02	.22	.22	-.15	-.23	.14	.09
Victory	Personal tax burden	-.45	.38	.41	.17	-.35	.00	-.17	.29	.50
Vote change	Personal tax burden	-.13	.56	.36	-.01	-.17	.15	.30	.25	.26
Victory	Personal benefit	.00	.19	.41	.17	-.18	-.14	-.33	-.14	.00
Vote change	Personal benefit	.14	.13	.19	.20	.07	.28	.08	.26	.09
Victory	First-year tax	.71	.72	.41	1.00	.34	.00	-.16	-.27	.23
Vote change	First-year tax	.26	.34	-.07	.00	.28	-.08	.08	.07	.26
Victory	Last-year spending	-.30	-.54	.21	.00	-.51	.53	-.28	-.73	-.91
Vote change	Last-year spending	.14	-.49	-.42	.15	-.15	.20	-.24	.07	-.28
Victory	Absolute ratio	.30	-.54	.00	.00	-.35	.14	-.17	.00	-.50
Vote change	Absolute ratio	.49	-.40	.28	.07	.09	-.07	-.08	.19	-.19
Victory	% ratio	.14	-.54	.00	.00	-.35	.14	-.17	-.14	-.50
Vote change	% ratio	.28	-.40	.28	-.07	.23	.00	.15	.07	-.10
Number of states		28	28	26	28	27	28	24	28	22

cients are rarely significant, and they are inconsistent in their direction (positive or negative). A coefficient of .30 would be about the minimum necessary to establish a relationship, but few of the statistics reach this level.

These results are contrary to all of the rules of political folklore. Governors who lead in increasing taxes do not suffer at the polls significantly. Conversely, governors who are cautious in their revenue programs in fear of a "tax revolt" are not particularly rewarded for their restraint. The impact of spending programs is also limited. Neither the relatively extravagant nor the comparatively penny-pinching state executives gain obvious electoral support for their labors. The voters do not express their financial demands by making consistent and meaningful distinctions among governors on the basis of state fiscal policies. The governors apparently have considerable discretion. While they cannot ignore the electoral impact of their budgets, they are not compelled politically either to restrict taxes or to expand spending.

The figures also provide some indication of the politically most desirable time to raise taxes or spending. Governors who concentrate their tax increases in the first year of their terms tend to be successful, confirming the hornbook rule, but the relationships are not strong or fully consistent. Contrary to the original supposition, however, it also appears best to concentrate spending increases in the earlier part of a gubernatorial term. Such action may be necessary for two different reasons. Early spending increases may be advantageous because time erases the voter's memories of the governor's extravagance. Alternately, the benefits of state spending may not become apparent to the voter for some time. An early sowing of increased governmental services may be necessary for state executives to reap the political harvest in the next election.

Though the overall relationships are not convincing, there is a suggestive temporal shift in the electoral consequences of state fiscal politics. It appears that low taxes were politically profitable until 1956, while high spending has become more advantageous since 1958. However, because of the generally low level of the coefficients, the statistical evidence is not conclusive.

A temporal shift is indicated by the changing direction of the coefficients in Table [1]. In the earlier period, positive correlations occurred more than twice as often as negative figures. Political rewards were associated with frugal government. In the contests beginning in 1958, the situation has become considerably different, and negative figures are more common than positive numbers. High taxers and spenders no longer seem vulnerable at the polls. Indeed, the simple factor of victory at the polls is particularly likely to be associated with a liberal fiscal policy in the later era.[12]

The apparent change in the political impact of governmental finances may result from new attitudes on the part of the voters. The electorate may well have become newly aware of the impact of state budgets, with rising governmental costs. While all of the states taxed 2.3 per cent of the gross national product in 1946, and spent but 1.8 per cent of the country's wealth, they received 3.7 percent in 1962, and spent 3.8 per cent.[13] Yet even increased attention does not explain the greater electoral tolerance of spending governors.

The outcome of an election is only partially dependent on awareness of state finances. More decisive in determining victory is the general trend toward one of the parties. A Republican or Democratic swing elects both spenders and savers of the winning party, while the individual's record can have only a marginal effect. Nationwide trends explain the temporal shift in gubernatorial elections. As Table [2] evidences, the period from 1948 to 1956, when low-taxing governors were favored, was also a period of Republican dominance. In 1958, a period of Democratic supremacy began,

TABLE [2] Party Fortunes in Gubernatorial Elections of 37 States

Year	Number of Victories		Median Vote (%)	
	Democrats	Republicans	Democrats	Republicans
1948	14	14	49.2	50.8
1950	6	22	45.2	54.8
1952	6	20	45.5	54.5
1954	13	15	49.0	51.0
1956	13	14	49.6	50.4
1958	20	8	52.6	47.4
1960	12	12	50.1	49.9
1962	14	14	50.0	50.0
1964	14	8	54.0	46.0

coinciding with the success of high-spending executives.

Democrats are more prone to extend governmental programs, although not all spenders are Democrats, and not all Democrats are spenders.[14] The recent change to a Democratic advantage in state elections therefore largely accounts for the new relationship between increased spending and electoral victory. The earlier Republican dominance similarly accounts for the past success of governors who limited new taxes and spending. It is possible that the causal relationship should be reversed. Greater voter acceptance of state spending could lead to Democratic party victory, as earlier public support for low taxes might have brought Republican preeminence. This line of argument, however, seems to assume too much voter generosity and awareness to be plausible. The shift to the Democrats is almost certainly the result of party, not fiscal, factors.[15] The earlier discussion

---

[12] There are more than twice as many positive as negative coefficients involving "victory" in the 1948–56 period. In the later time the positive coefficients are less than one-third the number of negative figures.

[13] Frederick Mosher and Orville Poland, *The Costs of American Government* (New York: Dodd, Mead, 1964), pp. 157, 165.

[14] Although no detailed study is available, it may be significant that the range of annual percent spending increases is greater for Democratic than Republican governors in three of the four elections since 1958, and similar to or higher than the Republicans' in all years except 1948. For national party differences consistent with this assumption, see Herbert McClosky *et al.*, "Issue Conflict and Consensus among Party Leaders and Followers," *American Political Science Review*, Vol. LIV (June 1960), pp. 406–427; and Lewis A. Froman, Jr., *Congressmen and Their Constituencies* (Chicago: Rand McNally, 1963), chap. 9.

[15] The importance of national trends in congressional elections similarly is evidenced by Donald Stokes and Warren Miller, "Party Government and the Saliency of Congress," in Angus Campbell *et al.*, *Elections and the Political Order* (New York: Wiley, 1966), chap 11, and Milton C. Cummings, Jr., *Congressmen and the Electorate* (New York: Free Press, 1966).

of the 1962 Wisconsin election reinforces the point.[16] Voters choose parties primarily and policies secondarily.

The results of state elections again demonstrate the pervasive influence of partisanship. Previously, we have learned how individual voters view the world of politics through partisan eyes and how the choice of party is crucial in the innovation of national policy. In gubernatorial politics as well, voters' preferences are channeled through parties. The direct control of government action is unlikely. Electoral influence must be indirect, through popular endorsement of policy-oriented politicians.

WHAT MAKES A DIFFERENCE?

Our general analysis indicates that there is no strong and unidirectional relationship between tax or spending increases and electoral results. Voters do not evidence a consistent concern for fiscal issues. Moreover, their party preferences complicate their policy choices. Within the general pattern, however, some factors may make a marginal difference. It would be useful, therefore, to separate or "control" some of these factors, to see if any stronger relationships become evident.

For this purpose, the states involved in each election were divided into two groups on each of the following dimensions: (1) Democratic or Republican governors at the time of election; (2) competitive states;[17] (3) Democratic or Republican victory in the state in the current or preceding presidential election; (4) high or low personal income; (5) presence or absence of incumbent candidates; (6) two- or four-year terms; and (7) outcome of the previous election, either continuation of the same party in power or a party turnover. The relationship of politics and finances is then calculated separately for each group.

Only one measure of each variable was used in this analysis. Political success was considered vote change, as previously defined. The index of tax or spending increases was the per cent annual increase. This measure was chosen as the one least affected by the wealth of the states or the differences between two- and four-year terms. The correlation coefficient is *Yule's Q*, explained in the appendix, which varies from 1.0 to −1.0. The results are presented in Table [3].

Financial policies affect governors of the two parties in a different manner. Although neither partisan camp is greatly affected by tax increases, a Democrat is more likely to run ahead of his party's national trend by limiting new spending. Republicans evidence the opposite relationship. They are more likely to run ahead of the national GOP if their spending increases are relatively high.[18]

These results, although of a low magnitude, indicate similarities in the practical situation facing governors of both parties. To run ahead of his party, a governor should act contrary to the common public impression. A Republican, belonging to a party which is regarded as more concerned with economy, can lead his fellow partisans by being relatively generous with public monies. A Democrat, whose party is regarded as more extravagant, can exceed the national trend by frugality.[19]

The outcome of elections, as we have seen, is largely dependent on overall swings. Marginal differences from these trends, however, can be gained by policies which broaden a state executive's coalition beyond that normally associated with the party. Frank Lausche established his position as Democratic governor of Ohio by his conservative fiscal policies, whereas Earl Warren twice won re-election as Republican governor of California by a liberal spending program. The relationships between the presidential vote in a state and taxation confirm this analysis. In states carried by Democratic candidates for the White House, governors surpass the national trend by frugal policies, while Republican states on the national level tend to give

---

[16] See Chapter IV, pp. 78–80, *supra*.

[17] The competitive states are those ranked 1 to 19 in gubernatorial competition by Richard Dawson and James Robinson, "Inter-Party Competition, Economic Variables, and Welfare Policies in the American States," *Journal of Politics*, Vol. 25 (May 1963), pp. 265–287. Minnesota, which is not included in their study, is also considered competitive. The other states, as well as Nebraska, are considered less competitive.

[18] Even the total figures are still quite low, and the correlation could occur by chance more than one out of five times. These results, however, do indicate that the recent success of the Democrats is not due to voters deliberately casting their votes for high spenders.

[19] For images of the parties, see *The American Voter*, chaps. 3, 10, and Opinion Research Corporation, *Public Opinion Trends—Their Meaning for the Republican Party* (1965).

Variables	1948	1950	1952	1954	1956	1958	1960	1962	1964	Total
					Election Years					
					(coefficients of correlation)					
Democrats:										
Taxes	.00	.85	−.38	−.33*	−.50	.00	−.14	−.38	−.28	−.09
Spending	.00	.85	−.38	1.00*	−.50	.00	−.14	.14	.28	.14
Republicans:										
Taxes	−.67	.14	.00	−.25	.00	.60	.78	−.14	.33	−.01
Spending	−.38	−.38	.00	.09	.47	−.60	−.50	−.14	.33	−.13
Competitive:										
Taxes	−.38	.60	−.72	.00	−.28	.60	.00	.00	−.90	−.17
Spending	.14	.60	−.72	.60	.28	.00	.00	.60	−.50	.11
Noncompetitive:										
Taxes	.45	.47	.00	−.47	−.14	.47	−.60	−.80	.20	−.08
Spending	.85	.00	.00	.47	.45	.00	.00	−.47	.78	.30
Dem. president:										
Taxes	−.38	.61	.00*	.00*	.00*	.00*	.38	.38	.28	.16
Spending	.14	.14	.00*	.00*	.00*	.00*	.88	.38	.28	.26
Rep. president:										
Taxes	−.14	.45	−.38	−.22	−.15	.14	−.72	−.60	.00*	−.22
Spending	−.14	−.14	−.08	.36	.15	−.14	−.72	−.22	.00*	−.08
High income:										
Taxes	−.38	.89	−.28	.14	.14	.14	−.67	−.38	.60	−.05
Spending	−.76	.61	−.28	.61	−.38	−.40	−.67	.14	.00	−.13
Low income:										
Taxes	−.67	.45	−.60	−.67	−.60	.14	−.50	−.14	−.38	−.37
Spending	.45	−.14	.00	−.14	.60	.45	.20	−.14	−.38	−.03
Incumbents:										
Taxes	−.38	.00	.22	−.92	−.38	.45	.20	−.25	.28	−.15
Spending	.00	.00	−.22	−.60	.61	−.22	−.50	.42	−.28	−.04
Nonincumbents:										
Taxes	−.80	.92	−.80	.00	.00	.22	−.14	−.33*	.00	.00
Spending	.00	.60	.00	.60	−.60	−.38	−.94	−.33*	.00	−.20
Two-year term:										
Taxes	.50	.11	.71	−.11	−.22	.38	−.38	−.38	−.14	−.07
Spending	.50	−.30	−.11	−.11	.22	.00	−.38	.61	.45	.10
Four-year term:										
Taxes	.80	.64	−.20	−.50	−.84	.00	−.20	−.14	−.84	−.15
Spending	.00	1.00	−.20	.20	.64	−.38	−.20	−.67	−.20	.04
Continuity:										
Taxes		.61	.85	−.50	−.11	.50	−.47	.00	−.50	.08
Spending		.28	−.14	−.18	−.54	−.30	−.80	.00	−.50	−.36
Reversal:										
Taxes		1.00*	1.00*	−.33*	−.38	.64	.50	−.47	−1.00	.33
Spending		1.00*	1.00*	−.33*	.38	−.20	1.00	.47	.78	.53

*Five or fewer states.

marginal support to more extravagant gubernatorial candidates.

There are limited, but intriguing, differences between the more and less competitive states as well. Voters in the more competitive states are apt to support governors associated with larger tax increases and are not greatly troubled by spending increases. In the less competitive states, governors are barely affected by tax increases, but earn rewards for restrictions in state governmental expenditures. There is, in brief, a greater possibility of political gain for governmental welfare programs in competitive states.

These differences suggest alternative strategies for governors in varying political environments. In competitive states, politicians would seek votes by spending programs of mass benefit and devote less attention to the tax burden. Unsure of office, the parties would seek to appeal to the large number of lower-income voters in their fiscal programs. The costs of government will not be resented by the mass of voters if a substantial share is paid by the well-to-do. State spending will be of political benefit where the spending is widely distributed.

In the less competitive states, a different strategy would be appropriate. In these states, the "have-nots" of society have less opportunity for influence. The absence of two parties of relatively equal strength makes it difficult "to carry out sustained programs of action, which almost always are thought by the better element to be contrary to its immediate interests. This negative weakness thus redounds to the benefit of the upper brackets."[20] Politics in the less competitive states can be expected to be more controlled by economic elite groups, and successful politicians will be more prone to serve their interests. While these elites may not resent tax increases, which are often a regressive burden on lower-income groups, they are more likely to seek and politically reward spending limits.

When we examine the states with wealth controlled, we find that low-income states are more willing to accept tax rises and high-income states are more receptive to spending increases. Because there are relatively fewer taxpayers in poorer states, these voters may be willing to support governors who raise taxes on other people. The leading, but clearly exceptional, example is that of Huey Long, who won strong popular approval of his "share the wealth" program. The tolerance for spending in high-income states may reflect the

greater demands voiced by prosperous citizens with "rising expectations" of universal education, modern highways, and extensive recreational facilities. The outcry which greeted Ronald Reagan's effort to impose tuition in California's universities reflects the wealthier voters' concerns, and their pressures on governors to maintain public spending.

Correlations in the last three groupings provide some tentative guides to wise political action. Incumbents are better able to defend a record of tax increases, while new candidates are advisable for a party responsible for spending increases. There is apparently some political safety in a four-year term, for governors with longer tenure appear to benefit from higher taxes. Finally, governors of a party reelected to office are most likely to succeed in future contests when they increase spending. State executives elected in a party turnover would be better advised to limit taxing and spending.

These differing strategies are of marginal, not overwhelming, importance. Our detailed correlations do not show direct voter control over state fiscal policy, even when important factors are analyzed separately. We find, rather, that governors have considerable discretion within the limits of the electorate's partisanship. The political situation of different states does make some strategies more attractive than others. The reactions of the electorate must be considered, for popular resistance to taxes or popular demands for new spending may have an effect at the polls. Still, these effects are neither obvious nor immediate, and politicians have considerable room for maneuver. There is no iron law of state politics or state finances.

THE MEANINGS OF STATE ELECTIONS

Clear electoral mandates are rare in gubernatorial contests. There are some technical reasons for the absence of any clear and direct relationship between fiscal policy and electoral success. By using a measure of total taxes, we lump together levies of greater and lesser political sensitivity. Voters may react to a state sales tax, while being hardly aware of minerals severance imposts. Similarly, some expenditures are more likely to win voter attention than others. State spending for welfare is widely distributed and debated, while the promotion of tourism is neither visible nor contentious. Our data may also be somewhat inaccurate, with

[20]V. O. Key, Jr., *Southern Politics* (New York: Knopf, 1949), p. 308. The argument was further developed by Duane Lockard, *New England State Politics* (Princeton: Princeton University Press, 1959), chap. 12. It has since been criticized by Dawson and Robinson, *Op. cit.*, and Thomas W. Dye, *Politics, Economics and the Public* (Chicago: Rand McNally, 1966), and defended by John N. Fenton, *People and Parties in Politics* (Glenview: Scott, Foresman, 1966), chap. 2.

items disguised or deferred through accounting devices.[21]

The fundamental problems involved in the explanation of state elections, however, are political, rather than technical. We have not found simple relationships because the relationships are not simple. The meaning of elections is complex, often contradictory, and can rarely be explained as a direct association between ballots and fiscal policy. The "buzzing, blooming confusion" of the political world is evident in institutions, in the voter's perceptions, and in campaigns.

The complexity of American institutions ... limits governors and voters. State chief executives do not fully control their own administrations. Separation of powers, decentralized administration, and the proliferation of public authorities create rival power centers. Their competition makes it difficult for the citizen to focus his attention and appropriately to distribute rewards and punishments for state taxing and spending. Institutional separations are often broadened by political fissures. A governor of one party may co-exist with a legislature and elected administrative officials of the opposition. Furthermore, at least until recent reapportionment, a governor might be more responsive to the urbanized areas of a state, while the legislature was biased in favor of rural districts. The responsibility for fiscal policies becomes quite clouded in these circumstances.[22]

At the same time, governors are in the middle of a complex federal system; they cannot isolate their states from the actions of superior and subordinate governments. National taxation limits the opportunities for state revenue; national fiscal policies stimulate or retard a state's prosperity; and national grants-in-aid allow increased state expenditure without increased internal taxation. Local communities collect a portion of state revenues and demand a rising proportion of state expenditures, while they increase their own taxes and spending. Governors are not formally responsible for national or local policies, but in the noncentralized American system of federalism, they cannot avoid involvement or some political culpability.

The chief executives are also involved, or entrapped, in a political party and will inevitably share in their party's electoral fate. National politics affects state elections, not infrequently overwhelming other influences. The fiscal records of the governors have only a marginal effect on the vote. National tides can sweep in or submerge both the frugal and the free-spending. An autonomous state politics does not exist.[23]

Voter perceptions further complicate the governors' political problems. The most important political object to the electorate is the national party. The voter's reactions to the nature of the times or the provision of group benefits is commonly a broad and undifferentiated judgment on all politicians grouped under a partisan label. His fire is a fusillade of buckshot over the entire electoral terrain, not a rifle bullet precisely aimed at fiscal culprits. If unhappy with the Democrats, even economy-minded Democrats will not totally escape his wrath. Opposition to the Republican party will damage all of the GOP's candidates, whatever their fiscal policies.

The electorate, furthermore, cannot be expected fully to distinguish the different levels of the federal structure. The impact of taxes and spending is a total impact, not one in which the voter carefully separates national, state, and local finances. An increase in an individual's withholding tax may cause resentment of his state's governor, even when new taxes have actually been imposed by local or national governments. Conversely, the governor may receive credit for a new school or highway even when the major part of the cost has been paid by municipal or federal agencies.

Even if the voter does concentrate on state budgets, his goals are not necessarily constant nor coherent. He may wish tax relief in one year, but be more concerned with new state services at another election. In many cases, both goals are wanted. Thus, "taxation to finance welfare programs meets opposition among those who favor welfare pro-

[21] The statistical methods employed can also be criticized. Rank-order correlation is relatively simple, but it ignores the exact differences among the ranked data. Using only two or three categories for each variable also limits the degree of comparison possible. Because of the peculiarities of this method, a small change in the number of states in any cell can effect a drastic change in the coefficient of association. The small number of cases in any year also limits the generality of the findings.

[22] See V. O. Key, Jr., *American State Politics* (New York: Knopf, 1956), chaps. 3, 7.

[23] See Key, *American State Politics*, chap. 2, and Judson L. James, "American Political Parties as Executive-Centered Coalitions" (mimeo, 1967).

grams even more frequently than among those who oppose them. . . . The same people simultaneously want increased expenditures and reduced taxes."[24] Given such contradictions, no clear electoral relationship is likely between political success and gubernatorial fiscal programs.

Finally, individual campaigns will affect the electoral importance of taxes and expenditures. In many state elections, these questions are not presented to the voters, or are not perceived by them. Attention may be limited to the personal character, associations, and abilities of the candidates. Any discussion of the incumbents' records may center on scandals or substantive policy, rather than on financial matters. National and even international issues may intrude. In the 1966 campaign, for example, news commentators stressed the importance of segregation in Alabama, scandals in Massachusetts, presidential politics in Michigan, and campaign funds in Pennsylvania.[25] While these may be appropriate issues, their emphasis clearly dilutes the impact of budgetary questions.

For these many reasons, tax and spending policies are not controlled through state elections. Even when they are important, there is no indication that popular resistance to taxes is the predominant fiscal consideration. The diversity of state politics is illustrated by the last three elections in our largest states, California and New York. In 1958, Democrat Pat Brown and Republican Nelson Rockefeller were elected governors of these two states, in each case reversing party control of the executive branch. In each case as well, their campaigns had been waged partially as attacks on the previous administration's extravagance, but largely on other issues. Brown was also aided by the strong Democratic tide created by the 1958 recession. Once in office, each of the governors adopted a budget of over $2 billion, balanced through some quarter-of-a-million dollars in new levies and increases in the state income tax. After compromises and amendments in the state legislatures, both governors' programs were adopted.

In 1962, Brown and Rockefeller were reelected.

California, soon to be the most populous state, had already become the nation's leader in spending. The state's campaign, however, centered not on finances, but on Richard Nixon's presidential ambitions, other national issues, and political extremism. In New York, Rockefeller's tax record was a more central issue, but its impact was reduced by such personal questions as his divorce and remarriage. To meet the criticisms of his financial record, the Governor pledged no new taxes in his second term.

In the following four years, the budgets of the two states rose considerably, to $3.9 billion in New York and $4.6 billion in California. Rockefeller withdrew his no-tax pledge and resorted to bonds, accelerated tax payments, and eventually a state sales tax. Brown also made use of extensive borrowing and accelerated payments and sought a withholding system for income levies as part of a program of "fiscal reform."

Each governor ran for a third term in 1966, and each defended his past budgets by pointing to achievements such as the Feather River water project in California or the Medicaid program of New York. Finances were an issue in each state, but there were other factors. In New York, Rockefeller apologized to the voters for the "blooper" of his no-tax pledge, and attributed the deficit in state revenues to a lagging national economy. Narcotics control, "bossism," and splinter parties complicated the situation. In California, the candidates' personalities, student activity at Berkeley, and race relations received predominant attention in an election seen as a national test of conservative sentiment. While taxes were debated, the focus was on local, rather than state, revenues. In November Rockefeller won, but Brown was defeated.

These two cases illustrate the difficulty in interpreting gubernatorial elections in a single-minded way or finding them a "mandate" for lower taxes or increased spending. Simple relationships and simple explanations are restrained by the diversity of American institutions, the national tides of party politics, and the multiplicity of state issues. Complexity is created as well by the voter, who does not mechanically respond to financial allurements. The conventional assumption is that taxes are particularly unpopular and politically dangerous. The record indicates, however, that the electorate can understand and accept the need and

[24]V. O. Key, Jr., *Public Opinion and American Democracy* (New York: Knopf, 1961), pp. 168–169. See also Robert Axelrod, "The Structure of Public Opinion on Policy Issues," *Public Opinion Quarterly*, Vol. XXXI (Spring 1967), pp. 51–60.
[25]American Broadcasting Company, *Factbook: Elections 1966.*

uses of public revenues and spending. An account of a Rockefeller street campaign speech is enlightening:

As the Governor spoke, a man in his shirtsleeves came out of a tavern, The Inn, and called: "I want to know what you're going to do about the state income tax. It's bad news."

"Let me tell you about pure water. I know you don't bother with it," Mr. Rockefeller said, as the crowd laughed.

"Taxes, taxes!" the man continued to shout.

The Governor said that the taxes paid by the man helped children go to school, and the crowd applauded. The man retreated to The Inn. He declined to give his name. [26]

Voters will often bear taxes when they are convinced of the value of state services, just as they will often reject state services when they appear wasteful. To return to our original hypothesis, there is no inevitable "taxpayers' revolt," if we judge by the empirical evidence presented here. Limits on state taxation are not necessarily imposed by the voters. In fact, the opposite relationship is quite common. High spending can be politically advantageous.

Even if invalid, however, the belief in a taxpayer revolt can still be important in restricting state action. Politicians necessarily must make some assumptions about the electoral consequences of their behavior. Their commitments and actions are conditioned by the reactions they expect from the voters. If governors believe they will be electorally punished for taxing and providing services, they will not tax nor provide services. The governor's reading of the public will is as vital as the true content of that testament.

The politician is the crucial link in voter influence over public policy. The electorate does not mandate policy, but it accepts or rejects the officials who initiate policy. Politicians are not severely restricted by decisions at the polls, but neither can they fail to protect the voters' vital interests. In state politics, governors have discretion to limit or raise taxes and spending, as their conception of the public's needs and desires indicates. The electoral consequences are uncertain, depending on the governors' commitments, the voter's changing concerns, and the quality of party competition. If this uncertainty prevents any sim-

ple explanation of politics, it does provide an opportunity for meaningful dialogue between elected and electors.

The evidence of state elections is consistent with our earlier discussions of theory, institutions, and voters. Empirical evidence from presidential and gubernatorial contests is similar. On neither level do the voters prescribe specific governmental action. Initiatives in public programs do not follow directly from popular mandates. The impact of elections on policy, therefore, must be sought through their indirect effects. If the voters do not determine policy, they still may influence it through their choice of candidates and parties. Our evidence indicates that the crucial decisions are made by the elected, not the electors. The actions of these officials, in turn, may be related to their campaign pledges, as stated in party platforms. . . .

APPENDIX

Below are explanations of the techniques used in this chapter.

VOTE CHANGE

In each year, the vote for a given candidate is considered the number of percentage points (calculated to one decimal place) by which he exceeded or trailed the median percentage received by all of his party's gubernatorial candidates in the given election year. (To avoid complications from negative figures in the computer program, a constant of 50.0 percentage points was added to all figures.) The vote change between elections is then defined as the change in this deviation from the party average. As an illustration, suppose a candidate received 55 percent of the vote in successive elections, while his party's national average fell from 55 to 50 percent. His vote change would be: $(55 - 50) - (55 - 55)$, or $+ 5$. Symbolically, where c represents the candidate, p his party, and subscripts 1 and 2 successive elections, then:

$$\text{Vote Change} = (c_2 - p_2) - (c_1 - p_1)$$

GOODMAN-KRUSKAL GAMMA

This statistic measures the association between two sets of data arranged to constitute ordinal variables. An ordinal variable is one in which the data are grouped into classes with higher and lower values, but the intervals between the classes are not specified. "Ordinal scales permit discussion of

[26]*New York Times*, September 21, 1966, p. 37. The account of the Brown and Rockefeller administrations is drawn from various articles in the *Times*.

'moreness' or 'lessness,' but they make no assumptions as to how much more or less."[27]

The procedure is illustrated, using the data in Table [4], by calculating the association between changes in the vote and percentage increases in taxes for 28 gubernatorial elections in 1950. Six steps are involved:

1. Arrange the deviations from the national party trend in order, from the highest deviation above to the highest deviation below the trend, as in the horizontal rows of Table [4].
2. Divide this array into three groups, with an approximately equal number of states in each group. When victory is defined as the measure of political success, only the two categories of victory and defeat are employed.
3. Arrange the percentage increases in taxes in order, from the lowest to the highest, as in the vertical columns of Table [4]. It is important that the orderings be in the direction predicted by the hypothesis.
4. Divide this array into three groups.
5. Construct a 3 × 3 table, counting the number of states which fall into each of the resulting nine cells.
6. Calculate *gamma*, by the formula:

$$G = \frac{f_a - f_i}{f_a + f_i}$$

in which, "to compute f_a we multiply the frequency in each cell by the frequencies in all the cells that lie both below and to the right of it. By adding these products together, we obtain f_a.... To compute f we multiply the frequency in each cell by the sum of the frequencies in the cells which lie below and to the left of it and add these products."[28]

In this case, f_a is equal to:

$$5(6 + 3 + 2 + 4) + 1(2 + 4) + 2(3 + 4) + 6(4) = 119$$

and f_i is equal to:

$$2(6 + 1 + 2 + 3) + 3(2 + 3) + 2(1 + 3) + 6(3) = 65$$

[27] Linton C. Freeman, *Elementary Applied Statistics* (New York: John Wiley, 1965), p. 7.

[28] Freeman, chap. 8 and p. 85. The original source of this statistic is Leo Goodman and William Kruskal, "Measures of Association for Cross Classifications," *Journal of the American Statistical Association*, Vol. 49 (1954), pp. 733–764.

TABLE [4]. Vote Change and Percent Increase in Taxes, 1950*

Vote Change	Percent Increase in Taxes Since Last Election		
	−18.1 to 6.6	6.8 to 24.7	27.6 to 273.6
9.8 to .5	5	2	2
.2 to −5.2	1	6	3
−5.5 to −17.6	3	2	4

*The number in each cell is the number of states with the designated vote change and percentage tax increases.

By the formula above,

$$G = \frac{119 - 65}{119 + 65} = \frac{54}{184} = .29$$

There is a moderate relationship in 1950 between tax increases and political results. Governors who were relatively stringent in their tax programs were likely to improve their electoral performance compared to other candidates of their party.[29]

The same procedure is used for the analysis of spending. In the analysis of both first-year taxes and last-year spending, the financial data are ranked from high to low. Concentrating taxes in the first year, or spending in the last year, will therefore result in a positive coefficient if these actions are truly related to political success. In the calculation of the spending-taxes ratio, the absolute and percentage increases in spending in a term are divided, respectively, by the absolute and percentage increase in taxes. After they are ranked from low to high, they are correlated with the political variables.

YULE'S Q

This measure, mathematically a special case of *gamma*, is used in the second set of correlations. The small number of cases in each group permits use of only 2 × 2 tables. Each coefficient represents the correlation of vote change and percent annual tax increase for the designated group in the designated year. For all election years combined, a gross measure of association can be obtained by

[29] This result is not very impressive. A test of significance indicates that a similar coefficient might occur by change as often as one of five times. See Freeman, chap. 13.

TABLE [5] Vote Change and Tax Increase, Democratic States in 1950*

Vote Change	Percent Annual Increase in Taxes	
	−9.0 to 6.6	6.7 to 68.4
2.9 to 4.4	5	1
−4.6 to −17.6	2	5

*The number in each cell is the number of states with the designated vote change and annual percentage tax increase.

combining the figures from individual elections to achieve a grand 2 × 2 table. This total coefficient is listed in the last column of Table [3].

The procedure for calculation is similar to that for *gamma*, except that each array is divided into two, rather than three, groups. The coefficient of association is derived through the formula.[30]

$$Q = \frac{ad - bc}{ad + bc}$$

in which a, b, c, d correspond to the four cells of the table, and ad and bc are the diagonal products. An illustration of this statistic is provided by Table [5], which shows the relationship, for Democratic gubernatorial seats in 1950, between vote change and percent annual tax increases. In this case,

$$Q = \frac{5(5) - 1(2)}{5(5) + 1(2)} = \frac{23}{27} = .85$$

The relationship is strong, although the small number of cases limits its significance.

[30] See M. J. Moroney, *Facts from Figures*, 3rd ed. (Baltimore: Penguin Books, 1956), pp. 264–266.

ELECTORAL DECISION AND POLICY MANDATE: AN EMPIRICAL EXAMPLE
Leon D. Epstein

In terms of a theoretical model Robert Dahl has persuasively argued that elections cannot tell us much about the preferences of majorities and minorities, "beyond the bare fact that among those who went to the polls a majority, plurality, or minority indicated their first choices for some particular candidate or group of candidates." These first choices, he argues, can rarely be interpreted in a national election "as being equivalent to a majority of first choices for a specific policy." Elections, Dahl believes, are "ineffective as indicators of majority preference," although they are crucial for controlling leaders.[1] The reasoning is elegantly simple and lucid. Some of the voters electing a candidate may not agree with a given policy of the candidate but choose him for other reasons and in spite of, or unaware of, the particular policy disagreement. The thrust of the argument is against the responsible party school of political scientists who would have each slate of candidates clearly committed to sharply defined policy positions and so convert elections from mere candidate decisions to policy decisions as well.

The difficulties of combining policy and candidate choice are here to be illustrated by a specific empirical example related to Dahl's theoretical formulation. The example happens to be one in which circumstances were probably more favorable for policy choice than those which Dahl hypothesizes. For one thing, our case is a state election rather than a national election, rightly assumed by Dahl to involve more diverse and complex policy choices. Second, a single policy question dominated the election campaign to an unusual degree. And third, there is, as will be shown, a sense in which voter preferences on this policy question seem to have crucially affected the election result. If in these circumstances there are still important difficulties in the way of saying that the election decided a policy question, Dahl's argument will have been especially strongly supported by our example.

The case at hand is Wisconsin's gubernatorial election of 1962. The policy question is whether the state should raise additional revenues by increasing its income tax or by extending its sales tax. Data are mainly from a statewide survey of 759 respondents, chosen in a clustered area probability sample, by the Survey Research Laboratory of the University of Wisconsin.[2] Unfortunately, the survey was conducted six months after the

Source: Reprinted by permission from *The Public Opinion Quarterly* (Winter 1964), pp. 564–572.

[1] Robert A. Dahl, *A Preface to Democratic Theory* (Chicago: University of Chicago Press, 1956), pp. 130, 127, and 131.

election of November 1962. While we ought to assume that respondents' recollections suffer from the passage of time, the survey's gubernatorial vote division is within a percentage point of the actual election returns. And on tax questions respondents were about as likely to be aware of the policy disagreement in the spring of 1963 as in the preceding fall, since the state legislature was still engaged in sharp and well-publicized debate on the relative merits of income and sales taxes.

A little of the Wisconsin background must be noted.[3] Wisconsin had several years of nearly even two-party competition before 1962. A Democrat (Gaylord Nelson) was elected governor in 1958 and 1960, and he was running, successfully as it turned out, for the United States Senate in 1962. Another Democrat (John Reynolds) was elected attorney general in 1958 and 1960; he was running for governor, successfully too, in 1962. But in all three of these elections Republicans continued to control the legislature (both houses except in 1958) but without sufficient majorities to override a governor's veto. Their candidate for governor (Philip Kuehn) had run well in 1960 and was widely expected to win in 1962. Throughout these years of Democratic control of the governorship and Republican control of the legislature, the principal issue was tax policy. Democrats insisted that any additional revenue come from the income tax, Wisconsin's traditional source ever since the Progressive Era early in the century. Republicans, after hesitation and internal division, advocated that a sales tax be added to the state's revenue-raising methods so that the income tax would not have to be increased. During Nelson's second term as a Democratic governor, 1961–62, a sales tax was finally enacted in Wisconsin but only on selected items, excluding food and clothing in particular. For the governor to sign even this, which he did as part of a compromise to obtain funds for his program, was regarded as a retreat from traditionally

progressive opposition to the sales tax. John Reynolds, then the Democratic attorney general, denounced the compromise and began his campaign for governor on the basis of seeking the repeal of the selective sales tax. In this he was heartily endorsed by Democratic party activists. On the other side, the Republican candidate for governor (Kuehn) was backed by his party in a campaign based on the extension of the selective sales tax to a general sales tax (with a credit refund of benefit to low-income groups when filing their income tax returns).

A sharper important policy disagreement is hard to imagine in American politics. Each candidate took a firm position, and his position was linked to a traditional ideological perspective on a matter of familiar and intimate concern. The Democratic candidate attacked the proposed tax on food and clothing, and the Republican defended it as the means of providing state services without driving industry out of Wisconsin by raising income tax rates. The two candidates faced each other on this issue in the only television debate of the campaign.

The other features of the election should be observed. Wisconsin's voters were very evenly divided between the two parties. As measured by our survey, there was a small Democratic margin in response to a question about general party preference, with more independent answers than usual in similar national surveys,[4] and there was an almost exactly even Democratic-Republican response (with many saying "Depends") to a question about usual preferences for state and county offices. Therefore, it is not surprising that in the gubernatorial election, between two clear partisans, the result should have been a margin, for the Democrat, of only 12,000 votes out of more than one and one-quarter million total votes cast. This leads to the second additional point. The turnout was slightly more than half the potential electorate, as compared with nearly three-quarters in the presidential election of 1960, and we know from our data that the lower off-year turnout means that those of higher status (in education, income,

[2] The data used here, along with a great deal more, are presented more fully in *Votes and Taxes*, a monographic study of the 1962 election published in 1964 by the Bureau of Government, Extension Division, University of Wisconsin.

[3] Deeper immersion in the nature of the state's politics may be sought in the author's *Politics in Wisconsin* (Madison, University of Wisconsin Press, 1958), and in James R. Donoghue, *How Wisconsin Voted 1848–1960* (Madison, University of Wisconsin Bureau of Government, 1962).

[4] The 15 percent classified as independents in the Wisconsin survey was higher than any independent percentage reported in seven national surveys, 1952–58, employing similar questions and a similar index. Angus Campbell, Philip E. Converse, Warren E. Miller, and Donald E. Stokes, *The American Voter* (New York: John Wiley, 1960), p. 124.

TABLE 1. Usual Voting Preferences for State and County Offices
in Relation to Tax Preferences (in percent)

	Usual Voting Preferences[a]				
	Rep. (255)	Depends (164)	Dem. (255)	Don't vote (77)	All (759)[b]
Fairer tax[c]					
Sales	46	30	25	21	33
Income	45	57	65	64	56
Depends, neither, don't know	9	13	10	15	11
Total	100	100	100	100	100
Increase[d]					
Sales tax	54	43	33	34	43
Income tax	33	43	57	40	44
Don't know	13	14	10	26	13
Total	100	100	100	100	100

[a]"Voting preference" is derived from answers to this one question: "Over the years, which party's candidates for state and county offices have you usually voted for?"

[b]Total of 759 includes eight respondents not tabulated under voting preferences because information was not ascertained.

[c]Answers were in response to this question: "As a matter of principle, which form of tax would you say is the most fair to everybody, the sales tax or the income tax?"

[d]Answers were in response to this question: "If it is decided that the state absolutely needs to raise more money, would you favor getting it by increasing the sales tax some way, or by increasing the income tax and doing away with the sales tax?"

and occupation) are overrepresented.[5] So, as we will indicate, are those citizens who seem likely to be aware of a policy question like taxation.

FINDINGS

Which of the two taxes Wisconsin voters preferred is a first consideration. Although respondents by a large majority did not want more money to be raised by any new or increased taxes, they were nevertheless asked their preferences, in two separate questions, between sales and income taxes. The results (last column of Table 1) in response to the question about which tax is fairer in principle are significantly different from those in response to which tax should be increased if the state needed more money. While the latter shows a virtually even division of opinion, the preference in

principle is very strongly for the income tax. To both questions, responses predictably vary with party preferences (Table 1). Democratic voters are more favorable to the income tax than are Republican voters, although the margin is not so great on the second question as on the first. Democratic voters are more solidly for their favored tax than are Republicans, and this is especially so with respect to fairness preferences. Democrats regard the income tax as fairer by a margin of over 2½ to 1, while Republicans are evenly divided. At least as significant, however, is that among both groups of voters, even among the more committed Democrats, a large minority prefers the tax position adopted by the opposing party. This comes to exactly one-third of the Republicans and one-third of the Democrats in answer to the second question.

Perhaps these voters did not even know that their parties had different tax positions from their own. A large minority, it is clear from Table 2, could not have known of any such difference be-

[5]These high-status groups are more heavily overrepresented in Wisconsin's off-year turnout than in the presidential elections reported generally for nonsouthern states. *Ibid.*, p. 478.

TABLE 2. Identification of Parties with Taxation Stands, Voters and Nonvoters (in percent)

	All (759)	Voters (446)	Nonvoters (271)	Others[a] (42)
Identify Republicans as for sales tax	54	63	41	33
Do not identify Republicans as for sales tax[b]	46	37	59	67
Total	100	100	100	100
Identify Democrats as for income tax	44	52	32	26
Do not identify Democrats as for income tax[c]	56	48	68	74
Total	100	100	100	100

[a]Includes don't remembers and others not ascertained.

[b]Includes all those who responded to the question about which party was for the sales tax by saying anything but Republican. Possible replies were Democratic, both, neither, and don't know.

[c]Includes all those who responded to the question about which party was for the income tax by saying anything but Democratic. Possible replies were Republican, both, neither, and don't know.

cause of an unawareness of party positions. Confining attention to column 2 of that table and so overlooking the nonvoters, whose knowledge is even less, we observe that over one-third of the voters could not identify the Republicans as for the sales tax and that almost half could not identify the Democrats as for the income tax.[6] Perhaps, however, the first of these findings ought to be turned around to emphasize that the bulk of

[6]Even these proportions are fairly high relative to proportions that, in other studies, correctly perceive party differences on national issues of long-standing public visibility. Such correct perceptions are regularly less frequent than the simple holding of opinions. *Ibid.*, pp. 179–181, 184–185, and 211; and Bernard E. Berelson, Paul F. Lazarsfeld, and William N. McPhee, *Voting* (Chicago: University of Chicago Press, 1954), pp. 218, 227.

the electorate did possess the crucial information. Almost two-thirds of the voters knew that the Republican party was for the sales tax, which more clearly than the income tax was the campaign issue. Still, while this portion of the electorate might include those concerned enough to base their gubernatorial votes on the tax issue, there are many others who simply could not have knowledgeably cast their ballots on the tax issue even if they had wanted to do so.

Generally, as would have been expected from the association of party and tax preferences, the pro—sales tax voters favored the Republican candidate by about 2 to 1, and the pro—income tax voters favored the Democratic candidate by about the same margin (Table 3). But note well that a large number of voters for each candidate did not

TABLE 3. Tax Preferences and Vote for Governor (in percent)

	Voted For				
	Kuehn (Rep.)	Reynolds (Dem.)	Other*	Total	(N)
Prefer, as fairer in principle:					
Sales tax	44	18	38	100	(250)
Income tax	19	35	46	100	(426)
Favor increasing:					
Sales tax	40	22	38	100	(323)
Income tax	17	37	46	100	(333)

*Includes nonvoters.

agree with his tax policy. To be precise, when Table 3 is turned on end, it is found that one-third of the voters for the winning Democratic candidate preferred to increase the sales tax rather than to accept their candidate's proposed income tax increase.

A closer, narrower look at tax preferences and voting is afforded by an analysis of those respondents who stated explicitly that they had voted for governor on the tax issue. The number (109) who gave taxes as the most important reason for their vote is a surprisingly high proportion, over one-quarter, of the voters. Of these tax-issue voters, 80 percent, not just near two-thirds as for all voters, identified the Republican party as for the sales tax, and 71 percent identified the Democratic party as for the income tax. More of them, 58 percent, chose the Democratic than the Republican candidate. Did this group then provide the critical increment of votes to elect the Democrat? To try to answer this question, our numbers begin to appear too small for reliability, but they do suggest the strong possibility of such a critical increment. Of course, we cannot assume that all of those who reported voting for the Republican or the Democrat because of the tax issue would not have voted the same way in any event. Rather, we should conservatively assume that those who usually vote Republican and those who usually vote Democratic would have done the same in this election. Thus, looking at our tax-issue voters in Table 4, let us disregard the usual Republicans who voted for the Republican candidate and the usual Democrats who voted for the Democratic candidate. True,

this excludes the bulk of each candidate's voters. But it leaves the Democratic candidate with a greater number of tax-issue voters drawn from a combination of the other party and the non-attached group. He not only has more tax-issue voters altogether, but he has more from outside his party's usual voters than does his Republican opponent. The significance of this is borne out by the more complex breakdown of Table 5. Here tax-issue voters are compared with voters who had given some reason other than taxes to explain their gubernatorial vote. The Democrat won a higher percentage of tax-issue voters than non-tax issue voters in both the Republican and the "Depends" categories of usual party preference.

Accordingly, since the gubernatorial election was decided by less than a percentage point and since the winning Democratic candidate appears to have won somewhat more than that percentage as a result of the tax issue, the election was, in this sense, decided by voter preferences on a given policy question. Of course, the election could equally well have been decided by any other policy or by any other matter, including the personality of the candidates. Taxes, however, were the most prominent issue, and both the winning and losing candidates thought that it had been critically determining. The Democratic winner could, therefore, be expected to claim a political mandate for his tax policy although he faced a Republican legislature which also claimed a mandate for its tax policy.

TABLE 4. Relation of Those Who Voted for Governor on Basis of Tax Issue* and Usual Party Voting Preference for State and County Offices (in percent)

| Usual Vote | Because of Tax Issue Voted For | | |
	Kuehn (Rep.) (46)	Reynolds (Dem.) (63)	Total (109)
Republican	65	9	33
Depends, etc.	22	34	28
Democratic	13	57	39
Total	100	100	100

*"Those who voted for governor on tax issue" are the respondents who replied with tax issue statements when asked, with respect to the gubernatorial choice, "What were the most important reasons you voted for this man rather than for his opponent?"

TABLE 5. Usual Voting Preference and Tax Issue Salience in Relation to Vote for Governor [in percent]

| Usual Voting Preference | Voted For | | | |
	Kuehn (Rep.)	Reynolds (Dem.)	Total	(N)*
Republican:				
Tax issue voter	83	17	100	(36)
Non-tax issue voter	88	12	100	(135)
Depends:				
Tax issue voter	33	67	100	(30)
Non-tax issue voter	48	52	100	(60)
Democratic:				
Tax issue voter	14	86	100	(43)
Non-tax issue voter	13	87	100	(113)

*Excludes respondent who voted for governor but whose usual voting preference for state and county offices was not ascertained.

The result, incidentally, was another compromise, in which the sales tax was extended to more items, without being made general, and the income tax rate was slightly increased.

COMMENTARY

Putting aside the fact that the separation of powers worked in Wisconsin, as it often does elsewhere in the United States, to prevent any gubernatorial mandate from being completely effective, what inferences about the relation between candidate and policy choices can be drawn from Wisconsin's election of 1962? In discussing these inferences, let us assume that the admittedly tenuous findings support the view that tax-issue voting gave the Democrat his critical margin of victory. Even so, it must be plain from the data already presented that the margin thus produced was far from the same thing as a majority preference for the Democratic tax policy. It is not that the margin was very small, making it difficult to claim a popular mandate for anything; the margin would almost have to be small to permit one to say, as seems possible here, that any one policy issue decided the election. More to the point is the demonstration that the winning candidate's majority included a large minority who disagreed with his tax policy and many more who voted for him for reasons not connected with tax policy. To assert that even this election, centered though it was on a policy, provided a clue to the majority's preference on that policy is to give a totally unwarranted authority to a small portion of the winner's majority. This small portion consists only of those who voted for the Democrat because of the tax issue, and would not apparently have voted for him otherwise. Such voters were not just fewer, by a great deal, than the usual Democratic voters constituting the bulk of the Democratic candidate's majority, but they were also considerably fewer than the number of the Democratic candidate's voters who disagreed with the tax policy held by the candidate and by the critical incremental voters who elected him.

In this respect, our case illustrates empirically the difficulties that confront the interpretation of candidate election as a decision on policy. Within no logically defensible democratic theory can a small minority determining the election by their policy preferences be said to provide majority support for the policy at issue.

This section addresses the problems of the governor upon assuming and exercising the powers of his office. We follow him through the transition period, to the choice of his staff, to working with the legislature and the bureaucracy. And it is here we begin to run into discussions of the governor's role, which usually call for reform. Terry Sanford urged, "Make the chief executive of the state the chief executive in fact," and continued:

The governor, by his very office embodies his state. He stands alone at his inauguration as the spokesman for all the people.... He must, like the President of the United States, energize his administration, search out the experts, formulate the programs, mobilize the support, and carry new ideas into action.... Few major undertakings ever get off the ground without his support and leadership. The governor sets the agenda for public debate; frames the issues; decides on the timing; and can blanket the state with good ideas by using his access to the mass media.... The governor is the most potent political power in his state.[1]

A bedsheet list of proposals for reform usually follow such calls, and in the past few decades many particulars of these proposals have been fulfilled.

Yet the underlying theme of this book is that despite the call for more potent and powerful governors, and despite the achievement of many of the called for reforms, there are still serious constraints on the governor which may be outside the power of the reformer and the governor to overcome. The limits to what the governor, although potent and powerful in his office, can accomplish are still considerable.

The most obvious constraint is in the perceptions of just what a governor is and what he can do if given "the tools." Sanford portrays a chief executive who is hamstrung and waiting to be freed, and whose public demands that he do the things we all know must be done. Although there is evidence of governors attempting to obtain the needed funds, administrative structure, and then guiding the state government in specific actions, the picture too often is one of a governor still unable to control or direct activities, even some of those supposedly under his direct control. Departments of administration, budget offices, and planning offices have evolved to aid in "control" problems, but the problems, to a great extent, lie elsewhere in the system: The governor is really at-

[1] Terry Sanford, *Storm over the States* (New York: McGraw Hill, 1967), pp. 188, 185.

SECTION 2
GOVERNORS AND POLICY FORMULATION

tempting to gain control over federal programs in his state and cope with various problems and activities at the local level. Officials at these other levels have their claims to legitimacy and power which too often lead to confrontation politics with the governor versus these various actors. He can be given "the tools" within his own domain, but these may not and probably do not allow him to gain control over what happens at other levels of government. He may be the chief federal systems officer in the state, but this is equally as restricting as it is enhancing a role for him to fulfill.

A second broad constraint lies in the actual prospect of the governor taking action on the various problems he faces. In government taking action is translated into decisions, programs, and dollars, and each of these has its own political costs for the governor. Although decisions to take or not to take action delight some, they anger others, and sources of previous support are alienated. The enmeshing of programs into the bureaucracy brings a new type of politics to bear. What were once open lines to the governor are now closed or severely constricted, as the bureaucracy sets to its administrative task. Probably more important in this situation are the new open lines which the bureaucratization of programs allows; causes lost with the governor can be won once the program is placed within the agency. And, most obviously, financing programs and agencies leads to tax-related questions, never popular issues. All translates into votes, or better, the loss of potential votes, so the governor and his aides must think long and hard on the tradeoff between governmental action and votes.

Another constraint lies within the minds of men and in the structure of governmental programs as they often view all governors and states as being alike and equal. Therefore, what is good for one state must be good for the others. Similarly for that which is bad. For example, the urban problems of the Boston-Washington metropolitan belt, and their proposed solutions, are often translated into the national norm. Thus, national programs aimed at urban problems too often bring a basic northeastern bias to their guidelines, often to the detriment of the states and the governors in the hinterlands.[2]

Similarly, those who would reform bring the same basic list to each and every state without analyzing the possible consequences. The American states, as several articles in this volume suggest, are at varying levels of development, and this leads to variations among the states with regard to policy output, the configuration of the government components, certain political aspects, and, most important, the problems they must address. Thus, the same reform or program requirement will have varying effects from state to state depending on the state's particular blend of characteristics. A certain change in the governor's ability to perform may bring political and governmental forces into better balance in one state, but lead to a serious imbalance in another. Further, the actual need for change varies considerably among the states, and priorities set at the national level or for several states may actually be disruptive to the individual state-by-state priorities.

Finally, the twentieth century has seen the rise of the stronger executive movement: Governmental reform and political action have aimed at giving the chief executive more power.[3] Along with this has grown the myth of the chief executive's being able to right the wrongs of the day, only if given the chance. As Sanford emphasized, "He embodies the state"—that is, all that is good about the state. But, as Cronin has so well pointed out for the presidency,[4] this sets too great an agenda for one man to cope with: It suggests a certain "religiosity" about the office.

The governor, like the President, cannot be all things to all men: He cannot right all the wrongs if given the tools. He cannot chart the way into the future with the assuredness that the chart will be followed, let alone be correct. He does not have the moral power to sway those who deviate. He cannot do this because he does not have the power even to control to a great extent that which goes on around him within our fragmented political and governmental systems. He cannot do this because the very process that empowers him is based on the divisive power of politics.

[2] Daniel J. Elazar, "Megalopolis and the New Sectionalism," *Public Interest*, Spring 1968, pp. 67–85.

[3] Herbert Kaufman, "Emerging Conflicts in the Doctrines of Public Administration," *Public Administrative Review*, Vol. L (December 1956), pp. 1057–1073.
[4] Thomas Cronin, "The Textbook Presidency," a paper delivered at the 1970 Annual Meeting of the American Political Science Association, Los Angeles, California, September 8–12, 1970.

In summary, we often ask of the governor more than he can or wants to give. When he does not satisfy our expectations, which is a forgone conclusion, we retaliate as best we can through our views and our votes. The limits to what he can achieve lie not only within the system of government and politics, but also within men—the governors and the people.

CHAPTER
4
TRANSITIONS

In politics transition is usually thought of as the period between being elected and taking the oath of office. Only recently has there been any systematic and rigorous studies of this crucial period when new priorities are set and new personnel to run government are chosen, and when, in general, there is a change in the mood and tone of government, which makes new directions in policy and administration possible.

This chapter includes excerpts of most of the studies of transition in gubernatorial politics. Norton Long, in "After the Voting is Over," depicts the mood and nature of transition. Several later studies have developed more rigorous conclusions about transitions in one party settings as well as transfers of power in an interparty setting.

These studies suggest some major refinements in the notions of politicians and administrators about transition. For one thing, the transition period is not limited to the interval between election day and inauguration. Its duration is political rather than structural, and its impact on policy and administration lasts much longer than the formal transition period. And the initial impact of change in political leadership on change in policy and personnel may have been overestimated. Rather than wholesale change in personnel and dramatic policy shifts, the studies suggest more incremental change as state government adjusts to new leadership or as new leadership adjusts to state government.

AFTER THE VOTING
IS OVER
Norton E. Long

After the voting is over the search for the new definition of the situation goes on. There is, of course, no single objective definition of the situation which presents itself for recognition. In part the definition of the situation is created, is imposed by those having the power and the wit to do so. In part, the social situation and the socialized expectations and rules of interpretation provide limits to the range of alternatives and powerful

Source: Reprinted from "After the Voting Is Over," *Midwest Journal of Political Science* [Vol. 6, No. 2 (May 1962), pp. 183–200], by Norton E. Long by permission of the Wayne State University Press.

cues to action. The definition of the situation comprises not only the frontier scouts' interpretation of a sign, the guests' sense of drawing-room rules, but also the players' agreement that the one-eyed jacks shall be wild or that the game will be touch football. In one sense, the actors are searching for an objective definition to which they can intelligently relate their own behavior; in another, they are trying to create or to get created for them a definition of the situation which will permit them to function. The search of individual and institutional actors in its totality may be regarded as composing a social search process through which definitional consensuses are created, preserved, and changed. Campaign, election, and development of a new administration are aspects of a social technology by which adaptive change occurs within a stable system.

The process that stretches at least as far back as the preliminary preprimary negotiations and struggles, and has its roots in the working of the local political culture, passes for the moment out of the stage where the voters' action at an election is of crucial importance. That hurdle is over, past history to be reminisced about as part of the folklore of politics and a source of claims by various actors for rewards based on their supposed contributions to the campaign and on commitments of the candidate.

The campaign itself leaves a heritage of organization and oratory. The oratory provides enterprising members of the press, the protagonists of particular interests, opponents, and fellow partisans with texts to urge the logic and the duty of specific measures. For the candidate and part of his entourage, some, at least, of the oratory provides an island of commitment in a sea of uncertainty—these things at least we are bound to do. While much of the effort of the campaign is to present a shifting target, uncommitted on the issues that might adversely affect any important block of votes, after the election the absolute of a binding commitment provides the essential string in the political solution around which a program can crystallize. It is like the all-important first sentence of the essay which, once written, gives direction and momentum to the piece.

FROM CAMPAIGN TO OCCUPATION

The heritage of organization from the campaign provides the initial cadres of the political army of occupation. Much of the subsequent course of events stems from the motley nature of this volunteer army stiffened by a few professionals who constituted the shock troops of the electoral campaign. Discipline of a force composed mainly of unpaid volunteers, self-appointed officers, guerrilla bands with private purposes, enthusiasts for particular causes, and the mercenaries of the full time professional feudatory chieftains is rarely satisfactory.

The lowest and frequently the highest common denominator of the host is a many motived opposition to the ins. The boundary problem presents its peculiar difficulty during the campaign and even further difficulties after the election. Who is and who is not a member of the organization, and what rank or legitimate field of competence he possesses, is frequently painfully obscure and a matter of controversy. Attendant to this obscurity is the postelection problem of what commitments have been made and how they are to be honored.

The openness of the campaign organization, its need of volunteers, its fear of giving any offense, and the sheer lack of structure and commonly shared knowledge of definite membership rules encourage and invite the entrance into the organization of the most diverse kinds of actors. Many of these must at a later date be painfully combed out of the organization's hair. The normally unbureaucratized nature of the campaign organization in a sense furthers the process of the social search for a new definition or redefinition of the situation. The diverse actors who penetrate the loose campaign organization are frequently carriers of a wide range of ideas and proposals. The loose mesh of the campaign organization's screening process permits the entry of actors that at a later and more bureaucratized stage of the process would be screened out. This early looseness, then, permits a limited process of social experimentation to go on. The lack of well-defined purposes and structure is functional for a degree of innovation. The madhouse of the campaign viewed as a confused hurly-burly by its more orderly minded participants in which nobody knows what is going on, everybody is in everybody's way, and everything is a moment to moment reaction to the day's press and the hour's crisis is a significant interval in the social process in which mutation can occur. The soft, plastic state of the campaign organization is transferred to the top echelons of the government for a considerable period after the electoral transfer of power.

While the candidate is taking his well-earned vacation following the good news of election night, and his personal staff is cleaning up the bills, writing the thank you letters, and speculating and politicking over the offices to be filled, the disintegration of the existing administration, already evident if the campaign appeared hopeless, goes on apace. A none too covert search on the part of actors inside and outside the government for the terms of accommodation ensues. All the diverse personnel of the campaign organization to whom they have access become potential sources of needed information. The use and wont of the previous administration with which working relations have adjusted are crumbling and their continuance is in doubt. The folklore of elections and some of the rhetoric of the campaign support the belief that the election will make a difference. What difference and to whom become absorbing questions. Adequate sources of uncertainty absorption are in high demand to calm nerves and permit the uninterrupted continuance of customary routines.

While by and large most people know the election is not going to make any serious difference to them, many are unsure. What is statistically true in general may be fatally untrue in particular. Again, for the preexisting hardened routines, the period of transition to and settling down of the new administration represents a softening and even temporary relaxation of their grip. Upward mobile types, careerists, adventurers, the protagonists of previously disapproved programs all fish in the troubled waters of change. Many, of course, silently pursue their customary safe routines till they take the measure of the occupying forces. Nonetheless, some, impelled by curiosity, opportunism, and perhaps the sheer operating necessity of knowledge, seek to determine the difference the new administration will make. Nor is it possible for their informants to say merely we can't tell you; the executive-elect hasn't told us, and privately we doubt that he knows. Partial definitions of the emerging new situation and policies are offered from a variety of sources. Those who feel they cannot live with uncertainty search for access to a spokesman on whose authoritative interpretation they can rely. While some refuse to speak, many others do so freely. The new administration's positions are variously defined, as the vacuum human nature abhors is filled by rumor, gossip, and unauthorized statement. In this process

the dope stories and speculations of press, radio, and television play their part. In fact their importunity is one of the more effective social goading devices to secure program definition and decisions.

UNSTRUCTURED CHANGE

The structure of politics resembles a drama which is only partially defined as to roles and script. However, it is sufficiently well defined to force the actors to meet certain temporally defined deadlines, and as a folk art form it is presumed to have fairly stable audience expectations concerning performance that ought not to be slighted. The political columnist who doubles as retailer of inside dope and as art critic along with the older professionals or putative professionals serves as *arbiter elegantiarum* to the novices. For most who are entering high office, the office they are entering (if not all public office) implies a new and unknown role to be faced with as much fear of *gaucherie* as the drawing room and the ball. Unlike the socialization of the new recruit to most organizations, who is taught by his superiors and his equals, the political executive is taught by his inferiors and those doubtfully loyal to him, among whom he fears he must feel his way. Unlike other trades and professions, politics in the American subculture is rarely learned by formal apprenticeship and most often by a purely oral tradition. Written materials beyond the political gossip column, when read at all, are largely treated as sources of inside dope rather than as data for scientific problem solving. In this respect, much of our politics resembles a continuous performance of the Battle of Bull Run with new actors for each show and a minimal build-up of knowledge from the experience.

If the natives of the government bureaucracies and other interested parties are anxious and need to know what the new executive will do, this is an anxiety he shares with them. For he too must know what he proposes to do and must learn to play and to create the novel part to which he is now committed. How does one learn to play politics? Normally the way we learn how to behave in an organization is through the advice, admonitions, blows, and other sanctions of those already there. There will be blows and there is advice for the executive, but it comes differently to one whose entrance is at the top and whose socialization must take place under the conditions of his peculiar status position and relative isolation.

A major manifest function of the replacement of the top echelon of a political structure is to give new or altered direction to the organization. This suggests a clear incompatibility with the learning process by which a new entrant is successfully digested into the existing organization. What is wanted is a significant break, though by no means a complete break, with continuity. This the wholesale top replacement partially achieves.

The newly elected executive is like an assembly hand at a conveyor belt with forced options constantly coming up to which he must respond. While it would be carrying the figure too far, perhaps, to compare his situation to that portrayed by Charlie Chaplin in *Modern Times*, the image it conveys has its point. The tempo of the belt may relax or the spacing of the forced options may widen, but the drama is always moving, though sometimes deceptively. Play or assembly line, either figure contains the essential notion of a set of predetermined, built-in deadlines that must be responded to and met.

In the seemingly largely unstructured situation, elements of structure—inauguration, choice of cabinet, legislative program, budget, end of session, time for vetoes, these and many other compulsions to act—force responses in time. They are parts of the built-in structured social technology of the political culture that keep the actors in bounds and move the action along. In addition to the structured elements that are set in motion for the executive-elect and the other official actors by the election, there are, of course, the multitude of predictable and unpredictable matters that thrust themselves and are thrust on their attention, some officially relevant and others officially irrelevant but compelling nonetheless.

Before the executive-elect has taken over his office, and haunting him through his vacation, is the choice of his cabinet. This choice is difficult where it is a choice, since the executive elect, though knowing many people, rarely knows the right people to form a cabinet. The search for the definition or redefinition of the situation enters a critical stage with the selection of the cabinet. The campaign organization of course might have solved this. Indeed, in the textbook ideal of the well-structured party system with its worked out hierarchy and apprenticeship training and its accepted design for allocating offices and rewards, the task would theoretically be so limited as to be rela-

tively easy. But this theory is miles apart from American practice. The executive-elect may have a friend or two whom he can cajole into sharing his troubles—a friend or two who will not too violently offend against the supposed requirements of their offices. Beyond this he is at the mercy of the judgment of others as to whether a possible is possible, fills the image of the job, is acceptable to those to whom he must be acceptable, is likely to be loyal, and, most important, can be persuaded to accept.

LOOKING FOR CLUES

The choice of the cabinet is a stylized clue to the intentions of the new administration. The cluster of interests involved in each agency's operation, the party and factional claims, and the interpretation and impact of the media play a major role in the folk political science that provides the rationale of choice beyond the personal factors involved.[1] The members of the cabinet are, except for a few, unbound to their chief by ties of friendship and frequently unbound even by ties of party loyalty. Their choice has been dictated by the felt necessity to meet a supposed publicly expected image and to satisfy the claims, enforceable or not, of interests that have vested in the selection. As is often the case in politics, there is no sure answer to what the public or any public expects or to what this or that group really demands or can enforce. Choice must be based on hunch, partial information, folklore, and perhaps more significantly on the unplanned but real screening process that objectively limits and determines the perceived available options. This screening process is made up of the actors, their information, their definitions of the situation and the relevant technology, and their access to the executive. Much more could be detailed about how this human artifact emerges to sort the stimuli and attend to them and how the stimuli are transmitted. Suffice it to say at this point, the difference that makes the difference is the collection of properties that make the informal group around the executive expose him to some, shield him from others, and fail so to do in the cases where they do. In all this his intentions play

[1] By folk political science I mean the common sense notions of how politics works as opposed to an empirically verified body of knowledge.

a part, both his overt and actual intentions and those far more often imputed to him. But of sheer necessity much that goes on in his name or in the name of his office reflects the independent decisions of undirected subordinates.

The staffing of the cabinet is likely to be the first major symbolic step toward defining the situation. This step will receive major media attention and be acted on by many as a piece of persuasive evidence of the executive's choice among alternatives and directions. That individual cabinet selections may be highly fortuitous does not detract from their effect of commitment. Once the plunge is made and the man is chosen, for a time at least the executive will find the cost of abiding with a mistake more bearable than admitting to having made it. In fact, so painful is the admission publicly and personally that considerable ingenuity and effort will be made to learn to live with a bad choice and circumvent its effects. At best the behavior of even known individuals in new and unfamiliar roles is difficult to predict. The choices of many cabinet members, made on secondhand information with an eye to the newspaper mediated public impact of the choice and its acceptability to powerful groups, can rarely be based on a sufficiently reliable estimate of the job performance.

The cabinet is frequently regarded as an institution that should be but somehow never is. Outside of utopian parliamentary conditions, the collection of individuals chosen for widely varying reasons rarely becomes an effective group. Neither do its members become an intimate friendly council of the chief executive, nor do they form a tightly knit group with common political aims. For a long time the head of each agency must concern himself with his agency, as his chief must with the general government. If he is not brought in as a trusted friend of the executive the mutual relations must be worked out as each learns to play his role and as they develop mutually acceptable conceptions of their roles, goals, and the situation confronting them. In the beginning the unknowns are many.

The new cabinet member has two stable sources of coherent direction to guide him: his external institutional affiliation and sponsorship, and the bureaucracy of his agency. Beyond this in time he is likely to feel the pressure of the executive's personal staff and the overhead agencies.

In the ordinary case, the new cabinet officer in all but the lines of his chief's special interest and concern will be obliged to work out his own mandate within the constraints of the situation as he perceives it. He too will be confronted by an in box and an out box with the importunate demand that he read and sign or merely sign so the work can go on. The ongoing current of the normal flow of departmental affairs will carry him along, an increasingly unresisting prisoner of accepted routines. It is easy to go with the system and hard to buck it.

In his separate office in his separate building the department head, himself an increasingly busy man, finds few occasions to interact with his chief, a very busy man and one difficult of access. The formal occasions of cabinet meetings provide little effective communication. Frank talk is rare. The usual contact is to request authority or funds, or because of trouble. The executive hopes that somehow his department head will handle the problems in his department and reflect credit on the administration, above all keep himself and his department from a political row or a public scandal.

Although the department head might wish for explicit marching orders from his chief rather than this perilous freedom, he is not left to his own devices. All the issues that confronted his predecessor, every promise made in the campaign, the wishes of legislators and pressure groups, and the claims of the faithful press in upon him. In addition to the routine come the decisions—the appointments that he, like his chief, in turn must make and the budgetary decisions that he will either face or duck by accepting the decisions of his predecessor.

The ideological and the heavily motivated arrive breathing fire. Change seems not only manifestly desirable but relatively easy. Sooner or later they discover that the system they are trying to direct or alter is as resistant as a tar baby or may even kick back as viciously as a mule. Many administrators dream of an organization as responsive to their desires as a car with its steering wheel, brake, and accelerator. The dream is, of course, of a utopia. However, it has this pointed analogy for the administrative organization. The car functions well only on the existing highways, and at top speed only on the main ones. The temptation to travel these and these alone grows as one becomes officewise and tires.

SYSTEM TO MANAGE

The newcomer to office frequently forgets that he is dealing with a system. This system, if it is to have any stability at all, must be highly resistant to change. Change within it is possible—even incremental change of it—but revolutions come hard and require extraordinary energy and circumstances.

At the level of the secretary or the director's office there is a deceptive appearance of power and flexibility. Power is mostly in terms of following the direction of the system's own moment of inertia, sometimes in slightly shifting it, but rarely except in conditions of breakdown in radically altering it. The bureaucracy of the department is an iceberg that shows deceptively little of itself at the level of surface visibility. Beneath the surface lies its mass. This mass, unlike an iceberg of course, lies in its interconnections with the rest of the society. It is through these interconnections that the agency has its mesh and effect on society. Like any vital relation it is two way and controls the controllers. The Pentagon's problems with military bases and the manufacturers of military hardware are only an extreme example of the grip that the enmeshing system exerts. The struggle for agricultural change, so frequently looked at in terms of morality, economic principle, or even plain guts, gains more sympathetic understanding from a realization of the range and significance of behaviors that policy change would entail and the leverage available for such change.

Department heads are frequently disappointing because they are, as it is called, captured by their organization. The alternative to becoming captured at least to a considerable degree is to remain an alien and dubious pearl in the bureaucratic oyster. As a member of the political army of occupation the department head may attempt denazification. He will usually, like the military, find it necessary to use native technicians of doubtful loyalty and principles. In addition, like all occupiers who in a sense rule from without, he must seek a fifth column among the natives who will cast their lot with him. His own troops are too few. But even where an admiral and his retainers can be induced for "the good of the service" to break with the bureaucratic resistance and join with the civilian wreckers, his influence will moderate and brake as well as facilitate the exercise of power. In the extreme case, a secretary of state

may bypass his department and leave it largely unemployed. Even here, however, massive routines continue of which the secretary may remain ignorant and whose consequences are nonetheless significant though ignored.

The necessity of the department heads grappling with their departments, and as a price of real contact being in turn grappled by them, makes them seem alien, obstinate, and weak willed to the chief executive. His public image of power and his own early illusions produce an initial sense of frustration and weakness, if not incompetence, in the face of the insufficiently appreciated, if not unexpected, resistance of the system to lighthearted attempts at its alteration. The useful department head must at least in good part be captured by his department and the configuration of interests it represents or remain alien to it. The price of remaining alien is not to use it, to be ineffective, or in the extreme case to destroy it with the aid of hostile forces and go on or build anew.

The cost of any of these courses is, at least in the short run, the antagonism of the friendly constituencies of the agency, and press reports of conflict, disharmony, and failure. An easy appearance of vigor can chiefly be attained by forceful programmatic emphasis on those activities which are presently popular. Given the frequent political ambitions of department heads, their frequent identification with existing friendly agency constituencies, and their limited loyalty and identification with the chief executive, it is not surprising if such a course of short-run popularity recommends itself to them.

In a sense, the department head is the front-line foreman of the administration connecting it through the bureaucracies with the society it seeks to manipulate and by which it is itself manipulated. For this reason the department heads, even those who are personal friends of the chief executive, become estranged from him—become objects, important levers of the government which themselves must be manipulated if his peculiar purposes are to be achieved.

For reasons suggested, the formal cabinet cannot be the kitchen cabinet or the unofficial family of the chief executive, though individual members of it may have ambiguously personal relations with him and personal standing with and access to the unofficial family. The term "family" is expressive and significant. In fact, there is almost a contradiction in the term "official family." This is the basic clue to the failure of the cabinet to become a family. It cannot, because its members are there because of their official, not their family position. The one or two friends in the cabinet carry ambiguous roles in the family and in their departments. Are they official members or family members in office?

The basis of the family relationship is personal, one of personal trust and loyalty. It is poles apart from officiality. The chief executive needs this family of personal rather than official friends to extend and protect his personality through an unbureaucratized medium of personal trust. Personal trust is the medium of the family. Official responsibility is the medium of trust of the bureaucracy. The chief executive and the department head alike demand an entourage, an immediate family whose relation to them is personal rather than official. This produces a characteristic phenomenon of our politics, a family surrounding the top executive mediating most of his relationships with the organized bureaucracy.

The family is like a scrub team of baseball among a group of friends in which the roles are played because of an appeal to personal friendship rather than to any internalized role conception or concern with audience expectation. To change the figure, there is always the danger that one of the children in the game, growing bored or angry, will pick up his dolls and go home. And quite seriously for the stability of the family, there is always another much more real home to go home to. For it is characteristic of much of the American political subculture that the higher one goes up the governmental hierarchy the less certain would be the response to the question, is your real job here or back where you come from? The lowly clerk in Washington or Springfield would be far clearer that his real job, his life fate was with the government than the executive nominally responsible for a whole department or the paladins of the chief executive's household.

This produces the politics of limited commitment by the unbureaucratized strata at the top for whom the job and the relations elsewhere are still a real, ever present alternative and a powerful directing force—a fact that produces what Aaron Cicourel has sensitively observed as the army camp atmosphere of the capital, in which many of the draftees go home weekends on passes or at least

out on the town to scandalize the natives. This limited commitment of the top stratum produces that unbureaucratized plasticity through which innovative impulses from without can be transmitted to the more hardened structure beneath. It is importantly, though not exclusively by any means, through this top component of plasticity that the search procedure operates by which the system is organized to receive some, though by no means all, of the impulses for change developing within it. Plasticity is, of course, not the exclusive property of this top stratum. There are conditions under which other government components are unbureaucratized and dynamic.

UNBUREAUCRATIZED STAFF

The chief executive's family is perhaps the most unbureaucratized element in the government. There is functional differentiation, a press secretary, a legal adviser, a hill man, a patronage secretary, and the like, but the characteristic that is most typical and most maddening is that of everyone meddling in anything and everything and the jack-of-all-trades nature of the family members. As a family, of course, every member is concerned with the fate of the family, which is uniquely connected with the fate of the head of the family. Thus, on any subject there are many opinions and diverse advice for the chief to listen to and choose among. The one dominant common basis that all opinions and advice are supposed to have is loyalty to the head of the family as an operating absolute.

The peculiar characteristic of at least many of the members of the family is their mobility, freedom, and accessibility. They are unburdened with bureaucratic responsibility. Some, though by no means all, have the leisure to be idea men, to think about program, and to solicit and receive the views of those screened out by the formal channels of the departments. In the classic sense they are staff. The press secretary, the legal advisor, the hill man, and the patronage secretary may be so overwhelmed with the insistent routine with which they must cope that they are in danger of becoming captured by the externally imposed flow of business. In fact, both the assembly line and the unprogrammed crisis to which they must so largely attend dull their creativity and separate them from others who have the leisure to be idea men but who also have the attendant insecurity of having no routine business to keep them employed and in the main apparent flow of action and *the Man's* attention.

The fluidity and amorphousness of the family are in a curious way one of its greatest assets, probably because they permit it to retain its paramount characteristic—personal loyalty to the head and loyalty to one another as family members. Where the family role has hardened into ongoing officiality, as with the Bureau of the Budget in the Executive Office, the President's men cease to be his men and become Bureau men. They cannot form members of the family. They have degenerated into officials with loyalties of an ongoing institutional sort replacing the older devotion to the chief.

The family, because of its lack of officiality and because it is not a natural family, is a psychologically costly affair. The relations, being highly personal, must be tended like friendship and a love affair. Feedback costs to sustain the interpersonal structure of trust are heavy. A day away, and doubt hangs heavy as to how one stands. This is not only the uneasiness of the courtier in the uneasy competition round the throne, it is also and more a set of valued personal relationships subject to constant stress. It is small wonder that members of the family seek escape in officializing their roles, and others are simply burned up. Those with the heavy demands of urgent routine or the routinized crises of the press are protected by the anodyne of fatigue.

But these too are bitterly hurt by the sense of personal failure or by criticism from the chief in connection with the unavoidable misfortunes that always occur. The tension of the family, its almost childlike rivalry for parental approval and affection are sources of great dynamism. The brotherhood in personal loyalty to the chief, for all its costs has its peculiar if evanescent warmth. The composition of this dynamic uninstitutionalizable institution is of particular significance for the nature of the regime, since both the quality of the thinking and the range and kind of top level access will be determined by it.

One might hypothesize that over time during the course of an administration the sheer psychological costs of maintaining a family would bring about crystallization into officiality and routine, that the family would harden into the staff around the general and the court would institutionalize. This should logically attend the loss of creative

energy in the new administration as it ages and accepts a particular definition of the situation as its own. The plastic top of the government, replacing the previous administration, in its turn hardens into defined bureaucratized routines.

Along with the choice of cabinet and key officials after the vote is over, an early besetting task of the chief executive and the early members of his family is the inaugural ball. The literature of a republican and blindly male-oriented social science neglects the importance of the court and women in the affairs of state. If one weighed the man hours and anxiety displayed over the inaugural ball and the expediental division of status symbols its invitations represent, one would find a work load that explains much of the frequent failure to get ostensibly more important matters decided at an early date. Mansion and White House have a lady, a first lady in fact but not usually appreciated in theory. The social affairs associated with the court—aspects of the chief executive's function, though frequently scoffed at—evidence a major role that is often undervalued. The republican monarch falls heir even at the level of mayor and clearly at that of President and governor to an integrative role. Politics, with all that is dishonorable in it, is still the fount of honor.

Politics as a system of honor is the title to an unpenned essay about a very real subject. A major problem of the chief executive is so to conduct himself as to be able to fill that part of the public expectation—elite and vulgar public expectation and even yearning—for the dispenser of honor and the setter-on of high tasks. It is a far cry from Arthur and his knights to Eisenhower and his businessmen or Kennedy and his professors. But politics, if it be only high enough and if its chief actor but know how to play the democratic kind, still ennobles. And society despite the split between the hierarchies—social, economic, cultural, and political—still responds to the deep cultural heritage of political primacy. The integrative role goes beyond the capacity to summon businessmen to the mayor's committee or the Department of Defense; it involves the capacity to claim the sacrifice even to the endangering of life of the ordinary citizen. So deep is the yearning for a monarchical uncertainty absorber who can both resolve doubts by a courageous act of will and give meaning to dull lives by proclaiming a Holy Grail that the management of this aspect of the chief executive's presentation of self is a major though often neglected source of power. A fact that he must learn. The texts frequently deplore the combination of ceremonial with practical chief executive in American politics. They forget that a real king, even a democratic one, gives more meaning to ceremony than can be squeezed out of a constitutional monarch of the most ancient lineage. The ill-considered democratic contempt so pleasingly expressed by Mark Twain in his *Connecticut Yankee* misses the critically important integrative function of ceremony and the need for a court.

In all the conflict of the competing departments and institutionally embodied interests that work through the government, like economic interests in a market, there is a need for a shared symbolism of common interest and common goals. This is the function of the latent "Society" the chief executive evokes and leads.

The court and the women present problems as well as fulfilling functions. There are works on the business executive's wife, but the literature on the wife of the public man has yet to develop the same seriousness. Here again is a difficult role that new incumbents have to learn and create. Among the many trials the chief executive and his family must face, few are more difficult than those occasioned by the frictions between palace and executive office. The strain on the first lady without the anodyne of work to dull the barbs of press and gossip is ill appreciated, and its effect through her on her husband even less. The war of nerves is not just an international phenomenon. As a special source of access and a psychological force on the chief executive, the palace and all that it implies is a major factor in shaping action. Like the chief executive's office family, the palace too goes through its *Sturm und Drang* before settling into a supportable if uneasy routine.

The conventions of the American political subculture demand with increasing insistence that the chief executive formulate a program and thereby in a major way define the situation for all the participants. In this respect the executive is, like Hobbes's sovereign, the source of order without whose forceful intervention a limited anarchy ensues. Friend and foe alike demand that he define the situation so that the players may know the nature of the game to be played. Even the adversary cooperation of the opposition requires that he set the target for them to shoot at. The press insists that he furnish a score card consisting of his musts so they can report the game. The built-in requirement that he propose a budget and that some kind of a State of the Union message be delivered provide compelling points in time when he must perform his basic function of uncertainty absorption and provide at least his tentative *definition of the situation*.

There are many reasons why the chief executive is reluctant to respond to the pressure for decisive clarifying action. The habit of the campaign is largely one of calculated ambiguity and platitudinous blandness. The easy criticism of the ins, fixed as they were in the immobility of the responsibility and power of office, changes into all the difficulties of action. The lack of knowledge which even seems to assist the campaign engenders doubt and hesitation in office. The problem of the nature of the social reality receives an unwonted attention. The epistemology of power traps thought in a doubt that may be more Hamlet-like than creative.

Friends and foes and even administration members wonder what the executive has in mind, what the strategy is. The differing, unchecked and sometimes uncheckable interpretations disrupt the possibility of effective cooperation except at those levels of routinized action which, like the functions of the body, go on unaffected by all but the most severe paralysis of mind.

FOUR MAJOR DOUBTS

Four major sources of doubt plague those who would like to cooperate as friends, limited allies or opponents, neutrals of varying degrees or outright foes.

First there is doubt as to the chief executive's intentions. What are his real goals? Second, there is uncertainty as to his capabilities. What cards does he hold? Third, there is doubt as to the relevant and efficacious technology. Is the folk political science correct as to the efficient relationship of means and ends? And fourth, what is the objective truth about these matters with respect to the other parties involved?

This leads to competing explanations of the executive's action or inaction. He has no guts. He is indecisive. He is naïve. He is getting bad advice. He doesn't know the score. He has a deep strategy. He is perfidious. He doesn't have the cards, the opposition does. All these and many more interpretations compete to explain his and others' actions or inactions.

Every attempt to probe the truth in particular is met with an array of uncertain and often hopelessly untestable answers concerning some or all of the essentials. Since action is forced, the common-sense definition of the situation must be adopted even by those who have checked it out and found it wanting in one particular case after another. This lack of a sufficiently structured objective situation makes the political arena resemble a shared field in which the players cannot get together on just which of the many games they might play is actually going to be played. The ignorance of *Kriegspiel* is confounded by the lack of any agreement that the laws of chess should apply or that an impartial umpire should define the objective situation for the players.

The picture of uncertainty and ignorance can be replaced by one of the most boring security in the recurrence of expected routines and the utter predictability that tomorrow will be much like today. A few echelons down the bureaucratic ladder, use and wont prevail. While the doubts above may titillate some, the old timers have little hope and less fear. All depends on the perspective. Does one concentrate on the dubieties of change or the massive continuities of the ongoing system?

Since much of the new executive's time is taken up with appointments, speeches, and the incredible amount of busy work of the office, the budget —the program in dollars—is likely to be largely the incrementally arrived at spending program of the past. What holds for the chief executive holds even more for the department heads. Without trained, knowledgeable staff it is difficult and dangerous to meddle. The trained budget professionals have a figure lore that defies easy mastery. Members of the "family" try to intervene, tapping special sources of university, pressure group, and esoteric information—trying on occasion to get the real dope from knowledgeable friendly natives. By and large this search for where the new chief executive can express his or his party's individuality is met with severe constraints in what seems to be the short run inflexibility of the situation. Where innovation is most likely is frequently where it is least desired and politically most unattractive. The necessity of facing up to inescapable objective problems such as taxation compels the painful act of politically costly choice.

The vagueness and all-promising position of the campaign constricts itself by a process of successive eliminations and alterations to the legislatively feasible course of the present moment.

Just as the loose campaign organization has to be painfully altered to fit the differing necessities of office, so the campaign oratory designed to appeal to a multiple and frequently contradictory electorate goes through a winnowing and reshaping that transforms it into a legislative program. What is designed to appeal to the electorate can hardly ever be a feasible action program.

The process by which the legislative program is developed is a complex interaction of many factors. First and foremost there are the massive continuities of departmental programs and budgets. By and large when these are taken care of, the executive for the first time fully realizes how limited is his freedom of action. The dollars are scarce or even nonexistent for new program. Even the maintenance of existing program may entail the unpopular resort to new taxes. Group after group whose support was accepted or sought during the campaign urge their claims. Legislators whose support will be needed urge measures on whose effective furtherance their own political lives depend. Agency on agency present compelling cases for building, for salary adjustments, for staffing, for new legislation. Other levels of government urge administration sponsorship of their legislative demands. Out of this welter of conflicting and competing claims the administration is compelled by public expectation, enforced by the press and other institutions, and the conventions of the political culture, to select a set of measures that will constitute the administration's program. Along with the budget, this provides a significant contribution of order to the otherwise anarchical situation that prevails in the absence of adequate unity of purpose backed by power.

While the continuities of the departments provide the bulk of the budget, the family of the executive work up the unique list of measures that constitute the administration's program. This constitutes the score card by which they hope to be judged and through whose passage they hope to make the "record"—the record on which the executive and his party will later run. This is the major integrating initiative and it provides most of the conscious unifying logic of the session. Many other initiatives from legislators and groups will, of course, occur, but none will be equally comprehensive. The dialogue between the executive and the legislature will be carried on over these matters in open session and in the lobby and the executive office. Much of the dialogue will be for the sake of a public whose attention to it in the press and the other media is a constant concern. The interpretations of the public and the public's reaction are a major determinant of the conduct of the parties. Here the soothsayers of public opinion have a role like the augurs of old. The peculiar mechanism by which anticipation of legislative action, legislative action, and executive and legislative anticipation of relevant voter action combine to screen the grist of measures and proposals is a crucial part of the social technology of controlled innovation. Stripped of the rhetorical packaging the program of one administration must be much like its predecessor or intolerable strain would be put on the system.

Yet innovation and adaptation occur through a dynamic within the system and a dynamic of the system. For the most part, the changes are incremental and piecemeal over time, and almost imperceptibly changes in degree may work changes in kind; changes within the system may produce changes of the system.

The voting provides the symbols of legitimacy to a government composed of an elected executive and his entourage and a legislature. It provides an increment to the folk political science of voter behavior. This folk political science provides no certain congruent definition of the situation for the executive and the members of the legislature. However, despite many differences there are considerable shared common sense definitions of the relevant political reality that permit friendly and adversary cooperation. The uncertainty of voter behavior of the campaign is replaced by the certainty of the election. The overmastering new uncertainty is the terms of legislative acceptance of the administration's program. This arena for sparring and struggle, though partially closed, is conducted by executive and legislators with an eye to probable relevant voter reaction. This reaction is shrouded in all the uncertainty of the folk political science and its multiple meanings and interpretations for the actors.

The architecture of the maze (the proper object of our study) is only partially discernible as yet. But its compulsions are probably the most durable elements on which a predictive social science can be built.

GUBERNATORIAL TRANSITION IN A ONE-PARTY SETTING

Thad L. Beyle
and
John E. Wickman

During the 1960s, there were a total of 157 gubernatorial elections in the states. Every two or four years state government goes through a period which is potentially, if not actually, one of change in leadership and direction. The transition period can bring a redefinition of the whole structure of governmental and political rewards and punishments. While uncertainty may be a fact of political life, the transition expands the boundaries of uncertainty to include once-established policies, programs, positions, and roles. Everyone concerned with government waits expectantly for clues as to the depth and direction of change.

Party labels provide the most visible, if not readily interpretable, indicator of new directions. However, only 54 gubernatorial elections in [the 1960s] brought a turnover of the party in power, while 103 represented either the reelection of an incumbent or a change of leadership within a single party. In 15 states, one party . . . controlled the governorship throughout [the] decade, some for several decades; and in an additional 21 states, elections brought partisan change only once in the 1960s. To the external observer, the ramifications of a change of leadership within one party are perhaps more difficult to anticipate than movements across party lines. To those involved in the ongoing activities of state government, the "problems" of transition are perhaps less well defined.

The fact that only a relatively small proportion of gubernatorial elections involve party change suggests a weakness in the current literature on transitions. Explicitly in case studies, and implicitly in more general treatments, emphasis has been placed on transitions wherein the governorship

Source: Reprinted by permission from *Public Administration Review*, Vol. 30, No. 1 (January/February 1970), pp. 10–18.

passes from one party to another.[1] However, transitions within a single party are at least as frequent and need to be examined more fully. What are the characteristics of a transition in which partisanship is "held constant"? The experiences of Kansas and North Carolina in 1964 suggest some initial answers to this question.

During these two intraparty transitions, the authors were present in the governors' offices: Wickman in Kansas, and Beyle in North Carolina. Both participant observers were focal points in the transition process, the former as liaison for the governor-elect, the latter as the single holdover from the old administration to the new.[2] While breadth of perspective was perhaps foregone in viewing the transition from the office of the governor itself, increased access and immediacy were surely gained.

THE POLITICAL SETTING

Both Kansas and North Carolina have long histories of one-party dominance, extending back to the turn of the century. In recent years, both states have experienced an increase in the strength of the minority party, as evidenced by voter registration and the electoral success of some of the

minority candidates. However, the major conflicts over office have taken place between factions in the dominant party. In Kansas, the basic divisions among Republicans have historically followed geographic and population lines, with some economic interests being represented. Traditionally, the governorship, with its prestige, power, and patronage, had been the central vehicle for reducing factional rivalries once the election was over. In North Carolina, divisions within the dominant Democratic party, in the 1960s, seemed to resemble a liberal-moderate-conservative split. While these terms cannot be equated with national or general ideological counterparts, they do provide a useful distinction between the three factions in North Carolina Democratic politics, which have been vastly more competitive than friendly in the last decade.

The 1964 gubernatorial election reaffirmed the strength of the dominant party in each of these two states. In Kansas, incumbent Governor John Anderson was succeeded by fellow Republican William Avery. Likewise, in North Carolina, Governor Terry Sanford and his successor Dan Moore were Democrats. Yet the degree of interfactional hostility in the two states in 1964 differed markedly. The gubernatorial primary in Kansas had been a heated, six-way contest. When Avery emerged as the Republican nominee, he consulted with representatives of rival factions and made a concerted effort to smooth out disaffections. Since the incumbent Anderson had not sought reelection, his willingness to cooperate with Avery was not inhibited by electoral battle scars. Indeed, Anderson's own trying experiences in 1960 made him especially mindful of the need for concert between the incumbent and governor-elect.[3] The

[1] See, for example, Charles Gibbons, "Transition of Government in Massachusetts," *State Government*, Vol. XXXIV, No. 2 (Spring 1961), p. 100; Clark D. Ahlberg and Daniel P. Moynihan, "Changing Governors—and Policies," *Public Administration Review*, Vol. XX, No. 4 (Autumn 1960), pp. 195–204; and Norton Long, "After the Voting Is Over," *Midwest Journal of Politics*, Vol. VI, No. 2 (May 1962), pp. 183–200.

[2] Wickman was active in the Kansas campaign and served as the governor-elect's liaison to the incumbent, and for a short period as administrative assistant. Beyle was in the incumbent governor's office in North Carolina, concerned with planning, program development, and intergovernmental relations. He was held over in a similar position in the new administration. Both authors were recipients of NCEP Faculty Fellowships for the period involved, and hence were not dependent upon state appropriations for their positions. The authors were decidedly interested observers of the transition process, and worked with no research design to structure observations in advance. Yet while interview and sampling methods would have been desirable, more formal procedures would have removed them from central positions in the administrations. For further discussion of the problems of participant observation, see Morris S. Schwartz and Charlotte Green Schwartz, "Problems in Participant Observation," *The American Journal of Sociology* (January 1955), pp. 343–353. James A. Robinson has also explored this in an unpublished paper, "Internships, Participant Observation, and Research" (April 1965).

[3] George Docking (Democrat), Governor of Kansas from 1956 to 1960, was a perfect example of an individual whose general attitude made the work of transition most difficult. In interviews conducted with former Governor John Anderson, several members of Anderson's staff, and one member of Docking's staff, it was made quite clear that no help was given to the incoming Republican governor. The Docking administration was one of the few in the history of Kansas which destroyed its papers on leaving office. On this point, see the letter from Gene Sullivan, Governor Docking's executive assistant, to the state archivist, Robert W. Richmond, dated June 28, 1961, in the files of the Kansas State Historical Society, Topeka, Kansas. Mr. Sullivan indicated that all files were destroyed at Governor Docking's order, before the administration left office.

North Carolina situation provided a strong contrast. Since none of the three candidates in the Democratic primary had received a majority of votes, a runoff primary was held. This direct clash between the liberal candidate, backed by Governor Sanford, and Moore's moderate faction left bitter antagonisms, not easily laid aside for the sake of "a smooth transition." So while a cooperative relationship existed between incumbent and governor-elect in Kansas, the North Carolina milieu was one of mutual distrust and hostility.

INTRAPARTY TRANSITION: SOME OBSERVATIONS FOR TESTING

The following observations flow from a comparison of the authors' experiences and understanding of the transition periods in Kansas and North Carolina. These are not intended as generalizations applicable to all transitions. Rather, these observations are advanced both as a description of two cases of intraparty transition, and as possible hypotheses for testing and refinement in other states.

1. *The duration of the transition period is politically, rather than structurally defined.*

Transition did not occur between election and inauguration days, or even for several weeks on either side of these dates. Instead, the transition process seemed to last a minimum of one year to one-and-a-half years in these two states. It began with the opening of the political campaign and extended throughout the first legislative session of the new administration.

While the tempo of transition activity increased in relation to the proximity of the election, it was nonetheless apparent in the early portion of the campaign. The old administration began to lose its maneuverability and control over the activities of several state agencies. Individuals, groups, and agencies began lining up behind particular candidates, making overtures toward what was hoped would be the new administration. While a similar chain of anticipated reactions may be intrinsic in transition, it is perhaps highlighted in a one-party state, where the primary is the de facto election.

After the general election, the pace of the transition process accelerated, with the establishment of liaisons and initial appointments. Soon after inauguration, the budget was due. In Kansas, the governor-elect was required to submit his budget less than 100 days after the election, while in North Carolina, the document went to the printer in mid-December. However, the preparation of the budget, the fiscal cement of government, was a process largely completed under the old administration—and begun before the new administration was even voted into existence.

Just as transition clearly did not begin on election day, it extended well beyond the inauguration. Throughout the first legislative session, the new administration was attempting to have its own innovations adopted, while insuring legislative support for regular state activities. Moreover, executive-legislative jousting tended to feed back on the appointment process. To fill key administrative positions too early in the administration would reduce the governor's bargaining power, by depriving him of appointive inducements for winning over individual legislators. This type of bargaining strategy was used in North Carolina with several agency appointments, including the Department of Motor Vehicles. Yet these delayed appointments protracted transition still further, as new directors adjusted to their roles and departmental activities.

While time boundaries of transition are difficult to delineate, transition seemed to begin with the opening of the gubernatorial campaigns and end when the legislators left the state capital. Thus, political considerations set the pace.

2. *Change in personnel during the transition is initially small and confined to the top levels of the administration.*

As discussed above, delays in appointments were used as gubernatorial tools vis-à-vis the legislature. However, slowness and low incidence of personnel change was also a function of time constraints and lack of competence and trusted individuals to fill specific positions. Other scholars have noted the tendency for noncongruence between campaign and administrative personnel.[4] Many who were drawn to the goal of winning elections and who excelled in campaign strategy were neither equipped for, nor desirous of administrative appointments. Consequently, those new individuals who were recruited as part of the administrative team were spread over more territory than their job specifications might have indicated. In effect, they took on much of the administrative burden

---

[4]This "deviation" from the responsible party model is noted, for example, in Long, *op cit.*, p. 187 ff.

later to be assumed by further appointees. The massive state bureaucracy, controlling the routine of state government, persisted virtually unaltered by transition.

3. *Alterations in the pattern of communication supplement personnel change, and induce a shift in "mood" or "tone."*

While transition brought little physical change in agency personnel, new patterns of unofficial interaction often developed. From the governor's perspective, directors and other high-ranking agency officials were seen as unknown quantities, unless they had openly worked in the campaign. If it was sensed that they had ties with the old administration, yet replacement was not feasible, the governor turned to someone in the agency whose loyalty was assured. This individual became the unofficial contact in the agency, until the director proved himself trustworthy or was replaced. For example, in North Carolina, the assistant director of the Personnel Department became Governor Moore's contact, remaining the key figure in the department until a new director was chosen. In several agencies in which directors who were closely associated with the Sanford administration had resigned, high career-level personnel were selected as contacts and given acting directorships. Later these individuals were appointed agency directors, after proving their competence and loyalty. Such changes in contact patterns had clear repercussions for the power configurations within the agencies. So while actual personnel change was negligible, shifts in tone were apparent.

In Kansas, the change in communication patterns was perhaps more generalized. While the outgoing administration had a reputation, either real or fancied, for a lack of communication, Governor Avery made a special effort to change this mood after inauguration. He instituted frequent contacts with agency heads to obtain their views on current or potential problems. Many agency heads who had not been consulted at any time during the previous administration now felt free to recommend changes to the governor. Thus, Avery's alteration of the communication pattern served to set a mood of responsiveness, which contributed to an increased flow of information throughout the administrative network.

Similarly, the tone of interaction between the governor and other elected officials was altered by

new communication patterns. Governor Avery held weekly breakfast meetings with his executive council, consisting of the elected officials. All save the attorney general and lieutenant-governor had served more than one term in their posts. Yet the new governor set a mood for communication which the others soon reciprocated. In North Carolina, the separately elected state treasurer had been viewed as a political antagonist of the old administration; however, the same individual became a close and frequent advisor to Governor Moore.

Thus, while personnel remained largely constant, inclusions and exclusions in the communication patterns altered the tone of relationships in the new administration.

4. *During the transition period there is a tendency for relationships in the executive to revert to more formalized channels.*

In the old administration, an unofficial substructure of relationships had formed over time: The governor learned which lines of authority and communication worked and which agencies could get a job done. This network did not necessarily correspond to the formal lines of the organization chart, but followed patterns of mutual trust. When the new governor assumed office, he had a certain coterie of appointees and contacts whose loyalty was established, as was noted above. But in agencies lacking such loyal and trusted personnel, he tended to revert to formal channels, working through the director or agency head to the specified job holder. Old patterns of behavior were thus disrupted between and within agencies, as these rigid lines were superimposed over the informal relationships of the old administration.

This change could be most subtle, causing serious ramifications for those who did not recognize it. The antipoverty program in North Carolina was a case in point. Under the Sanford administration, the program operated out of the governor's office, bypassing the director of the Department of Administration, in whose office the program was officially located. The head of the program was a political neophyte, given the position for just that reason. With the transition, he continued to operate as he had before, ignoring the signals of the new administration and failing to go through regular channels. This aggravated the director being bypassed, puzzled the governor as reports came directly to him from an unknown source, and made the antipoverty personnel most insecure and doubtful of support from the new administration. As the head of the poverty program persisted in this basic error, decisions came to be made elsewhere, through the "normal" channels of the department director and his assistants. This only led to more insecurity and a growing lack of communication between the antipoverty agency and Department of Administration. Insensitivity to the shift from informal to formal relationships in transition resulted in more disruption in the poverty program than was necessary.

In reverting to formal lines of authority, the new governor was attempting to gain administrative control in the face of uncertain loyalties and limited information. This procedure would be modified over time, as the new executive developed his own substructure of informal relationships.

5. *Changes in governmental activity as a result of transition are incremental.*

This point has been implicit in much of the previous discussion. The vast machinery of state government was tinkered with, and some functions and dollars were redirected in part. Yet the support of individuals, groups, the legislature, and other agencies served as an effective counterforce to change. Moreover, most state government activity was established by statute, and by such immovable considerations as federal grant-in-aid requirements, earmarked taxes, and the budget itself.

Such systematic inertia often resulted in changes of form, but not substance. In North Carolina, the Sanford administration had developed the Good Neighbor Council, an ad hoc agency in the Department of Administration established by executive order, with the purpose of maintaining peace in race relations. The new legislature attacked this agency, refusing to grant an appropriation for its continuance. Yet funds were granted the governor to conduct a similar activity out of his office; and he did so, with the same personnel, goals, and even the same agency name.

The budget also provided great policy continuity, locking programs into dollar commitments.[5] In Kansas, the emphasis of Governor Avery's new budget was more on achieving greater fiscal responsibility from the agencies than on expensive innovations. The time element was crucial, with the new governor being required to submit his budget soon after inauguration. In such a situation investments in on-going programs are rarely overturned. Changes in the North Carolina budget were similarly minor. There were some additions reflecting gubernatorial interest, such as funds for alcoholic rehabilitation clinics, and some minor reductions indicative of a "wrist-slapping" for the agency involved. Yet significant shifts were absent. Continuity is built into the state governmental system to a far greater degree than campaign rhetoric would suggest.

6. *Many of the approaches to problems by the new administration are more in the nature of "theory testing" than predesigned solutions.*

Despite preelection emphasis on programmatic change, the new administration tended to move from crisis to crisis, problem to problem, developing ad hoc solutions. This was due, in part, to the newness of some of the participants to the government process, as opposed to the campaign trail. While such newcomers were most likely to be innovative,[6] their lack of experience necessitated a trial-and-error approach. Moreover, those who were veterans of previous administrations had to adjust to changes in the nature of problems and governmental tools for dealing with them. This was especially true in the early 1960s, when so much new government activity was initiated throughout the federal system under the Kennedy-Johnson administrations. Subjectively, to those entering as the new administration, there was great change, measured by new federal programs, new federal agencies, and different emphases in goals under these programs.

To deal with such external changes, new hunches and theories had to be tested, with little foreknowledge of probable consequences. The State Planning Task Force in North Carolina was such a trial measure. This body was established in the Department of Administration, not only to plan, but also to administer some of the new programs, including the Appalachian, Anti-Poverty, and Outdoor Recreation programs, cutting across normal

---

[5]The relationship between incrementalism and the budget is most notably explicated in Aaron Wildavsky, *The Politics of the Budgetary Process* (Boston: Little, Brown, 1964). The federal analogy appears to hold on the state level.

[6]Long discusses the "plasticity" and innovative potential of the executive family that the new governor brings to office, *op cit.*, p. 193 ff.

administrative boundaries. This approach, using a small, high-level task force grouped around particular programs, was devised and announced as an innovation in state government. It was to be tested for two years, and then formalized if successful.

7. *The basic problem of transition is one of communicating interests and directions, both between the old and new administrations, and within the new.*

Differences between the transitions in North Carolina and Kansas underscored the centrality and highly political cast of the problems of inter- and intra-administration communication. In North Carolina the incumbent and incoming administrations had long been enemies in the political world, generating animosities not easily overcome. The basic element of trust, essential to clear and credible communication of intent, was lacking; instead, mutual suspicion prevailed. The outgoing Sanford administration feared that the programs it had established would be undone, while the Moore entourage suspected political motives in every move and suggestion from the incumbents. When the old administration spent its last days appointing supporters to various positions as part of its reward system for loyalty, this seemed to be loading the deck to the Moore people. The situation but added to the ongoing tension built up by transition. Not only was open contact lacking, but in some cases there was individual fear that proximity to the other administration would somehow be contaminating.

In Kansas the Avery administration was not confronted with significant political opposition once the election was over, since incumbent Governor Anderson had not campaigned for a third term. Yet the new administration still had difficulty conveying its intentions, and bringing these in line with habits of mind and behavior nurtured in the previous executive's terms. It was not possible to anticipate bureaucratic responses to programs in terms of known political alignments. Instead, a lack of receptivity to gubernatorial objectives was often cloaked in terms of "expertise" versus inexperience. While this made agency opposition more difficult to diagnose, it was perhaps easier to overcome since it lacked the factional roots of antagonisms found in North Carolina. Governor Avery's vigorous efforts to establish open communications greatly facilitated clarification of directions and

transmission of needed information. Yet even in this almost classic model of cooperation in transition, there was frequently a slowdown of activity when distrust was aroused. Moreover, in both Kansas and North Carolina the very number of necessary messages between the old and the new, and within the new administration resulted in overload and communication breakdown.

Of the many elements entangled in transition, the key variables seemed to be time, politics, and control. These factors both contributed to the problems to be resolved through the communication process, and set the parameters within which that proce s c uld take place.

CONCLUSIONS

Although it has been suggested elsewhere that transition "contains no purely political overtones,"[7] the authors' experiences in Kansas and North Carolina suggest the opposite: that the common denominator of transition is politics, pervading all attendant activities. With respect to one-party states, Coleman B. Ransone's observation is apropos: "The governor is elected in an atmosphere of factional politics and he continues to operate in that atmosphere in his dealings with the legislature, with his department heads, and with other members of the executive branch."[8] Mutual antagonism, rooted in electoral confrontation, attends both intraparty transitions between rival factions and the party turnover situation in competitive states. Yet it is easy to overstate the centrality of such opposition and the extent to which they create the problems of transition. Incrementalism in personnel and policy change, budget constraints, entrenched habits of the old administration, and narrowly defined bureaucratic norms—all these factors contribute to what might be called systemic inertia. The state executive is an ongoing system when the new governor enters the scene. Any major, or even minor, redirection at one point in the system would lead to a series of repercussions throughout. Balfour's dictum suggests itself: Whichever party is in office, the conservatives are in power. The functioning system is by nature a conservative entity. So while the very term "transi-

[7]Kenneth O. Warner, "Planning for Transition," *State Government*, Vol. XXXIV, No. 2 (Spring 1961), p. 103.
[8]Coleman B. Ransome, Jr., *Office of the Governor in the United States* (University, Ala.: University of Alabama Press, 1956), p. 94.

tion" denotes change, perhaps the greatest challenge to the incoming governor is one of inducing change. He must work under an often accurate assumption that his objectives in transition are not necessarily those of the incumbent administration, department heads, career bureaucracy, or legislature. Thus, his goal becomes one of exercising power in Dahl's terms, of getting someone to do what they would not otherwise do.[9] Factional or partisan rivalries may make this task more difficult, but they do not create it. In the one-party transitions in Kansas and North Carolina, where the salience of factions differed greatly, the fundamental problem of eliciting cooperation remained the same.

All too frequently, impediments to a smooth transfer of power have been viewed as essentially structural and administrative. The new governor is seen as handicapped chiefly by a lack of funds for staff, material, and office space, and inadequate procedures for securing information.[10] Some states have responded with legislation providing greater access to information for the newly elected governor. Yet the structural-administrative approach to facilitating smooth transition is inadequate in itself, and cannot substitute for comprehensive action on the part of the executives involved. Governor Avery of Kansas commented that the relationship between the incumbent and governor-elect varies from individual to individual; unless both parties are willing to cooperate freely, the transition cannot progress effectively, regardless of what other arrangements have been made.[11]

The incoming and outgoing governors can exert a strong influence upon the attitudes of the career civil service and upper-level appointees, who may really carry the greatest burden in transition. As Henry has indicated in his work on presidential transitions,[12] an alert chief executive, vitally concerned with making the transition a smooth one, is himself the key factor in its success. We suggest that the same is true at the state level. The governor who consciously seeks to establish coopera-

tion, through both formal and informal communication channels, can best overcome structural and partisan impediments, and insure a smooth and efficient transition.

COMMENTS

Thad Beyle's and John Wickman's observations on intraparty gubernatorial transitions ("Gubernatorial Transition in a One-Party Setting," PAR, January/February 1970) were of particular interest to me because of their considerable congruity with some of the findings of a study of interparty gubernatorial transition in which I recently participated.[13]

Beyle and Wickman offered seven observations flowing from their "experiences and understanding" of Kansas and North Carolina transitions, carefully (perhaps too cautiously) hedging their incisive comments by the following qualification: "These [observations] are not intended as generalizations applicable to all transitions. Rather, these observations are advanced both as a description of two cases of intraparty transition, and as possible hypotheses for testing and refinement in other states" (p. 11).

Their foci of interest in gubernatorial transitions were somewhat different from my own emphasis on the budget process during the change between the administrations of California Governors Edmund G. Brown and Ronald Reagan in 1966 and after. However, in the course of interviews with public officials aimed at defining the context and limits of my own work, broad consideration of the transition was necessary. The resulting data provide an interesting supplement to Beyle and Wickman which may be of interest to readers of this Review. No more than they, do I offer proven generalizations; my remarks are also in the nature

Source: Reprinted by permission from Public Administration Review, Vol. 30, No. 4 (July/August 1970), pp. 467–470.

[9] Robert Dahl, "The Concept of Power," Behavioral Science, Vol. II, No. 3 (July 1957), pp. 201–215.

[10] Gibbons, op cit., p. 100.

[11] From an interview with Governor William Avery by John Wickman, December 27, 1966.

[12] Laurin L. Henry, Presidential Transitions (Washington, D.C.: The Brookings Institution 1960).

[13] The John Randolph Haynes and Dora Haynes Foundation supported a research project in California gubernatorial transition at the University of California, Davis, under the general direction of Professor Richard W. Gable. My own research leading to a doctoral dissertation focused on the budget and budget process during transition ("When Governors Change: The Case of the California Budget," Davis, Calif.: Institute of Governmental Affairs, 1969).

of "observations." But in a yet fresh and developing field it seems that corroboration and/or disconfirmation between and among similar studies cannot usefully remain limited to rigorously developed conclusions.

"1. *The duration of the transition period is politically, rather than structurally defined.*" The California experience during the Brown/Reagan transition certainly supports the notion that transitions may be defined by political—rather than structural—limits. The transition began prior to the election. While in theory Governor Brown could have won reelection, a number of crucial political actors early looked beyond the day of reckoning to the possibility of a change in administration. And they planned for it. For example, the Reagan campaign organization was sufficiently optimistic (and well financed) to concern itself with the following year's legislative program more systematically than it might have done had it perceived the electoral race to be very close. Further, in postelection interviews with selected career civil servants in the Department of Finance, some respondents disclosed that prior to the election they had begun to try to anticipate the new budget "culture" that might emerge if (when?) a new governor assumed office.

"2. *Change in personnel during the transition is initially small and confined to the top levels of the administration.*" Beyle's and Wickman's point is highly applicable to the California interparty transition. Governor Reagan's administration was plagued for some time after the election with difficulties in making key appointments to departmental and staff positions. As one crucial instance, the day after the election Governor-elect Reagan had 12 weeks until he would have to submit a budget to the legislature. But he did not manage—though he tried—to find a Director of Finance (*his* man on the budget) and get him on the job until seven weeks had passed. Meanwhile, converted campaign aides and a few new staff members tried to learn how to control 100,000 plus civil servants and a $5 billion plus per year budget. The state bureaucracy by and large carried on with relatively little actual interruption by the new administration.

"3. *Alterations in the pattern of communication supplement personnel change, and induce a shift in 'mood" or 'tone.'*" Both as governor-elect and shortly as governor, Ronald Reagan seemed to search for incumbent officials ("political" and career) whom he could trust. His task was perhaps more difficult than that of a governor in a smooth intraparty change, for his administration carried a public aura of conservative Republicanism which the state bureaucracy was quite unaccustomed to observe in the governor's office. Yet, Governor Reagan found officials upon whose "neutral competence" he began to depend. More specifically, in connection with the budget, he made an effort to discern the character and competence of top civil servants in his Finance Department. Could he trust them to work for his financial goals as they had done for those of his liberal predecessor? Apparently, the Governor was satisfied with what he saw and heard in that department.[14]

"4. *During the transition period there is a tendency for relationships in the executive to revert to more formalized channels.*" Evidence exists to suggest that some of the informal relations between units of the Department of Finance and the governor's office that had characterized the Brown administration were interrupted, at least temporarily, as Governor Reagan took office. The Office of Program and Policy Planning provided an example of this phenomenon. Governor Brown's office had employed the career civil servants of this Finance Department unit for the development of major portions of its legislative proposals. But after Governor Reagan's inauguration, the warm relations that the Office of Program and Policy Planning had had with the previous administration contributed to its being characterized by an unsavory taint from the perspective of the new governor.

"5. *Changes in governmental activity as a result of transition are incremental.*" The incremental

[14]This observation derives from conversations with Finance Department personnel rather than with the governor, and in that sense is one-sided. A supporting note should probably accompany remarks about the Department of Finance. In this agency, as in most others in California state administration, the governor dispenses very little "patronage." He has authority to appoint a director of finance (who serves "at his pleasure"), and the director may make two further "political" appointments. The rest of the department serve under merit civil service rules. Within the Department of Finance, thus, the governor has three of *his* men to oversee a multibillion dollar a year budget process. Such a situation not only points to the cruciality of the political appointments, but also to the importance for the governor of harmonious relations with decision makers among the career employees.

quality of the California transition may be seen clearly by reference to the budget. At first, Governor Reagan energetically sought substantial deviation from the normal incremental pattern of expenditure growth in state government. Yet the results of his efforts during his first two years in office (measured by appropriations) scarcely appear abnormal in the light of a ten-year growth trend. Despite constitutional entrenchment of California's "executive budget," which appears to grant the governor considerable financial authority, the empirical "budget system" deprived the governor of much actual control by such well-known devices as special funding, permanent appropriations, earmarked revenues, etc.[15]

"6. *Many of the approaches to problems by the new administration are more in the nature of 'theory testing' than predesigned solutions.*" The "theory testing" characterization of the early period of Governor Reagan's administration is also an item of congruity between California and the Kansas/North Carolina of the Beyle-Wickman report. One illustration grew out of the time squeeze on budget submission that Governor Reagan faced (see above, remarks under observation number two) combined with his goal to reduce expenditure proposals. The budget was essentially completed by the time that the new administration arrived in Sacramento, but Governor Reagan did not want to be bound by a financial program not of his own design. Early in January he called for a 10 percent across-the-board slash in expenditures for each department whose funding was under his direct control. Such a move was an experimental, emergency step, aimed at producing quick results. This decision placed the onus upon the administrative departments to identify those elements of their programs they could afford to cut or to protest that 10 percent was too large a proportion to lose. Governor Reagan's action was the target of

[15]I discuss certain structural features of the "budget system" in "When Governors Change: The Case of the California Budget," *op. cit.*

much criticism—from expected sources, such as the opposition party and many administrative agencies, as well as from some people concerned with the proper practice of public budgeting. The essential point here is that the new administration tried a budget technique as the trial half of a trial-and-error sequence by novitiates in government.

"7. *The basic problem of transition is one of communicating interests and directions, both between the old and new administrations, and within the new.*" Lessons from the California experience again lean in the same direction as the observations made about intraparty transitions. Of course, mistrust is probably expected between old and new administrations when a party transfer occurs. But the problem of "communicating interests and directions" within state government remained for at least several months after the inauguration. Perhaps the shift from a liberal Democratic governor to an allegedly conservative Republican chief executive created an exaggerated aura of change. Some conservatives may have looked for liberals under every administrative rock, and some liberals may have overreacted. Even the use of simplistic political labels such as liberal and conservative can impede clear and frank communications. Evidence to sustain serious reflection on these propositions was revealed during interviews with both governor's staff and career servants in several departments.

Findings in the California gubernatorial shift thus support Beyle's and Wickman's appreciation of gubernatorial transition as strongly characterized by political considerations. Transition, as public administration more generally, is not adequately considered by mere reference to the impersonal mechanics of shifts in superiors and subordinates. Transition is foremost the sum of human activity and attitudes within a boundary defined by a pre- and postelection concern with change and continuity in government; it is only secondarily a concept satisfactorily covered by reference to the structural context in which those activities and attitudes occur.

Alan Evan Schenker

CHANGING GOVERNORS—AND POLICIES
Clark D. Ahlberg
and
Daniel P. Moynihan

While it appears mankind has ever lived in a time of transition, the problem occurs in state government but every two or four years. Doubtless its onset varies with each occurrence: for some administrations it comes quietly, an awakening of powers; for others it is a troubled, foreboding period, reflecting the darkening winter skies that accompany it.

For still others it begins with a crash of understanding. This is the way it began for the Harriman administration in New York State. The scene took place in a New York City hotel, five weeks after the election of 1954. For a month Harriman and his advisers had been furiously at work drawing up a "bold and adventurous" legislative program designed to alert the country that a resurgent Democratic party was back in power in New York if not yet in the nation. In Albany, the new governor's budget director designate and his aides had spent the same period going over the state's finances, intent on getting a picture of the financial situation and a view of ongoing state programs. On the Saturday in question the two groups met. The budget director reported there were no surplus funds for new programs nor would existing taxes produce sufficient revenues to meet even the ongoing program costs. There was in fact a deficit; there had been one for nearly every year since the end of the war. The discussion of new programs would have to be recessed while they talked of new taxes.

Harriman's program advisers reacted with open incredulity if not hostility. The meeting broke up in an impasse. The revenue problems that preoccupied the budget staff had hardly occurred to the program staff. The two points of view met head on and for the moment the work of the incoming administration came to a standstill. But its transition period had begun.

Popularly the period of transition is viewed as the time of the new broom sweeping out the old mess, refurbishing the executive mansion with fresh ideas and new men. In reality it is frequently

Source: Reprinted by permission from *Public Administration Review* (1960), pp. 195–205.

a time of disadvantage and difficulty for the new governor in his relations with the legislature and within his own branch of government. The danger, from the point of view of effective government at the state level is that these disabilities will become permanent, that the new governor will lose entirely his opportunity to gain leadership over the government at just that moment when he is commonly thought to be enjoying the "honeymoon" phase of his administration.

In New York State two changes in government have recently taken place in comparatively rapid succession. In 1954, after twelve years of Republican governor Thomas E. Dewey, the Democrat, Averell Harriman, was elected. Four years later he was in turn succeeded by a Republican, Nelson Rockefeller. The events of these transitions, occurring in the context of relatively constant political conditions elsewhere, reveal a number of the factors at work during such a period in New York.[1]

The theme running through each of the events that follow is the difficulty of change: the difficulty of devising new programs, of financing them, of winning support for them, of implementing them. Concern with political transition has long been directed to the task of providing stability and continuity to the processes of government. Clearly the newer task is to provide, as it were, an innovative element that will correspond to the function of government as an instrument of change and adaptation in a society constantly demanding both.

THE PROBLEM OF THE OUT PARTY

The Republicans in the New York State legislature have more or less a permanent majority: Al Smith declared it unconstitutional for the Democrats to control the legislature and they have in fact done so for but three years of the twentieth century and then by accidents of national politics. Since 1942, however, the party division has been more geographic than ideological. Both the Democrats and Republicans are more or less impregnable in their respective strongholds. Their legislators generally represent the largely similar constellation of interests of the political establishments of large metropolitan areas. Notably since the ascendancy of the

[1] The authors, as members of the Harriman administration, write with a background of much fuller knowledge of the events of the transition from Harriman to Rockefeller.

"modern" Republicans, brought about by Governor Dewey, there has been little sharp ideological conflict between the two groups in the legislature.

The Republicans, however, retain exclusive control of legislative business, allowing the Democrats little more than token participation and, to some minds, receiving only token opposition. (It is common for the budget to emerge from the finance committees without the minority members ever being given the opportunity to vote on reporting it out.) Having few strong ideological conflicts, the Democratic legislators generally acquiesce in their impotence. What little legislative patronage they get is used for local party purposes and the appointees generally offer little technical competence.

Given this situation, during periods of Republican governors the Democratic party almost completely loses touch with the affairs of the state government. By contrast the Republicans have available at all times a large legislative staff which serves the Republican state committee as well as the majority in the legislature. A Democratic gubernatorial candidate is left almost entirely on his own in developing campaign issues and, if elected, administrative programs. Except for the minority leaders and their counsel, no Democrat associated with the legislature provided Harriman assistance of any significance during the 1954 campaign or its immediate aftermath. The Democratic platform and campaign statements were drawn up principally by returnees from the Democratic administration in Washington using what information they could glean from the New York City government and the various interest groups. Apart from the traditional charges of economic decline and government corruption, the platform followed closely the pattern and subject matter of the Republican program: Where the Republicans tended to take credit for having implemented the most recent increments in the various ongoing programs, such as unemployment insurance and civil rights, the Democrats tended to propose the next.

In only three instances were major new proposals made in the Democratic platform: "Assumption of responsibility by the State for the care of the chronically ill, as now done in the case of tuberculosis and mental illness"; a state minimum wage of $1.25; and a referendum on direct state aid for school construction. Whatever the merits of these proposals, they would have raised so many

difficulties—the first would have required a vast increase in state expenditures—that once in office the Harriman administration changed them so completely as to constitute new approaches. Where the Democratic policy-makers had struck out on their own they completely lost touch with what they came to regard as reality once in office.

In contrast to Harriman in 1954, Rockefeller in 1958 had access to abundant sources of program information and ideas as a result of his party's position in the legislature. The Republican legislative leaders, supported by expert and experienced staff, had maintained a vigorous opposition to Harriman, accumulating in the process an impressive stockpile of information and some issues. Midway through the Democratic administration Rockefeller was made head of a state commission concerned with revision of the constitution. This provided him a year-and-a-half to assemble a staff, to inform himself on state problems and proposals for correcting them, and to appear before the voters in a responsible and nonpartisan manner. When Harriman tried to put an end to this in 1958 by refusing to approve the continuation of the commission, it was reestablished as a legislative body.

When the campaign arrived Rockefeller's top commission staff became his top campaign staff (as it later became his official staff). In rapid succession he issued a series of policy statements and speeches covering every major issue in state government, even discussing the need for a new state social insurance program to protect every wage earner against the danger of catastrophic medical expense. As events had it, a sharp economic recession and a development within the Democratic party led Rockefeller to concentrate on the issues of economic decline and political bossism—much the issues that had dominated Harriman's 1954 campaign—but at the same time Republican Rockefeller easily outdistanced Democrat Harriman as a proponent of more government action to the point of winning the last-minute support of the state's most "liberal" newspaper.

Rockefeller's election by 573,000 votes was a startling upset in the year of an historic Democratic sweep. It was brought about in measure by a heavy defection of voters from the liberal wing of the Democratic party—a movement certainly encouraged by the impression of vigor which Rockefeller was able to give as a result of the information and staff support he received from the legislature.

Clearly, a party lacking a vigorous legislative wing is handicapped in a gubernatorial campaign. If successful withal, it is likely to enter the transition period with little hard information concerning the task ahead.

By contrast, a party with too powerful a legislative wing will incline to be too little responsive to the policy objectives of even their own governor. Here the difficulty of changing policies arises from the absence of political necessity rather than from the shortage of technical ability and information.

FACING THE LEGISLATURE

The new governor takes office only to find he must share power. The legislature, experienced, entrenched, indispensable, is there waiting for him. Having won the mandate of the people for his program, the governor now finds he must ask permission of the legislature to enact it. Conflict is inevitable: If there is a difference of party, the conflict is public and pronounced; if the parties are the same, a kind of family quarrel ensues, no less bitter for being more private.

With Harriman's election the Republican legislative leaders assumed a new importance and independence; both promptly became candidates for the 1958 gubernatorial nomination. Reinforced by a number of Dewey officials who took staff posts in the legislature, they commanded unusual, perhaps unequaled, knowledge of the New York State government processes. After announcing their own legislative program a day before the Governor's Annual Message, they promptly moved to dispute his gloomy view of state finances.

FINANCES: THE CHALLENGE TO HARRIMAN

For his part, Harriman challenged the powerful and widely accepted image of his predecessor, Thomas E. Dewey, as a prudent, pay-as-you-go fiscal manager. Although the Democratic platform had challenged this image, asserting "for the last nine years the State has been spending far in excess of its income," it is doubtful that even those who wrote the plank really believed it—as witnessed by their first reaction to the report of their own budget director which confirmed it. During the campaign, Harriman declared there would be no need to increase income or business taxes in order to meet the needs of the state and its communities. His running mate even proposed reducing income taxes.

On recognizing the true fiscal condition, the new Governor declared in his opening budget message that the state had been operating at a deficit for all but two years of the postwar period. To restore the balance of state finances, Harriman called for a general tax increase of $127.6 million, including the ending of the year-to-year tax forgiveness which amounted to some $48 million. He declared this necessary to avoid an approaching deficit in the capital construction fund and to provide for "mandated" increases in state services. The Republican leaders, appropriately shocked, charged revenues were underestimated.

Almost immediately Harriman began to soften his stand. He had been elected during the 1953–54 recession; unemployment, which reached almost 6 percent of the work force in the fall of 1954, dropped off to just over 4 percent by mid-1955. As the session progressed, revenue estimates were revised upward $31 millions, a development of little significance in terms of the state needs or its fiscal problems but nonetheless the subject of widespread Republican comment. This contributed, late in February, to Harriman's decision to postpone the effective date of his proposed motor fuel tax increase until the beginning of the following calendar year. This cut out for 1955–56 one-half his tax package. At the same time the "freeze" on new construction was withdrawn. A month later he agreed to a modified series of Republican-sponsored income tax reductions for "hardship cases" which he had earlier indicated would be vetoed unless accompanied by measures to replace the revenue loss.

In the end Harriman got not quite 30 percent of the new tax revenues he proposed and then only by use of his veto power to end tax forgiveness legislation. However, as a result of the economic upswing, the revenue yield from the state tax structure was $17.5 million more than he had predicted would result from the adoption of his entire new tax program. The revenue estimates approved by the new budget officials had failed badly to gauge the dimensions and significance of the economic recovery. The next year Harriman proposed a new type of personal income tax forgiveness and a reduction in the unincorporated business tax, thus ending even the tax gains he obtained in 1955 by means of his veto.

Rockefeller's campaign in 1958 was marked by the number of new programs and projects which he proposed. Although Harriman's staff privately estimated they would cost $2,468,150,000 over a four-year period, he, like Harriman in 1954, indicated there would be no need for tax increases to pay for them. Early in the campaign he stated there would be no need even for Harriman's gas tax increase which by then the GOP legislative leaders and state chairman had agreed would be necessary. Rockefeller declared he would expand "needed social services" by pursuing policies of economic growth which would increase state revenues "without increasing the burden on the individual taxpayer." However, a national recession had once again reduced state revenues and new taxes were needed when Rockefeller took office. Most new programs had to be set aside.

Echoing Harriman, Rockefeller began his first budget message with the announcement that "New York is faced with the most serious fiscal problem of more than a generation." Like Harriman he blamed his predecessor but, again in parallel, the legislature was not long in blaming him. Before the session was concluded, the governor's authority had been dramatically shaken by a legislative revolt as had not been seen for a generation.

Finding himself in a situation seemingly identical to Dewey's, with the same legislative leaders, finance committee chairman, budget director *et al.*, Rockefeller promptly restored the quasi-parliamentary practice which Dewey had instituted of weekly meetings with the legislative leaders to agree on the course of action for the coming legislative meetings. In this way a budget was drawn up calling for $277 million in new taxes, including the gas and Diesel fuel taxes Harriman had sought four years earlier. Though a Draconic measure, there was clearly little expectation of difficulty: the Republicans had the votes; in twelve years Dewey's budget had been cut but once. As if to emphasize that it would be easy, the gas tax increase was put through on a straight party vote before the new budget was even submitted. Within weeks, however, this masterful procedure was reduced to shambles.

Three factors seem to account for this. First, the public reaction was very bad, ranging as one upstate paper put it, "from rage to resignation." This was the aftermath of a Republican campaign which talked of tax cuts and new programs, not tax increases. Harriman had had a similar reaction of disbelief, particularly from the press. Second, the Republican legislature, after four years of vigorous opposition to "High Tax Harriman," found it difficult to adopt so suddenly a new attitude to finances and, at the same time, to revert to its former subservience to the governor. Dewey had put an end to twenty years of Democratic rule in Albany; Rockefeller became the head of a party whose legislative leaders regarded the Republicans as the normal holder of executive authority and felt no unusual obligation to him as the current incumbent, particularly as he was ideologically far to the left of most of his party in the legislature. Third, in an unusual election development, the Democrats managed to retain the office of state comptroller. This gave them a center of informed opposition, much as would be provided by an active and well-staffed legislative party.

Within a week of the budget message, the *New York Times* reported mounting opposition among Republican legislators to the governor's proposals. The Democratic comptroller spearheaded the attack with the charge that the proposed revisions in the income tax were regressive and, further, would yield from $80 to $107 million more revenue than the governor estimated. This charge, although promptly challenged, was supported by a detailed economic analysis and gained increasing acceptance. In time it was taken up by the Republican majority leader of the Senate and the leaders of what became known as "the Budget Revolt." On February 27, the *New York Times* reported that the revolt had been joined by sufficient Republican assemblymen to defeat the Rockefeller budget.

Weeks later, but only after the elimination of the Governor's proposed forgiveness of the 1958 tax on capital gains, an increase of tax credit for individuals from $10 to $25 to counter the "soak-the-poor" charges of the Democrats, and a $40 million cut in the budget itself which the Governor had agreed to accept, the legislature finally passed the administration tax program—by a margin of two votes.

Pursuing the Harriman parallel to the point of destiny, Rockefeller's revenue estimates blew up on him as well. He, too, had been elected at the peak of a recession. The unemployed percentage of the work force dropped from 7.4 percent in the autumn of 1958 to 5 percent in the spring of 1959 and continued to drop. With the business recovery and the effectiveness of withholding taxes, money came rolling in. The state completed the 1959-60 fiscal year without using the $133 million in bond funds that had been programed and with an actual increase in its cash assets. In June 1960, within two months of the close of his first fiscal year, Rockefeller suddenly announced a $120 million increase in his second year revenue estimates and promised a $90 million tax cut on 1960 personal incomes. But already on the preceding day the Senate majority leader had announced that the Republican members of the Senate had unanimously pledged themselves to a 10 percent tax cut in 1960-61, an objective they had sought in the legislative session just ended but which the Governor had blocked.

As a result of the Harriman and Rockefeller transitions, the balance of executive-legislative power in New York State had come to a more nearly even point than at any time since the establishment of the executive budget system by Alfred E. Smith in 1927.

FINANCES: THE LIMIT ON INNOVATION

This New York State experience suggests that the range of practical policy choices open to new governors is limited by the financial commitment of existing programs and the relative inflexibility of state revenues. This essentially determines the difference between state and national politics. Change costs money. In New York, where some 60 percent of all noncapital state expenditure goes as aid to local government and 75 percent of state operating funds are required to run institutions, not much money can be had by cutting back existing programs. Capital programs provide the best opportunity, but even here it takes twelve to eighteen months to slow down (or step up) a capital program. As matching federal capital grant programs increase, significant cuts in this area may become too "expensive" to contemplate.

During both the Harriman and Rockefeller transitions, such fiscal considerations were dominant. Both governors were elected during a recession and took office before the extent of the recovery was discernible. Both found new taxes required to finance the ongoing government, and both abandoned election objectives of stepped-up state programs to deal with a revenue crisis. The national economy, both on the downturn and the upsurge, fixed the limits of the real policy alternatives for these new governors as must be true in nearly all states.

This also points to the crucial importance in the New York State experience of a knowledge of the state's financial problem as a basis of policy planning in the campaign period. Harriman did not have the necessary staff, the legislative assistance, or a budget document which provided this information when he won in 1954. Rockefeller had this financial data but failed to use it or thought it unwise to do so. Hence neither winning candidate prepared the voters in advance of his election for the fiscal policy he eventually adopted. Instead, each campaigned on the basis of new programs and new services to be financed by a resurgent state economy which he promised to bring about.

Finally, this experience would support Balfour's dictum that whichever party is in office the conservatives are in power. This has rarely been more evident than in the transitional phase of the Harriman and Rockefeller administrations when the boldest innovators were reduced to "marginalistic incrementalism"—or whatever the Russians would call it—by the automatic and built-in increases in the cost of the ongoing government programs and the money shortage resulting from an economic downturn.

CHALLENGE TO THE CHIEF

In New York as elsewhere a number of important activities are carried out by officials whose terms of office extend beyond that of the governor who appoints them. A new governor almost never starts with control over these activities and may for some time find himself dealing with executive agencies which are actively hostile.

The Dewey administration, which had known for some time that 1955 would bring a change of governor if not of party, took the precaution of ensuring that most of these agencies would remain Republican for some time. The terms of the Thruway Authority members, just taking over direction of the world's longest limited access highway, were staggered to ensure Republican control throughout the succeeding administration. The Power Authority, engaged in the enormous enterprise of harnessing the St. Lawrence and Niagara Rivers, was scheduled to remain Republican for three years; the Public Service Commission was tied up for four. In fact, Rockefeller found most of the commissions and authorities still in the hands [in which] Dewey had left them though this may not have been true had Harriman anticipated defeat. With a Republican legislature to support them, these agencies constituted an important opposition enclave within Harriman's executive branch.

This problem was acerbated for Harriman by uncertainties about the neutrality of the state civil service. In New York, as in Washington, the government had grown enormously during the 1940s. Harriman found a civil service greatly expanded by the Republicans, including large groups that had entered state service by special devices. Eisenhower was confronted with a similar situation in 1953. The Dewey civil servants had become accustomed to working with the Republican legislators and found the habit hard to break, which gave rise to further suspicions, as did the fact that many of the Democratic legislators regarded these civil servants as "Dewey men."

The situation was made still worse for the Democrats by the fact that the Republicans were scheduled to control the Civil Service Commission for the first half of Harriman's four years. This would have prevented the creation of exempt jobs at the high civil service level which enables a governor to underpin his commissioners with deputies and aides in whom they have confidence. The anomaly of this situation was such that the Republican chairman of the commission resigned in order to give the new Governor a freer hand in organizing his administration.

When Rockefeller succeeded Harriman he found a civil service but little changed from that which Dewey left, and correspondingly a source of less apprehension, but even so a Democratic member of the Civil Service Commission was persuaded to resign in order to give the new Governor control over his personnel department, thus repeating and perhaps establishing the sensible practice begun in 1955.

In the best of circumstances, power can easily slip away from a governor during the transition period, as in the case of Harriman and the State University. After much Democratic pressure (this was one of the rare issues on which the Democrats were active during the Dewey era) the University was begun somewhat tentatively in 1948; a permanent board of trustees was not authorized until 1954, and it had not been appointed by the time

of Harriman's election. This gave him an opportunity to identify himself and his party with a new institution of great importance and increasing political significance in an area of crowded colleges. However, in the context of a rumor that Dewey would call a special legislative session to confirm the appointments, and as a courtesy to the outgoing Governor, Harriman agreed to accept the recess appointment of a board of fifteen permanent trustees, of whom only one was chosen by him. The board chairman, chosen by Dewey and redesignated by Harriman, was an active Republican political leader who had served as state comptroller and lieutenant governor under Dewey. The chairman seized the initiative in January by calling for a $250 million bond issue for the State University together with a program for student loans and increased state scholarships awarded on the basis of need. As the Governor's annual message had contained no proposals of any kind relating to the State University, and with the budget at the printers, this proposal filled a vacuum. In time the Harriman administration proposed and pushed for more state scholarships based on need and for the State University bond issue but it could not claim exclusive credit for them. Eventually the board chairman emerged as Rockefeller's chief supporter for the gubernatorial nomination and thereafter as one of his closest campaign advisers and one of his first appointees as governor.

A New York governor has far less problems with overlapping term commissions than do most heads of states. He appoints nearly all department and agency heads. Even so, the State Power Authority, the Public Service Commission, the State Education Department, the Department of Social Welfare, and the State Thruway Authority all remained outside Governor Harriman's direct control through most of his administration. The most visible and frequent consequences were minor political opposition, withholding of information, and nonresponsiveness, but seldom with respect to any real policy issue or program objective. There is admittedly too little data to justify a firm conclusion, but we would question the wisdom of this method of policy insulation on the state level.

STRANGE BEDFELLOWS
Both Harriman and Rockefeller recruited and kept on personal staffs of pronounced liberal views. In each administration, policy formulation was or is

in the hands of persons considerably to the left of their party's center. These ideological differences tend to be associated with more general group differences. Thus, of Harriman's seven principal staff aides, five were Protestant, two Jewish. None was Catholic, although Catholics predominate in the New York Democratic party, and only one was a regular party man. By contrast, of the twelve department heads originally appointed by Harriman, seven were Catholic, four Jewish and only one, a "nonpartisan" holdover from Dewey, was Protestant. Five of the seven who were Catholics and two of the four who were Jewish were party regulars.

An instance, of small matter but considerable significance, of the type of misunderstanding that can arise in such circumstances occurred early in the Harriman administration. As liberal Democrats, personally and ideologically involved with the conduct of foreign affairs under Roosevelt and Truman, Harriman and his staff were perhaps more easily aroused by the loyalty issue as it emerged during the McCarthy period than by any other current political conflict. This sensitivity was sharpened when the legislature raised the issue with regard to two of the Governor's most trusted cabinet aides. One of the first orders of business in the new administration was to revise what were regarded as exaggerated state security regulations. Several months later the Governor and his staff learned in the newspapers that one of the new department heads, a regular Democrat, was requiring all applicants for licenses issued by his agency to fill out questionnaires regarding membership in subversive organizations, a practice never previously required and clearly contrived with the object of getting political "mileage" out of the communist issue. This was the type of measure which brought fire to the eyes of liberals at that time. The department head promptly withdrew his order, but the episode illuminated the gulf of understanding on certain issues which separated the two wings of the administration team.

Governor Rockefeller's personal staff is drawn principally from the liberal wing of his party, while his cabinet ranges across most of the Republican spectrum. In this situation, essentially identical to Harriman's, it would be no cause for surprise if similar tensions were to arise.

In line with their tendency to ideological differences, party regulars present the familiar problem of dual loyalty—to their political sponsors as well as to the administration. Quite apart from any substantive difficulties, such persons rarely have a highly developed sense of the importance of working for or through the governor—far less through the governor's pink-cheeked staff. The regulars frequently find themselves more easily working directly with the legislature, and are, of course, much more readily distracted by matters of importance to the locality from which they happen to come.

DIFFICULTY IN GRASPING THE REINS

With rare exceptions, the new cabinet appointees of the Harriman administration came to their posts with little knowledge of their program assignments. They were not well prepared to assist the new governor in framing his first legislative program and appeared to have much difficulty with the notion that he would assess their performance more with regard to the new ideas they produced than the quality of their administration of ongoing programs. Lacking confidence in their own information, they tended to embrace the "policy view" of the career civil service, which was often sound but seldom sensitive to the governor's view or that of his party. Nor was it responsive to the governor's need for original proposals, tending rather to produce extensions of the programs of the previous administration.

It appears that the Rockefeller administration has attempted to avoid this difficulty by looking outside the government for new ideas. At least one Rockefeller cabinet member has commented that he spends more of his time discussing his programs with outside advisers to the governor than in consultation within the government. This could be regarded as an extension of the existing practice in New York of relying heavily on temporary state commissions for new policy proposals. If it eliminates the problem of developing a creative career service, it may also tend to produce wild ideas on the one hand and decidedly dull civil servants on the other.

Contrary to frequently held opinion, a governor cannot always appoint men who will be loyal both to him and to some ideal of service beyond party. Nor is the number of party appointments necessarily a measure of political independence or lack of it. New York State government finds it difficult to attract first line talent to appointive posts. Although New York pays as good or better salaries than the federal government, Harriman was never able to attract to Albany an adequate supply of the type of persons who would willingly serve in Washington. It became a recognized rule that a less-than-adequate party nominee need never be accepted unless there were no better candidates available, but frequently there were none. Asked what were the de facto qualifications for a particular class of legal patronage, one of Harriman's secretaries wistfully replied: "Five years' unsuccessful practice of the law." Alternatively, this situation encouraged the hiring of young persons with limited experience but considerable promise, often at comparatively high salaries.

One consequence of the difficulty of recruiting qualified officials, particularly in the seven or eight weeks between the election and inauguration, is that a number of the key personnel of the preceding administration are given the opportunity to stay on for varying periods under the new regime. New commissioners without prior experience are inclined to regard an incumbent deputy or counsel or other experienced appointive officials as indispensable to their own transition. The tendency was marked in the Harriman administration, much less so during the Rockefeller transition when many former Dewey officials reappeared at once and even larger numbers were available.

In the Harriman administration this practice appeared to impede the achievement of control by the governor rather than to ease it. The very efficiency of holdover deputies and legal counsel served to postpone for many new officials the actual date of coming to grips with their duties. A career service such as New York's embodies more than enough competence needed for day-to-day affairs and inclines to place considerably more than enough emphasis on the value of continuity in policy and program. In these circumstances a "throw the rascals out" policy is likely to have long-term advantages for the new governor that outweigh the short-run value of avoiding early mistakes.

PROPOSALS

The recent New York state experience with transitions points to the curiously decisive problems of this transition period. At least four suggestions may have value in other situations.

1. *The state fiscal situation can and should be made known to the new governor.*

The New York practice of inviting the new governor to have his budget director participate in the budget hearings that normally begin a week after election is clearly of value. It enabled both Harriman and Rockefeller to present major tax programs which were largely of their own making, for in both cases the incumbent director dropped out of the process once the hearings were completed.

A complete and comprehensive budget document and comparable financial reports can contribute to a responsible political campaign. In New York state, lack of these materials prior to Harriman made it difficult if not impossible to talk intelligently about the state's financial problem. Perhaps of greater interest is the fact that the data were available in 1958 but were not used until after the campaign.

Insofar as this recent New York experience is relevant, it also points with great emphasis to the importance of revenue estimates. A professional civil service staff of quality, both in the state tax department and budget division, applied advanced techniques but failed badly to gauge the revenue significance of the 1954-55 and 1958-59 economic upturns on the yield of the state tax structure. A more accurate estimate might have transformed the character of the transition periods of both Harriman and Rockefeller. Here is a specific opportunity for improvement within the scope of professional public administration. Similarly, it points to the difficulty of constitutional procedures such as New York's which require that the budget be submitted to the legislature on or before the first day of February. Printing schedules mean that the budget must be completed by mid-January—too soon for the administration to master its details and, more importantly, too soon to make use of the all-important revenue indications that appear at the end of the calendar year. Much could be said for delaying the submission of a new administration's first budget for a period beyond the customary date, perhaps, in a case such as New York's, until the middle or end of February.

This further points to the importance of the pre-inaugural period as a time of preparation. Certainly this period should not be shortened. Rather, there is a need for developing practices that will assist the governor-elect to make the most of the fleeting weeks available to him. The informal practice in New York of engaging certain of the governor-elect's aides as paid budget consultants made available professional assistance on most satisfactory, noncommittal terms.

2. *The governor's role in routine government business, particularly legislative business, should be institutionalized to provide continuity without overwhelming the executive during his first months.*

As much as half the thousand and more bills passed by the New York legislature each year are departmental measures of a nonpolitical character. The necessity to act on these measures seriously burdened Harriman's staff during his first legislative session. This came at a time when the legislature (and perhaps some of the departments as well!) yielded to the familiar temptation to try to slip by the new Governor measures which would not pass the scrutiny of more experienced eyes. To alleviate this situation in the future the Harriman administration instituted the practice of pre-clearance by the Budget Division of all departmental legislation. Before any such measures were introduced, they were studied, approved and logged by the Division, acting as a staff unit for the Governor's counsel. This system provided the incoming Rockefeller administration with a complete record of all departmental legislation prefiled for the forthcoming 1959 session, as well as a system for reviewing and coordinating all such measures throughout the legislative period. It gives the new governor at least a fighting chance in his opening duel with the legislature.

3. *Each party should have a vigorous legislative wing which fully participates in the legislative process.*

The only thing that corrupts more than power is lack of it. An effort should be made to avoid the continuous dominance of one party in legislatures. New York is roughly divided between New York City and the rest of the state. The legislature for the city is twenty-five to one Democratic; the legislature for the state is as permanently Republican; neither is as good as it could be, and the source of difficulty in both is the absence of a vigorous minority.

This situation almost certainly could be helped in New York State by the innovation of a bipartisan legislative council and staff which would ensure that minority as well as majority members would have access to information on government issues and programs and which would in that measure make an informed opposition at least possible. While the legislative council may not have

lived up to its full potential, when you are in the basement so far as a bipartisan staff is concerned, as is the New York State legislature, the only way you can go is up.

4. *The career service should be responsive to the problems of transition.*

The practice begun by the Republicans and continued by the Democrats of turning over the civil service commission to the new governor is a sound step. Nothing does greater harm to the career service than to wall it off, as against a natural enemy, from the influence of the chief executive. First impressions remain. If the first impression a governor has of his civil service is that of a hostile and vigilant garrison entrenched behind statutes which he must somehow breach, both are in for troubled careers. Directions of the civil service should be turned over to the new governor promptly as his greatest source of strength during the period of transition—and as one of his principal responsibilities throughout his administration.

Correspondingly, the time of transition is one of great opportunity for the civil servant who will come forward with ideas and proposals. The tendency is to stay out of sight. It is a rare bureau chief who is ready for his new commissioner with a summary of the laws affecting the department or a list of suggestions for new legislation or for implementing the more viable campaign commitments of the victorious party. Those who are ready rarely regret it. Their rewards are fully their due, for a civil servant is never more valuable, surely, than when he is abetting the processes by which the citizenry choose to have things done differently. The important role the civil servant plays in contributing to responsible social change should be emphasized in training for public service.

The professionalization of government service and the concept of "permanent status" are marks of a complex society. Yet there is wanting a greater awareness among civil service career staffs of the essentially conservative consequences of such arrangements, most particularly in areas of government not subject to the pressures of social conflict. This traditional strength of the career service is its greatest weakness when it results in the tendency to resist change and adjustment wherever the values of elected officials conflict even slightly with established professional and career service values. Engineers, educators, doctors, social workers, nurses, to mention but a few, were among the groups most resistant to suggestions for change and quickest to sense "politics" where the slightest adjustment or shift in emphasis was proposed. Thus the prospect emerges that the ease of transition in administration will be in inverse proportion to the professionalization of the bureaucracy: hardly the outcome sought by the merit system, but doubtless a commentary on American professional education as a preparation for public service.

CHAPTER 5

THE GOVERNOR AND HIS STAFF

Very little attention has been given to the staffing of governors' offices. Yet the professional policy advisors and legal assistants who serve the governor are key persons in state governments, and as one article in this chapter points out, a competent staff is an essential ingredient of a successful gubernatorial tenure.

While studying governor's offices for the Study of the American States and the Institute on State Programming for the 1970s, the editors found that the extent and expertise of governors' staffs vary considerably among the states. In the smaller states, the governor's office may consist of no more than an administrative assistant and several clerical-secretarial helpers. In larger states, the governor most likely will have not only administrative and legal assistants but also policy experts on a broad range of state functions and processes. The size of the state is not the only variable that determines the nature of the governor's staff. In states where governmental functions have been organized around broad and coordinated functions, governors have less need for staff experts in policy areas and often rely on cabinet officers in the administrative departments for policy advice. The need for staffing is greater where reorganization has not taken place. Most of the states now have departments of administration or equivalent agencies where the management functions of budgeting, planning, and purchasing are located, and governors uniformly rely on such departments for these highly technical and sizeable functions.

The size and nature of the staff often are affected by a governor's personal style as well as the other factors mentioned. Claude Kirk, when he was governor of Florida, had more professional public relations men than most governors. In fact, it was possible for Floridians to visit the governor and have their picture taken shaking his hand on several days of the week.

A great deal has been written about presidential staffing and the Executive Office of the President. Presidential aides, the men on the President's personal staff, are often depicted by journalists as more influential than presidential appointees to key administrative positions. The matter of who is more influential is often raised in the foreign policy arena vis-à-vis the president's foreign policy advisor and the Secretary of State.

The same questions might be raised in connection with executive leadership at the state level.

How influential in policy and administration is the governor's administrative assistant, his legislative liaison, his legal advisor, his staff specialists in education and urban affairs? Where are these staff assistants recruited at the state level and what expertise do they bring to state executive leadership? The essays in this chapter address these questions in dealing with the consequences of staff organization and behavior in the governors' offices.

GOVERNORS' STAFFS—BACKGROUND AND RECRUITMENT PATTERNS
Donald R. Sprengel

The focus of this paper is on the development of a gubernatorial staff profile based upon demographic and experience characteristics and on uniformities in staff recruitment patterns among the states. Demographic profiles have long been of interest to students of political elites, particularly since the perceptive work of Matthews popularized the approach.[1] Since then, research has consistently demonstrated basic differences between social characteristics of political elites and those of the general public. The middle- and upper-class bias of political elites is by now well established for it can be easily demonstrated that elites are better educated, more affluent, and more prestigiously employed than the mass of citizens. Given this variance, we need not compare staff demography with that of the general population since the findings would likely be redundant of prior analysis. Rather, the question might more profitably be put whether the profile of gubernatorial staffs differs in any significant fashion from that of other political elites. In the analysis which follows an effort has been made to draw upon the wealth of elite data available in comparing age, education, and occupation patterns.

Source: Reprinted with the permission of the author and the publisher from *Gubernatorial Staffs: Functional and Political Profiles* (Iowa City, Iowa: Institute of Public Affairs, 1969), chap. 2.

[1] Donald R. Matthews, *The Social Background of Political Decision Makers* (Garden City, N.Y.: Doubleday, 1954).

AGE

Table [1] presents age distribution data for a number of political elites and reveals a striking disparity between gubernatorial staffs and the others. Some 54 percent of the staff people are under age 40, nearly double the proportion of any other elite grouping. The median age statistic serves to dramatize this marked difference among the elites. In a study of presidential staffs from 1939 to 1967, Alex Lacy found that presidential staff members were an average 46 years old at the time of appointment and that 31 percent were under age 40.[2] While these figures are not directly comparable to gubernatorial staffs (age at time of appointment versus age at time of interview), nonetheless it is interesting to note that the two elites with the highest percentage of individuals under age 40 are the executive elites.

This condition inevitably stimulates a quest for explanation. Three highly speculative explanations have been chosen for discussion: salary, personal loyalty to and association with the governor, and political and career opportunism. A study by Elmer Cornwell and his associates conducted in 1966 found that staff salaries are competitive with those of the higher civil service positions; "75 percent of the professional staff receive in excess of $10,000 a year; 46 percent receive between $10,000 and $15,000; 29 percent receive more than $15,000."[3] These salary levels are fairly attractive, and the argument can be advanced that they would be more of an inducement for a younger person. If one considers that older persons are generally settled in career positions of equal or better remuneration, they would be unlikely to exchange the relative security of that position for one as politically and temporally tenuous as that of a staff person. It should, however, be noted that individuals frequently reject the security of private positions in favor of political ventures. United States senators, congressmen, and for that matter governors would be prime examples.

In Table [1], it can be observed that except for state legislators, the other categories are either professional or highly prestigious (as in the case of

[2] "The White House Staff Bureaucracy," *Transaction* (January 1969), p. 51.

[3] "Professional Staff for Governors' Offices Subject of Questionnaires," *Newsletter of the Bureau of Government Research*, University of Rhode Island, September 1968.

TABLE [1] Age Distribution of Selected Elites*

Age	Governors' Staff	State Legislators	State Administrators	City Managers	Federal Political Executives	GS-15-18
39 or less	54%	29%	13%	16%	17%	6%
40–49	29	32	28	51	41	39
50–59	13	22	35	22	30	44
60 and over	4	17	24	11	12	11
	100%	100%	100%	100%	100%	100%
Median age	38	48	53	43	48	50
	(226)	(469)	(933)	(1014)	(1041)	(559)

*The data are from the following sources: Legislators—John C. Wahlke et al., *The Legislative System* (New York: John Wiley, 1962); state administrators—by permission of Deil S. Wright and Richard McAnaw from their study code book; city managers—by permission of Robert P. Boynton from an unpublished study; federal political executives—David T. Stanley et al., *Men Who Govern* (Washington, D.C.: The Brookings Institution, 1967); GS-15-18—David T. Stanley, *The Higher Civil Service* (Washington, D.C.: The Brookings Institution, 1964). Column titles in all subsequent tables refer to these sources unless otherwise indicated; figures in parentheses represent the number of respondents. In some cases interpolation of the data has been required to make them comparable; while the error margin in such cases is small, nonetheless the reported figure is not necessarily precise.

federal political executives). Being closest in age to state legislators is suggestive of an alternative explanation. Attitudinal studies of legislators have revealed the ambition or opportunity motive among younger legislators, that is, they perceive the legislature as a means to further their careers; relatively few regard the legislative position as terminal. In short they are "on the make," and legislative office is consciously viewed as a rung on the career ladder. A similar attitude might be suggested here: Are younger staff personnel ambitious, particularly politically ambitious? Data reported elsewhere in this chapter reveal that 32.3 percent of the respondents anticipate some future political venture. When correlated with age, 84.9 percent of these respondents are under age 40, evidence which strongly supports the suggested possible explanation. Because of the moderate size of the ambition groups, however, this explanation can only be viewed as partial.

Besides ambition and salary, another plausible explanation rests in motivation emanating from personal and political relationships with the governor. Other data reported in this chapter reveal that 69.1 percent of the respondents had worked in the governor's election campaign, and that 51.3 percent had had other personal relationships with the governor prior to his assumption of office, excluding the election campaign. Younger staff tend to group in the former statistic, older staff in the

latter. The transfer of campaign aides to staff positions confirms a trend noticeable in presidential staffing. "The two Presidents since 1939 who first came to office straight from elections and not because of another President's death—Eisenhower and Kennedy—drew heavily from their original campaign staffs."[4] The tendency is reasonable to expect in that campaign staffers would be familiar with the executive's work habits, thought processes, and attitudes; becoming settled in an office routine would be correspondingly easier. Interesting also is the fact that of those respondents expressing political ambition, 72.2 percent were active in the governor's election campaign, but only 58.3 percent had had prior personal relationships with the governor. The argument might be advanced that the ambitious perceive the rising star of the governor as a mechanism to further their own careers.

All the foregoing is, however, exceedingly speculative; additional data are required to establish motivational patterns for staff assignment. The suggestions of salary, ambition, and personal motivation may, however, be key variables in explaining the relative youth of executive staffs.

EDUCATION AND OCCUPATION
A generally unsubstantiated but popular and cynical commentary on gubernatorial staffs pictures

[4]Lacy, *op. cit.*, p. 52.

TABLE [2]   Education Levels of Selected Elites

Education Level	Governors' Staff	State Legislators	State Administrators	City Managers	Federal Political Executives	GS-15-18
High-school graduate or less	9%	19%	14%	7%	7%	2%
Some college	20	26	21	18	18	13
College graduate	24	55*	24	21	75*	38
Graduate study	13	xx	xx	23	xx	12
Graduate degree	34	xx	40	31	xx	33
Other/NA	0	xx	1	0	xx	2
	100%	100%	100%	100%	100%	100%
	(226)	(469)	(933)	(1014)	(1041)	(559)

*Figure represents total for college graduate, graduate study, and graduate degree.
Unknown distribution indicated by xx.

them as political hacks and general incompetents. This qualitative generalization can be challenged on the basis of educational attainment and professional expertise of the staff. Table [2] presents comparative data on educational levels. Seventy-one percent of the staffers have earned a minimum of a bachelor's degree, substantially higher than either state legislators and state administrators, equal to city managers and federal political executives, but beneath federal career executives. Gubernatorial staffs exhibit a slightly lower level of educational attainment than do presidential staffs, about three in four of the latter having earned a college degree and over one-half an advanced degree.[5] On the basis of this evidence the conclusion is inescapable that staff personnel are extremely well educated. The data reported here are somewhat less impressive than that found by Cornwell and his associates; their data indicate that 63 percent of the staff have had postgraduate study as compared to the 47 percent found here. Except for a differing time period for the two studies, no other explanation for this discrepancy is immediately apparent.

As a further indication of the objectively apparent competence of gubernatorial staffs, one might

[5]*Ibid.*, p. 51.

TABLE [3]   Occupations of Selected Political Elites

Occupation	Governors' Staff	State Administrators	State Legislators
Law	17%	19%	36%
Journalism	16	5	4
Public relations	6	*	2
Public administration	7	2	6
Business	10	9	32
Finance	2	4	12
Secretarial/clerical	8	*	xx
Other	22	40	8
None/no answer	12	21	xx
	100%	100%	100%
	(226)	(933)	(469)

*indicates less than 1%.
xx indicates unknown.

examine the occupations which staff personnel profess. The data in Table [3] show occupations of elites in state political systems—staff, legislators, and administrators. Lawyers, the omnipresent jacks-of-all-trades of politics, predominate among the occupational categories presented. This concentration is not unexpected, the role of the lawyer in politics having been long established; regardless of the type of elite, they have been present in substantial numbers. An interesting pattern among staffers centers on the number of persons recruited from journalism, public relations, and public administration, occupations which suggest the importance of image-related activities as compared to administration as a definition of the staff role. Some 22 percent of the staff personnel identify their occupation as either journalism or public relations; these data are supportive of the . . . role of the staff in image creation and projection.

GENERALISTS AND SPECIALISTS

Education and occupation are offered as an index of the degree of competence and specialization in staffs. To bring this latter aspect—specialization—into sharper focus and to determine the extent to which generalists or specialists dominate educational patterns, a series of additional questions was used. Because of the generalist connotation implicit within the staff position, the questionnaire attempted to ascertain how many staff members possessed at least one degree in either political science, journalism, or public administration. The responses indicate that of those respondents who were college graduates (N = 159), 22 percent possessed at least one degree in political science, 14.5 percent at least one degree in journalism, and only 7.5 percent at least one degree in public administration. The dominance of politics and media relations over administration is clear.

The generalist aspect of staffs is one of the conclusions of the Cornwell study; only 36 percent of their respondents were identified as specialists. To tap this dimension, the respondents in this study were asked if they possessed any special qualification, experience, or information in any particular subject area. The results may be found in Table [4]. While the data reveal that staff members are slightly more specialized than found to be the case in the Cornwell research, nonetheless, a clear majority could not identify any specific area of special competence. On this basis the generalist

TABLE [4] Specialized Areas of Staff Competence

Percent	Specialized Area Response
4.4	Budgeting, finance, taxation, economics
7.5	Law enforcement, corrections, judicial administration, civil rights
8.9	General administration, government
2.7	Recreation, tourism, natural resources, conservation, industrial development
6.2	Political-public relations
4.9	Intergovernmental relations, community development
2.2	Health, education, welfare
7.1	Multiple response
3.5	Other
52.6	None/no answer
100.0%	
(226)	

notion of gubernatorial staffs is affirmed, although a somewhat diverse specialist emphasis can be observed. . . . Focusing on general administration and political-public relations, those staff members giving multiple responses were redistributed according to individual category of response. As a result, 11.1 percent felt exceptionally well qualified in general administration, and 12 percent felt qualfied in political-public relations. The differences in the responses are admittedly marginal, but they do serve to emphasize two features of staff competence. First, competence is widely distributed as to area and fosters the impression that the majority of staff people are generalists as opposed to specialists. Second, the image related public relations function is of at least coequal importance with that of administration.

POLITICAL BACKGROUND

Ample evidence has been accumulated by political scientists that political leaders and political elites are a markedly different breed than the average citizen not only in demographic detail but also in political life. Membership in an elite is not accidental; it is the result of a progression of political experiences having an early beginning and extending late in life. Elites possess a history of political awareness, involvement, and commitment far more activist than the general public. Their families have been politically active; many of their parents have held political office. They are introduced to politics at an early age, and the interest thus generated finds expression in a variety of political activities. With these generalizations in hand, the questions for this study are: What political genesis characterizes gubernatorial staffs, and does it differ from other elites? To explore this question, data were gathered on political socialization, the mechanics of involvement, partisanship, and prior political experience.

To test the, by now, commonplace assumption that political elites are introduced to, become interested in, and take an active role in politics early in their lives, a closed-ended question sought to determine the time period when the respondents first became interested in politics generally. Table [5] presents the distribution of responses. By age 18, 43.8 percent of the respondents had developed an interest in politics. The responses are roughly comparable to data available in other elite studies. The factor that explains much of this early socialization, as is to be expected, concentrates in the influence of the family. Family involvement in politics was cited singly by 15.5 percent of the respondents, and another 19 percent cited that they had "always been interested"; of these two groups, 94.3 percent had developed an interest in politics before age 21. Of the 24.3 percent of the respondents who cited multiple causes for their interest, an additional 15.5 percent cited family involvement and 9.7 percent that they were "always interested." In conglomerate terms, 31 percent cited family involvement as a cause and 28.7 percent were always interested; the combined total for these two categories, eliminating overlap between responses of both family involvement and always interested, is 51.3 percent. A trend is also discernible regarding the impact of particular political events as a contributing factor in generating interest; 20.4 percent cited a political event as the single factor. While the influence of family domi-

nates socialization through adolescence, political events themselves assume increasing importance as one moves along a time dimension. Events are the dominant causal characteristic in the over-age-21 categories.

While the impact of family and political events on socialization is clear, the manner in which the respondents first became *actively* involved is also clear-cut and follows a similar age distribution pattern. First active contact with politics is most frequently the product of assisting in a political campaign; 35.4 percent gave this as the single event while another 15 percent offered it as one of a multiple of reasons. Wyner makes a similar observation in his study of staff in fourteen states. Of second, but still of significant importance, was recruitment by a political party, a group, or friends (singly by 15.5 percent and as one of several by 9.3 percent). The citation of assisting in a political campaign and being asked was the most frequent multiple response. In the post-21 age groups, these two factors remain strong, but are secondary to appointment to office as the initial political contact; such is particularly true of businessmen. It is worthy of note, too, that newspaper reporters tend to socialize later in life, and the event that causes first interest is most frequently their assignment to cover political events.

A final correlation was drawn between the time of first interest and whether the respondent had had any relatives active in politics. The result is as expected—those respondents who had direct relatives active in politics tend to socialize earlier than do those whose family was inactive. Again the influence of family is apparent. In all, 21.7 percent of the staffers had direct family who had held public or political party office, 11.9 percent at the local level and 11.1 percent at the state level. Almost 16 percent had held elective or appointive executive positions, and 7.1 percent had held party positions. It should be noted that officeholding by immediate family is a rather severe criterion for family involvement in politics. The extent to which political discussions took place in the home or parents worked in or contributed to a political campaign are, perhaps, better indicators of the political environment. Nonetheless, the data can be interpreted to indicate that staff personnel mature in highly politicized environments.

Socialization studies have also demonstrated that the family is the primary determinant of political

TABLE [5] Time of First Interest in Politics

Percent	Time of First Interest
15.9	Childhood or grammar school (up to 13 years)
27.9	Adolescence or high school (ages 13–17)
21.2	College or equivalent period (ages 18–21)
13.3	After age 21, but before becoming active in politics
17.7	After age 21, at the time of active involvement
0.4	Other
3.6	No answer
100.0%	
(226)	

party identification, and that this identification is remarkably stable over time. If staff members emerge from a highly politicized environment, then party identification should reflect stability over time and be somewhat consistent with parental party identification. The partisanship of the respondents broke down as follows: 43.8 percent Democratic, 48.7 percent Republican, 5.8 percent Independent, 1.3 percent Wallace Democrat, and 0.4 percent other. Asked if they had ever belonged to a party other than the one to which they now belonged, 87.6 percent responded they had *always* been an identifier with their present party. Equal numbers (2.7 percent each) had changed parties because (1) they could no longer accept their previous party's philosophy, or (2) because of the candidacy of a particular individual (John F. Kennedy in five of six cases). The stability of party identification can be further characterized by parental party identification; 67.9 percent stated that both they and their parents belonged to the same political party.

EXPERIENCE IN OFFICE

Like other elites, staff personnel have had extensive experience in public and political party office. A politically experienced staff is an obvious asset to a governor, particularly in terms of being able to gauge the political costs and consequences of decisions and to deal with other political actors on familiar terms. Data were collected on three types of experience: elective or appointive public office, political party office, and administrative assistant experience, especially that in a governor's office. Table [6] reveals relevant statistics for each of the three types of experience as well as a total figure. Over 38 percent of the respondents have held some type of political position, with elective and appointive public office being the most prominent.

The experience data were analyzed according to level (federal, state, and local) and type (executive, legislative, and judicial). Elective public office is about evenly divided between the local and state levels; only one respondent had held national elective office. Elective legislative experience is about double the rate of executive, although such a ratio might be considered low given the numerical superiority of legislative positions over elective executive in the political system as a whole. Experience in appointive public office has been overwhelmingly in the executive branch, again as would be expected given the structure of the political system. There are simply more appointive executive than appointive legislative positions. Appointive executive experience has been almost exclusively at the state level.

Respondents also indicated a moderate degree of experience as administrative assistants or, more aptly phrased, staff personnel. This experience has been primarily executive in nature at the state level and almost exclusively legislative at the national level.

Of special interest are those individuals who have served on the staff of any other governor: 18.1 percent of the respondents have had such experience. Three of these 41 individuals had served on staffs in at least two states. All three are Republicans appointed by a Republican governor; the remarks of one respondent would indicate that deliberate lending or borrowing of the staff person was involved. . . . There is no evidence of interstaff transfer among Democratic governors. The 41 individuals are spread among 22 states, 9 Republican governors appointing 20 individuals for a ratio of 2.2 each and the 13 Democrats appointing 21 for a ratio of 1.6. With the exception of Pennsylvania where a large number of former Governor Scranton's personnel were retained, the phenome-

---

TABLE [6] Percent Having, Mean, and Median Years of Political Experience, by Type

Percent Mean, and Median	Elective or Appointive	Administrative Assistant	Political Party	Total, All Experience
Percent with experience	24.3% (226)	11.1% (226)	19.9% (226)	38.1% (226)
Mean years of experience	6.5 (55)	4.4 (25)	4.9 (45)	6.8 (86)
Median years of experience	4.0 (55)	4.0 (25)	4.0 (45)	5.0 (86)

non of appointing individuals with prior staff experience is largely a border and southern state phenomenon. Of the 13 states in these regions for which data are available, 12 have staff people with prior experience; the remaining 10 states are scattered without regional configuration. Speculatively speaking, this concentration may be the result of the regional political culture, largely dominated by one political party and possessing a distinct style of factional politics that would make prior experience of great value to a governor.

Sixty-three of the respondents had held some office in a political party; at one time or another, 77.8 percent of these held office at the local level, 60.3 percent in state party office, and 3.2 percent at the national level. Given the role of the governor as party leader, personnel versed in internal party dynamics would be a resource of great potential importance. Such staff people are employed by the governors of 26 states.

POLITICAL AMBITIONS

Since staff people have held a wide assortment of public and party offices, which is indicative of overlapping and interchangeable roles, inquiry was made as to future political plans. As cited earlier . . . , 32.2 percent of the respondents admitted to political ambitions. These ambitions are directed to all levels of government, but concentrate most heavily at the state level (49.3 percent). About equal numbers mentioned state legislative and state executive positions. National political ambitions were held by 17.8 percent of the respondents. Another 8.2 percent aspired to local office, and 34.3 percent admitted ambition but were indefinite as to level of government or type of office. Due to multiple responses, these figures amount to more than 100 percent. Only two respondents indicated any desire to pursue office in a political party.

Another interesting sidelight of these data emerged as the result of an impressionistic hunch. Ambitious respondents were grouped by state and correlated with ambition factor for the governor derived from actual candidacies in the 1968 election, roles played in the 1968 national party conventions, and newspaper speculation and reports. It is obvious that ambitious staffs were more than matched by ambitious governors who included two presidential hopefuls, four persons mentioned as vice-presidential possibilities, and

two United States senatorial candidates. Evidently, ambitious staff perceive a shared political fate with an ambitious governor.

These ambitions, however, do not carry a corresponding imminence about them; 84.6 percent of the respondents declared an intention to continue on the staff for the duration of the governor's term. Of the 27 respondents who intended to resign, only 1 was leaving to seek elective public office, 10 were being appointed to other positions, and 11 were leaving for an undetermined reason. On the basis of his research, Wyner enumerates five factors involved in staff turnover: (1) better opportunity elsewhere; (2) promotion to an administrative position; (3) corruption; (4) personal inefficiency due to poor political judgment, an inability to work with people or groups, or plain incompetence; and (5) political or ideological incompatibility.

This low intention of turnover rate is indicative of two things: first, that the staff have a commitment to remain, perhaps based on personal loyalty to the governor; and second, that this loyalty takes precedence over political ambition. The turnover rate itself has been moderately low. The bulk of the respondents (72.6 percent) have held staff positions since the early days of the administration, 15.5 percent having joined the staff before the governor assumed office, 40.3 percent at the time of inauguration, and 16.8 percent soon thereafter. Wyner found a similar stability among staff personnel; 75 percent of the complement were original appointments, a factor which he contends leads to behavioral and operational stability. Long tenure and low intention of turnover appear to be two characteristics of staff employment, both of which suggest the value of pursuing the hypothesis that personal loyalties are a major component in staff recruitment and behavior.

PATTERNS IN THE RECRUITMENT PROCESS

Social and political background characteristics do not purport to explain completely why specific types of individuals are recruited for gubernatorial staffs. At best they constitute only one, dangerously close to deterministic, aspect of the recruitment process. While special educational and occupational skills and adroitness founded on political experience can be important considerations, they need not be fundamental. The politically sensitive and personally intimate nature of the staff position requires a close working relationship with the governor. Persons attuned to the work habits, thought processes, attitudes, and expectations of the governor are essential to a smoothly functioning staff operation. This operational necessity delimits to some degree the available sources of labor. Friends of long standing, political associates, business colleagues, and employees—these and similar sources would appear to be the motherlode of talent and skill.

SOURCES OF STAFF

Two sets of questions are implicit here and require exploration. First, what sources do governors tap for their staff? We have already examined professed occupations, but the question focuses more specifically on the position held immediately prior to joining the governor's staff. Second, what associational patterns existed between the governor and his staff before the former's assumption of office, especially those associations that would contribute to an immediate working rapport?

Table [7] presents the percentage distribution of positions held by the staff prior to their staff employment. The large number of responses in the unknown category limits the ability to generalize from these data. Assuming nonetheless a proportionate distribution of the unknowns among the categories cited, about one-third of the staff personnel are recruited from the private sector, about one-quarter are garnered from government service, about one-fifth were already on the governor's staff, and one-seventh were in the service of the previous governor. These proportions are roughly comparable to those found by Lacy in his study of presidential staffing. Comparison of occupational categories between presidential and gubernatorial staffs is also suggestive. The former have been recruited from a diversity of fields; although large numbers possessed law degrees, relatively few were dependent upon a legal practice for their livelihood.

The Presidents tended to recruit their staff members from different fields . . . . Roosevelt recruited primarily from government and from journalism—getting about a quarter from each. Truman got about half from government. Eisenhower recruited a third from the business world. Kennedy got about two-thirds of his people from government (most with previous staff experience) and the universities. Johnson, too, relied primarily on government service (again mostly staff men) and the business world.[6]

Interesting differences emerge when the recruitment data are controlled for the political party of the governor. Democratic governors rely somewhat more heavily upon the private sector, government, and defeated candidates for staff; Republican governors draw larger percentages of recruits from the previous governor and from their own personal coterie. The suggestion is latent but nonetheless strong that Democratic and Republican governors differ in their recruiting styles, in that the former recruit on the basis of a personal coalition, while Republicans do so on the basis of an electoral coalition. Personal coalitions represent people with long-term familiarity with the governor in a variety of relationships, while electoral coalitions reflect short-term political and advisory relationships formed most frequently just prior to the governor's campaign for public office.

There is little evidence of recruitment by the governors directly from the political party organization. If the political party is not a major source of staff, what influence does party identification have on the recruiting process? How partisanly pure are staffs? No Democratic governor appointed a Republican identifier to his staff, although 6.1 percent were defined as independents. Democrats, however, comprised 7 percent of the Republican gubernatorial staffs (9 of 128 appointees). It is interesting to note where these appointments occurred. Eight of the nine respondents were in two border states, both of which elected Republican governors for the first time in recent memory. Whether this facet can be attributed to the lack of an indigenous Republican supply of potential staff or a conscious attempt to build an

TABLE [7] Position Held Immediately Prior to Staff Position

Percent	Position Held
19.9	Private sector (business, professional)
14.6	Other governmental
12.4	On staff prior to inauguration
9.3	With previous governor
2.2	Defeated candidate for political office
0.9	Other
37.2	Unknown
3.5	No answer
100.0%	
(226)	

[6] *Ibid.*

electoral coalition based on some factions of the Democratic party remains an open question.

PATTERNS OF ASSOCIATION

In general, Democrats appoint Democrats, Republicans choose Republicans, and both recruit in dissimilar proportions from the same sources. Have these appointees had any relationships with the governor prior to his assumption of office, and is there any difference between Republican and Democratic governors in this regard? Table [8] gives percentage distributions according to the number of years the respondent has known the governor aside from the time spent on the staff as controlled for the governor's political party. It is immediately apparent that Democratic governors have been acquainted with a larger proportion of their staffs for a longer period of time than their Republican counterparts. This tendency supports the notion that Democrats recruit personal coalitions for staff while Republicans recruit an electoral coalition. On this basis the less-than-one-year category would reflect individuals who have become acquainted with the governor during his campaign for office and do not mirror any long-term personal association. The category one to five years can be interpreted to include the period in which the governor began to organize his drive for the office; while certainly more familiar with the governor than the former group, the association

would be pragmatically related to the pursuit of the highest state office. The last two categories more truly reflect long-term acquaintance patterns. The distinction between personal and electoral coalitions as a basis for staff recruiting is the basis for this interpretation. When these groupings are controlled for job position, a pattern emerges indicating that those individuals who have had no or very short acquaintance with the governor hold, respectively, secretarial/clerical jobs or less sensitive assistant-to-an-assistant type positions in the larger states. It is evident, too, that key staff positions are not entrusted to individuals who have not had a long acquaintance with the governor; such critical positions require as a prerequisite an intimate understanding of the governor personally and attitudinally.

Not only the length but also the type of association or acquaintance is important. The data in Table [9] describe the type of association controlled for the party of the governor. While Lacy found in his study of presidential staffs that the majority of the staff appointees had had no significant working or personal relationships with the President prior to appointment, the reverse is true of gubernatorial staffs; 51.3 percent expressed some prior association with the governor. The variance apparent between Democratic and Republican staffs is neither striking nor significant, but this conclusion must be tempered using the aggregate statistic on the *number* of respondents having had any prior association. An appreciably higher percentage of Democratic staff (61.1 percent to 47.5 percent) indicated some manner of prior acquaintance. The reason for accepting the total figures as the more realistic is that the data on type of association are artificially inflated in the Republican column due to a small number of re-

TABLE [8] Total Years Staff Has Known Governor Before Inauguration, by Political Party of the Governor

Years Known	Democrats	Republicans	Total
None	18.4%	24.8%	22.0%
Less than 1	7.1	11.2	9.4
1 to 2	7.1	12.8	10.3
2 to 3	4.1	10.4	7.6
3 to 4	12.3	7.2	9.4
4 to 5	8.2	5.6	6.7
5 to 10	16.3	16.0	16.2
More than 10	26.5	12.0	18.4
	100.0%	100.0%	100.0%
Data Regrouped by 5-Year Intervals			
Less than 1	25.5%	36.0%	31.4%
1 to 5	31.7	36.0	34.0
5 to 10	16.3	16.0	16.2
More than 10	26.5	12.0	18.4
	100.0%	100.0%	100.0%
	(97)	(126)	(223)

TABLE [9] Type of Association Prior to Inauguration, by Political Party of the Governor

Type of Association	Democrats	Republicans	Total
Personal friend	14.7%	17.2%	15.5%
Family friend	6.3	4.1	4.9
Social	32.6	24.6	27.0
Business	22.1	18.0	19.0
Advisory	16.8	21.3	18.6
Political	31.6	26.2	27.4
Total, any relationship	61.1%	47.5%	51.3%
	(95)	(122)	(217)

spondents citing multiple types of association. While it is obvious that there exists no meaningful difference in the *type* of association staffs have had with their respective governors (in fact they are quite congruous), nonetheless the aggregate statistic does reinforce the contention (moving up from suggestion) that recruiting styles do vary between Democratic and Republican governors.

It has thus far been demonstrated that Democratic governors recruit their staffs from the same generic sources as Republicans but vary in degree of emphasis, that Democratic staffs tend to have known the governor for longer periods of time before assumption of office, and that Democratic staff tend to have had more prior associations. What is needed to force the issue is a correlation between the number of years the respondents had known the governor prior to inauguration as controlled for party with the type of association. If, as we suspect, recruiting styles do vary and reflect personal coalitions in the case of Democrats and electoral coalitions for Republicans, then those respondents serving Democratic governors should tend to have long-term (more than five years) associations across the board, while those serving Republican executives should exhibit a higher percentage of short-term associations, particularly in the advisory and political categories. These two categories are particularly crucial since short-term advisory or political associations are reflective of electorally based interaction. Table [10] presents the relevant data. It is apparent from the table that the data tend to support the hypothesis. Only

12.5 percent of the Republican staffs had any political association of longer than ten years, and only 15.4 percent had advisory relationships of the same duration, as compared to 26.7 percent and 25 percent, respectively, for Democratic staffs. Democratic staffs also show a fairly consistent pattern in all groupings. Apparently then, Democratic governors exhibit a greater tendency to recruit staffs that have had long-term, personal associations than do Republicans; this pattern is reflective of a variation in recruiting style.

Attention might also be focused on the extent to which current staff were active in the governor's primary and general election campaigns. The data on primary campaigns must be accepted with serious reservation; not all governors faced meaningful primary opposition, if any at all; the statistics, therefore, are potentially meaningless unless taken as an indication of early commitment. Some 55.2 percent of the staffs did take a role in the primary campaign, 71 percent of these as members of the governors' personal primary campaign staffs. The other 29 percent were active only in terms of localized or general assistance, i.e., clerical, secretarial, local organization, precinct work, envelope stuffing, etc.

With reference to the general election, 69.1 percent indicated some involvement, 72.3 percent of these on the governor's personal campaign staff. This assistance took the form primarily of strategy and planning, but also included speech writing, press relations, finance, and scheduling. When the campaign activity data are sorted according to the

TABLE [10]   Years Staff Has Known Governor Prior to Inauguration As Controlled for Party, by Type of Association

Years Known	Social	Political	Business	Advisory	Personal Friend	Family Friend
Democrats						
Less than 1	9.7%	10.0%	4.8%	12.5%	0.0%	16.7%
1 to 5	41.9	36.6	28.6	37.5	35.7	0.0
5 to 10	12.9	26.7	23.8	25.0	7.1	16.7
More than 10	35.5	26.7	42.8	25.0	57.2	66.6
	100.0%	100.0%	100.0%	100.0%	100.0%	100.0%
Republicans						
Less than 1	17.2%	6.2%	13.6%	11.5%	9.5%	0.0%
1 to 5	24.1	50.0	27.3	42.3	33.3	20.0
5 to 10	24.1	31.3	36.4	30.8	28.6	40.0
More than 10	34.6	12.5	22.7	15.4	28.6	40.0
	100.0%	100.0%	100.0%	100.0%	100.0%	100.0%

governor's political party(see Table [11]), interesting differences result. While Democratic staffs were generally more active in both the primary and general election campaigns, the result is reversed when the active respondents are sorted according to the type of assistance rendered. While more Democrats provided *some* sort of assistance in the electoral process, Republican staffs tend to have contributed time and talent more on the candidates' personal staff. In other words Republican governors tend to retain as staff more of their key campaign advisers and assistants than do Democrats. Once again, the data demonstrate a tendency on the part of Republican governors to recruit an electoral coalition as staff.

In 16 of the 40 states included in the study, the governor's campaign manager is also a member of his executive office staff. Whether or not the campaign manager remains on the staff after inauguration appears to be completely random. The 16 campaign managers are equally divided between Democratic and Republican governors. There are no regional configurations, and the fact is independent of the governor's political ambitions as demonstrated in the political events and specula-

tions of the 1968 election year. Nor are the campaign managers, for the most part, politically ambitious themselves. As was said, the pattern would appear random.

METHOD OF RECRUITMENT

Having discussed social and political campaign associations, the duration of noncampaign associations, and the sources of staff recruitment, attention turns to the actual sequence of events by which the individual was appointed to the staff. These data are to be found in Table [12].

Slightly more than half of the respondents were asked by the governor to join or were already on his staff. Those asked by the governor tend also to be those respondents who have known the governor for some period of time and who have had other associational linkages. Those not falling into either of these two categories tend to be recruited by others on the staff or through the good offices of an intermediary. Individuals soliciting the position themselves break about even between those who knew or had associations with the governor and those who did not. Perhaps most striking is the high level of comparability between Democratic and Republican governors; while differences have been noted in other facets of staff recruitment, the actual sequence of events does not vary, even controlling for length and type of prior associations.

SUMMARY OF THE FINDINGS

The perplexity and sheer volume of data covered thus far can probably best be understood in capsulated form; therefore, a summary statement is in order. Gubernatorial staffs are comparatively quite young; 54 percent are under age 40 and the me-

TABLE [11] Type of Activity in Election Campaigns, by Political Party of the Governor

Activity	Democrats	Republicans	Total
Any assistance in			
Primary			
Yes	60.4%	51.2%	55.2%
No	39.6	48.8	44.8
	100.0%	100.0%	100.0%
	(96)	(127)	(223)
Election			
Yes	74.0%	65.4%	69.1%
No	26.0	34.6	30.9
	100.0%	100.0%	100.0%
	(96)	(127)	(223)
Personal staff in			
Primary			
Yes	68.0%	72.3%	71.0%
No	32.0	27.7	29.0
	100.0%	100.0%	100.0%
	(50)	(64)	(114)
Election			
Yes	69.8%	74.4%	72.3%
No	30.2	25.6	27.7
	100.0%	100.0%	100.0%
	(63)	(78)	(141)

TABLE [12] Method by Which Recruited, by Political Party of the Governor

Method of Recruitment	Democrats	Republicans	Total
Asked by governor	38.8%	38.4%	38.5%
Recommended by staff	13.3	13.3	13.3
Already on staff	12.2	12.5	12.4
Solicited job himself	9.2	10.8	10.1
Recommended by others	6.1	5.8	6.0
Staff of prior governor	9.2	8.3	8.7
Other responses	11.2	10.9	11.0
	100.0%	100.0%	100.0%
	(98)	(120)	(218)

dian age is 38. They also are quite well educated, 71 percent possessing at least one college degree. Occupationally speaking, law, business, and journalism are dominant elements and the majority of the respondents are engaged in high prestige occupations. Slightly less than half of the respondents profess any degree of special competence, a fact that indicates the degree of specialization among staff members. In general, the high status bias of political elites also applies to gubernatorial staffs. A number of other variables including party, section of the country, and size of state were correlated with these staff characteristics, but no meaningful relationship emerged.

Like other political elites, staff members become interested in politics at an early age, primarily through family involvement. Younger staff experienced first active involvement by means of a political campaign, whereas older respondents were usually asked to become active by friends, a group, or a political party. A large percentage of the respondents had family who held public or party office, which is indicative of the highly politicized background of staff people. Party identification, as would be expected, is remarkably stable over time and reflects the influence of the family in early identification.

Staff people, too, have had widespread political experience; 38.1 percent of the respondents indicated some prior elective or appointive public office, party office, or an administrative assistant position. This experience level does not include those individuals who had served previously on a governor's staff; some 18.1 percent indicated service on the staff of another governor. While these individuals are scattered among the forty states in the study, there is a distinct border and southern state flavor to the distribution.

Staff members are also politically ambitious with 32.3 percent indicating some future political plans. These plans, however, have little immediacy about them; 84.6 percent of the respondents indicated their intention of remaining with the governor until the expiration of his term of office. In terms of commitment to remain on the staff, it is also interesting to note that 72.6 percent of the staff have been with the governor from the beginning of his term.

Recruitment patterns, too, reveal some interesting trends. About a third of the staff are recruited directly from business, another quarter from gov-

ernment, a fifth were already on the governor's staff when he assumed office, and a seventh had served the previous governor. Democratic governors select more of their staff from the first two of these sources and Republicans more from the latter two. This fact motivated a search for variations in the recruiting process based on the political affiliations of the governors, which search structured the remainder of the chapter. Partisanship itself is a distinct element in the recruitment process. No Democratic governor appointed a Republican to his staff, but 7 percent of the Republican appointees were Democrats. This phenomenon occurred primarily in two border states which had elected a Republican governor for the first time in recent history.

The type of person recruited for the staff also tends to be a long-term acquaintance of the governor; 40.7 percent had known the governor for at least four years prior to his becoming governor. Democratic governors tend to have had associations of longer duration with their staffs than do Republican chief executives; this finding suggests that the former recruit staff on the basis of personal factors while the latter select on the basis of electoral factors. The pattern of personal relationships staff personnel have had with the governor also confirms the different style in recruiting. Some 51.3 percent of the respondents had had some prior association with the governor before his assumption of the office. Here, too, more respondents serving Democratic governors (61.1 percent) have had prior association than have those serving Republicans (47.5 percent). This, too, substantiates a differential style in recruiting. When length of association is controlled for party and correlated with the type of association, the data again demonstrate the electoral coalition in Republican staffing and the personal coalition in Democratic staffing.

The associational pattern also spills over into electoral assistance. While 54.4 percent of the staff had taken part in the governor's primary campaign, it should be remembered that not all the governors were forced to undertake a primary fight. The data thus should be viewed with some suspicion. On the other hand, all the governors experienced a general election campaign, and in this regard 68.2 percent of the staff took an active part. Republican staff who participated in the election campaign tend to have held positions on the governors' personal campaign staff to a greater extend than Democrats. This, too, supports the notion of an electoral coalition on GOP staff.

The actual sequence of events by which the respondents were approached to become members of the staff indicates that the governor himself is the primary recruiting officer; 37.2 percent of the appointees fall into this category. An additional 12.8 percent were recommended to the governor by existing staff, and 11.9 percent were already in the governor's employ.

From this mass of data we may extrapolate four generalizations. First, gubernatorial staffs are quite similar to other political elites in the United States; only age would appear as a deviating factor. Second, staff personnel are highly politicized individuals. They have had early and extensive political experience, in terms of both themselves and their families. Third, the associational pattern and length of time that some staff have known the governor suggests a recruitment pattern that is highly selective. The basic source of talent for the governor includes those persons whom he has known for some time, who have had prior associations with him, and who have played significant roles in his primary and general election campaigns. Fourth, the data indicate distinct differences between Democratic and Republican governors in the type of person recruited for a staff position. Democrats tend to seek personnel on the basis of a personal coalition, Republicans on the basis of an electoral coalition. . . .

STAFFING THE GOVERNOR'S OFFICE
Alan J. Wyner

Like other political executives, governors require staff assistance to cope with their many responsibilities. An essential ingredient of a successful tenure is a competent and loyal staff. Yet, the composition, and behavioral characteristics of gubernatorial staffs is a neglected topic in the literature of public administration in the states. This essay describes four characteristics of gubernatorial staffs—recruitment, removal, staff role perceptions, and perceptions of job satisfaction—and suggests several consequences that flow from particular staff organizations and behaviors.

For the most part, only the professional staff members receive consideration in the following discussion. Clerical-secretarial employees exact a minimal amount of attention. The occupational designation "clerical-secretarial" suggests a common and acceptable referent, but the category of "professional staff" requires a short explanation. Professional staff members are those who possess some authority for planning and decision making in the governor's office about either substantive areas of the governor's responsibilities, or organizing the offices and governor's agenda. Confusion on this point arises because sometimes an individual in a governor's office has the title "secretary," but is clearly not primarily performing clerical tasks, and, therefore, is classified as professional; e.g., the governor's personal secretary is often responsible for arranging his agenda and is considered a professional in that sense.

RECRUITMENT
A natural starting point for a discussion of gubernatorial staff is the recruitment process. Recruit-

Source: Reprinted by permission from *Public Administration Review* Vol. 30 No. 1. (January/February 1970), pp. 17–24.

Data for this analysis is extracted from a larger study of 14 governors' offices conducted from January to June 1966. Relying primarily, but not exclusively, upon those who served as both full-time staff members as well as trained observers, the research project collected data on several aspects of gubernatorial behavior. The 14 sample states cannot be named because the governors were promised anonymity for their cooperation. Along several dimensions it appears that a representative sample of states was selected. The National Center for Education in Politics and its director, Bernard C. Hennessy, sponsored the project, and James A. Robinson helped the author plan and conduct the research. . . .

ment is taken to mean not just the initial acquisition of staff, but, in addition, the prospects for retaining those appointed to staff positions. Topics explored in this section, then, include the previous backgrounds of staff members, nature of their appointments, and length of staff tenure.

Almost invariably, gubernatorial assistants possess previous political experience. Most staff members participate in election campaigns, either for the present governor or some other person in the same political party, prior to their gubernatorial service. Several staffers' first association with their governor occurs during his campaign for office. However, every staff has at least one member whose association with the governor predates the first campaign. Oftentimes, it is the governor's personal and confidential secretary. Not uncommon are personal secretaries retained by the governor for as many as 15 years. Retention of some staff by a governor as he moves from position to position, whether public or private, provides him with a sense of continuity and confidence in his ability to manage both his schedule and policy program.

As in other phases of politics, the governor's office attracts many lawyers. Unfortunately, the exact proportion of staffs who are lawyers by training is not available, but a conservative estimate would place the number at about 50 percent of all key staff personnel. The press of purely legal matters does not necessitate all those lawyers. Only one individual in the office is usually assigned the task of providing legal counsel. However, lawyers' inclination for political involvement means that a number of them attach themselves to governors or gubernatorial candidates.

A significant minority of staff members hold advanced degrees, approximately 20 percent. Larger states, and thus larger offices, exhibit a marked tendency to recruit personnel with advanced degrees in many different areas, ranging from professional planners to engineers to political scientists. To take advantage of their specialized skills, these individuals are usually assigned specific "program" tasks in contrast to other office members who become "generalists."

Journalism was a common occupational background, and journalists easily number as many as, or more than, the number of "academic" type personnel. Skills the journalist can contribute are obvious. Their training, for instance, has taught them to write appealingly and understandably to the kind of audiences with whom a governor must deal. This must be contrasted with the usually ponderous style of the academic. Therefore, journalists often write speeches, maintain relations with the state press corps, and perform other public relations tasks.

Staff composition is not usually a reflection of the governor's successful electoral coalition.[1] However, the position of staff aide requires successful interaction with those coalition members who are important to the performance of his job and, therefore, offensive attitudes or behavior toward important segments of the governor's supporters is obviously not tolerated.

Staff appointments are overwhelmingly personal appointments of the governor. This must be contrasted to both the situation in which the political party or important campaign supporters have the deciding influence in naming staff personnel and the likelihood of civil servants staffing the governor's office. Neither of these two possibilities occurs very often. Before taking office, governors apparently learn the value of key staff personnel entirely of their own choosing, because the naming of their initial staff reflects their personal wishes. Why is this so important? The governor is a politician and presumably interested in party affairs, so why not involve the party in staff selection? Alternatively, one could advance a plausible argument about the value of staff continuity and, thus, civil servants might seem appropriate for staffing. The crux of an answer revolves about the necessity for intense staff loyalty to the governor. Ahlberg and Moynihan state the case against party men this way:

In line with their tendency to ideological differences, party regulars present the familiar problems dual loyalty—to their political sponsors as well as to the administration. Quite apart from any substantive difficulties, such persons rarely have a highly developed sense of the importance of working for or through the governor . . . .[2]

Civil servants, protected by civil service legislation, would likely develop a loyalty to the governor*ship* and not necessarily to the incumbent governor. Also, so many of the tasks required of staff per-

[1] See Clark D. Ahlberg and Daniel P. Moynihan, "Changing Governors—and Policies," in Frank Munger (Ed.) *American State Politics* (New York: Thomas Y. Crowell, 1966), p. 162, for a discussion of this point.

[2] *Ibid.*, p. 163.

sonnel are immersed in state politics that it would be difficult for theoretically apolitical civil servants to perform adequately in the upper ranks of the office.

In addition to loyalty, the substance and style of a governor's operations is an important issue. No governor wants his staff disagreeing *too* sharply with him on content of policy and the manner in which he wants to perform his role. While not foolproof, agreement is more likely if the staff is of his own personal choosing.

Construing the preceding to mean that political parties have absolutely no influence in naming personnel is wrong. Although not necessarily public knowledge, instances are on record of a party chairman's concern about a new, inexperienced governor leaning to a strongly worded "suggestion" that a specific individual be placed on the staff. It is more common, however, for the party to play a determining role only in naming certain kinds of staff members—the secretarial-clerical help. Governors use these positions as opportunities to reward the party faithful, and in this sense patronage is involved in staff appointments.

Civil service or the merit system also plays a limited role. Some large offices have civil servants in positions such as "supervisor" of secretarial-clerical help. A few instances were also uncovered in which receptionists, switchboard operators, and general helpers were retained by incoming governors on their own volition—these people were not protected by civil service. Note that these roles are not policy oriented, but extremely helpful in operating an efficient office. Retaining this kind of personnel provides continuity and elementary, but important, help for a new governor.

The original assertion still stands. Governors choose their staff personnel, and especially the key ones, based on criteria of their own making. The specifics of these criteria are still unknown, and await further research, but previous experience and personal compatibility are obviously important.

A consistency that emerges from a state-by-state examination of data about staffs is the extended tenure of professional staff members. With the exception of one sample state, all offices contain at least 50 percent or more of their original professional staff members; the mean figure is 75 percent of original staff. What accounts for this relatively low rate of personnel turnover? The manner in which the staff is first recruited appears to account for most personnel continuity. Potential staffers are highly motivated politically and, as pointed out previously, often have worked for the governor in his campaign. Moreover, the governor is able to choose his staff with a minimum of "interference" from outside sources, and this usually produces a staff loyal to him personally. If one is inclined to politics, and state politics in particular, no other spot in state government can compete with the governor's office for the sheer excitement and opportunity for active participation in the state's affairs. Nothing of consequence in state politics remains outside the purview of the governor's office for long. Factors such as these help explain why gubernatorial staff members remain on the job in large numbers.

As a consequence of the small personnel turnover, a continuity and consistency in staff decisions tends to develop. By no means does this imply stagnation. Rather, it allows both governmental and nongovernmental (interest groups, for example) personnel to develop expectations about the policies, actions, and operational style of the governor and those in his office who must do most of the detailed work. This probably has very advantageous consequences for the governor's office and the whole state government. The stability in key gubernatorial staff positions—with its consequent stability in behavior—leads to a stability in the expectations held by others, and, thus, helps the whole governmental process to function without major disruptions in one of its most important parts. This line of reasoning rests on the assumption that the governor's office is the key agency in most state governments today.

REMOVAL

Although an apparent longevity in staff tenure exists, some staff members do depart. Why? The first group who chooses to leave are those staffers who decide, by themselves, that better opportunity, financial or otherwise, awaits them elsewhere. They leave of their own accord and with no hard feelings, although with some disappointment on the governor's part.

Next are those who leave at the governor's suggestion, whether that be implicit or explicit. All states allow governors to hire and fire their own professional staff without restrictions.

For instance, during the course of an administration, a governor may fervently wish he had a trusted and loyal friend in a particular executive department or agency. Governors may ask one of their own staff to accept a position in an executive department. By no means are these transfers thought of as demotions, but rather as a continuation in a different setting of the staffer's help to the governor. In these instances, the governor will pick a staff member in whom he has complete confidence and, in effect, will send him over to a department to be "his man" there. While this strategy can cause difficulties, it seems to work for staff members known to have the governor's backing and confidence. However, when a governor tries the same technique with a staff member he is merely trying to remove from his office for one reason or another, he will oftentimes run into several balking department heads who simply refuse to accept the displaced person.

Aside from a transfer to an executive department, what are some reasons why a governor might wish to remove an individual from a staff position?[3] The possible reasons for gubernatorial displeasure leading to a staff member's removal can conveniently be summarized into three categories. Within this context it is important to remember that staff members are not usually fired but removed. This distinction is explained and illustrated below.

Topping any list of reasons for removal is corruption. In some cases it may be more appropriate to say corruption that has become public. No governor tolerates a staff member who has been shown publicly to be involved in corrupt practices or in situations of obvious conflict of interest. In all but one sample office, it is clear that any staff member implicated in conduct labeled corrupt would remain an aide to the governor about one minute.

The second, and by far most prevalent reason for staff removal is lack of personal capability. At least three types of inability cannot be permitted: (1) poor political judgment; (2) inability to work with the groups and individuals called for by the job; and (3) an insufficient, for the job, mental capacity. Obviously, people who fall into one of

these categories should not have been on the staff in the first place. They are usually a mistake, but some governors are hard-pressed to admit that they made the error. As a result, these people are often kept in the office longer than efficiency standards would permit.

Finally, a problem stems from those who become staff members and then a political or ideological incompatibility with the governor or other personnel is discovered. Some differences in political outlook are tolerated because they provide the governor with a range of advice. However, the permissible variance is limited. Extreme differences in political ideology cause problems in office relations, morale, and program development, and are not condoned.

Only in rare instances are staff personnel ever fired outright. The consequences arising from such an act would probably cause more trouble than if the staff member had been allowed to remain in the office. Of course, the exception is the rare instance in which the governor must fire a staffer because of illicit activities. Publicly firing a staff member is an open admission by the governor that either he made a mistake in hiring the man or that serious dissension prevails in his office. To say the least, politicians are not prone to admissions of this type. Other reasons, though, also explain why a staff member is not fired. The unwanted member most likely has knowledge of certain matters of controversy that either the opposition or the press would find exciting. Therefore, one tries to avoid firing a person, because the antagonism that individual will probably hold toward the office and governor, coupled with his store of information, may make him dangerous to the governor. Another factor mitigating against precipitous dismissal is the tendency in the office, as in any occupation, to look after one's colleagues. Firing a man most likely ruins his career, and this is a responsibility not many people feel comfortable taking.

So instead of firing an unwanted staff member, one of two avenues of removal are used. If the staff member is willing, a job may be found for the man in private industry or in the state political party. Governors usually have sufficient "connections" to arrange such transfers. However, cases arise in which the staff person refuses to leave and will not leave without creating an undesirable situation. The not so subtle technique of ostracizing him from official and social relations in the office

[3]I am indebted to Peter Kobrak for giving needed precision to the list of possible reasons why a staff member might be asked to leave the office.

is then employed. Unable to withstand the tension for long, a "resignation" is eventually submitted.[4]

ROLE PERCEPTIONS

Professional staff members in ten of the sample states were asked: "What do you think should be the role of a governor's staff?" A question such as this can elicit two types of answers. First, answers that simply repeat the functions each staff member performs in his everyday work could reasonably be expected. In this case we might have expected, for instance, replies to mention such functions as answering mail, writing speeches and press releases, talking to agency heads. Alternatively, it is also plausible to anticipate answers that take a more general approach; to show a concern with concepts of role and role performance. The latter pattern of answers was received in the overwhelming majority of cases.

A listing of the most common responses to this question illustrates the terms in which staff members think of their jobs. Individual staff members were not asked to rank-order their replies, but based on a tabulation of the frequency with which each response was reported, the replies can be presented according to their popularity. From office to office strikingly similar replies were noted.[5] Size of the state or office did not seem to influence the normative role concepts held by staff members. The following summaries are not direct quotations but rather a paraphrasing of replies.

1. *Organize information for the governor.* The first part of this role involves research. Next is a screening process in which decisions must be made by the staff about what information the governor will see. The process is necessitated by the large number of "bits" of information and ideas coming into the office coupled with the severe demands on the governor's time.

2. *Create a favorable image of the governor.* Because almost all governors want to be reelected, or move to another office, it is necessary that the public maintain a favorable image of the man dur-ing the time he is in office and making controversial decisions. A desire to be liked and to be popular is present even in those governors not seeking another office. Interestingly, not only the press secretaries but all members of the staff were concerned with this role of public relations. Performance of this role by staffers means that they must be willing to stay in the background, while all the time watching the governor get credit for some of their own ideas and speeches.

3. *Handle details.* The staff should dispose of minor problems and make minor decisions in order to avoid flooding the governor's already tight schedule. As one staff member put it, "The staff should handle the details and leave the governor to look after bigger and better things." The amount of detail the staff attends to depends upon the working style of the governor.

4. *Take the blame for any mistake.* To preserve the good image of the governor, the staff must be willing to assume responsibility for any decisions that produce a negative reaction. It is necessary to protect the governor from too much criticism, and the staff thus siphons off the critics. During the course of a governor's normal activity he must make decisions that he knows in advance will elicit critical remarks and possibly negative editorials in the state's newspapers. To help alleviate this kind of problem, the office often uses this tactic: If the decision or action is felt to be critical or involving "bad news" for some part of the state or some important clientele group, the press release or announcement from the office will go out over the signature of one of the governor's assistants. If the reaction to the announcement is too strong, the governor can always reverse himself by claiming that the matter had not been brought to his attention, but had simply been handled by his staff, and "of course," they made the wrong decision.

5. *Coordinate the activities of the state executive branch.* Some staff members mention this as a primary responsibility; usually those members of the staff with the title of director of administration or a similar title. The degree of success achieved in the performance of this role is questionable.

6. *Serve as a complaint bureau for the public.* The governor receives many complaints, inquiries, and citizens' problems; some can be handled in the governor's office but many must be directed to

---

[4] This kind of "resignation" can also backfire and cause problems because of the individual's animosity, but it is harder for him to cause trouble than if he were fired outright. "After all, the man wasn't fired, *he* resigned," is the usual defense offered by the office if trouble arises.

[5] A few other replies could be listed, but they received only one mention, and the roles listed by the article were all mentioned more than once.

other agencies. One of the functions of the staff, it was reported, should be to assist those persons making complaints or having problems in their relations with the state government. This role dovetails nicely into the public relations goal of the staff.

One potential staff role remains conspicuously missing from almost all the replies—planning for future problems and contingencies. Only two staff members, in different states, mentioned planning of any kind. Is there something about the recruitment process of staff members that prevents people with an interest in non-day-to-day problems from becoming members of a governor's staff? Or, do the everyday demands on the staff prevent even the best-intentioned member from looking past the short-range future? A little truth probably exists in both these possibilities. The demand of meeting everyday schedules is grueling, and usually prevents attention to anything but the immediate future. Staff members become conditioned to think in terms of the immediate. Indeed, some offices seem to operate on a continual crisis basis. Yet, when a break in the routine occurs, such as when the governor is out of the state, personnel often do not know how, or do not want, to take advantage of the relief in order to ponder the difficult and abstract problems that will face the state in the not-so-immediate future. This is partially true because little political payoff seems to result from long-range planning by governors' offices.

Governors were asked a complementary question about their staff: "What do you think should be the proper role of a governor's staff?" Responses from nine governors can be used here; the rest either did not reply or their answers were not applicable. While some governors seemed to stress particular aspects of staff work, e.g., research, responses by governors to this question varied little among states. In addition, governors replied to the question in the same terms as their own staff members. Each staff and gubernatorial response in the nine states was ranked according to frequency, and a correlation of .87 was observed between the two rankings. The correspondence between staff and governor *within* each state was also high, but the exact correlation was not computed because of the very small N involved. Apparently an impressive degree of role consensus permeated the offices.

Finding agreement on staff role requirements is not very surprising. In fact, our eyebrows would have been raised if the results had pointed in the opposite direction. Given that governors can hire and fire or remove staffers without legal restriction and with "only" political repercussions to consider, coupled with the very personal nature of staff recruitment, one would expect to find consensus about staff roles. That it is present also suggests that governors seek compatibility among their immediate colleagues.

SATISFACTION WITH JOB AND RATING OF THE OFFICE

Are office members satisfied with their jobs? Job satisfaction has an important bearing on the office's operations. As Simon, Smithburg, and Thompson suggest:

An organization lives on the contributions of its members. The members make their contributions because of satisfactions they receive in return. We have seen that these satisfactions may be of many kinds, of which money in the form of wages or salaries is only one. . . . A change in the satisfactions that an organization provides its members is important to the organization in several ways. First, if there is a great decrease in satisfactions a member may refuse to contribute any longer—he may leave his job. . . . Second, a decrease in satisfactions may lower morale, and consequently lower the contribution the individual is willing to make to the organization.[6]

The data indicate a very high level of job satisfaction. To be sure, there are always the minor exceptions in every office, such as the one typist who complained about everything continually. However, looking at each office as a whole, the members seem satisfied with the tasks they are asked to perform. This does not imply, of course, satisfaction with the outcome of these tasks, but merely satisfaction with the job itself. Only two states harbored an office staff that seemed somewhat "disgruntled," and, in practical terms, either bored or overworked, professionals being the former and secretaries the latter.

This finding—of high job satisfaction—correlates with other results. We also found evidence of extreme personal loyalty to the governor, a willing-

[6] Herbert Simon, Donald Smithburg, and Victor Thompson, *Public Administration* (New York: Knopf, 1959), p. 111. These authors have borrowed from and developed the ideas of Chester I. Barnard, *The Functions of the Executive* (Cambridge, Mass.: Harvard University Press, 1940).

ness to work long, hard hours, and, as indicated above, a low level of personnel turnover among gubernatorial staff. All of these are indicative of job satisfaction. People who work for governors are highly motivated individuals who apparently take pride and satisfaction in performing their responsibilities.

Given the high level of job satisfaction, it would also seem likely that office members would rate the governor's office near the top in any comparison with other statehouse offices. This was our finding. Terms such as "best office in the state government," "vastly superior," "rates very high," were used by staffs in comparing the governor's office to other offices. Pride in the office is a common attribute.

The presence of two "deviant" cases helps substantiate the claim that job satisfaction is related to a high rating for the governor's office by the staff. In both these states—which bear no similarity to geography or office organization—it was reported that the staff was "moderately" satisfied. An undercurrent of constant complaining was present in these offices. These were the offices referred to above as "disgruntled." In both these offices, and this is the interesting point, the staff rated the office "only average," not outstanding." or "maybe second." Thus, a decline in job satisfaction seems related to a decline in office rating.

OUTSIDERS' VIEWS

To gain a somewhat different perspective, perceptions of the governor's office were sought from "outsiders," that is, newspapermen, lobbyists, and other statehouse office personnel. An examination of these data provided an entirely different picture from that presented above. Even the use of a charitable coding scheme produced no more than 5 governors' offices, from the 14 sample states, that deserved classification as "highly respected" or "very efficient" according to the opinions of various outsiders. The rest were referred to with such tongue-in-cheek comments as "doesn't elicit wild enthusiasm" or the straightforward remark that the staff was simply "incompetent." Most offices were not held in high esteem by outsiders.

Before attempting to offer some explanation of this finding, it is important that a methodological note be entered. Data on this point was collected by interns who were working in the governor's office. Quickly, they became identified as representatives of the governor. They could not talk to people around the capital posing as mere observers or disinterested parties. Respondents were well aware of the intern's staff position. Therefore, any response by outsiders to a question about the governor's office must be conditioned in some way by the respondent's knowledge of the intern's position. A plausible assumption is that most outsiders will not want to make derogatory remarks about the governor's office to a member of that office. Accordingly, we expected the results of this outside inquiry to show almost unanimous acclaim for the governor's office. Such was not the case. Thus, the validity of the present data is enhanced. If replies to the intern's inquiry of outsiders were mostly positive in nature, we would have had to dismiss them as mere reaction to the intern and his position with the governor. But the presence of so many negative responses lends credence to the validity of the findings.

What accounts for the generally negative image of the governor's office held by outsiders? Why did we hear so many comments such as "not very talented men," or "extremely difficult to contact"? Several reasons may be tendered. First, the outsiders who offered opinions about the governor's office are people who in the normal course of business frequently want something from the office, whether it be news releases, support for a bill, or a larger budget allocation. Invariably, they will be frustrated in their pursuits; all they request will not be made available. Turning the situation around, the office often wants something from these outsiders, and this causes annoyance at the least. A governor's staff is busy and it cannot devote time and attention to matters of interest to all outsiders. This too will lead to troubled relations and, thus, a poor image. Finally, governors are the focal point of action in state government today and as such they must make decisions and act on them. Friction as a result of gubernatorial decision making is inevitable and is also a contributing factor to the generally poor image of the office held by many outsiders.

These reasons may be plausible, but they must not be taken as excuses. An objective measure of the equality of work performed in the governor's office might reveal that the poor image held by these outsiders is justified. Unfortunately, such a measure is not available. Instead the opinion is offered that any highly motivated, generally intelligent, and hard-working group of employees—such as those found in the governors' offices—will develop a sense of pride and protectionism in any discussion of their office. For this reason, staffers give almost uniform praise to office operations. A feeling of superiority is probably a functional feature of the office organization—it reinforces the belief that important, necessary, and top-quality work is being performed and thus contributes to job satisfaction. At the same time, it is understandable that outside, and sometimes competing, groups and individuals might not agree with the staff's perception of the office.

An established feature of modern government is the increasing predominance and activity of political executives. Practically, this often means burgeoning demands are placed on the staffs that surround these executives. Knowledge about staff characteristics and behavior becomes more important. This paper represents a small attempt to probe into the world of staff behavior; more attention is needed.

CHAPTER
6
THE POLITICS
OF
LEADERSHIP

Despite the attention given in this volume to the governor's newer roles in federal programs, his major job involves traditional roles and responsibilities. Like the President, the governor is known primarily as chief legislator, director of budgets, and, even more than the President, as chief personnel officer—appointing many boards and commissions.

Malcolm Jewell, a student of state legislative politics, contends that governors today are judged largely on their job as chief legislator. "Unless his administration has been plagued by unusually serious scandals, the administrative successes or failures of a governor are neither visible nor interesting to the voter," Jewell says, and thus governors are judged on the success of programs which they submit to state legislatures.

This chapter deals with some more traditional roles of the governor—his success as a leader in the politics and policies of his own state, at the state level. We are interested in his influence with the legislature, his control of administration, and his power over expenditures.

Influence and power have been the subject of much scholarly discussion. Although power should be distinguished from influence for some purposes, often they are used interchangeably to denote a relationship between people. Used this way, power usually means "The capacity of one actor to do something affecting another actor, which changes the probable pattern of specified future events."[1]

It is this concept of power and influence that Jewell and Sarah P. McCally use to analyze gubernatorial leadership in state legislative matters. Jewell says that legislative accomplishments vary widely among states and among governors of the same state. He asks what are the most effective techniques of leadership or influence: the matter of party discipline, the expert in personal negotiation, or the leader in public opinion? McCally tests the governors' power or influence over their legislative parties by observing their success with vetoes. The best relationship she found had nothing to do with past events, such as the size of the governor's vote or the size of his party's legislative majority. The best predictor of a governor's success with his own party members was how well he did in a subsequent primary election. Although

[1] Robert A. Dahl, "The Concept of Power," *Behavioral Scientist*, Vol. 2 (July 1957), pp. 201–218.

few would dispute that a governor facing a legislature composed of a majority of his own party clearly has an advantage over one who must deal with a majority in opposition, this indicates that gubernatorial power and influence are more complex than simple arithmetic or party lineups.

In addition to power as influence, the amount of formal power a governor has is often used in measuring gubernatorial leadership or potential leadership. Governors of the 50 states vary in the amount of formal power bestowed upon their offices. Some have longer tenure potential, greater formal control of the budget, and more appointment power. Some have simple vetoes and others, line item vetoes. In both legislation and administration, the principal question of gubernatorial leadership is: Can the governor govern? Are his powers adequate to the tasks he faces?

Joseph Schlesinger, who has written several articles on the formal powers of governors, contends that formal powers are important as indicators of potential influence. For example, McCally's finding of how well a governor does in subsequent primary elections may point to the importance of tenure, or the ability of a governor to succeed himself in office, as a measure of his potential influence with the legislature. Likewise, the question of whether a governor has the power to govern may mean, from Schlesinger's perspective, that the more formal power a governor has the more he should be able to implement his program.

But the concept of formal power creates problems. It is the contention of many that most governors' powers are substantial but probably inadequate to enable them to govern comprehensively. Yet it has been contended that the governors of certain southern states, who rank low in formal powers, are in fact extremely powerful within their own political systems.[2] And there is the question of which formal powers are the most important. The ones Schlesinger employs in his power index, or others? Students who wish to know what some governors have had to say on this score might consult the article "The Governor's Formal Powers: A View from the Governor's Chair."[3]

[2] Robert Highsaw, "The Southern Governor—Challenge to the Strong Executive Theme," *Public Administration Review*, Vol. 19 (Winter 1959), pp. 7–11.

[3] *Public Administration Review*, Vol. 28 (1968), pp. 540–545.

Gubernatorial leadership deals with concepts which are elusive and difficult to measure with specificity. Thus the articles in this chapter are precise and more rigorous than some. But, hopefully, the reader has already seen the need for dealing with power and influence in such a manner.

THE GOVERNOR
AS A
LEGISLATIVE LEADER
Malcolm E. Jewell

A governor is judged today largely on the success of his legislative programs. Unless his administration has been plagued by unusually serious scandals, the administrative successes or failures of a governor are neither visible nor interesting to the voter. The gubernatorial candidate's platform is composed largely of legislative promises—whether he offers more money for education, the enactment of a merit system, or the lowering of taxes. To the extent that issues determine elections, a governor is judged by the legislative promises he has kept or broken, and this often means he is judged by his success or failure as a legislative leader. As Duane Lockard has said: "People increasingly speak of a law being 'passed by the governor.' In sarcasm the storekeeper tosses coins into a can labeled 'Sales Tax' and says, 'A penny for the Governor.' "[1]

There are some states where the governor usually meets little resistance to his major legislative programs, where the legislature often seems to play a subservient role. Most of these states are in the South, where a single-party system often predominates, and where the frequent constitutional limitation to a single term makes it impossible to determine the relationship between legislative success and victory at the polls for the governor seeking reelection.

Our objective is not simply to recount the frustrations that governors face today as legislative

Source: Revised by the author and reprinted with his permission from "State Decision Making: The Governor Revisited" in Wildavsky and Polsby (eds.) *American Governmental Institutions* (Chicago: Rand McNally, 1968).

[1] Duane Lockard, *The Politics of State and Local Government* (New York: Macmillan, 1963), pp. 367–368.

leaders or to chronicle individual tales of failure. From state to state the pattern varies, and even in a single state governors vary widely in their legislative accomplishments. What can explain these variations in gubernatorial effectiveness? Is a governor's success determined by the political environment within which he must work? If techniques of political leadership are determining, which are most effective? Who most successfully commands legislative support: the master of party discipline, the expert in personal negotiation, the leader of public opinion?

THE POLITICAL ENVIRONMENT

A governor may face any one of three political situations: He may command a party majority in the legislature of a two-party state. He may find the opposition party in control of one or both legislative branches. He may govern in a one-party state, where the absence of a substantial opposition party eliminates the possibility of *party* leadership in the legislature. Political leadership has such different meanings in two-party and one-party states that we can most usefully discuss these two situations separately, though recognizing that some states fall into an intermediate category of emerging two-party systems.

A model two-party system is one in which there is frequent alternation of power and in which the governor regularly has a party majority in both houses. This is an elusive model, in practice. During the 1947–68 period, there was no state that had some alternation in party control of the governorship or the legislature that completely escaped divided government. There are several reasons for a partisan division in government. When one party has long been in the minority, it may not have enough organizational breadth and enough good candidates to elect a legislative majority when its gubernatorial candidate wins. In recent years this has been the Democratic experience in Maine, New Hampshire, Vermont, Kansas, North Dakota, and Iowa, for example. The Republican party has faced the same problem in Maryland, Kentucky, Arkansas, Florida, Oklahoma, and West Virginia. A party may have its strength so localized in one area that it cannot elect a legislative majority despite gubernatorial victories; the Michigan Democratic party, for example, has been handicapped because its strength was primarily in the Detroit area. Midterm elections may destroy a governor's majority in the legislature because his coattails are missing, his administration has lost popularity, or his party organization is weak.

V. O. Key, Jr., calculated that during the 1930–50 period, Democratic governors faced a Republican majority in at least one branch of the legislature 51 percent of the time and Republican governors confronted opposition majorities 18 percent of the time in 32 two-party states.[2] From 1952 through 1966, for 28 two-party states, the figures were 59 percent for Democratic governors and 43 percent for Republican governors.[3] For many years malapportionment of state legislatures was one of the most important causes of divided government. In a number of northern states it preserved Republican control of one or both houses even when Democratic governors won substantial victories. In some border and southern states malapportionment was beginning to handicap the Republican party. The drastic changes in apportionment standards during the 1960s resulting from the *Baker* and *Reynolds* decisions eliminated malapportionment as a significant cause of divided government. The growth of the Republican party in many southern and border states during the 1960s, however, has increased the proportion of divided government situations that occur during Republican administrations.

A governor whose party normally has a minority in the legislature faces certain fundamental problems from the outset. He must temper overtly partisan appeals, rely more heavily on public opinion, distribute patronage to both parties, and constantly base his tactics on the necessity of ultimate compromise with the opposition party. All of the tools of party leadership are dulled because they cannot be used with maximum effectiveness, but these tools still have utility. Particularly if the governor's party controls one house or has a large minority in the legislature, he is able to bargain with the opposition from a position of considerable strength *if* he can depend on unified support from his own party in the legislature. Very often, then, the successful governor must be effective both as a partisan leader and as a bipartisan leader.

[2] V. O. Key, Jr., *American State Politics: An Introduction* (New York: Knopf, 1956), pp. 58–64.
[3] Malcolm E. Jewell, *The State Legislature* (2nd ed.; Random House, 1969), pp. 12–16.

THE GOVERNOR AND PARTY ORGANIZATION

In a two-party state a governor's party leadership may be based on sources external to the legislature as well as on his relationships to legislators. One of the potentially most important sources of a governor's power is a strong state party organization. The strength of party organizations, and thus their potential value to a governor, varies greatly from state to state. Lockard has suggested several criteria of strong party organizations: "clearly identified and continuous leadership; leadership control up the ladder of promotion; centralized party finances and centralized operation of party campaigns; great party influence in the making of legislative policy." By contrast, weak organizations are characterized by "wide factional cleavage; frequent conflicts over nominations, little centralized control over promotion for the ambitious; little party leadership influence in the making of legislative policy."[4]

The governor's leadership depends not only on the existence of a strong organization but also on his ability to control it; one does not automatically follow from the other. Governor Mennen Williams, in alliance with leaders of organized labor, captured control of the Michigan Democratic party and built it into a strong organization; he commanded strong support from Democratic legislators. Party organization has been traditionally strong in New York, and Governor Dewey's legislative success was due in considerable measure to his firm hold on the party machinery. Governor Rockefeller has had greater difficulty in gaining and maintaining influence over the Republican party organization. The high level of voting unity by Democratic legislators in Rhode Island has been based in part on the tight control maintained over the party by a few leaders who, at least until recently, have been able to control nominations and avoid contested primaries. The power exercised by Mayor Richard Daley in Chicago assures a Democratic governor of legislative support on most issues from Cook County Democrats, as long as he maintains good relations with the mayor. When a governor does not fully control the party machinery, but is dependent on powerful allies, his position may become precarious. Governor Mike DiSalle had considerable difficulties with the Ohio

[4] Duane Lockard, *op. cit*, p. 188.

legislature in part because of a feud with the party leadership in Cuyahoga County (Cleveland).

The governor who wins nomination by defeating an entrenched organization is likely to find his political authority over the legislature weakened. Fred Hall won the Kansas governorship in 1954 as an outsider, fought with limited success to gain control of the party organization, and at the end of his two-year term was defeated in the primary. He was handicapped in his relationships with the legislature by his inability to command party control and by the loyalty of many legislators to his opponents in the party hierarchy. Governor Chester Bowles of Connecticut was less dependent on the state party organization than most Democratic governors, and consequently did not have full support from the party leaders in his dealing with the legislature. Governor Frank Murphy won the Michigan governorship in 1936 on the strength of his own personal campaign and Franklin Roosevelt's coattails. Murphy was not an experienced leader in the state party, he did not try to control and strengthen party machinery, he lacked rapport with Democratic legislators, and his legislative record suffered as a result.[5]

The Democratic party in Massachusetts offers a good example of a weak, splintered organization. According to one account:

There is no state-wide party organization that delivers the votes, but rather dozens of small squabbling factions built around individual candidates and colorful personalities like the late Governor James Michael Curley, immortalized in *The Last Hurrah*.[6]

V. O. Key has attributed the plight of the Massachusetts Democratic party largely to the growth of the primary:

Gradually whatever cohesiveness the organization ever possessed became inadequate to curb the tempting opportunity to fight out differences in the primary. In fact, in due course even the factional elements of the party be-

[5] Rhoten A. Smith and Clarence J. Hein, *Republican Primary Fight: A Study in Factionalism* (New York: Holt, Rinehart & Winston, Case Studies in Practical Politics, 1958), pp. 3-12; John A. Perkins, *The Role of the Governor in Michigan in the Enactment of Appropriations* (Ann Arbor: University of Michigan Press, 1943), p. 155.

[6] John P. Mallan and George Blackwood, "The Tax That Beat a Governor: The Ordeal of Massachusetts," in Alan F. Westin (Ed.), *The Uses of Power* (New York: Harcourt Brace Jovanovich, 1962), p. 288.

came so ineffectively linked with the voters that the outcome of primary contests, at least for the lesser offices, became almost a matter of chance.[7]

Duane Lockard has pointed out, however, that the relative strength of Republican party organization in that state suggests that other factors than the primary may also be involved in splintering the party.[8]

Robert Wood and Bradbury Seasholes have described how this party system affects the Massachusetts governor:

... many of the twentieth-century governors have risen swiftly in the party, created enmity, and sometimes taken short cuts in their pursuit of high office. At any rate, none of the recent governors have relied on party organizations exclusively for their campaigns, and some scarcely used them.

Moreover, once a governor was in office, efforts to build up the state party apparatus have generally been disappointing. ... None could see any immediate use of the party machinery important enough to warrant a major effort to reorganize or streamline its operations while they were serving as governor.[9]

This conclusion applies to governors of both parties. Though the Republican organization is stronger, most of the recent Republican governors have relied more on their own popularity and personal organization than on party organization in winning elections.

Though generalizations are risky, most of the party organizations in the Northeast and Midwest are relatively strong. The organizational strength is enhanced where the use of primaries is minimized, where party machines remain strong in large metropolitan centers, where sufficient patronage exists to cement party ties. It is weakened in some of these states by traditionally wide-open primaries and regional or ethnic divisions in the parties. Even where the organizational machinery is potent, there may be divisive struggles to control it—as there have been in one or both parties in nearly every northeastern and midwestern state at some time within recent years. Further west, in the Plains, Mountain, and Coastal states, party organization tends to be weaker, a less valuable prize for a governor to control, because there are fewer metropolitan party machines, weak party loyalties among the voters, and often wide-open primaries. Many of these are states where progressivism left its mark, and the anti-party tradition has had lasting effect.

NOMINATIONS AND ELECTIONS

Potentially one of the most powerful sanctions a governor might have as a party leader would be the ability to assist or obstruct legislators seeking renomination or reelection. In a few states with strong party organization the governor occasionally exercises such power. In Connecticut, where the primary is seldom used to challenge the endorsements of local caucuses, the state leadership can often persuade the local party to deny renomination to a recalcitrant legislator. In New York, where the local party is strong and the primary is weak, there is a similar pattern of cooperation between state and local party organizations.[10] In such states the number of legislators denied renomination is small, but the potential use of this sanction is a significant reason for the high degree of party cohesion in the legislature.

In states where the primary assumes greater importance, it is rare to find the governor openly involved in the legislative primary. During gubernatorial election years the governor has his hands full with his own race. The strongest argument against the governor's involvement is that the probable risks appear to outweigh the possible gains. The governor recognizes that he would be flying in the face of tradition and anticipates that local reaction would range from apathy to hostility. In the absence of a strong party organization the governor may lack allies at the local level who can be depended on to carry out a campaign for

[7] Key, *op. cit.*, p. 158.

[8] Duane Lockard, *New England State Politics* (Princeton: Princeton University Press, 1959), p. 125. Note the roles of Democratic and Republican governors with respect to party organization in Illinois described by James B. Holderman, "The Modern Governor: Limits of Effectiveness," in *The Office of Governor* (Urbana: Institute of Government and Public Affairs, University of Illinois, 1963), pp. 57–59.

[9] Robert C. Wood and Bradbury Seasholes, "The Image of the Governor as a Public and Party Leader: The Disintegration of an Image—Reflections of Five Governors," in Robert R. Robbins (Ed.), *State Government and Public Responsibility, 1961: The Role of the Governor in Massachusetts*, Papers of the 1961 Tufts Assembly on Massachusetts Government (Medford, Mass.: The Lincoln Filene Center for Citizenship and Public Affairs, Tufts University, 1961), p. 93.

[10] Lockard, *New England State Politics*, pp. 297–302; Warren Moscow, *Politics in the Empire State* (New York: Knopf, 1948), pp. 170–176.

his endorsee. Unless the chances for success look good, a governor will avoid trying to purge a legislator for the simple reason that failure will guarantee that legislator's hostility in the next session. In Colorado the governor may be able to work behind the scenes to influence the choices made by the powerful preprimary party conventions, which have sometimes been able to block the renomination of a maverick legislator. The convention system is highly decentralized, however, and there is no certainty that the delegates to the convention held in each district will respond to the wishes of the governor.[11]

We might expect a governor to campaign vigorously for his party's legislative candidates in the general election—particularly where they are legislators who have loyally supported his program or where they are running in closely contested districts. Such intensive gubernatorial efforts are infrequent, probably because they appear unwise or unnecessary to the governor. In states where there is reason to expect an opposition majority in at least one house of the legislature, the governor may not want to antagonize opposition legislators by a personal campaign against them, a campaign that he may believe is fruitless. This may temper a governor's campaign even when there is some prospect of winning a legislative majority. One writer has noted Adlai Stevenson's tactics in 1950:

Stevenson, campaigning for a Democratic legislature in 1950, hurled no charge of "worst" against the Republican Senate of the Sixty-sixth General Assembly; never did he attack his opponents by name; so that when his bid failed . . . he was not required to pay a ruinous forfeit to the victors.[12]

The governor may believe that a campaign for his legislative ticket in a gubernatorial election year is unnecessary because voters so often cast a straight party ticket. His chance of winning a legislative majority is clearly dependent on his success in rolling up a large majority in the gubernatorial election. In Indiana, where there is two-party competition for most legislative seats, during three elections—1948, 1952, and 1956—a majority vote was cast for the same party in both gubernatorial

and lower house races in 88 percent of the counties. Nine percent favored the winning gubernatorial candidate and the opposing party's legislative candidate, and only 3 percent favored the losing gubernatorial candidate and the other legislative candidate.

The election of state legislators in a two-party state is closely related to the governorship. Straight party voting assures this relationship in a gubernatorial election year. In off-year elections the vote for legislators is, at least vaguely, a vote of confidence in the state administration, though the outcome may be affected by national party trends. This fact is recognized by legislators as well as by the governor, and it helps explain why the governor seldom finds it necessary to participate directly in legislative primaries or elections. Lacking the independent stature and the long-established reputation that most congressmen have, the legislator in a competitive district recognizes that the voter's judgment of the governor will largely determine his own political fate. The legislator in the governor's party has a personal stake in the governor's success. This does not necessarily create tight party cohesion in the legislature, but it creates a fundamental attitude of party loyalty among many legislators in two-party states. It provides an incentive for voting for those measures that are central to the governor's program and the success of which are crucial to his prestige.

It may be significant that two of the clearest examples of vigorous gubernatorial campaigns for legislators were carried out by third-party governors in the 1930s who lacked a solid party base in the legislature. Philip LaFollette, campaigning as a Progressive in Wisconsin in 1936, compiled a legislative score for each incumbent legislator and publicized it when visiting his district. He campaigned for Progressive candidates and against the "17 reactionary Senators" whom he blamed for defeating much of his program in the previous session.[13] Campaigning in 1932 on a Farmer-Labor ticket in Minnesota, where the legislature is nonpartisan, Floyd B. Olson made a similar effort to elect legislative candidates pledged to his program.[14]

[11] Curtis Martin and Rudolph Gomez, *Colorado Government and Politics* (2nd ed.; Boulder, Col.: Pruett Press, 1964), pp. 79–80.

[12] Kenneth S. Davis, *A Prophet in His Own Country* (Garden City, N.Y.: Doubleday, 1957), p. 351.

[13] David Carley, "Legal and Extra-Legal Powers of Wisconsin Governors in Legislative Relations," *Wisconsin Law Review* (1962), pp. 36–37.

[14] George H. Mayer, *The Political Career of Floyd B. Olson* (Minneapolis: University of Minnesota Press, 1951), p. 117.

THE GOVERNOR AS PARTY SPOKESMAN

Perhaps the governor's most important party role is that of spokesman. In an age when the techniques of reaching and persuading public opinion have assumed such importance, the governor has no rival in his ability to command public attention, nor can anyone effectively challenge his right to speak for the party. As his party's choice for the highest office in the state, the gubernatorial candidate in his campaign assumes the responsibility for defining the issues and making commitments that form the basis for his legislative program. The issues that have become part of the governor's personal program are likely to be given highest priority by his party in the legislature.

The first step that the gubernatorial candidate takes may be to gain a hand in writing his party's platform. He can define the issues more sharply in his campaign if the platform is an asset rather than a liability. If the governor has been unable to dictate the platform, he has considerable freedom to depart from it, because of his position as party leader. Governor Warren in his 1950 campaign in California followed the somewhat unusual course of defining which planks in the Republican platform he would adopt as his own.[15] Philip La-Follette in Wisconsin and Floyd Olson in Minnesota took great care to determine the content of the third-party platforms on which they ran; the ideological orientation of the Progressive and Farmer-Labor parties made those platforms more important, and perhaps more vulnerable to attack, then the average party platform. LaFollette in particular devoted great care to drafting and editing his party's platform in order to produce a detailed document of his purposes. In Wisconsin the impact of the governor on the party platform can be measured with unusual precision because there are two platforms: one drafted by the voluntary endorsing convention before the primary and one drafted by the statutory convention between the primary and the election. As an example, when Walter Kohler, Jr., was nominated in 1950, he requested and obtained a number of specific changes in the original platform. Kohler's attitude toward the platform is probably typical of most governors: "I believe that the governor should be the chief architect of the platform, especially for the first time he runs."[16]

The governor's role as a party spokesman does not cease at the end of the campaign, but it becomes merged with his role as a leader of bipartisan public opinion. Though a governor seldom commands the public interest and attention that the President enjoys, the same tools of communication are available to him: the press conference, radio and television broadcasts, and innumerable speeches across the state. The governor has repeated opportunities to speak, to capture the headlines; if he wishes, he may capitalize on these opportunities to focus attention on his legislative program. The same techniques and opportunities are available to all governors, but there is great variety in the skill and imagination with which governors use them. The most renowned governors of this century have been men who were able to lead public opinion. This has been a trademark of New York governors—Smith, Roosevelt, and Rockefeller, for example—and men like Earl Warren in California, Adlai Stevenson in Illinois, and Woodrow Wilson in New Jersey. Governor Mennen Williams of Michigan was typical of recent governors who have employed a wide variety of communications techniques: television reports, a weekly newspaper column, and constant trips across the state during which his activities ranged from formal speeches to square dances. Williams has warned that "once you get too far ahead of the people you become ineffective and your legislative and administrative programs then tend to lag."[17]

It is difficult to define exactly what effect gubernatorial leadership of public opinion has on the legislature. Legislators are geographically close to their constituents, but constituent mail is frequently thin on the major issues confronting the legislature. The legislature, like the congressman, must often depend more on community leaders, pressure groups, and newspapers that quite imperfectly reflect the viewpoints of the public. In the absence of adequate research on the public opinion process at the state level, we may hazard a guess that the legislator responds to the governor's initiative when he senses public interest in and sup-

[15] Coleman B. Ransone, Jr., *The Office of Governor in the United States* (University, Alabama: University of Alabama Press, 1956), p. 168.

[16] Carley, *op. cit.*, pp. 41–45.

[17] G. Mennen Williams, *A Governor's Notes* (Ann Arbor: Institute of Public Administration, University of Michigan, 1961), p. 7.

port for the governor's public statements through his haphazard contact with community and group leaders. At times the governor who is gifted in sleight-of-hand may create the impression that he has popular support simply by seeking it through a bold and articulate campaign. Public opinion leadership is an important variable in determining a governor's legislative success, important because some governors have been much more skillful than others in this leadership role.

Leadership of public opinion outside the legislature is not an effective substitute for skillful handling of legislators. Foster Furcolo of Massachusetts is a notable example of a governor who relied primarily on public opinion. He held weekly press conferences, spoke widely across the state, and made use of all the free radio and television time available. He relied heavily on seminars and conferences with civic leaders. He had great confidence in his ability to sell his programs to citizens through a variety of public appearances. In the words of an observer, "Foster Furcolo saw himself above all as a tribune of the people."[18] But Furcolo was aloof from the party organization, ill at ease with politicians, and unskilled and uncertain in bargaining sessions with legislators. His legislative record was a frustrating one and his gubernatorial career ended in defeat in the primary after four years. Publicity is an important weapon in the governor's hands, but a weapon of limited range. Many legislators, and often legislative leaders, are protected from it by one-sided partisan makeup of their districts, which guarantees reelection, and their local popularity, which assures renomination. Such men may follow public opinion, but they do not have to. Working outside the legislature, the governor may generate political strength and public support great enough to affect the legislative environment. To focus this support on specific legislative measures the governor usually needs to work directly with legislators.

THE GOVERNOR AND LEGISLATIVE LEADERS

No factor is more important in determining a governor's legislative success than his relationship with the legislative leaders of his party. When that party is in the majority, these leaders—and particularly the House speakers—have broad powers to appoint committees, assign bills to committees, and guide

[18]Mallan and Blackwood, *op. cit.*, pp. 298–299.

deliberations on the floor. Moreover, these are the governor's spokesmen and representatives in the legislature. If they are ineffective or uncooperative, the governor is seriously handicapped. If he tries to bypass or undermine his leaders on one bill, he damages the effectiveness of their leadership on other legislation. The position of the governor is very much like that of the President: He must accept his legislative leaders for better or worse, once they have been chosen.

The governor has greater opportunities than the President to influence the choice of legislative leaders, however, because the tenure of these leaders is usually less than it is in Congress. The relatively short tenure of speakers in the lower houses of legislatures is illustrated by a survey of 28 two-party legislatures for the period from 1947 through 1970 (covering twelve two-year terms). There were six state legislatures in which a new speaker was chosen every two years, and nine others where the usual term was two years but some speakers served four-year terms. There were eleven states where a two-year or four-year term was normal, but one Speaker (or occasionally two) had served a term of six, eight, or ten years. Two states had speakers with long terms of service; one in Rhode Island served from 1941 to 1964, and one in New York served from 1937 to 1960.[19]

If the governor's party has just won a majority or if the speaker or floor leader in the previous session is no longer in the legislature, the governor has the best opportunity to influence the choice of leaders. He may find that it is necessary to work behind the scenes in support of his candidate, to avoid appearing to dictate to the legislature and to minimize the loss of prestige if his candidate should not be chosen. Although the governor's influence over the choice of leaders is usually limited to members of his own party, in two recent cases the Illinois governor has reached across party lines. In 1959, when the Democrats held a House majority, Republican Governor Stratton

[19]These 28 legislatures had some alternation in majority party control of at least one house of the legislature from 1947 through 1968. The reference to a term of a certain number of years for a speaker means an uninterrupted term. If the same man is elected speaker again after an interruption it is counted as the start of a new term. Data for 18 one-party legislatures are found later in the paper. (Two nonpartisan legislatures and Alaska and Hawaii are omitted.)

swung Republican voters to elect as speaker a down-state Democrat who had only a minority of Democratic votes for the post. Two years later despite a narrow Republican majority, Democratic Governor Kerner gained the election of the same down-state Democrat as speaker when several Republicans in the House failed to appear for the vote.[20]

A governor's influence may depend on his own concept of gubernatorial prerogatives. A student of the Wisconsin governorship has described the contrasting approaches of two governors there:

Walter Kohler took no active part in the organizing of the legislatures which served during his three terms. This was true in spite of the fact that both houses in all three sessions had significant Republican majorities. . . .

Not a single speaker in Kohler's three terms was friendly to his program. Consequently, it is not surprising to note that his program had its greatest difficulty in that house. . . .

Philip LaFollette, on the other hand . . . did everything possible to install his choices for legislative office. But even LaFollette, knowing well the strong tradition of legislative supremacy in Wisconsin, was reluctant to admit to personal intervention. . . .

LaFollette had his men in each legislative post available to the Progressives. . . . Wherever and whenever the Progressives had a majority, the governor's program was safe because the whole legislative machinery was under executive control.[21]

When a governor is confronted with a legislative leader in his party who is seeking reelection, he faces another type of dilemma. If he tries to effect the election of someone else, the governor may, at best, divide the party and, at worst, fail and be confronted with a hostile leader. If, on the other hand, the governor acquiesces in the reelection of an incumbent, he will get a leader who can probably get things done in the legislature but who may act independently of the governor or even at cross purposes to him. The Democratic leader for many years in the Massachusetts Senate was John Powers, who owed his great political strength to a quarter-century of experience in the legislature, during which time he did countless favors for legislators and gained the personal loyalty of members in both parties. This broad base of political strength made his opposition to Governor Fur-

colo's tax program in the late 1950s particularly damaging, but also made it impossible for the governor to seek his replacement. In the neighboring state of Rhode Island the combined power of the speaker and the Democratic floor leader in the House (who between them had over eighty years of legislative experience before they retired) was so awesome that no Democratic governor would try to challenge them.

In California, where party ties have been traditionally weak, the campaign for the speakership often lasts several months before a session starts, it extends to members of both parties, and it involves intensive bargaining over committee assignments. The role left for the governor to play may be minimal. During the 1961 session of the California Assembly, majority leader Jesse Unruh collected signed pledges of support for the speakership from a majority of members and left Governor Pat Brown with little choice but to accede to his election at the start of the 1962 session.

Once legislative leaders have been chosen, it can be assumed that frequent conferences between the governor and his party's leaders will be routine. The effectiveness of these conferences, however, depends on the loyalty of the leaders to the governor and his skill in personal relationships. The governor must make his views known to the leaders fully and early enough in the life of any particular measure to have the best chance for influencing its course. He must also listen to advice, because the skillful legislative leader will know the temper of the legislature and be able to estimate what legislation is possible.

OTHER CHANNELS TO THE LEGISLATURE

While he must work primarily through his party's legislative leaders, the governor has several other channels of communication with the legislators. In the relatively few legislatures where important decisions are made in party caucuses the governor may participate directly or through a representative. An example is Michigan, where Governor Williams took a personal part in caucus deliberations. In Connecticut John Bailey served for several years as the Democratic governor's spokesman in caucuses. During Philip LaFollette's administration in Wisconsin, the Progressive party members held regular caucuses, usually attended by the governor. "The caucus undoubtedly was a key factor behind the relentless display of party unity on vote after vote after vote." The Republican caucus

[20] Thomas B. Littlewood, *Bipartisan Coalition in Illinois* (New York: McGraw-Hill, 1960).

[21] Carley, *op. cit.*, pp. 333–334.

during Governor Walter Kohler's administration in Wisconsin was a less effective, less binding institution, but the governor frequently visited the caucus and believed that his presence served a useful purpose.[22] Where the political environment and the legislative leadership are conducive to strong caucuses, this institution provides the best means for continuing gubernatorial influence over the decisions of his legislative party. The governor trying to innovate such procedures runs the strong risk, however, that his efforts will be counterproductive. Where the caucus is weak or meets infrequently the governor may find that a personal appearance before a committee hearing is a productive device.

There are many opportunities for informal, private conferences with legislators. During the closing days of a legislative session these may consume a large proportion of the governor's time. The governor may argue the merits of his legislation, appeal to party loyalty, or negotiate bargains involving various kinds of patronage or the pet bills of individual legislators. Skill in face-to-face negotiations, in developing conpromises, in minimizing the patronage costs of legislative victories is a prerequisite of the successful governor. Legislators appreciate personal attention and, although time consuming, individual meetings may be more productive than larger formal meetings. Some governors have found it useful to meet with legislators prior to or early in the session while the legislative program was still in the planning stage. Wood and Seasholes offer the following cautionary note from their interviews with Massachusetts governors:

No amount of effort at legislative liaison, in the governors' judgment, compensates for not "belonging." Lengthy conferences with individual legislators, open houses, elaborate social occasions, repeated conferences with legislative leaders, formal appearances before legislative committees, informal meetings with the committees—none of these seemed to help the governors who were "outsiders." Obviously other factors were relevant here—personalities, programs, parties—but with these taken into account, legislative service still seems critical. . . . [23]

In some of the larger states the governor's staff includes a legislative secretary; in the remainder, staff members are likely to devote much of their time to legislative matters during the session. Staff members represent the governor at committee meetings and caucuses. They keep him informed about the progress of important bills in the legislature. They keep the legislative leaders and often the rank-and-file informed about the governor's views on legislation. The governor may delegate to them some of the task of persuasion and the dispensing of patronage and favors. In a large state, where the demands on the governor's time are greater, a larger proportion of the legislative oversight is left to the staff. Employees in various state agencies may be borrowed by the governor's office to perform legislative liaison functions. In some cases staff members may work in close collaboration with lobbyists who support the governor's legislative program. In a large state where patronage is extensive, one or more of the governor's assistants may devote himself largely to this function. The staff must advise the governor concerning the wide variety of bills presented to him for signature or veto.[24]

The staff members who handle legislative liaison occupy a delicate position. As Governor Mennen Williams has pointed out, they "must have the legislature's confidence as well as the governor's."[25] They must be judicious in making commitments in the governor's name, and tactful in applying pressure to legislators. They must be diplomatic in working with the elected legislative leaders to avoid impinging on their scope of activity. A staff member who has served in the legislature can be most valuable, particularly if the governor has not had such experience.

THE GOVERNOR'S RESOURCES IN A TWO-PARTY STATE

On the surface, the governor in a two-party state seems to have substantial advantages over his counterpart in a one-party state, but a combination of circumstances often contrive to reduce this advantage. Party organization is not consistently strong in two-party states. Moreover, a governor often rises to power without the help of established party leaders, and, as a consequence, he may be unable to utilize the party machinery to influence the legislature. The wide-open primary in some states has contributed to loose party organization and independently nominated governors. Some

[22] Carley, *op. cit.*, pp. 285, 312.
[23] Wood and Seasholes, *op. cit.*, pp. 89–90.
[24] Ransone, *The Office of Governor in the United States*, chap. 10.
[25] Williams, *op. cit.*, p. 10.

governors discover that their legislative party has an established pattern of cohesive roll-call voting, while in other cases there seems to be no such cohesion. The pattern of cohesion tends to be stronger in the larger industrial states where, typically, the Democratic party (and especially the Democratic legislative party) is rooted in metropolitan areas and the Republican party draws its strength from outside the metropolitan areas. In other words homogeneity of a legislative party's constituencies reduces the pressure on legislators to become mavericks. A governor confronted with a heterogeneous party, lacking in legislative cohesion and programmatic unity, finds that his most polished tools of party leadership have minimum effect.

The governor is his party's spokesman, but this does not give him a significantly greater impact on public opinion than is possible for the governor of a one-party state. Any governor's potential impact on opinion is great; his personal skills, his charismatic qualities, and perhaps his public relations advisers determine how great that impact is in practice. Patronage—in the form of jobs, contracts, and other favors—is available in some degree to all governors. Governors of two-party states have no greater share of patronage, and in some of the major two-party states the governor has relatively limited power to use patronage. Patronage tends to be more important as a gubernatorial tool in many of the one-party states.

The resources available to the governor in a two-party state are varied and in some cases seriously limited, but he has one liability which most one-party governors are spared—an organized opposition. When the opposition party has a majority in one or both houses, the problems faced by the governor are obvious. Less obvious, but worth emphasizing, is the fact that the existence of a continuing organized opposition party, even in the minority, insures that a number of legislators will be invulnerable to most or all of the weapons or all of the weapons of gubernatorial influence. The opposition party has the organization structure and the motivation to maintain cohesion in the legislature. It is seeking to build a legislative record, which sometimes may require cooperation with the governor and sometimes opposition to him. The opposition may be seeking to discredit the governor by blocking those legislative programs on which his prestige depends. The opposi-

tion may remain united in order to maximize its bargaining power with the governor for its own preferred bills or for the benefits of patronage. Whenever the opposition party in the legislature is strong enough to take advantage of disunity in the governor's party, the governor faces a potential power struggle on every bill he sends to the legislature.

THE GOVERNOR AS PARTY LEADER IN A ONE-PARTY STATE

The more completely a legislature is dominated by a single party, the less organized and cohesive that legislative party is likely to be. Consequently, the governor in a one-party state cannot depend on the party loyalty of a legislative majority. There are few if any legislators who link their political fortunes with his, or who expect their reelection or renomination to be dependent on the governor's success or their alliance with the governor. Nothing the governor does is likely to help or hurt the legislator at the polls, and both of them realize it. In many southern one-party states the governor is limited to a single term which makes it difficult for him to form cohesive factions to support him in the legislature. A one-term limitation handicaps a governor's attempts to dictate the choice of his successor or to discipline rebel legislators at the polls. In trying to organize a legislative majority, the governor has a number of resources at his disposal, but these do not usually include any significant support from state or local party organizations.

There are some one-party states in which the party organization is of greater importance to the governor. In Kentucky, for example, one of the governor's assistants usually acts as de facto party chairman, serving as a coordinator for local party leaders, a contact man for patronage, and a mediator of local party disputes. Kentucky is also one of the few states in which the governor, during Democratic administrations, has tried to influence the outcome of legislative primaries. During the gubernatorial primary in Kentucky the candidates rarely pay any attention to legislative primaries. But several recent Democratic governors have supported candidates in a large proportion of midterm legislative primaries. The Democratic party in Kentucky has been divided into factions, and the governor, as the leader of one faction, has supported legislative candidates who were loyal to that faction and could be counted on to support him in the legislature. His support of candidates has often been effective because he could command the assistance of party workers in his faction. Although gubernatorial support of legislative candidates has usually been unpublicized, in 1965 Governor Breathitt publicly supported a number of candidates in senatorial primaries—in most cases successfully—during his factional struggle with Lieutenant-Governor Waterfield for control of the senatorial party.[26]

Louisiana is another state in which slating arrangements between gubernatorial and legislative candidates were common during the period of deep factional divisions in the Democratic party. These slating arrangements were most common during runoff primaries, and were limited to certain parts of the state.[27] In other one-party states, such as Tennessee, Texas, and Alabama, factions loyal to the governor have appeared from time to time, but they have been transitory in nature and uneven in effect, and they have rarely resulted from any intervention by the governor in legislative primaries.

If the one-party governor usually lacks a loyal political faction in the legislature, he also lacks an organized opposition. There is no group with the organizational structure or the motivation to play the role of the opposition with consistency. As Lockard has said, in describing the New Hampshire legislature when it was dominated by one party, the governor "operates in a power vacuum. . . . That the governor does not have to deal with strongly cohesive parties is in a sense a factor enhancing his power."[28] Operating in a power vacuum, the governor has available many of the tools of a governor in a two-party state and sometimes greater freedom to use them.

If factions do develop in the legislature, the governor's faction is likely to be more effective and enduring than any opposition faction because the governor has more resources at his command. In Kentucky, for example, it has been common for

legislators in an opposing faction, even those whom the governor has tried to defeat in a primary, to support the governor's program because they see nothing to be gained and much to be lost by persistent opposition.

There are sometimes examples in one-party states of opposition factions winning legislative control and blocking a governor's program. This is unlikely to occur unless the opposition is united by a common interest—geographic, socioeconomic, or ideological. During Governor Folsom's first term in Alabama, he fought a continuing and often losing battle against the rural, black-belt coalition which dominated the legislature with the help of an outdated apportionment.[29] Despite his dominance of the legislature in later years, Huey Long often lost his battles during the first few sessions of the Louisiana legislature as he sought to make major changes in the socioeconomic structure of the state. Since that time Louisiana governors have usually been able to command a dependable factional majority in the legislature.[30] During the period when the Florida legislature was dominated by a clique of legislators representing small rural counties, a series of governors who were more responsive to urban needs saw their programs repeatedly being defeated in the legislature.[31]

It should be pointed out that in many southern and border states the Republican legislative party has become strong enough to threaten Democratic dominance. One consequence is that factionalism within the Democratic party has begun to decline. Another consequence is that Democratic governors are less likely to be able to win the support of Republican legislators by offering patronage or other favors—a practice that in some states had kept the Republican party weak and ineffective. As the Republican legislative party begins to develop more numerical strength and also more cohesion, the Democratic party is likely to gain in cohesion also and to provide the Democratic governor with more consistent support.

The governor in a one-party state, like his counterpart in a two-party state, is looked upon as a

[26]Malcolm E. Jewell, *Legislative Representation in the Contemporary South* (Durham, N.C.: Duke University Press, 1967), pp. 56–75.

[27]*Ibid.*, pp. 76–92, and Allan P. Sindler, "Bifactional Rivalry as an Alternative to Two-Party Competition in Louisiana," *American Political Science Review*, Vol. XLIX (1955), pp. 641–642.

[28]Lockard, *New England State Politics*, p. 74.

[29]Ransone, *The Office of Governor in the United States*, p. 186.

[30]Allan P. Sindler, *Huey Long's Louisiana* (Baltimore: Johns Hopkins Press, 1956).

[31]William C. Havard and Loren P. Beth, *The Politics of Mis-Representation* (Baton Rouge: Louisiana State University Press, 1962), chaps. 5 and 7.

party spokesman. Candidates increasingly run in the primary election on some kind of a platform, which may be developed further and publicized more if there is also a general election campaign. Voters and legislators often believe that the winning gubernatorial candidate has received a mandate for his program that deserves some respect. As Ransone has said, "the people have come to regard the platform of the successful candidate in the Democratic primary [in Southern states] as something more than a pious hope."[32] A student of Virginia politics has attributed the legislative failure of one governor there partly to his failure to present a program during the primary campaign.[33] The governor's campaign platform often forms the basis for the governor's first message to the legislature, which in turn often serves as the principal agenda for the legislature.

THE GOVERNOR AS LEGISLATIVE LEADER IN ONE-PARTY STATES

Any governor needs the support of legislative leaders, and some of the clearest examples of a governor's control over the selection of leaders are found in one-party states. A survey of tenure in the speakership for eighteen one-party states from 1947 to 1970 shows somewhat less frequent changes in the speaker than in two-party states. This is partly because there are no changes in party majorities to force the removal of a speaker. There were two states choosing a new speaker every two years and four others where most speakers served two years and some served four. In three states a four-year term was normal but some terms were shorter; these were all states where the governor dominated the selection process. In five states the speaker usually served two to four years, but one man had served from six to ten years in succession. Finally there were four states, Mississippi, South Carolina, Virginia, and Georgia, in which one man had served throughout at least half of the twenty-four year period, and usually much longer.

It is quite common in many one-party states for the governor to select one or more legislators to serve as his floor leaders. These men may be regarded as the governor's spokesmen rather than as the leaders of any party or faction in the legislature. In addition, in several one-party states, it has been traditional for the legislators to accept the governor's choice as the speaker in the House and the elected presiding officer in the Senate. In Alabama this has traditionally been the governor's prerogative, and when the lieutenant-governor has been out of step with the governor, the Senate has sometimes taken away his right to choose committee members.[34] In Kentucky the Democratic governor has traditionally selected the speaker of the House, the president pro tem of the Senate, and the floor leaders. The willingness of Kentucky legislators to accept this advice was summed up by one of them in 1966 when the governor was unusually slow in announcing his choice: "I wish he'd just go ahead and tell us who he wants. That's what we're all waiting for." When a Republican governor took office in 1968, Republican legislators followed precedent and turned to him for advice on the choice of floor leaders.[35] Governor Faubus of Arkansas had close supporters serving as presiding officers and chairmen of key committees. In two states where the governor has traditionally selected the leadership, there are signs of legislative resistance. The Tennessee governor in 1965 needed some votes from the minority Republican party to win a majority for his choice as presiding officer of the Senate. In 1967 the Democrats in the Georgia House reelected the speaker (who had already served eight years) before Governor Maddox had had an opportunity to suggest his choice for the position.

In Florida there is usually a prolonged contest for speaker, and the choice is made so far in advance of the session that an incoming governor has no opportunity to influence the outcome. In Texas the candidates for speaker of the House carry out an extensive campaign and seek pledges of support from legislators and legislative candidates during the primary; the results of the legislative primaries may determine the outcome. If the contest is close, an incoming governor may be able to exercise some influence over the result if he works discreetly behind the scenes.[36] Of course,

[32] Ransone, *The Office of Governor in the South*, p. 68.
[33] George W. Spicer, "Gubernatorial Leadership in Virginia," *Public Administration Review*, Vol. I (1941), pp. 441–457.

[34] Hallie Farmer, *The Legislative Process in Alabama* (University, Ala.: Bureau of Public Administration, University of Alabama, 1949), pp. 185–191.
[35] Malcolm E. Jewell and Everett W. Cunningham, *Kentucky Politics* (Lexington: University of Kentucky Press, 1968), pp. 238–239.
[36] Clifton McCleskey, *The Government and Politics of Texas* (Boston: Little, Brown, 1963), pp. 123–125.

in states like South Carolina, Virginia, and Mississippi, where legislative leaders have been entrenched in power for many years, governors have found it necessary to get along with the incumbent rather than trying to pick a successor.

In many one-party states it is common for the governor to become personally involved in negotiations with legislators. This may be more necessary because the governor cannot rely on party loyalty and cannot use such devices as a party caucus to win support for his program. Governors rarely follow the example of Huey Long, who frequently appeared on the floor of the Louisiana legislature to supervise its activities and lobby for his bills. But they may be found testifying at committee hearings or talking informally to legislators in the corridors of the capitol building. More often, of course, they meet with legislators in the governor's office. One reason for direct negotiations by the governor is that legislators often expect the governor to meet with them personally. Some Texas legislators were critical of Governor Connally because, despite his public advocacy of a legislative program, he was seldom willing to participate personally in legislative negotiations. One source of Governor Faubus's success in Arkansas was that he not only met frequently with legislators but took an interest in their political problems and avoided pressure tactics that would hurt them in their relationships with constituents.[37]

The governor in a one-party state cannot appeal to the party loyalty of legislators, but he has other bargaining techniques available. In one-party states, particularly in the South, the various types of patronage seem to be more important gubernatorial tools than is true in many two-party states, both because party leadership is less important and because there are often fewer restrictions on the governor's use of patronage. Several southern states lack comprehensive merit systems. In several the governor has control over highway systems both for patronage purposes and for determining the allocation of funds to specific purposes. In some southern states, such as Louisiana, the governor has extensive power to fill vacancies at the local level. In Virginia the governor controls a board that sets local salaries. In some southern states there are only limited legal restrictions on the letting of contracts. In some one-party states, however, the governor's control over patronage is severely limited because the governor cannot directly appoint the heads of major agencies, such as the highway department.[38]

There are never enough jobs to go around, of course, and many of those that are available must be given to local political leaders rather than to legislators. The governor may be able to decide which county will get a new highway or the resurfacing of an old one, a new or improved park, hospitals, community colleges, and a variety of other projects and services that are of great importance to constituents. Legislators very much want to be able to take credit for getting such projects and improvements for their district. On the other hand, the governor may have to take into account a number of other factors, such as the suggestions of advisory committees or the advice of federal agencies that share in the financing, when he decides on the location of a project. One of the most difficult tasks of any governor is to use the various kinds of patronage that he controls—both jobs and projects—in such a way as to gain the maximum support among legislators for his program.

THE VARIABLE DEMANDS ON THE GOVERNOR

American governors vary not only in their constitutional and political powers but in the demands made on them by the citizens of fifty widely varying states. The authors of one study on gubernatorial leadership have pointed out that "Evaluation of performance tends to depend not on absolute volume of accomplishments but rather on volume of accomplishments relative to public program demands."[39] In states where these demands have grown most rapidly, the image of the governor has been most seriously jeopardized. The demands for new and improved state services, in education, welfare, and highways particularly, and the demands of local government for help have grown throughout the country. Every governor has experienced the growing demand, but it has been most urgent in the major industrial states with their expensive metropolitan centers. In the less densely populated or less industrialized states of the South and West the demands have been more moderate.

[37]Alex B. Lacy, Jr. (Ed.), *Power in American State Legislatures* (New Orleans: Tulane University, 1967), p. 23.

[38]Robert B. Highsaw, "Southern Governor—Challenge to the Strong Executive Theme," *Public Administration Review*, Vol. XIX (1959), pp. 7–11.

[39]Wood and Seasholes, *op. cit.*, p. 81.

When demands are made on government, they are made on the governor. He has become the focus of attention, the center of conflict in state government. The role that the public expects the governor to play is usually an impossible one. It fails to take into account the power of other actors in the state political process. The public is usually ignorant of the limitations imposed on the governor by the constitution, the division of authority with other elected officials, the weakness of party organization, the shortage of skilled legislative leaders. The public does not realize how seriously a governor is handicapped when the opposition party has a legislative majority; in fact a large proportion of the public may not even be aware of that division in government when it occurs. The demands made on government vary from state to state, but in all states these demands are focused on the governor.

Another variable affecting the governor's legislative leadership results from the fact that the governor and the legislative majority sometimes represent different constituencies and consequently are sensitive to conflicting demands by the voters. This is more likely to be true when there is partisan division in government, when the parties are homogeneous and issue oriented, or when the conflicts among demands for limited tax resources become intense. When all of these conditions prevail, as in Michigan, the stage is set for deadlock between the governor and the legislature. While divided partisan control of government increases the chances of deadlock, such a division creates fewer problems in those states (such as the Mountain States) where the parties lack ideological unity and do not represent sharply contrasting constituencies.

On the other hand, if a single interest or a single type of constituency is dominant in the state, there may be a minimum of conflict between governor and legislature. In some of the most rural states, this fact helps to explain the low-pressure politics and the smoothness of gubernatorial-legislative relations that are frequently found. Just as a few deeply divisive issues may undermine cooperation between the governor and the legislative majority, agreement on a major issue may enhance cooperation. In some southern states agreement on segregation legislation has been a unifying theme in the legislature. This brought unity to the legislature in Louisiana, so often divided on socioeconomic issues.[40]

The contrast can be stated in different terms. In many northern, industrial states recent governors have responded to the demands of urban constituents for change, change which usually involves enlarging the role of government and increasing the tax burden. The governors have sometimes succeeded in their legislative programs but have often had to compromise or retreat in the face of resistance by legislators representing other constituency interests. In many southern and some western states the governors, under less pressure, have made fewer proposals for change; there has been less conflict between governor and legislature, more consensus on the conservative programs needed for the state.

The similarity of interest between governor and legislature in some states has made legislators inclined to accept the bills proposed by the governor. They recognize that these are not likely to damage the interests of their constituents. Under these conditions legislators are likely to focus their attention on the needs of their localities. Some of these needs can be met by the governor, and his ability to do so gives the legislators additional reasons for supporting his program. Some local needs can be met only by local legislation. In some states, such as Kentucky, the governor and legislative leaders keep a tight hold over local legislation, facilitating its passage in return for voting support on major legislation. In other states, like Alabama, the leadership follows a "hands-off" policy with regard to local bills. The legislature passes without controversy any local bill on which the legislators from the particular county are agreed. There is an implicit agreement between governor and legislators: The governor receives support for statewide legislation that does not drastically change the status quo, and the legislators have a free hand to take care of the legislative needs of their counties.

In the years ahead the demands on state government and on the governor for new programs and services will continue to grow. At the same time these pressures will become more conflicting, as

---

[40] For example, during a special session held late in 1960, the Louisiana Senate considered 20 bills and resolutions concerning school segregation; it passed 8 unanimously and 12 with an average of 4 opposing votes.

the variety of group interests increases in a more complex society. In the last decade, for example, it has become increasingly clear that within metropolitan areas there are sharp conflicts between the interests of the central city and those of the suburbs. Governors of southern states face greater problems of legislative leadership because new groups are gaining legislative power—suburbanites, Republicans, and black voters.

Will the resources of gubernatorial leadership keep pace with the demands of the governor? It is possible to strengthen the governor's constitutional powers, but progress in this direction has been agonizingly slow in most states. The growth of merit system and greater federal controls over state spending have made the use of patronage more difficult. Skillful governors may be able to find better ways to utilize the media, and especially television, in order to influence public opinion. The growth of two-party systems will increase the importance of party leadership but will not necessarily make the governor a more effective party leader. Although divided government may decline in northern states, it is likely to become more common in those southern states where a two-party system is just emerging. Reapportionment should decrease the likelihood that a governor and a legislative majority represent fundamentally different constituencies, and consequently it should eliminate some of the worst examples of persistent deadlock between the governor and the legislature. On the other hand, reapportionment seems to be increasing the proportion of relatively independent legislators who are less willing to give unquestioning obedience to party discipline. It is probably accurate to conclude that the success of a governor depends more than ever before on his personal skill as an innovator, a leader of public opinion, a negotiator, and a politician—in the best sense of that term.

A COMPARISON OF THE RELATIVE POSITIONS OF GOVERNORS
Joseph A. Schlesinger

Since the governor's role is central to administrative-political relations, an assessment of the relative position of the governors in the several states is necessary. We have come to speak of "strong" and "weak" governors. Here we shall examine a number of major organizational devices which observers often think define the strength of the governor, rate the governors according to each, and then combine the various ratings to obtain an overall measure of the relative political impact of the governors upon the administration of the states.

One element which defines the influence of one administrator over others is status. It is, however, a factor difficult to quantify. The organizational chart of a state is largely a definition of the relative status of individuals, departments, and agencies. In part, status may be defined as who appoints whom, but it also derives from the placement of agencies within larger entities. An agency head beneath the governor is expected to consult with him. If an agency is a unit within a larger department, then it is to be expected that its head will consult with others in the same department and will report to the head of the overall department. An organizational chart is, therefore, a statement of formal communication channels and the influence which derives from control of information.

While the organizational chart is overtly a statement of who has the power to tell others what to do, it is also a chart of the incentive system of the state. We have argued elsewhere that an official is as much driven by his ambitions as by those forces or individuals which have put him into his present place.[1] The organization of the state is the means whereby those ambitions are defined. A finely graded bureaucracy which constantly holds out the hope of promotion is most capable of controlling the behavior of its members. The more extensively an organization seeks to control the

Source: Reprinted by permission of the authors and publisher from Herbert Jacobs and Kenneth Vines, *Politics in the American States*, 2nd edition. Copyright © 1971 by Little, Brown and Company (Inc.).

[1] Joseph A. Schlesinger, *Ambition and Politics: Political Careers in the United States* (Chicago: Rand McNally, 1966).

behavior of its members, the more refined must be the status system, as in the case of military organizations.

In most of the states the organizational status system is not very clearly defined, a fact which affects the behavior of administrators. An agency head whose unit is one of many in a large department may temper his devotion to his own agency because he hopes to be promoted to department head. The more independent the agency, the more he is likely to devote himself to internal goals exclusively. No doubt the resistance of agencies and their clientele to the integration of their departments with others rests upon some awareness of its policy consequences.

Status is also defined by pay. The governor outranks all other political executives. The discrepancy between the governor's pay and that of other executives does vary greatly. One exception to the salary-status system should, however, be noted. In many states the members of administrative boards may be unpaid or may be simply reimbursed for expenses. In Delaware most administrative agencies are headed by such unpaid boards.[2] When the state does not provide the salary incentive for men charged with executing its policies, it is difficult not to conclude that the nongovernmental employers of such officials find their influence increased. The existence of such a method of employment is another sign of the extent to which the state governments are not neatly closed systems but are bound up with the group structure of their states. The boundary between the government office structure and society is never so clean that officials are free of external influence. But what is characteristic of the states is the extent to which a customary device for defining the boundaries of an organization from its environment—the use of salaries and wages to define to whom an official is responsible—can also be extended to the larger society and economy.

Let us turn now to some aspects of the governor's administrative position which can be measured.

TENURE POTENTIAL

We have already noted that governors typically enjoy short terms of office which may reduce their

[2]Paul Dolan, *The Government and Administration of Delaware* (New York: Thomas Y. Crowell, 1956), pp. 94–95.

TABLE 1. The Governor's Tenure in Office Compared with That of the Secretary of State, 1914–58

| Average Tenure (in years) | Distribution of States | | | |
| | Governor | | Secretary of State | |
	N	%	N	%
Under 3	3	7	0	0
3.0–3.9	15	31	4	10
4.0	12	25	4	10
4.1–4.9	5	10	3	8
5.0–7.9	13	27	8	20
8.0–9.9	0	0	8	20
10.0 plus	0	0	12	32
	48	100	39*	100

*Number of states with an elective secretary of state.

Source: Turnover figures for governors and secretaries of state derived from state manuals and blue books.

influence. When the governor's tenure is compared with the tenure of the other elected executives we can see that he is at a further disadvantage.

Compared with the secretary of state the governor can expect to be in office only a short time. Whereas in the period from 1914 to 1958 no governor could expect an average of eight or more years in office, over half of the secretaries of state could; and in twelve states the typical secretary's term ran to over ten years. A similar relationship can be found for the other minor executive posts, with the exception of lieutenant-governor and attorney general which are also positions of high turnover. Since ambition is probably related to opportunity, the possibility of long tenure for lesser elected officials helps determine the extent to which they can be controlled by a governor or anyone else through their career expectations.

The term of office for governors ranges today from two to four years, although it has been as short as one year. Together, the length of term and the stipulations on reelection state the likelihood of long tenure for governors. In Table 2 the states are ranked according to tenure potential for the governor. Note that all four-year-term states have a higher rating than any two-year-term state, regardless of restraint on reelection, in accord with experience. Much the longest tenure is found in those four-year-term states which permit reelection. It is in these states that we would expect a governor to last long enough in office to put his mark on the state administration.

TABLE 2. The Governors' Tenure Potential, 1969

Four-Year Term, No Restraint on Reelection (5 points)*

California	Massachusetts	North Dakota
Colorado	Michigan	Utah
Connecticut	Minnesota	Washington
Hawaii	Montana	Wisconsin
Idaho	Nevada	Wyoming
Illinois	New York	

Four-Year Term, One Reelection Permitted (4 points)*

Alaska	Maryland	Ohio
Delaware	Missouri	Oklahoma
Louisianna	Nebraska	Oregon
Maine	New Jersey	Pennsylvania

Four-Year Term, No Consecutive Reelection
(3 points)

Alabama	Kentucky	Tennessee
Florida	Mississippi	Virginia
Georgia	North Carolina	West Virginia
Indiana	South Carolina	

Two-Year Term, No Restraint on Reelection (2 points)*

Arizona	Kansas	Texas
Arkansas	New Hampshire	Vermont
Iowa	Rhode Island	

Two-Year Term, One Reelection Permitted (1 point)*

New Mexico	South Dakota

*The points are used for the construction of the General Power Index, Table 7.

Source: The Book of the States, 1968–1969, p. 133.

The shortness of the governors' tenure is due to various factors. Most important is the American attitude which rejects long tenure for chief executives. The attitudes which led to the Twenty-second Amendment of the federal Constitution restricting a President to two terms have produced similar restraints on the terms of governors. Apart from governors, elective state treasurers and auditors frequently have limited terms, which reflects the constitution writers' distrust of those put in charge of the state's monies. Yet lesser officials often overcome the constitutional restraint by the practice of rotation, as in Colorado where the state treasurer and auditor frequently alternate over a series of elections. On the other hand, there are no instances where governors have circumvented the constitutional intent, evidence that the formal restraint upon the chief executive has popular support. The closest to an actual circumvention of a constitutional limitation was the election of George Wallace's wife, Lurleen, to succeed him as Alabama's governor in 1967.

Despite popular support, the consequences of formal restraints upon the governors' tenure are by no means clear. The governor who cannot run for reelection undoubtedly has limited control over the personnel who can hope to outlast him. On the other hand, the governor himself is freed from the control of the gubernatorial electorate and can carry on his administration with greater flexibility. The unexpected behavior of some southern governors is probably related to the fact that restraints on gubernatorial tenure are characteristically a southern rule. Therefore, it is not always easy to predict from his campaign how a southern governor will react to the civil rights crisis. In 1958, S. E. Vandiver, Jr., was elected governor of Georgia on a strong segregationist platform which pledged that no school would be integrated while he was governor.[3] Nevertheless, in 1961 he lent the power of his office to further peaceful integration of the University of Georgia.

Vandiver's subsequent behavior in aiding integration may be interpreted as a result of the need to change his constituency, if he wished to continue his political career. Unable to succeed himself as governor he had no place else to go in Georgia politics. The road to the [U.S.] Senate was effectively blocked. Both of the state's senators, Russell and Talmadge, were powerful figures and, in any event, Vandiver was related by marriage to the former and had been a campaign manager for the latter. With the election of John Kennedy as President, Vandiver was pushed strongly for Undersecretary of the Army, an appointment civil rights groups managed to block because of his campaign stands. But the experience pointed the way to future national office.[4]

Vandiver's behavior contrasts with that of Orval Faubus of Arkansas, a state which allows its governors reelection. Considered a moderate, Faubus nevertheless in 1956 sparked the first major crisis over school integration. He was reelected five times, breaking a long-standing two-term tradition for Arkansas governors.

It is true that in most of the states where a gov-

[3] *New York Times*, January 11, 1961.
[4] For a critical discussion of the effects of limitations on succession, as well as other aspects of the governor's powers, see Gove, "Why Strong Governors?", *National Civic Review*, 53 (March 1964), pp. 131–136; and Robert B. Highsaw, "The Southern Governor–Challenge to the Strong Executive Theme," *Public Administration Review*, Vol. XIX (Winter 1959), pp. 7–11.

ernor may not succeed himself he may run for reelection after an interval. But the politics of such reelections are a good deal more complex than in the case of an incumbent governor, and they are not a common occurrence. The most prominent examples are James E. "Kissin' Jim" Folsom of Alabama, A. B. "Happy" Chandler of Kentucky, Theodore G. "The Man" Bilbo of Mississippi, Earl K. Long of Louisiana, and Gifford Pinchot of Pennsylvania. In seeking reelection to the governorship after an enforced interval, a strong personality is undoubtedly an essential asset.

RECENT IMPROVEMENTS IN THE GOVERNOR'S TENURE POTENTIAL

The decade of the 1960s has seen a considerable improvement in the tenure potential of governors. Between 1960 and 1969 the number of states giving four-year terms to their governors jumped from 19 to 29. According to our point score for tenure potential the average for all states went from 3.26 in 1960 to 3.68 in 1969. The increase in potential does appear to be reflected in an actual trend toward increased tenure. Looking at a sequence of decades since the beginning of the republic we can see that the number of years spent in office for governors serving in the 1950s begins to approach the experience of a typical governor in the first decade of the nineteenth century. Yet we must conclude that still the greater proportion of these recent governors (69.5 percent) serve at most four years. It is indeed a significant departure that governors such as Mennen Williams in Michigan or Nelson Rockefeller in New York can serve twelve or more years. The increase in tenure for most governors, however, appears marginal.

THE POWER OF APPOINTMENT

The most widely appreciated means of controlling officials is the power to name them. Presumably, if a person can name an official, not only is the official beholden to him, but that person can also hope to affect the administration by naming someone whose values are close to those he wishes to implement. A sign of the diffusion of administrative control in the American state is the diversity of ways in which men are named to offices. As we have seen, many are popularly elected. The governor, with varying degrees of freedom, may name others. Then, again, boards or commisions may name the agency head.

We can measure a governor's appointive power by defining the extent to which he is free to name the heads of the major agencies. Taking sixteen principal functions and offices we can score each according to the relative influence, in formal terms, which the governor has over the appointment of the head of the function. The scale of values runs as follows:

5: Governor appoints alone

4: Governor must obtain approval of one house of the legislature

3: Governor must obtain approval of both houses of the legislature

2: Appointment by a board, of which the governor is a member

1: Appointment by an agency or individual other than the governor

0: Executive is popularly elected

The range, then, is a statement of the likelihood that the governor can influence the administrator on the basis of formal appointive powers alone.

For each of the sixteen major functions the governors have been rated and the score for each function totaled. Since not all states have each of the sixteen functions, the index has been converted into a percentage of the possible maximum rating in a state. Thus, if a governor rated a 5 for all of

---

TABLE 3. Tenure in Office of Governors
(figure is percentage of all governors who served during the decade)

Number of Years Spent in Office of Governor	1800–1809	1820–1829	1850–1859	1870–1879	1900–1909	1920–1929	1950–1959
10 plus	14.3	3.5	0.8	0.0	1.3	1.0	4.0
5–9	16.1	14.0	5.6	11.8	8.5	15.1	26.5
3–4	30.3	40.2	40.4	49.1	54.5	53.5	50.3
1–2	39.3	42.3	53.2	39.1	35.7	30.4	19.2
N	56	92	124	154	154	185	151

Source: Joseph A. Schlesinger, "The Governor's Place in American Politics," *Public Administration Review,* Vol. XXX (January/February 1970), p. 4.

TABLE 4. The Appointive Powers of the Governor

State Rankings

5 Points[a]	4 Points[a]	3 Points[a]	2 Points[a]	1 Point[a]
73 Tennessee	50 Arkansas	44 Alabama	37 Maine	29 Texas
72 Pennsylvania	50 California	44 Missouri	37 Oregon	27 Colorado
69 Hawaii	50 Connecticut	44 Washington	35 Nevada	26 Georgia
68 New Jersey	49 Idaho	43 West Virginia	35 Wisconsin	26 Mississippi
64 Indiana	49 Kentucky	42 Alaska	34 Louisiana	25 Delaware
59 Massachusetts	48 Michigan	42 Nebraska	33 New Hampshire	25 North Dakota
58 New York	48 Minnesota	42 Rhode Island	33 North Carolina	24 New Mexico
56 Maryland	47 Ohio	41 Utah	32 Kansas	21 South Carolina
56 Virginia	46 South Dakota	40 Iowa	31 Wyoming	20 Oklahoma
55 Illinois	46 Vermont	39 Montana	30 Florida	17 Arizona

The figure for each state is based on the governor's powers of appointment in sixteen major functions and offices. It indicates the degree to which the governor can be assumed to have sole power over the sixteen functions or offices.[b] For each function, the index is scaled according to the governor's powers of appointment according to the following formula:

$$\text{Index} = \frac{\text{Values of } P_1 + P_2 + P_3 \cdots (100)}{\text{Maximum Values of } P_1 + P_2 + P_3 + \cdots + P_n}$$

where $P = 5$ if governor appoints

  4 if governor and one body approves
  3 if governor and two bodies approve
  2 if appointed by director with governor's approval or by governor and council
  1 if appointed by department director, by board, by legislature, by civil service
  0 if elected by popular vote

and where subscript indicates the chief administrator for each of the sixteen major functions and offices.

[a]The points are used for the construction of the General Power Index, Table 7.
[b]Functions are: Administration and Finance, Agriculture, Attorney General, Auditor, Budget Officer, Conservation, Controller, Education, Health, Highways, Insurance, Labor, Secretary of State, Tax Commissioner, Treasurer, and Welfare.
Source: The Book of the States, 1968–1969, pp. 136–137.

the functions in his state, he would get a 100. If, on the average, he rated a 4, i.e., he appointed everyone with the approval of one house of the legislature, then he would rate an 80. A rating of 60 would mean that he appoints on the average with both houses' approval, and so on.

The ranking of the governors shows a great range, going from 73 in Tennessee to a low of 17 in Arizona. States such as New Jersey and New York which, along with Tennessee, have had major state constitutional revisions in the last thirty years also rate highly. States such as Illinois and Virginia which pioneered in administrative reforms in the first part of the century rank highly, too.[5] Thus the rating is a good reflection of the extent of the impact of the dominant trend in management reform on the several states.

A better idea of what the rankings mean can be

[5] Leslie Lipson, *The American Governor, from Figurehead to Leader* (Chicago: University of Chicago Press, 1939).

had from looking at selected states. The reasons why Tennessee ranks as high as it does are first, the governor (with the exception of three public utilities commissioners) is the only elective officer; second, most of the other positions are filled by him without the need of legislative approval. Even here, however, there are major officers chosen not by the governor but by the legislature itself—the secretary of state, the treasurer, and the controller. At the other extreme, Arizona's governor has weak appointive powers not only because such positions as secretary of state, attorney general, treasurer, and auditor are popularly elected, but also because the major functional departments such as agriculture, labor, health, and the like are headed by men appointed by boards and commissions. North Dakota's governor has weak appointive powers because, in addition to the usual elective offices, such positions as tax commissioners and the commissioners of agriculture, labor, and insurance are also elective.

The ratings given here of the governors' appointive powers are necessarily indicative only of gross differences. Not all offices and functions are equal in importance, nor do the values of our point scale have any inherent validity. As we noted earlier, there is a historical difference between the older elective offices and the newer functions of great importance which are more often appointive. So it is probably more important for a governor to appoint a welfare director than a state auditor, or even a secretary of state. Of all the older elective offices it is probably the attorney general's which is most important because the judgments and legal advice he is called upon to give may have great political importance. Attorneys general, along with lieutenant-governors, are the minor elected executives who have effectively been able to use their posts to advance to the governorship or the U.S. Senate. In this connection it is interesting to note that the earliest state official resistance to the 1954 desegregation decision of the Supreme Court was among southern attorneys general, a fact which Krislov has attributed to their aspirations for local office.[6]

It is worth noting that state executives are quite sensitive to the influence of the appointing power. Deil Wright questioned department heads in all fifty states and found a strikingly positive relation between those who were appointed by the governor and their perception that they were controlled by the governor and also their preference for such control.[7] Popularly elected department heads, in contrast, were least likely to see or prefer having the governor with much influence over their agencies.

Again, it is well to look at the governor's appointive powers within the total context. While the power to appoint is an obvious means of controlling subordinates, once the appointment is made the influence fades rapidly unless it is backed either by the use of power to remove or preferably by control over future appointments. Even when a governor can remove an official he is constrained by the wrangle which would result. It is a power to be used only as a last resort. Far more effective is control through the hope for reappointment or for advancement. Here lies the significance of political parties in state administration. For, while governors may come and go, a party organization has a memory which enables future governors to reward administrators for past services.

That governors may indeed expect to influence ambitious administrators is indicated in a study of Swinerton of the agency heads of six states.[8] He found that the more ambitious agency heads tended to view their function as aiding the governor in carrying out his program. Agency heads whose career goal was primarily to remain in that particular office tended to have less of a governor-oriented view of their function.

Party organization may modify our ratings in another respect. In our scale we have rated elective positions as those over which the governor is likely to have the least influence. This is true only to the extent that the individual does not owe his nomination and election to the governor. In a competitive state it is not at all unlikely that a governor or candidate for governor will be closely involved in the selection of his party's candidates for lesser state offices, and to the extent that they can ride his coattails they are as dependent on him as any formal appointee. Of course, to the extent that the lesser official develops independent electoral support, as we have already pointed out, the governor's influence is lessened. However, it is also likely that men who run for elective offices are sensitive to political protocol and will conflict with a governor only if they feel it will aid their political ambitions.

CONTROL OVER THE BUDGET

One important control over administrative agencies is the power of the purse. The power to give and withhold operating funds may transcend weaknesses in the appointive power. In general, the power is shared by the governor and the legislature, most states having placed the authority to prepare the budget in the hands of the governor. We can define the governor's strength again on a five-point scale according to the extent to which the budgetary authority originates with him.

5: Governor has the responsibility for preparing

[6] Samuel Krislov, "Constituency Versus Constitutionalism: The Desegregation Issue and Tensions and Aspirations of Southern Attorneys General," *Midwest Journal of Political Science*, Vol. III, (February 1959), pp. 75–92.

[7] Deil S. Wright, "Executive Leadership in State Administration," this book.

[8] E. Nelson Swinerton, "Ambition and American State Executives," *Midwest Journal of Political Science*, Vol. XII (November 1968), pp. 538–549.

the budget and shares it only with persons appointed directly by him

4: Governor has the responsibility but shares it either with a civil service appointee or an appointee of someone other than himself

3: Governor shares authority with legislature

2: Governor shares authority with another major elected official (no contemporary examples)

1: Governor prepares budget only as a member of a group, usually of other elected state officials or members of the legislature

As may be seen from Table 5, most states today give the main authority for budgetary preparation to the governor. Note also that diffuse control exists in many states. For example, it is common practice to "earmark" funds for particular purposes, such as gasoline taxes for highways. Then, too, many states finance special projects such as highways, bridges, and power resources through tolls and fees. Such devices provide the agencies concerned with an independent income, further reducing the governor's control.

THE VETO POWER

Finally the governor's formal strength may be defined by his power to veto bills passed by the legislature. While not strictly speaking a control over administration, it is a means by which a governor can prevent administrators from going over his head and obtaining support from the legislature. This is particularly true when the governor has the item veto or the power to veto a particular item of an appropriation without being forced to accept or reject the entire bill.

As in the case of budgetary powers the governors are typically strong with respect to the veto. Most

---

TABLE 5. The Governors' Budget Powers

Full Responsibility (5 points)*

Alabama	Maryland	Ohio
Alaska	Massachusetts	Oklahoma
Arizona	Michigan	Oregon
California	Minnesota	Pennsylvania
Delaware	Missouri	South Dakota
Georgia	Montana	Tennessee
Hawaii	Nevada	Utah
Idaho	New Hampshire	Vermont
Illinois	New Jersey	Virginia
Iowa	New Mexico	Washington
Kentucky	New York	Wisconsin
Maine	North Dakota	Wyoming

Shares with a Civil Service Appointee or with Person Appointed by Someone Else (4 points)*

Colorado	Louisiana	Rhode Island
Connecticut	Nebraska	
Kansas	North Carolina	

Shares Authority with Legislature (3 points)*

Arkansas

Shares With Another Popularly Elected Official (2 points)*

No example

Shares with Several Others with Independent Sources of Strength (1 point)*

Florida	South Carolina
Indiana	Texas
Mississippi	West Virginia

*The points are used for the construction of the General Power Index, Table 7.

Source: The Book of the States, 1968-1969, pp. 144-152.

TABLE 6. The Governors' Veto Powers

Very Strong (5 points)*: Item Veto Plus at Least 3/5 of Elected Members of Legislature to Override

Alaska	Louisiana	North Dakota
Arizona	Maryland	Ohio
California	Michigan	Oklahoma
Colorado	Minnesota	Pennsylvania
Delaware	Mississippi	Utah
Georgia	Missouri	Washington
Hawaii	Nebraska	Wyoming
Illinois	New Jersey	
Kansas	New York	

Strong (4 points)*: Item Veto Plus Majority of Elected Members of Legislature to Override

Alabama	Kentucky
Arkansas	Tennessee

Medium (3 points)*: Item Veto Plus Majority or More of Legislature Present to Override

Connecticut	Montana	South Dakota
Florida	New Mexico	Texas
Idaho	Oregon	Virginia
Massachusetts	South Carolina	Wisconsin

Weak (2 points)*: No Item Veto, but Special Majority Required to Override

Iowa	Nevada	Rhode Island
Maine	New Hampshire	Vermont

Weakest (1 point)*: No Item Veto and Simple Majority Required to Override, or No Veto At All

Indiana	North Carolina	West Virginia

*The points are used for the construction of the General Power Index, Table 7.

Source: The Book of the States, 1968-69, pp. 62-63.

enjoy an item veto which requires an extraordinary majority of the legislature to override. Some, however, lack such a power, and in some states either a majority of the total membership of legislature or even a simple majority of those present can override the veto. These provide us with a five-point scale of veto powers in the accompanying table.[9]

As in the case of all formal powers, the veto must be considered within the total political context. Despite the fact that he has no veto, the governor of North Carolina does not appear weaker in relation to the legislature than other southern governors. Most governors can dominate their legislatures on matters of policy because if the governor is weak in formal powers, the state legislatures are still weaker as instruments of policy leadership. Legislatures have only the barest capacity to provide any kind of oversight of the state administration. Frequently the legislative leadership itself is chosen by the governor, as in Tennessee, a fact which makes meaningless the presumed "weakness" of his veto power.[10]

A GENERAL INDEX OF THE GOVERNORS' FORMAL POWERS

To arrive at a general rating of the governors' formal powers we have combined the four measures of each governor's strength already presented: his tenure potential and his appointive, budgetary, and veto powers. The maximum possible rating is 20, found only in New York, Illinois, and Hawaii. The lowest rating is 7, found in Texas. The median score is 15. Although each measure is independent of the others, they appear to go together. Formal powers for the governor are cumulative and their adoption undoubtedly reflects similar, overall views of the governor's role.

A cursory examination of the general ratings shows that there is a relation between the size of the states and the formal strength of their governors. Texas is the only populous state where the governor's formal strength is low. All of the urban giants—New York, Illinois, California, Pennsylvania, and New Jersey—have ratings at the top. Indeed, the nine states with a formal power index of

19 and 20 contain almost 42 percent of the total population of the United States.

Undoubtedly, the many factors which account for the variations in population among the states account for the variations in their formal power index. Factors related to the size of the states relate to the power index in the same manner. Therefore, the higher the proportion of urban population in a state, the higher the formal power index.

The fact that the formal strength of the governor is positively associated with the size of the state suggests that, as the complexity of a state increases, the governor's need for explicit means of control over his administration also increases. We have already pointed out that there is not necessarily a relation between the formal devices for administrative control and the influence which the governor wields. Within the context of their own states the governors of Mississippi and North Dakota may have as much, if not more, influence as do the governors of New York and Illinois. A governor trying to oversee the spending of a $6 billion budget has a much harder task than one dealing with a budget of $150 million. The terms "state" and "governor" mask differences in administrative problems not unlike those which separate the small neighborhood dress shop from the larger department store.

Apart from differences in the size of the operation the government of the small rural state looms much larger on the economic horizon than that of the industrial state. An industrial, urbanized state has separate and sizable aggregates of wealth and population. The president of a major manufacturing concern, the head of a labor union, and the mayor of a metropolitan center can compete with a governor. On the other hand, in a state with no large cities and only minor industries there is no figure as important as the governor. Thus, if a governor of New York had to work with the administrative apparatus of Mississippi he would be helpless in competition with its varied interests. Yet it is a mistake to infer that the governor of Mississippi is helpless. The minor jobs, the contracts, and the patronage which a Mississippi governor dispenses provide him with the influence over legislators, administrators, and interest groups which his formal powers appear to deny him.[11] For a New

[9] For an earlier classification see F. W. Prescott, "The Executive Veto in the American States," *Western Political Quarterly*, Vol. III (January 1950), pp. 98–112.

[10] On the relationship of the governor to the Tennessee legislature, see John Wahlke *et al.*, *The Legislative System* (New York: John Wiley, 1962), pp. 56–59.

[11] On the Mississippi governor, see Highsaw, *op. cit.*, p. 9.

	Budget powers	Appointive powers	Tenure potential	Veto powers	Total index
New York	5	5	5	5	20
Illinois	5	5	5	5	20
Hawaii	5	5	5	5	20
California	5	5	5	4	19
Michigan	5	5	5	4	19
Minnesota	5	5	5	4	19
New Jersey	5	5	4	5	19
Pennsylvania	5	5	4	5	19
Maryland	5	5	4	5	19
Utah	5	5	5	3	18
Washington	5	5	5	3	18
Ohio	5	5	4	4	18
Massachusetts	5	3	5	5	18
Wyoming	5	5	5	2	17
Missouri	5	5	4	3	17
Alaska	5	5	4	3	17
Tennessee	5	5	3	5	17
Idaho	5	3	5	4	17
North Dakota	5	5	5	1	16
Kentucky	5	4	3	4	16
Virginia	5	3	3	5	16
Montana	5	3	5	3	16
Nebraska	4	5	4	3	16
Connecticut	4	3	5	4	16
Delaware	5	5	4	1	15
Oklahoma	5	5	4	1	15
Alabama	5	4	3	3	15
Wisconsin	5	3	5	2	15
Colorado	4	5	5	1	15
Louisiana	4	5	4	2	15
Georgia	5	5	3	1	14
Oregon	5	3	4	2	14
Nevada	5	2	5	2	14
Arizona	5	5	2	1	13
South Dakota	5	3	1	4	13
Maine	5	2	4	2	13
Vermont	5	2	2	4	13
Kansas	4	5	2	2	13
Arkansas	3	4	2	4	13
Iowa	5	2	2	3	12
New Hampshire	5	2	2	2	11
Rhode Island	4	2	2	3	11
New Mexico	5	3	1	1	10
North Carolina	4	2	3	1	10
Mississippi	1	5	3	1	10
Indiana	1	1	3	5	10
Florida	1	3	3	2	9
South Carolina	1	3	3	1	8
West Virginia	1	1	3	3	8
Texas	1	3	2	1	7

TABLE 7. A Combined Index of the Formal Powers of the Governors

TABLE 8. Governors' Power Index Related to Selected Social and Political Characteristics of the States

(a) Distribution of Total Population in U.S., 1960

Power index	No. of states	Percent of total population
18–20	13	52.3
16–17	11	12.0
13–15	15	15.9
7–12	11	19.8

(b) Distribution of States According to Percentage Urban, 1960

Power index	Over 75%	60–74%	45–59%	Under 45%
18–20	6	7	0	0
16–17	1	1	6	3
13–15	0	9	3	3
7–12	2	3	2	4

(c) Distribution of States According to Degree of Party Competition[a]

Power index	1st Quartile (most competitive)	2d Quartile	3d Quartile	4th Quartile (least competitive)
18–20	6	6	0	0
16–17	3	2	3	2
13–15	2	2	6	5
7–12	1	2	3	5

(d) Distribution of States According to Percentage of National Leaders Coming from Them[b] (1900–1958)

Power index	2.5% plus	1.0–2.1%	0.42–0.84%	0.0
18–20	8	3	1	0
16–17	2	3	2	3
13–15	0	2	7	6
7–12	3	3	2	3

[a]The measure of party competition is that in Richard I. Hofferbert, "Classification of American State Party Systems," *The Journal of Politics*, Vol. 26 (1964), pp. 550–567. Does not include Alaska and Hawaii.

[b]Distribution of sources of national leadership, J. A. Schlesinger, *Ambition and Politics: Political Careers in the United States* (Chicago: Rand McNally, 1966), p. 24.

York governor such patronage in a vast domain would be a crushing burden; he needs the order which formal, hierarchical controls help provide.[12] However, should the rural state governor obtain these controls he might well have an excess of power. Perhaps this explains the resistance of rural, particularly one-party rural, states to the arguments for administrative reform.

But there are also political factors to be considered. Political indices as well as the factors of size relate to the power index. The more highly competitive states tend to concentrate power in the hands of the governor. There is, too, a direct relation between the extent to which a state contributes to the national leadership corps (defined as presidential candidates and appointees to the cabinet and Supreme Court) and the formal power index. These political characteristics are, of course, also related to the size of the state and its degree of urbanism. Yet party competition may be the critical factor—the need for parties to make their mark in a competitive political situation. The principal aberrations from the graduation of power according to size are those states out of line in terms of competition as well. Thus, one-party Texas has a weak governor, while the highly competitive but thinly-populated mountain states of Utah, Montana, and Wyoming have strong governors.

[12]For a discussion of the difficulties faced by a New York governor in gaining control of that state's administration, see Clark D. Ahlberg and Daniel P. Moynihan, "Changing Governors—and Policies," this book.

THE GOVERNOR AND HIS
LEGISLATIVE PARTY

Sarah P. McCally

When the dust settles following the reapportionment upheavals, the traditional problems of legislative policy-making will remain. This process is divided between the governor and (with due respect to Nebraska) the two legislative houses, with the governor generally taking the lead. A governor represents the totality of interests within his party. No single legislator or faction represents as wide a variety of interests as the governor. The governor proposes and vetoes and normally plays an even greater legislative role in state government than the President in the national government because of the infrequent sessions, low seniority, lack of statewide influence or prestige, and inadequate staff of the legislators. The governor's legislation is geared to please his statewide constituency and, depending largely upon his degree of control over his party, is passed, modified, or rejected.

What affects the ability of the governor to control his legislative party is a question seldom asked and rarely investigated except by the harassed occupant of the executive mansion. This is surprising, since the definition of party responsibility is closely related to executive control. By common agreement, a definition of party responsibility would include the ability of the party to control nominations, to present a united front in the election and thereafter to discipline the legislators to uphold the program of the executive in order to make a good record for the next election.[1]

Those who investigate the behavior of legislative parties in the interest of party responsibility equate the latter phenomenon with party voting loyalty. The loyalty rate of legislators on party votes is not the same animal as their degree of support of administration bills. Executive request legislation has received little attention from scholars. We will set this distinction aside for the moment in order to examine the factors which have been claimed to cause party responsibility or voting loyalty, as it has been defined for research purposes. The two characteristics of interparty conflict and intraparty cohesion in legislative situations are the major conditions for party responsibility as recently restated by Thomas A. Flinn.[2]

If interparty conflict means that the governor's party has a reasonable chance of obtaining a working majority of the legislature, this variable has immediate surface appeal as a condition for gubernatorial control. With the resources at his disposal, a governor can forge party agreement on legislation which is vital to his program. He will be disadvantaged if his party has a permanent minority position in the legislature, for he will have to use his resources to bargain with the opposition. If he has an overwhelming percentage of seats in the legislature he may be unable to control rival factions. It is the expressed hope of proponents of reapportionment that governors with new majority parties will bring about promised reforms; but it is doubtful that the possession of a majority in a competitive legislature guarantees that the governor's program will be passed. Enough exceptions come to mind to cast suspicion on this as a controlling variable. His success in statewide competition for the governorship may play a part in his influence over his legislative party.

Intraparty cohesion indicates unity which can be forged either by power resources or by ideological agreement. Students of legislative voting loyalty commonly assume that cohesion results from similarity of districts within a party's legislative contingent. If legislators from similar districts vote alike because they have the same interests to defend, then the most unified party would be one in which the districts were most similar. From the governor's point of view, the most loyal legislators would come from districts which reflect the characteristics of his statewide constituency. Yet one need not dig too far into the study of power structures to discover that they are not necessarily fed by ideological agreement. Organizational rivalries, personal ambitions or sidepayments need not follow demographic differences. Reapportionment will bring about increased suburban representation within both parties, but new demands, rather than increased cohesion, may result from suburban fac-

Source: Reprinted by permission from the *American Political Science Review*, Vol. 60 (December 1966), pp. 923–942.

[1] Committee on Political Parties, American Political Science Association, "Toward a More Responsible Two-Party System," *American Political Science Review*, Vol. 44 (September 1950), Supplement.

[2] Thomas A. Flinn, "Party Responsibility in the States: Some Causal Factors," *American Political Science Review*, Vol. 58 (March 1964), p. 60.

tions with increased legislative voting strength to use at the bargaining table.

The discussion to this point has been intended to show that satisfactory operational definitions of competition and cohesion must be formulated before these concepts can be used to test the governor's control over his legislative party. A review of the research related to these concepts may aid the quest for accuracy of definition.

COMPETITION AND COHESION: PREVIOUS RESEARCH

There have been several probes in the areas of party competition and cohesion and their effect on legislative voting behavior. Malcolm Jewell compared several competitive states with respect to the degree of voting loyalty with the parties, using all the roll-call votes in a session.[3] His findings do not confirm the hypothesis that party competition for control of the legislature can of itself explain party voting loyalty. Furthermore, since party voting loyalty did not vary with the degree of statewide competition for governor, this variable was also rejected as a meaningful explanation. Since neither statewide competition nor legislative competition could explain the voting behavior he witnessed, Jewell turned to intraparty cohesion for an explanation. He advanced the proposition that there is more ideological cohesion within the parties of urban states because he discovered a higher degree of party loyalty in urban than in rural states. Jewell did not consider the strength of the state party organization as a factor in legislative voting loyalty.

It was Duane Lockard's major thesis that close party competition at the state level produces party voting loyalty in the legislature. However, the connecting link in this causal chain is party organizational strength.[4] Lockard comes closer than Jewell to affirming the party-responsibility school's two major conditions of party competition and party cohesion. Jewell and Lockard agree on the measurement of party competition either as a statewide vote for governor or President or as competition for a legislative majority but disagree over its effect on legislative voting loyalty. Lockard claims that competition produces cohesion which in turn produces voting loyalty. Jewell finds no direct correlation between competition and loyalty although he states that a certain type of competition—urban-rural competition—produces ideological cohesion followed by voting loyalty within the parties. The two writers disagree on the measurement of cohesion, one defining it as party organizational strength, the other as ideological agreement, but both claim it influences voting loyalty.

A different research approach, which tends to reaffirm the importance of electoral competition and organizational cohesion, is that of Wahlke and his associates, who interviewed legislators in four states in an attempt to determine the influence of many outside variables affecting their roles.[5] They found that political career patterns and orientations are likely to be shaped by the degree of competition in a given system. Also, the varying degrees of the particular party's organizational strength and morale may be an important factor affecting the legislators' career patterns and orientations. The authors state that party organizational strength is probably related to degree of competition between the parties, but, as the case of California Democrats in one direction and Ohio Democrats in another direction indicated, it may also operate independently of it. Another major determinant of legislative behavior was the relative strength of the majority and minority with the legislature.

---

[3] Malcolm E. Jewell, "Party Voting in American State Legislatures," *American Political Science Review*, Vol. 49 (September 1955), pp. 773–791. Jewell chose eight competitive states and limited his research to sessions in which the party balance in the legislature was reasonably close, for he assumed that there would be less party voting even in strong two-party states during the years of one-sided legislative control. He discovered, however, that the three states with the highest levels of party loyalty had long records of Republican legislative control, with only a few Democratic years, while the Democrats frequently held large legislative minorities and (except in Pennsylvania) won control of the governorship. In the states with a closer balance between the parties in the legislature, a lower level of party unity was found. He used all the roll-call votes in a session and paid no attention to their sponsorship.

[4] W. Duane Lockard, *New England State Politics* (Princeton: Princeton University Press, 1959). In the then essentially noncompetitive states of New Hampshire, Maine, and Vermont, policy-making was primarily a function of the dominant party in the legislature. The factions within this party, both inside and outside the legislature, determined the fate of legislation. In the competitive states of Massachusetts, Connecticut, and Rhode Island, Lockard discovered considerable discipline in both legislative parties. He used votes on which there was disagreement between the parties.

[5] John C. Wahlke *et al.*, *The Legislative System* (New York: John Wiley, 1962).

Another area of research assumes that legislative voting behavior is a result of ideological cohesion brought about by the economic composition of the districts represented by the individual legislators. The more alike the districts are within each party, the more ideological cohesion and therefore voting agreement exists. On the other hand, the theory goes, the more diverse the districts within the party, the more disunity because of lack of ideological agreement.[6] Thomas Flinn tested this theory of party unity based on similarity of district in the Ohio Assembly of 1949 and 1959. He concluded that differing constituencies do not give rise to intraparty voting disagreement and that policy differences between the parties are not due to differences in the composition of the legislative parties in terms of constituencies represented.[7]

This theory of constituency influence has been used with more success in explaining the deviant members of the legislative party. It cannot account for average party loyalty, but it can account for a few of the deviant cases. Duncan MacRae attempted to measure the comparative effectiveness of party power and constituency interest over the roll-call voting of the individual legislator on issues chosen to reflect class differences.[8] Both Thomas R. Dye and Thomas A. Flinn give some support to the theory that constituency economic pressures affect the extremes in party loyalty.[9]

The degree of competition in a constituency measured singly or in combination with economic characteristics has been offered as an additional variable affecting the extremes in legislative voting loyalty. It is assumed that members with comfortable margins are a more loyal group than those from competitive districts because they are freed from constituency pressures and hence can vote the party line without fear of voter retribution. On the other hand, the legislators with close races will reflect the interests of their constituencies—be they for or against the party line. Thus the most deviant legislators are to be found from competitive atypical districts. The findings are not conclusive and differences exist with respect to the variables between parties, between legislative bodies and between sessions.[10]

The study of the deviant members of a state legislative party suffers from lack of justification. No one in the party-responsibility school would require a "party line" vote on all issues on which the majority of both parties are opposed. Taking all votes on which there is substantial disagreement may not be a true test of party responsibility. It does not separate the votes which the administration wants passed from those on which the administration has taken a hands-off policy. The leadership of each party tolerates deviations in party voting as long as the necessary vote is achieved.

The studies reviewed so far confirm the warning that the evidence sifted governs the results achieved. Three definitions of competition have been used: state, legislative, and constituency, with conflicting results. Three definitions of intraparty cohesion have been used: structural, statewide ideological, and similar-constituency. The roll calls chosen to test the theories have ranged from the total number to those which represent party conflict to those which are of economic importance. The reason for this may be that there has not been an operational definition of party responsibility upon which researchers can agree. With respect to legislative policy-making, party responsibility can be defined as the ability of the governor

---

[6]David R. Derge, "Metropolitan and Outstate Alignments in Illinois and Missouri Legislative Delegations," *American Political Science Review*, Vol. 52 (December 1958), pp. 1051–1065. Since this study, it has been acknowledged that party is a more important determinant than rural-urban conflict, and the subsequent studies have dealt with the presumed relationship between similarity of district and degree of ideological cohesion within the party contingent.

[7]Flinn, *op cit.*, p. 63.

[8]Duncan MacRae, "The Relationship Between Roll Call Votes and Constituencies in Massachusetts," *American Political Science Review*, Vol. 46 (December 1952), pp. 1046–1055. MacRae maintained that those legislators who come from districts which are most typical of their parties tend to show highest party loyalty on roll calls. Those who come from districts atypical of their party tend to cross party lines more often. We do not know whether the roll calls selected by MacRae were administration-supported measures or whether deviations were sizable enough to prevent passage.

[9]Thomas R. Dye, "A Comparison of Constituency Influences in the Upper and Lower Chambers of a State Legislature," *Western Political Quarterly*, Vol. 14 (June 1961), pp. 473–481; Flinn, *op cit.*, pp. 64–69. Both

writers used all party opposition votes whether or not the issues were economic. Dye measured voting deviation and Flinn measured voting support.

[10]MacRae, *op. cit.*; Dye, *op. cit.*, p. 477; and Samuel C. Patterson, "The Role of the Deviant in the State Legislative System: The Wisconsin Assembly," *The Western Political Quarterly*, Vol. 14 (June 1961), pp. 460–472.

to command enough votes in the legislature to pass his legislation. The major question to be asked is: What affects the ability of the governor to get his legislation passed?

THE USE OF VETO VOTES TO MEASURE GUBERNATORIAL INFLUENCE

Because we are interested in measuring the influence of the governor in the legislative process, two traditional methods of identifying significant partisan roll calls are not appropriate. Neither Lowell's party vote nor Rice's index of likeness [11] takes into consideration the raw number of votes necessary to pass legislation. Both indices assume that partisan activity can be identified by comparing the percentage of members of each party (or group) who agree or disagree. But the passing of legislation is not purely mechanical. The proponents do not have unlimited favors to pass out to supporters. Because of this they make marginal calculations, procuring enough votes to pass their measure, but no unnecessary surplus. Most bills require for passage a majority of those voting. If the party of the sponsors of legislation has an overwhelming percentage of the legislature (80 percent, for example), the bill needs the affirmative vote of only 63 percent of their party members in order to pass. If the other party is unanimous in opposition, the index of likeness would approximate 40 percent. This is far from complete disagreement, and those looking for roll calls which exhibit partisanship might disregard it entirely. However, a great deal of partisanship was present. Does a party which needs only 63 percent of its members to pass legislation and gets it show any less partisan activity than a party which needs and gets 100 percent?

William H. Riker developed an index of significance which *does* take into consideration the minimum votes necessary for victory on a roll call; [12]

but it gives less indication of partisan activity than the previous two indices, and in fact completely obscures party. A vote of 50–50 could mean two highly disciplined parties, two widely split parties, or one split majority party and a cohesive minority party.

The above three measures will have to be discarded as not appropriate for our use. They are not valid indicators of party activity except in legislatures where the party split is approximately 50–50; and they cannot distinguish between trivial and important legislation except in a mechanistic way.

We want to test the governor's influence over his party on measures which are important to him. The most satisfactory way would be to test the influence of the governor on administration bills— those bills which the governor wants passed. This would provide the best test of the party in power— the ability to get its program passed. The governor's position is clear. If the administration bills could be identified, the roll-call votes on this legislation would provide a clear indication of the behavior of the parties on issues of major importance. David Truman used this type of legislation for the Eighty-first Congress. He automatically included votes on sustaining presidential vetoes, votes on presidential reorganization plans, and (in the Senate) votes on the confirmation of presidential nominations and the ratification of treaties. Other votes were included if the public record revealed an express presidential preference concerning the precise content at stake in the vote. [13]

The identification of governor's program bills for the seven legislative sessions for each state during the period (1946–60) proved to be too difficult. In the attempt, the Legislative Reference Bureaus of 35 northern states were contacted and asked to send lists of administration bills for each session. With the exception of Pennsylvania, Nevada, Wisconsin, and Oregon, for which lists of administration bills for some sessions were sent, the only help came in the form of suggested procedures to be used in identifying the administration bills. In all of the states, the governor presents a program message to the legislature in which he outlines the substance of the program he wants passed for the session. This is usually translated into administration bills which are often introduced by the gover-

[11] A. Lawrence Lowell, "The Influence of Party upon Legislation in England and America," *Annual Report of The American Historical Association for 1901*, Vol. I (Washington: American Historical Association, 1902), p. 323; and Stuart Rice, *Quantitative Methods in Politics* (New York: Knopf, 1928), pp. 209–211.

[12] William H. Riker, "A Method for Determining the Significance of Roll Calls in Voting Bodies," in John C. Wahlke and Heinz Eulau (eds.), *Legislative Behavior* (New York: Free Press, 1959), pp. 377–384. He defined the most significant roll call as one in which (1) all members vote, and (2) the difference between the minority and the majority is the minimum possible under the voting rules.

[13] David B. Truman, *The Congressional Party* (New York: John Wiley, 1959), p. 327.

nor's party leaders in the house or senate or by legislators whom the governor may specify. In the states in which this is an ironclad custom, the name of the party floor leader attached to a bill may identify it as an administration bill. This is the case in Connecticut, Illinois, Indiana, Massachusetts, New York, and West Virginia. For the bulk of the states, however, no foolproof procedures exist for the identification of program bills.[14]

As a substitute for votes on administration bills, votes on vetoes were used because, as with administration bills, (1) the position of the governor is clearly stated and (2) the governor's party leaders would exert maximum influence to see that the veto was sustained. The veto calls for a vote of confidence in the governor. In most cases he uses it sparingly, more as a threat than an actuality, so that when a veto does come before the legislature, the greatest amount of party activity attends it.

One might question why a governor who had considerable influence in his legislative majority would ever allow unapproved legislation to slip through. In this regard, it must be remembered that the governor recommends for passage only a small amount of the total legislative product. If offensive legislation is called to his attention, he may threaten to veto it if passed and must do so enough to give credibility to his threats. Cases have arisen in which the governor vetoed a bill in his program because it was altered substantially in the legislative process. Furthermore, it is possible for the minority party to gain enough support to pass a bill on which the governor has taken no stand, whereupon the governor might send it back with a veto message if it is not in his conception of the "public interest."[15]

Table 1 gives the number and substance of vetoes used in the 58 house sessions on which this research rests.[16] These sessions are broken down by percent of seats of the governor's party. The Democratic sessions follow a pattern we would expect. There are more vetoes when a party has a hopeless minority position than when it has 40 to 70 percent of the legislature. There are also more vetoes when the party has an overwhelming percent of the legislature, and therefore may have less control over its own members. The Republicans, however, show the reverse of the expected. We cannot say, therefore, that the number or substance of the vetoes are related in any significant degree to the party balance in the legislature. It is interesting to note that the largest number of vetoes on taxation come from Democratic governors whose legislative parties are hopeless minorities.

After choosing veto votes as the most efficient indicators of the influence of the governor, we need a measure which will indicate the degree to which his party supported him on these issues. Rice's index of cohesion is not suitable because it is not directional.[17] It does not indicate whether the majority supported or opposed the governor. It may be that the party was more cohesive in opposition to the governor than in support. In this

must be remembered that the governor vetoes frivolous as well as major substantive legislation. For instance, the one veto of the late Governor Stevenson which was put to a roll-call vote in the Illinois Senate in 1949 was S.B. No. 93, an act to provide protection to insectivorous birds by restraining cats. (Illinois, *Journal of the Senate*, 1949, p. 541). In the following session of 1951, on the other hand, the one veto roll call was on S.B. No. 102, an act to protect against subversive activities. (Illinois, *Journal of the Senate*, 1951, pp. 1946–50). Regardless of the substance of the veto, the roll-call vote puts on record the degree of party support the governor can muster. Not all veto votes are taken by roll call, but the assumption is that most votes of real controversy are recorded in this way.

[16] As an additional test of the ability of a governor to have his veto upheld against opposition, the following screening procedure was used: (1) 80 percent or more of the legislature must vote on the veto; and (2) There must be 10 percent or more of those voting in disagreement. We hoped in this way to reject low-interest, low-tension vetoes. A large percentage of these are technical vetoes. In California, for instance, this method cut 185 out of 189 roll-call votes in the seven sessions studied. It seems logical that in a state where so little party voting exists, a governor's veto may be the only check on hasty and ill-advised legislation.

[17] Rice, *op. cit.*, pp. 208–209.

[14] As a second try, all the governors from 1946 to 1960 were contacted and asked for lists of program bills from their personal files. In all, 101 governors were contacted and replies were received from 72. Only one governor had such a list: Governor Williams of Michigan sent his worksheet "Priority Points of Democratic Legislators and Governor Williams" for 1960. A considerable amount of strategy was admitted by some governors. Some declared the necessity of including certain items in a message as an aid to secure the enactment of legislation more seriously sought. Capital newspapers could provide the type of information needed. Usually capitol reporters either know specifically what measures are aimed at enacting part of the governor's program or make their own evaluations in covering the legislative session.

[15] The substantive importance of these vetoes varies. It

TABLE 1. Number and Substance of Vetoes According to Percent of
Seats of the Governor's Party in 58 House Sessions[a]

Percent of Seats	Class I Party Interest[b]	Class II Substantive	Class III Taxation	Class IV Procedural	Total	No. of Sessions	Average Per Session
			Democratic				
0–39.9	3	22	11	25	61	14	4.4
40–54.9	1	7	2	0	10	5	2.0
55–69.9	1	3	0	8	12	7	1.7
70–	2	3	1	0	6	2	3.0
Totals	7	35	14	33	89	28	
			Republican				
0–39.9	2	1	1	3	7	4	1.8
40–54.9	2	5	1	6	14	4	3.5
55–69.9	0	14	5	14	33	9	3.7
70–	1	25	1	10	37	13	2.8
Totals	5	45	8	33	91	30	

[a]The states and number of sessions are: Arizona (2), Calif. (1), Colorado (1), Conn. (1), Delaware (1), Idaho (2), Illinois (1), Indiana (3), Iowa (2), Kansas (3), Maine (3), Maryland (2), Mass. (6), Mich. (5), Montana (1), Nevada (1), N. H. (2), N. Y. (1), N. D. (1), Ohio (6), Oregon (2), R. I. (2), S. D. (1), Utah (1), Wisc. (6), Wyo.(1).

[b]The four categories of vetoes involved the following issues:

Class I   Party interest
    Elections and reapportionment
    Appointments
    Legislative procedure and organization
Class II   Substantive
    Fish and game laws (conservation)
    Labor
    Appropriations for other than those listed
    Veterans affairs
    Welfare, health, education
    Business regulation
Class III   Taxation
Class IV   Procedural
    Civil service
    State administration
    Local administration
    Judicial and legal

case the index would be misleading. For instance, in the Arizona House session of 1949, the majority Democrats voted 39 to 8 to override the governor's veto on H.B. No. 71, which would have removed the supervision of real estate from the state.[18] The percent of cohesion is 83. (If this is converted to a scale of 0–100, the index of cohesion becomes 66.)

INDEX OF ADMINISTRATION SUPPORT
What we need for our purposes is an *index of administration support* which measures the degree

to which the governor's party members support him. For a single roll call, the index is obtained by dividing the number of votes cast by the party members who voted for the governor by the total number of party members who voted. When several vetoes were used, the average index was the arithmetic mean of the indices derived for the various roll calls in the session. David Truman used this type of measure for the Eighty-first Congress.[19] Using the example from Arizona men-

[18]Arizona, *Journal of the House of Representatives*, 1949, p. 638.

[19]Truman, *op. cit.*, p. 60. Truman used the arithmetical mean of the legislators' *individual* administration support indices as the average index for the session.

tioned above, the index of administration support would be 17.

INDEX OF ADMINISTRATION SUCCESS

Neither the index of cohesion nor the index of administration support indicates whether the governor was successful in obtaining enough votes from his party to win. If he has an overwhelming percentage of the legislature, the number of votes necessary to win does not form a large percent of his party. An index of cohesion or administration support takes no account of the percentage of the governor's party which must support him in order to pass his legislation. For instance, in the Iowa House session of 1953, the majority Republicans had an index of cohesion of .59 and an index of administration support of .41 on a veto.[20] Neither figure would make one suspect that the governor was in good shape, but the governor needed only 36 percent of his party to uphold his veto, and thus was comfortably over his margin. The *index of success* is obtained by dividing the percent of those who voted in favor of the governor by the percent of his party votes he needed in order to uphold his legislation. One-third-plus-one of those elected is the usual requirement for upholding the veto. The index of success is a ratio of percents instead of votes because when the governor's party had fewer than 34 percent of the seats in the legislature, it was assigned 100 as the requirement on the minority party. One maverick makes it impossible for the governor to make his quota. The arithmetic mean of the individual indices for success was used in order to obtain an average index for a session.

I substituted the veto votes for votes on administration bills to make it possible to use many more sessions in my analysis. I assumed that the governor would receive the same support on vetoes that he would receive on administration bills. Table 2 compares the index of support for veto votes with the same index applied to votes on administration bills for seven state sessions for which lists of program bills had been supplied by the governors or methods of identification of program bills had been related. In all cases except two, the program bills received a higher index of support than the veto bills. The two sets of support indices have a correlation of 7.1. The first guess might be that passing program legislation is more important to a governor than having his vetoes upheld. The second guess might be that the animosities which develop over program legislation might be ironed out by the time the vote reaches the floor, whereas a veto comes to the house directly in the form of a message from the governor, and the anger of those who voted for the measure may not have been assuaged.

If our assumption is correct that a governor does not use his limited supply of favors to obtain more votes than he needs, it is logical for him to receive a different degree of support for roll calls on vetoes for which he needs only 34 percent of the house than for program legislation for which he needs 50 percent of the house. On this basis, we would expect the index of success to be about the same for the governor for both sets of votes. The index of success was previously defined as the ratio of the percent he needed to pass (or uphold) his bills (or vetoes) to the percent he received. If the governor has the influence and resources to obtain what he needs, and if he calculates at the margins, he should be equally successful with program bills as with veto votes. Comparing the two indices of success state by state, we note that the governor was more successful with the veto than with program legislation in four sessions. In only two sessions, however, did he receive over 100 percent on one success index and under 100 percent on the other. In both cases his success was well over 90 percent on the other index. The index of success on vetoes can be fairly confidently used to indicate the governor's success on program legislation. The correlation between the two indices is .63. The index of success has the disadvantage of requiring 100 percent of any legislative party which does not have the required minimum number of seats for victory. This imposes a hard task on a hopeless minority party. Seldom is even the most cohesive party unanimous. One or two mavericks carry more negative weight in a minority or bare majority party than in a party which has votes to spare. Although the index of success would seem to be a better measure of gubernatorial influence than the index of support, it does not do as reliable a job of predicting the comparative influence of the governor on program bills and vetoes on a session-by-session basis. This may be due to the inaccuracy of measurement just mentioned.

[20] Iowa, *Journal of the House of Representatives*, 1953, p. 1234 (H. B. 123, relating to exemptions for debts).

TABLE 2. Comparison of Roll-Call Votes on Program Bills and Vetoes with Respect to
Indices of Administration Support and Success for Seven House Sessions[a]

State, Session (Party, % Seats)	Mean Index of Support	Percent of Party Needed[b]	Mean Index of Success	Mean Index of Cohesion[c]	No. of Roll Calls
Connecticut, 1955 Democratic, 33%					
Program	94.6	100.0	94.6	94.6	2
Vetoes	89.4	100.0	89.4	89.4	2
Wisconsin, 1957 Republican, 67%					
Program	80.5	75.9	106.0	83.7	8
Vetoes	68.4	50.8	135.0	73.1	12
Oregon, 1959 Republican, 45%					
Program	72.2	100.0	72.2	80.4	18
Vetoes	74.2	100.0	97.5	83.2	6
Nevada, 1953 Republican, 38%					
Program	68.7	100.0	68.7	81.2	7
Vetoes	55.6	97.7	56.9	69.8	3
Wisconsin, 1951 Republican, 76%					
Program	65.6	67.5	97.2	97.2	6
Vetoes	52.3	46.2	113.0	52.3	1
Massachusetts, 1959 Democratic, 60%					
Program	75.7	82.5	91.8	84.0	8
Vetoes	40.2	54.1	74.0	62.7	12
Massachusetts, 1957 Democratic, 55%					
Program	84.9	91.0	93.3	84.9	10
Vetoes	89.7	58.7	153.0	89.7	1

[a]Program bills were "screened" in the same way as vetoes.

[b]States differ with respect to the percentage of votes needed to uphold vetoes. In some states, the one-third required is based on total membership; in others, on those present. In Connecticut, a majority present could uphold the veto. (As of 1965, one-third of the members are needed to uphold).

[c]This is the percent of those voting who took the majority position on roll calls. It is not converted to a scale of 0–100.

The index of cohension was given for comparative purposes only. Note that in Nevada 1953, in
Wisconsin 1951, and in Massachusetts 1959, the
party was more cohesive in opposition to the governor than in support. When the states are compared, as they will be in the rest of this study, it is
more important to know that the governor was
135 percent successful on a veto than that he received 68.4 percent of his party. In Wisconsin in
1957, the 68.4 percent meant that the governor
was 135 percent successful, whereas in Nevada
in 1953, the governor received 68.7 percent of
his party on program legislation and was only
68.7 percent successful.

SOME CORRELATES OF GUBERNATORIAL INFLUENCE

Because there is so little agreement as to the appropriate measures to be used for electoral competition or intraparty cohesion, several indicators of
each concept were used in the initial analysis.[21]

[21]With respect to measuring interparty competition
see: Robert I. Golembiewski, "A taxonomic Approach to
State Political Party Strength, I," *Western Political Quar-
terly*, Vol. 11 (September 1958), pp. 499; V. O. Key, Jr.,
American State Politics: An Introduction (New York:
Knopf, 1956), p. 98; Austin Ranney and Willmoore
Kendall, "The American Party Systems," *American
Political Science Review*, Vol. 48 (June 1954), 477–
485; Coleman B. Ransone, *The Office of Governor*

This procedure has been suggested recently by Richard F. Curtis and Elton F. Jackson.[22] The use of multiple indicators is called for when the researcher has definite theoretical concepts which he wishes to relate but for which he is unable to obtain or defend "single, unambiguous, direct, operational definitions."[23] Examining the effects of several indicators on gubernatorial influence will postpone the choices among them until the individual associations have been observed.

A survey was made of the vetoes in the entire universe of 476 legislative sessions held in 34 states outside the South during the period 1946–60.[24] All the senate and house sessions (76 house sessions; 64 senate sessions) in which there were one or more veto roll calls were used in the research. The vetoes were, of course, subject to the screening procedure described in footnote 16. Altogether, 525 votes were used.[25]

_____

in the United States (University, Ala.: University of Alabama Press, 1956), pp. 12–94; Joseph A. Schlesinger, "The Structure of Competition For Office in the American States," *Behavioral Science*, Vol. 5 (July 1960), pp. 197–210; and William H. Standing and James A. Robinson, "Inter-Party Competition and Primary Contesting: The Case of Indiana," *American Political Science Review*, Vol. 52 (December 1958), pp. 1066–1077. For measures of party cohesion based on primary voting see: V. O. Key, *op. cit.*, pp. 109–118; and Joseph A. Schlesinger, *How They Became Governor* (East Lansing: Governmental Research Bureau, Michigan State University, 1957), p. 27.

[22] Richard F. Curtis and Elton F. Jackson, "Multiple Indicators in Survey Research," *American Journal of Sociology*, Vol. 68 (September 1962), pp. 195–204.

[23] *Ibid.*, p. 195.

[24] The eleven southern states were not included because they did not offer sufficient two-party competition to be directly comparable with the northern states. Nebraska and Minnesota were excluded because their legislatures are elected on a nonpartisan basis. New Mexico did not publish a record of the legislative proceedings during this period.

[25] The following information was collected for the 140 legislative sessions and processed on an IBM 709 Computer.

I. Independent Variables
  A. Electoral Competition
    1. The mean percent of the vote for the seven elections preceding the session won by the governor's party.
    2. The percent of the preceding seven elections won by the governor's party.
    3. The percent of alternation of control of office between the parties for the preceding seven elections.
    4. The governor's of the presession vote.

Table 3 gives the results for 58 house sessions which followed a gubernatorial election. It seemed reasonable to assume that a governor might have more control over legislators elected concurrently, rather than in midterm, or on staggered terms as in many senates. The results of the product-moment correlations between the variables of competition, party structure and legislative behavior run contrary to the expectations of previous hypotheses and offer the following findings of speculative interest.

(1) State-wide electoral competition does not appear to be a major explanatory factor of legislative discipline. In only three cases do we get a correlation higher than .30 between electoral competition and legislative behavior, and two of these correlations are not in the anticipated direction. If competition produces disciplined parties, as the party-responsibility theorists suggest, we should expect a negative correlation between percent of the electoral vote and amount of support and success. The mean percent of the electoral vote over the past seven elections is more highly correlated with the degree of support and success of the governor than are the other measures of competition, and in the anticipated direction. A plausible explanation is that the correlation is caused by the lack of discipline of traditional majority parties over the previous 14 to 28 years.

_____

    5. The governor's percent of the postsession vote.
  B. Party Structure
    1. The governor's percent of the total primary vote both presession and postsession.
    2. The governor's "winning percentage" of the highest two primary candidates both presession and postsession (as in Joseph A. Schlesinger, *loc. cit.*).
    3. The governor's percent of the highest two primary candidates both presession and postsession.
  C. Control of the Legislature
    1. Percent of seats held by the governor's party.
    2. Absolute number of seats held by the governor's party.
    3. Average percent of the seats held by the governor's party over the previous six sessions.
II. Dependent Variables
  A. Index of support
  B. Index of success
  C. Index of cohesion. (This is based on a scale of 50–100. It is not converted to a scale of 0–100.)

TABLE 3. Product-Moment Correlations Between Certain Variables of Party Competition and Structure and Legislative Behavior Variables of Support, Success, and Cohesion Within the Governor's Legislative Party in 58 House Sessions[a]

Measures of Party Competition and Structure	Index of Support		Index of Success		Index of Cohesion	
Electoral vote						
Mean percent of gubernatorial vote– 7 elections	$-.38^b$		$-.15^b$		$-.23^b$	
Percent of elections won by governor's party	$-.28$		$.26$		$-.25$	
Percent of alternation	$-.02$		$-.22$		$-.05$	
Percent of presession vote	$-.05$		$.25$		$-.02$	
	Gov.	Party[c]	Gov.	Party[c]	Gov.	Party[c]
Percent of postsession vote	.27	.06	.22	.29	.18	$-.05$
Over 50%	*.32	$-.11$	*.36	.20	.23	$-.28$
Under 50%	$-.19$	.03	$-.02$	.14	$-.09$	$-.03$
Primary vote						
Before: governor's % of total	.26		.02		.15	
Winning % of highest two	.25		.02		.16	
% of highest two	.25		.01		.17	
Incumbent	.39		$-.03$		.32	
Nonincumbent	.16		.13		.07	
After: Governor's % of total	.60		.49		.17	
Winning % of highest two	.46		.37		.21	
% of highest two	.61		.49		.18	
After: Candidate's % of total	.54		.15		.36	
Winning % of highest two	.52		.27		.37	
% of highest two	.50		.13		.32	
Legislative seats						
% of seats–governor's party	$-.60$		.20		$-.49$	
Over 50%	$-.45$		$-.05$		$-.36$	
Under 50%	.09		.46		.10	
Absolute number of seats	$-.12$		.31		$-.15$	
Average percent six sessions	$-.55$		.22		$-.45$	

[a]These sessions are the same as those in Table 1.

[b]For all correlations higher than .30, $p \leq .05$ for a two-tailed test except for those correlations asterisked. For those, $p \leq .10$ for a two-tailed test. Correlations above .40 in magnitude are underlined for convenience.

[c]The vote for the post-session is the vote for the governor or for his replacement.

This modest negative correlation may indicate that, over a long period, lack of competition will produce lack of cohesion. Competition in any single election does not appear to produce cohesion. The gubernatorial election success of the governor following the legislative session is positively correlated with his support and success in the legislature. This may be an indication of a major effort on the part of the governor to consolidate his party for a decisive win. In the 14 year period within which the legislative sessions fall, the gubernatorial elections became more competitive. During that period in 24 of the 32 states outside the South the election results were within 45–55 percent. The eroding of the traditional majority party and the close competition which followed may have brought about the positive correlation between the legislative support and the electoral record of the governor, both indicative of his personal efforts. These correlations are not high, and do not support the theory that electoral competition produces legislative support or success due to the efforts of the governor to make a vote-getting record for the next election.

(2) Intraparty cohesion on the state level has a high positive correlation with the support and

success of the governor in the legislature. The highest correlations are obtained between the governor's primary percentage after the legislative session and the degree of loyalty he receives from his legislators during the session. The high correlation between outside party cohesion and legislative loyalty would seem to support the theory that the outside party organization generates discipline in the legislative party. The *direction* of this influence needs to be explained, since the legislative discipline predates the organizational cohesion. One would expect that the primary of an *incumbent* governor held before an election in which both he and the legislature ran concurrently would correlate as highly with legislative loyalty as his primary after the session was over. This expectation is based on the assumption that the strength of the governor's faction as measured by his ability to make a strong primary showing is reflected in his ability to induce his legislative party to back him. Surprisingly, this is not true. As Table 3 shows, even with incumbents it is the postsession primary which correlates most highly with support and success.

Correlation does not indicate causation, and we ponder whether it is the legislative success which affects primary results, or whether both indicators are part of a general control exercised by the governor. The latter hypothesis makes more intuitive sense. In that case the progression of events would start with the efforts of a governor to build support within his party, both electoral as well as legislative, to help him win the next primary and election. With his supply of rewards and punishments and his own ability and effort, he forges a coalition to stand by him at primary time. The degree of his success is measured both within the legislature and by the primary results. Additional evidence can be garnered to support this interpretation of the results. The correlations between party structure and primary voting for the three remaining categories of legislative sessions included in the study are presented in Table 4. They are even higher than those previously reported for the 58 house sessions. Of particular interest is the fact that the governor's success with his party increases as the election approaches. The senates and houses elected midway through the term of a four-year governor produce extremely high indices of success. The assumption that the governor wields his maximum influence over legislators elected concurrently with him appears to be in error. His influence grows as the time for election approaches. His strategy is oriented toward the next election, and the strength of the coalition he builds is measured both in legislative and primary support.

The governor's success in receiving the necessary votes to pass his legislation is a more personal matter than his degree of support. While the index of support has a correlation of well over .40 in most cases with the primary fortunes of the party's next candidate, the index of success was not correlated highly with the primary success of the party's candidate. Success is correlated with the strength of the individual governor, and not with the strength of the leadership faction of the party. It would appear that the strength of the leadership faction within the party has a definite relationship to legislative support, but that the personal efforts of an incumbent governor who plans to run again make the difference between support and success.

Comparison between the index of cohesion and those of support and success shows that cohesion is not as highly related to the governor's primary and election as the other variables. This is to be expected, since a party which was completely opposed to the governor would be assigned an index of 100 percent, as would a party which completely supported him. Cohesion does not measure the direction of loyalty within a party, but only the extent of agreement among its members.

Common sense also suggests that the percentage of seats a governor's party holds in the legislature would affect his support and success. Assuming that governors calculate at the margins and do not expend more rewards or punishments than necessary to gain support for their projects, we would expect a high negative correlation between the percentage of seats a governor has and the percentage of his party which supports him. This is confirmed by the statistics in Table 3. Fifty percent of the seats was used as a break-point to investigate this relationship further. Again the results show that the size of the governor's majority affects his support. If he has under 50 percent of the seats, there is little relationship—presumably the governor works to rally all of his party members behind him, or the

TABLE 4. Product-Moment Correlations Between Gubernatorial Primary Results and Support, Success, and Cohesion Within the Governor's Legislative Party for Designated Sessions [1]

Primary Vote	Index of Support[a]	Index of Success[a]	Index of Cohesion[a]
Forty-two Senates Elected Concurrently with the Governor[b]			
Before session:			
Governor's % of total	.23	.08	.08
Winning % of highest two	.24	.08	.12
% of highest two	.24	.08	.13
After session:			
Governor's % of total	.71	.48	.48
Winning % of highest two	.63	.48	.55
% of highest two	.67	.45	.46
After session:			
Candidate's % of total[e]	.40	.03	.26
Winning % of highest two	.40	.03	.28
% of highest two	.30	−.04	.19
Eighteen Houses Elected Midterm[c]			
Before session:			
Governor's % of total	.21	−.12	.12
Winning % of highest two	.21	−.12	.12
% of highest two	.19	−.15	.11
After session:			
Governor's % of total	.63*	.82	.69
Winning % of highest two	.32	.70	.42
% of highest two	.64*	.71	.67
After session:			
Candidate's % of total[e]	.39	.15	−.03
Winning % of highest two	.28	.16	.04
% of highest two	.36	.20	.05
Twenty-two Senates Elected Midterm[d]			
Before session:			
Governor's % of total	.08	−.20	−.13
Winning % of highest two	.24	.07	.12
% of highest two	.03	−.23	−.20
After session:			
Governor's % of total	.69	.89	.47*
Winning % of highest two	.56*	.86	.47*
% of highest two	.72	.85	.42*
After session:			
Candidate's % of total[e]	.51	.40	.19
Winning % of highest two	.47	.44	.17
% of highest two	.48	.41	.14

[a]Correlations above .40 in magnitude are underlined for convenience.

[b]For all correlations higher than .30, p≤.05 for a two-tailed test.

[c]For all correlations higher than .50, p≤.05 for a two-tailed test, except for those correlations asterisked. For those, p≤.10 for a two-tailed test.

[d]For all correlations higher than .50, p≤.05 for a two-tailed test except those asterisked. For those, p≤.10 for a two-tailed test. All correlations between .40 and .50 have p≤.10 for a two-tailed test except those asterisked. For those, p≤.20 for a two-tailed test.

[e]This is the party candidate, who may be either the governor or his replacement.

deviations which do occur do not show any consistent pattern. If he has over 50 percent, he does not work for as many votes and the correlation is negative. This finding is important to bear in mind when comparing different parties with respect to indices of cohesion or loyalty. Legislative voting is not a "rally-'round-the-flag-boys" type of support, but a carefully calculated operation in which energy is not expended unnecessarily to force conformity among party members whose votes are not needed to pass. Part of this strategy may be a planned pattern of deviations, in which those whose constituencies or philosophies make it uncomfortable for them to support certain measures are allowed independence. As the majority hovers close to the 50 percent level, however, deviations are not tolerated because every vote counts.

Before we assume that this strategy is crowned with accomplishment it is necessary to consider the factor of success. Success is the ratio of the percent of the party the governor received to what he needed. We would think that the more seats the governor had to spare, the more successful he would be. This is not the case. There is a low negative relationship between the number of seats over a majority and success. Apparently an excess of seats is not in the governor's favor. A more logical breakpoint might fall somewhere about 55 percent, with extra seats an advantage until then. Thereafter, the surplus may generate rivalries within the house that the governor cannot control. This finding may modify the total strategy assumption related above. The governor may be able to handle a modest majority, but when his party has an overwhelming majority, coalitions form against him which he cannot undermine by his traditional stock of rewards and punishments.

The absolute number of seats was correlated with the indices of support and success as a control over the assertion that it is the percentage of seats rather than the raw number of seats which affects the governor's support and success. The control proves this assertion to be true. The *success* of the governor is advantaged slightly by a larger numerical contingent in the legislature (the difference between .31 and .20). For instance, a governor with 36 percent of a 100-member legislature may have a harder time in obtaining the necessary one-third vote than a governor who has 36 percent of a 200-member legislature. The first

governor can tolerate two defectors and the second, four defectors. This advantage is not large, however, and percentage of seats remains a good indicator.

So far the legislative behavior of both parties has been grouped together. Table 5 affords a comparison between the two parties. The major reason for the differences can be laid to the larger majorities which the Republicans traditionally hold in these legislatures.[26] The mean scores for the 3 types of legislative competition for the 58 sessions are:

	Republicans	Democrats
Percent of seats of governor's party	67	46
Absolute number of seats	83	58
Average percent for six sessions	64	39

This explains why the mean index of support for the Republican Party is lower. The Republicans do not need as many votes to pass legislation. It was necessary for the Democrats to mobilize all of their party members to sustain a veto 40 percent of the time while the Republicans needed unanimity only 14 percent of the time. Thus there was no spread over 100 percent success to distinguish one particularly successful Democratic governor from another. The measure of success makes the Democratic party appear less loyal than the Republican, but this is an accidental and misleading by-product of the method. We proceed with the assumption that the Democratic party would behave the same as the Republican with respect to success *given the same opportunities.*

A MODEL OF GUBERNATORIAL INFLUENCE
THE LINEAR REGRESSION MODEL

So far we cannot assess the relative weights to give to the independent variables of party structure and competition in explaining their effect on gubernatorial influence. If we assume a linear model for explaining a single dependent variable such as gubernatorial legislative success as the sum of separate effects from several independent variables

[26] An additional reason for the high negative correlations between the first two electoral variables and support for the Democrats is that there are high positive correlations between the electoral and house seat measures for the Democrats but not for the Republicans. Thus the variables for elections may be measuring the same phenomena as seats.

TABLE 5. Product-Moment Correlations Between Variables of Party Competition and Structure and Legislative Behavior Variables of Support, Success, and Cohesion Within the Governor's Legislative Party in 58 House Sessions by Political Party[a]

Measures of Party Competition and Structure	Index of Support		Index of Success		Index of Cohesion	
	Republicans M = 62.4	Democrats M = 80.5	Republicans M = 113.9	Democrats M = 100.2	Republicans M = 77.3	Democrats M = 88.0
Electoral vote						
Mean percent of gubernatorial vote—7 elections	−.03[b]	−.55[b]	.33[b]	−.12[b]	−.18[b]	−.18
Percent of the elections won by governor's party	.06	−.42	.41	−.05	−.19	−.15
Percent of alternation	−.28	.11	−.45	.11	.06	−.20
Percent of the presession vote	−.24	.11	.21	.27	−.24	.23
Percent of the postsession vote—governor	.31	.24	.30	.21	−.08	.24
Percent of the postsession vote—party[c]	−.06	−.08	.37	−.06	−.30	−.06
Primary vote						
Before: Governor's % of total	.29	.14	.14	−.08	.26	−.11
Winning % of highest two	.34	.08	.17	−.12	.27	−.11
% of highest two	.36	.06	.16	−.13	.29	−.13
After: Governor's % of total	.59	.55	.74	.28	−.05	.13
Winning % of highest two	.51	.04	.68	−.10	−.03	.05
% of highest two	.58	.54	.68	.28	−.08	.12
After: Party candidate[c] Percent of total	.47	.59	.06	*.39	.35	.34
Winning % of highest two	.51	.48	.14	*.34	.28	.28
% of highest two	.50	.46	.12	*.33	.28	.26
Legislative seats						
Percent of Governor's party	−.59	−.50	.22	.05	−.49	−.16
Absolute number of seats	.09	−.10	.37	.23	.09	−.16
Average percent 6 sessions	−.40	−.56	.33	−.03	−.40	−.18

[a]These sessions are the same as those in Table 1. There are 30 Republican sessions and 28 Democratic sessions.

[b]For all correlations higher than .35, $p \leqslant .05$ for a two-tailed test except for those correlations asterisked. For those, $p \leqslant .10$ for a two-tailed test. Correlations above .40 in magnitude are underlined for convenience.

[c]The party vote for the postsession is the vote for the governor or his replacement.

such as primary support and percentage of seats in the legislature, multiple regression analysis helps us to estimate the size of such effects. For each individual session, the residual difference between the actual and predicted value of success can be calculated and subjected to further analysis; for the group of sessions, the squared multiple correlation coefficient indicates the percentage of gubernatorial success which can be explained by the model.[27] Coefficients in such regression models may be interpreted in either of two ways. The b-coefficient before each independent variable in a regression equation indicates the direction and amount of change in gubernatorial success associated with a unit change in only that one variable. When each of the variables has been standardized, different versons of the b-coefficients called beta-

[27]A good explanation of the technique appears in Hubert M. Blalock, *Social Statistics* (New York: McGraw Hill, 1960), chap. 17–19. For two applications see Donald E. Stokes, Angus Campbell, and Warren E. Miller, "Components of Electoral Decision," *American Political Science Review*, Vol. 52 (June 1958), pp. 367–387; and Hayward R. Alker, Jr., "Dimensions of Conflict in the General Assembly," *American Political Science Review*, Vol. 58 (September 1964), pp. 642–657.

weights are appropriate. These beta-weights tell how much each independent variable contributes toward explaining success when its potential contribution has been equalized and when all the other independent variables have been held constant. Beta-weights are comparable; b-coefficients are not. The b-coefficients, on the other hand, have the advantage of concreteness. They are more likely to remain stable in different samples having unequal variances than the beta-weights.

From an analysis of the intercorrelations between independent variables correlating between independent variables correlating most highly with the dependent variables of support and success, several were chosen for the regression subject to the restriction that they not be intercorrelated at higher than .50 level themselves.[28] One exception was made in the case of the majority factor, which has a correlation of .84 with the percentage of seats a governor's party controls. This variable has

potential importance because of the many advantages which accrue to a governor who has a majority. The speaker is from his party as well as the chairmen and majorities of committees. The speaker controls the membership of committees and the assignment of bills. This gives the governor, through the speaker, a control over legislation which he does not have with a minority, in which the leadership positions are in the hands of the opposite party. In order to check the supposition that the majority variable has an independent contribution to make in explaining support and success, I did not include this variable in the initial regression.

Since it is the primary record of a governor who runs again which has the highest correlation with support and success, 34 house sessions preceding an incumbent's election campaign were used to provide the data.[29] The regression estimates for support and success are [below].[30]

Index of Support for the governor's party (R = .66 with the majority variable; R = .66 without the majority variable)

$$\text{Sup.}_i = 58.6 - .13 \text{ G.E.}_i + .66 \text{ Prim.}_i - .71 \text{ Seats}_i + 1.9 \text{ Maj.}_i \quad \text{With the majority variable}$$
$$\quad\quad\quad (0) \quad\quad (.03) \quad\quad\quad (.36) \quad\quad\quad\quad (.50) \quad\quad\quad\quad (.04)$$

$$\text{Sup.}_i = 57.4 - .12 \text{ G.E.}_i + .65 \text{ Prim.}_i - .67 \text{ Seats}_i \quad \text{Without the majority variable}$$
$$\quad\quad\quad (0) \quad\quad (.03) \quad\quad\quad (.35) \quad\quad\quad\quad (.47)$$

Index of Success for the governor's party (R = .55 with the majority variable; R = .47 without the majority variable)

$$\text{Suc.}_i = 1.2 - .57 \text{ G.E.}_i + 1.4 \text{ Prim.}_i - .38 \text{ Seats}_i + 38.2 \text{ Maj.}_i \quad \text{With the majority variable}$$
$$\quad\quad\quad (0) \quad\quad (.09) \quad\quad\quad (.54) \quad\quad\quad\quad (.19) \quad\quad\quad\quad (.38)$$

$$\text{Suc.}_i = 23.3 - .37 \text{ G.E.}_i + 1.4 \text{ Prim.}_i + .44 \text{ Seats}_i \quad \text{Without the majority variable}$$
$$\quad\quad\quad (0) \quad\quad (.06) \quad\quad\quad (.53) \quad\quad\quad\quad (.22)$$

[28] The regression equation for explaining a governor's index of support (Sup.) was $\hat{\text{Sup.}}_i = K + b_1 \text{G.E.}_i + b_2 \text{Prim.}_i + b_3 \text{Seats}_i + b_4 \text{Maj.}_i$. In this equation the i subscript may indicate any of the 34 sessions being analyzed. K is an appropriate constant; G.E.$_i$ equals the governor's percent of the postsession election; Prim.$_i$ equals the governor's percent of the postsession primary vote; Seats$_i$ equals the percent of seats the governor's party has for the session; Maj.$_i$ equals one if the governor's party has 50 percent or more of the House, zero if it does not. K equals zero when the explanatory variables are standardized. A similar equation was used for explaining a governor's index of success (Suc.).

[29] The states and number of sessions used are: Republican: R.I. (1), Maryland (1), Idaho (1), Oregon (1), Illinois (1), N.H. (1), Mass. (1), Wisconsin (3), Kansas (1), Ohio (2), and Michigan (1). Democratic: Maine (1), Ohio (3), Conn. (1), Iowa (1), Kansas (2), Michigan (4), N.Y. (1), Nevada (1), California (1), Colorado (1), Mass. (2), Montana (1), and R.I. (1). There were 16 sessions in which the governor had a minority of the legislature: (4 Republican: 12 Democratic). There were 18 sessions in which he had a majority: (10 Republicans: 8 Democratic).

[30] In these equations b-coefficients are given with the independent variables; beta-weights are given below them in parentheses. Beta-weights are obtained by multiplying a concrete b-coefficient times the standard deviation of its independent variable and dividing by the standard deviation of the dependent variable.

The coefficients and the multiple correlation coefficients serve to test succinctly a number of hypotheses and answer a number of questions about the relative contribution of electoral competition and party structure to gubernatorial support and success. We will first interpret the unstandardized b-coefficients in the explanatory models. The addition of the majority variable to the other independent variables makes an appreciable change in the value of R in the equation for success, but no change in the value of R in the equation for support. Apparently, holding a majority of seats in the house and the ability to organize its procedures barely affects the negative relationship which exists between the percentage of seats and the support of the governor. The results in Table 3 indicate that this negative relationship can be interpreted in either of two ways: (1) Legislative support is a matter of gubernatorial strategy. The governor makes marginal calculations concerning the votes needed to pass his legislation and does not try to marshall excess votes. Therefore as the proportion of seats held by the party goes up, the proportion of party votes needed to pass legislation goes down. (2) Excess seats are a liability to a governor. As the proportion of his party seats in the house rises, rivalries are generated which a governor cannot control. Therefore gubernatorial support falls as the percentage of seats rises.

Nor does the possession of a majority change the positive relationship which exists between the governor's primary showing and his support. With or without a majority of the legislature, a stronger governor gets higher support on upholding his vetoes; the weaker governor less support. This indicates that a strong governor can make use of the advantages which come to him as a result of majority control while a weak governor cannot. It may indicate that a strong governor calculates at the margins, but can counteract rivalries which develop with a large majority. The success equation clarifies many of these queries and will be considered next. The index of success controls for the "strategy" interpretation since, by definition, it is the percentage of party votes received out of the party votes needed.

The addition of the majority variable to the regression equation for success makes a noteworthy increase in the value of R. It changes the independent influence on the equation of the percentage of seats from positive to negative. Without the addition of the majority variable, it appears that the higher the percentage of seats, the more the governor is advantaged. The addition of the majority variable indicates that when the governor has a majority of the seats, however, extra seats over this majority become a disadvantage. Before the addition of the majority variable, the b-coefficient for seats indicated that the governor needs excess party seats to be successful. His success in getting the percentage of his party he needs is aided by increasing the number of seats in his party up to a certain limit. Probably a few seats over a majority are to his benefit. This explains the positive relationship which existed before the addition of the majority variable. With the addition of this variable the independent effect of the percentage of seats changed. The negative influence of seats over a majority indicates the attrition which excess seats brings to even the strongest governor. Thus the "rivalry" explanation for the negative relationship between seats and party support must account for the negative relationship between excess seats and success, since we have controlled for the "strategy" interpretation in our measure of success.

The equation for support which includes the majority factor tells us that a one percent increase in the postprimary support of the governor causes a .66 percent increase in his index of support. On the other hand, a one percent increase in the governor's legislative party contingent causes a .71 percent loss of support by the governor.

The equation for success which includes the majority factor indicates that receiving 80 percent in a primary vote is worth three times the advantage of having a majority in the legislature in terms of the ability to get the necessary votes to sustain a veto. In other words, possessing a majority of the legislature is not an automatic guarantee that vetoes will be upheld. It is the impact of a popular governor which contributes much more to the equation for success. A 1 percent increase in the general election support leads us to expect a little over one-half of 1 percent decrease in legislative success. While this looks like an influential variable, it must be remembered that the election returns rarely swing outside of the 45–55 percent range, so the actual effect of this variable is minimized.

The preceding examination of the unstandardized b-coefficients in the explanatory models confirms the hypothesis that there is an appreciable difference between the effects of the same independent variables on gubernatorial support and their effects on success. In the equations for support, defined as the percentage of the governor's party which voted to support him, the influence of his strength in the outside party amounted to only half as much as it did in the equation for success, the measure of his ability to get the votes he needed. On the other hand, the influence of the percentage of seats in the legislature was twice as much in the first support equation as in the first success equation. This indicates that most governors make marginal calculations based on the votes needed to pass, but that the governors who are successful in achieving what they need are those who are also in control of the outside party.

The comparison between the variables would be on a more equitable basis if we used the beta-weights. The use of beta-weights corrects for the fact that there are differences in range and variability involved in measuring the independent variables. We measure changes in the dependent variable in terms of standard deviation units for each of the other variables, a method which assures us of the same variability in each of these variables. These beta-weights can be presented by means of a bar graph. The direction in which a bar extends from the midline indicates the direction of the variable on support and success. If it extends to the left, it is exerting a negative force on the dependent variable; if it extends to the right, it is exerting a positive influence on the dependent variable. The length of the bar indicates the magnitude of a variable's force on support and success.

These beta weights are compared in Figure 1, which gives the direction and degree of change in both support and success brought about by the standardized variables. From the comparison one can see that the gubernatorial election does not affect the support or success of the governor to a very great degree. The primary accounts for more positive change in the success index than any other variable and affects support to a very large degree. Success, which indicates whether or not the governor received the deciding number of votes to uphold his veto, is more closely allied with the governor's postsession primary vote than is support, which is simply his percentage of support by his own party, unrelated to whether or not he got what he needed. A comparison of the relative contribution of the percentage of seats and majority factors confirms the previous findings. The fact that a governor has a majority has very little to do with his support, which is affected in the high negative by the percentage of seats. Success, however, is much more affected by the possession of a majority than by the percentage of seats. This may indicate the contribution of such organizational factors as the speakership and control over committees, or it may indicate, more simply, that the governor has sufficient votes to uphold his veto if he works on it.

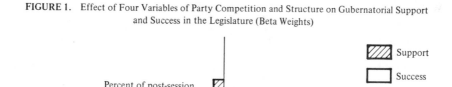

FIGURE 1. Effect of Four Variables of Party Competition and Structure on Gubernatorial Support and Success in the Legislature (Beta Weights)

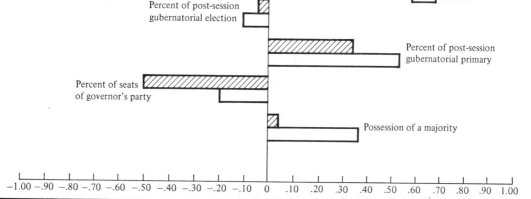

R AND THE RESIDUALS

The multiple correlation (R) is given with each regression equation for support and success. The nonsquared multiple correlation coefficient associated with the support equation is .66, which is higher than any of the single correlations between an independent variable and the dependent one.

Squaring this correlation shows that about 44 percent of the governor's support can be explained by a linear model using the independent variables we have chosen. A multiple correlation of .55 is also "respectable" as an indication of the correlation between the actual and predicted values of success. That these multiple correlations are fairly high

TABLE 6. Actual and Predicted Values for Support and Success for the 34 House Sessions

State	Session	Governor's Party	Support Actual percent	Support Predicted[a] percent	Support Percent- age[c] Error	Success Actual percent	Success Predicted[b] percent	Success Percent- age[c] Error
\multicolumn{9}{c}{Governor's Party with Less than 50% of the House Seats}
Rhode Island	1959	R	100	90.0	+11	100	90.8	+10
Maryland	1951	R	65	91.0	−29	65	90.2	−28
Ohio	1951	D	54	97.7	−45*	54	103.0	−48*
Maine	1955	D	97	100.0	−04	97	102.8	−06
Ohio	1953	D	79	99.8	−21	79	104.9	−25
Idaho	1959	R	93	81.3	+15	110	80.6	+36*
Connecticut	1955	D	89	84.4	+05	89	78.3	+14
Iowa	1957	D	87	94.2	−08	87	101.9	−15
Kansas	1957	D	98	93.1	+05	98	99.8	−02
Michigan	1949	D	95	90.4	+05	103	102.0	+01
Michigan	1951	D	98	94.0	+04	98	103.7	−05
Michigan	1953	D	100	93.2	+05	100	100.5	+00
New York	1955	D	100	81.7	+22	118	85.7	+27
Michigan	1957	D	100	76.5	+31*	112	77.6	+44*
Kansas	1959	D	100	86.9	+15	116	103.0	+13
Oregon	1959	R	78	73.7	+06	100	70.5	+42*
\multicolumn{9}{c}{Governor's Party with More than 50% of the House Seats}
Illinois	1957	R	42	56.0	−03	55	40.0	+30
Nevada	1947	D	95	61.6	+54*	143	92.4	+35*
Ohio	1949	D	41	73.6	−44*	44	112.0	−61*
California	1959	D	87	73.8	+18	118	122.2	−03
Colorado	1957	D	38	77.0	−51*	62	126.5	−50*
Massachusetts	1949	D	96	82.9	+16	144	126.5	−14
Massachusetts	1957	D	90	80.1	+12	153	130.0	+18
New Hampshire	1949	R	95	59.2	+60*	166	93.7	+77*
Massachusetts	1947	R	96	78.6	+22	175	137.2	+27
Montana	1949	D	98	77.5	+26	182	131.5	+38*
Wisconsin	1957	R	68	72.9	−07	135	131.3	+03
Rhode Island	1947	D	100	60.2	+66*	142	102.9	+38*
Kansas	1955	R	18	41.5	−57*	38	68.2	−44*
Ohio	1957	R	29	47.4	−39*	45	80.3	−44*
Wisconsin	1953	R	66	66.5	−01	143	125.3	+14
Wisconsin	1951	R	52	65.0	−20	113	122.0	−07
Ohio	1947	R	36	53.0	−31*	67	113.4	−41*
Michigan	1947	R	40	53.0	−25	103	120.8	−15

[a]For each session the equation for support including the majority variable was applied.

[b]For each session the equation for success including the majority variable was applied.

[c]The formula for the percentage error is:

$$\frac{\text{actual value-predicted value}}{\text{predicted value}} \times 100$$

*The sessions under- or overpredicted by over 30% are asterisked.

even when the indices we have used are rather crude is quite encouraging. As indicators of legislative support and party structure the veto votes and postsession primary results are at best approximate.

An analysis of the residual differences between actual and predicted values for the sessions reveals several reasons why the Rs were not even higher. Table 6 gives the residuals for the 34 house sessions. The model for support was close to being correct in 24 out of the 34 sessions. The model for success is not quite as accurate, predicting within 30 percent of the actual success in 21 out of 34 sessions. The over-or underpredicted sessions serve to lower the correlations between the actual and predicted values.[31] There are several possible explanations for the deviant sessions. Local factors not amenable to interstate comparisons may account for some of the cases. The effects of constituency interests upon the behavior of the individual legislator have not been considered in this paper. The role perceptions of the legislator may account for deviations. Further research on the deviant cases is clearly indicated.

STRENGTHS AND LIMITATIONS OF THE LINEAR REGRESSION MODEL

The linear equations which were presented represent an attempt at both economy and accuracy of prediction. They have the advantage of indicating when certain variables are only spuriously correlated with the dependent variables, although the "independent-dependent" interpretation of the regression model ignores the more complicated interdependent and nonadditive causal interrelations of the variables involved.[32] For instance, we know

that the degree of success in the primary after the session has a high positive correlation with gubernatorial success in the legislature. It can hardly cause this because it comes later in point of time. We used the postsession primary to indicate the cohesion of the party structure outside the legislature. Like malaria's high positive correlation with marshes via the mosquito, there is undoubtedly a causal connection between legislative discipline and primary success. We have assumed throughout this paper that the governor provides this causal connection through his efforts to consolidate his party to win in the primary and in the election.

A SUGGESTED CAUSAL MODEL

Based on the findings we have just presented, a model of gubernatorial influence would give the most weight to the ability of the governor to form winning coalitions both within and outside the legislature. There may not be a time lag here. The two processes probably occur simultaneously. Instead of the legislative party being an independent entity, it is subject to the direction and influence of the governor's coalition within the electoral organization. The fact that the two variables of legislative party support of the governor and primary cohesion are so highly correlated indicates that the governor provides the connecting link. Correlations between legislative performance and primary results of the party candidate were not as high. Also, it was the primary *following* a session which correlated most highly with the legislative success of the governor, indicating that influence builds upon a future reward, rather than a past success.

Within most states outside the South, enough competition exists for either party to consider winning the election a possibility. In Figure 2 the broken line indicates the influence of the variable of statewide competition upon the governor because this variable is potentially strong, but cannot be used as an effective predictor of the cohesion of most of the states in the North whose election competition is within the 40–60 percent range. Because either party can win, competition for the party nomination is keen. Active and potential factions exist within both parties. The governor must compete for the nomination and, in order to do so, he starts building a coalition within the party which will be large enough to assure him of an uncontested primary nomination, or at least guarantee victory in the primary election. This faction, we hypothesize, includes members of the legisla-

[31] Multiple correlation represents the zero-order correlation between the actual values obtained for the dependent variable and those values predicted from the equation. If all of the points are on a least-squares line in a scattergram, which is a geometrical interpretation of the equation, the actual and predicted values will coincide and the multiple correlation will be unity. The greater the scatter about the line, the lower the correlation between the actual and predicted values.

[32] A way of deciding between alternative models of the causal interrelationships among variables has been elaborated by Hubert M. Blalock, "Correlation and Causality: The Multivariate Case," *Social Forces*, Vol. 39 (March 1961), 246–251. It was used by Warren E. Miller and Donald E. Stokes, "Constituency Influence in Congress," *American Political Science Review*, Vol. 57 (March 1963), pp. 45–56.

FIGURE 2. Causal Relationships in the Model
of Gubernatorial Influence

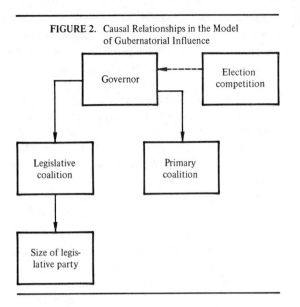

ture who come from areas where the governor has organization support. With his supply of resources the governor can "pay" other legislators to back him. The model does not separate the legislative from the electoral party, but considers it to be a partner in the forming of party coalitions which later battle in the primary.

Within the legislature itself, a variable which has a great deal of weight upon the success of the governor in building his faction is the size of the legislative party. If the governor has an overwhelming majority, he has trouble building a coalition large enough to pass his legislation. The excess may fall prey to rival factions who can gain a strong enough foothold to entice a deciding number of potential supporters from the governor's coalition. Insofar as reapportionment is able to make it possible for either party to gain control of the legislature in a state in which the electorate is fairly evenly divided between the parties, the handicap of excess seats will be diminished. The governor will find his legislative party more manageable with his supply of limited resources.

CONCLUSIONS

There are several avenues of future research which lead from these findings. The only factors which have been considered are state-level factors which bear an influence on the governor's support. At best we were able to explain only 44 percent of the support with these factors, and the predictive value of the equation cannot be improved unless

we know more about the following components of gubernatorial influence:

1. The amount and availability of economic resources such as jobs and contracts and their effect on the ability of the governor to form coalitions;
2. The personal basis of gubernatorial coalitions as a possible reason for the lack of permanence of controlling coalitions within the party;
3. The bases for permanent coalitions within a political party which can outlive any one governor; and
4. The economic and social components of a coalition and the effect on coalition building brought about by a diversity of economic interests within a party;
   a. The relationship of constituency economic interests upon the success of the governor. (Flinn discovered that members from constituencies more typical of the party supported the party position more often[33]); and
   b. The relationship of constituency economic interests upon the failure of the governor to pass his legislation. (There is more agreement among researchers that variance in party loyalty can be related to constituency characteristics.)

The ability of the electoral party organization to influence the voting loyalty of the legislators is unquestionable. Further test borings into the resources which feed successful gubernatorial coalitions should be of interest to those who claim that a party should be able to pass its program.

[33]Flinn, *op. cit.*, pp. 61–66.

AGENCY REQUESTS, GUBERNATORIAL SUPPORT, AND BUDGET SUCCESS IN STATE LEGISLATURES
Ira Sharkansky

This is a study of the budget success of state administrative agencies. Although a number of recent studies provide valuable information about environmental influences on state and local govern-

Source: Reprinted by permission from the *American Political Science Review*, Vol. 62, (December 1968), pp. 1220–1231.

ment expenditures, relatively little is known about the factors that affect the budgets of individual administrative units.[1] Existing studies typically focus on the state as the unit of analysis, and report findings about the correlates of state (or state plus local) government expenditures in total and by the major fields of education, highways, public welfare, health, hospitals *et al*. The United States Bureau of the Census provides an invaluable service for this scholarship by collecting state and local government data and ordering it into categories that permit state-to-state comparisons. When political scientists and economists rely exclusively on Census Bureau publications, however, they preclude an attack on certain aspects of the expenditure process. In order to report data by the comparable fields of education, highways, public welfare etc., the Bureau of the Census rearranges the expenditures made by individual state agencies.[2] As a result we know little about the factors that affect the budgets of individual agencies. And because it is the agency's budget that is the focus of budget-making, we have no systematic information about many of the influences that might affect government expenditures. Chief among the unknowns are the influence of each agency's budget request in the expenditure process, and the support given to the agencies by the governor.

Much of the existing literature on government budgeting suggests the importance of incremental decision rules. Officials who review agency requests in the executive and legislative branches are said to have too few resources for a comprehensive examination of each agency's program. Studies of federal budgeting reveal that appropriations committees generally accept each agency's "base" of previous expenditure, and focus their attention on the requests for new funds.[3] Congress holds down the growth rate of most agency budgets, typically to within 10 percent of their existing budget.[4] The common explanation for incremental budgeting cites the difficulties associated with a comprehensive review of each agency. Legislatures have much else to do beside reviewing past and present expenditures. To reopen past budget decisions each year would broaden the scope of political controversy. Decision makers can limit their task by accepting their own past evaluations about each existing program, and by focusing their current inquiries on those items that an agency seeks for the first time, or those which the agency hopes to increase well beyond the limit of past funding.[5]

A principal task of this study is to identify and measure some likely mechanisms of incremental budgeting in state governments. By looking at the *requests* of 592 agencies in 19 states, the *response of the governor* to agency requests, and the *action of the legislature*, it will assess the importance of incremental routines in each of these states. Then it identifies certain characteristics of each state that influence the nature of its budget procedures. The study proceeds at two levels of analysis. It first reports the results of 19 separate within-state analyses that show relationships between measures of agency success in the legislature and measures of budget size, agency acquisitiveness and gubernatorial support. Secondly, it uses these 19 states as the units of analysis, and defines the importance of certain environmental conditions for these rela-

[1] See, for example, Thomas R. Dye, *Politics, Economics and the Public: Policy Outcomes in the American States* (Chicago: Rand McNally, 1966); Glenn W. Fisher, "Interstate Variation in State and Local Government Expenditures," *National Tax Journal* Vol. 17 (March 1964), pp. 57–64; Seymour Sachs and Robert Harris, "The Determinants of State and Local Government Expenditures and Intergovernmental Flow of Funds," *National Tax Journal*, Vol. 17, (March 1964), pp. 75–85; Elliott R. Morss, J. Eric Fredland, and Saul H. Hymans, "Fluctuations in State Expenditures: An Econometric Analysis," *Southern Economic Journal* (April 1967); Richard E. Dawson and James A. Robinson, "Interparty Competition, Economic Variables, and Welfare Politics in the American States," *Journal of Politics*, Vol. 25 (May 1963), pp. 265–289; and Ira Sharkansky, "Economic and Political Correlates of State Government Expenditures: General Tendencies and Deviant Cases," *Midwest Journal of Political Science*, Vol. 11 (May 1967), pp. 173–192.

[2] Most state governments have several administrative units with educational responsibilities, for example, and their titles and program responsibilities vary considerably from one state to another.

[3] Otto A. Davis, M.A.H. Dempster, and Aaron Wildavsky, "A Theory of the Budgetary Process," *American Political Science Review*, Vol. 60 (September 1968), pp. 529–547.

[4] Richard F. Fenno, Jr., *The Power of the Purse: Appropriations Politics in Congress* (Boston: Little Brown, 1966), Chapters 8 and 11.

[5] Charles E. Lindblom "Decision-Making in Taxation and Expenditure," in *Public Finances: Needs, Sources and Utilization* (Princeton: National Bureau of Economic Research, 1961), pp. 295–333.

tionships among agencies, the governor and the state legislature.

TECHNIQUES AND EXPECTATIONS

The complexity and individuality of state government budgets represent formidable barriers to comparative analysis. Because state budgeting proceeds with a variety of separate funds whose labels and components vary from state to state, and because the official documents vary widely in the quality of information they contain, it is necessary to eliminate over half of the state governments from this analysis. The budget documents and financial reports of 19 state governments meet the essential criteria of providing an agency-by-agency record of current expenditures; the agencies' initial requests for the coming budget period;[6] the amount recommended by the governor for each agency,[7] and the sum appropriated by the

legislature. The 19 states come from each major section of the country and range in population size from Texas and Illinois to Vermont and Wyoming. They range in economic well-being (measured in per capita personal income) from Illinois and Indiana to West Virginia and South Carolina. For each major agency in these states two measures of budget success are defined. These are the dependent variables for the within-state analysis of agency budgets:[8]

Y_1: The percentage of the agency's request for the coming budget period appropriated by the legislature (short-term success)

Y_2: The percentage of current expenditures appropriated by the legislature for the coming budget period (success in budget expansion)

The first dependent variable is labelled short-term success because of its concern with one budget period. It simply measures the success of each agency in getting from the legislature what it announces as its goals. The second dependent variable measures the willingness of the legislature to provide each agency with an increase over its current budget. Thus, it measures the increment of growth enjoyed by each unit. In most of the states there is not a significant coefficient of simple correlation between the two measures of success, indicating that they are distinct aspects of the budgetary process.

The independent variables for the within-state analysis of agency budgets are:

X_1: Agency request for the coming budget period (budget size)

X_2: Agency request for the coming budget period

---

[6] The states included in this study—and the nature of the findings—may be affected by the requirement of separate indications for the agency's budget request and the governor's recommendation. One tenet of certain administrative reformers prescribes that public agencies *not* submit their own budget requests to the legislature. Instead, they should submit their requests to the chief executive, who should then review each agency's budget in the light of his whole program, and submit his own recommendations for each agency to the legislature. Presumably the legislature will consider only these budget recommendations of the executive, and thereby force each agency to operate within the budget limits set by the leader of the "administration team." A number of states have adopted these budget procedures, and their budgets show only the governor's recommendation for each agency. Our sample, in contrast, may be overly representative of states with "unreformed" budget procedures.

The "budget period" employed is the fiscal year or the biennium, depending upon the usage prevailing within each state. Although the use of a single year or a biennium varies from one state to another, this should not have a material effect on the findings insofar as the principal findings grow out of correlation coefficients that are calculated separately for each state. The particular years employed in the analysis of each state are indicated with the name of each state in Table 1. In each case, the most recent budget period was employed for which complete data was available. A small number of additional states publish budgetary information that would qualify them for this type of analysis. They are not included here, however, because the appropriate documents were not available.

[7] In some cases it is a budget review board, rather than the governor *per se*, that is directly responsible for the recommendation to the legislature. In each case, however, it is reported by observers native to the state that the governor's role is critical in the recommendations.

[8] All of the findings reported below for the within-state analysis of agency budgets reflects data about the "general fund" for those states that segregate the "general" fund from the "total" fund. For most states, the designation of "general" fund pertains to those moneys subject to state legislative appropriation. For those states showing both general and total fund accounts, the correlation analyses were performed twice: once with each account. However, the findings from the two analyses were not so different as to warrant separate reporting here. For each state, agencies requesting at least $500,000 were included. These are considered the "major" agencies. Supplementary appropriations are excluded from the legislature's appropriation due to lack of data. In the case of one state for which supplementary appropriations were available, the within-state analysis of agencies was run with and without the supplementals; the differences in findings appear inconsequential.

as a percentage of current expenditures (agency acquisitiveness)

X_3: The governor's recommendation for each agency as a percentage of its request (short-term support)

X_4: The governor's recommendation for each agency as a percentage of its current expenditures (support for budget expansion)

Due to the alleged conservatism of governors and legislators who review agency budgets,[9] it is expected that measures of budget size and acquisitiveness will show negative relationships with the measures of short-term support and legislative success; incremental budget reviewers should cut budgets that threaten to grow. But because an expansionist request is probably a requirement for an increase in appropriations, there are likely to be positive relationships between the measure of acquisitiveness and gubernatorial support and legislative success in budget expansion; it is probably the agencies that ask for the largest increases that receive the largest increases, even though their final appropriation is reduced substantially below their request. Because state legislators have limited investigatory resources and are poorly prepared by training or background for budget reviews,[10] it is expected that the governor's recommendation will serve as an important cue for their decisions. The measures of gubernatorial support should therefore relate closely to the measures of legislative appropriations.

Coefficients of simple correlation are computed separately for each of the 19 states, and provide measures of association between the dependent and independent variables.[11] With these correlations, we shall also perform a causal analysis to test for the relative importance of the agencies' requests and the governor's recommendations in the decisions of the legislature.

Once we have correlation coefficients that express the prevailing relationships between agency acquisitiveness, gubernatorial support and budget success for each state, we shall employ these coefficients as dependent variables in another inquiry that focuses on the state as the unit of analysis. There we shall consider several aspects of governmental structure, political characteristics, and economic resources as potential influences on relationships between agencies, the governor and the legislature. The independent variables for the state-by-state analysis are:[12]

S_1: Schlesinger's index of the governor's potential for tenure in office[13]

S_2: Schlesinger's index of the governor's veto power[14]

S_3: Ranney's measure of two-party competition[15]

S_4: Number of elected state executive officials

S_5: Percentage of voting-age population casting ballots in a recent statewide election[16]

S_6: Total state government expenditures per capita[17]

S_7: Total state government debt per capita

S_8: Per capita personal income of state residents

[12] Several other variables were considered, but excluded in this report because of their failure to add anything of importance to the findings reported below. Those excluded are:

a. Schlesinger's index of the governor's formal budget powers
b. Schlesinger's index of the governor's formal powers of appointment
c. Schlesinger's aggregate index of the governor's formal powers
d. Ranney's measure of Democratic party strength
e. Biennial compensation paid to members of the state legislature
f. State expenditures per capita for personal services
g. Total population of the state
h. Number of state government departments with elected heads

[13] Joseph A. Schlesinger, "The Politics of the Executive," in Herbert Jacob and Kenneth N. Vines, *Politics in the American States* (Boston: Little, Brown, 1965), p. 229.

[14] *Loc. cit.*

[15] Austin Ranney, "Parties in State Politics," in Jacob and Vines, *op. cit*, p. 65. The measure of competition used here equals the difference between each state's score on Ranney's index of Democratic party strength and .5000, with the result inverted so that high scores indicate high interparty competition.

[16] The data pertain to the 1964 election for U.S. Representative.

[17] The figure used is total general state government expenditures per capita in 1966.

[9] Cf. Thomas J. Anton, *The Politics of State Expenditure in Illinois* (Urbana: University of Illinois Press, 1966), chaps. 5, 6.

[10] Malcolm E. Jewell and Samuel C. Patterson, *The Legislative Process in the United States* (New York: Random House, 1966), pp. 251 ff.

[11] The data used in this study meet two of the primary assumptions of correlation analysis: the distribution of each variable approximates normality; and all two-variable relationships are linear.

It is expected that a governor with long tenure potential and extensive veto powers will have a relatively strong position vis-à-vis the agencies and the legislature. Such governors may take a hard line in cutting agency budgets, and succeed in providing the legislature with its major budget cues. Intense party competition and high voter turnout often work in favor of high expenditures.[18] Under conditions of high turnout and competition, therefore, acquisitive agencies should be able to elicit the most support from the governor and the legislature. Where there is a large number of separately elected executive officials, it is expected that acquisitive agencies will use them as allies and have a better chance of getting the governor and legislature to approve their budgets. And because independent executives may compete with the governor in supporting agency budgets, the states with numerous elected officials may be those where the governor's recommendations are least potent in the legislature. Where state resources are as yet uncommitted, agencies may draw on the "slack" for their budgets.[19] Therefore, the states with low per capita expenditures and debt, but high per capita personal income should offer the most hospitable environments for acquisitive agencies.

Recall that the dependent variables of the state-by-state analysis will be correlation coefficients determined by the within-state analysis of agency budgets. After describing the results of the within-state analysis, we shall specify the dependent variables for the second inquiry.

FINDINGS: THE CORRELATES OF AGENCY BUDGET SUCCESS

Administrative agencies and the governor play more consistent roles than the legislature in the state budget process. In each of the 19 states the major agencies requested a sizable increase (15 to 53 percent—over their current appropriations for the coming year, and the governor pared down the increase in his recommendations (by 4 to 31 percent). Table 1 shows the percentage changes occurring at each major stage of the budget process by states; it indicates that major agencies requested an average 24 percent increase over their current budgets, and that the governor's recommendation trimmed an average 14 percent from their requests. The legislature's final appropriation for these agencies typically remained close to the governor's recommendation, but varied from a cut of 8 percent below his recommendation to an increase of 19 percent above his recommendation. Six of the legislatures cut agency budgets below the governor's figure, and 11 appropriated more than the governor asked. In only one case, however, did a legislature (in Nebraska) give more money to the agencies than they had requested themselves. The average legislative grant for the coming period was 13 percent below the agencies' request, but 13 percent above the agencies' current budget.

The governor's support appears to be a critical ingredient in the success enjoyed by individual agencies in the legislature. In 16 states there is a significant positive correlation (shown in Table 2) between the governor's support and short term success,[20] and in 14 of the states there is a similar relationship between the governor's support and success in budget expansion. A contrary finding appears only in the case of Nebraska, where a negative coefficient of .54 links the governor's recommendation with the legislature's appropriation. In 1965, the Nebraska legislature was unique in acting consistently in opposition to the recommendations of Governor Frank B. Morrison. A reading of Nebraska newspapers during that period suggests that gubernatorial-legislative antagonism over the budget was part of a larger dispute that grew out of a tax conflict. The conservative Democratic governor opposed any new taxes, while the Republican leadership of the legislature sought the establishment of a state income or sales tax. Perhaps in an effort to force the governor's acceptance of a new tax, the legislators voted more funds than the governor recommended for the major agencies. (see Table 1). The legislature was especially generous with those agencies which has suffered a budget cut in the Governor's office (see Table 2).

The acquisitiveness of agency requests plays an important role in the budget process. There is a significant negative relationship between acquisi-

[18]See the works of Dye and Dawson and Robinson, cited in note 1.

[19]The concept of "slack" is explained in Richard M. Cyert and James G. March, *A Behavioral Theory of the Firm* (Englewood Cliffs, N.J.: Prentice-Hall, 1963), pp. 36 ff.

[20]A test for significance is not, strictly speaking, applicable because the units of analysis are not chosen at random to represent a larger population. Nevertheless, the tests for significance provide a convenient device to denote relationships that are "sizeable."

TABLE 1. Annual Percentage Changes by Stages in the Budget Process of Major Agencies, by State

State, Showing Years of Budget Analyzed and Number of Agencies	Agency Request as Percent of Current Expenditure	Governor's Recommendation as a Percent of Agency Request	Legislature's Appropriation as a Percent of Gov's Request	Legislature's Appropriation as Percent of Agency's Current Expenditure	Legislature's Appropriation as a Percent of Agency Request
Florida, 1965–67, N = 39	120	90	93	109	84
Georgia, 1965–67, N = 26	153	86	100	139	87
Idaho, 1967–69, N = 23	119	93	92	109	86
Illinois, 1963–65*, N = 37	118	83	102	108	85
Indiana, 1965–67, N = 47	123	83	103	112	86
Kentucky, 1966–68, N = 28	120	90	93	109	84
Louisiana, 1966–67, N = 32	121	90	101	110	91
Maine, 1965–67, N = 17	114	85	108	109	92
Nebraska, 1965–67, N = 10	122	87	119	124	104
North Carolina, 1965–67, N = 61	120	84	105	112	87
North Dakota, 1965–67, N = 21	124	74	111	111	82
South Carolina, 1966–67, N = 29	117	96	104	116	99
South Dakota, 1967–68, N = 25	136	82	98	109	80
Texas, 1965–67, N = 41	128	82	104	117	86
Vermont, 1965–67, N = 17	121	87	106	115	91
Virginia, 1966–68, N = 57	120	92	100	114	91
West Virginia, 1966–67, N = 43	125	88	92	101	81
Wisconsin, 1965–67, N = 26	115	96	98	111	94
Wyoming, 1967–69, N = 13	133	69	109	112	75

*The Illinois data comes from the Appendix of Thomas J. Anton's *The Politics of State Expenditure in Illinois* (Urbana: University of Illinois Press, 1966). All other data come from the official budgets and financial reports of the states.

TABLE 2. Coefficients of Simple Correlation Between Measures of Budget-success in the State Legislature and Independent Variables, by State

	Correlations Between Short-term Success and:			Correlations Between Budget Expansion and:		
	Budget size	Agency Acquisitive-ness	Governor's short-term support	Budget size	Agency Acquisitive-ness	Governor's support for expansion
Florida	.03	−.63*	.77*	−.04	.50	.71*
Georgia	.02	−.82*	.93*	−.12	−.09	.92*
Idaho	.04	−.80*	.72*	−.14	.74*	.79*
Illinois	.03	−.51*	.79*	−.04	.81*	.81*
Indiana	.04	−.27	.86*	−.04	.99*	.99*
Kentucky	.06	−.77*	.80*	−.14	.07	.19
Louisiana	.00	−.48*	.72*	−.09	.04	.54*
Maine	.24	.18	.75*	.25	.64*	.74*
Nebraska	−.09	.51	−.54	−.06	.79*	.43
North Carolina	−.04	−.20	.99*	−.05	.93*	.99*
North Dakota	.17	−.80*	.94*	−.16	.42	.87*
South Carolina	.00	−.17	.36	−.05	.81*	.75*
South Dakota	.00	−.70*	.63*	−.15	.58*	.48*
Texas	−.25	−.06	.52*	−.10	.95*	.89*
Vermont	−.12	−.61*	.58*	.24	.37	.46
Virginia	.07	−.27*	.19	−.02	.81*	.60*
West Virginia	.01	−.65*	.61*	−.09	.22	.26
Wisconisn	−.08	−.28	.67*	−.06	−.10	.16
Wyoming	−.18	−.70*	.94*	−.13	.18	.92*

*Significant at the .05 level (see note #20).

tiveness and short-term success in 12 states and a significant positive relationship between acquisitiveness and success in budget expansion in 11 states. The legislature is most likely to trim the budgets of agencies that ask for large increases, but it is only these acquisitive agencies that can hope for a large increase to remain after the legislature has acted. The acquisitiveness of the agencies is also a factor in the governor's recommendation. Table 3 shows significant negative relationships between acquisitiveness and the governor's short-term recommendations in 14 states, and significant positive relationships between acquisitiveness and the governor's recommendation for budget expansion in 14 states. Both the governor and the legislature may be using similar decision rules: Do not cut the agencies that ask for little or no increase; but do not recommend a budget expansion for those agencies that ask for little or no increase. Short-term cuts are made in the budgets of acquisitive agencies, but the acquisitive agencies stand the best chance of enjoying a substantial budget increase.

The absolute size of agency budget requests does not appear to influence the decisions made by the governor or legislature. Tables 2 and 3 show generally weak or inconsistent correlations between budget size and the governor's recommendations or the legislature's appropriations. Budget reviewers in the governor's office and the legislature are using procedures that serve to minimize the increments of budget growth; they are more likely to respond to the increment of change that is requested (i.e., agency acquisitiveness) than to the sheer size of the request.

Because agency acquisitiveness shows similar relationships with both the governor's recommendation and the legislature's appropriation, one is tempted to ask if the legislature responds directly to the agencies' acquisitiveness, or merely to the governor's recommendations. The alternate explanations are conveniently depicted and analyzed with the techniques of causal inference.[21] The

[21] The techniques are explained in Hubert M. Blalock, Jr., *Causal Inferences in Nonexperimental Research* (Chapel Hill: University of North Carolina Press, 1964), pp. 64 ff.; and demonstrated in Donald J. McCrone and Charles F. Cnudde, "Toward a Communications Theory of Demcoratic Political Development: A Causal Model,"

TABLE 3. Coefficients of Simple Correlation Between Measures of Gubernatorial Support and Independent Variables, by State

	Between Short-term Support and Correlations		Between Support for Expansion and Correlations	
	Budget size	Agency Acquisitive-ness	Budget size	Agency acquisitive-ness
Florida	.04	−.80*	−.03	.22
Georgia	.08	−.86*	−.05	−.11
Idaho	.45*	−.70*	−.03	.99*
Illinois	.07	−.52	.00	.85*
Indiana	.10	.13	−.04	.99*
Kentucky	.18	−.94*	.02	.04
Louisiana	.12	−.82*	−.05	.37*
Maine	.08	.22	.09	.75*
Nebraska	−.23	−.59	−.27	.76*
North Carolina	−.05	−.20	−.06	.94*
North Dakota	−.01	−.84*	−.34	.39
South Carolina	.06	−.30	−.02	.77*
South Dakota	.02	−.75*	−.11	.71*
Texas	−.10	−.63*	−.04	.93*
Vermont	−.16	−.67*	.36	.85*
Virginia	.12	−.56*	−.05	.71*
West Virginia	.16	−.57*	.03	.57*
Wisconsin	−.03	−.61*	.07	.88*
Wyoming	−.15	−.82*	−.09	.28

*Significant at the .05 level (see note #20).

alternate linkages and the computations associated with them are reported in Figure 1 and Table 4. The results support the inference that the legislature responds more often to the governor's recommendations than directly to agency acquisitiveness. In the case of short-term success, the data support this for Florida, Georgia, Illinois, Louisiana, Nebraska, North Carolina, North Dakota, South Carolina, and Wyoming. Only in the cases of South Dakota, and Virginia does the legislation seem to respond primarily to agency acquisitiveness. In the remaining states the findings suggest that the legislature is responding to a combination of gubernatorial recommendations and agency acquisitiveness. Similar findings appear in the causal analysis of budget expansion. Georgia, Idaho, Kentucky, Maine, North Carolina, North

American Political Science Review, Vol. 61 (March 1967), pp. 72–79. In this causal analysis, the author is following the convention of inferring a linkage to be absent if the difference between expected and actual findings are less than the difference for the alternative model, and if the difference between expected and actual findings is less than .10.

Dakota, Vermont, West Virginia, and Wyoming show legislative reliance primarily on the governor's recommendation, while only South Dakota, Texas, and Virginia show legislative response primarily to agency acquisitiveness.

For most of the 19 states, it is a combination of incrementalism and legislative dependence on the governor's recommendation that shapes the budgets of major agencies. Both the governor and the legislature respond to the agencies request for increments above their present expenditures, and their response serves to minimize budget growth. Also, most legislatures weigh the governor's recommendations heavily in their own decisions. Without a favorable recommendation from the governor, an agency is unlikely to enjoy any substantial increase in its appropriation.

THE CORRELATES OF AGENCY-GOVERNOR-LEGISLATURE RELATIONSHIPS

An examination of the correlation coefficients in Tables 2 and 3 indicates that states vary in the nature of budget relations among agencies, the governor and the legislature. Although agency

TABLE 4. Differences Between Relationships Expected on the Basis of Causal Inferences and Actual Relationships

	Short-term Success				Program Expansion			
	Expected	Actual	Difference	Model Inferred	Expected	Actual	Difference	Model Inferred
Florida								
$r_{AL} = r_{AG}r_{GL}$	−.62	−.63	.01	#1	.16	.50	.34	#3
$r_{GL} = r_{AG}r_{AL}$	.50	.77	.27		.11	.71	.60	
Georgia								
$r_{AL} = r_{AG}r_{GL}$	−.80	−.82	.02	#1	−.10	−.09	.01	#1
$r_{GL} = r_{AG}r_{AL}$	.71	.93	.22		.01	.92	.91	
Idaho								
$r_{AL} = r_{AG}r_{GL}$	−.50	−.80	.30	#3	.78	.74	.04	#1
$r_{GL} = r_{AG}r_{AL}$	.56	.72	.16		.73	.79	.06	
Illinois								
$r_{AL} = r_{AG}r_{GL}$	−.41	−.51	.10	#1	.69	.81	.12	#3
$r_{GL} = r_{AG}r_{AL}$	.41	.79	.38		.69	.81	.12	
Indiana								
$r_{AL} = r_{AG}r_{GL}$	−.11	−.27	.16	#3	.99	.99	.00	indeter-
$r_{GL} = r_{AG}r_{AL}$	.04	.86	.83		.99	.99	.00	minate
Kentucky								
$r_{AL} = r_{AG}r_{GL}$	−.75	−.77	.02	#1	.01	.07	.06	#1
$r_{GL} = r_{AG}r_{AL}$	.72	.80	.08		.00	.19	.19	
Louisiana								
$r_{AL} = r_{AG}r_{GL}$	−.59	−.48	.11	#3	.20	.04	.16	#3
$r_{GL} = r_{AG}r_{AL}$	.39	.72	.33		.01	.54	.53	
Maine								
$r_{AL} = r_{AG}r_{GL}$	.17	.18	.01	#1	.56	.64	.08	#1
$r_{GL} = r_{AG}r_{AL}$	.04	.75	.71		.48	.74	.26	
Nebraska								
$r_{AL} = r_{AG}r_{GL}$	.32	.51	.19	#3	.33	.79	.46	#3
$r_{GL} = r_{AG}r_{AL}$	−.30	−.50	.20		.60	.43	.17	
North Carolina								
$r_{AL} = r_{AG}r_{GL}$	−.20	−.20	.00	#1	.93	.93	.00	#1
$r_{GL} = r_{AG}r_{AL}$	.04	.99	.95		.87	.79	.12	
North Dakota								
$r_{AL} = r_{AG}r_{GL}$	−.79	−.80	.01	#1	.34	.42	.08	#1
$r_{GL} = r_{AG}r_{AL}$	.67	.94	.27		.16	.87	.71	
South Carolina								
$r_{AL} = r_{AG}r_{GL}$	−.11	−.17	.06	#1	.58	.81	.23	#3
$r_{GL} = r_{AG}r_{AL}$	.05	.36	.31		.62	.75	.13	
South Dakota								
$r_{AL} = r_{AG}r_{GL}$	−.47	−.70	.23	#2	.34	.58	.24	#2
$r_{GL} = r_{AG}r_{AL}$	.53	.63	.10		.41	.48	.07	
Texas								
$r_{AL} = r_{AG}r_{GL}$	−.33	−.06	.26	#3	.83	.95	.12	#2
$r_{GL} = r_{AG}r_{AL}$	.04	.52	.48		.88	.89	.01	
Vermont								
$r_{AL} = r_{AG}r_{GL}$	−.39	−.61	.22	#3	.39	.37	.02	#1
$r_{GL} = r_{AG}r_{AL}$	.41	.58	.17		.31	.46	.15	

Table 4 (Continued)

Virginia									
$r_{AL} = r_{AG} r_{GL}$	−.11	−.27	.16	#2	.43	.81	.38	#2
$r_{GL} = r_{AG} r_{AL}$	.15	.19	.04		.58	.60	.02	
West Virginia									
$r_{AL} = r_{AG} r_{GL}$	−.35	−.65	.30	#3	.15	.22	.07	#1
$r_{GL} = r_{AG} r_{AL}$	.37	.61	.24		.13	.26	.13	
Wisconsin									
$r_{AL} = r_{AG} r_{GL}$	−.41	−.28	.13	#3	−.09	.16	.25	#3
$r_{GL} = r_{AG} r_{AL}$	.17	.67	.50		.14	−.10	.24	
Wyoming									
$r_{AL} = r_{AG} r_{GL}$	−.77	−.70	.07	#1	.26	.18	.08	#1
$r_{GL} = r_{AG} r_{AL}$	.57	.94	.37		.05	.92	.87	

acquisitiveness and the governor's recommendations generally show certain correlations with the legislature's appropriation, the strength (and occasionally the direction) of these relationships vary from state to state. By examining these variations it is possible to define the conditions under which the governor is severe or supportive in his review of agency budgets, and the conditions under which the legislature is particularly responsive to agency acquisitiveness and the governor's recommendations. The dependent variables of this inquiry are certain correlation coefficients from Tables 2 and 3:

$r_{X_2 X_3}$: The stronger the *negative* correlation between agency acquisitiveness and the governor's short-term support, the more the governor appears to be restraining the agencies' budget development

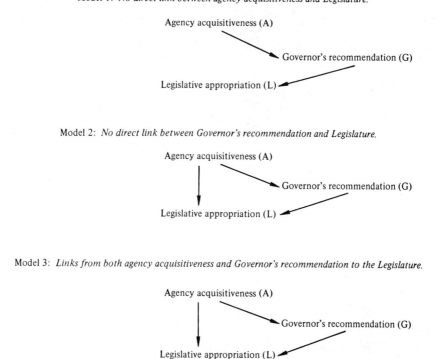

FIGURE 1. Alternative Causal Models for Relationships Among Administrative Agencies, the Governor, and the Legislature

Model 1: *No direct link between agency acquisitiveness and Legislature.*

Agency acquisitiveness (A)

Governor's recommendation (G)

Legislative appropriation (L)

Model 2: *No direct link between Governor's recommendation and Legislature.*

Agency acquisitiveness (A)

Governor's recommendation (G)

Legislative appropriation (L)

Model 3: *Links from both agency acquisitiveness and Governor's recommendation to the Legislature.*

Agency acquisitiveness (A)

Governor's recommendation (G)

Legislative appropriation (L)

$r_{X_2 X_4}$: The stronger the *positive* correlation between agency acquisitiveness and the governor's support for budget expansion, the more the governor appears to accept agency-initiated budget expansions

$r_{X_2 Y_1}$: The stronger the *negative* correlation between agency acquisitiveness and short-term success in the legislature, the more the legislature appears to be restraining agency budget development

$r_{X_2 Y_2}$: The stronger the *positive* correlation between agency acquisitiveness and budget-expansion in the legislature, the more the legislature appears to accept agency-initiated budget expansions

$r_{X_3 Y_1}$: The stronger the *positive* correlation between the governor's short-term recommendation and the legislature's short-term appropriation, the greater the gubernatorial-legislative rapport in short-term budget making

$r_{X_4 Y_2}$: The stronger the positive correlation between the governor's budget-expansion recommendation and the legislature's budget-expansion appropriation, the greater the gubernatorial-legislative rapport in budget-expansion

The independent variables for this analysis are introduced above. By examining correlation coefficients between the measures of agency-governor-legislature relationships and the measures of government structure, political characteristics and economic resources, it is possible to define certain state characteristics that support these behaviors.

FINDINGS: THE ENVIRONMENT OF AGENCY-GOVERNOR-LEGISLATURE BUDGET RELATIONS

The impact of the environment on agency-governor-legislature budget relations does not appear to be strong. Only a few of the correlation coefficients reported in Table 5 are strong enough to pass a test for statistical significance. However, by combining these significant relationships with those showing a magnitude of at least .30, it is possible to speculate about certain budget behaviors.

Two environmental characteristics associated with the governor's restraint of agency budget development are substantial veto powers and high state government expenditures.[22] Perhaps the threat of veto permits the governor to impose a severe review on the agencies when they submit requests to him. And the already-high expenditures may incline the governor against further large increases in state spending. Where the governor accepts agency requests for budget expansion, there tends to be a low state debt, high personal income, relatively intense party competition, and

[22] The correlations indicate that high scores on veto power and expenditures correspond with high *negative* relationships between agency acquisitiveness and the governor's short-term support.

TABLE 5. Coefficients of Simple Correlation Between Measures of Agency-Governor-Legislature Relationships and Independent Variables

	S_1: Governor Tenure	S_2: Governor Veto	S_3: Party Comp.	S_4: Elected Execs.	S_5: Voter Turnout	S_6: Expend/ Capita	S_7: Debt/ Capita	S_8: Personal Income/ Capita
rX_2X_3: Agency acquisitiveness and gov short-term support	.15	−.52*	.16	−.08	.16	−.34	−.05	.14
rX_3X_4: Agency acquisitiveness and gov support for expansion	−.04	−.20	.34	.07	.40	−.22	−.45	.33
rX_2Y_1: Acquisitiveness and legis, short-term appropriation	−.17	−.21	.07	.34	−.09	−.45	−.21	.15
rX_2Y_2: Acquisitiveness and legis, expansion appropriation	.09	−.27	.14	.20	.10	−.51*	−.50*	.24
rX_3Y_1: Gov. support and legis, short-term appropriation	.32	−.05	−.11	−.31	.08	.34	.21	−.06
rX_4Y_2: Gov. support and legis, expansion appropriation	.38	−.01	−.17	.18	−.11	−.07	−.45	.14

*Significant at .05 level (see note #20).

high voter turnout.[23] Perhaps low debt and high personal income permit the governor to support agency plans for expansion. And in a high participation-competitive party situation he may be inclined to seek electoral and legislative rewards by supporting innovative agencies.

Where the legislature restrains agency budget development there is relatively high state government expenditure and a low incidence of separately elected officials.[24] Like the governor, the legislature appears to resist an acquisitive agency in the face of already high expenditures. And with a scarcity of separately elected executives, agency heads may lack for politically independent allies who can promote their budget through the legislature. Where the legislature accepts agency-initiated budget expansions there tend to be low total state expenditures and state debt.[25] Thus, the condition of still-flexible resources seems to permit the legislature (like the governor) to give some support to acquisitive agencies.

Gubernatorial-legislative rapport on short-term success is high where the governor has considerable tenure potential, where there is a scarcity of separately elected executive officials, and where total expenditures are relatively high.[26] With high

tenure potential the governor may be able to elicit legislative cooperation on the expectation that he will remain in office for some time to come. The scarcity of separately elected executives may reduce the governor's competition with other powerholders for the legislature's attention. And the already-high expenditures may encourage the legislators to accept the governor's cues on the agencies' budgets. Where the governor and legislature show rapport in budget-expansion there is a similar high tenure potential and there tends to be a low state debt.[27] Perhaps the low debt constraint permits the governor and legislature to cooperate in the support of agencies that seek to expand their budgets.[28]

SUMMARY AND DISCUSSION

By means of separate correlation analyses within each of 19 states this article has defined certain relationships between administrative agencies, the governor and the legislature in state government

[23] The correlations indicate that low scores on debt, but high scores on party competition, voter turnout, and per capita personal income correspond with high *positive* relationships between agency acquisitiveness and the governor's support for budget expansion.

[24] The correlations indicate that high state expenditures and a low number of elected officials correspond with high *negative* relationships between agency acquisitiveness and short-term success in the legislature.

[25] The correlations indicate that low expenditures and debt correspond with high *positive* relationships between agency acquisitiveness and budget-expansion success in the legislature.

[26] The correlations indicate that high tenure potential and expenditures, but a low number of elected officials correspond with high *positive* relationships between the governor's short-term recommendation and the legislature's short-term appropriation.

[27] The correlations indicate that high tenure potential and low debt correspond with high *positive* relationships between the governor's recommendation and the legislature's appropriation for budget expansion.

[28] An examination of simple correlation coefficients among variables S_1–S_8 suggests that the relationships which appear most strongly in Table 5 are independent. Except for the expected relationships among turnout, competition and personal income, few of the variables show strong relationships with each other. Thus, the relationships in Table 5 involving the governor's veto, and tenure potential, and total per capita state expenditures and debt are not the product of any of the other independent variables considered in this study. The coefficients of simple correlation among the independent variables are reported here [see below]. A test with regression analysis lends support to the importance of many elected officials for the legislature's short-term support of acquisitive agencies and the importance of few elected officials for governor-legislative rapport on short-term appropriations; this independent variable (S_4) shows a regression coefficient of at least 1.5 times the standard error with the appropriate dependent variables, in the presence of all other independent variables.

	S_1	S_2	S_3	S_4	S_5	S_6	S_7	S_8
S_1 Governor's tenure	1.00	.06	−.34	−.32	.13	.19	.08	.30
S_2 Governor's veto		1.00	.20	.22	−.24	.20	−.28	.13
S_3 Party competition			1.00	.53*	−.87*	−.20	.15	−.65*
S_4 # elected executives				1.00	−.45	−.32	−.10	−.23
S_5 Voter turnout					1.00	.35	−.19	.50*
S_6 Expenditures/capita						1.00	.08	−.09
S_7 Debt/capita							1.00	−.27
S_8 Personal income/capita								1.00

*Significant at the .05 level (see note #20).

budgeting. A favorable recommendation from the governor seems essential for agency budget success in the legislature. The agency may influence both the governor's recommendation and the legislature's appropriation by the nature of its request. Acquisitive requests generally receive severe short-run treatment from the governor and the legislature, but an acquisitive strategy appears to be essential for a significant budget expansion. On the basis of separate causal analyses for each of the 19 states, it appears that the governor's recommendation is more directly important for the legislature of more states than is the acquisitiveness of agency requests.

The findings about the interaction of agency, gubernatorial, and legislative behavior help to substantiate several observations that have been made previously about executive-legislative relations and the budgetary process in American governments.[29] The reluctance of governors and legislators to support an acquisitive agency in the short term reveals the conservative bias that is built into incremental budgeting. Agencies that request little or no increase over their current budget are generally treated well by the governor and the legislature, while those seeking large increases suffer the greatest reductions in their requests. Yet an acquisitive strategy appears to be a prerequisite for a substantial budget increase. It is a rare occurrence for the governor or legislature to provide an agency with a sum larger than that it had requested. In part, this is a function of incremental budgeting. Executive and legislative budget-makers concentrate on the inspection and reduction of increments; they leave the development of incre-

ments to the agencies. At its heart, the reluctance of governors and legislators to innovate may reveal the difficult position of the generalists in their relations with agency specialists. The highly trained professional personnel in the agencies are most intimately aware of current programs and the new services that an expanded budget might produce. Chief executives and legislators have surrendered much of their innovative potential for a more limited role as reviewers of administrators' requests. And state legislators seem to have accepted a more limited supervisory role than the governors. The findings of greater importance for the governor's recommendation (rather than the agency's request) in the legislature's decisions indicates the legislature's dependence on the governor's budget cues. Perhaps this reflects the greater staff resources of the governor and the typically amateurish character of state legislatures. When they are compared to the professional analysts in the governor's office, legislators appear to have little experience in public budgeting, no professional training in a relevant discipline, an impossibly brief time to consider agency budgets and inadequate staff and clerical assistance.[30] State legislators have a desperate need for cues that will guide their budget performance and the governor's recommendation is usually the best cue available.

When the 19 states are examined for the characteristics that support various styles of relationships between agencies, the governor, and the legislature, the findings shed some new light on the influence of governmental and political characteristics of the states.[31] The veto and tenure powers of the governor help to strengthen his position with both the agencies and the legislature. Because of formal prerogatives, the governor appears to be in a more secure position when he reduces agency requests and makes recommendations to the legislature; the governors that have these powers are more likely to be severe in cutting agency requests and they are more likely to be successful in their recommendations to the legislature. In contrast, the presence of numerous separately elected executives appears

[29] See, for example, Arthur MacMahon, "Congressional Oversight of Administration: The Power of the Purse," *Political Science Quarterly*, Vol. 58 (June and September 1943), pp. 161–190, and 380–414; Warner Schilling, "The Politics of National Defense: Fiscal 1950," in Schilling *et al.*, *Strategy, Politics and Defense Budgets* (New York: Columbia University Press, 1962), pp. 1–266; Elias Huzar, *The Purse and the Sword* (Ithaca; Cornell University Press, 1950); Aaron Wildavsky, *The Politics of the Budgetary Process* (Boston: Little, Brown, 1964); Rufus Browning, "Innovative and Non-Innovative Decision Processes in Government Budgeting," a paper delivered at the Annual Meeting of the American Political Science Association, September 1963; Richard Fenno, *The Power of the Purse, op. cit.*; John P. Crecine, "A Computer Simulation Model of Municipal Resource Allocation," a paper presented at the 1966 Midwest Political Science Association Meeting.

[30] See Malcolm E. Jewell and Samuel C. Patterson, *op. cit.*, p. 251 ff.
[31] See the works by Dye, Dawson, and Robinson and Sharkansky cited in note 1; plus Richard I. Hofferbert, "The Relation between Public Policy and Some Structural and Environmental Variables in the American States," *American Political Science Review*, Vol. 60 (March 1966), pp. 73–82.

to benefit agencies at the governor's expense. In the states where there are many elected officials, agencies are more likely to get their acquisitive requests approved by the legislature, and the governor's recommendation is most likely to be altered in the legislature. Party competition and voter turnout also seem to strengthen the agencies' position. In states with heavy turnout and intense competition the governor is most likely to support the agencies' acquisitive requests, perhaps in an effort to assert his own identity as a program innovator. High levels of state government expenditure and debt work in opposition to agency budget aspirations. Where spending and debt is already high, both the governor and the legislature are severe in reviewing agency requests. This may be an outgrowth of incremental budgeting. The principal reviewers are conservative in their attitudes toward increases in expenditures, and they may be particularly wary of acquisitive agencies when existing state resources are already heavily committed.

Much of this book is addressed to the newer roles and functions which are occupying the time and attention of state chief executives. Many of these functions center around the governor's administrative and political roles in the federal system, including the coordination of federally funded programs at the state and local levels; the assistance that state agencies, under the governor's policy direction, give to cities, counties and multicounty regions under federal programs; and the growing number of national and regional associations and interstate compacts on which governors serve and which exert influence on national policy. These roles and functions have made the governor the federal systems officer at the state level.

For years this role was minimal and pinpointed in such organizations as the National Governors' Conference and regional governors' conferences. In recent years, however, gubernatorial involvement and responsibility in governmental programs and activity have increased greatly.

There has been a trend in federal legislation—for example, the Omnibus Crime Control and Safe Streets Act, the Comprehensive Health Planning Act, the Economic Opportunity Acts, the Land and Water Conservation Act—and regional development programs—for example, the Appalachian Regional Commission—to designate the governor as the chief federal planning and administrative officer in the state. A new governor must become aware of the newer roles and the fact that they provide him with additional powers rather than constricting his ability to govern.

An example of the administrative responsibility given to the governor in recent federal grant programs is the Omnibus Crime Control and Safe Streets Act of 1968. Section 203 of the Act states in part:

A grant made under this part to a state shall be utilized by the State to establish and maintain a State Planning Agency. Such planning agency shall be created or designated by the chief executive of the state and shall be subject to his jurisdiction.

Similar authority to designate the planning, coordination, and utilization of federal funds has been given to the state chief executive in the other programs mentioned above. While the planning and utilization of federally funded programs are functions which the governor will designate to planning agencies and line departments, there are several reasons why the governor and his immediate staff

SECTION 3
GOVERNORS AND POLICY IMPLEMENTATION

assistants maintain a close interest in the development of these programs at the state level. The governor usually is interested in seeing that state agencies and local governments pursue these programs. Federal aid is necessary to alleviate serious problems which states face and for which governors feel an executive responsibility. Governors are usually interested in seeing that the direction sought in federally funded programs is compatible with the state's overall goals. In addition, much of the responsibility for federal "grantsmanship" devolves to the governor because he can use the status of his office to influence the procedural and policy guidelines that accompany federally funded programs and he wants to see that programs work to the advantage of state objectives—as he defines them.

To say that such programmatic influence and leadership are possible in the gubernatorial office is not to imply that governors always succeed in establishing their own priorities or their states' priorities in intergovernmental programs. Many states continue to operate within ideological and programmatic guidelines established at the national level. The articles written for this section ask questions concerning the approaches governors have taken in the changing federal milieu and how effective governors have been in the new programmatic concerns of the past decade. In a number of program areas—including crime control, health manpower and facilities planning, education and the whole range of urban housing and transportation problems—approaches of the past decade leave little doubt that governors have increased resources and opportunities for policy-making and planning. In some areas, such as crime control and poverty programs, the slight role given to governors has not evoked a strong political response and involvement by the governors throughout the states. But in urban, health, and education policies, where their role necessarily has been increasing in importance, the concern and activity of governors has been more pronounced.

The first urban disorders of the 1960s were the occasion for increased, direct contact by the governors with the internal problems and policies of cities. Perhaps the first realization was that the agencies responsible to the governor were not equipped to deal effectively with urban constituencies and problems, and this led to the creation of a number of new departments at the state level —most notably departments of urban and community affairs. Where only four states had urban affairs departments at the beginning of the sixties, more than half did by the end of the decade. Only in states without sizable urban areas did governors have neither an urban department nor urban coordinators on their staffs.

And as transportation problems begin to mount, states are responding by enlarging their approach from the traditional State Highway Department or Commission to Departments of Transportation. Similar broadening movements seem to be afoot in the areas of human resources or social services and conservation and environmental protection.

The order of presentation in this section is not random. It represents the trends of gubernatorial concerns. As seen earlier, traditional bases of leadership strength are significant and old antagonists have not disappeared. But here we not only see the governor concerned with how to control or direct state government with the best of the management tools available, but we also follow him into several crucial areas for which he now has greater responsibility.

It could be that the most significant chapter is yet to be written: the governors and revenue sharing. Some of the trends pictured here will continue, others will be redirected. But at least the following presentations may give a glimpse as to how the governors might cope with so great a responsibility.

CHAPTER 7

GOVERNORS, FEDERAL GRANTS, AND NEW POLICY TOOLS

In recent decades the leadership tools on which the governor has traditionally relied have been joined by newer ones, among them grants-in-aid, planning, the computer, and systems analysis. While they vary in usage and applicability to the needs of governors and state governments, they undoubtedly are increasingly relied on by state officials who make decisions and implement policies.

During the 1960s, the number, size, and scope of federal grant-in-aid programs increased greatly in response to programmatic demands and needs at all levels of government. The development of these grants had many positive aspects, not the least of which was to give states, and governors, more flexibility and wherewithal to carry out programs. But the grants often highlighted basic weaknesses in the states. Control over governmental activities became even more impossible than before with the added freedom and flexibility which federal funds could often provide, and management over just what state government was doing became even closer to a myth.

Into this breach has surged the panaceas of the 1960s—PPBS, planning, coordination, the computer, data banks, issue analysis and systems analysis.

The articles in this chapter explore this overall situation by focusing specifically on the governor's relationships with grants, planning, and the new systems technology. We call them new policy tools, but have the uneasy feeling that as they presently exist they are less tools than they are the panaceas or reforms of the day. And our governmental and political history is replete with examples of yesterday's reforms becoming today's roadblocks.

GOVERNORS, GRANTS, AND THE INTERGOVERNMENTAL SYSTEM
Deil S. Wright

On more than one occasion in corridors of hotels housing the annual Governor's Conference the comment has been made, rather quietly, that the convention is actually a gathering of the chief "federal systems officers." Responses to this suggestive but imprecise description vary from "So what else is new!" to "That's nonsense!" Whatever interpretation is placed on the governor's intergovernmental role it seems indisputable that the chief executive is deeply enmeshed in a tangled web of intergovernmental program and policy relationships. These connections stretch from the central core to the farthest nook and cranny of our complex political system. Furthermore, these intergovernmental linkages are dense and intense for governors where the grant-in-aid policy tool is employed.

One illustration will suffice. Robert Wood, former Secretary of HUD, reports that an operational simulation of the Model Cities program "identified the governor as a key figure in the delivery program."[1] It should be noted and perhaps emphasized that Model Cities is primarily a direct federal-local program with appearances and even expectations that state government would have only an incidental or insignificant role. Yet a careful modeling of the components, requirements, participants, and relationships involved in Model Cities pinpointed the governor's critical role.

The Model Cities illustration provides both a justification and a starting point for discussing the position and perspectives of governors on grants-in-aid in particular and on intergovernmental relations in general.

GRANTS: PAYOFFS AND PROBLEMS

The position of governors in relation to the new federalism of grant-in-aid programs is anomalous and ambiguous. Since grants supply a major portion of state budgets it would border on political suicide for governors to oppose or refuse to accept them. Indeed, there are positive political payoffs from a governor's standpoint in obtaining as much federal aid as possible. Federal grants do help meet demands for services and, perhaps more important, are generally regarded by voters as a way of keeping state taxes down.

But grants have disadvantages because they restrict the range of policy choices open to the governor. In fact, restriction is inherent in the grant device, since each federal grant program stems from a *national* decision to promote certain aims on a *national* scale through the grant mechanism. Policy restraints on the governor operate not only between programs, but also within those particular programs that include several detailed grant categories or prescribe administrative standards sharply limiting flexible and effective use (from the governor's viewpoint) of grant funds.

An additional element of restraint on the governor comes from a combination of two factors: (1) pressure groups, either the traditional private lobbies or those composed of public officials, and (2) the fact that frequently the fields supported by grants are partially insulated from gubernatorial control through the device of a board or commission. Highways provide an example. Policy control in this area usually rests less with governors than with alliances of highway engineers at all levels plus construction contractors and cement and equipment manufacturers. The administrative consequences of grants-in-aid tend to reinforce the dispersion of powers away from the chief executive. In short, the governors' policy-coordinating role is often diluted or effectively blocked.

Coleman Ransone, in a succinct analysis of these cross-pressures, raised a central question being asked by most governors, "the new federalism—bane or boon?" Two of his conclusions were:

In practice, therefore, the governor finds that his policy decisions are conditioned by the policy decisions which have been made in Washington....

The governor, to a considerable extent, is bypassed in the line of communication and finds that his control over both policy and management of the agencies which administer these [grant] programs at the state level is weakened considerably.[2]

Grants-in-aid, then, contribute to the headaches governors suffer in performing their political and administrative leadership roles. At the same time they can serve as aspirin to alleviate state fiscal woes. Such is the paradox of the governor and grants.

PRIOR PERSPECTIVES ON GRANTS

What do governors think about grant programs? Unfortunately, the data are exceptionally limited. We lack, for example, any systematic analysis of the frequency and content of governors' testimony before congressional committees or their interactions with the President and cabinet officers.

Two surveys have solicited governors' views on a

[1] Robert C. Wood, "Needs and Prospects for Research in Intergovernmental Relations," *Public Administration Review*, Vol. 30, No. 3 (May/June 1970), p. 267.

[2] Coleman B. Ransone, Jr., *The Office of Governor in the United States* (University, Ala.: University of Alabama Press, 1956), pp. 249–250.

range of questions on grants-in-aid.[3] The first, sponsored by the House Subcommittee on Intergovernmental Relations in 1957, asked detailed questions in four functional areas: employment security, highways, public health, and welfare. The number of responses ranged from 20 to 30. Although some reservation exists about the extent to which the responses represent the views of the governors rather than of their program officials, it appears that all responses were cleared through the governors.

Regarding program adequacy, there was major sentiment favoring expansion in all four functional areas. Clear majorities were satisfied with federal supervision but a notable minority in three areas indicated some dissatisfaction. A substantial minority favored some transfer of responsibility, mainly in the direction of a greater state role. Questions regarding the need for legislative or administrative changes pointedly demonstrated the ambivalence present among governors with respect to grant programs. Almost uniformly, the governors noted that these kinds of improvements were needed—*at the federal level*. These views stand in sharp contrast to their support for program expansion and their general satisfaction with program responsibilities and federal supervision. The general response pattern, although dated and admittedly limited, documents the difficult position of the governor under the "new federalism."

The second survey, undertaken by the Senate Subcommittee on Intergovernmental Relations in 1963, queried 6,000 state and local officials, including all governors. The response rate was very poor generally (8 percent), and only 9 of the 50 governors responded. Not surprisingly, the responses fitted the pattern revealed by the earlier House subcommittee survey. For example, six of the nine governors mentioned additional functions that should receive grant assistance, and the same

number wanted reassignment of some responsibilities under grant programs to the states. Conversely, five felt that grants distorted the emphasis of state and local programs, and eight of the nine agreed that federal grant requirements hampered organizational flexibility at the state and local level. Responses to numerous other questions fitted a similar mold.

In general the governors acknowledged the political and programmatic advantages of grants but were quick to point out the financial and administrative problems that almost invariably accompanied them. The continued proliferation of grants by number and type has added to the latter complexities.

RECENT SELECTIVE VIEWS

The six-year span from 1957 to 1963 produced no sharp differences in governors' views on federal grants. A generally favorable posture toward grants was balanced by a recognition of their problematic aspects, with the former somewhat outweighing the latter. The lapse of another six years from 1963 to 1969 and the impact of "creative federalism" raised some question about the balance of gubernatorial opinion on grants: Did it still fall on the credit side of the ledger? The number of governors' views expressed on grants in 1969 was even smaller than in earlier years. Two governors, Rockefeller of New York and Rampton of Utah, testified before the House Subcommittee on Intergovernmental Relations. They spoke as representatives of the National Governors' Conference and of their individual states on pending grant reform legislation.[4] Excerpts from their statements to the subcommittee convey the content and strength of their criticisms of grants.

Governor Rockefeller:[5]
I would like to concentrate on two fundamental questions:

Is the present system of categorical grants-in-aid effectively meeting today's needs?

---

[3] The two surveys were quite different in terms of content and respondents covered. See *Replies from State and Local Governments to Questionnaire on Intergovernmental Relations*, Sixth Report by the Committee on Government Operations, U.S. House of Representatives, Eighty-fifth Congress, First Session, House Report No. 575, June 17, 1957, and *The Federal System as Seen by State and Local Officials*, a study prepared by the staff of the Subcommittee on Intergovernmental Relations of the Committee on Government Operations, U.S. Senate, Eighty-eighth Congress, First Session (Committee Print), 1963.

[4] For an analysis of grant reform proposals see American Enterprise Institute, *Grants-in-Aid Reform Proposals* (Washington, D.C.: Legislative Analysis No. 24, Ninety-first Congress, Second Session, December, 1970), 64 pp.

[5] Hearings before the Subcommittee on Intergovernmental Relations of the House Committee on Government Operations, *Grant Consolidation and Intergovernmental Cooperation*, Ninety-first Congress, First Session (Part 1), June, 1969, pp. 87, 89.

And, two, if given more flexibility, can, and will, the states and localities use federal funds more effectively?

There is a maze of programs—420 federal grant-in-aid programs. In the five years between 1963 and 1967 alone, some 240 new programs have been added, an average of about 48 programs a year.

The Department of Health, Education and Welfare has some 209 separate programs, including 17 types of welfare grants, 79 for education, and 80 for public health.

The splintering of grants produces a maze of plans, regulations and rulings. The 17 grants in welfare alone have led to 5,000 pages of federal program operating requirements. In the case of education grants, a state is required to submit 20 separate plans.

Now, I would just like to make a comment parenthetically regarding this, if I may. The complexity and number of these rules and regulations require a tremendous amount of skilled manpower just to conform to the regulations. Thus we are siphoning off skilled manpower to follow the detailed regulations.

In the case of the 20 separate state education plans, the difficulty is that each plan is unrelated to the other. The plans are required by different bureaus, and the separate grant programs each have different requirements. The result is that state operations become very splintered. And I am not quite clear myself as to who actually reads these 20 plans when they come down to Washington, and if they are read, what is done about them.

But we have to submit them, and it prevents us from trying to plan an overall approach to education on an integrated state and local basis.

It is my feeling that the categorical grants system is not geared to today's needs. The failure to meet today's needs is far more critical than the concern for administrative waste, which, of course, is a very real concern.

The need for a more comprehensive approach and for greater flexibility to meet functional requirements is vital, as is the need for flexibility to help state and local governments meet their fiscal crises.

Now, you might summarize the problems which states and local governments face within three separate categories:

First, is the financial crisis, a crisis of money in both state and local governments, and I am sure that one would add at the federal level.

Secondly, the need for a flexible, comprehensive approach to today's problems, at both state and local levels.

And, third is the fact that aid programs, one might say, are for fringe benefits. They ask for additions to ongoing programs, but do not contribute to the basic ongoing costs of the state and local governments, such as the cost of teachers' salaries, police, fire, sanitation—the basic services which we have to supply.

Historically, federal grants were used to prod and push states and localities to begin specific new programs. I think this was an eminently justified and farsighted point

of view on the part of the Congress, and it has had very good effect. However, with rare exceptions, federal programs are not available for the everyday burdens, the ongoing services I mentioned before—police, teachers, fire, sanitation, et cetera, with a shortage of funds, the moneys have to be taken from basic services to be used for matching for fringe-benefit services. In fact, due to federal matching requirements, state and local funds must be used for the new programs. State and local fiscal crises are due, however, to the rapidly rising cost of day-to-day public service.

The basic need today is for Federal support, not Federal stimulation.

Governor Rampton:[6]
Mr. Chairman, I have very little to add to what Governor Rockefeller said, except that the problems encountered by New York State in responding to federal programs are probably magnified in a small state. Our state government is smaller and considerably more simplified than either the government of the State of New York or the government of the United States, and for the limited number of state departments that we have that have to respond or who have the opportunity to respond to so many federal programs, it is very difficult.

We have another problem, too, in regard to categorical grants. The standards and guidelines of categorical grants, which are often rigid and very detailed, are set forth to meet the needs of the typical state, and the typical state, of course, is generally a larger state. Often these rigid guidelines will not meet at all the requirements of a smaller state with substantially different problems.

I prepared a bill and had it introduced into the last legislature to make a single department of state government administer all manpower programs and consolidate them. Well, about halfway through I got cold feet for fear that I was going to lose some Federal money by using this consolidating procedure, and so we substituted a bill providing for a coordinating committee to try to coordinate them.

But, of course, coordination, while it is sometimes the only answer that you can get, is never as successful as actual consolidation into a single department, which we could do if all of these 17 grants that we have came to us in a single block grant.

Several significant features of these statements should be clarified and emphasized. Governor Rockefeller makes at least four telling points concerning grants. First, the recent rapid growth in grants had produced a situation bordering on administrative chaos. Second, the criticisms of grants now extends well beyond administrative difficulties. Third, the broader issue is the failure of

[6]*Ibid.*, pp. 93–94, 97.

categorical grants, according to Governor Rockefeller, to meet "today's needs." Fourth, categorical grants are out-of-phase because (a) they finance "fringe benefits" rather than basic state-local services and (b) they are stimulative rather than supportive.

Governor Rampton not only concurs in the above points, but adds a few significant ones of his own. First, he contends that the problems posed by grants are greater for small states than for large ones. He sees grant guidelines and standards geared for "the typical state" which to his way of thinking is a large state. A second point implicit in this "typicality" observation are views about the underlying diversity and divisions among the states—e.g., "large" versus "small." Not only is there a hint of interstate competition over grants but also the more openly expressed feeling that grants have a substantive bias favorable to the large states. A third point emphasized by Rampton is the difficulty encountered by a governor in attempting to assert a policy-coordinating role. The illustration concerns manpower programs, but it could be extended to multiple grant authorizations in numerous program fields.

A final point of emphasis is Governor Rampton's mention of the block grant. This type of funding mechanism, contrasted with the categorical grant, has long been a figment of academicians' imagination and a gleam in the eyes of state and local officials, especially governors. Two recently enacted grant programs, Model Cities and Law Enforcement Assistance, are the first experiments with block grants.[7] The block grant is, in part, a response to the governors' call for "support" rather than stimulation.

If the statements of Governors Rockefeller and Rampton are reasonably representative of governors' opinions generally, then we have documented an important shift in state executive reactions to the "creative federalism" of the Johnson years. A few years ago the governors' position in the spider-like web of grant relationships seemed to be buoyed by the sticky cords that the governor could climb, pull, or otherwise manipulate, albeit with no small amount of difficulty. Currently governors seem to perceive their position in the web much more like that of a trapped fly, wondering whether they will escape before the federal spider swallows them or the entire web is torn asunder.[8]

DISCRETE AND COLLECTIVE ACTIONS

Grants-in-aid are the basis for a major subset of the totality of intergovernmental relationships experienced by governors. Precisely what proportion of all external contacts by the governor are prompted by grant matters is impossible to specify. One consequence of grant-induced relationships is an increased orientation of the governor toward Washington, D.C. In more informal parlance the process has been described as expanding governors' "Potomac pipelines."

Three brief items about these state-national links reveal the nature and expanding scope of these linkages. Former governor (of Florida) Farris Bryant testified that:

> The next to the last year I was in office, I sent the executive director of our state board of health to Washington on a year's leave of absence, badly as we needed him, just so he could learn how to operate with federal people. He has been a great help to us since that time. But you ought not to have to do that kind of thing to learn just how to get along and through this morass.[9]

A second bit of information about the governors and Washington is the fact that over one-third of the states have permanent offices and staff people located in the nation's capital. A sidelight on the problem of establishing state (and gubernatorial) representation in Washington was a recent episode in North Carolina. The governor's proposal to create a state-federal relations agency located in Washington generated some criticism, particularly from the opposition party. The matter was re-

---

[7]For discussions of the block grant, especially the Law Enforcement Assistance Act, see B. Douglas Harman, "The Bloc Grant: Readings from a First Experiment," *Public Administration Review*, Vol. 30, No. 2 (March/April 1970), pp. 141–153; Urban Data Service, International City Management Association, *The Safe Streets Act: The Cities Evaluation*, Vol. 1, No. 9 (September 1969), 46 pp.; The Urban Coalition and Urban America, Inc., *Law and Disorder: State Planning Under the Safe Streets Act* (Washington, D.C.: June, 1969), 27 pp.; American Enterprise Institute, *The Crime Control and Safe Streets Bill* (Washington, D.C.: Legislative Analysis No. 11, Ninety-first Congress, Second Session, September, 1970), 23 pp.

[8]A less ominous but still apprehensive theme on intergovernmental relations is found in the action-oriented statements of nine governors for a symposium on the American governor. See *Public Administration Review*, Vol. 30, No. 1 (January/February 1970), pp. 27–41.

[9]*Grant Consolidation* hearings, p. 241.

TABLE 1. Resolutions of the Governors' Conference by Type of Intergovernmental Action Recommended and Time Period, 1946–69

Type of Action	Number				Percentages			
	1946–1957	1958–1964	1965–1969	1946–1969	1946–1957	1958–1964	1965–1969	1946–1969
Less (or opposed to) national action	14	13	13	40	11	10	11	11
More (or favorable to) national action	38	55	54	147	31	40	47	39
More state action	43	52	36	131	35	38	32	35
More interstate action	20	12	5	37	16	9	4	10
More local action	8	4	6	18	7	3	5	5
Total actions	123	136	114	373	100	100	100	100
Total resolutions	90	109	99	298				

Source of resolutions: *State Government* (Council of State Governments, annual articles on the Governors' Conference).

solved by creating the office but keeping it "at home" in Raleigh, the state capital.

A third piece of evidence about expanding Potomac pipelines appeared in 1966 with the creation of a separate staff for the Governors' Conference and the locating of that staff in Washington. Previously the Governors' Conference had been served by the staff of the Council of State Governments with offices in Chicago. This new and active governors' "base in D.C." attempts to monitor, inform, and provide leverage for the state chief executives on federal policy developments affecting the states.[10]

Reference to the Governors' Conference calls attention to the resolutions passed at its annual sessions as a rich source of gubernatorial perspectives on the intergovernmental system. A fivefold classification scheme was used in examining the formal substantive resolutions passed at the Governors' Conference from 1946 through 1969. Table 1 presents the results of the coding process for 298 identifiable substantive resolutions (called "policy statements" after 1968). A total of 373 assignments to the intergovernmental action categories were made since it was possible (and frequent) that a single resolution called for more than one type of action. The tabulation is also subdivided by three time periods which correspond to particular break points in federal-state relations and also happen to include about 100 resolutions in each of the three periods.[11]

The percentage columns in Table 1 translate the resolution frequencies into proportionate terms for interperiod comparisons. For the full quarter-century period, however, a few general observations can be offered. The distribution for the 1946–69 period reveals that in a collective setting the governors' policy concerns were about evenly divided between calls for more positive action by the national government and advocacy of state responses to public problems. Somewhat more than one-third of all actions recommended fell in each of these two categories. Negative stances toward national action occurred with nearly the same frequency as resolutions urging interstate efforts—i.e., "horizontal" federalism. Recommendations urging local action, e.g., improved local law enforcement, were infrequent, they amounted to only 5 percent of all calls for action and about half of the frequency of positions of an antinational nature.

Perhaps the major conclusion from the long-term tabulation is the minor extent to which the Gover-

[10] For a discussion of the considerations and recommendations leading to the creation of the Governors' Washington Office see: National Governors' Conference, *Official Papers: Special Interim Meeting*, White Sulfur Springs, West Virginia, December 16–17, 1966 (Chicago, 1967), pp. 6–19. Other discussions of Washington office operations include Arlen J. Large, "Taming The Octopus," *The Wall Street Journal*, September 1, 1967, and Jonathan Cottin, "Washington Pressures: National Governors' Conference," *National Journal*, February 28, 1970, pp. 454–459.

[11] The author is indebted to Mr. David E. Stephenson for assistance in coding and check-coding the Governors' Conference resolutions. The coding reliability was 84 percent agreement. Acknowledgment is also made of support for this research from the University Research Council of the University of North Carolina.

nors' Conference has been a formal forum for barbs aimed at the national government. Only a states' rights "tithe" of about 10 percent has been levied against the national government in actions urged by the state executives. This finding gives credence and precision to the assertion by Glenn Brooks that "the governors have not invariably sought to turn back the invading national government at the borders of the states."[12] Indeed, a plurality of their recommended actions ask for greater national action.

A breakdown of the resolutions by the three time periods shown in Table 1 provides the basis for further comments and conclusions. A word might be said about the rationale for using periods that are unequal in years but nearly equal in resolutions and actions. The year 1957 was selected as a dividing line since that was the date of President Eisenhower's historic Williamsburg speech urging the "return" of functions to the states. The next cutting point, 1964, was chosen because it was the last Governors' Conference prior to the flood of grants under the Great Society and creative federalism policies.

The most marked feature of the percentages across the three periods is the rise in proposals for greater national action. These proposals increased from less than one-third in the first period to nearly half of the actions in the 1965–69 period. For the most part actions recommended in this category increased at the expense of declining attention paid by governors to interstate matters. One might sum up this trend by concluding that the Governors' Conference has become increasingly "nationalized." Currently nearly 60 percent of its policy statements are beamed toward Washington, with about half of all statements asking for affirmative national responses.

A decade ago a study of governors reported that perhaps 20 percent of a governors' time was occupied by national problems and relationships.[13] If the proportion of Governors' Conference resolutions relating to national action even partially reflects the amount of time governors spend on their Potomac pipeline duties, then gubernatorial-national relations have taken a quantum leap in a short span of time.

[12] Glenn E. Brooks, *When Governors Convene: The Governors' Conference and National Politics* (Baltimore: Johns Hopkins Press, 1961), pp. 167–168.
[13] *Ibid.* p. 161.

CONCLUDING COMMENTS

What are the implications of such a shift in role and orientation by governors, if indeed the change has been as great as our imperfect data would suggest? Can we identify the causes of the shift and take corrective action, if need be, to alter the pulls, the pressures, and the constraints on governors? What are some of the consequences of the presumed changes and are these consequences desirable? Even if proximate answers were available to these questions they would be beyond the intended scope and space of this discussion. We can do no more here than call attention to their significance and offer a concluding paragraph on the governor's intergovernmental role.

The grant-based intergovernmental "economy" has led to the ascendancy of administrative professionalism in state government and has combined with increases in the scope and velocity of government to alter the role and the perspectives of governors. We submit the hypothesis that the governor has become a greater coordinator, controller, connector, and compromiser than at any period in the past. This increased "administrator" role does not assume or assert that the governor's policy leadership and public-political functions have disappeared or have been displaced. It does posit that a highly concentrated effort is required from the governor simply to hold the state public service system together and make it work. It also supposes that grand and imaginative policy innovations by governors are less and less likely.

Is this the mold into which the governors of the 1970s are cast? Will they be content to fit it? Must we wait for the 1980s to give us the answer?

THE GOVERNOR, PLANNING, AND GOVERNMENTAL ACTIVITY
Thad L. Beyle
and
Deil S. Wright

For over 35 years, the call for executive-oriented state planning has been made—from A. E. Buck in the 1930s,[1] to the little Hoover Commissions in

[1] Arthur E. Buck, *The Reorganization of State Government in the United States* (New York: Columbia University Press, 1938).

the 1950s,[2] to the spate of state government reform publications of the mid-1960s.[3] The call is usually phrased in terms of providing the governor and the executive branch with an additional decision-making tool. But the nature of what planning is and can do varies considerably.

The response of the states first came in a slow and halting fashion, but recently the pace quickened. The questions to be addressed here concern the experience of the states with executive-oriented planning. How is planning related to the governor and his executive office? What type of assistance does planning provide to the governors? What variables relate to the performance of the state planning agency and its activities?

THE GOVERNOR AND STATE PLANNING[4]

The history of the state planning function indicates that initially (in the 1930s) these planning

---

[2] For example, see State of Utah, Commission on the Organization of the Executive Branch of the Government, *Report to the Thirty-sixth Legislature* (Salt Lake City: The Commission, 1966).

[3] See, for example, Chamber of Commerce of the United States, *Modernizing State Government* (Washington D.C.: The Chamber, 1967); Committee for Economic Development, *Modernizing State Government* (New York: CED, 1967); Terry Sanford, *Storm Over the States* (New York: McGraw-Hill, 1967); and various publications of the Advisory Commission on Intergovernmental Relations and the Council of State Governments.

[4] Portions of the analysis in this section were originally presented in Thad L. Beyle, Sureva Seligson, and Deil S. Wright, "New Directions in State Planning," *Journal of the American Institute of Planners*, Vol. XXXV (September 1969), pp. 335–339, and in a report to the Department of Transportation, "State Planning and Intergovernmental Relations," January 1970 (80 pp., mimeo).

Much of the data used throughout this analysis was obtained in conjunction with surveys conducted by the Institute on State Programming for the 70s. The Institute was an independent, nonprofit organization created in January 1967 to strengthen state government by stimulating comprehensive, long-range planning activities in all the states. It was funded by the Carnegie Corporation of New York and headquartered at the University of North Carolina (Chapel Hill). Former Governor Jack M. Campbell of New Mexico (1963–66) served as chairman of the institute.

As one its activities, the institute conducted a survey on "The Present Status, Effectiveness, and Acceptance of State Planning and Advanced Programing in State Government." The collection, tabulation, and analysis of the data was supervised in part by the authors. The survey

agencies were created primarily as separate and independent entities. By the 1950s, the original agencies had evolved into "economic development" or promotional units. Beginning in the late 1950s, a shift away from the economic development focus occurred. Part of this shift in focus was prompted by federal grant program requirements calling for plans and a planning process. Part was to fill a need at the state level—especially by governors.

As Table 1 shows, during the period 1960–69, thirteen states added state planning agencies, while 31 states changed the location of their agencies, with 11 maintaining existing arrangements. Considerable shifting in agency location also has been evident since 1969.

In line with current planning and reform theory, the trend is to place the planning agency in close proximity to the governor, either directly in his office or in his fiscal and management arm—departments of administration or finance. In 1960, only 5 states had their planning agencies located in or close to the governor's office; by 1971, 36 states had such an arrangement.

The beginnings of a new departure, establishing planning agencies in departments of community or urban affairs, was evident between 1965 and 1969 as three states opted for such an arrangement. These new departments are usually closely tied to the governor in personnel, programs, style, and power, and therefore appear to be serving as key gubernatorial agencies.

The establishment of the new community or local affairs departments is also a new trend. There were only four such departments in 1963. By 1970, there were 28, with several other states considering the possibility of such an agency. And at a

---

was conducted under a U.S. Department of Housing and Urban Development Planning and Research Demonstration contract awarded under the provisions of Section 701(b) of the Housing Act of 1954, as amended. Its components included: (1) field interviews with 18 governors and 677 persons involved in charting and reporting on the direction of all 50 state governments; (2) a detailed content analysis of enabling legislation for officially designated state planning agencies; and (3) supplementary questionnaires designed to verify and expand on information supplied by state planning agency officials.

Additional data for the 1971 location of agencies was provided by the Council of State Governments.

TABLE 1. Organizational Location of State Planning Agencies, 1960–1971

Location	1960		1965		1969		1971	
Governor's office	3 ⎫		11 ⎫		20 ⎫		29 ⎫	
Department of administration or finance	2 ⎭	5	2 ⎭	13	7 ⎭	27	7 ⎭	36
Department of community affairs	0		0		3		3	
Department of commerce, development, or planning and development agencies	23 ⎫		27 ⎫		13 ⎫		8 ⎫	
Independent planning agency	5 ⎭	28	7 ⎭	34	5 ⎭	18	3 ⎭	11
None of the above	4		1		2		0	
Total state planning agencies	37		48		50		50	

meeting in June 1970, the Council of State Governments reported that directors of 42 state departments of community affairs were in attendance.[5]

Considerable residue remained, however, from the practice of the 1940s and 1950s of placing planning in development agencies or in entirely independent agencies. The number of such state agencies increased from 28 in 1960, to 34 in 1965. Apparently the trend has been reversed. By 1971 only 11 states adhered to this practice. The moves were most significant in departments of commerce or development, which housed 27 planning offices in 1965, but only 8 by 1971. The rapid growth in the number of state planning agencies that are gubernatorial staff services has been accompanied by a concomitant decrease in the number of agencies located outside direct gubernatorial control.

In the summer of 1967, the Institute on State Programming for the 70s investigated the "Present Status, Effectiveness, and Acceptance of State Planning and Advanced Programming in State Government." Of concern to this reform-oriented Institute was the effect of location on the state planning agency's performance. Following visits to each of the fifty states, the staff was asked to judge whether the activities of the agency were relevant to the decision-making process in the state.[6] Their answers indicate that these shifts in agency location are significant (Table 2).

Twenty-three of the state planning agencies were considered relevant to the decision-making process in the survey; 14 of those were located under the governor's direct control and only 9 outside of his control. Of those considered not relevant, the relationship was reversed; 12 of 16 were outside gubernatorial control, leaving only 4 within direct gubernatorial control as performing not-relevant activities. As contemporary planning and reform theory would have it, planning has become a key staff function; to be relevant it needs to be located as close to the chief decision-maker as possible.

PLANNING AND STATE GOVERNMENT ACTIVITIES

If state planning is increasingly becoming gubernatorial in both location and orientation,[7] we need

[5] *State Headlines* (Washington D.C.: Council of State Governments), no. 70-7, March 30, 1970, and *Governors' Bulletin* (Washington D.C.: National Governors Conference), no. 70-23, June 5, 1970.

[6] The relevance of the state planning agencies activities to the decision-making process was determined on the basis of the field interviews in each of the 50 states during the summer of 1967. This judgmental variable is thus based on interviews with many actors within each state's system, plus some observations and evaluations of the agencies' performance.

[7] For illustrations of how governors and the planning function can work in tandem, see Thomas J. Anton, "State Planning, Gubernatorial Leadership and Federal Funds: Three Cases," in *The Office of Governor* (Urbana: Institute of Government and Public Affairs, University of Illinois, May 1963), pp. 63–79.

TABLE 2. Organizational Location by Relevance of
State Planning Agencies, 1967

Relevance to Decision-Making Process	Location		
	In governor's office, Dept. of Admin., Finance, or Budget	Outside governor's office, Dept. of Admin., Finance, or Budget	Total
Is relevant	14	9	23
Is not relevant	4	12	16
Not adequately determined	6	4	10
Total	24	25	49

to know what type of management tool is being developed to aid the governors. This requires an analysis of what state planning agencies are authorized to do by the legislative act establishing them, and what they actually do in practice. Just what is the role of the state planning agency as it moves closer to the governor?

The 1967 Institute of State Programming staff was asked to judge the priorities of action pursued for each state planning agency. Thirteen specific activities were derived from the responses, and these were examined to see if they were performed as a requirement in the basic legislation establishing the agency (mandated), or as a role the agency itself developed (nonmandated).[8] Table 3 presents data showing that these activities break down into four basic roles: preparation of plans; review and

[8] Legislative mandate was determined by a content analysis of the state planning agencies enabling legislation as of 1967. Actual performance is a judgmental variable based on field interviews in each state.

TABLE 3. Activities of State Planning Agencies

	Performed			Not Performed		
	Mandated	Not mandated	Total	Mandated	Not mandated	Total
A. Plan Preparation						
1. State physical or economic plans	18	4	22	19	5	24
2. Regional plans	1	13	14	4	28	32
3. Local plans	2	13	15	5	26	31
4. Capital works budget	8	3	11	8	27	35
B. Review and Coordinate						
5. State functional plans	18	9	27	10	9	19
6. Regional plans	10	16	26	10	10	20
7. Local plans	16	12	28	7	11	18
8. Federal grants	12	19	31	3	12	15
C. Advise						
9. Governor	31	6	37	8	1	9
10. Legislature	13	4	17	17	12	29
11. Other state agencies	13	3	16	22	8	30
D. Provide Information						
12. Governor	18	9	27	10	6	16
13. Legislature	8	3	11	15	17	32

coordination of plans developed elsewhere; advice to other actors and institutions in state government; and provision of information to the governor or the legislature.

Clearly, many state legislatures perceived the state planning agency's central role to be assisting in the decision-making process at the state level, primarily by advising and otherwise assisting the governor and others in the state executive branch. Although preparing plans was not overlooked as an agency role (especially state-level physical or economic plans), the legislature believed it more important that the agency review and coordinate state and local government planning—again an advisory role. Actual preparation of plans was not to be a primary function of many state planning agencies.

The Institute staff found that these agencies have performed their charge in a selective manner. For example, the governor is key actor in the world of the state planning agency, but, surprisingly, the legislature plays a much less significant role. And this bias holds despite the fact that basic legislation under which the agency operates calls on the agency to perform certain activities for the legislature. Of note also, is the fact that comparatively little effort is made to advise other state agencies.

Of great importance to the state planning agencies is their review and coordination roles. They are especially involved in the federal grant-in-aid process which burgeoned so greatly in the 1960s, and are also involved in reviewing and trying to coordinate plans of other governmental agencies and units.

The hierarchy of activities performed by state planning agencies is then as follows: (1) advising the governor, (2) reviewing and coordinating the planning activities of other governmental units, (3) actual plan preparation, and (4) working with the legislature. There is nothing in these data to alter our sense of the increasing chief-executive orientation of the state planning function.

PERFORMANCE IN PROGRAM AREAS AND POLICY SECTORS

In addition to the roles, activities, and processes in which state planning agencies are involved, the different programmatic or functional areas with which the planning agencies have some type of connection were examined. Twenty-four different program areas were identified, and were subsequently grouped into 4 broad policy sectors: (1) economic development, (2) human resources and environment, (3) transportation, and (4) other physical facilities.

Immediately apparent from Table 4 is the heavy emphasis that the state planning agency places on

TABLE 4. Policy Sector Involvement of State Planning Agencies by Number of Program Areas with Which the Agency Is Involved

| | Policy Sectors | | | | | | | |
| Involvement of State Planning Agency: Number of Program Areas | Economic development (7 functions)a | | Human resources and environment (5 functions)b | | Transportation (5 functions)c | | Other physical facilities (7 functions)d | |
	No. of states	Cumulative %	No. of states	Cumulative%	No. of states	Cumulative %	No. of states	Cumulative %
None	11	22	26	52	22	44	23	46
One	10	42	8	68	11	66	12	70
Two	13	68	9	86	9	84	7	84
Three	8	84	4	94	5	94	6	96
Four	3	90	3	100	2	98	0	96
Five	5	100	0	100	1	100	1	98
Six							0	98
Seven							1	100

aAgriculture; commerce; community and urban development; industrial and economic development; recreation and tourism; water resources and fisheries; zoning.

bEducation; employment; hospitals/health; housing; pollution (general).

cAirports; highways, roads, or streets; land-use or open space; transportation; and waterways.

dConservation; resources (general); forest/parks; flood prevention; public works; sewage systems; utilities.

the economic development function. While in a relatively large number of states the planning agency is *not* involved in human resources and environment (26), other physical facilities (23), and transportation (22), only 11 states were not involved in at least one area of economic development. The columns indicating the cumulative percentages show a relatively consistent intersector difference, with state planning agencies much more likely to be involved in more than one of the economic development program areas than they are in any of the other three sectors.

In fact, the other three policy sectors are distributed quite similarly in their spread among the program areas. It is the economic development sector that stands out. This emphasis can be interpreted as a holdover from the history of state planning in the 1930s and 1940s when planning agencies performed extensively in this area; they were often little more than economic promoters for the state. Wyner notes the persistence of this programmatic tendency among governors—i.e., many still see the state promotion role as one of their important duties.[9]

However, none of these four policy sectors is covered adequately. In fact, the data seem to indicate that state planning is spread rather thin over the sectors. For example, in the sector of greatest involvement, economic development, 21 states perform in none or only 1 of the 7 program areas. In 21 states, state planning agencies participate in 2 or 3 program areas, and only 8 state agencies are involved in 4 or more of the 7 functions. In the transportation sector, only 1 state planning agency is involved in all 5 program areas; only 17 are active in 2 or more functions.

Finally, we must note that the type of activity each agency performs in each of the broad sectors varies greatly across the components of plan preparation, review and coordination, advising, research and information, and others. This means that individual state planning agencies are operating under a diverse set of assumptions as to their role and involvement in the functions of state government. In short, as currently practiced, state planning seems to be taking a rather "scattershot approach" with no clearly agreed upon focus beyond that of assisting the governor. As a management

tool for the governor, state planning agencies have biases, gaps, and inadequacies which hinder their fulfilling a key executive function.

CORRELATES OF STATE PLANNING CHARACTERISTICS
THE STATE PLANNING AGENCY: OVERALL DIMENSIONS

Several questions remain to be considered. These concern patterns in the structure and functioning of state planning agencies that may be related to variables lodged outside the immediate world of the agency. And these variables reflect broader trends affecting all of the state government and its activities.

We selected seven "independent" variables and explored their relationship to many of the variables already discussed. The first four variables are economic and demographic characteristics of the states:

1. Per capita personal income in the state, 1965 [10]
2. Percent of population in urban places in the state, 1960 [11]
3. Percent of population in SMSA's in the state, 1960 [12]
4. Estimated population size in the state, July 1967 [13]

The fifth and sixth variables represent political characteristics of the governor's role:

[9] Alan Wyner develops this argument in "Governor—Salesman," *National Civic Review*, Vol. 56 (February 1967), pp. 81–86.

[10] This measure was derived from U.S. Bureau of the Census, *Government Finances in 1965–66* (Washington, D.C.: U.S. Government Printing Office, 1967), p. 52.

[11] This measure was derived from U.S. Bureau of the Census, *1960 Census of Population*; Vol. I, *Characteristics of Population* (Washington, D.C.: U.S. Government Printing Office, 1961).

[12] *Ibid*, parts 2–5. The Census Bureau definition of an SMSA is as follows. "Generally conceived, a metropolitan area is an integrated economic and social unit with a large population nucleus. Each SMSA contains at least (a) one central city with 50,000 inhabitants or more, or (b) two cities having contiguous boundaries and constituting, for general economic and social purposes, a single community with a combined population of at least 50,000, the smaller of which must have a population of at least 15,000. The SMSA includes the county in which the central city is located, and adjacent counties that are found to be metropolitan in character and economically and socially integrated with the county of the central city." U.S. Bureau of the Census, *Statistical Abstract of the United States: 1970*. (91st edition.) (Washington, D.C.: U.S. Government Printing Office, 1970), p. 839.

[13] This measure was derived from U.S. Bureau of the Census, *Current Population Report*, No. 380, (Washington, D.C.: U.S. Government Printing Office, 1968), p. 25.

5. Governor's formal powers, 1968[14]
6. Size of the governor's staff, 1968[15]

The seventh variable is an indicator of the varying fiscal base of state planning activities—i.e., the mix of federal and state funds. Termed "state effort ratio," it is defined as

7. Ratio of state to federal planning money for all purposes and all activities of the state planning agency, 1968[16]

Several separate "dependent" variables were selected to represent various features of the structure and functioning of state planning agencies. The first two variables were structural in nature, focusing on the agency itself and its director:

1. Organizational location of the state planning agency, (whether or not it is located in or near the governors office)
2. Previous governmental experience of the state planning agency director[17]

The third variable concerns the scope or comprehensiveness of the agency's activities, and is best stated as a question:

3. Is the state planning agency doing overall planning?[18]

The next three dependent variables concern the performance of the agency and are based on the judgment of the Institute staff. The first two re-

[14]This measure was derived from Joseph A. Schlesinger, "The Politics of the Executive," in Herbert Jacob and Kenneth Vines, *Politics in the American States* (Boston: Little, Brown, 1965), p. 229, and Thad L. Beyle, "Gubernatorial Power: A View from the Governor's Chair," *Public Administration Review*, Vol. 28 (November/December 1968), pp. 342–344.

[15]This measure was derived from Donald P. Sprengel, *Gubernatorial Staffs* (Iowa City: Institute of Public Affairs, University of Iowa, 1969).

[16]This measure was derived from a questionnaire sent to the directors of the state planning agencies from the Institute on State Programming for the 70s, January 1968 and from U.S. Bureau of the Census, *Government Finances in 1965-66*. The response rate to the questionnaire was 45 of 49 states with such directors at that time (92 percent), but for this analysis only 34 states' data were usable.

[17]*Ibid.* All 45 responding states were included in the analysis.

[18]This measure was derived from the Institute on State Programming for the 70s' field interviews in each of the 50 states during the summer of 1967, and is thus a judgmental variable.

late how other actors in state government perceive the agency and its activities, while the third relates the agency's performance to the decision-making process in the state.

4. Extent to which other state government officials are aware of the state planning agency and its activities[19]
5. Extent to which state government officials accept state planning[20]
6. Relevancy of the state planning agency's activities to the decision-making process

The last two dependent variables represent the more dynamic aspects of the agency in its bureaucratic setting: How free from the winds of political change is the agency director? What is source of agency funds? Is the ability of the agency to obtain funds through the state budgetary process greater than its ability to obtain federal funds? Or is the reverse true?

7. Tenure of the director of the state planning agency[21]
8. State Planning Agency Effort Ratio[22] (this is the same as number 6 of the independent variables)

While there are variations in the relationships between specific independent and dependent variables, several broad themes appear in the data presented in Table 5. First, and perhaps most significant, is the nexus of strong governor-larger gubernatorial staff-more urban and metropolitan state-planning agency lodged close to the governor and conducting fairly significant activities. Or, more simply, urban and metropolitan state-strong governor-active planning agency. This is consistent

[19]*Ibid.* The awareness of state government officials to the state planning agency and its activities was determined on the basis of the field interviews in each of the 50 states during the summer of 1967, and is thus a judgmental variable.

[20]*Ibid.* The acceptance of state planning by state government officials was determined on the basis of the field interviews in each of the 50 states during the summer of 1967, and is thus a judgmental variable.

[21]This measure was derived from a questionnaire sent to the directors of the state planning agencies from the Institute on State Programming for the 70s, January 1968. All 45 responding states were included in this analysis.

[22]*Ibid.* The data for the total state government expenditures is from U.S. Bureau of the Census, *Government Finances in 1965-66*, pp. 34–39.

TABLE 5. **TABLE 5.** Means of Economic, Demographic, and Political Variables in Relation to State Planning Characteristics

Planning Characteristics	Independent Variable						
	Per capita personal income 1965 ($'s)	% Population urban, 1960	% Population in SMSAs 1960	Population size, 1967 (millions)	Formal powers of the governor 1968	Size of governor's staff, 1968	State planning effort ratio, 1968[b]
Means for all 50 states	$2,571	61.8%	48.4%	3.9	13.2	8.2	1.6
Organizational Location							
Governor's office (25)[a]	2,649	64.4	55.1	5.0	13.1	11.0	2.4
Not in gov's. office (22)	2,516	58.2	41.0	3.0	13.7	5.5	.9
Experience of SPA Director							
Other governmental (29)	2,617	64.0	51.4	4.1	13.1	8.4	1.4
No other governmental (16)	2,530	57.4	40.4	3.0	13.4	6.2	2.0
SPA Performing Overall Planning							
Yes (11)	2,764	64.3	58.0	4.7	15.0	9.9	2.0
No (28)	2,466	61.1	46.7	3.7	12.5	6.9	1.8
No judgment (10)	2,673	59.5	40.1	4.1	13.4	10.2	.8
General Awareness of SPA							
High (8)	2,770	66.8	61.8	3.2	15.2	10.5	.9
Moderate (22)	2,620	65.0	53.1	4.3	13.4	8.3	2.7
Slight or none (18)	2,445	55.7	38.0	4.2	12.3	7.5	.8
General Acceptance of State Planning							
High (9)	2,587	64.0	57.8	5.9	15.1	13.8	1.4
Moderate (21)	2,631	62.9	51.6	3.5	13.7	7.3	2.2
Low (14)	2,576	60.0	39.4	3.4	13.1	6.6	1.0
Relevancy							
Relevant (23)	2,677	63.3	49.8	3.7	13.3	8.6	1.3
Not relevant (16)	2,563	62.2	51.9	5.2	12.6	8.9	2.2
Not determined (11)	2,362	57.7	40.4	2.7	11.7	6.2	1.4
Tenure of State Plan Director							
Two years or less (29)	2,619	61.3	45.9	3.6	13.1	7.8	1.3
More than two years (16)	2,528	62.2	50.4	3.8	13.6	7.2	2.3
SPA Effort Ratio, 1968[b]							
Less than .05 (17)	2,545	57.9	37.0	3.1	12.6	6.9	
.05–1.0 (11)	2,511	60.5	43.1	2.1	11.6	5.6	
More than 1.0 (15)	2,744	66.8	60.9	6.1	14.9	11.2	

[a]The numbers in parentheses indicate the number of states in each category of the dependent or row variable upon which the means for the independent variable are calculated. An exception occurs in the last column, planning effort ratio, where missing data causes the number of cases to be slightly and systematically smaller. The data in the cells represent the means of the independent variables for the different categories of each dependent variable.

[b]This measure is derived by dividing the total expenditure from all sources and all activities of the state planning agency by the total state government expenditures.

with the concept of the urban or metropolitan governor,[23] who is involved in more of the problems of his state (and indeed his state may have more problems), and who needs the greater staff capability that planning provides.

[23]Robert C. Wood first suggested that governors were increasingly becoming urban or metropolitan oriented in "The Metropolitan Governor" (unpublished doctoral dissertation, Department of Government, Harvard University, 1949). This argument is extended by Joseph A. Schlesinger in "The Politics of the Executive," *op. cit.*

Second, is the interesting finding that planning agencies close to the governor rely to a significant extent on "hard-money" state funds (2.4 state/federal ratio), while those outside the governor's direct control rely more on federal funds (0.9 state/federal ratio). Proximity to the governor provides both a fiscal support base at the state level and a type of constraint that reduces the ability and possibly the need to conduct certain more expensive and expansive activities.[24] As agencies become more remote from gubernatorial constraints they may also be able to negotiate more freely for outside (federal) funding. This may also reflect the program orientation of federal funds, as opposed to the greater staff orientation of state funds.

However, with a slightly different but incomplete data base (31 states), and relating fiscal support to agency location and relevancy of activities, the impact of relevancy is apparent.[25] (See Table 6.) While agencies outside direct gubernatorial control do have considerably greater average support scores, there are equally significant differences in support between agencies performing relevant activities (1.20) and those not doing so (0.69). Thus, while proximity to the governor places constraints on these staff agencies, the agency's own perfor-

mance serves to expand the bounds of at least the fiscal constraints.

Third, there appears to be a "push-pull" model at work in the states. The most developed or urbanized states are pressed by circumstances to pursue planning rather vigorously and are "pushed" to use their own funds to a greater extent to achieve the necessary planning effects. Those states less urbanized, and thereby with seemingly fewer problems (i.e., less "push") appear to be "pulled" into such planning efforts by the availability of federal planning grants. There is no less need for planning in either case—only the source of the impetus varies.

This "push-pull" model is seen clearly in the state planning-effort ratio data. The significant break for the ratio is at the 1:1 point in the federal-state mix on agency funds—i.e., between those who rely more on federal funds (below 1.0) and those who rely more on state funds (more than 1.0) to finance state planning agency activities. States that rely most on state funds are richer, more urban, considerably more metropolitan, and twice the size of the other states. They also have stronger governors with much larger staffs. Greater emphasis on federal support relates to poorer, less urban and metropolitan states and to weaker governors with smaller staffs. Also note that agency directors with shorter tenure relied more on fed-

[24] Beyle, Seligson, and Wright, *op. cit.*, p. 338.
[25] *Ibid.* pp. 338–339.

TABLE 6. Average Support Level of State Planning Agencies by Location of Agency and Relevance to the Decision-Making Process

State Planning Agency Relevant to the Decision-Making Process	In Governor's Office or Departments of Administration, Finance, or Budget		Outside Governor's Office or Departments of Administration, Finance, or Budget		Totals	
	N^a	Average support[b]	N^a	Average support[b]	N^a	Average support[b]
Is relevant	6	.60	4	2.00	10	1.20
Is *not* relevant	3	.33	10	0.80	13	0.69
Not adequately determined	6	.66	2	0.50	8	0.63
Totals	15	.60	16	1.06	31	0.84

[a]Number of states within that category.
[b]Average support score for states within that category. Individual scores obtained by dividing total general state expenditures into state planning agency expenditures for the fiscal year 1965–66. To categorize these percentages, a 3 was assigned to the 1 state where the percentage was above 0.25 percent; a 2 was assigned to 6 states where the percentage ranged between 0.15 percent and 0.25 percent; a 1 was assigned to the 11 states where it ranged between 0.05 and 0.14 percent; and a 0 was assigned to 13 states where it was below 0.05 percent. Data on state government expenditures were developed from U.S. Census Bureau, *Government Finances in 1965-1966* (Washington, D.C.: U.S. Government Printing Office, 1967), Chart 18; and the data on state planning agency expenditures were developed from American Society of Planning Officials, *ASPO Planning Advisory Service* (Chicago: ASPO, April 1967), Report No. 221, Table 17. Data on the latter were available on only 31 states.

eral funds than did those with longer tenure. This indicates that new directors move toward available federal planning funds to obtain more immediate "program mobility," while the older directors fall back on state funds, some of which may be replacing or picking up activities or programs aided originally by federal grants. So within the cross-state "push-pull" pattern, individual agency directors are able to play on the availability of federal planning monies to "pull" their agencies along.

The "push-pull" model represents one possible causal type of interpretation of the results. There may be others, but this one is the most intuitively attractive despite inadequate data to test it or alternative models. It is a complex model with its interweaving of demographic and political variables and federal involvement. All interact on agency performance. This complexity also speaks strongly to the diversity in our federal system as different patterns accrue át different developmental stages among the states.

THE STATE PLANNING AGENCY:
FISCAL SUPPORT
This series of correlates concerns the relative level of fiscal support that state planning agencies receive. The proportions of agency expenditures to total state government expenditures were grouped into four categories: very high, high, moderate, and low. The means for the seven independent variables for these categories are presented in Table 7.

It is instructive to view the data *in toto* for each of the columns, as the pattern is so consistent. The states that are both highest and lowest in relative support for state planning agencies are also the richer, more urban and metropolitan larger states. They are also the states with stronger governors and larger gubernatorial staffs. The states that have only less than moderate levels of support are poorer, less urban and metropolitan, and smaller in population size. These same characteristics are apparent in the governors' power in these states, and a similar pattern holds for the size of the governors' staffs.

In the column concerning the ratio of state to federal planning monies, there is a very significant trend: As the level of the state's fiscal commitment to state planning decreases, the proportionate use of state-derived funds increases. To put it in a slightly different way, federal funds appear to be more attracted to higher fiscal-support-level states.

The findings from Table 7 suggest the role of unusual idiosyncratic factors in determining fiscal support for state planning. Highly developed states lie at both ends of the fiscal support ratio, indicating that something other than developmental variables such as size, wealth, and urban complexity are at work. In other words, support for planning does not automatically flow from need. It flows from a specific commitment. And consistent with the previous analysis, this means gubernatorial commitment.

TABLE 7. Means of Independent Variables for Levels of Fiscal Support

Planning Fiscal support Level	Independent Variables						
	Per capita personal income, 1965	% Population urban, 1960	% Population in SMSAs 1960	Population size, 1967 (millions)	Formal powers of the governor 1967	Size of governor's staff, 1968	State planning effort ratio, 1968
Very high (8)*	$2879	70.3%	57.6%	3.6	14.2	10.9	1.4
High (14)	2556	60.0	43.6	2.9	13.2	7.0	0.8
Moderate (10)	2390	53.8	35.4	2.6	12.6	6.4	1.4
Low (12)	2669	65.3	54.8	6.2	13.0	8.8	3.1

Very high = .20% or more of state general expenditures for planning
High = .10–.20% or more of state general expenditures for planning
Moderate = .05–.10% or more of state general expenditures for planning
Low = .01–.05% or more of state general expenditures for planning

*The numbers in parentheses indicate the number of states in each category of the dependent or row variable upon which the means for the independent variable are calculated. An exception occurs in the last column, planning effort ratio, where missing data causes the number of cases to be slightly and systematically smaller.

THE STATE PLANNING AGENCY:
POLICY SECTORS

In this section the analysis is extended by applying the seven independent variables to the four policy sectors of (1) economic development, (2) human resources and environment, (3) transportation, and (4) other physical facilities. (See Table 8.) We consider the states in categories of how many of the program areas within the policy sectors they were involved in: none, one, two, or three or more.

Economic Development. The 11 states in which the planning agency is not involved in the economic development sector are lower in income, much less urban and metropolitan, and smaller than the other states. They also have weaker gover-

nors with small staffs and are highly reliant on federal dollars for their state planning activities.

As the involvement in the economic development policy sector increases, the states also increase in wealth, urban and metropolitan character, population size, and power of the governor, except for those states most involved. The 16 states with agencies working in 3 or more functions depart from this straight-line trend across the independent variables, falling back to approximate closely the overall averages for all states on these variables.

We would be remiss in not repeating the earlier finding that state planning agencies have been more involved in the functions of this policy sec-

TABLE 8. Means of Independent Variables for Categories of Observed
State Planning Agency Activity for Policy Program Sectors

Policy Sectors: Degree of Program Involvement	Independent Variables						
	Per capita personal income, 1965	% Population urban, 1960	% Population in SMSAs 1960	Population size, (millions)	Formal powers of the governor 1968	Size of governor's staff, 1968	State planning effort ratio, 1968
Economic Development (7 functions)							
None (11)*	$2400	56.0%	37.2%	2.9	11.4	5.4	0.4
One (10)	2484	62.7	50.8	4.9	12.3	13.9	3.2
Two (13)	2708	66.6	61.3	4.5	14.5	7.5	1.6
Three + (16)	2633	61.2	44.1	3.6	13.9	7.1	1.4
Human Resources and Environment (5 functions)							
None (26)	2430	59.0	43.6	3.5	12.6	7.8	1.8
One (8)	2690	62.1	48.7	4.0	14.4	9.5	1.0
Two (9)	2804	65.5	53.3	4.3	14.2	8.2	0.7
Three + (7)	2663	66.8	59.3	5.1	12.7	8.0	2.8
Transportation (5 functions)							
None (22)	2482	58.3	43.7	3.7	12.8	8.2	1.8
One (11)	2516	60.9	45.4	3.7	14.0	7.1	0.8
Two (9)	2598	63.5	45.8	4.0	11.9	7.4	1.8
Three + (8)	2862	70.5	68.2	4.8	14.6	10.4	1.9
Other Physical (7 functions)							
None (23)	2430	59.6	45.6	3.9	12.9	8.3	1.6
One (12)	2625	65.9	53.1	3.9	12.8	8.2	1.3
Two (7)	2571	58.7	44.4	2.4	12.9	6.7	1.5
Three + (8)	2897	64.4	52.8	5.3	14.9	9.0	2.5
Means for all 50 States	2571	61.8	48.4	3.9	13.2	8.2	1.6

*Figures in parentheses indicate the number of states on which the means are based except for the effort ratio column. For this independent variable the number of cases is slightly and systematically less than the numbers indicated because of missing data.

tor than of any other sector. It may be for good reason because they are able to link their efforts with certain visible achievements. But, to the consternation of many thoughtful persons, these functions smack of "smokestack chasing" rather than increasing a state's fundamental economic health.

Human Resources and Environment. As the state agencies become more involved in the human resources and environmental sector they tend to be increasingly wealthier, more urban and metropolitan, and larger. There do not appear to be any significant patterns regarding the gubernatorial variables or the type of fiscal support the agency receives—except that states that are most involved in this sector rely to a great extent on state financing.

The basic implication is that as a state becomes larger and more urbanized, the state planning agency perforce tends to become more involved in this policy sector. Complexity leads to involvement in human and environmental concerns.

Transportation. Those state planning agencies with broadest involvement in transportation were located in the highest income, most urban, more metropolitan, and large states. Those with no such involvement were located in low-income, much less urbanized and metropolitan, and less populated states. The one- and two-function state agencies fell neatly in the middle of these extremes.

It is commonplace to note that greater concern for transportation occurs in the larger, more urban states. But it is of interest to find that the transportation activities of the state planning agencies also are more extensive in these more developed states. This is much akin to the finding in the human resources and environment sector and suggests that the relationship between these two sectors is closer than suspected. In other words, development per se leads to greater state governmental involvement in these two sectors as measured by the performance of the state planning agencies. We would suggest that since governors are using these agencies increasingly as a management tool, they become more involved in these two policy sectors as their states develop.

Other Physical Facilities. Patterns similar to the human resources and environment and transportation sectors appear to hold in this sector if we look only at the extremes—states involved in either none or three or more functions. Those state agencies with no involvement are low-income, slightly less urban, and considerably less metropolitan states. Those in three or more functions were wealthy, highly urbanized and metropolitan states, and by a considerable margin, the largest states. They were also located in strong-governor states that spent significantly more state than federal funds on their state planning activities. The one- and two-function states varied widely in their characteristics, presenting no clear pattern. Thus, those with the highest degree of development also tend to have state planning agencies quite involved in a broad range of physical facility planning. Those with a low development profile tend toward a limited range of involvement.

Conclusion. The most general finding in these data on the policy sectors is the tendency of state governments, as measured by the activities of their state planning agencies, to become involved in program areas in direct relationship to their level of development: The greater the developmental level, the greater the involvement. There also appears to be a progression of involvement in policy sectors tied to this developmental notion, as most state planning agencies become involved in the economic development policy sector first. At a later point in time, as the state becomes more complex, this initial involvement is broadened out to the three other policy sectors.

These findings reflect broader trends than what state planning agencies are doing. They indicate that the states have put more coordinated forethought, control, and follow-through in the economic development policy sector—at the expense of the other policy sectors. Programs have been developed and administered in these other policy sectors and in the various specialized agencies throughout the state government organization chart. But the overall coordination of planning for these activities has been missing as an aid to the governor. As the states develop, not only the state planning agency but also the governor becomes more involved in these policy sectors. This is the "push" side of the model posited earlier. The "push" is toward more coordinated state government policies achieved through the increased involvement and use by the governor of planning as a management tool.

THE GOVERNOR AND STATE PLANNING

This study has examined the recent development of one of the governors' management tools—state planning. State planning did not start from a policy management base, but during the 1960s the trend in this direction, as measured by close association with the governor, became an unmistakable reality. This is related to the general centralizing of the decision-making process which has been evident at all levels of government for several decades.[26] At the state level it has meant and should continue to mean enhancing the governors' ability to make decisions and control the direction of state government. And, in turn, it is gubernatorial commitment that makes planning an effective tool.

We also suggest that a "push-pull" model of governmental activities may aid in explaining certain governmental behavior patterns at the state level. Governmental activity is stimulated, or "pushed," by development in the state, such as urbanization, and government becomes involved in more programs as the state develops. Thus, governors and their planning agencies become involved in more diverse programs. Gubernatorial commitment combines with complexity to compel someone to chart a roadmap, raise the necessary funds and coalitions of support, and key the actors to action.

On the "pull" side, the federal government, through its various guidelines and fiscal grants, "pulls" less developed states along certain common paths such as planning. Here, governors and their planning agencies become involved in a greater mix of programs and activities at their developmental stage than would normally be anticipated due to the enticements and requirements of the federal government. More developed states are not necessarily "pulled" by such federal aids, but use them to aid or supplement programs already underway.

The diversity of our system must be recognized. To overlook it by reading each unit as equal is to depreciate the very strength and uniqueness of this diversity. The states, and their governors, are comparable in all aspects, but equal in only a few. To treat them equally whether governmentally, politically, or analytically, is to overlook a major factor of our system and possibly to misdirect the particular concern, whether it be program, election, or analysis.

THE GOVERNOR AND THE NEW SYSTEMS TECHNOLOGY
Robert L. Chartrand

Integrated forward planning, quantitative methods and man machine devices for the first time in American history make it possible for a governor to really direct, measure and control what takes place in his administration and thus to govern wisely, efficiently and effectively.

Orville Freeman

The annals of American history are filled with examples of governors who have successfully confronted the dual challenges of political responsibility and executive leadership. Even that remarkable collection of talents, Thomas Jefferson, found this confrontation a difficult one, and often felt that he was a glorified quartermaster general without the compensations of being able to indulge in philosophical research and theory. Today there is a need for assertive direction and decision-making as never before, as the perplexities facing the state executive continue to mount: population mobility, heightened complexity within our society, and the requirement to interact increasingly with the federal government, local jurisdictions, and other states.

In order to cope with this rising tide of demands, state governors, executive departments and agencies, and legislatures must be flexible and willing to effect organizational and procedural changes. Change has become a way of life, and a higher competence on the part of governmental leadership is required if the requisite services, and responsive priorities, are to be established. When viewed within this context, it is hardly surprising that innovative tools and techniques are much in demand, and that their application to the planning-programming-budgeting functions as well as the state's day-to-day operational programs is a matter of critical concern to the governor. The

---

[26] Herbert S. Kaufman, "Emerging Conflicts in the Doctrines of Public Administration," *American Political Science Review*, Vol. 5 (December 1956), pp. 1057–1073; Kaufman, "Administrative Decentralization and Political Power," *Public Administration Review*, Vol. 29 (January/February 1969), pp. 3–15. Witness also the Nixon administration's efforts to achieve more coordination at the federal level through implementing several of the proposals of the President's Council on Executive Reorganization (1970).

essence of the dilemma—and the opportunity—is contained in this commentary by the National Governors' Conference Committee on State Planning:

Every governor understands that we must develop more sophisticated ways of sorting facts, of facing issues, of opening options, to make better decisions if we, as states, are to continue as effective partners in our federal system. We must have means to survey where we are, what the gaps in our efforts are, what our goals should be, what the alternative means and ways to these goals are, what the costs and benefits are, what the relative priority between the various goals is.[1]

The relative independence enjoyed by state administrators, insofar as the intrusions of federal policies and programs were concerned, has been eroded increasingly during the past few decades. Tremendous sums have become available from the federal government through grants-in-aid, matching funds, or the direct implementation at the state level by federal entities which nonetheless affect state operations. In addition, local governments and regional development commissions often place demands upon the state planners and program managers which cause, either directly or tangentially, changes in priorities, funding, or the actual nature of services provided. This unprecedented and unrelenting pressure to cope with numerous and sensitive social, economic, and sometimes political problems—environmental pollution, transportation, housing, education, urban development—has forced state leadership to seek out all possible ameliorative options.

Among these are techniques and man-machine procedures collectively known as "systems technology": operations research, systems analysis, stimulation, model-building, and other quantitative methods of data handling. Quite distinct, but of high visibility and "presence," is the awesome array of equipment and "software" known as automatic data processing (ADP). The integration of this innovative technology into the state governmental structure is a continuing process with perturbations at many levels. However, both state and local governments throughout the nation are expanding their applications of the systems approach and ADP into an increasing number of management and program areas.

STATE ADMINISTRATION: STUDIES AND PERCEPTIONS

Evidence of the concern felt for the viability and effectiveness of state governments may be found in a variety of major studies, scholarly writings, and congressional hearings. While some of the older evaluations such as the Brookings report in the early 1930s understandably did not include any mention of new technology,[2] an increasing number of those undertaken in the past decade include at least some reflection of the existence of planning-programming-budgeting (PPB) and computers. Emphasis on the role of the governor, from two vantage points, is found in "A Study of American States," which was directed by former North Carolina Governor Terry Sanford (1965–67),[3] and the study undertaken by Deil S. Wright in the same time period, which utilized questionnaire responses by 933 department and agency heads from all 50 states.[4]

A report to stimulate comprehensive long-range planning by the states was prepared in 1968 by the Institute on State Programming for the 70s for the National Governors' Conference Committee on State Planning. Entitled *Relevance, Reliance, and Realism*, the report set forth a number of key considerations related to establishing effective planning mechanisms, and in a "Charge to the Governors" urged, among other things, the establishments of state PPB and management information systems.[5] Meanwhile, the State-Local Finances Project at the George Washington University was studying the adaptation of PPB procedures by 15 governments—the so-called "5-5-5 project"—at the state, county, and city levels. A report, *Imple-*

---

[1] U.S. Senate Committee on Government Operations, Subcommittee on Intergovernmental Relations, *Criteria for Evaluation in Planning State and Local Programs* (a study submitted by the Subcommittee, Ninetieth Congress, First session, July 21, 1967) (Washington, D.C.: U.S. Government Printing Office, 1967), p. v. (Foreword by Senator Edmund S. Muskie, quoting the goals set forth by the Governors' Conference Committee on State Planning.)

[2] Ferrel Heady, *State Constitutions: The Structure of Administration*, State Constitutional Studies Project (No. 4 in a series of background studies) (New York: National Municipal League, 1961), p. 29.

[3] Terry Sanford, *Storm over the States* (New York: McGraw-Hill, 1967).

[4] Deil S. Wright, "Executive Leadership in State Administration," this book.

[5] *Relevance, Reliance, and Realism*, 1968 report of the Committee on State Planning, the National Governors' Conference, July 22, 1968, p. 17.

menting PPB in State, City, and County, contains a survey of PPB implementation in the states. It was prepared in cooperation with:[6]

The International City Managers Association
The National Association of Counties
The National Governors' Conference
The National League of Cities
The United States Conference of Mayors
The Council of State Governments

The Council of State Governments also has periodically published its tabulations and comments on the use of ADP by the states.[7]

One of the most comprehensive studies of state use of computer technology and systems analysis was performed by the Special Subcommittee on the Utilization of Scientific Manpower of the Senate Committee on Labor and Public Welfare. Concurrent with the holding of extensive hearings during the 1965–1967 period, questionnaires twice were sent by the Special Subcommittee Chairman, Senator Gaylord Nelson, formerly the Governor of Wisconsin, to the governors of all 50 states, to mayors of the 22 largest cities, and officials of selected regional development commissions.[8] A detailed report entitled *Systems Technology Applied to Social and Community Problems* appeared in 1968, featuring the findings of the two Nelson surveys together with comparative data from the State-Local Finances Project and the Council of State Governments' questionnaire responses.[9]

Another congressional group that has looked into the role of PPB in state and local governmental operations is the Subcommittee on Economy in Government of the Joint Economic Committee. Early in 1970, a compendium of 12 papers on *Innovations in Planning, Programming, and Budgeting in State and Local Governments*[10] was published, emphasizing the experience gained by various subnational governments in developing PPB systems.

The narrative and statistical information derived from these studies, surveys, and analytical reports offers strong proof that many state governments are now irrevocably committed to the use of automatic data processing and systems methodology. This is but one manifestation, it would seem, of the states' determination to "move with the times" and retain—if not enhance—their independence and power within the fabric of contemporary federalism. Since a balance must be struck between fulfilling the commitments to the national government and the protection of the states' constitutionally derived power and responsibilities, no option should remain unexercised by the governors as they strive to serve the citizenry.

RESOURCES SELECTION AND APPLICATION

Having executive leadership and an organization capable of implementing decisions within a state has never been more essential than now. Interdepartmental disputes, lackadaisical leadership, and inertia at the program level are less tolerable today than in times past, and the strengthened position of the governor in most states allows a policy of accomplishment. In his classical work on

[6]Selma J. Mushkin, *et al.*, *Implementing PPB in State, City, and County* (Washington, D.C.: State-Local Finances Project of The George Washington University, June 1969), pp. 131–137.
[7]The Council of State Governments and Public Administration Service, *Automated Data Processing in State Government: Status, Problems, and Prospects*, 1965, 40 pp. Also see *Automation in State Government 1966–1967: A Second Report on Status and Trends*, 1967, 38 pp. plus appendixes. Both published in Chicago by the Public Administration Service.
[8]U.S. Senate Committee on Labor and Public Welfare, Special Subcommittee on the Utilization of Scientific Manpower, *Scientific Manpower Utilization, 1965–66* (hearings before the Special Subcommittee, Eighty-ninth Congress, First Session, November 18, 1965), 213 pp. Also see *Scientific Manpower Utilization, 1967* (hearings before the Special Subcommittee, Ninetieth Congress, First Session, January 25, 1967), 377 pp. Both published in Washington, D.C., by the U.S. Government Printing Office.
[9]U.S. Senate Committee on Labor and Public Welfare,

Subcommittee on Employment, Manpower, and Poverty, *Systems Technology Applied to Social and Community Problems* (a report prepared by the Science Policy Research Division, Legislative Reference Service, Library of Congress, for the Subcommittee, Ninety-first Congress, First Session, June 1969) (Washington, D.C.: U.S. Government Printing Office, 1969), 473 pp. Also see the commercial edition of this committee print: Robert L. Chartrand, *Systems Technology Applied to Social and Community Problems* (New York: Spartan Books, 1970), 478 pp. Hereafter referred to as *Systems Technology Applied to Social and Community Problems*.
[10]U.S. Congress, Joint Economic Committee, Subcommittee on Economy in Government, *Innovations in Planning, Programming, and Budgeting in State and Local Governments* (a compendium of papers submitted to the Subcommittee, Ninety-first Congress, First Session, August 29, 1969) (Washington, D.C.: U.S. Government Printing Office, 1969), 218 pp.

the American governor, Leslie Lipson offers this dictum:

Often the important thing in administrative matters is not *which* decision should be taken, but that *some* decision should be taken. Nowadays, the governor is there to render the decision.[11]

Closely related to the ability of the governor to perform in a meaningful decision-making role is the organization within the state government that executes his order and monitors ongoing operations. Much has been done to strengthen this vital support of the senior executive, as witnessed by the fact that 35 of the 50 states have established departments of administration in recent decades.[12] The range of services has varied widely, from records management and computer operations to the more recently emphasized long-range program planning and program execution control. In many cases, the changing stresses on society and its governing mechanisms, as reflected in a need for improved social services, environmental quality, planning and intergovernmental relationships, have led to reorganization, often of a sweeping nature. Between 1967 and 1969, twenty states reported that their governors had made recommendations to the legislatures concerning executive reorganization.[13]

As the governors and their advisors have sought to improve their management of the states' affairs, and in so doing have added professional systems analysts and operations research specialists to their permanent staffs, the question of where to place them, organizationally, has arisen. In an extensive interviewing of state government personnel in 1967, the importance of having such management counsel "close to the top" emerged as a fact of life.[14] While many of the "experts" were assigned positions in the budget-administration-finance realm, others were situated in state planning agencies or specific functional areas.

In broadening the inquiry as to where states have placed their in-house capabilities to include data-processing staff, the Nelson surveys' report shows:[15]

	No. of States
A. Special advisor for systems analysis or operations research	11
B. Line department for systems (or program) development	18
C. Assistant for planning-programming-budgeting	14
D. Computer programming group	24
E. Automatic data-processing facility	22

Regardless of the application undertaken, early development is a time of considerable sensitivity and turmoil. Often state officials will follow the lead of the federal government and industry in contracting with outside "think tank" or data-processing service bureau firms for assistance. These groups may serve only in an advisory capacity for a few months, or may be hired to maintain a continuing oversight until in-house personnel are recruited and trained. In other instances, certain categories of ADP support will be arranged for by having data services provided either through an on-line, time-sharing arrangement using a remote computer, or by a pickup-and-delivery service for such recurring items as payroll. It is interesting to note that in the report prepared by the New York State Business Advisory Committee on Management Improvement for Governor Nelson Rockefeller, the importance of reliance on industry technicians in the early phases is stressed, but the longer range need of the state is reflected in a separate proposal for the establishment of a Center for Advanced Studies, which could address the problems and changes affecting the state by utilizing "scientific management techniques."[16]

An overview of the states' development of systems analysis capability, as reported to the Nelson

[11] Leslie Lipson, *The American Governor from Figurehead to Leader* (Chicago: The University of Chicago Press, 1938), p. 244.

[12] *Modernizing State Government* (New York: Committee for Economic Development, July 1967), pp. 59–60.

[13] *State Executive Reorganization 1967–69*, RM-437 (Lexington, Ky.: Council of State Governments, October 1969), p. 2.

[14] Thad L. Beyle, "State Government Use of Management Techniques" (unpublished manuscript, June 28, 1968).

[15] *Systems Technology Applied to Social and Community Problems, op. cit.*, p. 176, fig. 40. Categories are not exclusive.

[16] New York State Business Advisory Committee on Management Improvement, *Report to Governor Nelson A. Rockefeller* (2nd annual report) (Albany: Business Advisory Committee on Management Improvement, May 1968), pp. 5–6. On September 14, 1970, Governor Rockefeller announced the establishment of a State Center for Governmental Policy Analysis.

FIGURE 1. Indications of Systems Analysis Capability by Function, 1968

[X—In-house capability; Y—out-of-house and in-house capability; Z—out-of-house capability]

States	Management Activities						Operational Program Activities																		
	Planning and Policies (1)	Personnel Management (2)	Interagency Activity (3)	Management Standards Control (4)	Equipment Selection (5)	Procurement Activity (6)	Legislatures (7)	Courts (8)	Financial (9)	Taxation (10)	Education (11)	Health and Hospitals (12)	Crime and Corrections (13)	Transportation (14)	Urban Renewal and Growth (15)	Science and Research Promotion (16)	Natural Resources (17)	Pollution Control (18)	Parks and Recreation (19)	Regulation of Commerce, etc. (20)	Labor and Manpower Services (21)	Utilities and Enterprises (22)	Welfare and Anti-poverty (23)	Social Security and Veterans (24)	Other (25)
Alaska	X	X	X	X	X	X	.	.	X	X	Y	Y	Y	Y	.	.	Y	.	Y	.	Y	.	Y	X	.
Arkansas	Y	X	X	Y	.	.	.	.	X	X	Y	.	Y	X	.	Y	Y	Y	Y	Y	Y	.	X	.	.
California	Y	Y	X	Y	Y	Y	.	.	Y	Y	Y	Y	Y	.	Y	Y	Y	Y	Y	Y	Y	Y	Y	Y	X
Colorado	X	Y	Y	Y	Y	Y	X	X	Y	Y	Y	Y	Y	.	X	.	X	.	.	X	Y	X	Y	.	.
Connecticut	X	X	X	X	X	X	.	X	X	X	X	X	X	Y	X	X	X	X	X	X	X	X	X	X	.
Idaho	Z	Y	Y	Y	Y	X	.	.	Y	Y	Y	X	.	Y	.	.	.	.	X	.	.	.	Y	.	.
Illinois	X	X	X	X	.	.	Z	.	X	.	.	X	X	X	X	X	X	X	X	X	X	X	Y	.	X
Indiana	X	X	Y	X	.	Y	X	.	Z	Y	Y	Y	X	X	X	.	Y	.	X	X	.	X	Y	.	.
Iowa	X	Y	Y	Y	Y	.	Y	.	Y	Y	.	Y	X	Y	Y	Z	Y	X	.	Z	Z	Y	.	.	.
Kansas	Y	.	.	.	.	.	.	N	Z	.	N	N	X	N	.	N	X	.	N	N	Z	.	Y	.	Y[a]
Maine	.	X	.	.	X	X	.	.	Y	Y	Y	Y	Y	X	.	.	Y	X	X	X	X	X	Y	X	.
Maryland	X	X	.	X	X	Z	N	.	X	X	Y	Y	Y	X	N	N	Y	Y	X	X	Y	.	Y	Z	.
Massachusetts	Z	X	Z	X	Y	Y	Z	.	X	Z	Y	Y	Y	Y	.	Y	Y	N	X	N	Y	Y	N	Y	.
Missouri	X	X	N	X	.	X	X	N	X	N	Y	Y	N	Y	N	.	N	.	N	N	Y	N	Z	Y	.
Nebraska	.	X	X	Y	.	.	Y	.	Y	X	Y	Y	Y	Y	Y	Y	Y	Y	Y	.	.	.	Y	.	.
New Mexico	Y	X	X	.	X	Z	.	.	X	X	Y	Y	Y	X	.	Y	X	Y	X	X	X	.	X	X	X
New York	Y	Y	X	X	Y	Y	Y	Z	X	X	Y	Y	Y	Y	Y	X	Y	N	Y	.	Y	Y	Y	.	.
North Carolina	Y	Y	Z	.	Y	Y	Y	X	X	X	Y	Y	Y	Y	Y	Y	Y	Z	X	X	X	X	Y	X	Y[b]
Ohio	X	X	X	X	X	X	X	.	X	X	X	X	X	X	Y	X	X	Y	X	X	Y	X	X	X	.
Oregon	X	X	Y	Y	Y	X	X	.	X	X	Y	Y	X	X	Y	Y	Y	Y	X	X	Y	X	Y	Y	.
Pennsylvania	X	Y	Y	Y	Y	X	X	Y	X	Y	Y	Y	Y	Y	Y	Y	Y	Y	Y	Y	Y	Y	Y	Y	.
Rhode Island	Y	Z	Y	Y	Y	X	Y	.	X	Y	Y	Y	Y	Y	Y	Z	Y	Y	.	.	X	X	Y	.	.
South Carolina	Y	Y	Y	X	X	X	.	Y	X	.	Y	X	Y	.	Y	N	Y	Y	Y	Y	X	Y	Y	.	.
South Dakota	.	.	.	.	.	.	N	N	X	Z	X	Y	Y	X	Y	Z	N	.	.	.	.	.	.	.	.
Texas	Y	Y	Y	Y	Y	Y	Y	Y	X	Y	X	X	Y	X	Y	X	X	Y	X	X	Y	Y	X	X	X
Utah	X	X	Y	Y	Y	X	Y	.	X	X	X	X	Y	Y	Y	Y	X	Y	X	X	X	.	Y	.	.
Vermont	.	X	Y	X	Y	X	.	X	X	X	N	N	Y	Y	N	.	N	.	.	N	.	.	Y	Y	Y
Washington	Y	Y	X	X	Y	X	Z	.	X	X	Y	Y	Y	X	Z	Z	X	Y	Y	N	Z	N	X	X	.
West Virginia	Y	.	Y	X	Y	X	Y	.	X	X	X	N	Y	Y	.	Y	X	Y	X	.	X	.	X	Y	.
Wisconsin	X	X	Y	X	X	X	X	X	X	X	Y	X	X	Y	X	X	X	X	.	.	X	.	Y	X	.

[a] Motor vehicle, liquor accounting and inventory.
[b] Liquor control board.

subcommittee in 1968, appears in Figure 1.[17] The 24 functional categories cover both management and operational program activities. Categories 1 through 6—related to management endeavors—warrant careful attention insofar as staffing is concerned: Rarely have the states relied solely upon out-of-house capabilities to perform these duties close to the seat of power.

In addition to the staffing problems, the states are hard-pressed to obtain funds for the testing of new methods or the provision of new ADP-supported services. Gradually the state administrators are learning that the introduction of computers does not necessarily mean a cost savings. Indeed, the new system may cost more, but in virtually every case the quality, and the variety, of service is increased significantly. Of course there are certain high-priority areas of activity where timeliness of response may be so critical that the question of cost becomes almost academic.

In funding systems-type programs and services, the states may use their tax revenue or qualify for federal assistance. During the five-year period 1965–69 the states reported spending a total of $56,685,394 on ADP and systems analysis, as

[17]*Systems Technology Applied to Social and Community Problems, op. cit.*, p. 170, fig. 37.

shown in Figure 2.[18] Expenditures by major cities are included to provide a better overall picture of subnational governmental expenditures in this pioneer developmental area.

The total expenditures for both states and cities were approximately $82 million, with over one-third of this amount reportedly spent for external consulting and ADP services. Because the figures provided often were "approximated," "projected," or "estimated," the total figure should be viewed only as a general indicator of state (or local) willingness to invest in systems analysis and ADP support.

The extent of federal government assistance has been randomly publicized and sometimes unappreciated by the public at large, but various departments and agencies have furnished the financial resources required to initiate, and sustain, systems-oriented or ADP-supported projects. More than half of the states responding to the Nelson questionnaires indicated that support for their programs was obtained from federal government sources, with the chief sponsors being:

Department of Housing and Urban Development (HUD)

[18]*Ibid.*, p. 176, fig. 41.

FIGURE 2. Total Funds Expended, 1965–69[a]

State	Number of Years Funded	Total	Cities	Number of Years Funded	Total
Alaska	3	$915,000	Chicago	3	$1,650,000
Arkansas	1	60,000	Cincinnati	4	3,370,000
California	2	1,881,000	Cleveland	2	5,200,000
Colorado	4	669,581	Denver	4	212,000
Connecticut	5	1,800,000	Detroit	3	1,141,602
Idaho	3	138,000	Kansas	3	205,000
Kansas	3	1,100,000	Los Angeles	5	4,230,718
Maryland	5	4,544,201	New Orleans	–	352,000
Massachusetts	5	1,450,000	New York	1	4,500,000
Missouri	3	1,565,000	Philadelphia	3	4,600,000
New York	5	28,700,000[b]	San Diego	1	225,000
Ohio	5	4,700,000	San Francisco	4	314,000
Rhode Island	4	925,000			
South Dakota	4	1,530,000[c]			
Texas	4	3,200,000[b]			
Washington	2	2,830,000			
Wisconsin	4	677,622			

[a]As reported to subcommittee in question IV of systems analysis questionnaire.
[b]Estimated.
[c]Data processing.
[d]Central systems staff only.

Department of Health, Education, and Welfare
(HEW)
Office of Economic Opportunity (OEO)
Department of Transportation (DOT)
Department of Justice (DOJ)
Department of Interior (DOI)
Department of Labor (DOL)
Department of Commerce (DOC)

To a lesser extent, the National Sciences Foundation (NSF), the Department of Defense (DOD), the Veterans Administration (VA), the Bureau of the Budget (BOB), and the National Institute of Mental Health (NIMH) also have provided financial support. Figure 3 depicts those functional areas, by state, which have been supported by these federal elements.[19]

Two interesting points are apparent from these data. First, there is further evidence of the segmental nature of most federal agency support of state governmental activity, i.e., DOT supports only transportation activities and DOL supports only labor-related activities. Second, is the importance of HUD in supporting management related activities at the state level, primarily through the "701" state planning assistance program.

As the states "gear up" to use the promising tools and techniques inherited from the aerospace and defense sectors, they often have the advantage of reviewing the experience of other users of this new technology, and can more accurately assess its benefits *and* limitations. Management today must be far more sophisticated than that of yesteryear, and the "tools of management"—which traditionally might carry the connotation of constitutional derivation and interpretation[20]—now include the full range of quantitative methods and new man-machine devices.

ACTION IN THE STATES

It is difficult, at best, to discover what steps the various states are taking in utilizing systems technology. In his first letter to the governors, accompanying the 1966 questionnaire, Senator Nelson pointed out that the subcommittee was "... particularly interested in techniques for the analysis of problems facing government and the development of alternative policies toward their solu-

tion."[21] Both the 1966 and 1968 questionnaires asked for the following information:

The planning and program areas in which the systems approach was being used
The type of systems performer (in-house or consultant)
Source of funding support, and amounts spent
Function and position of the systems capability within the governmental structure
Degree of benefit in terms of cost
Possible approaches for new Federal legislation

The 1968 questionnaire, developed after the holding of extensive hearings, was expanded to include a request for these items:

The federal agency or program that supported a systems activity
The inclusion of new programs or the termination of existing programs since 1966
Studies, reports, or other publications resulting from state and local government systems activities
The advantages and limitations of the use of systems technology

To facilitate the answering of the questions on such topics as staffing and sources of federal assistance, 24 functional areas were identified (as shown in Figure 3). These areas were divided into five major groupings, with Figure 4 indicating the extent of state and local activity by function for the two reporting periods.[22]

So diversified has become the state's use of computer technology and the systems approach that there has arisen an acute need for the creation of a *coordinated* system, allowing the most economic and efficient use of computer facilities and trained personnel. No longer can a state afford to have, for example, separate computers—each, in all probability, active only during daytime hours—supporting payroll, highway, procurement, personnel, and program oversight activities. Governors, senior administrators, and program personnel alike are learning by necessity how to share these electronic tools.

The scale of systems activity in state governments, as shown in the data collected during the

[19]*Ibid.*, p. 173, fig. 38.
[20]Heady, *op. cit.*, pp. 16–17.

[21]*Scientific Manpower Utilization*, 1967, *op. cit.*, p. 362.
[22]*Systems Technology Applied to Social and Community Problems*, *op. cit.*, p. 188, fig. 46.

FIGURE 3. Federal Agencies Support of System Analysis Activity (States)

State	Management Activities						Operational Program Activities																		
	(1) Planning and Policies	(2) Personnel Management	(3) Interagency Activity	(4) Management Standards Control	(5) Equipment Selection	(6) Procurement Activity	(7) Legislatures	(8) Courts	(9) Financial	(10) Taxation	(11) Education	(12) Health and Hospitals	(13) Crime and Corrections	(14) Transportation	(15) Urban Renewal and Growth	(16) Science and Research Promotion	(17) Natural Resources	(18) Pollution Control	(19) Parks and Recreation	(20) Regulation of Commerce, etc.	(21) Labor and Manpower Services	(22) Utilities and Enterprises	(23) Welfare and Anti-poverty	(24) Social-Security and Veterans	(25) Other
Alaska	HUD										HEW	HEW	DOJ	DOT			Int.		Int.		DOL		HEW		
Arkansas				HUD																			HEW		
California											HEW	a	a												
Colorado												b													
Connecticut[c]														DOT											
Idaho														DOT											
Illinois[c]																									
Indiana[c]			HUD																						
Iowa	HUD[d]										HEW	HEW		DOT							DOL		HEW		
Kansas									OEO		HEW	HEW		DOT	e	f			g			HUD			
Maine[c]																									
Maryland[c]																									
Massachusetts	HUD		HUD		DOL						HEW	HEW		DOT							DOL		HEW		
Missouri													b		b		d	b		b	b		b		
Nebraska											HEW	HEW													
New Mexico[c,h]																									
New York[c]																									
North Carolina														DOT		HEW									
Ohio														DOT									HEW		
Oregon				b																			b		
Pennsylvania[c]	i														j	f					k		l		
Rhode Island			HUD															Int.							
			OEO																						
South Carolina	HUD							HEW	HEW	DOJ	HEW	HEW			HUD	DOC	HEW	Int.		DOC	DOL	DOC			
South Dakota[c]																									
Texas	HEW										HEW	HEW	DOJ	DOT	HUD	NSF	Int.		Int.	DOC	DOL	DOC	HEW		
Utah	HUD										HEW	HEW	DOJ	DOT							DOL				
Vermont							HUD																		
Washington	BOB													n					Int.						
West Virginia[c]											b	b	HUD										b	m	
Wisconsin[c]																									

[a] NIMH.
[b] Did not specify source.
[c] Did not indicate Federal support.
[d] HEW, OEO, HUD, DOT.
[e] HEW, HUD.

[f] HEW, NSF, HUD.
[g] HUD, Int. (Bureau of Reclamation).
[h] HUD will support PPBS.
[i] HUD, DOD, DOT, EDA.
[j] HUD, DOT.

[k] Int. (Federal Water Pollution Control Adm.).
[l] HEW, OEO.
[m] HEW, V.A.
[n] DOT, Interior
[o] HUD, OEO.

FIGURE 4. Percentage of Active Respondents Employing the Systems Approach by Function (46 active respondents), 1966 and 1968

	1966	1968
I. Management and related activities— overall percentage	77	77
Planning and policies		
Financial		
Equipment selection		
Personnel management		
Taxation		
Procurement activity		
Interagency activity		
Management standards and control		
II. Services and transportation—overall percentage	60	59
Transportation		
Utilities and enterprises		
III. Social and economic development— overall percentage	57	61
Crime and correction		
Education		
Welfare and antipoverty		
Health and hospitals		
Urban renewal and growth		
Pollution control		
Social security and veterans' affairs		
IV. Utilization of resources—overall percentage	51	51
Parks and recreation		
Labor and manpower services		
Natural resources		
Science and research promotion		
V. Legal and regulatory—overall percentage	40	45
Legislatures		
Regulation of commerce		
Courts		

Nelson surveys—and substantiated by the investigations of the Institute on State Programming for the 70s, the State-Local Finances Project, and the Council of State Governments—shows a marked increase during the past five years. Figure 5 shows the number of states engaged in various levels of activity in 1966 and 1968,[23] with the graph revealing not only a higher "program density" per state reporting the use of ADP and systems analysis, but also an incremental increase in the number of states employing such technology.

Thus, the state governments are following the pattern that has been visible in the federal depart-

[23]*Ibid.*, p. 187, fig. 45.

ments and agencies—that of a modular development of ADP and systems methodology support commencing with the simple and graduating to the more complex tasks. Similarly, the state governments have moved apace with the national government in the development of better planning, programming, and budgeting procedures.

PPBS: THE NEW EXCELSIOR

The role of PPBS within a state government has been the subject of much debate, and has reflected the concern by administrators and economists alike that it may not be directly relevant for nor applicable to state governments. In discussing the potential "gainers" and "losers" at the state governmental level, should PPBS be introduced, William M. Capron, formerly Assistant Director of the Bureau of the Budget, points out that:

Even though in many states the governor has limited official power over large numbers of state programs, he does have influence, and PPBS can help him exercise that influence more effectively. Certainly it will help in those parts of the state budget over which he does have official cognizance. Those governors who really wish to govern can gain in their ability to do so by improving the kind and quality of information which informs the decisions that they must make.[24]

Decision-making, whether by the President or a governor, must depend on *information* that is reliable, relevant, and accessible. Which systems can provide this information? Is a PPB system, in the tradition developed by Secretary McNamara in the Department of Defense, a suitable vehicle for the states? Will "computerization" of critical planning, programming, and budgeting data have a deleterious effect on human governing?

If the initial assumption allows the selection of a PPB system to support the chief executive, and "taking with a grain of salt" the declaration that this is, indeed, "a very new and revolutionary system"[25] of program budgeting, then its actual insertion into state procedures warrants further

[24] William M. Capron, *"PPB and State Budgeting" Public Administration Review*, Vol. 19, No. 2 (March/April 1969), p. 156.

[25] Aaron Wildavsky, "The Political Economy of Efficiency: Cost-Benefit Analysis, Systems Analysis, and Program Budgeting," in Fremont J. Lyden and Ernest G. Miller (Eds.), *Planning, Programming, Budgeting: A Systems Approach to Management* (Chicago: Markham, 1967), p. 386 (quoting President Lyndon B. Johnson).

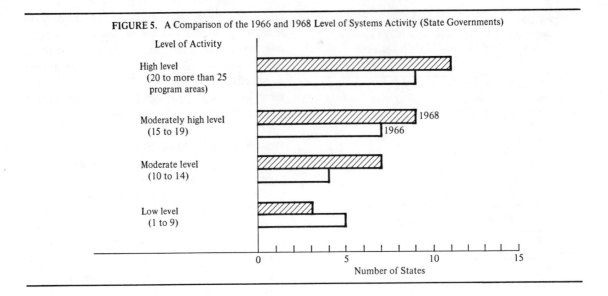

FIGURE 5. A Comparison of the 1966 and 1968 Level of Systems Activity (State Governments)

scrutiny and comment. Capron offers the opinion that:

The proposal to inject systematic analysis into state governments is not a proposal to substitute a computer for bureaucrats, department heads, or governors. . . . we are a very long way from being able to perform the kind of really satisfactory and rigorous analysis which someday we may hope to achieve. . . . [and] have too little understanding of such complex activities as, for example, public education . . . to make possible rigorous, comprehensive, and complete analysis. . . . many of us question whether we will ever develop analytic techniques and data which will permit us within a single comprehensive and rigorous analysis to make comparisons between widely diverse programs.[26]

Once again, the emphasis on the quality of information appears. Frederick C. Mosher notes that PPBS can, through providing key information to advisors, affect decisions in the "administrative maelstrom." The nub of the argument, in his words, might be summed up thus:

In an intellectualizing society and an intellectualizing government, *information* and its *analysis* are more than ever *power*. [Italics added.][27]

Before looking at developments in a few states which have led the way in developing or adapting PPB systems, it may be useful to review some of

the reasons for establishing this type of mechanism:

To focus attention on major issues for decision

To introduce analysis routinely into the comparison of alternative resource allocation

To provide information about future as well as current costs and benefits

To present agency budgets in terms of a meaningful activity structure

To save and focus the decision-making time of high officials

To make meaningful comparisons between government and private market programs[28]

Reportedly, the first state to institute a PPB system was Wisconsin, in 1959, during the administration of Governor Gaylord Nelson. Following the recommendations of the Hoover Commission in its *Task Force Report on Fiscal, Budgeting, and Accounting Activities*, the state began to take steps to establish a program-type budget. First, a consolidated department of administration was created in order to enhance the state's management process and its policy decision concepts. The governor, supported by a bipartisan legislative majority, successfully involved a group of business

[26] Capron, *op. cit.*, p. 157.

[27] Frederick C. Mosher, "Limitations and Problems of PPBS in the States," *Public Administration Review*, Vol. 19, No. 2 (March/April 1969), p. 163.

[28] Wilbur A. Steger, "On Implementing PPBS at the Local Level: Some Strategic Choices and Examples," in *Planning-Programming-Budgeting Systems*, papers presented at the PPBS short course held at the 1969 ASPO National Planning Conference (Chicago: American Society of Planning Officials, 1969), p. 42.

executives, which was charged with studying the state's administrative practices; these men formed task forces, each supported by an administrative analyst from the state budget office, which recommended that all agencies convert to program budgets. This position was strongly supported by a legislative interim committee (in 1962) and a citizens' committee appointed by the legislature (in 1964). Finally, after five years of hard work and an unusual degree of executive-legislative cooperation, new forms and instructions were prepared, and Governor Nelson prepared a directive outlining a three-part program to improve financial administration.[29]

In New York, a comparable chain of events occurred. Governor Nelson Rockefeller, in 1961, created a New York State Office for Regional Development which was charged with preparing a comprehensive development policy. The resulting document, *Change/Challenge/Response*, was published in 1964, and among the 15 recommendations were 2 concerning the role of the systems approach at the state level:

Systems analysis studies of the major functional action systems for providing the essential services and facilities provided by the state's population

A formalized integrated planning-programming-budgeting system[30]

In discussing these recommendations with Senators Nelson and Jacob K. Javits, Vincent J. Moore, Assistant Director of the Office of Planning Coordination of the State of New York, underscored the belief of the New York planners that

... the benefits of systems analysis approaches to functional planning would be realized only if a *formal* system existed to create the crucial *linkage* of the planning and budgeting functions. [Italics added.][31]

From these beginnings, then, the ranks of states using some type of PPBS approach swelled to 24 by the latter 1960s, with several others tentatively planning to take the step. While the name or location of the entity charged with PPB-related functions may vary—e.g., Governor Manuel Guerrero of Guam reports having an Office of Management Research, and Governor John A. Love of Colorado talks about his Management Analysis Office—there is a perceptible movement to trying out the new approach.[32] Imaginative projects such as the "5-5-5" effort have won plaudits from the gubernatorial incumbents,[33] and when coupled with a wider acceptance of the support role of computers, can lead to the development of a more effective, responsive state government. Some thoughtful persons now like to consider computer (and, by implication, systems) technology as a "counter agent" to the bureaucracy which tends to preserve the status quo.[34] The trend appears to be inexorable and of great promise for both the governors and the governed.

LOOKING TO THE FUTURE

With hard evidence in hand that the states' acceptance of the systems approach and ADP is of a lasting nature, it then becomes possible to consider the new potential for information formating, storage, retrieval, and transferability. Already there have been sweeping changes instituted by banks, transportation elements (e.g., airlines), credit card groups, and stock exchanges, to mention but a few. The emphasis is on *information exchange*, and the pressure is developing in many quarters to build what Governor Philip H. Hoff of Vermont called "a bridge of information" between the states,[35] and separate mechanisms for state-federal exchange. There is, although often in a tacit form, interdependence in policy and program development among the components of our federal system.[36] Asynchronous budget cycles, uncoordi-

[29] John W. Reynolds and Walter G. Hollander, "Program Budgeting in Wisconsin," in *Systems Technology Applied to Social and Community Problems, op. cit.,* Appendix H, pp. 321–326.

[30] Robert L. Chartrand, "Modern Management Analysis and Traditional Management Analysis: A Survey of the Impact," in *The Impact of the Management Sciences on Management Analysis.* Papers from the Fourth Annual Conference on Management Analysis in State and Local Government, October 23–24, 1967, Jug End Barn, Massachusetts, p. 12.

[31] *Scientific Manpower Utilization,* 1967, *op. cit.,* pp. 233–234 (remarks of Vincent J. Moore).

[32] *Systems Technology Applied to Social and Community Problems, op. cit.,* pp. 179–181.

[33] *Ibid.,* p. 181 (comments of Governor Warren Knowles of Wisconsin).

[34] Ida R. Hoos, "Automation, Systems Engineering, and Public Administration: Observations and Reflections on the California Experience," *Public Administration Review,* Vol. 26, No. 4 (December 1966), p. 313.

[35] *Systems Technology Applied to Social and Community Problems, op. cit.,* p. 183.

[36] For a discussion of this area, see Deil S. Wright, "Executive Leadership in State Administration," this book.

nated developmental plans affecting more than one state in a region, unnecessary and often harmful competition for limited federal funds—these conditions often spell the difference between progress and stagnation.

Problems *do* exist which must be faced up to and overcome. An analysis of the testimony by witnesses before the Nelson subcommittee and the ample commentary by governors and other state officials responding to its two questionnaires allows the enumeration of eight problems which must be solved before systems technology can have its full impact on government at all levels, and society in general.

1. Limited funds and lack of initial capital investment
2. Nonsynchronous budgeting cycles
3. Lack of management sophistication in understanding how to use systems technology
4. Inexperience in obtaining available Federal assistance, either monetary or consulting expertise
5. Tendency to develop fragmented management and program systems
6. Difficulty in obtaining qualified systems personnel, or retraining on-board staff members
7. Absence of enabling legislation which could provide the necessary initial impetus for corrective action
8. Difficulties caused by overlapping jurisdictional control[37]

The states and major cities, are creating those organizational, procedural, and legal capabilities and capacities which will allow them to cope with the problems of our times. Still other changes are advocated, including the creation of more regional development commissions, greater use of university resources—as exemplified by the midwestern academic consortium of 11 universities and its Council of Economic Growth, Technology, and Public Policy[38]—or the concept of a national Council for American Progress.[39] Assistance in implementing systems in the management and operational program areas should take the form of consulting services, direct financial subsidy, matching funds, training support, or enabling legislation, according to the Nelson respondents.[40]

The implication of the new systems technology for the governors is quite clear. Here is an array of weapons to help contain and eventually overcome the pressures and problems which now confront *all* states. The governor will have to play the visionary, as well as fulfill the velvet-and-steel role of the chief executive. There can be no wavering nor procrastination, nor any lasting penalty for creativity and courage, for the time is now.

[37]*Systems Technology Applied to Social and Community Problems, op. cit.,* p. 192.
[38]*Ibid.,* p. 141 (testimony of Dean E. T. Weiler).
[39]*Ibid.,* pp. 144–145 (testimony of Michael Michaelis).
[40]*Ibid.,* p. 177, fig. 42 for quantitative responses.

CHAPTER 8

IMPLEMENTING POLICIES IN THE STATES

There is a dearth of material when one looks for analysis of gubernatorial involvement in policy implementation. As this book, and the bibliography can attest, there is considerable knowledge about gubernatorial politics and power and on the politics of management and administration. There are also numerous case studies of particular governors facing particular problems at particular times and of certain governors' tenure in office; but few generalizations on the governors' relationship to policy implementation appear. Tom Dye's article attempts to provide an analytical base from which more general statements can be made.

We decided to move outside academic bounds and ask someone involved with governors in a policy sense to provide their views of how governors were indeed "implementing policies in the states." A Social Scientist who works as a private researcher and who has focused on state health delivery systems comments on this area. "Law and Order" is analyzed by North Carolina's special consultant for law enforcement and the Safe Streets Act. He has since moved on to be Director of Public Safety for a major urban county in Delaware but as the former President of the University of Massachusetts—and President just when that state began to reassume some of its responsibilities for higher education—he reflects on governors and higher education. Finally, a former urban reporter for a major New Jersey paper and that state's Associate Director of the Department of Community Affairs under Paul Ylvisaker, has put his experience in perspective.

These articles, flowing from personal involvement and experience, may in some way reorient the priorities some scholars suggest as being the most significant and important. While not as methodologically rigorous as other articles in this book, these selections raise and pinpoint areas of concern that should cause those of us outside the government to pause and rethink what, *in fact*, it means to be a chief executive of a state.

THE GOVERNOR AND COMPREHENSIVE HEALTH PLANNING
Nancy N. Anderson

The Partnership for Health Act of 1966 offered to the nation's governors a promise of increased resources for policy-making and planning, and opportunity for policy-making in the area of medical care and public health. It is appropriate now to compare promise with performance in order to ascertain whether there is, in fact, a useful gubernatorial tool in comprehensive health planning (CPH) agencies and bloc grants, the two more important provisions of the law. This evaluation cannot, of course, be accomplished with the specificity that each chief executive, knowing the state's particular health problems and governmental structures, could bring to the task; rather, what will be discussed is the mechanism of comprehensive health planning and the public role in what had been primarily a private, professional affair. Existing (admittedly superficial) evidence demonstrates that the governors have not taken full advantage of Partnership for Health. This is unfortunate because there are important reasons for gubernatorial involvement in comprehensive health planning, despite what many consider to be the inauspicious beginnings of the CHP agencies.

The act itself was a Great Society program passed by the Congress that also established Regional Medical Programs to link centers of learning and research to the hinterlands for purposes of better treating heart disease, cancer, and stroke; it was signed into law by a President who, in one of his yearly health messages, declared that good health should be the "right" of each American. There were five major provisions. Two called for federal funding of comprehensive health planning agencies, one in each state government, and several for the states' geographic sections (the state CHP agency and the areawide CHP agencies, sometimes called the "a" and "b" agencies after their designation in section 314 of the Public Health Service Amendments of 1966). In 1969, seven million dollars were appropriated, with grants ranging from $10,000 to nearly $500,000 going to the state CHP agencies. Two other provisions decategorized health grants-in-aid, which meant that Congress delegated the authority to specify on what health problems the funds should be spent to the states (under 413d) and (under 314e) to the

Department of Health, Education, and Welfare which was to review project applications submitted from all over the country. It was with funds appropriated for this latter decategorization provision that fourteen neighborhood health centers were established, but that is another story—about federal, not state, health policy-making and planning. The fifth provision of Partnership for Health set up project grants for training comprehensive health planners. We are concerned here with the establishment of state CHP agencies and the bloc grants made to the states to be spent "in accord with" whatever plans were to emerge from comprehensive health planning.

According to the usual custom, the Secretary of HEW wrote each governor asking him to designate a state agency as recipient of the grant to conduct comprehensive health planning. There was unusual interest in CHP as a gubernatorial resource, however, and the directors of every HEW regional office personally visited the governors of the region to discuss the potential of the new program. As a result of all the hoopla (including a highly visible about-face in Washington that took administration of the Partnership for Health Act out of an operating bureau of the Public Health Service and put it into the Office of the Surgeon General), the agency designed for comprehensive health planning in 16 of the states was one that was close to the governor—either a state planning agency, an office of administration or finance, or the governor's office itself. (This number includes eight situations where an early designation of the health department was reversed by the governor.) The proportion of states assigning CHP to the health department was smaller than usual. In contrast to CHP, for example, of the agencies designated as responsible for vocational rehabilitation planning, three-fourths were part of the state's division or bureau of vocational rehabilitation or in an independent commission, and one-fourth in a department of planning or development. The issue of agency designation foreshadowed an important debate relating to the governor's relationship to comprehensive health planning: Is the effort better undertaken by health professionals, and within a specific or "functional" agency, or should it be the responsibility of officials reporting directly to elected representatives, and be within a broader planning and policy capability? The issue is, of course, familiar to students of state government, being an instance of the debate over linking state planning to the governor directly or placing it within a department of commerce or development.[1]

The actual and potential gubernatorial role in CHP is analyzed from the perspective of a social scientist who has been observing comprehensive health planning from its beginnings. The data presented below were obtained from reports to the federal government made by each state CHP agency, generally in 1969. The information concerning expenditures of decategorized or bloc grants was supplemented by questionnaires completed by health department officials. Governors, or their immediate staff assistants, were not contacted directly, and consequently the evidence is more representative of the perspective of comprehensive health planners and public health officials than of chief executives. The resulting bias probably overestimates the importance of CHP within state government, since it was in the interest of its participants to do so. The evidence is inconclusive as well as underrepresentative of the governor's point of view, due to the difficulty of ascertaining from written documents what actually happens. With these caveats expressed, let us proceed to discuss the promise of comprehensive health planning.[2]

INCREASED PUBLIC ACCOUNTABILITY THROUGH CHP

There was much that was old hat about the Partnership for Health, the "feds" having long required the preparation of state plans to attest to the sobriety and morality of the expenditure of grant-in-aid funds. What was apparently new about the law were its intentions (sometimes a matter of inference, hence subject to disagreement): to broaden health planning beyond the customary concerns of health professionals, to counterbalance professional influence by providing for a consumer-dominated advisory council to the CHP agency, and to link these broader planning processes with budgeting a bloc grant.[3] The significance of these provisions becomes evident when they are compared with earlier health planning experiences.

Historically, much health planning that occurred before 1966 was undertaken by groups of practitioners in the same field (as in the AMA-sponsored Flexner Commission of 1910 which recommended reform of medical education) or by groups of professionals from various fields (as in the Wilbur Commission, comprising physicians and public-health representatives, which reported on medical care costs in 1932). In either case, the primary participants viewed the issue under study from the professional's perspective. To be sure, local health planning usually included community representatives—"laymen" in respect to health—and planning at the state level was generally conducted by officials within a public agency receiving federal health funds. So the public interest was presumably represented. Fact came to differ from theory, according to several studies, however, and much health planning still represented a dominantly professional outlook.

In the case of local or community health planning, the task may not appeal to nonprofessionals, busy with their own concerns, and many of the laymen who do remain involved become as vigorous advocates of the professionals' cause as the professionals themselves. A likely consequence is the limiting of what can be accomplished. Studies are undertaken to locate gaps in existing services, and recommendations concern adding new services; findings never point to the need for eliminating old services or otherwise trespassing on the participants' turf.[4] Hospital planning, another local planning endeavor, by and large protects the interests of hospitals. In a period where hospital expansion is needed, this is indeed a useful function. Facilities planning got its original impetus with the 1946 Hill-Burton legislation aimed at supporting increased construction of rural hospitals.

[1] Thad L. Beyle, Sureva Seligson, and Deil S. Wright, "New Directions in State Planning," *Journal of the American Institute of Planners*, Vol. XXXV (September 1969), No. 5, pp. 334–339.

[2] The data on CHP agency relationships and activities are coded from reports made by the agencies to the Division of Comprehensive Health Planning in the Department of Health, Education, and Welfare. All written materials were collected from the establishment of each agency through 1970. Coders were trained in content analysis techniques and categories for rating agency relationships and activities.

[3] This analysis of unique provisions in the Partnership for Health was originally presented in the writer's *Comprehensive Health Planning in the States: A Study and Critical Analysis* (Minneapolis: American Rehabilitation Foundation, 1968).

[4] Ralph W. Conant, *The Politics of Community Health* (Washington D.C.: Public Affairs Press, 1968).

Several decades later, however, many believe the existence of a small hospital in every community is a barrier to good medical care, comparable to the one-room schoolhouse before consolidated school districts were established. A study of eight metropolitan areas, four with hospital planning agencies, and four without, revealed a greater increase in the number of hospital beds per capita for the communities with planning agencies.[5] Now the same agencies are confronted with bed surpluses, a more difficult challenge for voluntary planning whose participants are largely hospital administrators.

Health planning within state agencies has been conducted by professionals who are protected from politics and isolated from the governor. A necessary reform a century ago, "private government," or "hidden hierarchies" of professionals, runs counter to today's cries for consumer involvement and public accountability.[6] Moynihan has attributed the Welfare crisis, for example, to the failure of professional social workers to report to elected officials the monumental change in the makeup of public assistance rolls (from rural, white widows, to urban, black, unwed mothers).[7]

The Partnership for Health Act was compatible with a trend to add more representative government and citizen involvement to the making of health decisions. It was enacted in a time of increased recognition that professionals could no longer be solely entrusted with getting health care to all who need it. Particularly people living in inner city and rural areas suffered because the professionals' own interests and ethics were well served by practicing under more favorable conditions. Further, there was new acknowledgment of the rights of the patient to participate in determining his medical needs; "doctor knows best" was becoming a less and less acceptable justification for health policies, concerning an individual, a community, or a state.

The unique provisions for the conduct of comprehensive health planning show how increased public accountability could perhaps be brought about. The scope of the planning was to be com-

prehensive, or broader than the jurisdiction of any one profession or agency. The advisory council to the CHP agency was to have a majority of consumers to counterbalance professional interests. Federal funds, now awarded as a bloc grant, could be spent in accord with a more comprehensive and consumer-oriented planning process.

The importance of the governor's role in realization of these intentions lies in his status as health layman and as an elected representative of consumers as well as providers. It was hoped that his involvement would give the health planning agency the purpose and power it needed to respond to health problems of the sixties and seventies. In turn, the agency was a capability with which the governor might recapture a role in health policy-making so frequently delegated in the past to professionals in state agencies. An examination of CHP agencies from 1966 to 1970 will suggest the extent to which governors have, in fact, been involved and the apparent usefulness of the capability to the state's chief executive.

A SLOW BEGINNING

Comparing the promise of comprehensive health planning with its performance over the four-year period 1966–70 is a risky business, even if it were possible to report impeccable data related to universal criteria of success. (Perhaps evaluation would not be so treacherous if funds to do so were not usually appropriated along with the enabling act, which, of course, assumes that the new program is a defensible expenditure). Our effort here will have to be contentedly limited to discussion of trends that may indicate the usefulness of CHP to the governors. These trends, in preview, seem to suggest that comprehensive health planning has not as yet been used by the governors as effectively as it might be.

The purpose in presenting evidence related to that hypothesis is not so much to test it as to illuminate untapped potential for gubernatorial leadership. (And this is not to imply that CHP has no other possible functions, although it is the author's opinion that the one under consideration here has major significance.) The information to be reported concerns relationships between CHP agencies and governors, activities of the agencies, and expenditures of the newly decategorized bloc grant. Before getting quantitative in this assessment of CHP, it is important to note what seems

[5] J. Joel May, *Health Planning: Its Past and Potential*, Perspectives Number A5, Chicago: Center for Health Administration Studies, 1967.

[6] Corrine Lathrop Gilb, *Hidden Hierarchies: The Professions and Government* (New York: Harper & Row, 1960).

[7] Daniel P. Moynihan, "The Crisis in Welfare," *The Public Interest*, No. 10 (Winter 1968), pp. 3–29.

to be a growing national disaffection with the Partnership for Health. Perhaps it is only waning delight in toys that are no longer new (health maintenance organizations and national health insurance now have the limelight) or our impatience with the time needed to build structures that will later facilitate better delivery of health services. Perhaps the author is misreading remarks dropped here and there, inside of the federal government and out. Notwithstanding, it is only fair—if not scientifically defensible to report that comprehensive health planning has not been favorably evaluated by those in Washington generally responsible for formulating national health policy and by increasingly vocal health consumer groups. The latter are more willing to go on record; the following criticism, quoted from a Health PAC newsletter, is more damning than many comments.

The Health Planning "movement," the most recent attempt to bring reason and light to America's nineteenth-century medical marketplace, is already showing signs of age and disillusionment. As hospital costs spiral and medical resources dry up, the once revolutionary concepts of planning and regionalization have settled down as harmless cliches.

The need to "rationalize" laissez faire medicine, even at the cost of long-dreaded government intervention, is now a commonplace theme for medical school graduation oratory. Government "intrusions" resulting from Kennedy/Johnson Health New Deal legislation have calmed the fears of all but the most rear-guard national health forces: The movement for planning and regionalization does not threaten to truly rationalize health services.

The need for planning became especially acute to many federal policy-makers after the passage of two financing bills—Medicaid and Medicare. Liberal medical advisors thought it would be prudent to follow up the federal dollars with some sense about health care organization. The results were the Comprehensive Health Planning Act (CHPA) and the Regional Medical Program (RMP). Both laws looked to the medical establishment—medical schools, voluntary hospitals and private insurance companies—for leadership towards the Brave New World of planned care. Both are failing fast.[8]

Although not all critics would be as blunt as Robb Burlage, the criticisms he voices seem to be common themes. The critics contend that comprehensive health planning has turned out to be nothing new; that its larger scope, consumer-dominated

[8] "The Great Planning Scandal," *Health PAC Bulletin* (July-August 1969), pp. 1–2.

boards, and decategorized grants have not been achieved, much less the more ultimate objectives of increased public accountability and better health care; instead, CHP is not much different from health planning programs that were begun well before 1966. What is needed, more and more will allow, is a look at some long-granted assumptions about the organization and financing of health services. This cannot be performed, the argument continues, by continuation of professionally-dominated or more strongly Establishmentarian planning, which is prevented by its very structures from considering basic changes.

Those closer to comprehensive health planning seem to be saying that it is too early to expect results and that the current preoccupation with planning processes and methods is a natural and necessary beginning. They would also attribute a slow beginning to limited resources, visibility, and influence.

Available quantitative data neither damn nor praise the Partnership for Health. They do suggest, in the first place, that the majority of CHP agencies have not been closely related to their states' chief executives. Contents of written reports were analyzed for mention of contact or association with a variety of state agencies, professional groups, and voluntary health associations, as well as with the governor and the legislature. The number of agencies describing relationships judged by trained coders to be "minimal (token)," "considerable," or "very close working relationship" are presented in Table 1.

Only 7 of the 48 agencies for which materials were available described what could be called a close working relationship with the governor. Five fell into the "considerable" category, and three into the "minimal," or "token," extent of relationship. These frequencies would seem pathetically small, considering the theoretical significance of comprehensive health planning for gubernatorial policy-making.

One also notes from these data the low incidence of close working relationships with other institutions. It turns out that the total number of reports of gubernatorial contacts is the fifth largest of all the possibilities tabulated; it is exceeded by relationships with the health department, the mental health department, the regional medical program, vocational rehabilitation planning agency, and mental retardation planning agency—in that order.

TABLE 1. State CHP Agencies Describing Relationships with Various Organizations[*]

Organization Relating to	Extent of Relationship			
	None	Minimal	Considerable	Very close working relationship
State health department	15	12	6	3
State mental health department	20	7	7	3
Regional medical program	20	7	9	3
State vocational rehabilitation pianning	23	9	4	2
State mental retardation planning	24	6	5	3
Governor	26	3	5	7
Areawide CHP	31	3	7	2
Voluntary health associations	31	5	6	1
Hospital associations	31	7	4	1
State planning agency	33	5	6	4
State department of education	34	6	3	1
Facilities planning	34	3	4	1
State OEO	36	5	1	0
State medical society	39	3	4	2
Legislature	39	2	2	2
Voluntary mental health associations	41	1	3	3
Professional associations	41	4	1	0
Hospitals	41	2	0	0

[*]Based on 48 agencies. These relationships were coded from descriptions in written reports made to DHEW by the agency. The agencies were not asked to describe relationships.

These findings would support two tentative conclusions. First, while a definite minority of CHP agencies are working as closely with the governor (as indicated by their own written descriptions of activities) as they are with many voluntary and professional associations, they are more frequently closer to other state agencies than they are to the governor. Second, the agencies do not very frequently report considerable or close working relationships with any institution; many of them seem to be working independently of other agencies, a phenomenon whose significance lies in the probability that these other agencies are sources of authority to get plans implemented. (One must also consider the possibility that relationships will be established as CHP agencies begin to have completed plans to implement.)

It is interesting to distinguish the characteristics of agencies describing some degree of relationship with the governor from those whose written materials contained no accounts of contacts with the governor.[9] The former agencies tend to have larger staffs, larger budgets, and more experienced directors. Interpreting this trend presents a chicken-and-egg problem: Do governors use the better equipped agencies, or do governors equip agencies they use?

The second kind of data—agency activities—is less obviously relevant to detecting the mutual benefits of CHP and gubernatorial policy-making, it does give a clue about the extent to which new topics are being tackled by health planners as well as the amount of progress they are making toward actually trying out new solutions. Readers may also make judgments from Table 2 regarding the relevance of the problems being planned to state government in general or to a particular state.

Table 2 shows most obviously the predominance of building health planning processes and developing health information systems among the activities for one year (1969 for most states) described in written reports. For example, all but 14 of the 53 agencies (including territories and the District of Columbia) on which data are available have been working on an information system. These are, of course, basic building blocks of a planning structure. Not as much progress has been made in substantive planning endeavors. Output (such as a report or recommendation) is reported

[9]These relationships were ascertained by analysis of variance.

in a total of 56 agency activities, but only 6 report that a change has been brought about. The data pretty well speak for themselves; few results were available by 1970. Whether they should be after a period of three years (allowing a first year for just getting an agency designated and initially staffed) is a more problematic judgment, involving two important questions: "What should their accomplishments be compared with?" and "Could the money have been better spent elsewhere?"

The most popular planning activities are related to health manpower and health facilities. These would seem to be similar to the concerns of earlier planning programs. Very few of the agencies are investigating patterns of health care delivery and financing health care, which are receiving considerable official, popular, and professional discussion. Again, this phenomenon should be interpreted in light of other considerations—most basically, the health issues in each state or territory.

The data on planning activities do not negate the criticisms leveled against the Partnership for Health, but neither do they invalidate the cautions that there has not been enough time nor enough resources committed to the effort. With regard to the governor and CHP, it would seem that there is as yet little evidence of increased public accountability through gubernatorial interest.

The CHP agency's impact on budgeting, therefore, becomes a crucial consideration, as this is, of course, a primary mode of gubernatorial leadership. It will be remembered that the Partnership for Health Act not only established planning agencies (areawide as well as state), but also untied the Congressional apronstrings from nine categorical grants-in-aid and proposed that these funds, to be henceforth awarded as a bloc grant, might be spent "in accord with" (that now-famous phrase) plans issuing from the CHP agency. What has actually happened to carry out legislative intent is no more ambiguous in this case than was the stated intent. Some would attach great significance to linking comprehensive planning to appropriation decisions, thus broadening the problems that are eligible for support and rationalizing the allocation process. Even if CHP is part of the health department which previously administered the federal funds under consideration, the CHP agency is charged with assessing *all* the state's health problems, including those not now touched by public health problems. Others posit that there was no intention to have CHP influence budgeting, and

TABLE 2. State CHP Agency Activities [*]						
	Level of Activity					
Type of Activity	None	Problem selected	Specific plan of action adopted	Organizational structure established to deal with problem	Preliminary activity reported	Output reported	Change brought about
Health planning process	3	1	1	5	19	23	1
Health information systems	14	0	2	11	22	4	0
Environmental health	22	2	4	13	10	1	1
Preventive health	49	0	1	1	1	1	0
Health manpower	16	1	3	12	14	7	0
Health facilities and equipment	19	1	3	12	15	3	0
Patterns of health care delivery	39	1	1	4	4	4	0
Financing health care	36	0	1	3	6	7	0
Specific diseases	38	1	0	6	7	1	0
Specific population needs	29	1	2	7	8	6	0
Provider education	33	0	1	1	3	13	2
Consumer education	32	0	2	7	9	3	0
Regulation relating to health	31	0	1	3	11	6	1
Mental health	40	0	2	7	4	0	0
Other	24	2	1	15	6	4	1

[*] Based on 53 agencies. These activites are only for one year for most states and thus do not represent all activities to date for the agencies; they were coded from reports to DHEW made by the agency.

that the bloc grant should be spent in such a way that it is not contrary to plans that have been developed. The argument tends to be academic in many states, either way, because, in fact, the CHP agency participation in budgeting is limited to issuing completed plans with which completed budgets can be compared by, perhaps, the HEW regional offices.

The state health departments were questioned by letter concerning CHP agency involvement in budgeting the decategorized funds. Preliminary analysis of their responses indicates minimal participation. Such a conclusion is in keeping with professional folklore about what is going on, but not trustworthy until the CHP agencies have also been contacted and both sets of answers thoroughly cross-tabulated.

Another indicator of Partnership for Health progress is the extent to which the decategorized funds are spent on problems different from those on which they had to be spent, by Congressional action, before 1966. Expenditures of federal health grants for the periods 1963–66 and 1968–70 were tabulated for each state, and the discrepancies between what would have been spent had the categories been maintained and what was spent, given decategorization was taken as a measure of increased flexibility. Thirty-seven percent of the funds spent in the period 1968–70 reflected new allocations, suggesting only a start toward making budgetary decisions at the state level of government.[10]

PROTECTING THE HEALTH CONSUMER

All that has been said to this point adds up to a commonly-professed planning theory—that planning is more powerful and more relevant to executive concerns if closely linked to the head of government (in this case, the governor)—and a commonly-expressed planning reality—that planning agencies often do not live up to expectation. The central issue has yet to be addressed. It is unfortunate that it cannot be addressed. In a paper discussing simply "the governor and comprehensive health planning," there is no way to answer for each governor a question that must be very

much on his mind: What is there about this program that demands my attention any more than all the other programs making similar promises? There is a way, however, to be more specific about possible functions CHP *can* serve for gubernatorial leadership, without assuming an advocacy position that this particular resource for health planning *will* do the job. The latter depends upon what the governor (and indeed the President) sees to be the state's responsibility in health, once a professional affair, now more and more a federal investment, as it depends also upon idiosyncracies of personalities, politics, and events.

Something about possible CHP functions has been suggested by the preceding analysis. We have seen more than simply a limited relationship between most governors and most agencies and a slowness in making plans and affecting budgetary decisions. There have been a couple of threads visible in the data, and a closer examination finds them woven through the discussion of previous health planning programs, illustrated mainly by facilities planning. These concern problems involving planning purposes and planning powers. Some of the presumed ineffectiveness of facilities planning has been attributed to limited powers, particularly in Conant's analysis of how difficult it is for professionals to make planning decisions contrary to their own interests.[11] It was also learned that many of the CHP agencies do not acknowledge working closely with operating programs, the governor, or the legislature—relationships from which could flow influence to get planning recommendations enacted.

Selecting planning purposes has been problematic according to critics of both facilities planning and comprehensive health planning, because if anything is to get done efforts must be focused on the solution of a problem. Constructing new hospital buildings in rural areas may be too narrow a goal; improving everyone's health to the highest level attainable is probably too broad to implement (at least in the short run).

The themes of power and purpose will be discussed in the limited context of the governor and CHP, and then only briefly. For it would seem apparent that to the degree comprehensive health planning is used as a gubernatorial resource, it will achieve at least some power and some purpose

---

[10] Further information can be obtained from Leonard Robins, "The Impact of Decategorizing Federal Programs: Before and After 314(d)," paper presented to the American Public Health Association, October 1970, Houston, Texas.

[11] Conant, *The Politics of Community Health*.

toward the general end of increased public accountability. The governor, therefore, can perhaps reduce the discrepancy between promise and performance if the discrepancy is not so large that he does not want to try. The crucial issue here is what CHP can do for the governor.

Three major health policy functions could be performed for the governor by a resource such as a CHP agency. First, the agency can conduct health-related gubernatorial responsibilities such as preparing legislative proposals and resolving current issues. Several CHP agencies have, for example, made studies to determine better ways to utilize state mental institutions or TB sanitariums. Second, the agency can analyze the health implications of a variety of state programs, including those within the health department, to determine their effectiveness in reaching policy objectives. Third, a CHP agency can function to protect health consumers more directly. It is on this last and less frequently discussed role for comprehensive health planning and the governor that we shall focus.

The need for consumer protection is the cry of many reformers in the early years of the 1970s, and their targets include the health industry, public and private. Lack of even presumed market forces and the special status of the health professional combine to overwhelm the consumer of health services perhaps more than the consumer of tangible goods, if not other human services. The student of state government might be interested in a hypothesis that adequate consumer protection from the inadequacies of a private system may be, in the long run, the fulcrum issue balancing mixed decentralization against a more centralized, publicly-owned health service. But the governor will probably be more taken with a similar hypothesis that consumer protection may be the major, if not the only, health issue demanding voter attention. Be that as it may, whether for historic or political reasons, protecting the health consumer seems to be a defensible planning purpose. It is certainly consistent with much of the Partnership for Health rhetoric, particularly, of course, the provision for a consumer-dominated CHP advisory council.

How to do this will be a bigger stumbling block than obtaining endorsement of the objective. The method of representing consumer interests in decision-making has so far received the most attention. In addition to putting consumers in a position to advise the planning agency, surveys and hearings have been sponsored to ascertain problems individuals have with keeping healthy and using health services toward that end. The planning agency also acts as a stand-in for consumer interests when it seeks to locate hidden health problems around the state. This approach is not difficult, although it is no small task to include and empower consumer participants.[12]

Another method of consumer protection concerns equity, a public responsibility since the New Deal if not long before, but one the states occasionally verge on abdicating to the federal government. Equal health opportunity involves at least making the location of health services accessible to all and insuring the ability to pay. The former is a familiar planning function; the danger is that comprehensiveness will be interpreted as much too broad for concern over the distribution of health services. (Note in this connection the argument over how much CHP is able to affect health by means other than improving medical care and public health.) There is the bigger hazard of trying to influence disparate pieces of a health program—for example, physicians separately from hospitals and clinics. At least two CHP agencies have been concerned with equal ability to pay for services because they have assisted the governor in preparing a plan for implementing Medicaid in those states. Referring back to Table 2, the reader will recall higher frequencies of involvement with health facilities (not programs, N.B.) than with financing health care, however.

An important challenge in regard to equity is the monitoring of the health of the state's citizens, particularly by geographic location, income, and age, in order that the efficacy and availability of services to various population groups can be continually observed. Several states are empowering CHP agencies (working with health departments) to license hospitals on the basis of need assessments; this development is but one means of consumer protection.

An equally important but less popular means of consumer protection involves not representing the consumer, or acting on his behalf—as in the two methods just discussed—but increasing the influ-

[12] Ellen Z. Fifer, "Health Planning Hang-Ups," *American Journal of Public Health*, Vol. 59 (May 1969), pp. 765–769.

ence of the consumer as a purchaser of services. Advertising is under scrutiny, and Ralph Nader contends that a new federal consumer protection agency should have information disclosure privileges. It is odd, in a way, that such controversies are generally considered irrelevant to health services. The governor and CHP could attempt to inform the consumer so he can more rationally select health services; together they could also investigate quality controls applied to services purchased with public funds for indigent consumers. The potential of pursuing such a purpose was first made evident to the writer in a study of nursing homes where it was found that the best predictor of poor quality nursing-home care was a high proportion of welfare patients. How relatively easy it would be to have a Duncan Hines system for nursing homes—at least easy when compared to other institutions dispensing medical care.

There is considerable opinion that increased equity measures and increased effective consumer demand will have little impact on health services unless they are organized differently. Comprehensive health planners have long been aware that reorganizing might be their real challenge; perhaps governors, like many Congressmen, still see the problem as one of financing, not organizing. In 1970, federal policy-makers began to make reorganization a more respectable planning objective by introducing the concept of the health maintenance organization, a generic term for a health care organization which is paid a fixed yearly sum to provide all services, including preventive and outpatient. Without debating the merits of the proposal (which at this writing had not been made statutory by amendment to the Social Security legislation but was influencing administration of federal health programs), its relevance for a state's efforts toward protecting the health consumer can be pointed out. It is relevant to the task of regional distribution: Licensing or other means of influencing where a so-called health maintenance organization locates should be an answer to the problem of new buildings but no staff, since the organization would be responsible for serving its specified consumer group. It is also relevant to helping a consumer purchase medical care wisely; the difference between selecting among organizations and selecting individually—as do most now—doctors and hospitals and clinics and laboratories is comparable to the difference between buying a Volkswagen and buying a chassis, a motor (that will fit in the trunk), paint, upholstery, and so on.[13]

Specific state actions that can be undertaken in behalf of better organized health services include most notably revoking laws preventing provision of care by organizations and purchasing care under Medicaid from organizations on a preferential basis.

SUMMARY

The Partnership for Health Act of 1966 promised the governor new resources for planning and increased authority over health expenditures. One implied purpose of the legislation was to increase public accountability of the health industry.

A review of comprehensive health planning agency materials, largely reports submitted to Washington, suggests that 7 of 48 agencies work closely with the governor; 6 of 53 agencies (more reports were available here) have seen change brought about as a result of their activities; and about one-third of decategorized federal health funds were spent differently from trends set before bloc grants were instituted.

The data and the general opinion that CHP has not achieved its potential cannot be interpreted with regard to the usefulness of the program to the governor, as this is an issue to be resolved within each state. It is proposed, however, that there are important functions CHP can perform to assist gubernatorial leadership: conduct health-related responsibilities, assess health implications of state programming and budgeting decisions, and increase consumer protection measures. The last function, being less often considered, is discussed in detail, and related to federal policies promoting health maintenance organizations.

[13] Statement by Robert H. Finch, Secretary of Health, Education, and Welfare on Medicare and Medicard Reforms, processed, March 25, 1970.

THE CRIME CONTROL ACT:
AN EXPERIMENT IN BLOC GRANTS

Harvey D. Miller

The Omnibus Crime Control and Safe Streets Act of 1968 (hereafter, crime control act) is a study in contrasts. Regardless of eventual outcomes in controlling and preventing crime and strengthening local response to the problems generated by crime, the act appears to be the forerunner of even more substantial efforts by the federal government to influence policies and directions of local governmental units through the use of state government as an intervening, and oftentimes controlling agent, where federal grants are involved.

But what of the impact of the crime control act upon the office of the governor? Does it contain enough dollar substance to invite the use of state executive power to control or at least lead the direction of local efforts in crime control? What is the nature of the act? Can the governor, if he chooses to do so, impose his will upon the administration of the Act and the distribution of funds to local units? If the governor does attempt to influence administration and distribution of funds, what can he buy and how can that control be enhanced so that it becomes a potent force in the already considerable stable of political nags that he can choose to ride?

Thus far, not much has been accomplished in the improvement of the processes of criminal justice through the funding of locally sponsored projects under the act. In the main, the impact of the crime control act upon the office of governor has been negligible. Indeed, its impact has been much like the hors d'oevres at a cocktail party—tasty, but hardly enough to constitute a full dinner.

LIMITED POLICY REACH

By design of law and tradition, governors have not intervened directly into problems generated by criminal activities except in a limited sense. In a number of states, the state police, highway patrols, bureaus of investigation, and the like have sharply defined original jurisdiction both geographically and by subject matter. Thus, with the exception of the legally defined jurisdiction by subject matter, the governor's role in the efforts of local government to control crime has generally been confined to judicial appointment powers, expressions of outrage at local occurrences or the posting of re-wards in particularly heinous crimes, and intervening, generally by invitation, in civil disorders or natural calamities.

However, there is a growing body of evidence that the crime control act is perceptibly altering the traditional state-local relationship in dealing with the problems of crime and criminal justice. In short, the modified bloc-grant approach of the act may be the reinforcing cement that strengthens "the keystones of the American governmental arch,"[1] as Elazer describes the state government's midway position vis-à-vis local-federal relationships. The crime control act, regardless of whether the processes of criminal justice are improved, represents a major effort by the national government to reestablish a truly federal relationship with the states. For with its passage in 1968, the U.S. Congress opted for a program in which potentially massive economic power, controlled in a large measure by the state governments, could be used to influence the processes of both state and local criminal justice.

The office of the governor of the subscribing state is mandated by provisions of the act as the key agency in its implementation. Thus, power— both economic and political (if these can ever be separated)—passes to the state. The "new" federalism bandied about by academics and politicians a few years ago is challenged by the crime control act, a product-oriented effort of the traditional national-state federal relationship.

The thrust of this article is not to suggest a monolithic conspiracy by state government to intervene in traditionally local concerns. It may reflect a particular bias on the part of the author that at this point in time there may, in fact, be few concerns, issues, or problems that are in themselves local. Be that as it may, the purpose of this article is to indicate that the modified bloc-grant approach to funding as outlined in the crime control act lends itself to a reinterpretation of federal-state-local relationships, and enhances the power of the office of the governor to influence these patterns. Crucial to this reinterpretation is the impact of the decisions made by the governors upon the administration of the act.

---

[1] Daniel J. Elazar, "The States and the Nation," in Herbert Jacobs and Kenneth N. Vines (Eds.), *Politics in the American States*, First Ed. (Boston: Little, Brown, 1965), p. 449.

The crime control act is the product of several years of searching by the administration and Congress for some method to improve the processes of criminal justice at the state and local levels. In its first two years of operation, the act has not offered enough empirical data to adequately test its impact upon the processes of criminal justice or the office of the governor. However, certain tendencies that are beginning to surface seem to offer substantial clues as to present and future impact in the areas mentioned.

The first year of the act (1968–69) was designated by the federal administrators as the planning phase; the time was allotted for the creation of the state administering agencies and the formulation of comprehensive state plans aimed toward improving the administration of criminal justice at the local level. Action money for the first year of operations was scarce; it consisted mainly of funds under section 307(b), which were allocated for riot control equipment and training and for improving police response to potentially threatening community situations. The remainder of the first-year funds ($68,000,000) was earmarked for the establishment of the various state planning agencies and a list of priorities developed at the national level, whose creation would assist local law enforcement agencies in improving their capacities to reduce the number and seriousness of crimes in their jurisdictions.

During the second year of the act (1969–70) project money began to flow to the states; it was allocated by the various state planning agencies to state and local units of government according, at least in theory, to the merit of the proposals submitted by local governments and the possible impact of these suggested programs upon the processes of criminal justice in the communities. In the early action stages of the act, it became immediately obvious that most funded projects would be successful, at least for the purpose of reporting to the federal administering agency, the Law Enforcement Assistance Administration (LEAA), for it soon became apparent to the law enforcement planners at the local and state levels that the reward system in grantsmanship is not too charitable to losers. Additionally, the requests for funding of local projects centered around police hardware and equipment needs and officer training. Consequently, on the shelves or in the books there was tangible evidence of success regardless of how it was measured.

Three factors—the nature of the act itself, the modified bloc-grant-to-the-states approach imposed by Congress which necessitated the creation of administering agencies by the states, and the proposals for action projects—coupled with the structures for arriving at decisions regarding allocation of funds to local units of government, offer some insights into the impact of the act and suggest that it may become considerably greater if and when Congress authorizes higher levels of funding and appropriates greater sums of money for action projects. (It is reasoned that before more money is appropriated, the value of past expenditures in improving the processes of criminal justice will have to be proven to the satisfaction of the Congress. And value will be proven even though the incidence of criminal acts is not lowered substantially, the processes of adjudication improved, or the successful habilitation of convicted offenders achieved. The first "iron law" of program funding through grants is to author an application that wins the approval of the funding agency. The second is that project success must be achieved on paper and, hopefully, in fact.)

GOVERNORS AND BLOC GRANTS

The presidential and congressional maneuvering that preceded passage of the act indicates the nature of the present and perhaps future impact of the bloc grant upon the office of the governor.

For several years prior to the passage of the act, crime, particularly street and organized crime, was one of the consuming passions of segments of the American public, the administration, and Congress. The Kefauver Commission focused public and political attention upon organized crime as an increasing drain on the resources of modern American society. *Crime in the United States, the Report of the President's Commission on Law Enforcement and the Administration of Justice*, which was released in 1967, and the various working papers associated with it, not only detailed the probable extent of crime in the United States but also offered several dozen general recommendations for federal, state, and local action to respond to problems raised by crime and juvenile delinquency.

Some spadework for federal entrance into local crime problems was performed by Congress between the Kefauver hearings and the passage of the crime control act of 1968. In 1965, Congress passed the Law Enforcement Assistance Act. An

Office of Law Enforcement Assistance was created as an adjunct of the Department of Justice, to administer a modest number of categorical "seed" grants for demonstration projects which, it was intended, would offer some improvement in local law enforcement and administration of justice. Under provisions of this act, grants of $25,000 were made available to each state that formed a Governor's Committee/Commission on Law Enforcement and Criminal Justice.

Most OLEA action grants were relatively small. Success of the funded projects was measured, not in terms of impact or improvements in the administration of criminal justice at the local level, but upon a system of quarterly financial reports to OLEA (coupled with narrative progress summaries relating to projects) which were compiled by the local project administrator. Some programs were demonstrated successes. Others were touted as unqualified successes. Reams of narrative summaries testify to this statement, although many projects became past history upon final funding by OLEA.

On these bases and from these experiences, President Lyndon Johnson, in 1967, submitted to Congress a crime control bill authorizing direct federal funding to local units of government for improvements in the several agencies concerned with the administration of justice. "Law and order" had become a dominant domestic theme in Congress. While the passage of some kind of crime control bill was never seriously in doubt, the form of funding became a crucial issue. Liberal Democrats favored categorical grants—direct payment from the federal agency to local units of government. Many Republicans and an assortment of southern Democrats opted for state government intervention in crime control through a system of bloc grants. Congressman William T. Cahill (R-NJ) gained approval of an amendment that transformed the administration bill into the bloc-grant approach. Although considerable opposition to this method became increasingly apparent in Congress, a compromise proposal requiring that a substantial portion of available funds be channeled by state administrators directly to local units of government assured passage of the act in 1968.

The act created the Law Enforcement Assistance Administration (LEAA) in the Department of Justice. Provisions were made for funding continuing projects of demonstrable value approved under the Law Enforcement Assistance Act of 1965, and Congress appropriated approximately $68,000,000

for LEAA for the 1969 fiscal year. The act provided for $100,000 to be made available to each state; the remaining 85 percent, after federal administrative costs were subtracted, was made available to the states according to their relative populations.

The act requires that each state establish a planning agency under the authority of the state's chief executive. The agency, variously named in the several states, is charged with the responsibility for the development of a "comprehensive" statewide plan for (a) the distribution of funds to local and state agencies; (b) the definition, development, and correlation of plans and projects for the improvement of state and local administration of criminal justice; and (c) the establishment of priorities for such improvements. The state planning agency is authorized to make grants to state and local law enforcement units (contingent upon the availability of funds at the federal level), with the local or state agencies to match 25 to 50 percent of the project costs. If the state fails to establish a state planning agency, grants may be made directly to local units of government upon submission of proper applications. However, in the absence of a state planning agency, all such applications must be evaluated and approved by the chief executive of the state and the evaluation must be submitted in written form to LEAA. At this time all states have chosen to establish planning agencies.

PLANNING SHAPED BY GOVERNORS

The governor has the authority to determine membership on the state law enforcement agency. In most states, the governor has shaped the character and nature of the law enforcement planning agency, and with his power of appointment, which determines who is to be represented in the agency, there has emerged a control system that can be overtly or covertly manipulated by the governor, if he wishes.

While of interest, the makeup of the agencies is of more importance when it is noted that the membership itself rarely determines agency policy. In fact, the agency members generally only affirm decisions already "blessed" by the full-time professional staff, which is theoretically employed by the appointed membership, but actually is appointed by and serves at the pleasure of the governor. From policy to funding, the agency membership rubberstamps the decisions of the professional staff. If the professional executive director of the state law enforcement planning agency favors a proposal of a state or local unit for funding, it is seldom vetoed by the appointed membership. If the executive director rejects a proposal or alters the amount of funding, his decision is generally affirmed by the committee or agency membership without question or comment.

Eighty percent of the states have subdivided the criminal justice planning process. Regional planning districts, as in the case of North Carolina, have been established to weld together the potpourri of proposals generated by local units of government. The regional planning districts generally conform to the boundaries of similar planning districts authorized by the state for the implementation of other federal-state or federal-local programs. Regional directors, much the same as the executive directors of the state law enforcement planning agencies, are often appointees of the governor. Most often, neither specialized skill in planning nor particularly deep knowledge of or interest in the processes of criminal justice are prerequisites for employment as a regional or state planning director. However, recently a definite trend toward employing knowledgeable and experienced criminal justice personnel as directors of planning has become apparent, although the governor's approval is frequently required before appointment is made.

Explicit in the act, both in its title and statement of declarations and purpose, is the intent of Congress that state and local governments should form a partnership to utilize federal, state, and local funds cooperatively to strengthen and improve law enforcement. Crime and the attendant social disorganization is primarily an urban problem. More than 3.8 million index crimes were committed in the metropolitan areas of the nation in 1967. This amounts to slightly more than 85 percent of *all* serious crimes reported in the United States. Consequently, it is readily apparent, if crime is an urban phenomenon, that the prime responsibility for crime prevention and control should be focused upon urban centers. Logically, state agencies administering LEAA funds should concentrate spending upon crucial target areas in which state-local cooperative efforts would improve the administration of criminal justice and assure the steady diminution of the rates of crime. Some states are operating programs that afford some cause for optimism. Arizona, Illinois, New York,

and Washington are states in which a measure of success seems assured. However, state, regional, and local plans in most of the remaining states appear to be mail-order catalog shopping lists of police desires rather than comprehensive, long-range plans. It is here, in the comprehensive planning phase and the subsequent allocation of funds on an individual project basis, that the influence of the respective governor's appointed representatives to the state planning agency should have its greatest impact; but in fact, decisions concerning planning and fund allocation are, by the nature of the agency, removed from them.

The National League of Cities (NLC) and the U.S. Conference of Mayors (USCM), although generally favorable to the intent of the act, predictably question the role of the states in its administration. While not directly critical of the office of governor, indirectly the governors are faulted as the act itself calls for the state planning agency to be created and designated by the chief executive of the state and to be subject to his jurisdiction.[2] In their analysis, the NLC and USCM conclude:

1. The planning process has not been effective in creating real, substantive state plans.... There is little relationship between plans and the actual distribution of funds for the projects....
2. The states, in their planning processes, have generally failed to take into account the specialized and critical crime problems of the major urban areas.... Significantly, this is a general defect in the plans recognized by LEAA itself, whose Police Operations Division, after reviewing state plans, noted with concern "... the failure of those states having large metropolitan areas, where from 25 to 60 percent of the state's crime is committed, to give separate treatment to the law enforcement situation in those areas."[3]

It is significant to note that the voice of state government does not agree with this statement. *State Government News*, published by the Council of State Governments, comments that, "Many states allocate a large percentage of their funds to metropolitan areas.... Arizona gave 63.8 percent to Tucson, Phoenix, Flagstaff, Yuma; ... Minnesota... 82 percent to Minneapolis, St. Paul, and surrounding counties; ... New Jersey... 53 percent to its five metropolitan areas; ... New

[2] Public Law 90-351, Section 203(a).
[3] *Street Crime and the Safe Streets Act: What is the Impact?* (Washington, D.C.: National League of Cities, February 1970), pp. 3-5.

York. . . 70 percent of its grants to its five metropolitan areas. . . ."[4] However, no mention is made of numbers or the nature of the population that reside outside of these selected metropolitan areas.

3. Despite general statements. . . .most states in the allocation of action dollars have neither demonstrated any real commitment to improve the criminal justice system, nor have they concentrated funds on programs in most critical need areas. . . . [I]n practice state dollar distributions have frustrated chances for coordination [of the diverse processes of criminal justice].

4. Regional planning units have often frustrated the capacity of individual cities and counties to gain expression . . . in state plans and action programs. . . .

5. . . .[The] bloc grant approach has interposed two new and costly layers of bureaucracy between the federal crime funds and their local application. . . . Delay in getting funds to local projects has been increased and not reduced. . . . [The] direction of the program has been toward increased concentration of power at the state level at the expense of the counties and cities. . . .[5]

STATE-LOCAL CONFLICT

Obviously, the conclusions of the National League of Cities reflect the strange "love-hate" relationship that has existed for many years between state governments and local governmental units. However, they also emphasize a critical fact as the governor works with the crime control act. Simply stated, the fact is that if the governor controls the staffing pattern of the state planning agency and the advisory council, he can determine the rationale that undergirds local planning and eventual funding of projects. If that rationale leads to a local response either political or personal, favorable to the state chief executive, rewards are purchased cheaply. Thus, local satisfaction rather than project merit becomes of primary importance. A "trade-off," either overt or covert, occurs by which all local units applying for funds are largely satisfied, but their appetites for "free" money are never wholly sated. Consequently, a city of 300,000 with a law enforcement budget of $6 or $7 million may receive $250,000 for action projects from the state planning agency and publicly tout the fundings of the program as a major ac-

complishment. An equally favorable impression of the state agency is created when a $10,000 project is funded for the eight-man police department with a total operating budget of $50,000 annually. Congressional intent as stated in the act is offset by geography and politically expedient allocation of funds. And yet the long-range costs are exorbitant. The favors of a few in the smaller unit are purchased at the price of 20 percent of the existing police budget in LEAA contributions. In the larger unit, even though crime is primarily an urban phenomenon, a relatively few dollars (approximately 4 to 5 percent of the total annual police budget) purchase a substantially greater amount of local support regardless of any project's impact in decreasing crime and criminality locally. Again, whether or not allocation of LEAA funds by the state administering agency is designed to win popular support is immaterial. The actual allocation process induces favorable local responses.

In summary, (a) the nature and intent of the crime control act, (b) specific requirement of the act that the chief executive of the state appoint the advisory council, (c) regionalization of the required planning process as an intervening layer of bureaucracy between the state agency and the local units of government, (d) quickly gained knowledge on the part of local law enforcement planners as to the kinds of projects currently in vogue at the state level, and (e) the fact that some states exhibit an uncertain commitment to the matching requirements of the act indicate areas wherein the power of the governor could be exerted. In the main, at this time, the uncertainties of federal funding and the slow pace of disbursement of funds at the federal level mitigate, to some degree, the impact of the act upon the office of governor as well as the impact of the governor's office upon the act. Additionally, levels of congressional funding of the act have not been substantial enough to evoke a wholly political response in state administrations. Only time will reveal if suggested funding at or near the $1 billion dollar annual level in subsequent years will alter the interest of governors in the administration of the act. It may well be that the future of bloc grants rests upon the manner in which governors respond to the Omnibus Crime Control and Safe Streets Act of 1968.

[4] "State Control of Crime Funds Boosts City Law Enforcement Efforts," *State Government News*, Vol. 13, No. 7 (July 1970).

[5] *Street Crime and Safe Streets Act*, pp. 3–5.

GOVERNORS AND HIGHER EDUCATION
John W. Lederle

Governors are giving increasing attention to problems of higher education. Even if they would like to leave these problems in the hands of university governing boards and administrators, the problems are so pressing and the financial demands brought about by burgeoning enrollments are so great, that the governors cannot avoid direct confrontation.

The confrontation takes place in an opinion climate that tends to view education as "independent of politics," or that holds that "formal education *ought* to be separated from government."[1] Professor Dwight Waldo cites several factors that support this independence:

"...a historic disposition to keep government small, and to disperse its powers and organs; a repugnance for politics as corrupt and tendentious, together with a special regard for education as having intimate, "sacral" qualities; a decision against an established religion, which meant that in the long period in which the dominant motives for establishing universities were religious, the universities would be formally nongovernmental, "private"; and the professionalizing of education in the past two or three generations, which has had the effect of creating an enormous vested interest in maintaining the fact of separation or the belief in separation."[2]

To the extent that this belief in the "independence of education" is reflected in state organization for higher education, it is not surprising that governors often feel that they are in a weak position to influence higher education policy.

In short, the governor, as the state's chief executive, is inevitably held responsible for actions or failings of public colleges and universities in the same way he is held responsible for those of other state agencies; but his ability to influence through organization is not as direct as for those state agencies located in the usual departmental hierarchy. Let us now examine the common organizational arrangements for higher education, after which we shall consider the executive budget process which represents a more effective gubernatorial control.

[1] Dwight Waldo, "The University in Relation to the Governmental-Political," *Public Administration Review*, Vol. 33 (March/April 1970), pp. 106–113, at p. 107.
[2] Waldo, *op. cit.*, p. 107.

GOVERNORS AND INSTITUTIONS OF HIGHER EDUCATION

Colleges and universities are usually governed by boards of trustees or regents, and it is customary for the governor to nominate members, often subject to confirmation by the upper house of the legislature. Sometimes the governor's appointing power is limited by a requirement that appointments be distributed between the political parties; sometimes he appoints only a fraction of the membership, the remainder being selected by the alumni, or gaining membership *ex officio* by virtue of holding some other, oftentimes elective, state office, such as that of Commissioner of Education, or Commissioner of Agriculture in the case of land-grant institutions. Ex officio trustees may or may not be responsive to the governor's views. In a few instances, boards are elective.

Because terms of board members usually exceed the governor's elective term and most frequently are overlapping, there is further reenforcement of the independence of the board of trustees from gubernatorial control. If a governor were to try to change the philosophy of a governing board through reconstitution of its individual membership, he would presumably be embarking upon a fairly long enterprise with little promise of success.

Yet as California Governor Ronald Reagan, who was first elected in 1966, has demonstrated, a persistent governor, starting off to change a board's philosophy with his first appointments, can, with a little luck, change a board's direction fairly quickly. After all, some board members die in office. Others resign after getting tired of academic boardsmanship in a day when almost every board meeting involves confrontations with student and faculty demonstrators. Being a member of the governing board of an academic institution has recently proved, in many instances, to be an arduous, time-consuming, and thankless job. There is evidence that it neither has the prestige nor is as much sought after as in the past.

It has been the rare governor who has used his power to make board appointments with the objective of profoundly changing educational policy. Moos and Rourke are probably right in saying

... governors have come to regard the selection of a high quality governing board as smart politics as well as sound administration. Regardless of how a university may be set apart legally from the direct administrative control of the governor, the successes and failures of the higher educational system invariably brighten or darken the public image of the governor. In a society that frowns at political favoritism, the appointment of unqualified persons as regents could scarcely improve the political standing of the governor.[3]

Frequently, the governor is himself an *ex officio* member of the board of major public institutions. It is doubtful whether this gives him any greater influence over educational policy. Even if he were not a member his views, should he choose to communicate them, would receive respectful attention. It is the rare governor who, as an *ex officio* member, consistently attends and votes at board meetings. Indeed, *ex officio* membership can be a matter of embarrassment, unnecessarily forcing him into the maelstrom of decision-making on controversial issues which he might better avoid, or, if necessary, handle on review after a failure to resolve the conflict at the institutional level. Then, too, some academic administrators recently have been perplexed by the necessity of organizing police protection for the state's chief executive when he comes on campus for a board meeting; minority groups may demonstrate against him on issues totally unrelated to academic concerns.

Governors customarily have little influence over college or university staff appointments, certainly not those on the teaching staff. Academicians would be quick to raise a cry of "politics" if political influence were brought to bear on teaching appointments. However, in appointing a president or top administrative officer who will have frequent dealings with the governor, a board does well to seek his views on the type of person needed if the appointee is to start off on the right foot. In such instances, the board must be careful neither to solicit specific nominations nor to authorize specific vetoes.

From what has been said, it is clear that governors have very little control over higher education through the formal channels of organization. Colleges and universities are not ordinarily organized under the state's departmental structure. Like regulatory boards and commissions and government corporations, college and university boards have a substantial degree of freedom and independence. The governor finds it difficult to dominate directly

[3] Malcolm Moos and Francis E. Rourke, *The Campus and the State* (Baltimore, Md.: Johns Hopkins Press, 1959), p. 240.

through the hierarchy if he has such domination in mind.

To the extent that institutional independence and autonomy is spelled out in the state's constitution, as in Michigan, Minnesota, and California, gubernatorial and legislative influence is even further reduced. Presidents of institutions thus enshrined in the constitution not infrequently refer to the institution as being a "fourth branch" of state government. But they also soon discover that the so-called "fourth branch" is not as "independent" as it might seem, for the executive and legislative branches control the purse strings. To be an inadequately funded "fourth branch" is not very satisfying.

THE GOVERNOR'S BUDGETARY IMPACT

It is not through the organizational hierarchy by itself, but rather through the executive budget process, that the governor makes his impact and gives significant leadership on major issues of higher education policy. While the legislature appropriates, it does so in the light of the governor's budget recommendations, and academic institutions are well aware of the fact that legislatures are reluctant to appropriate more than the amount in the governor's budget. Even when they do, the item veto may be an effective way to delete the legislative generosity. Hence it is crucial that the governor be won over. If he is supportive, nine-tenths of the battle has probably been won; if he is opposed, the battle may already be lost.

Questions of policy in higher education are frequently hot political issues, and college representatives may be able to see the governor personally about them, rather than be restricted to conferring with the budget officer or his junior staff associates. Decisions such as whether to establish a new branch of the state university or begin a new medical school have multimillion dollar implications, and academic institutions normally go to the "front office" to explain their problems and seek gubernatorial understanding and support. From the governor's viewpoint, expenditure requests need coordination at the budget division level, and, in the interest of preserving his limited time, most should stop there without the requesting agency reaching him for a personal presentation. From the agency's viewpoint, direct access to the governor is desirable to assure that he has at least heard the matter out, even though with his budget officer present. Governor Stratton of Illinois had a philosophy which would be popular with educational institutions. His belief was "that educational institutions—or for that matter any institution of the state—deserve the personal attention but not the personal direction of the chief executive."[4] He regularly allowed educators to make their cases directly, and he did not interfere in the details of administration. Not all governors have such an open door policy.

The degree to which academic institutions furnish backup for their budget requests will vary from state to state. Governors will be interested in the big picture, but budget officers may want information in considerable detail. To some extent, the kind of information required will also depend on the legislature. If a line-item budget is the practice, much detail will have to be furnished and explained.

In recent years, considerable attention has been given to the feasibility of using budget formulas for allocating funds to public colleges and universities.[5] For example, cost of instruction can be measured. The payroll for the teaching staff bears most directly on this. Student-teacher ratios can be developed as a method for allocating funds for additional staff to handle increasing student enrollments. But these formulas must be carefully designed. Obviously, the student-teacher ratio for a university with its graduate instructional and research and service responsibilities must vary from that of a teachers college with its fundamentally undergraduate role. State universities have frequently shied away from the formula approach, fearing rightly that unless developed with sophistication, formulas may unduly standardize or dilute out the quality factor, or reduce all institutions to a common level of mediocrity. There is a danger that in raising the support for community colleges or state colleges the university may be brought down in quality.

There is much merit in the pluralistic concept of higher education in the United States, which encourages each college or university to search independently for its own individual identity. Formulas tend to standardize and produce uniformity. Whatever the dangers, however, formulas do ap-

pear to be the wave of the future. When wisely developed, they can help to reduce the area of contention and can be important vehicles for securing adequate financial support. An understanding governor who appreciates the difference between the costs of graduate and undergraduate instruction, who is concerned about proper evaluation of institutional needs while preserving flexibility in internal institutional management, by supporting sound, discriminating formulas, can provide real policy leadership.

A second budgetary issue which has come to the fore recently involves the accounting for gifts, grants, and contracts, and particularly the receipts from contract overhead. Today, public institutions are beneficiaries of large financial support outside the state legislative appropriation structure. Unless these outside funds are included as part of the institution's revenue picture and expenditures therefrom are listed on the expenditure side, the governor and legislature have but a poor view of financial realities. It has become common to include these so-called "outside revenues" in accounting reports, and many states now require that anticipated income of this type be listed in the budget request, together with how it is intended to spend it. In a sense, this represents revenue to the state, not just to the academic institution, and it is important that its receipt and subsequent use be recorded in the public record. Naturally, the institution generating the funds feels some proprietary interest in their disposition, and would look with disfavor on their diversion to support academic expenditures that would otherwise be directly supported out of taxes. Governors seem more understanding of this than some legislators or budget officers who occasionally resent institutional primacy in controlling expenditure of these funds, even though there is full accounting afterward.

Eulau and Quinley, reporting on a recent survey of legislative opinion, found that legislators feel their control over appropriations is an inadequate control over public higher education.[6] At the same time, because they are members of part-time bodies, frequently poorly staffed and uninformed on details, legislators tend to look to the governors for guidance on educational policy. If the governor

---

[4] *Ibid.*, p. 237–238.

[5] For a detailed discussion of the use of budget formulas and cost analysis, see James L. Miller, *State Budgeting for Higher Education* (Ann Arbor, Mich.: Inst. of Public Administration, The University of Michigan, 1964).

[6] Heinz Eulau and Harold Quinley, *State Officials and Higher Education* (New York: McGraw-Hill,) p. 56.

has the item veto, as in California, his leadership role is reinforced.

MOVE TOWARD STATE-WIDE COORDINATION

The picture, then, has been one in which higher education is pluralistic, with each institution's governing board and academic administrators desiring to deal directly with the governor, who already suffers from too broad a span of control as administrative chief. In the typical state, community colleges, state colleges, and state universities are all separately organized under their own boards, or as separate college and university systems. Today, there is a very strong movement toward improved organization for higher education through some coordinative device that will reduce institutional autonomy and independence and assure better overall planning.

Unseemly competition among the institutions for limited state funds, the lack of statewide planning, duplication and overlapping of effort both on and off campuses, has led to the establishment of coordinating boards in state after state recently. While some effort has been devoted to voluntary coordination,[7] the wave of the future clearly is to take many broad educational policy decisions out of the hands of individual institutions and to place them under single boards with considerable coercive powers.

Logan Wilson, president of the American Council on Education, and himself a former president of the University of Texas, has written:

Our past assumption has been that the separated aims and activities of existing colleges and universities would somehow add up to the best educational interests of the nation. In my judgment, this is no longer a valid assumption. Higher education has become too complicated, too costly, and too important in the national welfare for its basic decisions to be made haphazardly.[8]

Lyman Glenny, who has devoted as much attention to coordination of higher education as any scholar, notes that there are three different types of coordinating systems.[9] One is a voluntary council of college and university presidents and board members. A second type is the single governing board for all the state's institutions. Finally, a growing number of states are imposing a coordinating board, with greater or lesser powers over the governing boards of individual institutions or systems of colleges and universities. State legislatures and governors are granting increasing powers to such coordinating boards, particularly in the areas of statewide higher education planning, budgets, and authorization of new programs at individual institutions. As the coordinating board develops respect and the authority of knowledge, even where its coercive powers are weak, it will more and more occupy a position between the individual institutions and the governor and the legislature, which heretofore dealt directly with each other.

The plain fact is that a single institution can never have the objectivity and overview required. Even the president of a long-time dominant state university is handicapped in providing educational leadership for the state. Despite the fact that he is at the apex of the hierarchy, his views will be construed as biased and his remarks as self-serving for his own institution. What state university fully recognizes the need for new community colleges, or is ready to accept graciously full colleagueship for a former state teachers college that is now striving to develop a multifaceted program and acquire the name of "university"? To assure the necessary objectivity, coordinating boards have been burgeoning recently. They are most frequently composed "either of a majority or a totality of citizen members who do not directly administer or govern any public institution."[10]

There is today widespread recognition of the need for statewide planning in higher education. A U.S. Office of Education study indicates that statutory or constitutional agencies have been established in 40 states to coordinate overall planning for higher education. It adds: "Seventeen of these 40 agencies also govern and regulate public institutions of higher education."[11] Governors and legislators have encouraged this movement and are giv-

---

[7]The leading advocate of voluntary coordination is M. M. Chambers who makes a stirring plea for it as against the governing or coordinating board approach. See M. M. Chambers, *Voluntary Statewide Coordination in Public Higher Education* (Ann Arbor, Mich.: The University of Michigan, 1961).

[8]Quoted by Lyman A. Glenny in W. John Minter (Ed.), *Campus and Capitol* (Boulder, Colo.: Western Interstate Commission for Higher Education, 1966), p. 28.

[9]*Ibid.*

[10]*Ibid.*

[11]Louise Abrahams, *State Planning for Higher Education* (Washington, D.C.: Academy for Educational Development, 1969), p. 2.

ing more and more credence to recommendations by coordinating agencies. Individual colleges and universities have often looked with suspicion on this new trend, fearing a loss of autonomy and that they will be cut off from direct contact with governors and legislators. As Logan Wilson has pointed out,

... it is pertinent to note that the initiative behind mandatory coordination in most states comes from outside rather than inside academic circles. In view of the entrenched tradition of institutional sovereignty, this is understandable, but the unfortunate aspect of it is that resistance to change often places educators in the role of passive observers rather than active participants in shaping the larger destinies of their institutions.[12]

It would appear that the splintering of policy initiative through separate approaches to the governor and the legislature by individual institutions is being modified in favor of policy coordination through governing or coordinating boards standing between the institutions and the executive and legislative branches.

INTEGRATION OF POLICY

Two other trends support integration of educational policy at a level above the institutions prior to gubernatorial and legislative review.

ROLE OF FEDERAL MONEY

One relates to increased federal participation in the financing of higher education. Governors and legislators alike hold the view that the increasingly horrendous demands for funds for higher education can only be met by vastly increased federal support.[13] Such support has been greatly expanded in the postwar period. Even seemingly well-financed private institutions such as MIT and Harvard have come to rely on federal funds for a substantial part of their operating budgets. When seeking federal contracts and grants, both public and private institutions frequently solicit support from the governor and from the state's congressional delegation. It is not unusual for a governor

to visit personally federal granting agencies and lobby on behalf of his academic institutions. Supporting letters and phone calls to Washington agencies by the governor and members of his staff are a daily occurrence.

Up to the present time, most federal funds have come directly to the academic institutions, bypassing the governor or his central staff agencies. Governors not only are looking to Washington for increased financial support, but also are seeking a greater say in their allocation within the state. Many of them join Governor Reagan of California in seeking an end to the "specific grant-in-aid approach presently used by the federal government."[14] Instead of categorical grants they would like the aid to come in the form of bloc grants, allocated to the state not to the individual institutions. Governor Don Samuelson of Idaho has said, "States know better where to apply educational funds."[15] On the same subject, Oregon's Governor Tom McCall asserted, "We could then use the money where the need exists, rather than where someone in Washington thinks it exists."[16] Gubernatorial influence is effecting a change, and there is a noticeable trend toward funneling federal funds through central state agencies, often a newly established coordinating board for higher education. This trend is a counterpart at the higher education level of the trend toward state departments of municipal affairs as coordinators and allocators of federal funds which have heretofore bypassed the state and gone directly to the individual municipalities.

THE PRIVATE-PUBLIC EDUCATION DILEMMA

The other trend that reenforces establishment of coordinating boards is the awakening recognition of the role of private or nonpublic colleges and universities in providing for state educational needs. Long financially independent, and proud of their autonomy and freedom from "political influence," many private institutions have come to the brink of bankruptcy. Others claim to see the handwriting on the wall, and reveal a great feeling of insecurity unless large new revenue sources are forthcoming. Whereas they once looked down upon public institutions as being politically con-

---

[12] Logan Wilson (Ed.), *Emerging Patterns in American Higher Education* (Washington, D.C.: American Council on Education, 1965), p. 33.

[13] Eulau and Quinley, *op. cit.*, pp. 83 ff.; see also Gene A. Budig, *Governors and Higher Education* (Lincoln, Neb.: Office of Chancellor, University of Nebraska, 1969), pp. 38 ff.

[14] Budig, *op. cit.*, p. 39.

[15] Budig, *op. cit.*, p. 39.

[16] Budig, *op. cit.*, p. 40.

trolled,[17] they now see state appropriations as their salvation. In recent years, they have shown little compunction about taking federal funds, but these have proved insufficient and have tended to be categorical or for physical plant. Given slight prospect for much further increase in tuition or in private giving, private colleges are beseiging the states for direct financial assistance. In state after state, private institutions have joined a common "association" with the objective of organizing a campaign to get state financial support. When the private education lobby makes its case before a higher education study commission, or the governor or the legislature, the number of in-state students being educated and the threat of impending bankruptcy are persuasive arguments for exploring avenues for assistance. Otherwise the educational burden they have been carrying may be unloaded on the taxpayer as a direct cost. Of course, in some instances (State University of New York at Buffalo), private institutions have been taken over directly by the state.

The sharp dichotomy between public and private institutions, so long stressed by the private institutions, is quickly vanishing in the face of the fiscal realities. Real statewide planning for higher education must include both private and public sectors, and the new coordinating boards are recognizing this. In New England, where three-quarters of the students attend private colleges, planning that ignores the private-sector contribution would be particularly futile. If Constitutional hurdles can be overcome, state aid to private institutions could be forthcoming. But private institutions may find they do not like to live in the goldfish bowl to which public institutions are accustomed. The quid pro quo for state aid may well be complete disclosure and opening of their books to public scrutiny. This is not the place to develop the variety of ways in which states are already aiding private institutions. This problem is on every governor's desk.

While new coordinating boards commonly have a mandate to develop plans that include private as well as public higher education, there is no inherent reason why private and public institutions cannot work together voluntarily. As in the case of five-college cooperation in the Connecticut Valley, where four private institutions—Amherst, Hampshire, Mount Holyoke, and Smith colleges—collaborate with the rapidly expanding University of Massachusetts, it will be found that students, faculties, and administrations can cooperatively create a common educational environment superior to that of any single institution. Such cooperation makes good sense. It is also good public relations for all concerned.

INTERSTATE APPROACHES

Opportunities for higher education cooperation not only exist between private and public institutions within a state, but also are even greater when higher education planning includes regional academic resources. Governors have been calling for more interstate cooperation and coordination, and when a local institution presses for funds to establish a new program, the governor is inclined to ask whether the need cannot be met by another institution in some other state in the region.

Three regional boards—the Southern Regional Education Board, the Western Interstate Commission for Higher Education, and the New England Board of Higher Education—are operating under interstate compacts ratified by member states and charged with fact finding and research on needs and problems of higher education in their regions as well as with the development of cooperative arrangements for technical, professional, and graduate education.[18] The attraction of this interstate approach lies in the possibilities for economy through sharing existing educational resources and avoiding undue duplication of costly graduate and professional programs. For example, students from one state where there is no medical school may be enrolled under a quota system in the medical school of a sister state. Ordinarily, the student pays in-state tuition rates, while the state of his

[17] It is paradoxical that many who have never attended a public college or university have a snobbish conception about deleterious gubernatorial and legislative political interference, and even doubt that public higher education can be excellent. As an innocent, educated entirely at a public institution, I recall my own shock when my first teaching assignment took me to a distinguished private university and I learned that the private institution was no more under the thumb of big business or the private establishment than my alma mater had been under the thumb of politicians.

[18] See Robert Kroepsch and M. Stephen Kaplan, "Interstate Cooperation and Coordination in Higher Education," in Wilson (Ed.), *op. cit.*, pp. 174–190.

residence pays an agreed upon additional contract rate to help cover the high costs of medical education. When a state is being pressured to establish a new school of veterinary medicine or architecture or social work, the regional board may be asked to study the issue and investigate its regional implications. Oftentimes, the sound solution proves to be a board-sponsored contract arrangement to assure a certain number of places for the state's residents in a professional school in a neighboring state. This is much cheaper than the establishment of a new school would be. It is better to have one good school than several undernourished ones of low quality.

The regional boards try to plan with both private and public institutions in mind. However, it is fair to say that private institutions tended to stand aloof until recently—when their financial difficulties led them to look more to public funding and encouraged development of better relations with public planning agencies. Both at formal meetings as well as at special conferences on higher education, regional boards bring governors, legislators, and college administors together for discussion of key issues. This is a most helpful way to develop mutual understanding. The southern body has been outstanding in building understanding and friendships between politicians and educators.

A NATIONWIDE APPROACH

Although only recently in operation, one other compact, nationwide rather than regional in scope, should be mentioned. In 1964, James B. Conant called for a formal interstate compact for educational policy to end educational "disarray" and "haphazard interaction" between state officials and educational leaders.[19] Conant emphasized "the need for educators and elected officials to get together, to understand each other, to work together when at all possible."[20]

Terry Sanford, who had just finished his term as Governor of North Carolina, took on the assignment of forwarding the compact idea, receiving Carnegie corporation and Danforth Foundation financial assistance in the enterprise. He broached the subject at the National Governors Conference in Minneapolis in July of 1965 and secured gubernatorial approval of the proposal in general terms. Nineteen governors were present at an organizational meeting at Kansas City the following September, and every state, as well as Puerto Rico and the Virgin Islands, was represented. There were some 50 state legislators and over 200 educators present, with the governors dominating the proceedings.

The compact establishes an Education Commission of the States, with seven representatives from each state including the governor, which meets annually. Its objective is to consider educational policy issues from the cradle to the grave, not just those of higher education. The Commission works through an executive committee and a professional staff. Its executive director is a former public-school superintendent, but staff responsibility for higher education is assigned to a distinguished former university dean and chancellor for higher education. As of the fall of 1969, forty states and three territories were members of the compact.

Because it has taken some time for the Commission to obtain its staff, there is no basis for assessing its impact. Because of strong gubernatorial support at its inception, and strengthened by Terry Sanford's fine hand in getting it off the ground, it offers great potential for educational leadership by governors. By bringing politicians and educators together at a forum for discussion of common problems and for sharing of state experience, it can be extremely helpful.

RISE OF THE JUNIOR COLLEGE

No discussion of the role of governors in higher education would be complete if it failed to deal with "the junior college phenomenon." While we are accustomed to focus on four-year colleges and on graduate and professional schools and universities, the fastest-growing institutions are the junior or community colleges. They have been sprouting like mushrooms in almost every state. Eulau and Quinley found that governors and legislators evaluate these institutions more positively than they do any of the other aspects of higher education covered in their survey.[21] The special treatment these colleges are given in allocating federal funds for construction of college buildings indicates that the Congress shares this high regard for two-year institutions.

[19] James B. Conant, *Shaping Educational Policy* (New York: McGraw-Hill, 1964).

[20] See Fred H. Harrington, "The Compact for Education," in Minter (Ed.), *op. cit.*, pp. 75–87.

[21] Eulau and Quinley, *op. cit.*, p. 113.

In a day when more students are graduating from high school and when an increasing portion of high-school graduates seek further education, the junior colleges help fill a crying need. Many four-year schools do not want to expand or are already too large, and also unlikely to accept curricular changes which would lead in a technical and vocational direction. If large numbers of additional students are to be educated, the governors believe that junior colleges will be less expensive than four-year institutions. Because junior-college students generally live at home, their educational expenses are reduced and educational opportunity is more accessible. For immature students, junior colleges ease the transition from high school to college. Not every bright high-school graduate is ready to face the complexities of a 25,000 student university. For many high-school graduates who have not demonstrated college potential, the so-called "late-bloomers," the junior college offers a second chance. The junior colleges thus serve as a screening system for many who initially would not meet the admissions requirements of four-year institutions.

Junior colleges have a strong political base. A legislator, being home-constituency oriented, takes a special and paternalistic interest in the junior college located in his district. More than one state university president has wished that he could find one legislator who would take the same interest in supporting university needs that each legislator seems to take in supporting "his" junior college. Because the state university belongs to all the people, it does not arouse the same personal dedication and interest of the part of individual legislators.

Issues of (a) coordination of junior colleges, (b) the appropriate mix of local and state financial support and control, (c) the inclusion of costly technical and vocational courses in the curriculum rather than simply a college transfer emphasis, and (d) requirements for admission, if any, are being faced in every state. Suffice it to say that the junior colleges have introduced a breath of fresh air, an innovative quality, into higher education. Community oriented, adapting the curriculum to felt needs, providing opportunity not only for recent high-school graduates, but also for those who have been out some time and feel the need to make a career change or update themselves, junior colleges have a bright future.

GOVERNORS AND ISSUES OF HIGHER EDUCATION

There is hardly an issue in higher education today that does not come to a governor's attention. Campus violence may force a decision on whether to call in the state police or the national guard. Student unrest may lead to a review of campus governance and consideration of student and faculty representation on the governing board. Issues of race relations move from simply assuring that there is no racial discrimination against blacks to examination of admissions policies with a view to "open admissions" and abandonment of College Board scores and middle-class evaluation devices which have made for unequal opportunity for higher education. Should tuition be increased at public institutions where low tuition has been the American tradition? How much can the state afford to spend on costly health science facilities, or on capital outlay generally to meet burgeoning enrollments? How about better space utilization, Saturday classes, and year-round operation? These are just a few of the issues governors are facing.

As higher education has moved into a central place in society and as a state activity, its problems inevitably demand the governor's attention. While most governors defer to the college administrators and governing boards, members of the campus community as well as citizens and taxpayers who do not like what the college is or is not doing are quick to call directly on the governor to act. The press, radio, television are all focusing on the campus for that's "where the action is."

In 1966, Samuel B. Gould, then President of the State University of New York, wrote: "Governors are identifying themselves with the cause of higher education as never before."[22] Fortunate in having the strong support of Governor Nelson Rockefeller, President Gould witnessed the dynamic growth of the State University of New York in size and quality. Governor Rockefeller first learned the facts and then bravely faced the financial consequences. That same year of 1966 saw the election of another governor, Ronald Reagan, who was to bring the state University of California system to a sudden day of reckoning. His first budget recommendation represented a drastic cut in university expectations and this pattern has continued. Crying out against campus unrest and violence, Rea-

[22] See Minter (Ed.), *op. cit.*, p. 8.

gan saw political advantage in attacking a university that only recently had been acclaimed as the finest state university and at least the equal of Harvard. Because the university's budget requests were cut all along the line, the University of California began to lose momentum. Staff morale suffered. It was surprising how quickly friends and alumni of the University of California began to lose faith in an institution that once had been their pride.

John Millett has observed "that the key person in the development of higher education policy in a state is the governor of the state. If a state has a governor who by reason of experience, conviction, or predisposition is inclined to make higher education a major interest, then legislation and appropriations for the development of higher education are likely to be enacted."[23] Moos and Rourke wrote: "The state governor today is the most prominent single official in a college's relation to state government."[24] If he is supportive, as Governor Rockefeller of New York has been, higher education will flourish. If he is antagonistic, as Governor Reagan of California has been, academic morale suffers and forward momentum is lost. Inevitably, the governor's views on higher education policies strongly influence educational opportunity and quality.

[23] See John D. Millet, "State Administration of Higher Education," *Public Administration Review*, Vol. 33 (March/April 1970), 101–106, at p. 105.
[24] Moos and Rourke, *op. cit.*, p. 234.

THE GOVERNORS AND THE
URBAN AREAS
John N. Kolesar

The civil disorders which erupted in the nation's black ghettos in the 1960s transformed "the urban crisis" from rhetoric to reality for most people. The transformation affected nobody more than the governors of the urban states.

Until the disorders, governors for the most part dealt with cities as integral units—complete molecular bundles of governmental problems and political structure. At the same time, mayors and city governments lived in a world of urban fragments—neighborhoods, racial blocs, ethnic groups, gangs, competing businesses, contending union locals, ward clubs, etc. Governors knew that all this diversity existed, but it was not part of their direct experience. They came to the cities as outsiders, wearing a convenient air of innocence. Once the disorders began sweeping the cities, governors were no longer able to maintain the distant viewpoint which had disguised all the bothersome detail of the urban crisis. Like astronauts who find that the bland white face of the moon is actually a treacherous terrain of mountains and canyons, the governors suddenly saw the city in a new way. Close-up, the formerly neat municipal molecules proved to be chaotic bundles of charged particles with enormous potential energy when stirred—energy that could no longer be contained within tidy municipal envelopes. Governors and their urban constituencies began to deal with each other in new ways.

THE MOLECULAR CITY
In the old days, before the disorders, few governors found it necessary or advisable to become involved directly in the problems or politics of the major urban areas. The typical big city had one-party or nonpartisan government. The mayor ran the government and a boss ran the politics; often mayor and boss were the same person. When the mayor-boss was as powerful as the late Frank Hague of Jersey City, he might exert great influence in selection of the governor. Even where the city did not have a Hague, its political structure usually had enough weight and unity to generate a protective magnetic field that repelled outside forces.

Any governor who hankered to penetrate into the interior of his urban areas' problems and politics could quickly find numerous good reasons for shifting his attentions elsewhere. To start with, big-city politics have never held much prospect of success for the outsider, part-timer, or overly fastidious. Few governors would risk the time, effort, or reputation for a genuine entry into big-city politics. In addition, governors and big-city mayors were usually different breeds of men, catering to different kinds of constituencies. For instance, it was a rarity for a mayor to be elected governor; he usually came equipped with the wrong kind of record and organization. As a result of all this, governors came to deal with their cities on an arms-length basis. Some preferred the even more sanitary distance provided by the proverbial ten-foot pole.

This separation between governors and big-city mayors was reflected in a kind of specialization in governmental policy and programs. Governors and state bureaucracies dealt with a categorical group of programs—highways, mental hospitals, higher education, agriculture, conservation, employment, etc.—which ostensibly had no particular geographical bias, but in fact avoided the more difficult urban problems. Hindsight indicates that the states' policies not only ignored urban problems, they may have aggravated them.

The cities, for a time, got along passably with the states looking the other way. They were thriving commercial centers with diverse populations, providing an array of public services unmatched in the suburbs and rural areas, growing with the railroads and heavy industry, and living decently off their local tax base. Occasionally, a mayor would grumble about the rural bias of state government and the cities' liberal, prolabor forces would do battle with the countryside's conservative, agrarian defenders. But when mayors really wanted help, they turned to Washington. And while governors complained in general about the federal government's growing intrusion in the states' internal affairs, they were not so self-reliant as to seek the state taxes or legislation needed to keep the Washington bureaucracy away.

THE ARRANGEMENT FAILS
The arrangement between governors and urban areas worked only as long as the big cities were on the upward slope of their economic growth curves. Once the cities started the downhill ride, the old methods served only to deepen the decline. The states and federal government stolidly implemented a transportation policy dominated by the automobile, diluting the cities' economic vitality and starting them on a case of chronic anemia. The cities' tax ratables began to spread outward, leaving behind unrewarding facilities devoted to the automobile—parking lots, freeway routes, widened streets, junkyards. The shrinking tax base generated a vicious spiral of rising tax rates that drove more taxpayers out. The cities' populations were replenished by poor black people from the rural South who needed more services and provided less revenue than their predecessors.

The old standard operating procedure of running

to Washington brought such programs as low-income housing, urban renewal, and welfare assistance. But these programs, harmless in small doses, proved extremely unwieldy when enlarged to even a fraction of what the national need called for. As a result, they were inordinately slow and complex. Often they consumed all the time and effort of a city's problem-solving staff and then delivered results long after they had any relevance to what the city needed. In the 1970s, cities were still demolishing and rebuilding facilities in urban renewal projects that had been engineered in the 1950s, when an earlier generation had seen things far differently. Low-income housing and welfare assistance, both humanely inspired programs, produced inhuman results when they reinforced the growth of the cities' ghettos.

A new tone of vehemence and desperation crept into the mayors' dialogue with the governors. But much of this was shrugged off as the usual poor-mouthing of local officials seeking to have someone else pay the tab for keeping city governments in the style they had become accustomed to.

THE POLITICAL LAG
As usual, changes in the political apparatus failed to keep up with the governmental realities. The cities had the misfortune to end their population growth just when the courts decided to enforce the "one man, one vote" doctrine. To make things worse, relatively few of the cities' newer residents took part in the electoral process, further reducing the urban areas' political weight.

To deal with the new situation, the cities attempted to rely on the old secret of political success—tight organization. In the short term, tight organization helped maintain the cities' political leverage. But the technique developed some dangerous long-term consequences. The coin of political commerce is gratitude; an organization expects it from those it serves and bestows it on those who serve it. But in the environment of the declining city the political establishments ran a large imbalance of gratitude: They imported more than they exported. The city political establishments had grown fat on the gratitude of opulent railroads, big commerce, and heavy industry, all of whom were either departing or declining. Smaller taxpayers might be called on to fill the gap, but they had more votes and fewer resources than the railroads, merchants, and industrialists. It could be dangerous to tap smaller taxpayers too hard, too often. Slimming down the establishment was a possibility, but it reduced the organization's ability to display gratitude.

In addition, city government became a complex activity that required competent professionals for its operation, making further inroads in the machine's ability to safely display gratitude to those who had served it usefully. The fruits of the bureaucracy gradually replaced the rewards of the machine.

Above all, the organizations felt the need for people who could be relied on to stick to the old truths. That meant the new immigrants with black and brown skins could not be freely admitted to the political organizations. An example of this kind of exclusiveness occurred in 1960 when the men running a national voter registration campaign as a major effort on behalf of John F. Kennedy found some Democratic city organizations that refused to cooperate in the face of the direst threats. The bosses feared for control of their machines.

Thus, efforts to strengthen the position of the organizations led to actions that caused a decline in the already low reputation of city politics, weakened the professional capabilities of city government, and alienated the racial minorities pouring into the cities. These effects were all exactly the opposite of what the times required. Politics, instead of providing the mechanism for adjusting government to changing needs, aggravated the shortcomings of urban government.

By the 1960s, the cities found themselves in a dangerous condition. They had fallen on bad times and everything they tried to do only made matters worse. And although action was harmful, inaction was unthinkable and probably un-American. A few prophets of gloom and doom foresaw an urban future of increasing instability, leading to some disaster. But most people's senses seemed numbed, muffled by a layer of faith in such principles as "things are never as bad as all that," "we always muddle through somehow," and "it's always darkest before dawn."

It was the black minorities in the ghettos, subject to the worst of the urban fates, who ripped away the fluffy layer of belief in comforting homilies. When alienated blacks took to the streets in anger and frustration, they tore the urban envelope from the inside. For the first time, large numbers of Americans realized the great danger the cities faced. Some of them sensed even more ominous implications for an entire society which was going urban with a vengeance. Governors and state governments had their heads forcibly turned toward the plight of the cities. As much as anyone, they had contributed to creating the crisis. More than most, they could do something about it.

FRAGMENTED CITIES

For many governors, the civil disorders themselves were their first occasions for direct contact with the internal problems and policies of their urban communities. When the state police and national guard were sent into cities, governors found themselves dealing directly with law enforcement on city streets. If they took as active a role as New Jersey's Governor Richard J. Hughes did in Newark in 1967, they could find themselves on the scene fulfilling literally their title of commander-in-chief of the state's military forces, meanwhile negotiating personally with black street leaders in hopes of restoring peace.

The aftermath of the disorders often found governors being drawn further and further into the internal affairs of their urban areas. Even where governors had only a peripheral involvement with the disorders, attempts to unwind the dangerous racial tensions drew state governments into new roles in dealing with their major cities. Frequently, the first reaction of mayors and other officials of cities hit by disorders was an old reflex— head for Washington. But existing federal programs and appropriations were too inflexible and slowmoving to respond with appropriate speed. Perforce, the city governments turned to the states.

Governors responded with what was at hand. In many instances, they had pitifully little to offer. State bureaucracies were not organized to serve at the urban neighborhood level. They were not even equipped to communicate effectively with neighborhood constituencies. Yet, neighborhood problems could not be referred back to the cities, as in days of old, because distrust of city governments was a major source of discontent in the ghettos. In some few instances, state bureaucracies such as employment service and welfare administration shared city government's bad name in the ghetto. Whatever the obstacles, most governors established some contact with neighborhood groups and tried to deal with their problems. The alternative was to close off the only recourse remaining to already alienated people.

In establishing contact with urban constituencies, a few governors had state agencies that could serve the purpose to some extent. The 1964 federal antipoverty legislation had created local community action organizations to act as umbrella agencies for conduct of the War on Poverty. These organizations provided an official outlet for the political aspiration of the black residents of cities. They had normal bureaucratic ties to state offices of economic opportunity, which frequently were attached directly to governors' offices. Another line of direct communication between governors and urban constituents was formed by the newly created community affairs departments which began springing up in many states in the mid-1960s. These agencies, orginally designed to coordinate a growing state interest in local government problems, were in their formative stages when the wave of disorders began. In the circumstance, they took an unexpectedly strong tack toward the concerns of urban areas, minorities, and the poor. They worked both through and around city governments. Their clientele was more diverse than the state offices of economic opportunity and thus they established more ambiguous relationships to the various components of urban communities. In theory, at least, they offered the hope of bringing city governments and community fragments together, ending what had become an adversary relationship.

Communication with fragments of the urban community frequently cast governors in the role of ombudsmen. Community and neighborhood groups frequently focused on municipal agencies, especially the police, as prime targets of their discontent. When they could not win satisfaction from mayors and city governments, they turned to the governors and state agencies. Most governors sought to respect traditions of municipal sovereignty, but rising racial and class tensions forced states to tread on the home-rule banner. A few states made efforts to institutionalize the ombudsman role. In Pennsylvania, neighborhood branches of the governor's office were set up to hear and satisfy complaints of ghetto residents. In New Jersey, at the governor's behest, the Department of Community Affairs in 1970 financed similar neighborhood offices in riot-threatened cities, although it put the offices under at least nominal control of the mayors. There were a variety of other groping attempts to fill the need for some mechanism that could act as a troubleshooter for the individual citizen caught in urban America's growing bureaucracy.

The content of the programs and policies the governors first brought to their urban constituents contained little that was new. Understandably, the first responses tended to be emergency, piecemeal steps aimed at cooling dangerous tension. There were a lot of borrowed ideas from the old federal handbook of urban programs, plus some newer wrinkles from the work of the antipoverty agencies and foundations. They led to a miscellaneous collection of well-intentioned social programs in the ghettos with an overlay of grants to match federal aid. Often, the most useful new state effort was in the housing field, though results were limited by the grim realities of finance. Great reliance was placed on funding programs through nonprofit corporations, a device that proliferated during the War on Poverty. This mechanism allowed neighborhood and other private groups to incorporate, receive state and federal funds, and operate programs of their own, bypassing mayors and city governments. While these programs had some temporary beneficial effect as tokens of state government's concern, few of them seemed to offer promise of long-term improvement in urban life.

DOWN TO FUNDAMENTALS

One weakness of the states' first efforts to deal with the urban crisis directly was that instead of acting like states, they tried to act like bigger, better cities or like a smaller, faster federal government. But once embarked on the job, the states could not long avoid issues that were central to their role in creating the conditions of urban life. They soon were brought face to face with their own tax systems, their school systems, their zoning laws, their planning and development controls. These were the fundamental state laws which had helped put the cities on the road to decline.

Changing such deeply embedded legal structures was politically hazardous work, but a surprising number of urban state governors had a try at it. Governor Nelson Rockefeller pushed through the New York Urban Development Corporation, the nation's most powerful state agency for physical construction of urban facilities. Governor Hughes of New Jersey overcame formidable opposition to create the Hackensack Meadowlands Development Commission, a unique regional agency with vast power to plan and develop a 30-square-mile area not far from Manhattan. Governor Francis W. Sargent of Massachusetts had the fortitude to call a one-year halt on freeway construction in the Boston area to afford time for a real look at what was being perpetrated in the name of transportation. He also won legislation aimed at forcing suburban and rural communities to do their part in providing sites for low-income housing. Governor Richard B. Ogilvie successfully fought for an income tax which considerably modernized Illinois' tax structure. Governor Raymond P. Shafer was unsuccessful in a similar effort in Pennsylvania, while Governor William G. Milliken of Michigan sought an even more ambitious statewide property tax for schools, coupled with reform of the educational system.

The governors' actions gave indications that the states were getting just a glimmer of a strategy for dealing with urban problems. No one had a blueprint, but there was the beginning of a list of some necessary ingredients: sensible tax systems; new ways of planning and regulating land-use; new methods for teaching school children and improved financial systems to pay the costs; revised urban government structures that shifted some powers downward to the neighborhoods and moved others up to counties and regions; transportation policies that recognized limits on the automobile's domain; new ways to provide the money and personnel for health care; and a legal system that was more reliable in catching criminals and more diligent in rehabilitating them.

UNCERTAIN POLITICS

As primitive as governmental strategy for urban areas was, political strategy was even more sketchy. The upheaval in the cities had left little of the old body of tradition standing. Urban political professionals lived in fear of white lashback and black lashback and of appearing too fearful of lashback. Race and ethnic conciousness welled up and made the simplest distribution of political spoils a grinding test of sensitivities. The black community began to show a dangerous split between militants, mostly young, and moderates, mostly older. Puerto Ricans and other Spanish-speaking minorities resented black domination of many urban programs and demanded separate but equal programs of their own. The major fear of people of good will was that cities would polarize along racial lines, with extremism permeating both camps. But election victories by such as Mayor John V. Lindsay in New York or black mayors in such divided cities as Cleveland, Gary, and Newark showed that the urban areas were not going extremist yet.

The new uncertainties of urban politics were particularly cruel to the Democratic party. Ever since Franklin D. Roosevelt had become the poor man's hero in the Great Depression of the 1930s, the Democratic party had based its considerable urban strength on a liberal coalition of white ethnic groups, black voters, and labor unions. But in the growing agony of the cities, liberals felt compelled to support black residents in their search for a fair shake. Such support put the liberals frequently at odds with the labor unions and white ethnic groups, threatening to tear up the Democratic party's urban structure and principles. By the end of the 1960s, Democratic governors had become all but extinct in the major urban states although there was a slight Democratic renaissance in the 1970 election. While election of Republican governors in the urban states was often taken as a sign of a conservative trend, the aftermath did not offer much supporting evidence. Many of the Republican governors proved to be at least the equal of the Democrats in progressive action on urban problems.

In election campaigns for governor, urban issues got two kinds of treatment—bland or divisive. A candidate who was willing to venture into plain-spoken extremism could avoid the sin of blandness, but ran the greater risk of being branded divisive. The more frequent technique was to be vague, on the theory there were no proven winners on urban issues and the less said the better. This disappointed those who wanted their elections to be forums for debate of major policy. Candidates strove for a tone of moderation mixed with a strain of toughness toward the lawbreaker. Each voter was left to complete the thought with his own favorite lawbreaker, freeing the candidate of any of the onus of sounding antagonistic toward blacks or Italians or whomever. With most candidates trying to sound moderate and vague on urban issues, elections had a tendency to be decided on other issues. This was not all bad, because it permitted governors to take office relatively free of foolish promises and commitments on urban affairs.

THE ELUSIVE UNDERLYING ISSUE

The fear of divisiveness and polarization was a strong one and led to a yearning for the ideal issue, one that would solve urban problems and bring the races and generations and classes together. The ecology was advertised as such a unifying issue. All races, generations, and classes presumably could support efforts to purify the environment. But not necessarily all the time, it turned out. Those trying to deal with the urban crisis soon began running head-on into those trying to deal with the ecological crisis, as for instance when the only site for integrated low-income housing in a community turned out to be a city park; when a state environmental department got fed up with a regional sewerage agency's constant pollution of major streams and tried to ban all construction in the area, threatening to shut down urban renewal and housing construction in several cities with large black ghettos; when a completed low-income housing project could not be occupied because an injunction had been issued stopping new sewer connections until a nearby river was cleaned up. Black leaders in the cities were particularly suspicious of the enthusiasm for ecology, for it had the earmarks of a diversion and they had had enough benign neglect. Clean air and water were nice, but they were no satisfaction to a man without a job or a decent house or a safe sidewalk.

The urban crisis, it seemed, would have to be met directly within its own terms. It challenged many of the basic policies of state government. Although the first state responses had been tentative and often inappropriate, some governors in the more urban states had launched efforts at real change in basic state policies. They had no assurance that political realities would permit the changes to be made, or that their authors would be spared retribution. But the government and politics of urban areas had come to hold more frightening specters than personal failure and defeat.

EXECUTIVE POWER AND PUBLIC POLICY IN THE UNITED STATES
Thomas R. Dye

This research explores the linkage between some major structural characteristics of state government and the content of public policies in the states. Specifically, the focus is upon the policy consequences of (1) the organizational structure of state executives, and (2) the formal powers of governors. What are the policy consequences of a fragmented state executive with many separately elected officials and independent boards, in contrast to a more streamlined executive organization? Does it make any difference in educational outcomes whether the chief educational officer in the state is elected, appointed by an independent board, or appointed by the governor? Are welfare benefits noticeably more liberal in states with an appointed welfare director in contrast to an independent welfare board? Does it make any difference whether the highway department is headed by an appointee of the governor or an independent board? What are the policy consequences of providing the governor with strong budgetary, appointive, and veto powers? Are there any significant differences in the public policies of states with strong and weak governors? Or are public policies primarily a function of the economic environment of a state—its wealth, industrialization, urbanization, and educational level?

In assessing the impact of structural variables on policies in the fifty states, we will inquire: (1) whether states with fragmented executive structures and weak governors pursue significantly different policies from states with streamlined executive structures and strong governors, and (2) whether any policy differences which are observed can be traced to these structural variables rather than other environmental factors. If the policies of states with fragmented executive structures and weak governors are noticeably different from the policies of states with streamlined executive structures and strong governors, and these policy differences can be attributed to structural rather than environmental variables, then we can infer that the structure of state government has a significant impact on state policies. However, if the policy choices of states with different structural characteristics and strong and weak governors do not differ significantly, or if differences which do occur are the product of environmental conditions rather than structural variables, then we must infer that the structure of state government is not an important determinant of public policies in the states.

Measures of public policy were selected from four of the most important areas of state activity—education, health and welfare, taxation, and highways. Education is the largest category of state spending, followed by health and welfare, and highways. The tax burden and revenue structure of the states was assumed to be an important policy area. Most of the policy variables combine state and local activities; this means we view local governments as integral parts of state political systems. Policy outcomes which depend in part upon decisions made at the local level are treated as attributes of state political systems. For example, the expenditure variables are based on *total* state and local expenditures, rather than just expenditures made by state government. To ignore local expenditures in the comparative analysis of state policy would be to overlook great variations among the states in their reliance upon state versus local levels of government for the provision of public services. The degree to which a state relies upon local governments for the provision of services or financial support is viewed here as a policy outcome of the state political system. The divisions of state-local responsibility in education, health, welfare, highways, and tax collection are considered as separate policy variables.

Most of the policy variables are *levels or amounts* of public service, and it is possible that results obtained with distributive or regulatory policies would be different. However, the rural-urban distribution of state highway funds and the percentage of highway revenues diverted to nonhighway purposes are two of the selected variables, and the relative reliance placed on state sales and income taxation are also considered. All of these variables would seem to involve distributive decisions.

A total of twenty-five policy variables were selected for analysis:[1]

[1] Actually, all operations were performed on a total of over 100 policy measures. The measures listed, and the analysis presented in this article concern only key, representative policy measures.

Education
  Public school expenditures per pupil in average daily attendance, 1960–61
  Average annual salary per member of instructional staff, 1961–62
  Pupil-teacher ratio: enrollment per member of instructional staff, 1961–62
  Drop-out rate: high school grads in 1963 as percent of ninth graders in 1959
  Percent of selective service examinees disqualified for failing mental test, 1962
  Average size of school district in pupils, 1961–62
  State participation: school revenues from state as percent of total school revenue

Health and Welfare
  Average weekly payment per recipient, Unemployment Compensation, 1961
  Average monthly payment per family, Aid to Dependent Children, 1961
  Average monthly payment, General Assistance, 1961
  Per capita state and local expenditures for health and hospitals, 1961
  Per capita state and local expenditures for welfare, 1961
  State participation: percent state expenditures of total expenditures for welfare, 1961
  State participation: percent state expenditures of total expenditures for health and hospitals, 1961
  Recipients of Aid to Dependent Children per 10,000 population, 1961
  Recipients of Unemployment Compensation per 10,000 population, 1961

Taxation
  Total state and local tax revenues per capita, 1961
  Total tax revenues as a percent of personal income, 1961
  State revenues as a percent of total state and local revenues, 1961
  Income tax revenues as a percent of total tax revenues, 1961
  Sales tax revenues as a percent of total tax revenues, 1961

Highways
  Per capita state and local expenditures for highways, 1961
  State participation: percent state expenditures of total expenditures for highways, 1961
  Percent of highway-user revenues diverted to nonhighway purposes, 1959
  Discrimination against urban areas in state highways expenditures, 1957–59

Previous research has shown that many of these policy variables are related to environmental variables, particularly those reflecting levels of economic development.[2] Urbanization, industrializa-

[2] See Richard E. Dawson and James A. Robinson, "Inter-party Competition, Economic Variables and Welfare Policies in the American States," *Journal of Politics*, Vol. 25 (May 1963), pp. 265–289; Richard I. Hofferbert,

TABLE 1. Economic Development and State Policy Outcomes

	Income	Industrialization	Education	Urbanization
Education				
Per pupil expenditures	.83*	.36*	.59*	.51*
State % educational expenditures	.88*	.64*	.57*	.69*
Average teachers' salaries	−.18	.26	−.37*	.06
Size of school district	−.43*	.19	−.50*	−.13
Teacher-pupil ratio	.54*	−.09	.60*	.40*
Dropout rate	−.46*	.13	−.70*	−.05
Mental failures	.80*	.30*	.67*	.55*
Health and Welfare				
Unemployment benefits	.74*	.26	.55*	.51*
ADC benefits	.76*	.39*	.43*	.58*
General asst. benefits	−.30	.16	−.42*	−.15
ADC recipients	.58*	.69*	.23	.39*
Unemployment recipients	−.01	.07	.08	.19
Per capita welfare expenditure	.56*	.39*	.42*	.45*
Per capita health expenditure	−.35*	−.15	−.17	−.11
State % welfare expenditure	−.08	−.07	−.15	−.30*
State % health expenditure	−.16	−.52*	.16	−.15
Taxation				
Per capita tax revenues	.76*	.23	.74*	.59*
Taxes relative to income	−.34*	−.08	−.24	−.28
State % taxes	−.15	.02	−.19	.03
Sales taxes	−.10	−.01	−.22	−.10
Income taxes	.02	−.51*	.36*	−.37*
Highways				
Per capita highway expenditure	−.15	.05	−.04	−.29*
State % highway expenditure	.07	.29	−.06	.42*
Highway fund diversions	−.24	−.15	−.16	−.11
Rural-urban distribution	.33*	.21	.20	.29

Note: Figures are simple correlation coefficients: an asterisk indicates a significant relationship. Economic development measures in all tables are: median family income; one minus the percent of work force in agriculture, forestry and fishing; median school year completed by the population 25 and over; per cent of population living in urban areas.

Source: U.S. Bureau of the Census, *Census of Population 1960* PCI-IC (Washington, D.C.: U.S. Government Printing Office, 1961).

tion, wealth, and adult education levels have been shown to be key environmental variables influencing a wide variety of state policy outcomes in education, health and welfare, highways, and taxation. The simple coefficients for the relationships between these economic development variables and twenty-five policy outcomes are shown in Table 1.

These economic-development, public-policy relationships present some problems in assessing the impact of structural characteristics of state govern-

"The Relation Between Public Policy and Some Structural and Environmental Variables in the American States," *American Political Science Review*, Vol. 60 (March 1966), pp. 73–82; Thomas R. Dye, *Politics, Economics, and the Public: Policy Outcomes in the American States* (Chicago: Rand McNally, 1966).

ments and state policy outcomes. This means that in any assessment of the *independent* effect of structural variables on public policy, we must endeavor to sort out the intervening effect of economic development. In order to isolate the effects of structural variables from the effects of economic development variables, it is necessary to control for these latter variables. This required that partial correlation coefficients be computed which would show the relationships between structural variables and public policy outcomes, while controlling for the effect of urbanization, industrialization, wealth, and education. If relationships between structural variables and state policies which appear in simple correlation coefficients disappear when economic development variables are controlled, then we must infer that there is no independent relationship between governmental structure and public policy among the fifty states. On the other hand, if correlation coefficients between structural variables and state policies remain significant, even after controlling for the effects of these environmental variables, then we may more readily infer that structural variables have an independent effect on state policy.

"FRAGMENTATION" OF STATE EXECUTIVES

The organizational structure of American state governments appears to reflect colonial thinking about "fear of the executive." Among the fifty states one finds many constitutional restrictions on a governor's term of office, his ability to succeed himself and his control over appointments and removals; the executive branch of many of the state governments is composed of a variety of separate boards and commissions, and there are long overlapping terms for the members of the boards and commissions. Jacksonian ideas about popular democracy led many states to elect rather than appoint a variety of executive officers.

Fortunately, for the sake of comparative analysis, the "fragmentation" of executive authority is not experienced uniformly by all the fifty states. There are wide variations from state to state in the number of elected state officers, and the number of executive agencies which are headed by elected officials, appointees, or independent boards and commissions. The Council of State Governments reports in 1965 that 2 states (Alaska and New Jersey) elected only their governor and lieutenant-governor, while Michigan elected 31 executive officers, commissioners, and board members; Texas, 33; and Nevada, 42.[3] The Council also reports that 2 states (Alaska and New Jersey again) had only 2 executive departments headed by elected officials, while Mississippi and South Carolina had a total of 13 executive departments headed by elected officials. Turning to specific agencies: 14 states had elected Public Utility Commissions while all other states handled this responsibility through appointed officials. In 6 states the education department was headed by an appointed official, in 23 states it was headed by an independent board, and in 21 states by a separately elected official. The health departments of 26 states are headed by an appointed official, but in 24 states they are headed by an independent board. The welfare departments of 29 states are headed by an appointed official, but in 21 states they are run by independent boards. One state (Mississippi), has an elected highway commissioner, while the highway departments of 26 states are headed by an appointed official and 23 states by a highway board. In short, there is sufficient variation among the states in the extent of executive "fragmentation" to permit systematic comparative analysis of the environmental correlates and policy consequences of such fragmentation.

In general, the fragmentation of executive authority in the American states is inversely related to measures of economic development. (See Table 2.) On the whole, wealthy, urban, industrial states have less "fragmented" executive structures than poor, rural, agricultural states. Perhaps the complexities of governing an urban industrial state require more streamlined executive structure, while rural agricultural states can continue in their apparent preference for Jacksonian democracy. There is a tendency for more agricultural states to elect more state officials, to elect more agency heads, to have an elected rather than an appointed public utility commission, to have an elected chief educational officer, and to have independent boards rather than appointed heads of their health, welfare and highway departments.

These relationships between economic development variables and structural characteristics are important to keep in mind when exploring the effect of these structural variables on public policy. The problem will be to sort out the effects of economic variables on policy outcomes from the effects of structural variables. For example, it may turn out that states which appoint their chief education official spend more for education than states which elect their top educational officer. But since we know that states with appointed educational heads tend to be wealthier than states with elected educational heads, it may be that wealth rather than the method of selecting their chief educational officer is the real determinant of educational expenditures. To identify the independent effect of a fragmented executive, it will be necessary to control for the effect of environmental variables.

[3]Council of State Governments, *Book of the States 1964-1956* (Chicago: Council of State Governments, 1965).

TABLE 2. Economic Development and the Fragmentation of State Executives

		Average of States on Measures of			
		Income	Industrialization	Education	Urbanization
Number of Elected Officials					
Less than 7	(N = 15)	$5,833	92.8%	10.7 yrs	63.8%
8–14	(N = 17)	4,989	89.7	10.5	59.4
15–21	(N = 18)	5,295	89.3	10.7	62.3
Number of Agencies with Elected Heads					
Less than 6	(N = 16)	5,836	93.6	10.7	68.6
6–18	(N = 16)	5,520	89.9	11.0	64.0
Over 18	(N = 18)	4,763	87.0	10.2	56.5
Public Utility Commission					
Appointed	(N = 36)	5,660	92.3	10.5	63.7
Elected	(N = 14)	4,562	84.4	10.2	56.5
Education Agency					
Appointed	(N = 6)	5,912	94.9	10.6	65.4
Board	(N = 23)	5,603	90.8	10.9	66.0
Elected	(N = 21)	4,918	83.5	9.8	55.8
Health Agency					
Appointed	(N = 24)	5,638	92.8	11.4	66.0
Board	(N = 26)	5,085	88.5	10.7	57.2
Welfare					
Appointed	(N = 29)	5,419	89.8	10.6	65.7
Board	(N = 21)	5,247	89.9	10.7	61.3
Highways					
Appointed	(N = 26)	5,380	92.0	10.3	63.6
Board	(N = 23)	5,299	89.3	11.0	62.0
Elected	(N = 1)	2,884	98.6	8.9	37.7

Source: Data on executive organization from Council of State Governments, *Book of the States 1964–65* (Chicago: Council of State Governments, 1965).

EXECUTIVE "FRAGMENTATION" AND PUBLIC POLICY

There is very little evidence to support the notion that executive fragmentation itself affects the content of public policy in the states. While states with fragmented executive structures pursue somewhat different policies than states with more streamlined executive branches, most of these policy differences are attributable to the impact of economic development rather than the structure of state executives. For example, Table 3 shows that there is some tendency for states which elect many agency heads to spend less money per pupil for education, to pay lower teachers' salaries, to provide lower welfare benefits, to have fewer unemployment recipients, and to pay a larger share of welfare costs with state rather than local funds. However, these relationships appear to be a product of the intervening effects of economic develop-

ment. That is, states with fragmented executives tend to be poorer, rural, and agricultural, and it is these environmental variables rather than executive fragmented itself which accounts for policy differences. The relationships between fragmentation and public policy which appear in simple correlations in Table 3 disappear when the effects of economic development are controlled. The partial coefficients show no significant relationships between fragmentation and public policy while controlling for urbanization, industrialization, wealth, and adult education. (In contrast, partial coefficients for the relationships between economic development variables and public policy remain significant after controlling for executive fragmentation; these coefficients are not shown here.)

Table 4 examines the specific policy differences between states having elected officials, appointed officials, or independent boards heading educa-

Table 3. Executive Fragmentation and Public Policy Outcomes

	Number of Elected State Agency Heads				
	Averages on policy measures			Simple correlation coefficient*	Partial correlation coefficient†
	Less than 6 (N = 16)	6–8 (N = 16)	More than 8 (N = 18)		
Education					
Per pupil exp.	442	406	360	−.43*	−.12
State % educ. exp.	42.2	30.3	47.7	.20	.08
Average teachers' salaries	5703	5459	4963	−.41*	−.08
Size of school district	3851	1767	3066	−.02	.16
Teacher-pupil ratio	23.8	23.7	24.5	.19	.07
Dropout rate	72.6	75.1	69.3	−.22	.08
Mental failures	14.8	12.0	19.4	.27	.14
Health and Welfare					
Unemployment benefits	33	32	29	−.34*	.19
ADC benefits	134	129	151	−.38*	−.03
General asst. benefits	61	54	43	−.38*	−.02
ADC recipients	190	154	200	.11	.07
Unemployment recipients	378	365	294	−.45*	−.11
Per capita welfare exp.	21	28	26	.27	.23
Per capita health exp.	22	21	18	−.24	.01
State % welfare exp.	84	85	96	.37*	.29
State % health exp.	69	60	64	−.17	−.03
Taxation					
Per capita tax revenue	205	212	186	−.22	−.16
Taxes relative to income	9.0	9.7	9.9	.36*	.24
State % taxes	62	55	68	.27	.13
Sales taxes	17	12	7	.22	.29
Income taxes	17	23	28	−.03	.01
Highways					
Per capita highway exp.	61	63	64	.06	.09
State % highway exp.	79	83	84	.17	.26
Highway fund diversions	6.6	3.5	5.8	.00	−.04
Rural-urban distribution	189	170	207	.27	.12

*Simple correlation coefficients between policy measures and number of elected agency heads; an asterisk indicates a significant relationship.

†Partial coefficients show the relationship between policy measures and number of elected agency heads, while controlling for urbanization, industrialization, income, and education.

tion, health, welfare, and highway departments. In educational policy, states with elected educational heads have somewhat lower pupil expenditures, and lower teachers' salaries than states with appointed educational directors or independent boards. But there are no other systematic differences between states with separate methods of selecting their chief educational officer. And it is probable that even these differences in pupil expenditures and teachers' salaries are a product of economic development. While regression analysis is somewhat less satisfactory with these dichotomous and trichotomous variables, nonetheless, the be-

havior of the simple and partial coefficients suggests that environmental variables and not the structural variables are more influential in determining policy outcomes.

An examination of contrasting health and welfare policy outcomes in states with appointed heads and states with independent boards suggests that the latter are more conservative in health and welfare benefits, in spending for health and welfare, and in numbers of recipients. However, these differences are not great, and here again it is probable that these differences are a product of the fact that wealthy, urban, industrial states are more

Table 4. The Method of Selecting Agency Heads and Public Policy Outcomes

Chief Education Officer

	Averages on policy measures			Simple correlation coefficient*	Partial correlation coefficient†
	Appointed (N = 6)	Board (N = 23)	Elected (N = 21)		
Education					
Per pupil exp.	440	410	379	−.22	.05
State % educ. exp.	41.1	38.2	42.8	.06	−.03
Average teachers' salaries	5903	5467	5083	−.30*	.11
Size of school district	3397	2774	2901	.03	.02
Teacher-pupil ratio	24.6	23.7	24.2	.00	−.05
Dropout rate	71.4	73.3	71.0	.05	.13
Mental failures	18.3	12.9	17.6	.06	−.08

Head of Health Department

	Averages on policy measures		Simple correlation coefficient*	Partial correlation coefficient†
	Appointed (N = 26)	Board (N = 24)		
Health				
Per capita exp. health	21	19	−.15	−.03
State % health exp.	67	59	−.19	−.28

Head of Welfare Department

	Averages on policy measures		Single correlation coefficient*	Partial correlation coefficient†
	Appointed (N = 30)	Board (N = 20)		
Welfare				
Unemployment benefits	31	30	−.10	−.25
ADC benefits	127	118	−.20	−.24
General asst. benefits	56	47	−.20	−.20
ADC recipients	190	170	.05	−.10
Unemployment recipients	378	325	−.21	−.21
Per capita exp. welfare	24	26	.06	−.05
State % welfare exp.			.15	.01

Head of Highway Department

	Averages on policy measures			Simple correlation coefficient*	Partial correlation coefficient†
	Appointed (N = 26)	Board (N = 23)	Elected (N = 1)		
Highway					
Per capita highway exp.	52	70	58	.28	.21
State % highway exp.	80	85	76	.21	.13
Highway fund diversions	7.0	3.7	0.1	.20	−.24
Rural-urban distribution	17.2	18.4	27.4	.11	.02

*Simple coefficients were computed with structural variables assigned weights as follows: 1–Appointed, 2–Board, 3–Elected, that is, in the direction of independence from the governor. An asterisk indicates a significant relationship.

†Partial coefficients show the relationship between structural variables and policy outcomes, while controlling for urbanization, industrialization, income, and education.

likely to have appointed heads and more likely to pursue liberal welfare policies. There are no significant simple or partial correlation coefficients between methods of selecting health and welfare department heads and health and welfare policies.

While independent boards are associated with *lower* health and welfare expenditures, just the opposite is true with highway expenditures. States with independent highway boards (and Mississippi with an elected highway director) spend *more* per capita for highways, assume more direct state responsibility for highway finance, and permit fewer diversions of highway funds. There are no discernable differences between states with appointed directors and states with independent boards in the rural-urban distribution of highway funds. Here again the association between independent highway boards and increased highway spending is probably a product of the fact that rural agricultural states spend more for highways and show a structural preference for independent boards.

While we cannot say that these structural variables have *no* impact on policy outcomes, they certainly do not appear to have as much impact as the economic development variables.

THE FORMAL POWERS OF GOVERNORS

Commentators on state politics typically speak of "strong" and "weak" governors. And certainly the power of governors in state politics seems to vary among the fifty states and even to vary from one administration to another in the same state. Yet it is very difficult systematically to describe variations among the states in gubernatorial influence, owing to our inability to find a suitable method of measuring and comparing political influence. Unfortunately, the theory and measurement of influence is not sufficiently advanced in our discipline to permit rigorous comparative analysis of executive influence. Probably the best that can be done in comparing executive power in the states is to focus on the formal powers of governors.

Joseph M. Schlesinger has compiled an index of the formal powers of governors in the fifty states.[4] This index considers the governor's tenure and ability to succeed himself, his appointive powers over executive agency heads, his responsibilities for budget preparation, and his power to veto bills passed by the legislature. The Schlesinger scale of values for a governor's "Tenure Potential" is as follows:

Four-year term, no restraint on reelection	5
Four-year term, one reelection permitted	4
Four-year term, unable to succeed himself	3
Two-year term, no restraint on reelection	2
Two-year term, one reelection permitted	1

The scale of values for appointive powers considers principal functions:

The governor appoints alone	5
Governor must obtain approval of one house	4
Governor must obtain approval of both houses	3
Appointment by board of which governor is member	2
Appointment by board or individual other than governor	1
Popularly elected	0

The governor's budgetary powers are scaled as follows:

Governor has responsibility for preparing the budget and shares it only with persons appointed directly by him	5
Governor has responsibility but shares it with civil servant or appointee of someone other than himself	4
Governor shares power with committee selected by himself, but from a restricted list (Indiana is the only case)	3
Governor shares authority with another official whom he does not appoint, the elected state auditor	2
Governor prepares budget only as a member of a group, usually other elected executives and legislators	1

The measures of veto power rely upon a four-point scale derived by F. W. Prescott.[5] Only in North Carolina is the governor given no veto powers; but in others, the veto may be restricted by limitations on the length of time that a governor may consider a bill after it is passed by the legislature, by permitting a simple majority to override the veto, or by requiring that a vetoed bill reappear at the next legislative session. The veto power may be strengthened by the item veto, by greater time

---

[4] Joseph M. Schlesinger, "The Politics of the Executive," in Herbert Jacob and Kenneth Vines (Eds.), *Politics in the American States* (Boston: Little, Brown, 1965).

[5] F. W. Prescott, "The Executive Veto in the American States," *Western Political Quarterly*, Vol. 3 (1950), pp. 98–112; also cited by Schlesinger, *op. cit.*

periods for the governor's consideration, and by the size of the majority needed to override a veto.

In addition to these evaluations of separate aspects of the governor's formal powers, it is possible to combine the four measures into a general index of the governor's formal powers. This combined index ranges from a low of 7 in Mississippi, South Carolina, Texas, and North Dakota, to a high of 18 in New Jersey and Illinois and 19 in New York. This does not necessarily mean, as Schlesinger points out, that within the context of their own states, the governors of Mississippi and North Dakota do not have as much influence as the governors of New York and Illinois. It means only that the governors of New York and Illinois need more *formal* powers to control the large complex bureaucracies in those states. Within their own borders, the governors of Mississippi and North Dakota are still central figures in their states' political system. It may be that patronage jobs, contracts, and petty favors provide governors of rural agricultural states with relatively more influence than the governors of urban, industrial states. Patronage and pork are probably less important in urban industrial states where governors need formal controls.

Schlesinger has already identified the environmental correlates of the formal strength of governors. He notes that there is a clear relationship between the size of the states and formal executive power: Texas is the only populous state where the governor's formal strength is low, while the nation's largest states—California, New York, Pennsylvania, Illinois, and New Jersey—all rank near the top in governor's powers. He also observes that formal governors' powers are related to economic development. As wealth, urbanization and industrialization increase, so also does the complexity of state administration and the need for formal executive control. Table 5 confirms Schlesinger's

observations about economic development and governors' power. Again it is important that we keep in mind the relationships between these environmental variables and the powers of governors, since environmental variables are also related to policy outcomes. This means that in order to sort out the impact of governors' formal powers on public policy, it will be necessary to control for the effect of these environmental variables.

GOVERNORS' POWERS AND PUBLIC POLICY
There is little evidence that a governor's formal powers significantly affect policy outcomes in the fifty states. While "strong" and "weak" governor states pursue somewhat different policies in education, health, welfare, highways and taxation, these differences are largely attributable to the impact of economic development rather than to the governor's power. Table 6 indicates that "strong" governor states spend more per pupil for education, pay higher teachers' salaries, have lower drop-out rates, pay higher welfare benefits, spend more per capita for health, collect more taxes, and rely more on local governments for revenues and services, than "weak" governor states. However, these relationships are clearly a product of the intervening effect of economic development; that is, a product of the fact that strong governor states are wealthy, urban, and industrial while weak governor states are not. The partial coefficients in Table 6 show no significant relationships between the governor's powers and public policy, while controlling for urbanization, industrialization, income, and adult education. In other words, the relationships between the governor's powers and public policy "wash out" when economic development is controlled. (The only exception is the relationship between the governor's tenure power and avoidance of income taxation; interestingly, the coefficient suggests that short-term governors are more likely to get state

TABLE 5. Economic Development and the Formal Powers of Governors

	Income	Industrialization	Education	Urbanization
Governor's				
Budget powers	.33*	.21	.20	.30*
Appointive powers	.39*	.27	.12	.24
Tenure potential	.49*	.36*	.39*	.30*
Veto powers	.34*	.10	.30*	.32*
Total power index	.60*	.38*	.37*	.44*

Note: Figures are simple correlation coefficients: an asterisk indicates a significant relationship.

Table 6. Public Policy and the Formal Powers of Governors

Public Policy Outcomes	Governor's Formal Powers									
	Budget		Appointive		Tenure		Veto		Total index	
	Sim.	Par.	Sim.	Par.	Sim.	Par.	Sim.	Par.	Sim.	Par.
Education										
Per pupil expenditures	.28	.23	.36*	.24	.27	.19	.38*	.26	.49*	−.04
State % educ. exp.	−.24	−.09	−.08	−.07	.15	−.03	.01	−.03	−.08	.05
Average teachers' salaries	.23	.13	.40*	.17	.39*	.13	.28	.15	.50*	.19
Size of school district	−.10	−.10	.07	−.08	.18	−.04	−.13	−.09	.01	.04
Teacher-pupil ratio	−.11	−.17	−.05	−.16	.04	−.13	−.23	−.18	−.12	.20
Dropout rate	.22	.10	.19	.10	.13	.07	.25	.08	.30*	−.04
Mental failures	−.25	−.08	−.11	−.06	.01	.01	−.10	−.02	−.18	.07
Health and Welfare										
Unemployment benefits	.29	.08	.29*	.07	.44*	.09	.35*	.08	.52*	.10
ADC benefits	.35	.15	.32*	.13	.26	.12	.26	.11	.46*	.02
General asst's benefits	.37	−.06	.38*	−.07	.26	−.10	.32*	−.07	.53*	.10
ADC recipients	−.25	−.02	−.02	.01	−.01	.02	−.14	.01	−.16	−.01
Unemployment recipients	.24	.12	.26	.09	.37*	.12	−.03	.06	.34*	−.02
Per capita welfare exp.	.18	.10	−.27	.05	.04	.09	.35*	.13	.07	.11
Per capita health exp.	.30*	−.09	.15	−.12	.41*	−.08	.17	−.12	.41*	.11
State % welfare exp.	−.24	.19	−.29*	.19	.01	.23	−.01	.21	−.24	−.04
State % health exp.	−.10	.12	−.03	.13	−.17	.10	.02	.16	−.12	−.08
Taxation										
Per capita tax revenues	.28	.04	.13	.03	.37*	.05	.36*	.05	.42*	−.05
Taxes relative to income	−.10	.07	−.27	.02	−.11	.07	.11	.05	−.17	−.08
State % taxes	−.40*	−.03	−.32*	−.01	−.12	.01	.01	.04	−.36*	−.21
Sales taxes	.00	−.20	.04	−.20	.08	−.17	−.27	−.25	−.03	.05
Income taxes	.05	−.29	.01	−.29	−.28	−.33*	.08	−.26	−.08	−.05
Highways										
Per capita highway exp.	.00	.01	−.17	−.02	−.10	−.02	.00	−.01	−.12	−.12
State % highway exp.	−.22	.05	.01	.08	.10	.09	−.32	.03	−.16	−.05
Highway fund diversions	−.09	.01	−.08	.01	.06	.03	.05	.02	−.03	−.17
Rural-urban distribution	−.03	.05	.08	.07	.08	.05	−.11	.04	−.04	.13

Note: Figures are simple and partial correlations coefficients; partial coefficients control for the effects of urbanization, industrialization, income, and education; an asterisk indicates a significant relationship.

income taxes passed than governors who can succeed themselves.) If these operations are reversed and one examines partial coefficients for the relationships between economic development variables and public policy (not shown here), one finds that controlling for the governor's powers does *not* wash out the effect of economic development variables. This lends additional evidence that economic development is more influential than the governor's powers in determining public policy.

ASSESSING EXECUTIVE INFLUENCE: MACRO- AND MICROANALYSIS

Comparative analysis of policy outcomes in the fifty states suggests that economic development variables are more influential than the organizational structure of state government or the formal powers of governors in determining a wide variety of important policy outcomes. On the whole, states with fragmented executive structures do not pursue noticeably different policies than states with streamlined executive structures; most of the policy differences which do occur turn out to be a product of socioeconomic differences among the states rather than a direct product of structural variables. Likewise, there are few systematic policy differences between states with "strong" and "weak" governors, when these terms are employed to describe formal governor's powers. Most of the policy differences which do occur are largely a product of the fact that the strong governor states are wealthy, urban, and industrial, while the weak governor states are poor, rural, and agricultural. Of course, it is conceivable that structural variables or governor's powers could have a more observable impact on some policy outcomes which were not investigated. Yet public expenditures for education, health, welfare, and highways, the liberality of welfare benefits, teachers' salaries and the quality of education, the tax burden and revenue structure, the rural-urban distribution of highway funds, and the degree of reliance upon state versus local governments in the provision of public service—all appear at face value to be important policy outcomes in state politics. Yet the organization of state government and the formal powers of governors seem to have little impact on these outcomes.

How do these findings compare with what we know about the effect of structural features and governors' powers on political processes *within* states? If these structural variables are relatively unimportant in determining policy outcomes, are they important in determining political relationships *within* states?

Deil Wright has reported that agency heads tend to prefer direct gubernatorial control of their agencies, in contrast to control by an independent commission or by the legislature.[6] Wright asked 933 agency heads in all fifty states a series of questions about governor versus legislative influence in executive administration. These agency heads felt that the governor was more sympathetic to the goals of their agency and less likely to reduce their budgets than was the legislature. The implication of Wright's survey is that an increase in gubernatorial control over state administration would increase public service levels, assuming that the perceptions of agency heads about benevolent governors is accurate.

Ira Sharkansky provides more direct evidence that the governor's formal powers affect budgetary allocations within states.[7] Sharkansky examined

the relationships between the budget requests of 592 agencies in nineteen states, the governors' recommendations regarding these requests, and legislative appropriations vis-à-vis agency requests and governors' recommendations. He was able to identify states where the governor's recommendations were closely adhered to by the legislature, and to distinguish them from states where the governor's recommendations were somewhat less influential. It turned out that the governor was more influential in agency-governor-legislative interaction in those states where he had long tenure and strong veto powers. Sharkansky concluded:

The veto and tenure powers of the Governor help to strengthen his position with both agencies and the legislature. Because of formal perogatives, the governor appears to be in a more secure position when he reduces agency requests and makes recommendations to the legislature; the governors that have these powers are more likely to be severe in cutting agency requests and they are more likely to be successful in their recommendations to the legislature. In contrast, the presence of numerous separately elected executives appears to benefit agencies at the Governor's expense. In the states where there are many elected officials, agencies are more likely to get their acquisitive requests approved by the legislature and the governor's recommendation is most likely to be altered in the legislature.

These findings about the relative influence of "strong" and "weak" governors *within* their respective states are not inconsistent with our findings that throughout the fifty states the public policies of "strong" and "weak" governor states cannot be systematically distinguished. We contend only that economic development levels in the fifty states are more influential determinants of policy outcomes than structural variables. However, within any particular state with a given level of economic development, the role of the governor in policy formations is still vitally affected by the formal powers at his disposal.

[6] Deil Wright "Executive Leadership in State Administration," *Midwest Journal of Political Science*, Vol. 11 (February 1967), pp. 1–26.
[7] Ira Sharkansky, "Agency Requests Gubernatorial Support and Budget Success in State Legislatures," *American*

Political Science Review, Vol. 62 (December 1968), pp. 1220–1231.

As V. O. Key Jr., so aptly said fifteen years ago, "The American people are not boiling with concern with the workings of their state governments."[1] Nor has this changed much since then. In November 1966, only 17 percent of a national sample indicated that they followed government and politics at the state level more closely than at any other level of government in the federal system. Another nationwide survey in March 1969 indicated a slight slippage on this question to below 15 percent.[2]

Yet much of the discussion in this book points to the fact that one actor at the state level, the governor, evidently does not suffer from such lack of interest. He has become a highly visible actor in the federal system, and must fight for his political life as he takes action on the various problems the state faces. He shoulders that which state government does, good or bad, despite the fact that his ability to actually control and direct action is constrained. To many, the governor is the state government, and state government means the governor.

In this section, the perceptions of several key actors in the governor's world are explored—the governors themselves, state administrators, and the public. Some of the constraints placed on the governor can be seen in these data; others are suggested. He is an actor often pushed into action from various sources, action that too often is unpopular and costs him support. And he receives little recompense in the day-to-day activities with which he must grapple, although they have so great an impact on the citizen—that is, education, welfare, and highways. He operates in politics and administration, but except for when these translate into such attractive policy issues as law and order, they do not greatly enhance his stature among the public.

Thus, the governor is in the anomalous position of being the total of state government, yet receiving little in return for his efforts. This may suggest that the governor has more leeway and flexibility vis-à-vis his broad public in many policy areas than

SECTION 4 VIEWS OF THE GOVERNOR'S ROLE

[1] V. O. Key, Jr., *American State Politics: An Introduction* (New York: Knopf, 1956), p. 3.

[2] The 1966 data are reported in M. Kent Jennings and Harmon Zeigler, "The Salience of American State Politics," *American Political Science Review* Vol. LXIV (June 1970), p. 525. The 1969 data are from the same survey reported on by Robert G. Lehnen in his article in this section.

might have been expected. Certainly he is a visible actor for his politics and position in the system. And he can receive public attention for his actions in certain key areas such as taxation policy and in such ephemeral areas as law and order. But for much of his charge, he and his efforts are not visible to the general public. Of course, a governor has more particular publics which do follow his activities very closely—such as the legislature, the bureaucracy, and the various interest groups. They care and watch closely, but they are not the governors' broad-based constituency—the one that votes.

PUBLIC VIEWS OF STATE GOVERNORS
Robert G. Lehnen

The way in which mass publics view the programs and administration of a state governor serves as a potential source of action and restraint on his capacity to achieve desired policy objectives. Though one of the more powerful elected positions, the office of governor is still severely circumscribed by the usual American practice of dividing authority and responsibility. In this context, the role of public opinion can be an important determinant of the governor's capabilities, for he holds a position relative to his state constituency that is the equivalent of the President's to the nation. Not all policy conflicts, however, are susceptible to the influence acquired by the governor from mass support or reaction. Those policies involving special interests, elite conflicts, and small payoffs—say, patronage appointments and special contracts—are generally not the type of policy activity where public opinion could greatly help or hinder his objectives. Other areas of policy outputs, though, seem particularly suitable to the "expansion of conflict."[1] Take such examples as public education and tax policies: Here the impact of these policies on masses is great, and the long-standing concern of citizens for these matters suggests that the mobilization of public opinion could have important consequences for policy outcomes.

There is a second perspective on the importance of public opinion that takes one beyond any immediate concern for policy outcomes. From this perspective, one accepts the evaluations of citizens of their political institutions and authorities as intrinsically important. The ability of citizens to "participate" in public affairs for the purpose of individual development as well as for improvement of the collective good has merit in and of itself. "Political participation," when conceived in quite broad terms, implies not only voting and electoral participation but also a general awareness of or psychological involvement in public affairs. Conditions such as political apathy and alienation are the antithesis of political participation. This perspective has its roots in centuries of political theorizing, the main focus being that the creation of good citizens also could achieve a good society. The two goals of good citizens and good societies are interdependent, but the fact that men become concerned with their public welfare and become involved in the affairs of politics has been judged to be both possible and desirable.

Although institutions of direct democracy and other explicitly participatory procedures are not common in the United States today, the general theme of this participatory approach still has relevance. For one thing, such matters as how interested and involved citizens are in political matters become important indicators for judging the political "health" of the society. If political decision-makers, especially state governors, act without creating concern or awareness among large publics, then one would judge the quality of state politics to be lacking, regardless of the merits of governors' policy goals and achievements.

In the essay below, we shall look at some indicators of public opinion in the nation as focused on the institution of state governor. The data presented will serve to expand the two basic themes suggested above—the potential role of public opinion in policy-making and the participation of citizens in political affairs associated with the governor's office. The raw material for analysis is the feelings, beliefs, and evaluations of governors across the land, but the interpretation of these "facts" is dependent on the above two perspectives.[2]

[1] E. E. Schattschneider, *The Semi-Sovereign People* (New York: Holt, Rinehart & Winston, 1960), chap. 1.

[2] The data are from the Southeast Regional Survey, a public opinion survey administered to a national sample of 1,504 adult Americans during March 1969. It was codirected by Thad L. Beyle and the author for the Department of Political Science, University of North Carolina, and was funded by a "Science Development Grant" awarded to the Department of Political Science and the University of North Carolina by the National Science

SELECTING A "PUBLIC" FOR ANALYSIS

In analyzing public opinion, it becomes necessary to specify precisely which publics are the focus of analysis. The concept of "public" involves defining that collection of individuals or the aggregate whose opinions are the point of analysis. Posing this definitional task suggests an interesting problem: Who, precisely, should be included in an analysis of public opinion about the governor? By implication, one can see that there are many publics, only a few of which may be of interest to the researcher and the reader. Shall we include nonvoters, children, and people who do not like politics? Voting studies usually focus on adult-aged voters; marketing studies look more at the potential consumer of a given product. The definition of the relevant public here is fairly broad: The generalizations are based on a representative sample of all adult-aged citizens residing in the continental United States during March 1969. It is necessary to take this broad approach, especially because of the concern with the "participatory" aspect of public opinion. All literate citizens, which are virtually all adults in the country, should participate, but do they?

The definition of the relevant public here excludes children and adolescents. Such an exclusion does not imply that the opinions of these individuals are not important. In fact, considerable current research is focused on the development and growth of political attitudes in this public.[3] The results of this research suggest important findings for the study of adult political attitudes. Because children, however, have only partially developed attitudes about political referents, the immediate questions concern what children do perceive and how they actually evaluate it.

A first theme developed from the study of children suggests that much of political life is just not salient for children. By "salient" one means a general awareness of political matters. To most Americans, which country last won the World Soccer Championship is not a salient piece of information. For many Americans, who won the World Series of Baseball is not part of their perceptual domain. So too with politics: Beyond the world of the practitioner, some students of politics, and a few interested laymen, the amount of political concern and interest drops off rapidly.

A second theme emerging from the study of children suggests that although little, if any, political information exists among the children, they, nonetheless, seek to make judgments about the political referents, and these judgments are overwhelmingly favorable. Fred I. Greenstein, in his early book *Children and Politics*, found that children are much more accepting of political authority than their elders.[4] This overwhelming acceptance of the "goodness" of political figures, however, is moderated somewhat with aging.[5] The third important conclusion is that children learn about some institutions before others. The President and the policeman are very much a part of the child's political perceptions. Later they develop an understanding of such institutions as courts and legislatures.

To summarize, the studies generally show children to have a selective amount of political information about particular institutions, especially executives such as the President and mayors, and that they judge such authorities to be benevolent. The perceptions of adults, then, need be considered in light of these findings.

ADULT VIEWS OF POLITICAL INSTITUTIONS: A COMPARATIVE VIEW

There are several ways to judge the amount of acceptance by citizens of the political institutions of the society. The approach used here compares how adults view five relevant political institutions in the United States: the President, the Supreme Court, the Senate, a local judge, and the state governor. Two concepts of acceptance are involved: the degree of trust the people have in the institution and the degree of power the institution is perceived to hold.

PERCEPTIONS TO TRUST

Table 1 reports the distributions of responses to a question about the trustworthiness of the five important political institutions. In looking at the re-

Foundation. I wish to thank James W. Prothro, Director of the Institute for Research in Social Science, and Angell G. Beza, Director of Research Services for the Institute, for their advice and assistance in the design of the project. Louis Harris and Associates conducted the interviews.

[3] Robert D. Hess and Judith V. Torney, *The Development of Political Attitudes in Children* (Chicago: Aldine Publishing Company, 1967), and David Easton and Jack Dennis, *Children in the Political System* (New York: McGraw-Hill Book Company, 1969).

[4] Fred I. Greenstein, *Children and Politics* (New Haven: Yale University Press, 1965), pp. 35–36.

[5] Torney and Hess, *op. cit.*, chaps. 2–3.

Table 1. Comparing the Levels of Trust for
Five Political Institutions

Political Referent (R)	% Trusting[a]	% Nonresponse
President	75%	14%
Governor of the state	67	14
Local judge	67	19
United States Senate	63	14
United States Supreme Court	60	10
Average for five institutions	66	14

Question: "R" can be trusted to do what is good for the
people. (Agree/Disagree/Don't Know-Not Sure)

[a]If A = the "agree" responses, D = the "disagree" responses, and N = the "don't know" and "not sure" responses, then

$$\% \text{ Trusting} = \frac{A}{A + D} \times (100)$$

and

$$\% \text{ Nonresponse} = \frac{N}{A + D + N} \times (100)$$

sults it becomes clear that the overall level of trust is reasonably high (66 percent) but not overwhelmingly so. The "percent trusting" represents the proportion of respondents who answered the question and gave an "agree" response. If a person did answer the question, it is evident that he was more likely to accept the trustworthiness of an institution rather than reject it.

The small variations, however, should be noted. First, the two executives—governor and President—have the highest levels of trust, but the President is somewhat higher (75 percent *versus* 67 percent). They are followed by the Senate and the courts. Surprisingly enough, the United States Supreme Court has the lowest level of trust (60 percent), while the local judge has the same level as the governor (67 percent).

Another way of considering the data is on the dimension of federal, state, and local. One finds that the state and local institutions (governor and local judge) have about as much support as the supposedly prestigious federal institutions—the Supreme Court and the Senate, but not as high as the President. In either case, the governor appears to be a relatively trustworthy political figure in the eyes of average citizens.

Table 1 also reports the percent of the total sample that did not make a judgment about the trustworthiness of these five institutions. Here one finds little difference in the level of nonresponse, but the courts represent the extremes. About one citizen in seven on the average does not judge whether a given institution is trustworthy (14 percent). If one sees the magnitude of nonresponse as a rough indicator of indecision and noninvolvement with political affairs, the governor appears to be no worse off in this regard than other institutions.

PERCEPTIONS OF POWER

A dominant view among political scientists is that political institutions have the capacity to apply binding sanctions. What distinguishes political institutions from other institutions in the society is their ability to legitimately apply force where necessary. If one chooses to resist the directives of a court, then the court may ultimately resort to force (police officers and incarceration) to gain compliance. Of course, the overt use of force tends to be the exception in day-to-day life, although the past decade has presented repeated instances where the authorities of one political institution or another have used overt sanctions to gain policy ends. Probably the most dramatic examples of late have occurred in civil rights demonstrations, civil disorders, and campus activities. One may not expect children to have developed a perception of the potential sanctions in society, but what can be said for adults? Has their increased political maturity brought them to the point where the power of political institutions is perceived, or can it be said that most citizens simply are not aware of the potential sanctions of political institutions?

Table 2 reports the distribution of responses to a statement about the potential sanctions of five political institutions: "A [political referent] has the power to get almost anyone to do what he wants them to." In no case did even half of the respondents agree with the statement; rather, the tendency was to reject the assertion of the statement. Two political institutions—the President and the United State Supreme Court—can be distinguished from the other three for their relatively high levels of perceived power. For these two institutions one finds that nearly half of those responding agreed with the statement. The statement is an extreme one—in the sense that, being absolute, it requires a certain amount of conviction to justify an "agree" response. The differences among the five institutions must, therefore, be interpreted in this light.

level of nonresponse to the statement on political power is, on the average, about the same. With the exception of the President, there is little difference among the institutions in the level of nonresponse, about one in seven respondents not making a definite judgment about whether the institution had power to control people's lives (14 percent). Thus, one gains a picture of state governors as one of the most trusted of political authorities, but they are perceived by their constituencies to have relatively low levels of power.

Table 2. Comparing the Perceptions of Power for Five Political Institutions

Political Referent (R)	% Perceiving Power[a]	% Nonresponse
United States Supreme Court	45%	16%
President	41	10
Governor of the state	27	14
United States Senate	24	15
Local judge	22	16
Average for five institutions	32	14

Question: "R" has the power to get almost anyone to do what he wants them to. (Agree/Disagree/Don't Know-Not Sure)

[a]If A = the "agree" responses, D = the "disagree" responses, and N = the "don't know" and "not sure" responses, then

$$\% \text{ Trusting} = \frac{A}{A + D} \times (100)$$

and

$$\% \text{ Nonresponse} = \frac{N}{A + D + N} \times (100).$$

The governor, the United States Senate, and the local judge all have about the same level of perceptions of power, somewhat lower than the Supreme Court and the President.

Although the level of agreement with the "power" statement differs considerably from that of the "trust" statement reported in Table 1, the

If one takes the data reported from the first two tables and presents them in the form of a graph (Figure 1), several patterns emerge. Each of the five points represents the position of an institution on the dimensions of trust and power perceptions. Points to the right, as most are, represent increased trust; points to the left, decreased trust. Moving higher in the graph, space represents increased power; lower, decreased power. The point labeled "average for five institutions" represents the average perceptions across the five institutions. The graph shows that the governor, United States Senate, and local judge are essentially viewed alike by the sample, whereas the President and Supreme Court show distinct patterns of response. The governor, Senate, and local judge are seen as slightly less powerful than might be expected given their level of trust; the President and especially the Supreme Court are seen as more powerful than might be expected given their levels of trust.

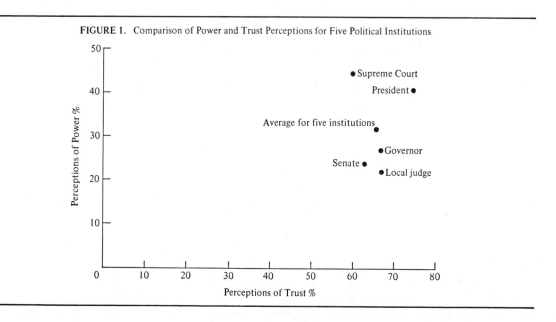

FIGURE 1. Comparison of Power and Trust Perceptions for Five Political Institutions

CONSIDERING THE SUBSTANCE
OF GOVERNORS' EVALUATIONS

To this point, only the latent and diffuse aspects of perceptions of state governors have been considered. The general levels of feelings of trust and beliefs about power represent years of experiences and political learning and, presumably, are not subject to rapid change. In particular, these levels are not solely dependent on the incumbents; instead, they are general predispositions toward the institutions and authorities. There is also an immediate, present-oriented aspect of perceptions— the reactions of our citizens to the day-to-day performances of their state governors—that deserves some consideration. What do people like and dislike about their state governors? How might the number and types of things liked and disliked about their officials differ across institutions? Are the activities of the governor of the state as salient, say, as those of the President?

Respondents were asked to describe for the Governor, President, and Supreme Court each what they particularly liked or disliked.[6] Respondents

[6] For state governors, the text of the questions was "Is there anything the Governor of [*Name of State*] has done lately that you like [don't like]? Would you please tell me about that?"

were then scored for the number and types of likes and dislikes for each of the three institutions. Figure 2 reports the distributions of likes and dislikes for the Governor, President, and Supreme Court. The most impressive fact revealed by this comparison is the rather high level of response given the questions about the governor. State governors actually received more comment than the President, and these two received considerably more response about their activities than did the United States Supreme Court. About 54 percent of the sample mentioned something about the President, while 57 percent commented about the governor; only 36 percent said anything about the Supreme Court. These results occurred during a time when the nomination of Justice Abe Fortas to be Chief Justice had been an issue and the propriety of his financial affairs was being raised.

It is also significant that the proportion of total respondents expressing "likes only" and "dislikes only" vary considerably by institution. While citizens tended to give either favorable or unfavorable comments only, the President received an overwhelming proportion of favorable comments. In contrast, state governors received more unfavorable comment than favorable, but, it might be added, not nearly as great a proportion of total

FIGURE 2. Patterns of Total Response About State Governors, the President, and the United States Supreme Court

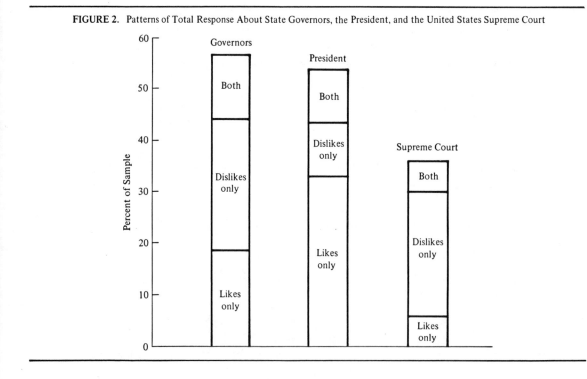

responses as did the Supreme Court. Thus, one finds the state governors to be a highly salient political authority, but the evaluations of their performances are an especially mixed collection of liking and disliking.

When one considers the range of things a national sample of respondents might say about their authorities, the list soon becomes unmanageably long. Some respondents mentioned a "dishonest face" or "attractive wife," while others mentioned such things as improving the schools or raising taxes. It was necessary in considering the content of the responses to make some preliminary distinctions between policy- and nonpolicy-related responses. The nonpolicy category included all mention of personal characteristics, party-related responses ("He's a Democrat"), and responses related to population groupings ("He's good for the poor people"). The policy-related category included all references to programs and functions of government, from education to highway construction. Figure 3 reports the distributions of likes and dislikes for each of the three institutions.

It is clear that respondents were able to and, in fact, did respond in policy terms more often than not. People studied tended to give about the same proportion of policy-related responses, regardless of the institution. Furthermore, whether the response was favorable or unfavorable made little difference in the proportion of policy-directed responses.

Although the programs and policies of governors do have impact on mass opinion, such a generalization is not totally correct without one important qualification. Figure 3 also shows that in no case did half of the sample express opinions about either their likes or dislikes.[7] The highest level of response occurred for favorable responses about the President (44 percent), yet about 56 percent of the sample gave no response to this question. Over 88 percent of the sample said nothing when asked about their favorable attitudes about the Supreme Court. Thus, to say that citizens respond to the policy-related activities and characteristics of a governor's administration is correct only if one realizes that most people do not find anything salient enough to make a comment about governors' activities.

[7]The "likes" and dislikes" bars in Figure 3 do not sum to the amount reported in Figure 2 because a respondent could express both likes and dislikes. Those respondents are classified as "both likes and dislikes" in Figure 2.

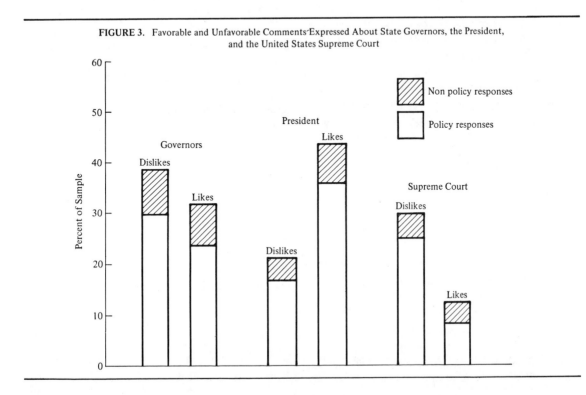

FIGURE 3. Favorable and Unfavorable Comments Expressed About State Governors, the President, and the United States Supreme Court

These response distributions are in marked contrast to the diffuse perceptions of power and trust reported earlier, where most everyone expressed an opinion. If one were to speculate, no doubt the rate of policy responses for specific likes and dislikes for a given institution would vary with short-term factors such as the political personalities involved, the programs introduced, and other historical events.[8] It would seem unlikely, however, to expect these immediate time-based responses to reach the frequency of response observed for the diffuse trust and power statements. Such factors suggest the limitations that governors must face if they are to use public opinion as a tool for achieving policy ends, for, given the short terms of governors and the generally few opportunities (biennial legislative sessions) they have to make large societal changes, these basic parameters of public opinion could be critical to the success or failure of many proposals and programs.

THE CONTENT OF LIKES AND DISLIKES

In classifying the responses within specific policy subgroups—welfare, civil rights, international relations, economic development, and taxation—there was an attempt to create comparable categories across the various institutions studied. After the coding of the responses was completed, however, it became apparent that the content of responses about the President and Supreme Court were quite different from those about state governors. In effect, this was dramatic evidence that the respondents had discriminated clearly on the level and type of institution they were evaluating. Table 3 represents various policy responses for state governors, combined into broad, encompassing groupings.

Certain issues dominated the state politics during 1969—specifically, taxes, spending, and law and order. Governors lost ground in popular eyes on some issues, while other policies worked more to their advantage. Notably, taxes and spending policies caused a net loss in opinion of 20.3 percent. In other words, there were over 20 percent more respondents who gave negative rather than positive comments relating to tax affairs. The governor picked up a net gain on law and order policies

Table 3. Likes and Dislikes Expressed About State Governors

	% Liking[a]	% Disliking	Net %[b]
Tax policies only	2.4%	13.9%	−11.5%
Tax and another policy	0.0	6.1	−6.1
Education policies	2.5	2.3	0.2
Spending policy	1.5	4.2	−2.7
Law and order policies	6.9	1.9	5.0
Other policy	8.1	2.5	5.6
Combinations of two mentions (at least one policy)	4.4	4.4	0.0
Other characteristics	8.1	8.2	−0.1
No response	66.0	56.5	9.5
	100.0%	100.0%	

Selected Likes and Dislikes Expressed About the United States Supreme Court

Law and order policies	1.7%	12.9%	−11.2%

[a]% Liking and % Disliking are based on the total sample.
[b]% Net = % Liking − % Disliking.

(5.0 percent) and on other policy considerations (5.6 percent). On education and other policy characteristics the difference was about zero.

Taxes and spending were rarely mentioned where the Supreme Court or President was concerned, clearly indicating that most Americans do not readily associate specific tax levels and spending policies with these federal institutions. Rather, it is an issue that has particular impact at the state level.[9] In contrast, the law and order issue, while virtually never mentioned in regard to the President, was the overwhelming source of unfavorable comment concerning the Supreme Court. The Court experienced a net loss of 11.2 percent on this policy alone. The issue of public order and criminal procedures then cut across the federal-state distinction, resulting in a net gain for the state executives, who are primarily responsible for enforcement policies, and a net loss for the Supreme Court, the source of many of these policies.

The data in Table 3 are suggestive also for what individuals did not comment about. Considering the wide range of outputs at the state level, it is interesting that the respondents mentioned few services and benefits, yet they were very much aware of the costs of government. Education is the exception, but regulation of business, highways, civil rights, and social-welfare programs—just to

[8]John E. Mueller, "Presidential Popularity from Truman to Johnson," *American Political Science Review*, Vol. 64 (March 1970), pp. 18–34, reports similar phenomena for the President.

[9]See Leon D. Epstein, "Electoral Decision and Policy Mandate: An Empirical Example," This book, for a case study of the effects of the tax issue in the 1962 gubernatorial election in Wisconsin.

mention a few—were rarely commented about, either in favorable or unfavorable terms. Of course, these generalizations are based on average responses of a national sample having many different governors as referents. There is no need to assume that any particular governor might use his personal (nonpolicy) appeal or some dramatic program to influence great numbers in his constituency. On the average, however, a state governor faces the prospect of having an inherent source of negative feeling toward his administration resulting from taxing and spending matters, and unless he has an issue such as law and order to create some positive response to his administration, it would seem unlikely that he could sustain, or even achieve, a favorable level of popular support for his administration.

KNOWLEDGE ABOUT POLITICAL AFFAIRS

Although several democratic theorists have suggested that participation in politics need go hand in hand with an awareness of political matters, translating this prescription into behavioral terms raises serious problems. For some theorists, the fact that many citizens seemingly disenfranchise themselves by not participating although no legal barriers exist is a serious deficiency. Other theorists fear mass participation without the proper foundation of political knowledge and involvement. They fear the potential consequences of such participation, both for the individual and the political system. Empirical studies, especially focused on the decision on whether and how to vote, have produced empirical evidence supporting both fears. Many citizens, in fact, do not become involved; others seem to participate regularly with what appears to some to be totally inadequate political information. One political scientist has commented on the rather pessimistic findings about citizen participation and knowledge by noting that what was lacking was not the citizens so much as the democratic theory. In particular, he noted that public opinion analysts were always attempting to "flunk" the electorate by demonstrating the scarce amount of citizen political knowledge (many of these analysts are college professors) rather than formulating a workable democratic theory.[10]

Although five knowledge questions were administered to the national sample, it was hardly the

[10]Schnattschneider, *op. cit.*, p. 135

Table 4. Indicators of Political Knowledge About Political Institutions

Question	% Giving Correct Answer[a]
Name the capital city of state	96%
Identify political party of governor	86
Name political party with majority in U.S. Congress	71
All of above	67

	Number of Correct Mentions					
	0	1	2	3	4+	Total
U.S. Senators	23%	19	20	13	25	100
U.S. Supreme Court Justices	50	22	15	8	5	100

[a]Percentages are based on the total sample.

purpose of these questions to "flunk" anyone. Rather, within the time and space limitations of a questionnaire, the questions were prepared to estimate the basic level and breadth of political knowledge in the sample. Unlike the "opinion" questions found in the interview, the answers to these five questions reported in Table 4 could be scored as "correct" or "incorrect." The questions range from those requiring elementary knowledge, such as the question about the location of the state capital, to rather difficult items, such as naming the Justices sitting on the Supreme Court. Virtually everyone could correctly identify his own state capital, but only half of the sample could identify at least one Justice sitting on the Supreme Court. The party affiliation of the state governor was a very salient fact for most citizens: 86 percent of the sample correctly identified his political party. One can contrast the response to this question with a similar one concerning the United States Congress, where 71 percent correctly identified the majority party. Two-thirds of the sample correctly answered all of the first three questions.

The identification questions were somewhat harder than the first three factual questions. They suggest that only a small percentage of the national sample has political information far beyond the simple requirements of "at least one correct identification." If one chooses a higher "cutting point"—say, at least three correct mentions—then more citizens would "fail" the test. In other words, the citizens seem to have basic levels of information about a range of political affairs, but the depth of this information is not very great for most people.

The range and depth of political information can become a critical factor in participation, depending on the particular political task at hand. For basic political activity, such as voting for governor, one would be hard pressed to suggest that the average citizen is inherently unqualified. If, however, one expected the average citizen to respond critically to public discussions of complex tax policy, the basic level of political learning could be judged as a severe limitation. A governor seeking to mobilize public opinion in some given direction needs to consider the capacity of mass publics to respond to his leads and suggestions: The basic knowledge levels and participation rates in his constituency can serve as both sources of restraint and potentials for action in a governor's attempt to use public opinion for attaining policy goals. If a governor restricts his public actions to broad, direct behavior, as in a campaign, he may be successful in creating a desired response. Unfortunately, many conflicts in state politics are not always susceptible to such gross treatment.

EXPLAINING PERCEPTIONS OF GOVERNORS

The electoral research of the last twenty-five years has produced two competing themes for explaining why people like and dislike political figures. The first explanation stresses the "stimulus-response" nature of the relationship between respondent and political figure. Individuals who perceive the characteristics or actions of a candidate simply evaluate him according to their own schedules of values. Should a candidate want to change this reaction, he must manipulate the stimuli—that is, change his behavior in some manner in order to create more favorable responses. The second approach, while not totally rejecting the first, emphasizes that the respondent is not a neutral agent receiving and interpreting stimuli. In a word, the stimuli from the political environment are subject to modification by the predispositions already existent in the respondent.[11] Thus, Republican

[11] See Bernard Berelson et al., Voting (Chicago: University of Chicago Press, 1954); Angus Campbell et al., The American Voter (New York: John Wiley, 1960), chap. 6; and Campbell et al., Elections and the Political Order (New York: John Wiley, 1966), chaps. 6–8.

voters might tend to judge an action of a Democratic governor more harshly than a similar one taken by a Republican governor. A Democrat may ignore the good characteristics of a Republican and the bad aspects of a Democratic governor. This latter approach may be called a "partisan-response" explanation.

To determine the extent of stimulus-oriented versus partisan-motivated responses to the activities of state governors, two aspects of the relationship of respondent to stimulus must be clarified. First, a "partisan" evaluation suggests that the respondent is knowledgeable of the governor's party affiliation, and in cases where the governor and respondent do not have the same party identification, the respondent can be expected to give more unfavorable and less favorable responses than under conditions of partisan agreement. Thus, correct knowledge of a governor's partisan commitments is a necessary condition in the partisan-response model.

In cases where the respondent is not aware of the governor's party, how might one interpret observed differences in response between party identifiers? If one makes the assumption that Republican and Democratic governors produce different sorts of political stimuli, observed differences between Republican and Democratic respondents would suggest that these differing stimuli are evaluated from differing schedules of values. Political party, in this case, is an approximation for the respondent's pattern of political values. If no differences between Republican and Democratic respondents exists, then the varying nature of the stimulus (Republican versus Democratic governors) has no apparent impact on citizen reactions.

The type of respondent knowledge about the governor's partisan commitments and his actual partisan alignment define four different conditions for studying the impact of the respondents' partisan attachments on his evaluations of gubernatorial activity: They are (1) knowledgeable respondents living in Republican states, (2) knowledgeable respondents living in Democratic states, (3) unknowledgeable respondents living in Republican states, and (4) unknowledgeable respondents living in Democratic states. The analytical problem is to determine in what way these three characteristics—knowledge of the governor's party identification, the governor's party identification, and the respondent's party identification—

	Partisan-Response Explanation			Stimulus-Response Explanations				
	Conditions: Respondents are knowledgeable of their governor's party affiliation, which is Republican.			*Conditions:* Respondents are not knowledgeable of their governor's party affiliation, which is Republican.		*Conditions:* Respondents are knowledgeable of their governor's party affiliation, which is Democrat.		
The Respondent Is A:	Rep[a]	Ind	Dem	Rep	Dem	Rep	Ind	Dem
Parameters for favorable response:	.084	.002	−.082	−.075	−.111	−.027	−.361	.154
Statistical tests:	$\chi^2 = 13.494, df = 3; p = .004$			$\chi^2 = 2.910, df = 2; p = .233$		$\chi^2 = 12.313, df = 3; p = .006$		
Goodness of fit test for favorable response model:	$\chi^2 = 2.860, df = 3; p = .119; \mu = .548$							
The Respondent Is A:	Rep[a]	Ind	Dem	Rep	Dem	Rep	Ind	Dem
Parameters for unfavorable response:	−.033	.053	.108	.126	.145	136	.248	−.069
Statistical tests:	$\chi^2 = 19.254, df = 3; p = .001$			$\chi^2 = 5.227, df = 2; p = .073$		$\chi^2 = 11.393, df = 3; p = .010$		
Goodness of fit test for unfavorable response model:	$\chi^2 = 3.969, df = 3; p = .265; \mu = .679$							

[a]Rep = Republican, Ind = Independent, Dem = Democrat.
See footnotes 12 and 13 for a description of the statistical technique used.

together or separately—predict the level of favorable and unfavorable response.[12]

A model of nine parameters was fitted to the data which adequately predicted the level of favorable and unfavorable response.[13] A summary of

the model and statistical tests for each response function may be found in Table 5. The general results of the model suggest that both the partisan-response and the stimulus-response explanations have support from the data at hand. To phrase the general findings another way, both appear to be operating but under quite different conditions.

PARTISAN-RESPONSE EFFECTS

Among knowledgeable respondents living in states with a Republican governor, there is direct evidence that citizens respond to the activities of the governor in a manner determined by their party identifications. Republican respondents, on the one hand, are much *more* likely to give favorable comments about their governors than either Independents or Democrats; Republicans are also much *less* likely to give unfavorable comments than either Independents or Democrats. Democrats, on the other hand, are *less* likely to give favorable comments and *more* likely to give unfavorable comments. The statistical tests show that these patterns most likely could not have occurred by chance factors introduced by the sampling procedures.

The statistical model fitted to the data on favorable responses about governors shows that the overall probability of favorable response was .548, or slightly over one person out of two. Republicans tended to respond at a higher rate than aver-

[12]Two linear models—one each for the probability of giving a liking and a disliking response—were fitted to the data by means of a general categorical data approach developed by the Department of Biostatistics, University of North Carolina. A weighted least-squares procedure, the weights being consistent with the variances of the Y scores, was used to fit the model to the data. See James E. Grizzle, C. Frank Starmer, and Gary G. Koch, "Analysis of Categorical Data by Linear Models," *Biometrics*, Vol. 25 (September 1969), pp. 489–504, and Ronald N. Forthofer, C. Frank Starmer, and James E. Grizzle, "A Program for the Analysis of Categorical Data by Linear Models," University of North Carolina, Institute of Statistics Mimeo Series No. 604 (January, 1969), for further details on this technique. I wish to thank Dr. Gary G. Koch of the Department of Biostatistics for his helpful assistance in fitting the models on which this analysis is based.

[13]The nine parameters are the general mean (1), the respondent's party identification under conditions of correct knowledge and Republican governor (3), the respondent's party identification under conditions of incorrect knowledge and Republican governor (2), and the respondent's party identification under conditions of incorrect knowledge and Democratic governor (3). The "goodness of fit test" reports how well the predicted and observed frequencies agree. The objective is to have a nonsignificant test. Variables having k categories are represented by (k − 1) parameters.

age (+.084), Independents, at about the average rate (+.002), and Democrats, below the average rate (−.083). The set of three parameters was statistically significant at the .004 level.

The unfavorable response model produced a different set of parameters. The overall probability of response was .679, somewhat higher than the overall probability of a favorable response. Democrats were above average in their unfavorable responses (+.108), Independents, also above average (+.053), and Republicans, below average (−.033). The set of three parameters was significant at the .001 level.

The partisan-response explanation was, however, not supported by the data for knowledgeable respondents living in Democratic states. In these states, the partisan attachments of the respondents made little or no difference in their tendency to comment about the good and bad aspects of their governor's performance. The statistical tests showed these parameters not to be significant, or, in other words, the observed differences were so small as most likely to result from chance factors unrelated to the respondent's party identification. Knowledgeable respondents with Democratic governors generally respond at the overall average rates of favorable (.548) and unfavorable (.679) response; it made little difference whether the citizen was a Republican, Democrat, or Independent.

There is no ready explanation of this rather interesting finding, but one observation comes to mind. The interviews were collected in the spring after the Republican party had successfully won a large number of new governorships in the 1968 elections. This special historical fact may be reflected in the partisan nature of response only for Republican governors. The actual patterns of response show that Republican governors were favorably influencing the groups who already were likely supporters (Republicans) and failing where the opposition was concerned (Democrats).

STIMULUS-RESPONSE EFFECTS

The stimulus-response explanation also has support from the statistical findings reported in Table 5. Among unknowledgeable respondents living in Democrat states, there is direct evidence that partisan affiliation of respondents makes a statistically significant difference in how they evaluate their governors. Although these individuals do not know the party of their governor, the Democrats

were most likely to give favorable responses followed next by the Republicans. Independents, however, were less likely to give favorable responses than either kind of party identifier. Notably, the partisan order is maintained between Republicans and Democrats, even though these respondents had incorrectly identified the party of the governor. Independents, though, do not maintain a place between the parties, but rather fall at the end of the partisan continuum.

The reversed pattern is also found for the unfavorable response model. Independents are most critical of their governors, having the highest level of unfavorable response; Republicans are next, and Democrats, the least critical.

Table 5 shows that Democrats are more likely (+.154) than the overall average to give a favorable response; Republicans, less likely than average (−.027), and Independents, least so (−.361). For the unfavorable response model, Independents are more likely to give critical comments (+.248), Republicans, next (+.136), and Democrats last (−.069). Both sets of parameters were statistically significant.

For unknowledgeable respondents living in Republican states, the parameters approach statistical significance but are not large enough to rule out chance factors.[14] It should be noted, however, that the same pattern of response is present for these parameters. Republicans gave more favorable comments and less unfavorable comments than Democrats.

To summarize, respondents, although lacking precise knowledge about the party commitments of their state governors, nonetheless respond differently to governors' programs, especially where Democratic governors are concerned. It is beyond the scope of this chapter to say precisely how the activities of governors are communicated to citizens or by what process the respondent synthesizes his perceptions with his partisan values. Regardless of the exact answer to these questions, it is clear that governors do have observable effects on the public opinion of their constituencies.

The behavior of Independents under these circumstances also deserves some comment. One can only guess at the meaning of "Independent" in this context; because many of these Democratic

[14] Independents could not be studied here because of too few cases.

governors were also southern governors, it is reasonable to speculate that these respondents are the core of opposition to traditional politics in these mostly one-party states. No doubt these respondents have values that are quite different from either a typical Democratic or Republican identifier, which in turn produces the distinct behavior observed from our model.

CONCLUDING STATEMENT

From the preceding analysis, one can argue that state governors on the whole do not appear in worse perspective than other major political institutions in America. This is not to say, however, that the position of governor does not carry some inherent limitations. Clearly, mass publics do not believe the governor has the power to carry out his programs, although they may trust him. On specific goals and policies governors desiring favorable public acclaim must confront the tax and spending problem, and the odds are that they will lose in the confrontation.

If a governor desires to maximize other program outcomes, he faces the prospect that the public will not perceive his goals and desires. If citizens do perceive them, the governor is more likely to impress people who tend to support him anyway—people of his own party. Partisan opponents and independents will probably have unfavorable reactions or, at a minimum, not give favorable support. An appeal to public opinion then most likely results in the mobilization of potential support rather than the conversion of opponents. Thus, public opinion is the governor's wealthy, jealous mistress—demanding of his attention, critical of his shortcomings, potentially dangerous to his position, but a necessary component for achieving many of his objectives.

THE WORLD OF STATE GOVERNMENT ELITES: GOVERNORS AND BUREAUCRATS

Thad L. Beyle
and
Robert E. O'Connor

Recent studies of public policy at the state level suggest that the most significant variables in "explaining" differences among the states are economic and environmental in nature.[1] With few exceptions,[2] political and governmental variables have been able to explain little of the state-by-state differences in policy—especially when the analysis is based on data subject to statistical manipulation. Yet, the "suspicion" remains that politics and government do make a considerable difference and that social scientists have been negligent, or often just plain wrong, in how they measure and analyze their impact. For if political and governmental variables are indeed insignificant, why is there interest and excitement over which candidate wins, which party controls, and how many programs are administered? These very questions support Hofferbert's suggestion that the study of state elites is a key area of study for the better understanding of policy in the states.[3] The role of state elites and their impact on policy may range from crucial to ephemeral, and vary among the states, but until these elites are investigated, the political variables cannot be set aside.

This study explores the perceptions of state gov-

[1] See, especially, Richard E. Dawson and James A. Robinson, "Inter-party Competition, Economic Variables, and Welfare Policies in the American States," *Journal of Politics*, Vol. XXV (May 1963), pp. 265–289; Herbert Jacob and Kenneth Vines (Eds.), *Politics in the American States* First Ed. (Boston: Little, Brown, 1965); and Thomas R. Dye, *Politics, Economics, and the Public* (Chicago: Rand-McNally, 1966).

[2] See, for example, Charles F. Cnudde and Donald J. McCrone, "Party Competition and Welfare Policies in the American States," *American Political Science Review*, Vol. LXIII (September 1969), pp. 858–866; John Grumm, "The Effects of Legislative Structure on Legislative Performance," in Richard I. Hofferbert and Ira Sharkansky (Eds.), *State and Urban Politics* (Boston: Little, Brown, 1971) pp. 298–322; and Joseph A. Schlesinger, "The Politics of the Executive," in Jacob and Vines, *op. cit.*, pp. 207–237.

[3] Richard I. Hofferbert, "Elite Influence in State Policy Formulation," *Polity*, Vol. II (Spring 1970), pp. 316–344.

ernors and high-level bureaucrats. The focus is on the particular concerns of the state elites and the actors and institutions most pertinent to them in dealing with these concerns. What characterizes governors' configurations of concerns and actors? Are their configurations different from those of state elites positioned in the possibly more secure confines of "the bureaucracy"? Does the evidence support the commonplace observation that the politician is more a generalist and the bureaucrat a specialist? Or does any division fall along different lines? Are certain environmental, political, or governmental phenomena related to these patterns?

THE DESIGN

Between October 1965 and March 1967, in connection with "A Study of American States," a series of ten questionnaires were sent to the governors of the fifty states.[4] Each questionnaire focused on a particular theme and contained several open-ended questions.[5] This questionnaire form called on the governor or his/her aides to pass the questionnaire to the person in state government best suited to answer the questions posed, except for those expressly answerable only by the governor or his immediate staff.

While the response level varied by questionnaire theme, the overall rate of return was 66.8 percent (334/500), of which 40.7 percent (136/500) were

returned over the signature of the governor or one of his immediate office staff. The data set is composed of a split sample of gubernatorial letters (40.7 percent) and letters from other state government personnel (59.3 percent).

There were few systematic variations in the level of response or the position of the respondent across the states as measured by 13 common environmental, economic, and political variables. Region did affect the rate of response ($p = .05$), so that northern states were more likely to be within the sample than southern or western states. And as the level of interparty competition increased across the states, there was a tendency for the response rate to be lower ($\tau_c = -.14$), a relationship most apparent in the responses to the questionnaire concerning boards and commissions, a most politically sensitive area in state politics. However, generally these relationships do not appear to have greatly skewed the distribution.

A coding scheme was developed which permitted classification of the letters into categories of type of concerns raised by the respondents and into categories of actors or institutions cited by the respondents as being pertinent to their world of state government.[6]

Table 1 reports the relationships to be examined in order to deal with the questions posed. The variables were selected to measure the impact of environmental, governmental, and political factors on these data derived from the questionnaires. Choice of these variables was made with an eye toward variety and commonality with other research on state government and politics.

[4] The study, directed by former North Carolina Governor Terry Sanford, was housed at Duke University and financed by a joint grant from the Carnegie Corporation and the Ford Foundation. The goal was to undertake a two-year study of the present condition and future potential of the American states, and to chart certain reforms or activities which might aid the states in better performing their role. See Terry Sanford, *Storm Over the States* (New York: McGraw Hill, 1967), for the report, suggestions, and activities of the study.

[6] The coding and analysis of these data were financed by a faculty research grant under the National Science Foundation "Center of Excellence" grant to the University of North Carolina at Chapel Hill.

[5] The questionnaires by theme and response rate were as follows:

Theme	Date Sent	No. of Responses	Governors
Constraints on the governor	October 1965	41	37
The state's role in the antipoverty program	October 1965	33	7
Comprehensive planning in state government	December 1965	47	12
Budgeting in state government–the governor and the agencies	January 1966	40	1
The role of boards and commissions in administration	February 1966	36	15
State revenues	March 1966	32	4
Urban affairs	April 1966	30	10
Interstate relations	July 1966	18	8
The governor and the transition	December 1966	29	26
Personnel systems	February 1967	28	16
		334	136

TABLE 1. Variables and Relationships to Be Investigated

A. Environment	D. Questionnaire Response	E. Concerns
1. Region[a]	1. Rate of return	1. Administrative
2. Population level[b]	2. Position of respondent–	2. Environmental
3. Level of urbanization[c]	governor/bureaucrat	3. Fiscal
4. Level of education[d]		4. Intergovernmental
		5. Legal
B. Politics and Government		6. Legislative
5. Level of party competition[e]		7. Political
6. Party of governor[f]		8. Social
7. Gubernatorial power[g]		9. Other
8. Size of governor's staff[h]		
9. Size of state bureaucracy[i]		F. Actors/Institutions
		1. Federal
C. Output Level[j]		2. State
10. State revenues		3. Local
11. State expenditures		4. Other actors
12. State and local revenues		5. Miscellaneous institutions
13. State and local expenditures		

[a]The states were assigned on the basis of the U.S. Bureau of Census regional criteria, with but one modification—moving Delaware from the South to the Northeast. This regional delineation has produced the most effective analytic results on certain questions of any others in current usage. See Thad L. Beyle and William Flanigan, "Comparative Regional Analysis of Partisanship in the United States," paper delivered at the 1970 Annual Meeting of the American Political Science Association, Los Angeles, California, September 8-12, 1970.

Region is employed in this study not as an explanatory variable, but for heuristic purposes. We are unwilling to accept any argument that region somehow causes variation, but we are willing to use regional data to attempt to identify possible causal factors (or interactions of factors) associated with regions. The states by region are as follows:

    Northeast (10)—Connecticut, Delaware, Maine, Massachusetts, New Hampshire, New Jersey, New York, Pennsylvania, Rhode Island, and Vermont.

    North central (12)—Illinois, Indiana, Iowa, Kansas, Michigan, Minnesota, Missouri, Nebraska, North Dakota, Ohio, South Dakota, and Wisconsin.

    South (15)—Alabama, Arkansas, Florida, Georgia, Kentucky, Louisiana, Maryland, Mississippi, North Carolina, Oklahoma, South Carolina, Tennessee, Texas, Virginia, and West Virginia.

    West (13)—Alaska, Arizona, California, Colorado, Hawaii, Idaho, Montana, Nevada, New Mexico, Oregon, Utah, Washington, and Wyoming.

[b]This measure was derived from U.S. Bureau of the Census, *Current Population Report*, No. 380 (Washington, D.C.: U.S. Government Printing Office, 1968), p. 25. Estimates as of July, 1967.

[c]This measure was derived from U.S. Bureau of the Census, *1960 Census of Population*, Vol. I, *Characteristics of Population* (Washington, D.C.: U.S. Government Printing Office, 1961).

[d]This measure was derived from U.S. Bureau of the Census, *Statistical Abstract of the United States: 1960* (81st edition.) (Washington, D.C.: U.S. Government Printing Office, 1960), p. 115.

[e]This measure was derived from Lester W. Milbrath, "Political Participation in the States," in Herbert Jacob and Kenneth N. Vines, (eds.) *op. cit.*, p. 40.

[f]This measure was derived from *World Almanac, 1967*, (New York: Newspaper Enterprise Association, Inc., 1966) p. 109.

[g]This measure was derived from Joseph A. Schlesinger "The Politics of the Executive," in Herbert Jacob and Kenneth N. Vines, (eds.) *op. cit.*, p. 229 and Thad L. Beyle, "Gubernatorial Power: A View from the Governor's Chair," *Public Administration Review*, Vol. 28 (November/December 1968), pp. 342-344.

[h]This measure derived from Donald P. Sprengel, *Gubernatorial Staffs* (Iowa City: Institute of Public Affairs, University of Iowa, 1969).

[i]This measure was derived from U.S. Bureau of the Census, *Public Employment in 1966* (Washington, D.C.: U.S. Government Printing Office, 1967), p. 11, standardized by level of population in state.

[j]This measure derived from U.S. Bureau of the Census, *Government Finances in 1965-66* (Washington, D.C.: Government Printing Office, 1967).

THE CONCERNS

Table 2 suggests that administrative, fiscal, and intergovernmental concerns are uppermost in the minds of both governors and bureaucrats. These concerns are expressed in a majority of letters from both types of respondents. Conversely, both governors and bureaucrats rarely express social or environmental concerns; in fewer than one letter

TABLE 2. Concerns of State Government Officials

	Governor		Bureaucrat		Difference		Total Sample	
					Governor higher	Bureaucrat higher		
	N	%	N	%			N	%
	104	76.5	173	87.4		10.9[a]	227	82.9
	98	72.1	167	84.3		12.2[a]	265	79.3
intergovernmental	72	52.9	136	68.7		15.8[a]	208	62.3
Legal	49	36.0	65	32.8	3.2		114	34.1
Legislative	46	33.8	56	28.3	5.5		102	30.5
Other	55	40.4	40	20.2	20.2[b]		95	28.4
Political	52	38.2	29	14.6	23.6[c]		81	24.3
Social	21	15.4	37	18.7		3.3	58	17.4
Environment	15	11.0	28	14.1		3.1	43	12.9
	136	100.0	198	100.0			334	100.0

[a]Significant at .01.

[b]Significant at .001.

All others are not significant.

[c]The percentages in these columns indicate which respondents mentioned a particular concern at higher levels, i.e., whether it was the governors or the bureaucrats who mentioned it at a higher rate.

in five are these newsworthy concerns mentioned. The conclusion is inescapable that comparatively mundane questions of administration, finances, and intergovernmental relations occupy the attention of state government elites to the relative exclusion of the more glamorous social and environmental concerns. The problems of maintaining the operation of state government predominate.[7]

Although the rankings of concerns are almost identical for governors and bureaucrats (Spearman's $\rho = .817$), there are significant differences in the degree of attention accorded to individual items. Not surprisingly, bureaucrats do pay more attention to administrative, fiscal, and intergovernmental matters than do governors; and governors are more than twice as likely than bureaucrats to mention political concerns. This may suggest that bureaucrats approach problems with a wholesome idealism, seeking solutions without regard to political pressures; or this may suggest a bureaucratic political naïveté sometimes dooming beneficial policies. Regardless of whether one favors a politically attuned bureaucracy, the finding remains that state bureaucrats currently are less concerned with parties, political pressures, and the like than are the governors.

Neither governors nor bureaucrats express much interest for social and environmental matters. Perhaps government elites have little opportunity actually to select issues to ponder, but must devote themselves predominantly to issues thrust upon them, issues of the day-to-day operation of the government. This may help to explain why social and environmental problems seem to be ignored until they reach crisis proportions, why governors seem to lose popular appeal during their terms of office just by being governor,[8] and why 13 incumbent governors were defeated in the 1970 primaries and general election.[9]

Table 3 reports the relationships between the nature of the governors' concerns and various state environment and political variables. Similar relations for bureaucrats are not reported because only 6 of 108 relations are significant at the .05 level for bureaucrats; this is precisely the number

[7]We are aware of the temporal nature of these data, as the letters were written in the mid-1960s. Undoubtedly, environmental concerns should be of greater importance now in the 1970s with all the recent activity and publicity. But for social concerns, certainly the mid-1960s were the height of "official" interest and action by governments at all levels as the antipoverty programs, aid-to-education, the civil rights movement, and the beginnings of civil unrest in our cities all dominated our domestic governmental agenda at one point or another during this period.

[8]This loss of popularity seems analogous to that suffered by the President. See John E. Mueller, "Presidential Popularity from Truman to Johnson," *American Political Science Review*, Vol. 64 (March 1970), pp. 18–34.

[9]See, particularly, the discussions of this point in the articles earlier in the book by James Clotfelter and William Hamilton, Gerald Pomper, and Stephen Turett.

TABLE 3. Concerns of Governors, by Independent Variables[a]

Independent Variables:	Administrative	Fiscal	Intergovernmental	Legislative	Political	Social	Environmental	Legal	Other
					Concerns				
Region		16.066			9.3572				
Chi square (3 df)		<.01			<.05				
Level of significance						.			
Population level						.217			
Urbanization						.146			
Education									197
Party competition	−.157	−.301			−.168				
Party of governor									
Chi square (1 df)								4.883	
Level of significance								<.05	
Gubernatorial power									.148
Size of governors' staff						.161			
Size of bureaucracy						−.140			.153
State revenues									
State expenditures									
State/local revenues	.149						.148		
State/local expenditures							.134		.208

[a]Figures are Kendall's τ values except for the relationship with the variables "region" and "party of governor" which are χ^2 as indicated. All relationships significant at the .05 level.

predicted if the data were random. Bureaucrats express similar concerns; differences among states in urbanization, party competition, government expenditures, and other political and social variables do not seem to affect bureaucratic concerns.

Governors, however, do tend to hold different concerns dependent upon state characteristics. Perhaps the elective nature of the office does predispose governors toward a sensitivity to the world outside their offices.

The governors in more populated and highly urbanized states appear to be more aware of social problems. Similarly, governors in states with higher state and local government revenues and expenditures appear to be more aware of environmental matters. However, there is a negative relationship between party competition and fiscal concerns: As party competition increases, which is related to larger populations and greater urbanization in a state,[10] the governors are significantly less likely to raise fiscal problems—highly volatile

[10]Donald P. Sprengel, *Gubernatorial Staffs* (Iowa City: Institute of Public Affairs, University of Iowa, 1969), pp. 34–36 and Elmer Cornwell *et al.*, "Professional Staff for Governors' Office Subject of Questionnaire," *Newsletter of the Bureau of Governmental Research*, University of Rhode Island, September 1968.

political issues. And, higher party competition is negatively related to the governors' lack of emphasis on administrative or political problems. Perhaps what is happening here is that governors are pushed by the growth level of the state into considering social problems, among others. Yet, increasing party competition encourages governors to avoid difficult administrative and fiscal questions where solutions to the social problems may lie.

Regional variations occur as southern governors are less likely to cite fiscal and political concerns than are their counterparts, especially in the Northeast. Much of this regional variation merely reflects the lower levels of party competition in the South.

ACTORS AND INSTITUTIONS

As was true in the case of their interests and concerns, governors and bureaucrats are very similar in their relative rankings of actors and institutions mentioned in the letters ($\rho = .806$). Table 4 reports that the governor and staff is the most frequently mentioned actor for both governors and bureaucrats. The fact that over 80 percent of letters mentioned the governor illustrates the overwhelming awareness which state elites seem to have of the governor and his/her staff. The pres-

	By governors		By bureaucrats		Difference		Total	
	N	%	N	%	Gover. higher	Bureaucrat higher	N	%
Actor/Institution	136	100	198	100			334	100
Federal	73	53.7	141	71.2		17.5c	214	64.1
President	8	5.9	2	1.0	4.9b		10	3.0
Congress	10	7.4	10	5.0	2.4		20	6.0
Supreme Court	6	4.4	2	1.0	3.4a		8	2.4
Specific federal agencies	34	25.0	41	20.7	4.3		75	22.5
Other federal	69	50.7	136	63.6		12.9b	205	61.3
State	129	94.9	181	91.4	3.5		310	92.8
Governor and staff	122	89.7	157	79.3	10.4b		279	83.5
Legislature	84	61.8	114	57.6	4.2		198	59.3
Dept. of administration	24	17.6	43	21.7		4.1	67	20.1
Budget office	16	11.8	53	26.8		15.0c	69	20.6
Planning office	13	9.6	32	16.2		6.6a	45	13.5
Other departments	83	61.0	120	60.6	0.4		203	60.8
Local	32	23.5	82	41.4		17.9c	114	34.1
Mayor	0	0.0	4	2.0		2.0a	4	1.2
Other local	32	23.5	81	40.9		17.4c	113	33.8
Extra- or intergovernmental	72	52.9	119	60.1		7.2	191	57.2
Interest groups	17	12.5	58	29.3		16.8c	75	22.5
Universities	13	9.6	50	25.3		15.7c	63	18.8
Consultants	12	8.8	43	21.7		12.9b	55	16.5
Political party	34	25.0	20	10.1	14.9c		54	16.2
Intergovernmental agency	17	12.5	21	10.6	1.9		38	11.4
Professional association	1	0.7	8	4.0		3.3a	9	2.7
Miscellaneous institutions	78	57.4	114	57.6		0.2	192	57.5
Other states	50	36.8	60	30.3	6.5		110	32.6
Reports	28	20.6	55	27.8		7.2	83	24.9
Constitution and statutes	34	25.0	34	17.2	7.8		68	20.3

aSig. at .05.
bSig. at .01.
cSig. at .001.
All others are not significant.

ence of the executive leader permeates discussion of all ten topics.

The second most frequently mentioned actor or institution is labeled "Other Federal," reflecting general references to the national government which could not be assigned to any specific agency or actor. Over half of the governors and almost three-fourths of the bureaucrats mentioned a federal actor or institution at least once. As actors or institutions at the local level were mentioned only half as frequently as those at the national level, state elites do seem to focus more toward Washington than toward cities, towns, and counties.

But the principal focus of state elites is on other state actors and institutions. The importance of governor and staff as the most frequently mentioned actor has already been indicated. Table 4 shows that other state institutions are also frequently mentioned. Majorities of letters of both governors and bureaucrats mentioned the state legislature; one in five letters cited the major gubernatorial management aids, departments of administration, or budget offices; and even the state planning office was mentioned in considerable numbers (9.6 percent of governors; 16.2 percent of bureaucrats). However, the tendency of bureaucrats to cite budget and planning offices more often than do governors corroborates earlier findings of this paper concerning the relatively more "political" nature of governors' perceptions, or at a minimum the more "administrative" nature of the bureaucrats' perceptions.

In addition to the high frequency of mentions of actors and institutions in one's own state, governors and bureaucrats both mentioned the experiences of other states in one-third of the letters. This tends to substantiate further the findings of Jack Walker concerning the patterns of communicating innovations through the states.[11]

The pattern of governors being more concerned with political institutions than are bureaucrats is clearly indicated by the differences in mentioning extragovernmental institutions. Bureaucrats are more likely to note interest groups, universities, consultants, and professional associations as relevant in dealing with the open-ended questions. Governors are over twice as likely to mention political parties than are bureaucrats. Perhaps the bureaucrat's world—enmeshed in interest groups, universities, consultants, and the planning and budget offices and in anticipating federal behavior—is really a world no less political than that of the governor. The bureaucrat's world is of the slightly different politics of the specialist.

Turning to the impact of environmental and political variables upon the behavior of the respondents, the finding is that the variables presented in Table 1 fail entirely to account for variation in actors and institutions mentioned. Although there is a great deal of variance in response frequencies, this variance is not correlated with any of the 13 variables.

CONCLUSIONS

This study has found that the speech-making world in which political, social, and environmental concerns predominate does not reflect the in-office world of state elites, a world in which administrative, fiscal, and intergovernmental concerns predominate. Similary, the rostrum world in which the President, Supreme Court Justices, Congress, and mayors are often mentioned is replaced by an in-office world of state legislators and state bureaus. The task of maintaining the functioning of

the government seems to retain the attention of both governors and bureaucrats.

This study has also found that there are significant differences in how state elites, as defined by their roles, do perceive their world of government and politics. Governors, vis-à-vis bureaucrats, are more likely to express political concerns and are more likely to mention federal political officials and political parties. Bureaucrats, conversely, are disproportionately likely to emphasize the more mundane concerns of government (administrative, fiscal, and intergovernmental) and to mention the state budget and planning offices, local officials, interest groups, professional associations, universities, and consultants.

Finally, economic and environmental variables commonly utilized in the more statistically based studies of state public policy explain little of the variation in state elite perceptions. A political variable, party competition, showed the strongest correlations, and elite roles, and pressures associated with particular elite roles, enhanced our understanding of variations in elite perceptions. This should not denigrate the many accomplishments of studies examining relations suggested by the Easton model,[12] but merely to suggest again that theoretically relevant areas of research, such as personality, structural demands, and roles, appear to warrant greater attention than they are currently receiving in the research in state government and politics.

[12] David Easton, *A Framework for Political Analysis* (Englewood Cliffs, N.J.: Prentice-Hall, 1965), or, more briefly, David Easton, "An Approach to the Analysis of Political Systems," *World Politics*, Vol. 9 (1957), pp. 383–400.

EXECUTIVE LEADERSHIP IN STATE ADMINISTRATION
Deil S. Wright

The issue of executive leadership in state and local government has been the fulcrum of debate among academicians and the focus of power struggles among public officials for most of the twentieth century. From the distant days of Seth Low and

Source: Reprinted from "Executive Leadership in State Administration," *Midwest Journal of Political Science*, Vol. 11, No. 1 (February 1967), pp. 1–26, by Deil S. Wright by permission of Wayne State University Press.

[11] Jack L. Walker, "The Diffusion of Innovations among the American States," *American Political Science Review*, Vol. 63 (September 1969), pp. 880–899.

Frank Lowden to latest state or local reorganization study commission the theme has remained essentially the same—concentrate power in the chief executive and hold him responsible! The standard solution to this "problem" has been the prescription of more power for the executive, although there have been noted and articulate dissents from this prognosis.[1] Herbert Kaufman has termed "executive leadership" one of the three doctrines permeating the history of public administration in the United States.[2] The other two doctrines, representativeness and neutral competence, Kaufman posits as preceding and overlaying the executive leadership doctrine. He also urges that the last mentioned doctrine had been in sharp conflict with neutral competence in recent years and is currently dominant, at least among political scientists.

In addition to Kaufman's analysis there is a much larger body of literature on state government that describes the primacy of the governor in state politics and administration. Writing in the late 1930s, Leslie Lipson argued that the governor's role had evolved "from figurehead to leader."[3] A decade ago Coleman Ransone completed a broad-ranging interview-based study of American governors that both updated Lipson's analysis and elaborated more broadly the governor's role in state political systems.[4] More recently the position of the governor has been appraised in short critical discussions. Malcolm Jewell expresses cautious optimism about the present and future

abilities of the governor to marshal the resources and manage the political complexities of state government in meeting popular demands and expectations.[5] Another observer, Joseph Schlesinger, is not as optimistic. He contends that the position of the governor, as well as the entire apparatus of state government, is one of "uncertainty" and "indeterminacy." These conditions, he suggests, can be traced to the "intermediary and ambiguous role of the state in the American political system."[6]

The preceding references are illustrative of the few critical and systematic efforts analyzing the governor's role in state government. They are valuable and insightful within their defined limits. We still lack, however, a deeper grasp of the relationship between the chief executive and the administrative process at the state level. One approach to this relationship is from the governor's standpoint; it is best implemented by interviewing governors, as Ransone did in his study. An alternative approach to studying this relationship is to survey top state administrators. This latter approach, employing a mailed questionnaire, was the one adopted to secure data reported and interpreted in this article. A brief discussion of the methodological aspects of the study appear as an appendix. Two additional comments are required here: (1) These data on the attitudes of 933 department and agency heads from all 50 states constitute a large and representative cross-section of top-echelon administrators at the state level, and (2) this discussion of executive leadership and state administration is only one of several major dimensions encompassed by the research.[7]

POLITICAL RELATIONSHIPS AND ADMINISTRATION

It is axiomatic that public administration proceeds within a political setting. This is particularly true at the state level. Here the governor and the legislature are the formal institutions of political control.

[1] F. W. Coker, "Dogmas of Administrative Reform: As Exemplified in the Recent Reorganization in Ohio," *American Political Science Review*, Vol. 16, No. 3 (August 1922), pp. 399–411, A. C. Millspaugh, "Democracy and Administrative Organization," in John M. Mathews and James Hart (Eds.), *Essays in Political Science in Honor of Westel Woodbury Willoughby* (Baltimore: Johns Hopkins Press, 1937); and Charles S. Hyneman, "Administrative Reorganization: An Adventure into Science and Theology," *Journal of Politics*, Vol. 1, No. 1 (February 1939), pp. 62–75.

[2] Herbert Kaufman, "Emerging Conflicts in the Doctrines of Public Administration," *American Political Science Review*, Vol. 50, No. 4 (December 1956), pp. 1057–1073; and *Politics and Policies in State and Local Governments* (Englewood Cliffs, New Jersey: Prentice-Hall, 1963), pp. 35–44.

[3] Leslie Lipson, *The American Governor; From Figurehead to Leader* (Chicago: University of Chicago Press, 1939), 282 pp.

[4] Coleman B. Ransone, Jr., *The Office of Governor in the United States* (University of Alabama Press, 1956), 417 pp.

[5] Malcolm Jewell, "State Decision-Making: The Governor Revisted," paper presented at the 1963 annual meeting of the American Political Science Association, New York City, September 4–7, 1963.

[6] Joseph A. Schlesinger, "The Politics of the Executive," in Herbert Jacob and Kenneth Vines (Eds.), *Politics in the American States: A Comparative Analysis* (Boston: Little, Brown, 1965), p. 208.

[7] A descriptive monograph covering most aspects of the study is in preparation and is planned for future publication.

To assess the respective roles and relationships of these two political actors to the administrative process we asked questions designed to measure the attitudes of state administrators toward these authoritative institutions. One question asked the agency head to judge which of these political actors, the governor or the legislature, exercised the greater control over the affairs of his department or agency. Money is an important means to the accomplishment of agency goals. A second question therefore inquired about the administrator's views on who had the greater tendency to cut agency budget requests, the legislature or the governor. We sought an additional and more generalized measure of the administrator's evaluation of gubernatorial versus legislative support of agency goals. Here we simply asked whether the governor or the legislature was more sympathetic to the aims and purposes of the administrator's agency. These three questions were intended to demark the perceptions of political controls by the state administrators.

The summary of marginal responses to these questions is provided in Table 1. The data relevant to generalized control and budget reduction reveal the lesser role of the governor in comparison with the legislature vis-à-vis state administration. Thirty-two percent of the agency heads felt that the governor exercised greater control; 25 percent thought that the governor tended to be more restrictive than the legislature on budget requests. The respective percentages responding in terms of greater legislative control and legislative budget reduction were 44 and 60 percent.

The primacy of the legislature in controlling administration at the state level has many ramifications and raises several questions. Since legislatures in most states meet only biennially, it is perhaps surprising to note the degree to which their noncontinuous impact reverberates through the administrative establishment. One might expect the continuity of the governorship contrasted with the discontinuous convening of the legislature to produce a more significant role for the state's chief executive than that accorded him in these findings.

It may be, however, that our notion of the discontinuous role of state legislatures with respect to the administrative process is a mistaken one. Legislative interim committees of a research or investigative nature, plus the very real possibility of continuous legislative oversight by one or a few

TABLE 1. Attitudes of American State Executives on Political Relationships[a]

	Percentages[b] (N = 933)
Who exercises greater control over your agency's affairs?	
Governor	32
Each about the same	22
Legislature	44
Other and N.A.	2
	100
Who has the greater tendency to reduce budget requests?	
Governor	25
Legislature	60
Other and N.A.	15
	100
Who is more sympathetic to the goals of your agency?	
Governor	55
Each about the same	14
Legislature	20
Other and N.A.	11
	100
What type of control do you prefer?	
Governor	42
Independent commission	28
Legislature	24
Other and N.A.	5
	100

[a]For the source of data and the survey instrument containing the precise wording of the questions see Deil S. Wright and Richard L. McAnaw, "American State Administrators: Study Code and Marginal Tabulations for the State Administrative Officials' Questionnaire" (Iowa City, Iowa: Department of Political Science and Institute of Public Affairs, January, 1965), mimeographed, 40 pp.

[b]Tabled percentages throughout this article may not add to 100 because of rounding.

important legislators, may be occuring to such an extent that our results accurately reflect continuous rather than discontinuous legislative control of state administration. Numerous observers have emphasized that individual congressmen and congressional committees are wont to tell administrators what to do in specific instances. The same pervasive legislative interest in administration is evidently present in several, if not most states as well as at the national level.[8]

[8]It was interesting to note that on a regional basis more administrators from the midwest reported greater legislative control than administrators in other regions, i.e.,

It is also possible that these results may reflect a particular response set on the part of state administrators. A substantial proportion (more than one fourth) of the responding administrators had legal training. This gives a strong law-oriented cast to our group of state executives. This law-oriented focus may have prompted many of our respondents to interpret the question of control largely in legal terms rather than in political or policy terms. Under such conditions the legislature, as law-giver, would most likely occupy a position of primacy.

The preceding qualification is negated to some extent by responses to the budget reduction question. Finances are central to program levels and policy directions and are less likely to be viewed in terms of law-oriented controls or anticipated negative reactions. In this sphere the legislature appears to exercise an even larger restrictive and containment role over state administration than on the dimension of generalized control.

Advocates of gubernatorial executive leadership will not be overjoyed by the results reported here. Since no trend data exist on gubernatorial versus legislative control we cannot document the effects of reorganizations designed to strengthen the position of the governor over state administration. We cannot, for example, confirm nor contradict Lipson's judgment of trends "from figurehead to leadership." But our findings a quarter-century after Lipson's thesis was advanced are inconsistent with his contention so far as the governor's present-day role as *administrative* chief. The governor apparently is not viewed as the primary power-wielder over state administrators.

We have attempted to delineate the perceptions of actual control over administration in state government. Perceptions of actual control may be usefully distinguished from other relational conditions and circumstances. Some of these other circumstances are:

1. perceptions concerning a positive orientation toward agency goals by governor and legislature in contradistinction to the negative implications of control and budget reduction;

2. preferred alternative conditions of control in contrast to the existing perceptions of control; and

3. objective, researcher-defined conditions of actual control contrasted with the subjective, administrator-perceived conditions of control.

Each of these circumstances deserves discussion and comment.

A measure of the political basis for positive orientations toward agency goals was obtained by asking the state executives: "Who do you feel is the more sympathetic to the aims and purposes of your agency or department? ( ) Governor ( ) Legislature." The tabulation of responses to this question also appears in Table 1. State administrators find the chief institutional basis of support for their program goals in the office of the governor. Over half of the executives believe that the governor is more sympathetic to their agency's goals; only one-fifth report that the legislature is more inclined than the governor to share their agency's aims and purposes. This finding documents the widespread and impressionistically held belief that the governor is the primary institutional means through which new or expanded state programs are advanced, advocated, and accepted. The data underscore the policy leadership role of the governor and reveal the specialized significance of the governor's position with respect to the administrative establishment. This leadership role persists despite the prior finding that from a control standpoint the governor's influence is exceeded by that of the legislature.

What is the relationship between perceptions of control and views concerning positive support? Do administrators who perceive the governor as the primary control agent over their operations also find him more supportive than the legislature of their agency's goals? What are the goal support views of administrators who felt they were under the primary control of the legislature? The tabulation presented in Table 2 reveals a strong association between the support and control variables.

Those under gubernatorial control obtain their chief support from that source. Of those under legislative domination, however, a majority obtain primary support from the governor. A similar pattern exists among administrators in the "each about the same" category. It seems evident that the administrators in these two majority categories are those who experience most acutely the vice-

---

53 percent contrasted with approximately 40 percent in the three other regions. The limited number of respondents from any one state (ranging from 7 to 27) makes individual state-by-state comparisons and conclusions hazardous at best.

TABLE 2. Control over Agency Affairs by Sympathy for Agency Goals, American State Executives

Agency Goals Greater Sympathy for	Greater Control over Agency Affairs		
	Governor	Each about the same	Legislature
	(percentages; number of cases in parentheses)		
Governor	81	52	52
Each about the same	11	29	13
Legislature	8	19	35
Total	100 (276)	100 (183)	100 (359)

grip in which our traditional separation of powers locks most top-level administrators. To borrow a phrase from voting studies, these are the "cross-pressured" administrators.

Perceptions of actual control, we suggested, could be distinguished from conditions of control preferred or desired by state agency chiefs. Under what control conditions or under whose primary influence would state executives prefer to operate? We tapped this attitude dimension by means of the following question: "If your state's governmental structure were to be reorganized and you were able to choose who should exercise the greater control over your agency, which of the following would you choose? ( ) Governor; ( ) Legislature; ( ) Independent Commission."

We had a special reason for posing the problem in this particular manner. Our preceding questions were presented in terms of legislative versus governor influence. In probing preferred control conditions we felt it necessary to offer the respondents a third alternative, independence of either primary legislative or primary gubernatorial control. We were cognizant of the strong centrifugal forces present in government agencies generally and at the state level in particular. We therefore included the alternative "Independent Commission" as one of the three institutional sources of control over the state administrator and as an indicator of the pressures for independence at the state level. In more general terms this option gave the respondent an opportunity to "take administration out of politics." Indeed, this motive force behind the neutral competence school was, as Kaufman has indicated, chiefly responsible for the proliferation of independent boards and commissions.[9]

The marginal responses to the preferred control question are indicated in Table 1. The most pre-

[9] Kaufman, "Emerging Conflicts . . . ," p. 1060.

ferred condition for state executives is under the primary control of the governor. While 42 percent of the executives selected this alternative, equally significant results are: (1) that less than a majority of the state administrators opted for gubernatorial control, and (2) that more than one-fourth (28 percent) preferred to function under the primary control of an independent commission. We have no standard for judging the requisite or appropriate degree of independence, if any, at the state level. But a figure in excess of one-fourth of all state agency heads favoring independence clearly identifies the extent to which there are strong centrifugal pressures fractionalizing state administration.

The sources of pressures for independence are many and varied. Interest groups, professional associations, popular election, and special methods of financing particular programs are only a few sources. We were not able to probe these and other sources of possible pressures toward independence within the limited confines of our questionnaire. It is important, however, to examine the relationships between preferred control and the other relational measures of perceived actual control, sympathy for agency goals, and budget reduction tendencies. The relationships between these variables are presented in Table 3.

Comparisons of the percentages across the rows for the governor and for the legislature categories

TABLE 3. Perceived and Preferred Political Relationships of American State Executives

Preferred Type of Control	Governor	About Equal	Legislature
	(percentages; number of cases in parentheses)		
Greater Control over Agency Affairs			
Governor	77	42	22
Independent commission	20	40	31
Legislature	3	18	47
Total	100 (294)	100 (188)	100 (394)
Greater Sympathy for Agency Goals			
Governor	58	45	14
Independent commission	28	30	31
Legislature	14	25	55
Total	100 (503)	100 (115)	100 (179)
Greater Tendency to Reduce Budget Requests			
Governor	53		42
Independent commission	27		29
Legislature	20		29
Total	100 (226)		100 (540)

in the cross-tabulations reveal exceptionally powerful associations between the first two "independent" variables and the "dependent" variable of preferred control. Only 3 percent of those presently under the primary control of the governor would prefer a shift to primary control by the legislature and 20 percent desire a change to dominance by an independent commission. The relationship is considerably attentuated in the case of the budget reduction—preferred control relationship.

Interesting and substantial defections occur among those administrators presently under the dominant influence of finding greatest goal sympathy from the legislature. About half (47 percent) of those under legislature control prefer to remain there; 22 percent indicate a desired shift to gubernatorial control while an even larger proportion, 31 percent, desire a shift to independent commission control. A similar pattern exists among administrators believing that the legislature affords greater support for agency goals. On the matter of budget reduction the shift away from the legislature is even more pronounced with only 29 percent preferring to remain under legislation control.

These data disclose powerful preferences for a shift away from legislative control at the state level. More importantly, however, these preferences for altered control do not accrue chiefly to the benefit of the governor. Rather, they are in the direction of independence from both gubernatorial and legislative control. In recognition of the governor's position as nominal head of state administration, we should acknowledge the clear majorities preferring to remain under the governor's primary control among those who find themselves currently under his primary control and among those who find him most sympathetic to their agency goals. Additionally, the governor is first choice for preferred control (1) among the administrators who perceive the governor and legislature about equal in terms of actual control and sympathy for agency goals, and (2) among administrators who find either the legislature or the governor more inclined to reduce their budget requests. In this latter instance it seems clear that the state administrator is left with almost no alternative but to opt for gubernatorial control in hopes of making the best of a bad set of circumstances. Further indica-

tion of the holding power of the governor among state administrators is disclosed by the data in Table 3. The pertinent figures are the respective percentages in the upper-left and lower-right cells of each of the three cross-tabulations: 77, 58, and 53; 47, 55, and 29. These percentages constitute the proportions appearing respectively in the governor-governor and legislature-legislature cells of the three tabulations. Two points merit comment. First, the variable most influential in orienting the administrators' attitudes in the direction of preferred control by the governor is the variable of actual control. Second, it is somewhat surprising to find approximate consistency and similarity among all but the first and last percentages, roughly in the neighborhood of 50 percent. This suggests, interestingly enough, that the retention of state administrators' allegiances (options on preferred control) is about a 50–50 proposition, with two exceptions. The first exception, the holding power of actual control by the governor, has been mentioned. The second exception, the 29 percent of those finding the legislature most restrictive on budget matters but preferring legislative control, might be called the losing power of state legislature. In other words, only this proportion of the state administrators are not disaffected or alienated from preferring legislative control by the fact that the legislature is more disposed than the governor to reduce their budget requests.

The findings outlined above suggests several provisional observations worthy of further reflection and subsequent investigation.

1. The challenges to the governor's primacy as chief executive are several and are potent insofar as state administrator's preferences are accurate measures of the challenges.
2. The lack of integration within the administrative establishment at the state level is clearly evident. Indeed, it is perhaps a misnomer to speak of *an* administrative establishment. There appear to be deep cleavages within state administration along the relational dimensions of perceived political control, fiscal control, goal congruence, and preferred types of control.
3. There are strong pressures bending administrator's preferences in the direction of independence from either primary gubernatorial or primary legislative control. The exact sources of

these pressures remain undetermined but their containment undoubtedly constitutes one of the major problems of state government today.

We might sum our findings to this point by indicating that Schlesinger's hypothesis about the "indeterminacy" of state government appears to be amply confirmed as far as state administration is concerned. This indeterminacy is perhaps best characterized in the author's words as "The unclear function of state administration, its varied character, and its relative freedom [and apparent desire] from public reckoning . . ."[10]

FORMAL STRUCTURE AND ADMINISTRATION

Do the state administrator's perceptions of control correspond closely with the degree of formal influence exerted by the governor on state administration? For objective indicators of the formal influence of the governor we have utilized two measures. One is the appointive powers of the governor; the other is an overall index of the formal power position of the governor developed by Joseph Schlesinger.[11] The former variable is based on the method of appointment indicated by the state administrator in his response to our questionnaire. Schlesinger's index is based on four components of the governor's position—tenure potential and appointment, budgetary, and veto powers. Schlesinger allocated a range of points for each of these four power dimensions and derived an index of governor's powers ranging from 19 (in New York) down to 7 (in Mississippi, North Dakota, South Carolina, and Texas). This rank-order index is used to relate the perceptions of control by state administrators to the governor's formal power position. In other words, we are testing the association between objective and subjective measures of control. (See Table 4.)

Are the formal powers of the governor positively associated with administrators' perceptions of gu-

[10]Schlesinger, *op. cit.*, p. 208.

[11]Schlesinger, *op. cit.*, pp. 217–229.

TABLE 4. Index of Formal Powers of State Governors[a] and Perceived and Preferred Political Relationships of American State Executives

	Formal Powers of the Governor			
	Strong	Moderate	Weak	Very weak
		(percentage; number of cases in parentheses)		
Greater Control Over Agency Affairs				
Governor	37	41	25	21
Each about the same	28	21	23	16
Legislature	35	38	52	63
Total	100 (261)	100 (194)	100 (232)	100 (184)
Greater Tendency to Reduce Budget Requests				
Governor	37	34	19	22
Legislature	63	66	81	78
Total	100 (227)	100 (164)	100 (211)	100 (157)
Sympathy for Agency Goals				
Governor	64	65	66	50
Each about the same	17	12	15	19
Legislature	19	24	19	31
Total	100 (227)	100 (178)	100 (219)	100 (163)
Preferred Type of Control				
Governor	49	49	41	29
Commission	27	29	33	32
Legislature	23	22	26	39
Total	100 (252)	100 (190)	100 (220)	100 (182)

[a]Source: Joseph A. Schlesinger, "The Politics of the Executive," in Herbert Jacob and Kenneth Vines (Eds.), *Politics in the American States* (Boston: Little, Brown 1965), pp. 217–229.

bernatorial control? The answer is a qualified yes. In states where governors have stronger formal powers, administrators acknowledge somewhat greater control by governors than in states where governors are weaker. The respective percentages are 37 and 41 compared with 25 and 21. The complement to this relationship is evident from the row percentages for legislative control. As one moves from the "strong" to the "very weak" categories, the proportion of administrators reporting primary legislative control rises from 35 percent to 63 percent. These results tend to confirm the long-held contention of reformers and reorganizers that formal powers and prerogatives of a governor *do* make a significant difference so far as administrator-perceived (actual) control is concerned.

Our interpretation of the percentages should recognize the comparative, rather than the absolute nature of the inferences. This qualification is important. Examination of the percentages for executives in states where "strong" governors hold sway reveals that the competition for control over state administrators is approximately a stand-off; 37 percent of the administrators report primary control by the governor, 35 percent report control by the legislature, and 28 percent indicate that control is equally divided. Here is further empirical confirmation of dispersed influence and powerful cross-pressures within administration at the state level. In this instance, however, our data disclose the presence and potency of these patterns in a political context where governors are the most powerful in a formal sense.

If these findings withstand challenge in their own right and are further confirmed by other research we may conclude that the net effect of structural reform and reorganization at the state level has *not* been to elevate the governor as *the* master of administrative management. Rather, the effects of strengthening the governor, based on the data from states where governors are stronger, has been to give him about an even chance in competing with the legislature for influence over the courses of action taken by state administrators. In a backhanded way this finding might be construed as a basis for advancing reorganization proposals that would strengthen the weaker governors. One frequent argument against such reorganization efforts is the cry of dictatorship, the charge that a more powerful governor will monopolize state government and state administration. Our findings

show that even in states where governors are the strongest they are far from having dictatorial, monopoly, or predominant control in the eyes of top state administrators.

The associations between the formal powers of the governor and administrators' views on other political relations run generally in the expected directions. (See Table 4.) The relationships are less pronounced than in the instance of perceived control. Perhaps the most notable feature is the subordinated role of the "very weak" governors regarding preferred type of control. Only 29 percent of the department heads in states with weak governors would prefer to be under the primary control of the governor in a reorganized setting. Lack of gubernatorial power evidently breeds disaffection and/or contempt for the weak governor.

The power of appointment is a much coveted prerogative in any system of government. Its significance stems largely from the pressured element of control attaching to the appointing privilege. Is there a close association between the method of appointment of state agency heads and their perceptions of control by the governor and legislature? We should recognize, however, that 14 percent (126) of the 933 agency heads fall outside the appointment category, that is, they were popularly elected. These officials were, as one would expect, mainly secretaries of state, treasurers, auditors, and attorneys general. These elected officials directly reflect the doctrine of representativeness in public administration as that concept has been elaborated by Herbert Kaufman.[12]

Among the 807 nonelected administrators, appointment methods were varied and widely distributed. The percentages appointed by the various methods were:

Governor only	16%
Governor with senate or council consent	29
Board or commission with governor's consent	11
Board or commission without governor's consent	19
Department head	17
Other and N.A.	8
	100%

The above figures underscore the limited and extensively shared role of the governor in the ap-

[12] Kaufman, "Emerging Conflicts . . . ," pp. 1058–1059.

pointment of top state administrators. Only one-sixth are appointed by the governor acting alone.

What of the association between appointment method and the several relational dimensions discussed earlier? If the gubernatorial power of appointment were extended more widely throughout state administration would there likely be a change in the perceptions and preferences of state administrators? Our data, presented in Table 5, permit us to make observations only on a cross-sectional basis. The "appointment categories have been arranged in approximate descending order of the governor's involvement in the appointment process, from appointment by the governor only to popular election of the administrative official.[13]

---

[13]Administrators appointed by department heads are omitted from this discussion since we were unable to ascertain the precise role of the governor in their appointment. The reason for the appearance of this type of appointment method—department head—in a survey of top state "agency heads" is the inconsistent administrative organizational pattern among the states. For example, in some states mental health is a separate department in its

There is a marked and consistent relationship between the manner in which a state administrator obtains his position and his perceptions of governor versus legislative control. The association is strong and positive between the degree of gubernatorial participation in appointment and perceived gubernatorial control. The more the governor is involved, the more he is perceived as having control; the less he is involved, the less he is perceived as having control. The extreme is reached with popular election. Only 9 percent of the elected administrators view the governor as having more control than the legislature over their agency's affairs. Proponents of the short ballot and of strengthening the appointive powers of the governor were "right" from the standpoint of their objectives and proposed reforms. The method of appointment does make a significant difference regarding executive leadership. In contrast to fiscal reforms, however, broadening the personnel (appointment)

---

own right but in many others it is organizationally located with a state health department and the mental health director is appointed by the health department head.

TABLE 5. Appointment Method and Perceived and Preferred Political Relationships of American State Executives

	Appointment Method				
	Governor alone	Governor with advice and consent	Board with governor's consent	Board without governor's consent	Popularly elected
	(percentages; number of cases in parentheses)				
Greater Control Over Agency Affairs					
Governor	57	41	28	15	9
Each about the same	18	26	30	30	11
Legislature	25	33	42	55	80
	100 (131)	100 (230)	100 (89)	100 (149)	100 (124)
Greater Tendency to Reduce Budget Requests					
Governor	35	29	37	24	17
Legislature	65	71	63	76	83
	100 (115)	100 (204)	100 (78)	100 (123)	100 (111)
Sympathy for Agency Goals					
Governor	80	70	66	58	33
Each about the same	16	18	16	18	15
Legislature	4	12	18	24	51
	100 (123)	100 (213)	100 (80)	100 (135)	100 (105)
Preferred Type of Control					
Governor	68	67	31	27	18
Commission	20	17	47	53	18
Legislature	13	16	22	20	65
	100 (126)	100 (227)	100 (87)	100 (144)	100 (114)

powers of the governor has been far more difficult to accomplish. The above findings reveal this limited progress and also emphasize the significance of the personnel dimension for executive leadership at the state level. A scanning of the percentages for the budget reduction and agency goal support variables tends to confirm the preceding observations. The positive associations between appointment method and gubernatorial influence on these two variables exist but are much less sharp and consistent, especially if elected officials are not considered. Varying appointment methods produce some differences in administrator's perceptions of the governor vis-à-vis the legislature on budget reduction and goal sympathy. But the variations, while substantial, are not as pronounced as in the case of the control dimension.

Large differences do appear, however, when preferred control is tabulated by appointment method. These differences can be observed in the final set of percentages in Table 5. Preference for gubernatorial control is, as expected, most divergent between the administrators who are popularly elected and those who are appointed by the governor alone or by him with senatorial consent. But a wide difference also exists between administrators in these latter two categories and those who are appointed by a board or commission (with or without the governor's consent). Less than one-third of the board-appointed administrators would prefer gubernatorial control whereas two-thirds of those appointed in some manner by the governor prefer gubernatorial control. The most popular option among the board-appointed agency heads is for primary control by an independent commission. Approximately half elect this alternative.

In broad terms these data can be meaningfully interpreted in the context of Kaufman's conflicting doctrines in public administration. Popular election at the state level enshrines the doctrine of "representativeness" for the most part in constitutional prescriptions. It is interesting to note how closely aligned and oriented these elected administrators are to the legislative body. The second sense in which Kaufman used representativeness—legislative supremacy over administration—is pointedly in evidence among these elected administrators. From the standpoint of executive leadership and popular election one is reminded of Max Weber's observation that if officials are elected instead of appointed discipline and control will be greatly weakened.[14]

Kaufman's doctrine of neutral competence is represented structurally by the appointive process involving boards and commissions. This institutionalized method of "taking administration out of politics" has notable consequences for the perceptions (and presumably conduct) of state administrators. Its most outstanding result is an undercutting of executive leadership and a strong preference to maintain this special organizational status. About one half of those administrators appointed by a board or commission prefer primary control over their agency's affairs by this institutional arrangement. The close proximity of the percentage distributions for board-appointed administrators appointed with and without gubernatorial consent suggests a further observation. The institutional protection and insulation of a board or commission effectively prevents the governor from gaining the administrator's loyalties (preferred control) although gubernatorial consent to a board appointment does appear to make some difference in perceived actual control, i.e., 28 compared with 15 percent.[15]

PUBLIC POLICY, POLITICAL RELATIONSHIPS, AND ADMINISTRATION

Today the persistent policy issues in public administration at all levels of government are between the pressures for program expansion versus the inertia toward the status quo. It therefore seemed desirable to probe the attitudes of state department heads toward the expansion of state programs and services. This was accomplished by using two questions, one set in the context of overall expansion of state services, the other in the context of expanding the administrator's own agency's services and programs. If an administrator favored some expansion, that is, he answered yes to the lead question, a follow-up probe inquired about the preferred extent or degree of expansion. Alternatives ranged from "0–5 percent" expansion

[14] Max Weber, *The Theory of Social and Economic Organization*, translated by M. Henderson and T. Parsons (New York: The Free Press, 1947), p. 335.

[15] For one of the few extended discussions of board and commission "independence" at the state level see James W. Fesler, *The Independence of State Regulatory Agencies* (Chicago: Public Administration Service, 1942), 72 pp.

to "more than 15 percent" expansion. Table 6 presents a tabulation of the responses to the two questions and probes.

State executives are evidently disposed to respond in favor of enlarging their own programs and those of state government generally. Such views do not approach unanimity, however, since rather significant proportions (24 and 30 percent respectively) do not favor any expansion of their own or their state's programs.[16]

What relationship exists between the program expansion preferences of administrators and their perceptions of control by the governor and legislature? The initial set of percentages in Table 7 provides the basis for observing that there is no apparent association. Nearly equal proportions of these under gubernatorial and legislative control are inclined against any expansion; a like situation is present in the categories favoring each of the varying degrees of program expansion. In other words, there is no concentration of sentiment for program expansion within a grouping of state executives that view themselves under the primary control of either the legislature or the governor.

There is no consequential variation in program expansion attitudes according to whether the governor or legislature is more disposed to reduce budget requests. Administrators' preferences for expanding their programs are not biased along lines of economy-minded governors or legislatures.

When we shift our focus from the dimension of actual control and examine executives' judgments

[16] A comparison of *desired* expansions by state executives with *actual* expansions of agency expenditures at the federal level is possible. Of the state executives who responded yes to the expansion question about two-thirds favored expansion of their own programs and expenditures by 10 percent or more. At the federal level nearly one half of the 444 cases examined by Aaron Wildavsky (37 domestic agencies over a 12 year span) showed appropriation increases of more than 10 percent in a single year. See, Aaron Wildavsky, *The Politics of the Budgeting Process* (Boston: 1964), p. 14. The legitimacy of such an inter-level comparison between desired and actual expenditure increases is open to challenge. It is justified on the similarity in the 1952–63 average annual percentage increase in state general expenditures and Federal nonmilitary budgeted expenditures. These average annual increases are 8.02 and 9.43 percent respectively. Derivation of the percentages is based on data from: U.S. Bureau of Census, *Census of Government: 1962* Vol. VI, No. 4, *Historical Statistics on Governmental Finances and Employment* (Washington: 1964), and *Governmental Finances in 1963*, G-GF63-No. 2, November 1964.

TABLE 6. Attitudes of American State Executives on Expansion of State and Own Agency's Services and Expenditures
(percentages; number of cases in parentheses)

Attitude Toward Degree of Expansion	Overall Expansion of State Services and Expenditures	Expansion of Own Agency Services and Expenditures
No expansion	30	24
Expand 0–5 percent	7	8
Expand 5–10 percent	19	16
Expand 10–15 percent	16	16
Expand 15 plus percent	18	31
Other and N.A.	10	6
Total	100 (933)	100 (933)

concerning general goal support we observe the presence of a slight relationship between expansionist preferences and a perception of the governor as more sympathetic to agency goals. The relationship is not strong nor statistically significant and the lack of a clear and consistent association tends to confirm our prior observation concerning the extensiveness of pressures for expansion. The policy pressures for expanding expenditures and services at the state level are evidently so great, as witnessed by the majority favoring expansion, that expansion is a permeating and preponderant goal throughout state administration. The extensiveness and apparent intensiveness of expansion preferences override the previously-documented cleavages in control over administration between the governor and legislature.

Parenthetically, we might also mention the results of further data analyses that have a bearing on interpreting the expansionist attitudes of state administrators. We tabulated these attitudes by four socioeconomic characteristics of the respective states in which the administrators held their positions. The characteristics were: urbanism, labor force engaged in manufacturing, labor force in white-collar occupations, and per capita income. In none of the cross-tabulations was there any consistent or significant association between these macrosystem socioeconomic characteristics and the micromeasured data of administrator attitudes. If any slight consistency could be discerned, it was that administrators from the least urban, lowest income, and lowest manufacturing and white collar states were a little more in favor of expansion than were administrators from states located at the other end of the spectrum on these variables. Aspirations for increased services are at least equal if not slightly more concentrated in the so-called "have-not" states. These attitudes may reflect a realistic assessment and a genuine commitment among administrators to meet the need for public services in these economically disadvantaged states.[17]

When policy attitudes are tabulated by preference for type of control in a reorganized state government a clear and statistically significant relationship is evident. The nature of this relationship is interesting and revealing. Administrators who prefer legislative control are more in favor of no expansion and less in favor of increases greater than 15 percent. The agency chiefs most in favor

of increases exceeding 15 percent and least in favor of no expansion were the executives who preferred to operate under commission control—independent of either primary legislative or primary gubernatorial control! This finding solidifies the conclusion advanced and partially confirmed in the preceding section regarding the strong centrifugal tendencies toward independence at the state level. In this particular instance we see the tendency demonstrated in terms of those desiring organizational independence (a degree of isolation or insulation from control by the governor and legislature) and preferring service and expenditure increases. This additional finding poses not only the problem of centrifugal tendencies but also the issue of the political responsibility of the administrators most disposed to expand their programs. Can and should such independence, characterized by one observer of the federal scene as the "discrediting" and "diffusion" of government, be tolerated at the state level where power is more fragmented than in the federal government?[18]

[17] The very slight relationship noted here may be the result of several uncontrolled and unknown factors, including the *lower* response rate from administrators in the low-income southern states. Response rates were generally in the 40-50 percent range in the South; elsewhere they ranged from 70 to 90 percent. Among the southern administrators who did respond, however, 40 percent favored expansion in their own agency's expenditures of "more than 15 percent." This percentage is higher than in any other region where the figures were 31, 33, and 28 percent for the Northeast, Midwest, and West, respectively.

[18] Herman Miles Somers, "The President, the Congress, and the Federal Government Service," in Wallace S. Sayre (Eds.), *The Federal Government Service* (Englewood Cliffs, N.J.: Prentice-Hall, 1965), pp. 85–88.

TABLE 7. Attitude on Expansion of Own Agency's Services and Expenditures and Perceived and Preferred Political Relationships of American State Executives

	Attitudes on Expansion of Own Services						
	No expansion	0–5%	5–10%	10–15%	15 + %	Total	Number of cases
			(percentages)				
Greater Control Over Agency Affairs							
Governor	25	8	16	19	33	100	276
Each about the same	24	7	19	19	30	100	193
Legislature	26	8	17	14	35	100	387
Greater Tendency to Reduce Budget Requests							
Governor	22	9	15	15	38	100	222
Legislature	25	7	17	18	33	100	529
Sympathy for Agency Goals							
Governor	20	9	19	18	34	100	488
Each about the same	28	7	10	16	39	100	121
Legislature	30	8	15	16	31	100	172
Preferred Type of Control							
Governor	22	9	18	18	32	100	369
Commission	19	8	13	20	41	100	250
Legislature	36	7	19	13	26	100	210

An alternative interpretation might be placed on the relationship between preferred control and agency expansion. Instead of viewing the relationship as a drive for independence among "expansionist" state administrators the association could reflect the lack of past political support from either the governor or legislature. The absence of such support, especially under board or commission organizational arrangements, could be both the cause and effect of the observed relationship. Little policy support from the governor or legislature produces conditions prompting administrators to be more desirous of substantial program expansions. The same limited policy support may have alienated administrators from the governor and legislature, pushing them in the direction of more reliance on and confidence in their own resources for policy support, e.g., from clientele groups, professional associations, and other organized interest groups.

CONCLUDING OBSERVATIONS

In this article we have briefly explored a few of the dimensions of executive leadership over state administration. A repetition of our findings is less necessary than an elaboration of their possible implications. These implications raise several questions that may be conveniently classified under two headings.

1. What are the implications of these findings for chief executives and "executive leadership" reformers? These one-point-in-time results constitute a benchmark regarding the progress made to date in bringing state administration under the aegis of the governor. The results also constitute a challenge to those concerned about executive policy coordination at the state level. The structural insulation of portions of state government under boards and commissions has produced demonstrably "independent" attitudes among state administrators. These inclinations toward independence pose a major challenge, some might say a threat, to the firmly held tenet of a politically responsible bureaucracy. Are not administrative officials revealing a substantial degree of political irresponsibility when one-third opt for a measure of independence from executive *and* legislative control over administration? And is there not a greater threat presented when the "independence-oriented" administrators are also those most inclined toward expansion of their programs?

We need to be cautious in our response. Political responsibility is obviously a complex concept, one that undoubtedly has several dimensions, both attitudinal and behavioral. Our attitudinal probings dealt only with preferred types of institutional control. It would be unwise and premature to judge harshly administrators' responsibility strictly in structural-institutional terms. Indeed, commitments to program accomplishment, clientele groups, administrative due process, and impartiality are other elements worthy of inclusion in the broad concept of political responsibility. Norton Long, for example, has argued that the bureaucracy itself is a more representative institution, both in democratic ethos and socioeconomic composition, than our legislative bodies.[19] His concept of representation is in sharp contrast to the representativeness doctrine elaborated by Kaufman. The latter has defined representation in structural terms, i.e., direct popular election of administrative officials and/or legislative supremacy over the administrative establishment. Long's concept of representation includes the normative orientations of the administrator as well as their socioeconomic and demographic personal characteristics.

Whatever the reform emphasis or focus in structural terms, it seems necessary to recognize additional elements in judging where and how to alter formal organizational arrangements. Neither structural symmetry nor reasoned simplicity can be or should be the only consideration guiding governmental reforms.

2. The problem of reform-related structural arrangements is closely associated with a second broad area in which our findings have some significant implications. It has been said that in any struggle for power, power gravitates toward the participant who can use it the best. This axiom can be imposed on our findings and interpreted in an intergovernmental context. What do our results suggest regarding the role of the states vis-à-vis local and national governments?

Recent commentators have contended that the states are now or soon will become mere administrative districts of the national government, dispensing funds but effecting little if any policy in-

[19]Norton Long, "Bureaucracy and Constitutionalism," *American Political Science Review*, Vol. 46, No. 3 (September 1952), pp. 808–818.

fluence.[20] Our findings do not bear directly on this point but in an indirect way we can make some pertinent observations. One main theme persistent through out survey findings (which go beyond the data presented here) is the strong pluralism and wide diversity present in state administration. Pluralism and diversity are present in the social backgrounds, personal characteristics, career patterns, and attitudes of the state officials.[21] These features are important factors operating against strong, effective state action, especially when it involves matters and relationships with other levels of government. If we grant a substantial degree of truth to the statement that power distributions in administration directly reflect power patterns at large, then York Willbern's analysis of political forces at the state level is accurate. Willbern contends that non-governmental constellations of power are much stronger at the state level than at the national or local levels and further, that "liberty" (by which he means pluralism or shared power) has tended to predominate as an important value in state government.[22]

Where do our results leave state government in this intergovernmental context? The results are not very favorable, at least from the administrative standpoint. There is the already-documented desire to substantially expand state services. Additionally, a majority of state administrators are prepared to accept activity and financing by any and all levels of government in various program areas. In very broad but somewhat oversimplified terms, we can say that the program orientations of state administrators appear to outweigh their commitments to state government as a unit of government. This tendency in administrative attitudes and loyalties has been given different terms: "functionalism," "vertical functional autocracies," and "programmatic values" are three examples.[23] In the latter instance, programmatic values were posited in opposition to "expediency" or unit-of-government values.[24] More recently, this phenomenon of administrator attitudes has been examined at the federal level with regard to federal grant-in-aid programs.[25] The conclusions reported there tend to mirror the results we have uncovered at the state level. When it comes to a choice between program considerations and intra- or intergovernmental coordination, administrators are not strongly inclined toward the latter choices. The long range consequences of these administrative tendencies at the state level are too imponderable for speculation. In the short run, however, unless these centrifugal forces are at least contained, if not rolled back, we are likely to see a further diminution of the general politico-administrative significance of state government.

METHODOLOGICAL APPENDIX

The data collection instrument for this research, a 4-page mail questionnaire, was sent to 1,357 elected and appointed state administrative officials in all 50 states. The names of the officials were obtained from *The Book of the States, Supplement 11: Administrative Officials Classified by Function.* This document, published by the Council of State Governments, listed the names of the state executives who headed functional departments and agencies as of July 1, 1963. Seventy-five different categories of agencies were listed and over 3,000 names of agency heads appeared under the categories.

[20] Arthur S. Miller, *Private Governments and the Constitution* (Santa Barbara, Calif.: Center for the Study of Democratic Institutions, The Fund for the Republic, 1959), 15 pp.; Ferdinand Lundberg, *The Coming World Transformation* (Garden City, N. Y.: Doubleday, 1963), 395 pp. For a further elaboration of Miller's position see, "The Constitutional Law of the 'Security State,' " *Stanford Law Review*, Vol. 10 (July 1958), pp. 620–671.

[21] Deil S. Wright and Richard L. McAnaw, "American State Executives: Their Backgrounds and Careers," *State Government*, Vol. 38, No. 3 (Summer 1965), pp. 146–153; Deil S. Wright and Richard L. McAnaw, "The Men at the State Capitol," *Nation's Cities*, Vol. 3, No. 11 (November 1965), pp. 21–26.

[22] York Willbern, "The States as Components in An Areal Division of Powers," in Arthur Maass (Ed.), *Area and Power: A Theory of Local Government* (The Free Press, 1959), pp. 70–88.

[23] Robert C. Wood, "A Division of Powers in Metropolitan Areas," in Maass (Ed.) *op. cit.*, pp. 53–69; Advisory committee on Local Government, Commission of Intergovernmental Relations, *An Advisory Committee Report on Local Government* (Washington: 1955), pp. 6 ff.; Edward W. Weidner, *Intergovernmental Relations as Seen by Public Officials* (Minneapolis: University of Minnesota Press, 1960), pp. 22 ff.

[24] Weidner, *op. cit.*, p. 22.

[25] *The Federal System as Seen by Federal Aid Officials*, Subcommittee on Intergovernmental Relations, U.S. Senate, 89th Congress, 1st Session (Washington, D.C.: U.S. Government Printing Office 1965), pp. 93–102.

THE GOVERNOR, A BIBLIOGRAPHY 1945-1970

BOOKS AND MONOGRAPHS

Abernathy, Byron R. *Some Persisting Questions Concerning the Constitutional State Executive* (Lawrence: University of Kansas, 1960). (Governmental Research Series No. 23.)

Allen, David J. *New Governor in Indiana: The Challenge of Executive Power* (Bloomington: Indiana University, Institute of Public Administration, 1965).

The American Assembly. *The Forty-eight States: Their Tasks as Policy Makers and Administrators* (New York: The American Assembly, Graduate School of Business, Columbia University, 1956).

Anton, Thomas J. *The Politics of State Expenditure in Illinois* (Urbana: University of Illinois Press, 1966).

Bell, James R., and Darrah, Earl L. *State Executive Reorganization* (Berkeley: Bureau of Public Administration, University of California, 1961). (1961 Legislative Problems No. 3.)

Belluch, Bernard. *Franklin D. Roosevelt as Governor of New York* (New York: Columbia University Press, 1955).

Bollens, John C. *Administrative Reorganization in the States Since 1939* (Berkeley: Bureau of Public Administration, University of California, 1947).

Brooks, Glenn E. *When Governors Convene: The Governors' Conference and National Politics* (Baltimore: Johns Hopkins Press, 1961).

Buechner, John C. *State Government in the Twentieth Century* (Boston: Houghton Mifflin, 1967).

Darrah, Earl L., and Poland, Orville. *Fifty State Governments: A Comparison of State Executive Organization Charts* (Berkeley: Bureau of Public Administration, University of California, 1961).

Davis, Kenneth S. *A Prophet in His Own Country* (Garden City, N.Y.: Doubleday, 1957).

Di Salle, Michael V. *The Power of Life or Death* (New York: Random House, 1965).

Eley, Lynn W. *The Executive Reorganization Plan: A Survey of State Experience* (Berkeley: Institute of Governmental Studies, University of California, 1967).

Fannin, Paul, McFarland, Ernest W., Goodall, Leonard E., and White, John P. *The Office of Governor in Arizona* (Phoenix: Bureau of Government Research, Arizona State University, 1964).

Flinn, Thomas. *The Governor and the Minnesota Budget* (New York and Indianapolis: Bobbs-Merrill, 1961). (Inter-University Case Program, No. 60.)

Gantt, Fred, Jr. *The Chief Executive in Texas: A Study in Gubernatorial Leadership* (Austin: University of Texas Press, 1964).

Graves, W. Brooke. *American Intergovernmental Relations: Their Origins, Historical Development and Current Status* (New York: Scribner's, 1964).

Graves, W. Brooke. *American State Government* (4th ed; Boston: Heath, 1953).

Heady, Ferrel. *State Constitutions: The Structure of Administration* (New York: National Municipal League, 1961). (State Constitutional Studies Project, Series II, No. 4.)

Herzberg, Donald G., and Tillett, Paul. *A Budget for New York State, 1956–57* (University, Alabama: University of Alabama Press, 1962). (Inter-University Case Program, No. 69.)

Hirst, David W. *Woodrow Wilson: Reform Governor. A Documentary Narrative* (New York: N.J. Van Nostrand Reinhold, 1965).

Hodges, Luther H. *Businessman in the Statehouse: Six Years as Governor of North Carolina* (Chapel Hill: University of North Carolina Press, 1962).

Hurst, James Willard. *The Growth of American Law: The Law Makers* (Boston: Little, Brown, 1950).

Illinois Assembly on the Office of Governor. *The Office of Governor: Final Report and Background Papers* (Urbana: Institute of Government and Public Affairs, University of Illinois, 1963).

Jewell, Malcolm E. *The State Legislature: Politics and Practice* (New York: Random House, 1962).

Kallenbach, Joseph E. *The American Chief Executive: The Presidency and the Governorship* (New York: Harper & Row, 1966).

Key, V. O., Jr. *American State Politics: An Introduction* (New York: Knopf, 1956).

Levin, Murray B., and Blackwood, George. *The Compleat Politician: Political Strategy in Massachusetts* (New York and Indianapolis: Bobbs-Merrill, 1962).

Liebling, A. J. *The Earl of Louisiana, The Liberal Long* (New York: Simon & Schuster, 1961).

Lipson, Leslie. *The American Governor: From Figurehead to Leader* (New York: Greenwood Press, 1968).

Littlewood, Thomas B. *Bipartisan Coalition in Illinois* (New York: McGraw-Hill, Eagleton Institute Cases in Practical Politics, 1960).

Lockard, Duane. *The New Jersey Governor: A Study in Political Power* (New York: Van Nostrand Reinhold, 1964).

Mayer, George H. *The Political Career of Floyd B. Olson* (Minneapolis: University of Minnesota Press, 1951).

Morey, Roy D. *Politics and Legislation: The Office of Governor in Arizona* (Tucson: University of Arizona, Institute of Government Research, 1965). (Arizona Government Studies No. 3.)

Moscow, Warren. *Politics in the Empire State* (New York: Knopf, 1948).

Ransone, Coleman B., Jr. *The Office of Governor in the South* (University, Ala.: University of Alabama Press, 1951).

Ransone, Coleman B., Jr. *The Office of Governor in the United States* (University, Ala.: University of Alabama Press, 1956).

Rich, Bennett M. *State Constitutions: The Governor* (New York: National Municipal League, 1960). (State Constitutional Studies Project, Series II, No. 3.)

Robbins, Robert R. (Ed.). *State Government and Public Responsibility, 1961: The Role of the Governor in Massachusetts* (Medford, Mass.: The Lincoln Filene Center for Citizenship and Public Affairs, Tufts University, 1961). (Papers of the 1961 Tufts Assembly on Massachusetts Government.)

Sanders, John L. *Report on the Office of the Governor of North Carolina* (Chapel Hill: Institute of Government, University of North Carolina, 1965).

Sanford, Terry. *But What About the People?* (New York: Harper & Row, 1966).

Sanford, Terry. *Storm over the States* (New York: McGraw-Hill, 1967).

Scace, Homer E. *The Organization of the Executive Office of the Governor* (New York: Institute of Public Administration, 1950).

Schlesinger, Joseph. *How They Became Governor: A Study of Comparative State Politics, 1870–1950* (East Lansing: Michigan State University Press, 1957).

Sindler, Allan P. *Huey Long's Louisiana* (Baltimore: Johns Hopkins Press, 1956).

Smith, Reed M. *State Government in Transition: Reforms of the Leader Administration, 1955–59* (Philadelphia: University of Pennsylvania Press, 1963).

Spence, James R. *The Making of a Governor: The Moore-Preyer-Lake Primaries of 1964* (Winston-Salem, N.C.: John F. Blair Publisher, 1968).

Sprengel, Donald P. *Gubernatorial Staffs: Functional and Political Profiles* (Iowa City: Institute of Public Affairs, 1969).

Walker, Harvey. *Executive-Legislative Relations* (New York: National Municipal League, Constitutional Studies Project, 1959).

Williams, G. Mennen. *A Governor's Notes* (Ann Arbor: Institute of Public Administration, University of Michigan, 1961).

ARTICLES IN BOOKS AND PERIODICALS

Ahlberg, Clark D., and Moynihan, Daniel P. "Changing Governors—and Policies," *Public Administration Review*, 20 (Autumn 1960), pp. 195–205.

"As Newsmen See the Conference," *State Government*, 31 (Summer 1958), pp. 173–177.

Backman, Ada E. "The Item Veto Power of the Executive," *Temple Law Quarterly*, 31 (Fall 1957), pp. 27–34.

Baker, Russell. "Best Road to the White House—Which?" *New York Times Magazine* (November 27, 1960), pp. 22 ff.

Baldwin, Thomas F., and Newton, Lowell. "State Governors and Broadcast News: A Survey of Facilities, Services and Attitudes," *Journal of Broadcasting*, 12 (Spring 1968), pp. 145–154.

Bane, Frank. "The Job of Being a Governor," *State Government*, 31 (Summer 1958), pp. 184–189.

Battle, John S. "Work of the Governor's Office," *Proceedings* of the sixty-fourth Annual Meeting of the Virginia State Bar Association, 1954, pp. 230–237.

Beyle, Thad L. "The Governor's Formal Powers: A View from the Governor's Chair," *Public Administration Review*, 28 (November/December 1968), pp. 540–545.

Beyle, Thad L. "State Executives," in Richard H. Leach (Ed.), *Compacts of Antiquity: State Constitutions* (Atlanta: Southern Newspaper Publishers Associations Foundation, 1969), pp. 27–34.

Beyle, Thad L., Seligson, Sureva, and Wright, Deil S. "New Directions in State Planning," *Journal of the American Institute of State Planners*, 35 (September 1969), pp. 334–339.

Beyle, Thad L., and Wickman, John E. "Gubernatorial Transition in a One-Party Setting," *Public Administration Review*, 30 (January/February 1970), pp. 10–17.

Bone, Hugh A. "State Constitutional Revision: A Review and a Strategy," *State Government*, 42 (Winter 1969), pp. 43–49.

Bosworth, Karl A. "The Politics of Management Improvement in the States," *American Political Science Review*, 47 (March 1953), pp. 84–99.

Botner, Stanley B. "Gubernatorial Succession–Question in Several States," *University of Missouri Business and Government Review*, 6 (March/April 1965), pp. 24–30.

Broder, David S. "What's the Best Road to the White House?," *New York Times Magazine* (September 22, 1963),

Brooks, Glenn. "The Governors: Often Winners in Past Presidential Sweepstakes, Their Future Is Now in Doubt," *Johns Hopkins Magazine*, 14 (November 1962), pp. 5–9.

"The Business of Being Governor," *State Government*, 31 (Summer 1958), pp. 145–149.

Caldwell, Lynton K. "Perfecting State Administration, 1940–1946," *Public Administration Review*, 7 (Winter 1947), pp. 25–36.

Carleton, William G. "The Southern Politician 1900 and 1950," *Journal of Politics*, 13 (May 1951), pp. 215–231.

Carley, David. "Legal and Extra-Legal Powers of Wisconsin Governors in Legislative Relations," *Wisconsin Law Review*, 1962 (January/February 1962), pp. 3–64, 280–341.

Clem, Alan L. "Popular Representation and Senate Vacancies," *Midwest Journal of Political Science*, 10 (February 1966), pp. 52–77.

"Comeback of the States," *U.S. News and World Report*, 67 (October 27, 1969), pp. 48–50.

Conner, J. E., and Morgan, R. E. "Governor and the Executive Establishment," *Academy of Political Science Proceedings* (January 1967), pp. 173–182.

Cornwell, Elmer E., Jr., Goodman, Jay S., and Cogger, Janice. "Professorial Staff for Governors' Offices Subject of Questionnaires," *Bulletin of the Bureau of Government Research*, University of Rhode Island, September 1968. pp. 1–2.

David, Paul T. "The Role of Governors at the National Party Conventions," *State Government*, 33 (Spring 1960), pp. 103–110.

Desmond, T. E. "To Help Governors Govern," *New York Times Magazine*, (June 2, 1957), pp. 14 ff.

Dye, Thomas R. "Executive Power and Public Policy in the States," *Western Political Quarterly*, 27 (December 1969), pp. 926–939.

Eley, Lynn W. "Executive Reorganization in Michigan," *State Government*, 32 (Winter 1959), pp. 33–37.

Epstein, Leon. "Electoral Decision and Policy Mandate: An Empirical Example," *Public Opinion Quarterly*, 28 (Winter 1964), pp. 564–67.

Eulau, Heinz and Koff, David. "Occupational Mobility and Political Career," *Western Political Quarterly*, 15 (September 1962), pp. 507–521.

Ewing, Cortez A. M. "Southern Governors," *Journal of Politics*, 10 (May 1948), pp. 385–409.

"Five Former Governors Appraise the Governors' Conference," *State Government*, 31 (Summer 1958), pp. 168–172.

Frost, Richard T. "The New Jersey Institutions Case," in Frost (Ed.), *Cases in State and Local Government* (Englewood Cliffs N.J.: Prentice-Hall, 1961), pp. 219–236.

Gantt, Fred, Jr. *The Governor's Veto in Texas: An Absolute Negative?* (Austin: Institute of Public Affairs, University of Texas, March 1969).

Garrity, Thomas A. "Separation of Powers Doctrine in New Mexico," *Natural Resources Journal*, 4 (October 1964), pp. 350–359.

Garvey, N. F. "Amenability of the Governor to Court Processes," *Howard Law Journal*, 7 (Spring 1961), pp. 120–144.

Gauss, John M. "The States are in the Middle," *State Government*, 23 (June 1950), pp. 138–142.

Gibbons, Charles. "Transition of Government in Massachusetts," *State Government*, 34 (Spring 1961), pp. 100–101.

Gove, Samuel K. "Why Strong Governors?," *National Civic Review*, 53 (March 1964), pp. 131–136.

Graves, W. Brooke. "Some New Approaches to State Administrative Reorganization," *Western Political Quarterly*, 9 (September 1956), pp. 743–754.

Gravlin, Leslie M. "An Effective Chief Executive," *National Municipal Review*, 36 (March 1947), pp. 137–141.

"Gubernatorial Executive Orders as Devices for Administrative Direction and Control," *Iowa Law Review*, 50 (Fall 1964), pp. 78–98.

"Gubernatorial Transition in the States," *State Government Administration*, 3 (December 1968), pp. 18 ff.

Hansen, R. H. "Executive Disability: A Void in State and Federal Law," *Nebraska Law Review*, 40 (June 1961), pp. 697–732.

Harris, Joseph P. "The Governors' Conference: Retrospect and Prospect," *State Government*, 31 (Summer 1958), pp. 190–196.

Harris, Louis. "Why the Odds Are Against a Governor's Becoming President," *Public Opinion Quarterly*, 4 (July 1959), pp. 361–370.

Havel, James T. "The Executive Veto in Kansas," *Bulletin of Governmental Research Center*, (Lawrence: University of Kansas, March 15, 1969) pp. 1–3.

Heady, Ferrel, and Pealy, Robert H. "The Michigan Department of Administration: A Case Study in the Politics of Administration," *Public Administration Review*, 26 (Spring 1956), pp. 82–89.

Highsaw, Robert B. "The Southern Governor–Challenge to the Strong Executive Theme," *Public Administration Review*, 19 (Winter 1959), pp. 7–11.

"How States Handle Governor Succession," *Congressional Digest*, 25 (March 1946), pp. 75 ff.

"How the States Provide for Disability," *Congressional Digest*, 37 (January 1958), pp. 4–5.

Jacob, Herbert, and Lipsky, Michael. "Outputs, Structure and Power: An Assessment of Changes in the Study of State and Local Politics," *Journal of Politics*, 30 (May 1968), pp. 510–538.

Jewell, Malcolm E. "State Decision-Making: The Governor Revisited," in Aaron Wildavsky and Nelson Polsby (Eds.), *American Governmental Institutions*, (Chicago: Rand McNally, 1968), pp. 545–565.

Jonas, Frank H., and Jones, Garth. "J. Bracken Lee and the Public Service in Utah," *Western Political Quarterly*, 9 (September 1956), pp. 755–765.

Kallenbach, Joseph E. "Constitutional Limitations on Re-eligibility of National and State Chief Executives," *American Political Science Review*, 46 (June 1952), pp. 438–454.

Kallenbach, Joseph E., "Governors and the Presidency," *Michigan Alumnus Quarterly Review*, 60 (Spring 1954), pp. 234–242.

Kammerer, Gladys M. "The Governor as Chief Administrator in Kentucky," *Journal of Politics*, 26 (May 1954), pp. 236–256.

Kammerer, Gladys M. "Kentucky's All-Pervasive Spoils Politics," *Good Government*, (July-August 1958), pp. 32–37.

Key, V. O., Jr., and Silverman, Corinne. "Party and Separation of Powers: A Panorama of Practice in the States," *Public Policy*, 5, (1954), pp. 382–412.

Lambert, Louis. "The Executive Article," in W. Brooke Graves (Ed.), *Major Problems in Constitutional Revision* (Chicago: Public Administration Service, 1960), pp. 185–200.

Langlie, A. B. "Responsibility of the States and their Governors," *State Government*, 29 (August 1956), pp. 144–145.

Lederle, John W., and Ahrens, Edmund G. "Executive Bill Clearance Procedure in Michigan," *Public Administration Review*, 15 (Summer 1955), pp. 205–209.

Lehman, Herbert H. "Albany and Washington–A Contrast," *New York Times Magazine*, (September 24, 1950), pp. 12.

Lipson, Leslie. "The Executive Branch in New State Constitutions," *Public Administration Review*, 9 (Winter 1949), pp. 11–21.

Long, Norton E. "After the Voting is Over," *Midwest Journal of Political Science*, 6 (May 1962), pp. 183–200.

Lowance, Carter O. "The Governor of Virginia," *The University of Virginia Newsletter*, 36 (February 15, 1960).

Luke, Sherrill D. "The Need for Strength," *National Civic Review*, 53 (March 1964), pp. 126–130.

McCally, Sarah P. "The Governor and his Legislative Party," *American Political Science Review*, 60 (December 1966), pp. 923–942.

McGeary, Morton N. "The Governor's Veto in Pennsylvania," *American Political Science Review*, 41 (October 1947), pp. 941–946.

MacKaye, Milton. "When Governors Get Together," *Saturday Evening Post*, 230 (May 10, 1958), pp. 923–942.

Macmahon, Arthur W. "Woodrow Wilson as Legislative Leader and Administrator," *American Political Science Review*, 50 (September 1956), pp. 641–675.

Mallan, John P., and Blackwood, George. "The Tax That Beat a Governor: The Ordeal of Massachusetts," in Alan F. Westin (Ed.), *The Uses of Power* (New York: Harcourt Brace Jovanovich, 1962), pp. 285–322.

Mileur, Jerome M. "The Politics of State Administrative Reorganization Studies," *Bulletin of the Bureau of Government Research* (University of Massachusetts, December 1967), pp. 1–4.

Mitau, "The Governor and the Strike," in Richard T. Frost (Ed.), *Cases in State and Local Government* ed. by Richard T. Frost (Englewood Cliffs, N.J.: Prentice-Hall, 1961), pp. 207–218.

Morey, Roy D. "The Executive Veto in Arizona: Its Use and Limitations," *Western Political Quarterly*, 19 (September 1966), pp. 504–515.

Morgan, Murray, "The Most Powerful Governor in the U.S.A.," *Harper's* 231 (October 1965), pp. 98–107.

Mosher, Frederick C. "The Executive Budget, Empire State Style," *Public Administration Review*, 12 (Spring 1952), pp. 73–84.

Mosher, Frederick C. "Limitations and Problems of PPBS in the States," *Public Administration Review*, 29 (March/April 1969), pp. 160–167.

Moynihan, Daniel P., and Wilson, James Q. "Patronage in New York State, 1955–59." *American Political Science Review*, 58 (June 1964), pp. 286–301.

Nixon, H. Clarence. "The Southern Legislature and Legislation," *Journal of Politics*, 10 (May 1948), pp. 410–417.

Olson, David J. "Citizen Grievance Letters as a Gubernatorial Control Device in Wisconsin," *Journal of Politics*, 31 (August 1969), pp. 741–755.

Pettigrew, Thomas F., and Campbell, Ernest Q. "Faubus and Segregation: An Analysis of Arkansas," *Public Opinion Quarterly*, 24 (Fall 1960), pp. 436–447.

Pomper, Gerald M. "Governors, Money and Votes," in *Elections in America* (New York: Dodd, Mead & Co., 1968), Chap. 6, pp. 126–148, 270–273.

Prescott, Frank W. "The Executive Veto in American States," *Western Political Quarterly*, 3 (January 1950), pp. 98–112.

Prescott, Frank W. "The Executive Veto in Southern States," *Journal of Politics*, 10 (November 1948), pp. 659–675.

Ransone, Coleman B., Jr. "Political Leadership in the Governor's Office," *Journal of Politics*, 26 (February 1964), pp. 197–220.

Ransone, Coleman B., Jr. "Scholarly Revolt in Dullsville: New Approaches to the Study of State Government," *Public Administration Review*, 26 (December 1966), pp. 343–352.

Rich, Bennett M. "The Governor as Administrative Head," in John P. Wheeler, Jr. (Ed.), *Salient Issues of Constitutional Reform* (New York: National Municipal League, 1961), pp. 98–114. (State Constitutional Studies Project, Series 1, No. 2.)

Rich, Bennett M. "The Governor as Policy Leader," in John P. Wheeler, Jr. (Ed.), *Salient Issues of Constitutional Reform* (New York: National Municipal League, 1961) pp. 80–97. (State Constitutional Studies Project, Series 1, No. 2.)

Scace, Homer E. "The Governor Needs Staff," *National Municipal Review*, 40 (October 1951), pp. 462ff.

Schlesinger, Joseph A. "The Governor's Place in American Politics," *Public Administration Review*, 30 (January/February 1970), pp. 2–10.

Schlesinger, Joseph A. "The Politics of the Executive," in Herbert Jacob and Kenneth N. Vines (Eds.), *Politics in the American States: A Comparative Analysis* (Boston, Little, Brown 1965), pp. 207–237.

Schlesinger, Joseph A. "Stability in the Vote for Governor, 1900-1958," *Public Opinion Quarterly*, 24 (Spring 1960), pp. 85–91.

Schlesinger, Joseph A. "The Structure of Competition for Office in the American States," *Behavioral Science*, 5 (July 1960), pp. 197–210.

Sharkansky, Ira "Agency Requests, Gubernatorial Support and Budget Success in State Legislatures," *American Political Science Review*, Vol. LXII (December 1968), pp. 1220–1231.

Simmons, Robert H. "American State Executive Studies:

A Suggested New Departure," *Western Political Quarterly*, Vol. 17 (December 1964), pp. 777–783.

Simmons, Robert H. "American State Executive Systems: A Heuristic Model," *Western Political Quarterly*, 18 (March 1965), pp. 19–26.

Solomon, Samuel R. "Governors, 1950-1960," *National Civic Review*, 49 (September 1960), pp. 410–416.

Solomon, Samuel R. "The Governor as Legislator," *National Municipal Review*, 40 (November 1951), pp. 515–520.

Solomon, Samuel R. "Master of the House: Recent Efforts Toward State Governmental Reform Give Promise of New Balance in Legislative-Executive Relations," *National Civic Review*, 57 (February 1968), pp. 68–74.

Solomon, Samuel R. "United States Governors, 1940–1950," *National Municipal Review*, 41 (April 1952), pp. 190–197.

Stratton, William G. "The Governors' Conference Through Fifty Years—and Tomorrow," *State Government*, 31 (Summer 1958), pp. 125–126.

Swinerton, E. Nelson. "Ambition and American State Executives," *Midwest Journal of Political Science*, 12 (November 1968), pp. 538–549.

Symposium, "The Governor's Views on Federal-State and State-Local Relations," *Public Administration Review*, 30 (January/February, 1970), pp. 27–42.

Titus, James E. "Kansas Governors: A Résumé of Political Leadership," *Western Political Quarterly*, 17 (June 1964), pp. 356–370.

Trachsel, Herman H. "The Governor and Administrative Organization," *Public Affairs* (University of South Dakota Research Bureau), 10 (August 15, 1962), pp. 1–4.

Trickey, David F. "Constitutional and Statutory Bases of Governors' Emergency Powers," *Michigan Law Review*, 64 (December 1965), pp. 290–307.

Turano, Peter J. "Constitutional Checks and Balances: Recent Use of Executive Veto in Michigan," *University of Detroit Law Journal* (October 1956).

Turett, J. Stephen, "The Vulnerability of American Governors, 1900–1969," *Midwest Journal of Political Science*, 15 (February 1971), pp. 108–132.

Warner, Kenneth. "Planning for Transition," *State Government*, 34 (Spring 1961), pp. 102–103.

Welsh, Matthew E. "The Role of the Governor in the 1970s," *Public Administration Review*, 30 (January/February 1970), pp. 24–26.

Wright, Deil S. "Executive Leadership in State Administration: Interplay of Gubernatorial, Legislative and Administrative Power," *Midwest Journal of Political Science*, 11 (February 1967), pp. 1–26.

Wyner, Alan J. "Governor–Salesman: Restrictions on Executives Have Caused Many to Focus on Industrial Promotion and Good Publicity," *National Civic Review*, 56 (February 1967), pp. 81–86.

Wyner, Alan J. "Staffing the Governor's Office," *Public*

Administration Review, 30 (January/February, 1970), pp. 17–24.

Wyner, Alan J. "Gubernatorial Relations with Legislators and Administrators," *State Government*, 41, (Summer, 1968), pp. 199–203.

Young, William H. "The Development of the Governorship," *State Government*, 31 (Summer 1958), pp. 178–183.

Young, William H. "Governors, Mayors and Community Ethics," *The Annals of the American Academy of Political and Social Science*, 280 (March 1952), pp. 46–50.

ORGANIZATION REPORTS

Committee for Economic Development. *Modernizing State Government* (New York: Committee for Economic Development, 1967), pp. 45–61.

Council of State Governments. *The American Governors: Their Backgrounds, Occupations and Governmental Experience* (Chicago: Council of State Governments, published periodically).

Council of State Governments. *The Book of the States* (Chicago: Council of State Governments, published biennially).

Council of State Governments. *Examples of Organization of the Governor's Office* (Chicago: Council of State Governments, 1962).

Council of State Governments. *The Governor and Public Information: Selected Methods Employed by Governor's Offices in Communicating with the Public* (Chicago: Council of State Governments, 1961).

Council of State Governments. *The Governors of the American States, Commonwealths and Territories: Biographical Sketches and Portraits* (Chicago: Council of State Governments, 1969). (Published periodically.)

Council of State Governments. *The Governors of the States, 1900-1966* (rev. ed.; Chicago, Council of State Governments, 1966).

Council of State Governments. *Gubernatorial Transition in the States* (Chicago: Council of State Governments, 1968).

Council of State Governments. *Issues in Gubernatorial Succession* (Chicago: Council of State Governments, 1969).

Council of State Governments. *Summary of Midwestern Governors' Conference* (Chicago: Council of State Governments, 1962– published annually).

Council of State Governments. *Proceedings of the National Governors' Conference* Chicago: Council of State Governments, 1908– ; (published annually).

Council of State Governments. *National Governors' Conference, 1908-1968* (Chicago: Council of State Governments, 1968).

Council of State Governments. *Reorganization of State Government* (Chicago: Council of State Governments, 1958).

Council of State Governments. *Reorganizing State Government: A Report on Administrative Management in the States and a Review of Recent Trends in Reorganization* (Chicago: Council of State Governments, 1950).

Council of State Governments. *Summary of Southern Governors' Conference* (Chicago: Council of State Governments, 1955– ; (published annually).

Council of State Governments. *Summary of Western Governors' Conference* (Chicago: Council of State Governments, 1945– ; (published annually).

National Municipal League, Committee on State Government. Model State Constitution with explanatory articles (New York: National Municipal League, 1948).

"Trends of State Government: As Indicated by the Governors' Messages," *State Government* (published annually in the spring or summer issue).

UNPUBLISHED MATERIALS

Bell, James R. "The Administrative Role of the California Governor" (unpublished Ph.D. dissertation, Department of Political Science, University of California at Berkeley, 1956).

Bellush, Jewell. "Selected Case Studies of the Legislative Leadership of Governor Herbert H. Lehman" (unpublished Ph.D. dissertation, Department of Political Science, Columbia University, 1959).

Beyle, Thad L., and Williams, J. Oliver. "New Governor in North Carolina: Politics and Administration of Transition" (unpublished report to the Governor's Office, Raleigh, North Carolina, 1969).

Black, Robert E. "Southern Governors and the Negro: Race as a Campaign Issue since 1954" (unpublished Ph.D. dissertation, Department of Government, Harvard University, 1968).

Botner, Stanley B. "The Office of Governor of Missouri" (unpublished Ph.D. dissertation, Department of Political Science, University of Missouri, 1963).

Carley, David L. "The Wisconsin Governor's Legislative Role: A Case Study in the Administrations of Philip Fox La Folette and Walter J. Kohler, Jr." (unpublished Ph.D. dissertation, Department of Political Science, University of Wisconsin, 1959).

Carone, Patrick A. "The Governor as a Legislator in West Virginia" (unpublished Ph.D. dissertation, Department of Political Science, Duke University, 1969).

Coor, Lattie Finch, Jr. "The Increasing Vulnerability of the American Governor" (unpublished Ph.D. dissertation, Department of Political Science, Washington University, 1964).

Crown, James T. "The Development of Democratic Government in New York State through the Growth of the Power of the Executive Since 1920" (unpublished Ph.D. dissertation, Department of Political Science, New York University, 1956).

Flinn, Thomas. "Governor and Legislature: A Case Study

in Political Decision-Making" (unpublished Ph.D. dissertation, Department of Political Science, University of Minnesota, 1957).

Gere, Edwin A., Jr. "Patterns of Federal-Regional Interstate Cooperation in New England" (unpublished Ph.D. dissertation, Department of Political Science, State University of New York, 1968).

Gibson, Juanita M. "The Office of Governor in Florida" (unpublished Ph.D. dissertation, Department of Political Science, University of Michigan, 1958).

Gibson, Lorenzo T. "The Role of the Governor in the Legislative Process: A Comparative Study of the Governor of Maryland and the Governor of Virginia" (unpublished Ph.D. dissertation, Department of Political Science, University of Virginia, 1968).

Gorvine, Albert. "The Governor and Administration: State of Nevada" (unpublished Ph.D. dissertation, Department of Political Science, New York University, 1952).

Harvey, Richard B. "The Political Approach of Earl Warren, Governor of California" (unpublished Ph.D. dissertation, Department of Political Science, University of California at Los Angeles, 1959).

Heslop, David A. "A Critique of Recent Theories of Executive Power" (unpublished Ph.D. dissertation, Department of Political Science, University of Texas, 1968).

Hester, Lewis A. "An Exploratory Study of the Florida Legislature's View of the Role of the Executive Branch of Government in the Enactment of Administrative Bills" (unpublished M.A. thesis, Department of Political Science, Florida State University, 1960).

Holmes, Jack E. "Party, Legislation and Governor in the Politics of New Mexico, 1911–1963" (unpublished Ph.D. dissertation, Department of Political Science, University of Chicago, 1964).

Ivy, Glenn H. "An Organization Structure for Gubernatorial Leadership in Texas State Government" (unpublished Ph.D. dissertation, Department of Political Science, University of Texas, 1970).

James, Judson L. "The Loaves and Fishes: New York State Gubernatorial Patronage, 1955–1958" (unpublished Ph.D. dissertation, Department of Political Science, Columbia University, 1967).

Kessel, John H. "Road to the Mansion: A Study of the 1956 Gubernatorial Campaign in Ohio" (unpublished Ph.D. dissertation, Department of Political Science, Columbia University, 1958).

Larson, Robert N. "The Governor's Council in New England" (unpublished Ph.D. dissertation, Department of Political Science, Boston University, 1960).

Lieberman, Carl. "The 1966 Gubernatorial Campaign in Pennsylvania: A Study of the Strategies and Techniques of the Democratic Candidate" (unpublished Ph.D. dissertation, Department of Political Science, University of Pittsburg, 1969).

Mills, Warner, Jr. "Ross Sterling, Governor of Texas" (unpublished Ph.D. dissertation, Department of Political Science, Johns Hopkins University, 1956).

Parker, Daisy. "An Examination of the Florida Executive" (unpublished Ph.D. dissertation, Department of Political Science, University of Virginia, 1959).

Rollins, Overman R. "The Power to Persuade: A Study of the Governor of North Carolina" (unpublished undergraduate thesis, Department of Political Science, Duke University, 1965).

Schlesinger, Joseph A. "Emergence of Political Leadership: A Case Study of American Governors" (unpublished Ph.D. dissertation, Department of Political Science, Yale University, 1955).

Simmons, Robert H. "The Washington Plural Executive: An Experiment in Interaction Analysis" (unpublished Ph.D. dissertation, Department of Political Science, University of Washington, 1962).

Sprengel, Donald P. "Legislative Perceptions of Gubernatorial Power in North Carolina" (unpublished Ph.D. dissertation, Department of Political Science, University of North Carolina, Chapel Hill, 1966).

Williams, Henry N. "The Legislative Process in Tennessee: With Special Reference to Gubernatorial Control" (unpublished Ph.D. dissertation, Department of Political Science, University of Chicago, 1951).

Wood, Robert C. "The Metropolitan Governor: Three Case Inquiries into the Substance of State Executive Management" (unpublished Ph.D. dissertation, Department of Government, Harvard University, 1949).

Wyner, Alan. "The Governor as Political Leader and Chief Executive" (paper delivered at the National Conference on Government, National Municipal League, Boston, November, 1965).

Wyner, Alan. "The Governor's Office: 14 Offices as Seen by Participant Observers" (unpublished Ph.D. dissertation, Department of Political Science, Ohio State University, 1968).

Young, Wayne F. "Oklahoma Politics: With Special Reference to the Election of Oklahoma's First Republican Governor" (unpublished Ph.D. dissertation, Department of Political Science, University of Oklahoma, 1964).

BIBLIOGRAPHIES

Chase, Karen A. *Reorganization of State Government: A Selective Bibliography* (Berkeley, Institute of Governmental Studies, University of California, 1968). 18 pp.

Citizens Conference on State Legislatures, *Selected Bibliography on State Legislatures* (Kansas City, June 1968). 39 pp.

Graves, W. Brooke. *American State Government and Administration: A State-by-State Bibliography of Significant General and Special Works* (Chicago: Council of State Governments, 1949). 79 pp.

Halevy, Balfour J. *A Selective Bibliography on State Constitutional Revision* (New York: National Municipal League, 1963). 177 pp.

Harmon, Robert B. *Political Science: A Bibliographic Guide to the Literature* (New York: Scarecrow Press, 1965), pp. 94–122.

Herndon, James, Press, Charles, and Williams, Oliver P. (Eds.). *A Selected Bibliography of Materials in State Government and Politics* (Lexington: Bureau of Government Research, University of Kentucky, 1963). 143 pp.

Hoppes, Muriel. *State Government: An Annotated Bibliography* (Chicago: Council of State Governments, 1959). 46 pp.

Press, Charles. *A Bibliographic Introduction to American State Government and Politics* (East Lansing: Institute for Community Development and Services, Michigan State University, 1964). 34 pp. Bibliographic serial No. 13.

Tompkins, Dorothy C. *Organization and Reorganization in State Government, 1958–1959: A Bibliography* (California Public Survey, Vol. 11, November 1959), pp. 185–195.

Tompkins, Dorothy C. *State Government and Administration: A Bibliography* (Berkeley: Bureau of Public Administration, University of California, 1954). 269 pp.

Yates, Marianne, and Gilchrist, Martha. *Administrative Reorganization of State Government, 1948–1952* (Chicago: Council of State Governments, 1948). 12 pp.

NAME
INDEX

SUBJECT
INDEX

Administrative agencies. *See* State administrative agencies.
Alabama, gubernatorial choice of legislative leaders in, 138
Appalachian Regional Commission, 185
Appointive power of governor. *See* Gubernatorial powers; State agency heads.
Arizona
  appointive powers of governor in, 145
  gubernatorial choice of legislative leaders in, 138
Arkansas, gubernatorial-legislative relations in, 139

Baker v. *Carr*, 128
Brown v. *Board of Education*, 41, 43, 44, 49
Budget
  as base for policy planning, 99
  completion during intraparty transition, 88, 90, 92–94
  complexity of, 171, 172
  control over administrative agencies, 146–147
  control over by governor, 146–147
  and formal gubernatorial powers, 255
  formulation of, 98
  gubernatorial-legislative conflict over, 97, 98, 99
  gubernatorial role in formulation of, 173, 174, 176–177, 180–181
  and higher education, 233–234
  incrementalism of, 85, 171, 176, 177, 182
  and need for increased taxes, 97, 98
  review of, 171, 172, 176, 182, 183
  and state administrative agencies, 146–147, 172–183
  submission of, 97, 98, 102
  and transition, 85, 90, 91, 95, 97, 98, 99, 100, 102, 103
  See also California; New York; Planning-Programming-Budgeting System; State fiscal policies

Cabinet. *See* State agency heads.
California
  budget in, 92–94
  campaign issues, in, 63
  fiscal policies in, 63
  gubernatorial influence on choice of legislative leaders in, 134
  higher education in, 232, 233, 239–240
  interparty transition in, 92–94

Campaigns
  gubernatorial
    communication tools in, 132
    image building of candidates in, 34–37
    important characteristics of, 33
    incumbent's position in, 32
    isolation from national trends of, 33
    issues in, 34, 98
    legislative support for candidates in, 96
    mass media in, 31, 33, 36
    policy planning in, 99
    Presidential support in, 38
    use of voter opinion polls in, 33, 34, 36
    value of issues in, 34
  legislative, gubernatorial campaigning in, 131
  See also Elections; Public policies; State fiscal policies; Voters.
Campaign issues, 34, 98
  as basis for legislative program, 132
  in New York, 96
  urban affairs as, 244–245
  See also New politics; State fiscal policies.
Campaign oratory
  as guide to action, 77
  as related to gubernatorial legislative programs, 85, 132
Campaign organization
  common denominator of, 77
  innovation within, 77
  lack of well-defined purposes of, 77
  participants in, 77
  recruitment of, 96
  unbureaucratic nature of, 77
  See also Gubernatorial staff.
Career patterns of governors
  advancement in federal political system, 9–17, 18
  changes in, 9–12
  effect of change in, 10
  factors affecting
    party organization, 11, 15–16, 17
    party system, 11, 13–15, 17
    structure of political opportunities, 11–13, 16–17
  as provider of order in political system, 10
  See also Political Party Organization.
Civil Rights Act of 1964, 37, 45
Civil service
  during transition, 100–103
  in New York state government, 100–103
  resistance to change in, 103
Colorado
  preprimary party conventions in, 131
  tenure of elected officials in, 143
Comprehensive Health Planning Act, 185
Comprehensive health planning, 218–226
  activities in, 223
  citizen participation in, 219, 220, 225
  consumer protection in, 225–226
  criticisms of, 221, 223–224
  gubernatorial role in, 219, 220, 221, 224–225, 226
  professionalism in, 218, 219, 220
  state agencies for, 218–219, 220, 221, 222, 223, 225
Connecticut, gubernatorial-party organization relations in, 129

and program success of governor, 126, 127, 133, 140–141

during transition, 88, 98, 99

in two-party states, 136, 138

See also Arkansas; Gubernatorial Power; Legislative leadership; Legislature; Louisiana; Michigan; Patronage; State fiscal policies, Texas.

Gubernatorial powers

appointment power, 127, 144–146, 252

appointments and administrative control, 281–284

budget control, 137, 146–147

concept of formal power, 127

factors affecting, 148, 149

increase in, 17, 185, 186

index of formal power, 148–150

index of governors' powers in states, 252–253

as indicator of potential leadership, 127

as influence, 126, 127

over legislative parties, 126

loss of during transition, 100, 102

restrictions on, 248

sources of, 129

strong executive movement and, 74

veto, 97, 147–148

See also Arizona; Budget; Legislative leadership; Legislature; New York; Political parties; Public policies; Public policy-making; State agency heads; Tenure; Veto.

Gubernatorial roles

as bipartisan public opinion leader, 132–133, 141

as chief budget officer, 95, 97, 98, 126

as chief executive, 40, 73

as chief legislator, 126

as federal systems officer, 2, 3, 4, 74, 185, 186, 187

as intergovernmental coordinator, 193

as legislative leader, 138, 140

in legislature, 151–170

in national politics, 9, 15–16

as negotiator, 141

as ombudsman, 243

as party leader in legislature, 136

as policy coordinator, 188, 191

as policy leader, 278

as state political party leader, 126, 130–131, 136–138

as political party spokesman, 132, 136, 138

as reformer, 73

See also Budget; Legislative leadership; Legislature; Political parties; Public policies, Public policy-making.

Gubernatorial staff

appointment of by governor, 119, 120

campaign supporters on, 119, 120

civil servants on, 119, 120

as compared with other political elites, 106–112

composition of as related to electoral coalition, 119

decision-making responsibility of, 122

definition of professional members of, 118

education of, 108, 117, 119

gubernatorial perceptions of staff roles, 123

job satisfaction of, 123–124, 125

journalists on, 119

lawyers on, 119

legislative duties of, 135

liberality of, 100–101

lobbyists and, 135

loyalty to governor, 112, 117, 119, 120, 124

outsider's opinions of, 124–125

political ambitions of, 107, 112, 117, 120

political party identification of, 111, 117

political socialization of, 110, 117

pre-election association with governor of, 107, 114, 116, 117

previous political experience of, 111–112, 117, 119

recruitment of, 113–116, 117, 118, 119, 120

relationship to governor of, 112–113

removal of, 120–122

roles of, 122–123

salary of, 106

size of, 105

socioeconomic backgrounds of, 106, 109, 116–117

specialization of, 109, 117, 119

tenure of, 112, 117, 120, 124

Gubernatorial transition. *See* transition.

Health planning. *See* Comprehensive health planning.

Higher education

budget for, 233–244

coordinating state systems for, 235, 236

factors reinforcing establishment of coordination of, 236

federal funding of, 236, 237

governors and issues of, 239–240

gubernatorial control over, 233–234

gubernatorial influence over, 233

gubernatorial roles in, 232

interstate planning for, 237–238

legislative control over, 234–235

and junior colleges, 238–239

national planning for, 238

organizational arrangements for, 232–233, 235

outside financial support for, 234

public and private institutions of, 236–237, 238

state planning agencies for, 235

Hill-Burton Act of 1946, 219

Illinois

higher education in, 233–234

legislative leaders in, 133–134

modernization of tax structure in, 244

Incumbent, definition of gubernatorial, 20

See also Campaigns; Elections; Vulnerability.

Indiana, two-party legislative campaigning in, 131

Influence

definition of, 126

power as, 126, 127

Interns, in governor's office, 124

Interparty transition

alterations in communications patterns during, 93, 94

California and, 92–94

change in personnel during, 93

decision-making during, 94

duration of, 93

formalized relationships during, 93

incremental change in governmental activity during, 93–94

New Deal-Great Society liberalism, 2
New Hampshire
  gubernatorial-legislative relations in, 137
  one-party dominance in legislature, 137
New Jersey, governors and urban affairs in, 243
New politics, 31–32, 132
  alternative meanings of, 31
  as component of vulnerability, 3
  as contributor to vulnerability, 31
  elements of, 3
  methodology of, 31, 32, 33
  use of methodology in gubernatorial campaigns, 35, 36
New York
  appointment power of governor in, 99, 100
  budget-making during transition in, 95, 97–99, 100, 102, 103
  campaign issues in, 63
  changes in government in, 95
  civil service in, 100, 102
  control of legislature in, 96, 103
  fiscal policies in, 63, 95, 97, 98
  Harriman administration in, 95
  legislative leaders in, 97, 98, 133
  legislative majority in, 95, 96
  legislative staff in, 96, 103
  local party organization in, 130
  party organization in, 129
  political parties in, 95, 96
  PPB in, 215
  transition period in, 95–104
  source of policy proposals in, 101
North Carolina
  antipoverty program in, 89–90
  Democratic party factions in, 87
  intergovernmental relations in, 191–192
  intraparty transition in, 87–92
  one-party dominance in, 87
  planning agency for crime control in, 230
  veto power, 148, 252
North Dakota, appointive power of governor in, 145

Ohio, gubernatorial-legislative relations in, 129
Omnibus Crime Control and Safe Streets Act of 1968, 185, 191, 227, 231
  See also Crime control act.
One-party states
  governor as legislative leader in, 138
  gubernatorial influence on re-election of legislators in, 136, 137
  gubernatorial-legislative relations in, 136–138
  See also Kentucky; Louisiana; North Carolina.
Opposition party, in legislature, 136
  See also Legislature; Elections.

Partnership for Health Act of 1966, 218, 220, 221, 223, 224, 226
Patronage
  as bargaining tool of governor in legislative relations, 139
  as gubernatorial tool, 136, 253
  See also Louisiana, Virginia

Party caucus
  gubernatorial participation in, 134–135
  in legislatures in one-party states, 139
Pennsylvania, governors and urban affairs in, 243
Planning. See State planning; State planning agencies.
Planning-programming-budgeting system, 187
  need for in state government, 205–207, 213–215
  as policy tool, 4
  problems of, 216
  use of in state government, 213–215
Policy. See Public policy; Public policy-making; Public policy implementation.
Political parties
  and preference on state fiscal policies, 59–61, 67–69
  presidential electoral position of, 14
  single-party system, 127
  strategies in presidential elections of, 13–15, 17
  strength of, 14
  two-party system model, 128
  and urban affairs, 244
  voter opinion of, 54, 62
  See also Legislature.
Political party organization
  changes in, 13
  criteria of strong, 129
  criteria of weak, 129
  definition of, 11, 15
  effect of primaries on, 129, 130, 135
  as factor in career patterns, 11
  factors affecting strength of, 130
  gubernatorial control of, 15–16, 129, 130
  gubernatorial influence in, 13–15
  gubernatorial relations with, 130–131
  influence in legislature of, 135
  in two-party states, 135
  leadership of, 129
  and legislative success of governor, 129
  See also Michigan; New York.
President of the U.S., public attitudes toward, 259–265
Presidential elections
  party electoral position in, 14
  strategic value of governor in, 13–15
  strategies of parties in, 13–15
Progressive Era, 11
Primaries
  effect of party organization on, 129, 130, 135
  legislative, 131
Public attitudes
  toward governor, 139–140, 258–269
  toward political institutions, 259–269
  toward political parties, 54, 62
  toward public policy, 263–265
  toward U.S. Supreme Court, 258–265
  See also State fiscal policies; Voters.
Public policies
  change in during transition, 96, 97, 98, 99
  effect of state politics on, 269
  and executive fragmentation, 248, 249, 254
  gubernatorial influence on, 254
  and gubernatorial powers, 245–255
  influence of voters on, 258